CHINA AND THE WTO

Examining the twenty years since China acceded to the World Trade Organization, this collection provides an original, systematic assessment of the opportunities and challenges that China has presented to the WTO. Offering in-depth analyses of the "two-way" relationship between China and the WTO, the contributions explore a range of key issues from the varied effects of WTO membership for China and the global economy to the responses of the WTO members to China's rapid economic growth. It presents diverse perspectives of leading scholars from multiple disciplines, including law, economics, political science, and international relations, as well as practical insights from senior policymakers from both China and the United States. This is an invaluable contribution to ongoing debates about the implications of the rise of China for global economic governance and enriches discussions of the wide-ranging implications of China's growing integration into the multilateral trading system, both now and in the future. This title is also available as Open Access on Cambridge Core.

HENRY GAO is a Senior Fellow at the Centre for International Governance Innovation and a Professor of Law at Singapore Management University. He sits on the Advisory Board of the WTO Chairs Program and the editorial boards of the *Journal of International Economic Law* and *Journal of Financial Regulation*. He has also published *Between Market Economy and State Capitalism: China's State-Owned Enterprises and the World Trading System* (2022).

DAMIAN RAESS is a Senior Researcher at the University of Bern specializing in International Political Economy. He has written extensively on globalization and labor, including China-led globalization. Coauthor of the Labor Provisions in Trade Agreements (LABPTA) dataset, he has provided consultant services for analyzing labor provisions in preferential trade agreements for the EFTA, the EU Parliament, and the World Bank.

KA ZENG is a Distinguished Professor of Political Science and Director of International and Global Studies at the University of Arkansas. Her research focuses on China's role in the global economy. She is the author or coauthor of *Trade Threats, Trade Wars* (2004), *Greening China* (2011), and *Fragmenting Globalization* (2021).

CHINA AND THE WTO

A Twenty-Year Assessment

World Trade Forum

Edited by

HENRY GAO

Singapore Management University

DAMIAN RAESS

University of Bern

KA ZENG

University of Arkansas

CAMBRIDGE
UNIVERSITY PRESS

CAMBRIDGE
UNIVERSITY PRESS

Shaftesbury Road, Cambridge CB2 8EA, United Kingdom

One Liberty Plaza, 20th Floor, New York, NY 10006, USA

477 Williamstown Road, Port Melbourne, VIC 3207, Australia

314–321, 3rd Floor, Plot 3, Splendor Forum, Jasola District Centre, New Delhi – 110025, India

103 Penang Road, #05–06/07, Visioncrest Commercial, Singapore 238467

Cambridge University Press is part of Cambridge University Press & Assessment, a department of the University of Cambridge.

We share the University's mission to contribute to society through the pursuit of education, learning and research at the highest international levels of excellence.

www.cambridge.org
Information on this title: www.cambridge.org/9781009291781

DOI: 10.1017/9781009291804

First published 2023

A catalogue record for this publication is available from the British Library

A Cataloging-in-Publication data record for this book is available from the Library of Congress

ISBN 978-1-009-29178-1 Hardback

CONTENTS

FIGURES

TABLES

CONTRIBUTORS

GRANT ALDONAS is an international lawyer and senior adviser with the Center for Strategic and International Studies. He previously served as U.S. Under Secretary of Commerce for International Trade, Majority Chief of International Trade Council to the U.S. Senate Committee on Finance, Principal Managing Director of Split Rock International, Inc., an international trade and investment consultancy he founded, and Executive Director of the Institute of International Economic Law at the Georgetown University Law Center, where he taught as an Adjunct Professor of International Law.

AXEL BERGER is Deputy Director (interim) at the German Institute of Development and Sustainability (IDOS). He works on the design, effects, and diffusion patterns of international trade and investment agreements, with a focus on emerging markets and developing countries. His other areas of research include the effects of an international investment facilitation framework, the impact of free trade agreements on upgrading within global value chains, and the role of the G20 in global governance. He teaches international political economy at the University of Bonn and regularly advises developing countries, development agencies, and international organizations on trade and investment matters.

IRYNA BOGDANOVA is a postdoctoral researcher and a recent Ph.D. graduate from the World Trade Institute, University of Bern. Her thesis, exploring the legality of unilateral economic sanctions under international law, was published as *Unilateral Sanctions in International Law and the Enforcement of Human Rights* (Brill, 2022). Previously, she was a legal trainee at the Appellate Body Secretariat of the World Trade Organization, worked as an international trade consultant at a leading European law firm in Brussels and as a legal and corporate affairs manager for a multinational corporation in Kyiv, Ukraine.

MANJIAO CHI is a Full Professor at the University of International Business and Economics (UIBE) Law School, Beijing. His research focuses on international economic governance, dispute settlement and global cooperation. He is the author of numerous books and articles, founding editor of the *Asian Yearbook of International Economic Law,* a frequent speaker at international conferences, and a visiting professor at leading law schools around the world. He has also served as Deputy Chair, the Academic Forum on ISDS; Co-Chair, ASIL Asia Pacific Interest Group; and Standing Council Member, Chinese Society of International Law. He delivered a course at the Hague Academy of International Law in 2021. He holds BA, LL.M and PhD in Law degrees.

THOMAS COTTIER is a Professor emeritus of European and International Economic Law at the University of Bern, senior research fellow and former managing director of the World Trade Institute, and Adjunct Professor at the University of Ottawa, Faculty of Law. He was a Deputy Director-General of the Swiss Intellectual Property Office and legal advisor to the Swiss Department of Foreign Economic Affairs. He served on the Swiss negotiating team of the Uruguay Round and on EFTA-EU EEA negotiations. He has been a member and chair of several GATT and WTO panels and currently serves on the MPIA pool of appeal arbitrators at the WTO.

MATTHEW S. ERIE (J.D., PHD) is an Associate Professor, Member of the Law Faculty, and Associate Research Fellow of the Socio-Legal Studies Centre at the University of Oxford. Professor Erie is trained in both law and anthropology and studies comparative Asian law, including the relationship between Anglo-American law and Asian law. His current research project "China, Law and Development," funded by a European Research Council Starting Grant (No. 803763), examines China's approach to transnational ordering through international law and the legal and regulatory systems of host states receiving Chinese capital.

SIMON J. EVENETT is a Professor of International Trade & Economic Development at the University of St. Gallen, Switzerland. He is also the Founder of the St. Gallen Endowment for Prosperity Through Trade, the institutional home of both the Global Trade Alert and the Digital Policy Alert. Professor Evenett was educated in economics at the University of Cambridge and Yale University. He is the author and editor of over 200 articles, book chapters, and volumes.

JOSEPH W. GLAUBER is a Senior Research Fellow at the International Food Policy Research Institute in Washington, DC and former Chief Economist at the U.S. Department of Agriculture. From 2007–2009, Glauber was the Special Doha Agricultural Envoy at the office of the U.S. Trade Representative where he served as a chief agricultural negotiator in the Doha talks. He served as an economic adviser at the so-called Blair House agreements leading to the completion of the Uruguay Round negotiations. He is the author of numerous studies on agricultural insurance, trade policy and U.S. farm policy.

JENNIFER HILLMAN is a Professor at the Georgetown University Law Center and the co-director of its Center on Inclusive Trade and Development. She is also a senior fellow at the Council on Foreign Relations. She previously served on the World Trade Organization's Appellate Body, completing her term in 2012. She has also served as a commissioner for the U.S. International Trade Commission and as both general counsel and chief textiles negotiator for the Office of the United States Trade Representative.

BERNARD HOEKMAN is Professor and Director, Global Economics, at the Robert Schuman Centre for Advanced Studies, European University Institute, where he is also the Dean for External Relations. He has held management positions in the World Bank working on international trade issues and served as an economist in the GATT Secretariat. A CEPR Research Fellow and ERF Senior Associate, he is a graduate of the Erasmus University Rotterdam and holds a Ph.D. in economics from the University of Michigan. His research focuses on commercial policy, trade in services, public procurement, global governance, and the WTO.

KRISTEN HOPEWELL is the Canada Research Chair in Global Policy in the School of Public Policy and Global Affairs at the University of British Columbia. She is the author of *Clash of Powers: US-China Rivalry in Global Trade Governance* (Cambridge University Press, 2020) and *Breaking the WTO: How Emerging Powers Disrupted the Neoliberal Project* (Stanford University Press, 2016). She is a Wilson China Fellow at the Wilson Center in Washington, DC.

SOO YEON KIM is an Associate Professor and Head of the Department of Political Science, the National University of Singapore. She holds a PhD (Political Science) from Yale University and BA (Political Science and International Relations) from Yonsei University. Her research areas include production networks, multinational firms, and trade agreements; and rising powers and economic governance. Recent publications: "High-Income Developing Countries, FDI Outflows and the International Investment Agreement Regime" (2021, with Yoram Haftel and Lotem Bassan-Nygate), *World Trade Review*; "Investment Commitments in PTAs and MNCs in Partner Countries," (2021) *Economics & Politics*; and *BRICS and the Global Economy* (2020, Editor, World Scientific Publishing).

SIMON LESTER is the co-founder of China Trade Monitor and WorldTradeLaw.net. He previously worked for the trade law practice of a Washington, DC, law firm; as a legal affairs officer at the Appellate Body Secretariat of the World Trade Organization; and at the Cato Institute's Center for Trade Policy Studies. He has written a number of law journal articles, policy chapters, and op-eds, and has taught courses on international trade law at American University's Washington College of Law, the University of Michigan Law School, and Melbourne University Law School.

JING LI is an Associate Professor of Economics at the Farmer School of Business at Miami University. He previously was on the faculty of South Dakota State University and Auburn University. He earned a PhD from the University of Alabama in 2006.

SIQI LI is an Associate Professor at the China Institute for WTO Studies, University of International Business and Economics, Beijing, China. She received her Ph.D. degree in 2015 and has been conducting WTO-related studies since then. Her articles have appeared in the *Journal of World Trade*, *China & World Economy*, and other international and Chinese peer-reviewed journals. She has conducted research for the Chinese government, including the Ministry of Commerce, the Ministry of Finance, and the Ministry of Agriculture and Rural Affairs.

WEI LIANG is Gordon Paul Smith Chair of international policy in the School of International Policy and Management at the Middlebury Institute of International Studies. Her research interests include the international political economy of East Asia, international negotiation and global governance. She is the coauthor of *China and East Asia's Post-Crises Community: A Region in Flux?* (Lexington, 2012), co-editor of *Challenges to China's Economic Statecraft: A Global Perspective* (Springer, 2019), *China and Global Trade Governance* (Routledge, 2013), and a number of journal articles and book chapters.

YE LIU is a Professor of Economics at Xiamen University. He obtained his PhD in 2003.

THOMAS SATTLER is an Associate Professor of International Relations at the University of Geneva, Switzerland. Before moving to Geneva, he was an Associate Professor at the London School of Economics & Political Science and an Assistant Professor at the University College Dublin. He also held visiting positions at the European University Institute, Central European University, and Trinity College Dublin. Thomas Sattler's research was published in journals like the *British Journal of Political Science*, *Comparative Political Studies*, *International Organization*, and the *Journal of Politics*. His PhD is from ETH Zurich, Switzerland.

TANJA SCHWEINBERGER is a postdoctoral researcher in the Department of Political Science at the University of Zurich and at the University of Geneva, Switzerland. She was an Asia Fellow of the Harvard Kennedy School Ash Center, United States of America. Her Ph.D. dissertation examined cooperation and conflict in U.S.-Chinese trading relations. She holds an MSc in International Relations from the London School of Economics and Political Science and a BA in Political Science from the University of Konstanz. Her single-authored manuscript "Mass public opinions toward trade balances" received the 2021 Best Graduate Paper Award of the International Political Economy Section of the International Studies Association. In autumn 2023, she will start a new position as Assistant Professor of International Political Economy at the University of Groningen in the Netherlands.

XINQUAN TU is Dean and Professor of the China Institute for WTO Studies at the University of International Business and Economics (UIBE) located in Beijing, China and Chair Holder of the WTO Chairs Program. He received his Ph.D. in international trade from UIBE in 2004. He was a visiting scholar at various institutions such as Johns Hopkins University, the WTO Secretariat, KIEP, the German Institute of International and Security Affairs, the Middlebury Institute of International Studies at Monterey, and Indiana University. His research and teaching focus on Chinese trade policy, the WTO, government procurement, U.S. trade policy, and U.S.-China trade relations.

ANQI WANG (PH.D.) is a research fellow at the World Trade Institute (WTI), University of Bern. Her research focuses on international investment law and dispute settlement. She used to work for the

International Institute for Sustainable Development (IISD) and the United Nations Conference on Trade and Development (UNCTAD) on issues of investment law and policy. She has also published articles concerning investment arbitration and investment policies. Her doctoral dissertation, which studies the most-favored-nation clause in investment law, was published as *The Interpretation and Application of the Most-Favored-Nation Clause in Investment Arbitration* (Brill, 2022).

CLARA WEINHARDT is Assistant Professor in International Relations at Maastricht University and a Non-Resident Fellow at the Global Public Policy Institute (GPPi) in Berlin. Her research interests combine questions of global trade governance with changing North-South relations, with an emphasis on global power shifts. Her work has appeared in, among other places, *International Studies Quarterly*, the *Review of International Political Economy*, the *Journal of Common Market Studies*, Routledge's International Political Economy Series, and Routledge's Global Institutions Series. She holds a Ph.D. in International Relations from the University of Oxford.

ROBERT WOLFE is a Professor emeritus at the School of Policy Studies, Queen's University, and a member of the Global Affairs Canada Trade Advisory Council. He was a foreign service officer for many years, serving abroad in Bangladesh and Paris-OECD, and in Ottawa in international economic relations. After completing a doctorate in Political Studies, he joined Queen's in 1995. He was a co-editor of the 2017 IRPP volume, Redesigning Canadian Trade Policies for New Global Realities. More recently he has published extensively on WTO reform.

XIAOZHUN YI is the chief advisor of the Network for International Trade and Investment System (NITIS) and served as a Deputy Director-General at the WTO from October 2013 to March 2021. Prior to becoming China's ambassador to the WTO in 2011, Mr. Yi was Assistant Minister and subsequently Vice Minister of China's Ministry of Commerce in charge of multilateral and regional trade negotiations and cooperation. He also worked as a diplomat at the Chinese Embassy in the United States for more than four years from the late 1980s to the early 1990s.

PETER K. YU (余家明) is Regents Professor of Law and Communication and Director of the Center for Law and Intellectual Property at Texas A&M University. Born and raised in Hong Kong, he previously held the

Kern Family Chair in Intellectual Property Law at Drake University Law School and was Wenlan Scholar Chair Professor at Zhongnan University of Economics and Law in Wuhan, China. He served as a visiting Professor of Law at Bocconi University, Hanken School of Economics, Hokkaido University, Tel Aviv University, the University of Haifa, the University of Helsinki, the University of Hong Kong, and the University of Strasbourg.

JINGJING ZHANG is a Lecturer in Law at the University of Maryland School of Law, and the founder of the Center for Transnational Environmental Accountability (CTEA). As the first litigation director of the Beijing-based Center for Legal Assistance to Pollution Victims (CLAPV), she won several milestone environmental lawsuits in the Chinese courts. She is currently working on transnational environmental and climate lawsuits in China's Belt and Road Initiative partner countries. She received her law degrees from Wuhan University and China University of Political Science and Law, and her Master's in Public Administration from Harvard University Kennedy School of Government.

WEIHUAN ZHOU is an Associate Professor, Director of Research, and Co-Director of the China International Business and Economic Law (CIBEL) Centre, Faculty of Law and Justice, UNSW Sydney. His research explores the most current and controversial issues in the field of international economic law, particularly the nexus between international trade law and China. He is co-Secretary of the Society of International Economic Law (SIEL) and sits on the Editorial Boards of the World Trade Review and the Journal of International Trade Law and Policy.

YINGGANG ZHOU is a Professor of Finance in the Department of Finance at the School of Economics and at the Wang Yanan Institute for Studies in Economics, Xiamen University. He obtained his Ph.D. in Economics and Finance from Xiamen University in 2001 and Cornell University in 2007.

HUAN ZHU is the co-founder of China Trade Monitor. Previously, she worked at the Cato Institute's Center for Trade Policy Studies, where she wrote a number of law journal articles, policy papers, and op-eds, and lectured on U.S.-Chinese trade relations. Zhu has a background in international economic law, intellectual property law, and comparative law. She holds an S.J.D. degree from the University of Kansas and an LL.M. from Ghent University in Belgium.

PREFACE

China's entry into the World Trade Organization (WTO) in December 2001 is a major landmark in the country's integration into the global economy as well as in the history of the international political economy. To evaluate the transformative changes of this event for China, its trading partners, and global trade governance, we brought together leading scholars and senior policymakers from various disciplines to participate in the book track of the World Trade Forum in November 2021, which was almost exactly at the time of the 20th anniversary of China's accession to the WTO.

While the event was held virtually due to the COVID-19 pandemic, we benefited greatly from the lively exchange among the participants and wish to thank all of them for their contributions, which resulted in this volume. We wish to thank the following individuals who took time out of their busy schedules to serve as external discussants of draft chapters and for their invaluable comments and suggestions: Frederick Abbott (Florida State University), Robert Basedow (LSE), Eddy Bekkers (WTO), Cosimo Beverelli (WTO), Donald Clarke (George Washington University), Manfred Elsig (WTI), Christian Häberli (WTI), Stuart Harbinson (WTO), Hosuk Lee-Makiyama (ECIPE), Petros Mavroidis (Columbia University), Ricardo Meléndez-Ortiz (ICTSD), Marcelo Olarreaga (University of Geneva), Rodrigo Polanco (WTI), Greg Shaffer (University of California, Irvine), Yeling Tan (University of Oregon), Peter Van den Bossche (WTI), Patrick Wagner (University of Konstanz), Ji Wenhua (UIBE), and Boliang Zhu (Penn State University).

ACKNOWLEDGMENTS

This volume would not have been possible without the support of the Robert Schuman Centre for Advanced Studies at the European University Institute (EUI) and the World Trade Institute (WTI) at the University of Bern and, in particular, of Manfred Elsig, Joseph Francois, Bernard Hoekman, and Peter Van den Bossche. Damian Raess is grateful for the financial support of the Swiss National Science Foundation Grant Agreements No PP00P1_198904 and, for the open access publication, No 10BP12_216907.

We further wish to thank Alexandra Eugster and Christian Steiger of the WTI for their excellent logistical support, as well as Marianne Nield, Rachel Imrie, and Sharon McCann from Cambridge University Press for their guidance throughout the entire process and continued support for the World Trade Forum.

In particular, we wish to thank Chris Hudson at Cambridge University Press for working with the designers to create the perfect artwork for the book, which shows the gate to the Gusu Garden in the courtyard of Centre William Rappard, with parts of the main building of the WTO in the background. Donated to the WTO by the Chinese government in 2013, the Gusu Garden is based on the traditional Chinese garden and represents a symbol of China's engagement and commitment to the WTO. The two Chinese characters inscribed at the top of the gate are "Enter" and "Win", which shows China's determination not only to win the battle of its accession negotiation, but also to win in international competition after accession. Together, the two characters form another term: "Wonderland", which was how China regarded the WTO, at least until the Gusu Garden was built.[1]

[1] See Henry Gao, China's Changing Perspective on the WTO: From Aspiration, Assimilation to Alienation.

Introduction

China's 20-Year Engagement with the WTO: Opportunities, Challenges, and Responses

HENRY GAO, DAMIAN RAESS, AND KA ZENG

The year 2021 marked the 20th anniversary of China's accession to the World Trade Organization (2001), an event that has stimulated the unprecedented integration of the world's largest transitional economy into the rules-based multilateral trading system. Since its entry, China has benefited significantly from enhanced trade flows made possible by its WTO membership, becoming the largest trader in goods and the second largest trader in services in the global economy today. Beijing's efforts to implement its WTO accession commitments have generated profound changes in its domestic regulatory framework in the areas of trade and beyond. At the same time, China's involvement in various WTO activities such as trade negotiations and dispute settlement has also changed the power dynamics within the WTO and presented unparalleled challenges to the functioning of the organization due to both the size of its economy and its unique economic model.

Outside of formal international economic institutions, China has actively negotiated bilateral investment treaties (BITs) and preferential trade agreements (PTAs) to secure expanded market access for Chinese goods, services, and capital. At the same time, Beijing's ambitious Belt and Road Initiative is increasingly subsuming much of China's economic (and political) involvement abroad (Ferdinand, 2016; Shaffer and Gao, 2020). While these developments have accelerated China's economic rise, transforming the country into the manufacturing center of the world and unleashing a global buying spree by Chinese firms, they have also provoked a strong backlash against Chinese influence (Colantone and Stanig, 2018; Raess, 2021). The ongoing trade war between the United States (US) and China, which, at the time of this writing in July 2022, has completed its fourth full year and still has no end in sight under the US administration of President Joe Biden, further speaks to the potential for the long-term strategic rivalry between the world's two largest economies in the years to come.

Looking back, the 20 years since China's accession to the WTO provide excellent opportunities to take stock of the implications of China's economic rise (for an assessment of China's first decade in the WTO, see Zeng and Liang, 2013). In particular, they raise important questions about the impact of WTO membership on China's domestic development, China's influence on the evolving global economic governance structures, and government responses in countries that are engaging China economically, responses that in turn shape global trade governance (for a broader evaluation of the country's trajectory in the international political economy, see Breslin, 2007; Zeng, 2019).

On the first question, contributing authors suggest that China's WTO accession has had a profound effect on the Chinese economy and society. Notably, WTO membership has stimulated China's phenomenal trade and economic growth. It has additionally prompted substantial domestic policy changes in China as the Chinese leadership sought domestic reforms to comply with multilateral trade disciplines and adverse WTO rulings in areas such as agricultural trade and intellectual property rights (IPR) protection. In the latter case, for example, the WTO's Agreement on the Trade-related Aspects of Intellectual Property Rights (TRIPS) has generated many benefits and incentivized the Chinese leadership to improve its IPR regime in an effort to encourage indigenous innovation. In the sensitive area of legal reform, efforts to implement its WTO obligations and commitments have introduced changes to the Chinese legal system. Even though barriers deeply entrenched in Chinese culture and society have impeded Beijing's ability to fully comply with its WTO obligations, China's growing integration into the rules-based WTO system has increasingly subjected it to WTO discipline in ways that have had transformative effects on Chinese society.

The domestic changes brought about by WTO membership have in turn increased China's economic clout and its weight in the global trading system, generating growing frictions between Beijing and its trading partners. Consequently, this volume additionally examines how China's rise has altered the power dynamics within the WTO. Contributing chapters suggest that China's status as both the second largest economy in the world and the largest developing country has heightened the tensions between its preference for special and differential treatment (SDT), on the one hand, and the organization's key underlying principle of reciprocity, on the other hand, precipitating heightened competition between the US and China that have threatened to derail major multilateral trade initiatives. This clash was further exacerbated by the growing divergence in the economic interests of China and developing and emerging economies. This latter set of conflicts has undermined the hope for solidarity among the Global South and introduced a new competitive dimension that further complicated the North-South divide which has impeded multilateral trade negotiations in the past. Overall, these developments highlight the challenges that China's emergence as a key player has posed to the WTO and their implications for the stability and viability of the multilateral trading system.

In view of the developments outlined above, how have governments and the public in major trading partners been responding to China's economic ascent? This volume engages this question and addresses reactions to the rise of China at both the government and individual levels. At the government level, frustrations with the difficulties of engaging China within the WTO have resulted in the revival of unilateral trade policies, as reflected in the recent trade war that Washington has launched against China. They have also led foreign governments to embrace the use of targeted, unilateral discriminatory measures to address trade concerns with China. Despite ongoing discussions of WTO reform, the substantial differences in the preferences and negotiation positions of the major players have continued to dim the prospect of multilateral trade cooperation. At the public level, China's economic rise has raised important questions about the degree to which attitudes toward China may be conditional on factors such as the presence of compensatory welfare and labor market policies or bilateral political relations.

Overall, this volume addresses the changes and continuities in China's role in the WTO by examining the following interrelated issues: (1) the political and economic implications of WTO membership for China and for the global economy; (2) China and global economic governance, including its role in WTO coalition building, dispute settlement, and discussions of WTO reform; (3) responses of WTO members to the economic rise of China; and (4) investment and technology issues related to China's WTO membership.

We adopt an interdisciplinary approach to tackling the above questions. In addition to approaching our main analytical tasks from the perspectives of multiple disciplines such as law, economics, political science, and international relations, the volume also draws on the contributions of senior policymakers from both China and the United States. Combining both theory and practice, it presents in-depth analyses and identifies the drivers and consequences of China's growing global economic integration. The research findings paint a rich picture of the processes, dynamics, and consequences of China's complex interactions with the WTO. They illuminate not only the opportunities and challenges presented by China's growing integration into the multilateral trading system but also ongoing debates about the implications of the rise of China for global economic governance.

I Main Themes of the Volume

We approach China's interactions with the WTO in the 20 years since its initial entry through the lens of "two-way" socialization which involves not only a process of "inducing actors into the norms and rules of a given society" (Checkel, 2005: 804; Johnston, 2001), but also efforts by agents to proactively influence the content and outcome of the socialization process (Sandstrom et al., 2013). In the context of China's relationship with the WTO, the theory predicts that China should not only be on the receiving end of international normative pressure but should also be able to exert its own influence on the evolution of global trade norms.

Indeed, China's growing participation in the WTO and other international economic institutions reflects the logic of such "two-way" socialization. On the one hand, China has been bound by WTO rules and has more frequently been brought to the WTO dispute settlement system than any other WTO members in the last two decades. Beijing's efforts to implement its accession commitments and WTO rules and rulings have led to domestic regulatory changes in the areas of trade, investment, and beyond.

On the other hand, however, China's WTO membership has also presented unparalleled challenges to the multilateral trade institution due to the sheer size of its economy, its status as a developing country, and its model of state capitalism (Mavroidis and Sapir, 2021; Wu, 2016). For example, China has sought to bring changes to the organization from within both by submitting its own proposals at the WTO and through coalition-building within the Doha Round negotiations (Gao, 2011; Tu, 2013). The economic ascent of China has additionally led to power shifts within the WTO, which some (e.g., Hopewell, 2020) argue have contributed to the crisis and relative decline of the organization. Such two-way interactions raise important questions about not only the impact of WTO membership on China but also China's influence on global economic governance.

Parts I–III of the volume directly speak to the above questions. Part I discusses China's perspective on the WTO, an issue that is rarely addressed in the mainstream literature in the West. Part II assesses the impact of the WTO on China in areas such as economic growth, the development of the rule of law, intellectual property rights protection, and agricultural trade, and seeks to identify both the incentives that the WTO membership has provided for trade and economic growth and the constraining effects of WTO rules on Chinese behavior. Part III in turn examines China's behavior within the WTO, focusing in particular on China's changing relationships with both the United States and the Global South as well as its role in WTO negotiations and its dispute settlement system.

In illuminating the two-way socialization mentioned above, we highlight the influence of both domestic and international politics on China's role in global economic governance (see in particular Part III). For example, while Hopewell (Chapter 8) emphasizes how China's development model and its self-identification as a developing country have posed serious challenges to US demands regarding special and preferential treatment, the chapters by Weinhardt and by Liang and Zeng (Chapters 9 and 10, respectively) in turn focus on how the increasingly divergent interests and preferences between China and other developing countries have complicated the existing divide among the major powers in WTO negotiations, further exacerbating the difficulties of effective multilateral trade governance. In addition, Hoekman, Tu, and Wolfe (Chapter 12) discuss how China's application to join the Comprehensive and Progressive Agreement for Trans-Pacific Partnership, by providing the necessary external pressure to break through domestic obstacles in sensitive areas such as non-trade issues, reform of state-owned enterprises, and data regulation, could potentially contribute to real WTO reform.

China's growing influence in the WTO has also provoked strong responses from its trading partners, which in turn have ramifications for global trade governance. This volume therefore additionally focuses on the responses and policy adjustments of countries that are engaging China economically (Part IV). Contributing authors consider not only individual responses to the rise of China's economic power but also the reactions of the U.S. government toward China's WTO accession as well as the policy measures adopted by foreign countries against Chinese exports since the Global Financial Crisis. For example, Raess (Chapter 13) shows that support for preferential trade liberalization with China among globalization losers is strongly conditioned by compensatory welfare policies (or belief in it). This evidence confirms the observed rise of protectionism and backlash against

China (e.g., trade wars) in countries with weak social safety nets or few labor protections. Hillman (Chapter 17) suggests that the perceived ineffectiveness of the WTO in engaging China has precipitated a turn by Washington toward the use of unilateral trade policy approaches in dealing with China's unfair trade practices in recent years. Such growing trends have contributed to the crippling of the WTO. Taken together, the chapters collectively illuminate the diverse responses at both the individual and government levels to China's rising economic clout since its WTO accession.

Finally, there exists a close relationship between trade and investment issues. Roughly one-third of global trade today is intra-firm trade among multinational corporation subsidiaries. Given the strong linkages between trade and investment issues, investment has been formally incorporated into the WTO framework through the Agreement on Trade-Related Investment Measures. Other WTO agreements such as the General Agreement on Trade in Services and TRIPS further include provisions relating to investment as they pertain to services and intellectual property rights, with the current ongoing negotiations on investment facilitation led by China more specifically targeting the issue. Investment issues have also increasingly been incorporated into free trade agreements, with NAFTA being the leading example. Furthermore, despite the relative decline of the WTO, foreign investment has continued to rise in recent years, with total global inward foreign investment increasing from $345 billion to $1,437 billion between 1995 and 2018 and global outward foreign investment rising from $361 billion in 1995 to $1,604 billion in 2017, before experiencing declines as a result of the pandemic after 2019 (UNCTAD statistics). China's growing prominence in the global investment landscape therefore calls for a better understanding of how the country's WTO membership has stimulated its investment growth.

Part V of this volume addresses this question. In Chapter 18, Erie and Zhang examine the evolution of China's domestic regulatory frameworks for governing inward and outward foreign direct investment (FDI), while Berger (Chapter 19) and Chi (Chapter 20) analyze China's international investment policy and its experience with investor-state dispute settlement and evaluate the degree to which it is a rule-taker, rule-breaker, or rule-maker within the system. Finally, non-reciprocal market access for investors and the issue of (forced) transfer of technology have been major sources of the US-China trade war and by extension of the WTO crisis (Chapter 22 by Cottier). The trade war has in turn served as a major push factor for Chinese firms' growing involvement in global production networks (Chapter 21 by Kim).

Overall, the volume highlights the changes that China's WTO membership has produced both at home and for the global trading community. On the one hand, the chapters in the volume provide excellent analyses of the multifaceted impacts of WTO accession on China's own development, not only in terms of economic growth but also in terms of the development of its rule of law, both broadly and more specifically in areas such as protection of intellectual property rights. On the other hand, the chapters also address the implications at the international level, which can be further broken into two strands: First, through its growing integration into the global trading system, China has taken on increasingly important roles in global trade governance, and the experiences it has gained in the trade arena have also found expression into other areas such as investment. At the same time, and second, China's growing role also generated concerns and sometimes backlashes in other countries. Initially, these concerns focused mainly on the economic impact of imports from China. Gradually, however, they shifted toward rules-related issues, especially when China started to take positions that some countries regarded as detrimental to their own interests or even threatening the core values behind the global trading system. In particular, in countries such as the US, the backlash has become so strong that it has led some to question whether it was a mistake to let China into the WTO in the first place (see the chapters by Aldonas and Hillman in this volume). Collectively, the chapters show that even though China can hardly be considered a rule-breaker within the WTO regime, its distinctive pattern of domestic development and divergent negotiation positions and preferences have resulted in growing friction with trading partners and threatened the viability of multilateral trade cooperation. Contributing authors additionally assess the effectiveness of the policies adopted by foreign governments to address the China challenge and explore the potential for strengthening cooperation to reduce conflict and increase the effectiveness of multilateral trade governance.

II Structure and Content

The book consists of five parts:

The first part (two chapters) sets the stage for the discussions by introducing Chinese perspectives on China's accession to the WTO. In Chapter 1, China's former WTO Ambassador Yi and his coauthor Li present China's official views on Beijing's record in implementing its WTO commitments and its involvement in WTO negotiations. Chapter 2 by

Gao provides the first-ever synthesis of China's changing perspectives on the WTO for the past 20 years and explores the reasons behind it. Putting China's interactions with the WTO into the larger geopolitical context, this chapter argues that Beijing's stance has evolved from aspiration, and assimilation, to alienation. These perspectives provide valuable insights for current discussions about how the global trade policy community can best adjust negotiation tactics to effectively influence Chinese behavior. Collectively, these two chapters provide invaluable accounts of Chinese perspectives, which tend to view Beijing as being exemplary in implementing WTO commitments and playing a constructive role in WTO negotiations. The two chapters also explain why China's perspective has evolved over time, especially in response to developments in the trading system that are regarded as unfair by China.

The second part (five chapters) proceeds to consider the political and economic implications of WTO membership for both China and the global trading system. In addition to examining the role of the WTO membership in fostering economic growth, promoting the rule of law, advancing intellectual property rights governance, and regulating export restrictions in China, contributing authors also consider its impact on global agricultural trade. By taking a "second image reversed" perspective that emphasizes the international sources of domestic changes (Gourevitch, 1978), this part helps to shed light on both the accomplishments and challenges that WTO membership has brought about to China and its trading partners.

In Chapter 3, Li, Liu, and Zhou utilize the synthetic control approach to assess the impact of WTO membership on China's economic growth. Specifically, the authors construct two control groups, including both donor pool A which consists of 9 economies that acceded to the WTO at least 5 years later than China, and donor pool B which includes 12 economies with similar WTO accession dates as China. This identification strategy enables the authors to address the counterfactual of what would have been the growth trajectory of China's economy in the absence of WTO membership and to assess the degree to which China's post-WTO growth is exceptional. The findings suggest that WTO membership has had a positive effect on China's economic growth, an effect that has become especially pronounced within ten years of accession.

The next three chapters in the second part further illuminate the "two-way socialization" between China and the WTO. Yu (Chapter 4) focuses on the interactions between the WTO and China's IPR regime. He details early efforts adopted by the Chinese government to bring its IPR regulations in line with the requirements of the WTO's TRIPS agreement. He further suggests that although Beijing's more recent IPR reforms were mainly motivated by a desire to promote indigenous innovation rather than responses to external pressure, it is not clear whether these improvements would have been possible within a short span of a decade in the absence of the positive incentives generated by the TRIPS agreement. This chapter additionally identifies areas in which progress in China's IPR protection has in turn positively affected developments within the global IPR regime, thus shedding light on the mutually reinforcing effects between China's domestic IPR landscape and global IPR norms.

China's WTO membership has also raised questions about the compatibility between its domestic legal system and the rules-based WTO system. Aldonas tackles this question in Chapter 5, documenting both the progress of and impediments to the development of the rule of law in China since its initial accession and their implications for the country's WTO compliance. The chapter further assesses the potential for using claims of non-violation nullification and impairment to address trade concerns with China to not only induce Chinese compliance with "the letter of law," but also ensure that Beijing meets the expectations of WTO members regarding the benefits of its membership. Similar to the Yu chapter, this chapter provides a good illustration of the "two-way socialization" involving the role of WTO jurisprudence in affecting legal changes in China, on the one hand, and the effect of domestic reforms in China on its WTO compliance, on the other.

In Chapter 6, Glauber turns to an examination of the impact of China's WTO accession on global agricultural trade. In addition to providing an overview of the evolution of China's agricultural trade in the two decades since its accession, this chapter highlights the tensions between Chinese government policies designed to support the agriculture sector such as domestic support and export restrictions on the one hand and WTO disciplines on the other, noting in particular the challenges that recent WTO disputes involving agricultural and food products have presented to China's compliance with WTO trade rules. The chapter concludes by documenting the disruptions that the US-China trade war has generated for trade patterns and discussing the outlook of China's agricultural trade and trade policy.

Bogdanova and Wang analyze in Chapter 7 China's use of export restrictions in the period from 2001 to 2021. They suggest that, during this period, China's approach has shifted from the elimination of export restrictions before and immediately after joining the WTO, to the selective use of export restrictions for domestic policy reasons until 2016, and finally to the strategic use of export restrictions as an instrument of geopolitical competition in more recent years. The chapter discusses the economic and political reasons for the shift and the consistency of the measures under WTO law and concludes with thoughts on the broader implications of such measures for the future of the multilateral trading system.

Part III of this volume shifts from discussions of the impact of the WTO on China to the country's role in the WTO. The first three chapters in this part highlight the tensions that China's self-identification as a developing country has generated for not only the WTO's key principles but also for China's relations with the Global South. For example, Hopewell (Chapter 8) argues that China's rise has accentuated the incompatibilities between the WTO's core principles of reciprocity and universality, on the one hand, and preferential treatment for developing countries, on the other. By emphasizing how the U.S. demand for the former and China's insistence on the latter have impaired core WTO negotiation functions, including the Doha Round negotiations and efforts to revitalize global rules, this chapter illustrates how the "China paradox" has fueled the U.S.-China power competition and created serious challenges to global trade governance.

The next two chapters (Chapter 9 by Weinhardt and Chapter 10 by Liang and Zeng) turn attention to the interactions between China and other developing and emerging economies within the WTO. A common theme that runs through these two chapters is that despite its self-proclaimed developing country status, the concrete differences in the negotiation preferences and approaches between the two have undermined their ability to act as a cohesive group. This has increased the fragmentation of the power structure within the WTO, further complicating the processes of multilateral trade negotiations. Specifically, Weinhardt assesses China's role in negotiations related to development issues through a detailed analysis of China's negotiation behavior in the WTO's Trade Negotiation Committee and Member perceptions of China's role. Her findings suggest that despite China's attempts to position itself as a developing country member, it has increasingly been perceived as both a partner and competitor of developing countries on issues such as agricultural subsidies and SDT. This new conflict line reinforced the old North-South divide and, along with the growing heterogeneity of developing country interests in the WTO, has magnified existing tensions within the WTO regime.

The Liang and Zeng chapter echoes the above argument. By tracing the involvement of China and the rest of the BRICS countries in two ongoing WTO negotiations, specifically, those relating to e-commerce and fisheries subsidies, the authors show that the divide between developed and developing countries that has frequently led to negotiation impasses in the past has given way to a more complex pattern of power configurations featuring competitions among developed countries, emerging economies less China, China as an outlier, and least developed countries. In the e-commerce negotiations, China's strong preferences for maintaining domestic regulatory sovereignty distinguished its position from those of Brazil and India. Along with the refusal by India and South Africa to join the talks, these divergent preferences have limited the group's ability to act as a coherent bloc. In the fisheries subsidies negotiations, China's insistence to be treated as a developing country and enjoy SDT despite its status as the largest subsidizer has impeded progress toward an agreement. Its negotiation position has been rejected by both developed countries openly and BIS (Brazil, India, and South Africa) subtly. The growing fragmentation of power within the WTO has therefore exacerbated the difficulties of multilateral trade negotiations.

The fourth chapter (Chapter 11 by Zhou) focuses on the important issue of China's involvement in the WTO dispute settlement mechanism. It argues that in spite of concerns about the incompatibilities between China's model of state capitalism and the rules-based WTO system, China has managed to maintain a generally good record of compliance with adverse WTO rulings and demonstrated a growing understanding of how to deal with them. While there remain areas of continued concerns with China's compliance record, these challenges are rooted more deeply in broader issues inherent in the WTO dispute settlement system. According to Zhou, these findings reinforce the importance of developing a well-functioning WTO dispute settlement system as a useful tool for managing the growing trade frictions between China and its trading partners.

The last contribution (Chapter 12 by Hoekman, Tu, and Wolfe) explores the potential for WTO reform which is vital to effective global trade governance through an examination of the positions of three leading players, that is, the United States, the European Union, and China on this issue. Based on analyses of an original survey of trade policy experts, this chapter reveals both the points of convergence and divergence among the three on issues such as transparency, plurilateral negotiations, SDT, subsidies, WTO operations, and dispute settlement. By shedding light on the perspectives and positions of the three largest economies, this chapter contributes to a better understanding of the alignment (or the lack of it) across the three which is indispensable to efforts designed to foster com promise and cooperation and facilitate the effective resolution of the problems of the WTO.

Overall, we can see that since its accession, China has been learning the culture of the WTO and, as it gradually mastered the rules of the game, it has started to better formulate its own positions, build coalitions, and exploit the loopholes in the dispute settlement system. While such an enhanced level of sophistication could occasionally make it more difficult for WTO members to reach deals, China has largely played a constructive role, and a negotiating approach that tries to work with China could still produce meaningful results, as the latest outcomes on fisheries subsidies and waiver on IP rights on the vaccine at the 12th Ministerial Conference have shown.

China's WTO accession has also had major impacts on its trading partners. Part IV (five chapters) addresses this issue by probing the responses of China's trading partners, including both governments and private citizens, to its economic rise. In addition to examining individual attitudes toward trade with China, including both trade cooperation generally and PTAs specifically, contributing authors also highlight trading partner actions targeting Chinese exports since its WTO accession as well as U.S. trade policy toward China going all the way back to the Clinton administration and up to the Trump and Biden administrations.

In Chapter 13, using original survey data, Raess investigates the power of economic and political models in explaining Swiss citizens' attitudes toward specific cases of preferential trade liberalization, contrasting individual determinants in the North-South and North-North PTA contexts (the China–Switzerland PTA and EU-Switzerland bilateral agreements, respectively). As North-South trade, particularly preferential liberalization with China, has stronger distributional effects and raises concerns about social standards, he expects and finds standard trade and partisan models to be more effective in explaining attitudes toward North-South than North-North PTAs. Specifically, the level of support for the Sino-Swiss PTA is significantly lower than that for the EU-Switzerland agreement among the losers of international trade. At the same time, compensatory welfare and labor market policies (or belief in it) strongly increase support for the Sino-Swiss PTA among losers. Finally, support for the China–Switzerland PTA is lower among left-leaning compared to right-leaning individuals, reflecting a rift between left and non-left parties over the desirability of the agreement.

The second study on individual attitudes, by Schweinberger and Sattler (Chapter 14), employs a survey experimental design to examine how the publics in the US, Germany, and Australia assess trade cooperation with different trading partner countries. China is increasingly viewed as a political adversary of the US and the West. The authors probe whether being an ally/adversary influences individuals' level of support for cooperative trade policy initiatives. The findings are that while reciprocity plays an important role in shaping individual attitudes toward trade irrespective of the identity of the trading partner, its impact is significantly reduced when the trading partner is an adversary such as China and Russia instead of an ally of the home country. The chapters by Raess and by Schweinberger and Sattler suggest that both domestic policies that compensate the losers of trade and the nature of political relations among trading partners are critical to revive or sustain bilateral trade cooperation with China.

Evenett (Chapter 15) draws on the Global Trade Alert Database to examine unilateral measures adopted by foreign trade partners targeting Chinese manufacturing exports since the Global Financial Crisis. While the chapter's main contribution is to document foreign governments' policy responses, the insightful interpretations of the findings yield highly instructive policy implications for the disciplining effect (or the lack thereof) of WTO rules and for the ability of the WTO to protect members' trade benefits. Given the rapid growth of China's exports since its WTO accession, the sheer size of those exports, and the disruptions to local labor markets in countries exposed to Chinese exports, or the so-called "China shock" (Autor et al., 2013), the author contends that reactions by trading partners were to be expected. The key question is whether the share of Chinese goods exports exposed to foreign trade distortions has been greater than for other countries. The analysis shows that this has indeed been the case, suggesting that China has been prevented from reaping the full benefits of its WTO membership. This might in turn temper China's willingness to take on more multilateral trade obligations in the future.

The last two chapters in this part (Part IV) turn to US government responses to China's growing economic challenges. While Lester and Zhu (Chapter 16) focus on the Biden administration's trade policy toward China, Hillman (Chapter 17) evaluates the argument that bringing China into the WTO reflects a failure of US policy. Specifically, Lester and Zhu assess the degree to which the Biden administration's trade policy toward China differs from that of the Trump administration and identify a set of factors, such as the debate between decoupling and recoupling, the role of the state in the Chinese economy, and the policy conflicts within the Democratic party, that may influence the former's approach as well as the future trajectory of US-China relations. Hillman in turn explains the discrepancy between many politicians' expectations of what China's WTO membership can deliver and what can realistically be achieved given China's WTO obligations. Viewing the rise of unilateral trade policy approaches in the United States as Washington's reactions to the rise of China and the perceived failures of the WTO, this chapter underscores the importance of embracing multiple approaches, including efforts to revitalize multilateral rules and to encourage bilateral and plurilateral dialogues, for addressing the competitive challenges China poses to US security and economic interests. These two chapters provide a nice contrast to the earlier chapters by Gao, and Li and Yi. On the one hand, they juxtaposed the changing perspectives of the US versus those of China: while for China, it only needs to follow the letter of its commitments; for the US, China also needs to follow the spirit of the WTO rules. On the other hand, these two sets of contributions reveal that neither the American nor the Chinese perspectives remain static. Instead, both have been evolving, not only in response to domestic politics but also more importantly, to the changing trade policies adopted by the other side. Any discussion of the evolution of a country's trade policies would not be complete without understanding this feedback loop.

While the above parts focus mainly on traditional trade-related issues, the last part (Part V) expands the scope of analysis further to investment governance, which often goes in tandem with trade and has become a hot issue in the WTO in recent years. Trade agreements nowadays increasingly include investment chapters and policymakers often use trade and investment policies interchangeably, as can be seen in China's Belt and Road Initiative to boost its foreign trade and investment despite restrictions employed by the US to deal with what they perceive as unfair trade practices by China. Moreover, investment also provides a good example of how China has been transplanting the negotiation skills it has acquired in the trade forum to other fora. In addition to examining the evolution of the regimes governing both China's inward and outward foreign direct investment and shifts in Chinese firms' investment patterns, contributing authors also analyze China's approach to BITs, its involvement in investor-state arbitration cases, and its position on investor-state dispute settlement. The review of China's role in the global investment regime suggests that it has generally been supportive of existing rules governing investment facilitation and that such preferences are frequently driven by a desire to promote China's foreign economic policy agenda. This part additionally evaluates the role of existing WTO law in regulating investment-related technology transfer and diffusion among China, the West, and other developing countries, highlighting how the similarities and differences in geopolitical, commercial, and ideological interests among the three shape the prospect of international negotiations on this issue.

Chapter 18 by Erie and Zhang compares the legal and regulatory regimes for governing foreign direct investment into and overseas direct investment (ODI) out of China. Drawing from an analysis of hundreds of Chinese normative documents, they find that, at a general level, China's FDI regime has transitioned from restrictive to lenient, whereas the ODI regime has evolved from lenient to restrictive. The authors note in particular that such discrepancies could generate detrimental environmental impacts on the overseas projects of Chinese firms.

In Chapter 19, Berger investigates whether China assumes the role of a rule-taker, a rule-maker, or even a rule-breaker in the international investment regime. After reviewing the evolution of China's international investment policy in four distinct phases, he argues that it has acted as a rule-taker by broadly accepting the templates of its treaty partners while sticking to a number of defensive lines. He concludes that the trend has continued in the current phase, despite new developments such as the signing of the China-EU Comprehensive Agreement on Investment and Beijing's active role in the WTO agreement on investment facilitation.

Berger's "rule-taker" thesis seems to be confirmed by Chi's analysis in Chapter 20, which provides a comprehensive study of China and the investor-state dispute settlement (ISDS) mechanism. Chi starts by reviewing ISDS cases involving China and the main legal issues and then proceeds to examine China's position on the ongoing ISDS reform, based on its position paper submitted to the United Nations Commission for International Trade Law (UNCITRAL) Working Group III. The chapter concludes that, despite the rising number of ISDS cases against China, China still supports ISDS and its further judicialization, including the addition of an appellate mechanism.

In Chapter 21, Kim analyzes the impact of the US-China trade war on the investments of Chinese firms. Through an examination of the investment patterns of Chinese firms between 2010 and 2020, this chapter notes that Chinese firms have shifted their investments away from the US to other countries and regions since the onset of the trade war. However, there have been less noticeable changes in the sectoral patterns and types of activities of Chinese investments. While the chapter focuses mainly on investment activities, its findings could also help inform the analysis of firms' trading activities in the future.

One frequent complaint against China's investment policies is the alleged forced transfer of technology, which is explored by Cottier in Chapter 22. After first noting that existing WTO law offers a broad and sound basis for regulating technology in domestic law, the chapter proceeds to discuss the emerging doctrine and principle of the common concerns of humankind and identify the following as potential areas of continued and enhanced bilateral and multilateral cooperation on technology and knowledge transfer: climate change mitigation and adaption, biodiversity, and combating global pandemics. The chapter concludes by calling the WTO to develop a proactive trade and investment-related agenda for negotiations enabling and supporting recognized common concerns of humankind.

Twenty years have elapsed since China's entry into the WTO. Compared to China's first decade in the WTO, the second decade has seen both changes and continuities in China's interactions with the organization. Noticeably, the second decade has witnessed rising tensions between China and its trading partners both inside and outside of the trade regime. Within the WTO, China's distinctive model of state capitalism and its self-identification as a developing country have increasingly put it on a collision course with major powers such as the United States. The growing divergences between its interests and those of developing and emerging economies have further undermined the solidarity among the global South, further exacerbating the challenges of effective multilateral trade governance. The mounting China challenge has additionally contributed to the crisis of the WTO and, outside of the organization, the rise of unilateral approaches that heightened the conflict between China and partner countries.

Despite growing tensions, however, there are also signs that the WTO has positively affected China's domestic development, albeit with ongoing challenges. Furthermore, as some contributors have pointed out, far from being a rule-breaker, Beijing has continued to operate within the parameters of existing global rules in areas such as WTO dispute settlement, the negotiation of bilateral investment treaties, or investor-state dispute settlement. In other words, there remain areas of cooperation between Beijing and the global trade community at a time when China and its major trading partners in the democratic world are entering into a period of sustained competition, rivalry, and conflict. Such a mixture of conflictual and cooperative dynamics is likely to persist in the coming years, accentuating the importance for the international community to find opportunities to sustain cooperation in a way that accommodates Beijing's development aspirations.

References

Autor, David, David Dorn, and Gordon H. Hanson (2013). The China syndrome: local labor market effects of import competition in the United States. *American Economic Review* 103(6): 2121–68.

Breslin, Shaun (2007). *China and the Global Political Economy.* New York: Palgrave Macmillan.

Checkel, Jeffrey T. (2005). International institutions and socialization in Europe. *International Organization* 59(4): 801–26.

Colantone, Italo and Piero Stanig (2018). The trade origins of economic nationalism: import competition and voting behavior in Western Europe. *American Journal of Political Science* 62: 936–53.

Ferdinand, Peter (2016). Westward Ho – the China dream and 'one belt, one road': Chinese foreign policy under Xi Jinping. *International Affairs* 92(4): 941–57.

Gao, Henry (2011). China's ascent in global trade governance: from rule taker to rule shaker, and maybe rule maker?. In Birkbeck, Carolyn D. (ed.), *Making Global Trade Governance Work for Development: Perspectives and Priorities from Developing Countries.* Cambridge: Cambridge University Press, pp. 153–80.

Gourevitch, Peter (1978). Second image reversed: the international sources of domestic politics. *International Organization* 32(4): 881–912.

Hopewell, Kirsten (2020). *Clash of Powers: US-China Rivalry in Global Trade Governance.* New York: Cambridge University Press.

Johnston, Alastair Iain (2001). Treating international institutions as social environments. *International Studies Quarterly* 45(4): 487–515.

Mavroidis, Petros C., and Andre Sapir (2021). *China and the WTO: Why Multilateralism Still Matters.* Princeton: Princeton University Press.

Raess, Damian (2021). The demand-side politics of China's global buying spree: managers' attitudes toward Chinese inward FDI flows in comparative perspective. *Review of International Political Economy* 28(6): 1555–81.

Sandstrom, Kent L., Kathryn J. Lively, Daniel D. Martin, and Gary Alan Fine (2013). *Symbols, Selves, and Social Reality: A Symbolic Interactionist Approach to Social Psychology and Sociology.* New York: Oxford University Press.

Shaffer, Gregory, and Henry Gao (2020). A new Chinese economic order? *Journal of International Economic Law*, 23(3): 607–35.

Tu, Xinquan (2013). China's position and role in the Doha round negotiations. In Ka Zeng and Wei Liang (eds.), *China and Global Trade Governance: China's First Decade in the World Trade Organization.* London: Routledge, pp. 167–88.

Wu, Mark (2016). The "China, Inc." challenge to global trade governance. *Harvard International Law Journal* 57(2): 1001–63.

Zeng, Ka (ed.) (2019). *Handbook on the International Political Economy of China*. Cheltenham: Edward Elgar.

Zeng, Ka, and Wei Liang (eds.) (2013). *China and Global Trade Governance: China's First Decade in the World Trade Organization*. London: Routledge.

PART I

Setting the Stage: Chinese Perspectives on China's Accession to the WTO

1

20 Years On

China's Role in the Multilateral Trading System

SIQI LI AND XIAOZHUN YI

Joining the WTO was a major challenge for China in 2001. The conditions for China being a WTO member were broad, deep and even demanding. For its WTO accession, China made significant concessions. Beyond general WTO commitments for all the WTO memberships, there were some tailor-made provisions incorporated into China's accession to the WTO agreement, stipulating certain WTO-plus obligations and WTO-minus rights (Qin, 2010). It was not easy for China to fulfil such a grand international obligation in its entirety. However, the Chinese government took the challenge of WTO accession as an opportunity to promote domestic reform and opening up and made great efforts in studying and implementing WTO rules.

I China's Overall Implementation of WTO Commitments

To assess whether China has fulfilled its WTO commitments, the legal documents signed by China at the time of its WTO accession shall prevail, that is Protocol on the Accession to WTO of the People's Republic of China[1] (hereinafter referred to as the 'Accession Protocol') and Report of the Working Party on the Accession of China[2] (hereinafter referred to as the 'Working Party Report'). To fully fulfil its WTO commitments, China has undergone a comprehensive process of tremendous legal adjustments, substantive market opening up on goods and services, and relevant commitment implementation on intellectual property rights and transparency.

[1] WTO. WT/L/432, available at: www.wto.org.

[2] WTO. WT/ACC/CHN/49WT/ACC/CHN/49, available at: www.wto.org.

(i) Legal Adjustments

The WTO is an international economic organization based on rules. In order to achieve the consistency between the domestic trade law system and the WTO rules, China began to prepare for the adjustment of domestic laws since 1986 when it began the negotiation of 'Returning to GATT'. By carrying out a large-scale review and revision of domestic laws and regulations after China joined the WTO in 2001, the Chinese central government has cleaned up more than 2,300 laws, regulations and departmental regulations, and the local governments have cleaned up more than 190,000 local policies and regulations (The State Council Information Office of the People's Republic of China, 2018). The relevant legal adjustments include: the general foreign trade law and legislative law, as well as specific laws and regulations concerning trade in goods and services, intellectual property and foreign investment.

(ii) Fulfilment of Commitments in Trade in Goods

1 Tariff and Non-tariff Barriers Cut

Annex 8 to the Accession Protocol[3] is the tariff concession obligations for China. According to the Schedule of Concessions, China would reduce the total import tariff rate to 9.9 per cent within the transition period of six years after China's accession to the WTO. So far, China has fully implemented its tariff commitments and reduced the total import tariff further to 7.5 per cent in 2020, as indicated in Table 1.1.

Besides, as of January 2005, China had eliminated all non-tariff measures such as import quota, import licence and specific bidding requirement, involving 424 dutiable products including automobile, mechanical and electrical products, natural rubber and so on. Instead of traditional non-tariff measures, tariff quotas were introduced on bulk commodities related to the national economy and the people's livelihood such as wheat, corn, rice, sugar, cotton, wool, wool top and fertilizer. The Ministry of Commerce announces the quantity, the proportion of state-owned trade, the application condition and the distribution principle, etc., of the specific products subject to tariff quotas in the form of governmental proclamation annually, ensuring the transparency of tariff quota administration and the consistency with the WTO rules.

[3] WTO. WT/ACC/CHN/49/Add.1, available at: www.wto.org/english/thewto_e/acc_e/completeacc_e.htm#chn.

Table 1.1 *Tariff rates of China 2001–2020*

	Simple average MFN tariff applied (%)		
Year	Total	Agricultural products	Non-agricultural products
2001	15.3	18.8	14.7
2002	12.0	18.1	11.4
2003	11.0	16.8	10.3
2004	10.4	15.6	9.5
2005	9.9	15.3	9.0
2006	9.9	15.2	9.0
2007	9.84	15.2	8.95
2008	9.8	15.2	8.92
2009	9.8	15.2	8.9
2010	9.8	15.2	8.9
2011	9.8	15.2	8.9
2012	9.6	15.6	8.7
2013	9.9	15.6	9.0
2014	9.6	15.2	8.6
2015	9.9	15.6	9.0
2016	9.9	15.5	9.0
2017	9.8	15.6	8.8
2018	9.8	15.6	8.8
2019	7.6	13.9	6.5
2020	7.5	13.8	6.5

Source: WTO World Tariff Profiles 2002–2021, www.wto.org.

2 Right to Trade

Before China joined the WTO, the approval system for granting foreign trade rights restricted sufficient participation of enterprises in foreign trade. Since 1 July 2004, the original approval system changed to the registration system for granting foreign trade rights, and the scope of traders in China expanded to individuals. China has fully fulfilled its WTO commitment to liberalize the foreign trade rights and has been greatly releasing the foreign trade vitality of private enterprises. In 2020, there are 531,000 enterprises participating in foreign trade in China, with an increase of 6.2 per cent as compared with the previous year. Among them, the total trade volume of private enterprises reached 14.98 trillion

CNY, accounting for 46.6 per cent of China's total foreign trade. This shows the top position of private enterprises in China's foreign trade. Besides, the total trade volume of foreign-invested enterprises reached 12.44 trillion CNY, accounting for 38.7 per cent of China's total foreign trade (Xinhua Finance, 2021).

3 Subsidies

China has accepted certain specific subsidy commitments upon its WTO accession. For example, China committed that 'subsidies provided to state-owned enterprises will be viewed as specific if, inter alia, state-owned enterprises are the predominant recipients of such subsidies or state-owned enterprises receive disproportionately large amounts of such subsidies'. Meanwhile, China has foregone some special and differential treatment under Articles 27.8, 27.9 and 27.13 of the Agreement on Subsidies and Countervailing Measures (ASCM) that provide more subsidy space for developing countries.

In addition, China has regularly notified to the WTO of its domestic subsidy policies in accordance with the notification requirements of the ASCM. As of 27 August 2021, China has notified its domestic subsidy policies seven times to the WTO, covering the period of 2001–2020, as is shown in Table 1.2.

4 Agriculture

According to Article 12 of the Accession Protocol, China shall not maintain or introduce any export subsidies on agricultural products. Meanwhile, according to Section 235 of the Working Party Report, China would have recourse to a *de minimis* exemption for product-specific support equivalent to 8.5 per cent of the total value of a specific agricultural product and a *de minimis* exemption for non-specific product support equivalent to 8.5 per cent of the value of aggregate agricultural production in the relevant year. Such a *de minimis* level is lower than the 10 per cent allowed for developing members.

According to China Trade Policy Review Report released by the WTO Secretariat in June 2018,[4] China's average MFN tariff rate for agricultural products in 2017 is 14.8 per cent, which is well below the average tariff rate of 56 per cent of developing members and 39 per cent of developed members. China's average tariff rate for agricultural products has been reduced to 13.8 per cent in 2020. Besides, China submitted the latest notification of

[4] WTO. WT/TPR/S/375, available at: www.wto.org/english/tratop_e/tpr_e/s375_e.pdf.

Table 1.2 *Notifications of subsidy policies by China to the WTO (October 2001–2021)*

Date of notification	Document number	Duration covered	Number of subsidy policies	Government level
13 April 2006	G/SCM/N/123/CHN	2001–2004	78	Central Government
21 October 2011	G/SCM/N/155/CHN; G/SCM/N/186/CHN	2005–2008	93	Central Government
30 October 2015	G/SCM/N/220/CHN; G/SCM/N/253/CHN; G/SCM/N/284/CHN	2009–2014	86	Central Government
29 July 2016	G/SCM/N/123/CHN/suppl.1; G/SCM/ N/155/CHN/suppl.1; G/SCM/N/186/CHN/suppl.1; G/SCM/ N/220/CHN/suppl.1; G/SCM/N/253/CHN/suppl.1; G/SCM/N/284/CHN/suppl.1	2001–2014	100	Local Government
19 July 2018	G/SCM/N/315/CHN	2015–2016	Central Government: 82; Local Government: 108	Central and Local Governments
19 July 2019	G/SCM/N/343/CHN	2017–2018	Central Government: 79; Local Government: 420	Central and Local Governments
27 August 2021	G/SCM/N/372/CHN	2019–2020	Central Government: 71; Local Government: 374	Central and Local Governments

Source: www.wto.org/english/tratop_e/scm_e/scm_e.htm.

Table 1.3 *Number of trade remedy investigations involving China, 1995–2020*

Investigation	Number of investigations against China	Proportion (%)	Number of investigations by China	Proportion (%)
Anti-dumping	1,478	23.46	292	4.63
Countervailing	189	29.91	17	2.69
Safeguard	400 (total investigations)	100	2	0.5

Source: www.wto.org/english/tratop_e/adp_e/adp_e.htm.

agricultural subsidies on 14 December 2018,[5] covering agricultural subsidies up to 2016. According to China's notifications, the green box subsidies were 1.31 trillion CNY, and the blue box subsidies were 39.039 billion CNY. The above two categories of subsidies are not subject to WTO subsidy commitments. In addition, China notified amber box subsidies for specific agricultural products, that is corn, cotton, rapeseed, rice, root crops, soybean, wheat, cattle, pigs and sheep, and notified amber box subsidies for non-specific agricultural products (25.759 billion CNY). Except for terminated amber box subsidies for corn, cotton and soybean, other amber box subsidies for specific agricultural products and non-specific agricultural products did not exceed the *de minimis* exemption level of 8.5 per cent.

5 Trade Remedies

After its WTO accession, China amended and enacted the domestic trade remedy laws in order to make the domestic laws and regulations consistent with the WTO rules. Meanwhile, China has been reporting to the WTO of the amendment of trade remedy laws and the implementation of trade remedy measures in a timely manner.

According to WTO statistics from 1995 to 2020, China was the top target country by foreign anti-dumping and countervailing investigations, but at the same time, China was very cautious to launch trade remedy investigations, accounting for a relatively low proportion of global trade remedy investigations, as is shown in Table 1.3.

In addition, China has accepted certain China-specific rules on trade remedies, including: (i) a special textile safeguard mechanism (which

[5] WTO. G/AG/N/CHN/47, available at: https://docs.wto.org/dol2fe/Pages/SS/directdoc.aspx?filename=q:/G/AG/NCHN47.pdf&Open=True.

expired on 11 December 2008)[6] and a transitional product-specific safeguard mechanism (which expired on 11 December 2013)[7]; (ii) WTO members are authorized to apply the 'surrogate country' methodology in anti-dumping cases against China for a period of 15 years following China's accession to the WTO[8] and (iii) WTO members are authorized to use 'external bench-mark' to determine subsidies in countervailing duty cases against China.[9]

6 Investment Measures

The WTO rules concerning investment measures are mainly embodied in two aspects: one is the Agreement on Trade-Related Investment Measures (hereinafter referred to as the TRIM Agreement) in relation to trade in goods, and the other is the General Agreement on Trade in Services in respect of trade in services.

According to Section 203 of the Working Party Report, China has to fully abide by the TRIM Agreement to cancel the foreign exchange balance requirements, trade balance requirements, local content requirements and export performance requirements. Furthermore, China has committed to provide national treatment to both foreign products and persons, while the normal WTO national treatment clauses only cover measures applicable to products.

In order to fulfil these commitments, China amended the Law of the People's Republic of China on Foreign-capital Enterprises, the Law of the People's Republic of China on Chinese-Foreign Equity Joint Ventures and the Law of the People's Republic of China on Chinese-Foreign Contractual Joint Ventures before China joined the WTO, eliminating the original investment requirements not conforming to its WTO commitments.

In addition to fulfilling its TRIM Agreement commitments, China also implemented the opening up policy for foreign investment on its own. On 3 September 2016, the Standing Committee of the National People's Congress issued the 'Decision on Amending the Four Laws Including the Law of the People's Republic of China on Foreign-capital Enterprises', stipulating that the original approval system for the establishment of foreign-capital enterprises, Chinese-Foreign Joint Ventures, Chinese-Foreign cooperative enterprises and Taiwan-invested enterprises shall be changed to the register administration when no special market access

6 The Working Party Report, Paragraph 242.
7 The Accession Protocol, Article 16.
8 The Accession Protocol, Article 15(a) and 15(d).
9 The Accession Protocol, Article 15(b).

administrative measures are involved. On 28 June 2018, China issued the nationwide Special Administrative Measures (Negative List) for Foreign Investment Access (Edition 2018) for the first time, providing that all kinds of entities can enjoy access to Chinese market equally except for those sectors and businesses that are covered by the Negative List. On 1 January 2020, China enacted the new Foreign Investment Law that replaced the three previous laws, that is the Law of the People's Republic of China on Foreign-capital Enterprises, the Law of the People's Republic of China on Chinese-Foreign Equity Joint Ventures and the Law of the People's Republic of China on Chinese-Foreign Contractual Joint Ventures, aiming to provide clarity on foreign investment policies. The new Foreign Investment Law consolidated the legal status of pre-establishment national treatment and negative list for foreign direct investment (FDI), showing the determination of China to open up market to foreign investment.

China's implementation of these commitments and further opening up on its own have created an open and fair competition environment for foreign investment in China. After joining the WTO, the FDI in China has increased from US$46.88 billion in 2001 to US$136.32 billion in 2017, with an annual growth rate of 6.9 per cent (The State Council Information Office of the People's Republic of China, 2018). Comparing a sharp drop in FDI globally, the FDI in China has rose to US$144.37 billion with an increase of 4.5 per cent in 2020. In the same year, the FDI in the service sector reached 776.77 billion CNY with an increase of 13.9 per cent, accounting for 77.7 per cent of total FDI in China. Meanwhile, the FDI in high-tech manufacturing sector increased by 11.4 per cent and FDI in high-tech service sector grew by 28.5 per cent (MOFCOM, 2021).

China's improvement on investment environment has gained recognition from foreign enterprises. According to China Business Climate Survey Report 2021 published by American Chamber of Commerce in China, 61 per cent of the American enterprises surveyed list China as the primary investment destination and show confidence about China further opening its market. Eighty-three per cent of the American enterprises surveyed respond that they are not considering shifting business outside China (AmChamChina, 2021). The Business Confidence Survey 2021 published by the European Union Chamber of Commerce in China points out 'the resilience of China's market provided much-needed shelter for European companies amidst the storm of the COVID-19 pandemic'. Sixty-eight per cent of European companies in China are optimistic about growth, and 60 per cent of European companies plan to expand their business in China in 2021 with nearly 10 per cent increase compared with that of 2020.

Seventy-three per cent of European companies still report positive earnings, with another 14 per cent breaking even. A quarter of European manufacturers intend to further onshore some of their supply chains into China, with 4 per cent attempting to fully onshore (European Chamber, 2021).

(iii) Fulfilment of Commitments in Trade in Services

In accordance with Annex 9 to the Accession Protocol, China committed itself to opening up 100 sub-sectors in nine major sectors of trade in services by 2007. The number of sectors China committed to open was significantly above the average (54 sub-sectors) of developing countries and close to that (108 sub-sectors) of developed countries. Such a level of commitment was regarded as 'the most radical services reform programme negotiated in the WTO' (Mattoo, 2003).

In terms of opening up service market, China has implemented a series of market opening measures in major service sectors including banking, insurance, securities, tourism, telecommunication, education, medical service and construction. By 2019, banks from fifty-five countries and regions have set up offices in China, and banks from all six continents have set up business establishments in China. The total assets of foreign banks in China reached 3.48 trillion CNY and their annual net profit reached 21.613 billion CNY (Xinhua Finance, 2020). By 2020, foreign insurance institutions have set up 66 foreign-funded insurance institutions, 117 representative offices and 17 professional insurance intermediaries in China, with total assets of 1.71 trillion CNY (China Economic Net, 2021). In addition, from 1 April 2020, the restriction on foreign ownership of securities companies has been lifted and the proportion of foreign ownership in securities companies can be up to 100 per cent.

(iv) Fulfilment of Commitments for Protection of Intellectual Property Rights

Intellectual property right (IPR) protection has always been one key issue for China, which is also the area where other countries have concerns about China. After China's accession to the WTO, in order to fully fulfil its WTO commitments and keep the domestic IPR laws in line with the WTO rules, China has successively amended the Trademark Law, Patent Law and Copyright Law several times, and has promulgated the Regulations for the Protection of Layout design of Integrated Circuits and amended the Regulations for the Protection of Computer Software.

In terms of law enforcement, China has re-established the National Intellectual Property Administration and set up intellectual property courts and specialized adjudication institutions to enhance law enforcement and punishment for IPR cases, providing effective civil, administrative and criminal remedies for IPR holders. From 1998 to 2020, the National Intellectual Property Administration published the White Paper on China's IPR Protection annually. China's progress on IPR protection has been widely recognized by foreign communities. According to China Business Climate Survey Report 2020 published by American Chamber of Commerce in China, 69 per cent of American enterprises surveyed believe that China's IPR protection has been improved. The Business Confidence Survey 2020 published by the European Union Chamber of Commerce in China shows that 67 per cent of the European enterprises surveyed rate the effectiveness of China's laws and regulations on IPR protection as 'excellent' or 'adequate'.

(v) Transparency

Transparency is a basic principle of the WTO. China's transparency obligations are mainly stipulated in Article 2(c) of the Accession Protocol and Sections 331 through 336 of the Working Party Report. After China's accession to the WTO, it has completed the following tasks in fulfilling the transparency obligations: (1) Enhancing transparency in the Legislative Process. China has formulated, promulgated and implemented the Legislation Law of the People's Republic of China, the Regulations on Procedures for the Formulation of Administrative Regulations and the Regulations on Procedures for the Formulation of Rules. These laws and regulations contain provisions on transparency and stipulate the uniform implementation of national laws and regulations. (2) Regularly issuing publications of trade-related laws and regulations. The official publications of China to promulgate trade-related laws, regulations and measures include the Gazette of the Standing Committee of the National People's Congress,[10] the State Council Gazette,[11] the Catalogue of laws in force issued by the National People's Congress,[12] China Foreign Trade and Economic Cooperation Gazette,[13]

[10] Available at: www.npc.gov.cn/wxzlhgb/index.shtml.

[11] Available at: www.gov.cn/gongbao/2021/issue_9346.htm.

[12] Available at: www.npc.gov.cn/npc/c30834/202101/170eaa5d4a994214aaf88e5dfac97665.shtml.

[13] Available at: www.mofcom.gov.cn/article/b/g/.

the Proclamation of the People's Bank of China,[14] the Proclamation of the Ministry of Finance[15] and so on. In addition, China committed to translate all foreign trade laws into one of the WTO official languages, while the general transparency obligation in the WTO agreements only requires members to publish trade laws and regulations in their own national languages. (3) Designating national Enquiry Points. The Chinese government has established the 'WTO Enquiry Point'[16] within the Ministry of Commerce to provide information for public queries related to the WTO. In addition, the Chinese government has established the 'WTO/TBT-SPS Notification and Enquiry of China' website[17] under the General Administration of Customs to publish technical trade measures and answer public inquiries. (4) Undergoing a special transitional review mechanism operated annually since China's accession to

Table 1.4 *China's notifications to the WTO 2001–2021*

Notification theme	Number of notifications
Agriculture	57
Anti-dumping	58
Customs valuation	8
Import licensing	27
TRIPS	28
Regional trade agreement	44
Rules of origin	22
Safeguard	17
SPS measures	1,415
Trade in services	125
State trading enterprises	7
Subsidies and countervailing measures	39
TBT measures	1,804
Textile	36
Trade and development	8
Total	3,695

Source: www.wto.org/english/thewto_e/countries_e/china_e.htm#OTHNotDocs.

14 Available at: www.pbc.gov.cn/tiaofasi/144941/144959/index.html.
15 Available at: www.mof.gov.cn/gkml/bulinggonggao/czbgg/.
16 Available at: http://chinawto.mofcom.gov.cn/.
17 Available at: www.tbt-sps.gov.cn/page/cwtoz/Indexquery.action.

the WTO, with the final review taking place in 2011 to examine the first 10 years of China's WTO membership.

Besides the above transparency measures, China has been conscientiously fulfilling its notification obligations. As of 18 August 2021, China had submitted 3,695 notifications to the WTO, as detailed in Table 1.4.

II China's Contribution to the World Economy and Trade

(i) China Acts as a Driving Force for the World Economy

Although China made significant concessions upon WTO accession, accepted certain tailor-made obligations and gave up some special and differential treatment for developing countries, China still has been honouring its WTO commitments, expanding market access, improving business environment and making positive contribution to world trade and economic development.

China's implementation of WTO commitments and its broader opening up policy have accelerated its integration into the world economy and made it a critical part of global value chains. China is now the second largest economy in the world, with a dramatic increase of GDP from US$1.339 trillion in 2001 to US$14.723 trillion in 2020.[18] The GDP value of China represents 17.4 per cent of the world economy in 2020. Meanwhile, China has become the leading trading nation. From 2001 to 2020, China's exports rose by nearly 8.74 times from US$266.1 billion to US$2,590.6 billion, while imports climbed by nearly 7.44 times from US$243.55 billion to US$2,055.59 billion (Figure 1.1). It presents a striking example of how opening an economy can boost productivity, the adaptation of modern technologies and international competitiveness.

In addition, China's integration into the world economy was marked by huge waves of FDI focusing on manufacturing for export and, increasingly, for its enormous and rapidly growing domestic market. The inflows of FDI to China totalled US$144.4 billion in 2020, representing an annual increase of 5.8 per cent since 2001.[19] Increasing numbers of foreign enterprises have established research and development centres, manufacturing factories and marketing branches in China, stimulating China's trade from foreign-owned subsidiaries as well. Following the surge in inflows of FDI, China's outward FDI has increased rapidly. In 2020, China's

[18] The World Bank website, available at: https://data.worldbank.org/indicator/NY.GDP.MKTP.CD?locations=CN. The GDP data is in current US$ term.

[19] The National Bureau of Statistics of China, available at: www.stats.gov.cn/tjsj/tjgb/ndtjgb/.

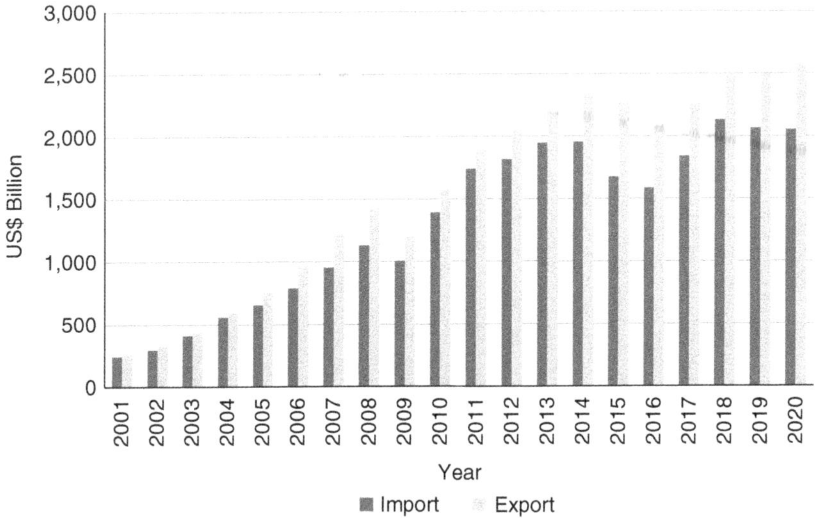

Figure 1.1 China's annual foreign trade, 2001–2020
Source: UN Comtrade Database, available at: https://comtrade.un.org/data/.

outward FDI reached US$110.2 billion, with an annual increase of 18.91 per cent since 2005 (Figure 1.2).

In return, China's dramatic growth has been a critical driving force for the world economy. Despite the weakened world economy following the 2008 financial crisis, the Chinese economy remains the single largest contributor to the world economic growth, contributing nearly 30 per cent of global growth on annual average. In the wake of current COVID-19 crisis worldwide, China became the only major economy in the world to achieve positive economic growth in 2020. According to the World Bank calculation, the world economy has declined by 3.593 per cent, with China's economic rebound by 3.1 per cent.[20] Being the first to gain the momentum for recovery, China has made contributions to stabilizing the global supply chain and driving the world economy to recover.

China's deeply embedded position in global value chains is broadly benefiting other countries. First, China has quickly gotten involved in the global supply chain and successfully upgraded from low-end industrial products that are resource-intensive and labour-intensive to

[20] The World Bank website, available at: https://data.worldbank.org/indicator/NY.GDP.MKTP.CD.

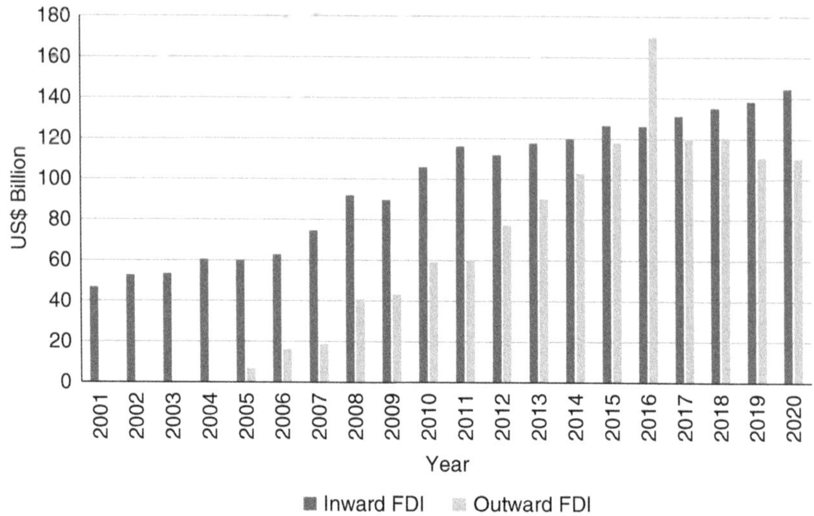

Figure 1.2 China's inward and outward FDI, 2001–2020
Note: The inflows of FDI data represent the actual use of FDI and does not include the FDI in banking, securities and insurance sectors. The outward FDI data can be traced back to 2005 and does not include the FDI in financial sector.
Source: The National Bureau of Statistics of China, available at: www.stats.gov.cn/tjsj/tjgb/ndtjgb/.

more sophisticated industrial products that are capital-intensive and technology-intensive. As the world largest exporter, the share of high-technology manufactures in China's exports has been growing from next to nothing in 1980 to 31 per cent in 2019.[21] Second, China is a major consumer market with the world's largest middle-class consumers. As the fastest growing economy with strong demand for raw materials, advanced machinery and consumer products, China has become an even more important source of global demand, stimulating other economies' growth. Third, China's industrial upgrading and expanding trade will lead to further specialization and increased efficiency in world markets, and its increasingly educated labour force will become a force for global innovation, which have benefited developed and developing countries alike (The World Bank and Development Research Center of the State Council, the People's Republic of China, 2013).

[21] The World Bank website, available at: https://data.worldbank.org/indicator/TX.VAL.TECH.MF.ZS?end=2020&name_desc=false&start=2007.

(ii) China Plays a Constructive Role in Multilateral Trading System

China's significant rise has changed other countries' perceptions of what is at stake in the global trading system. As China rises as a global power, it is naturally expected that China should play a larger role in global institutions (Wolfe, 2015). For decades, China has gradually translated its trade ascendancy into significant influences in the WTO.

As a firm supporter of the multilateral trading system, China's contribution to the WTO is obvious to all. First of all, China's WTO membership has contributed to making the WTO a relevant and truly global organization. Without China, with its 1.3 billion people and enormous market as a major trading nation, the WTO would be incomplete (Sun, 2011). On the one hand, China's accession to the WTO set a good example for the WTO to encourage more developing countries to join. Following China's accession, Cambodia, Vietnam, Laos and other developing countries became WTO members later on. On the other hand, China's active participation in WTO negotiations and its strong support for the legitimate positions of the least developed countries (LDCs), African, Caribbean and Pacific Group of States, the African Group and other groupings of developing countries make the WTO more inclusive, representative and legitimate. Since China's accession, the WTO membership has expanded from 143 to 164 members, with most of the 'recently acceded members' being developing countries. The participation of developing countries has led to the WTO leadership being more balanced (Li and Tu, 2018).

Second, China has taken an active part in key aspects of the WTO since its accession. Regarding the WTO negotiation function, China is an important contributor to the successful conclusion of the Trade Facilitation Agreement (TFA) and has voluntarily given up some preferential treatment of TFA for developing members. For example, China did not designate any Category C measures and agreed to implement 94.5 per cent of the measures immediately upon ratification. All of its Category B measures were fully implemented by January 2020.[22] China has been participating in all 'Joint Statement Initiatives' (JSIs) including

[22] The TFA includes three categories of implementation time frames. Category A includes provisions that the WTO member will implement by the time the Agreement enters into force, Category B includes provisions that the WTO member will implement after a transitional period following the entry into force of the Agreement and Category C includes provisions that the WTO member will implement on a date after a transitional period following the entry into force of the Agreement and requiring the acquisition of assistance and support for capacity building.

negotiations on Investment Facilitation for Development, E-commerce, Services Domestic Regulation as well as Micro-, Small- and Medium-Sized Enterprises. China is also the driving member to promote the Informal Dialogue on Plastics Pollution and Environmentally Sustainable Plastics Trade.

Regarding the WTO judicial function, China has seriously implemented WTO dispute rulings. Since the establishment of the WTO in 1995, as of August 2021, WTO members have initiated 605 dispute cases in total, among which the USA and the EU are the most active members. The USA initiated 124 cases (20.5 per cent of the total) as complainant and was sued by 156 cases (25.8 per cent of the total) as respondent. The EU initiated 105 cases (17.4 per cent of the total) as complainant and was sued by 88 cases (14.5 per cent of the total) as respondent. China is at the third position, initiating twenty-two cases (3.6 per cent of the total) as complainant and being sued by forty-seven cases (7.8 per cent of the total).[23] If we only calculate the dispute cases since China's accession to the WTO in 2001, as of August 2021, the number of disputes initiated by the USA and the EU was 55 and 49, and the number of disputes targeting the USA and the EU was 100 and 55, which are much higher than the number of cases initiated by or targeting China. Regarding the implementation of WTO dispute rulings, during 1995–2020, the WTO issued twenty-five arbitration decisions authorizing retaliation against non-compliant respondents in nineteen dispute cases according to Article 22.6 of the Understanding on Rules and Procedures Governing the Settlement of Disputes. The relevant non-compliant respondents are the USA (18 arbitration decisions), the EU (5 arbitration decisions), Brazil (1 arbitration decision) and Canada (1 arbitration decision). China has never been targeted by any WTO arbitration decision authorizing retaliation, reflecting China's good implementation record of WTO dispute rulings.

Third, China has taken an active part in various development assistance and aid for trade programmes of the WTO. For example, China and the WTO signed a Memorandum of Understanding in 2011 to establish the China's LDCs and Accessions Programme. This programme is aimed at strengthening LDCs' participation in the WTO and at assisting acceding governments in joining the WTO. In addition, China and African countries have jointly launched the Initiative on Partnership for Africa's Development to provide technical and financial assistance to support

[23] The WTO website, available at: www.wto.org/english/tratop_e/dispu_e/dispu_by_country_e.htm.

Africa's pursuit of prosperity and stability. Many developing countries have identified China as an important South-South development partner and source of financing.

III China's Recent Efforts in Promoting WTO Joint Statement Initiatives

China has been active in promoting the WTO negotiating function through creative ways. One specific illustration is that China was a driving force behind the launch of JSI for Investment Facilitation for Development (Wolff, 2021) and mobilized wide support from WTO members.

Cross-border investment is an important driving force for economic growth. However, the existing international investment rules are dominated by bilateral and regional agreements, which are characterized by fragmentation and complexity. In recent years, the international communities have been working on promoting the formulation of multilateral investment rules. In September 2016, G20 leaders reached the Guiding Principles for Global Investment Policymaking at the Hangzhou Summit.

Building on the outcome of the G20 Hangzhou Summit, China took the lead in introducing the topic of investment facilitation into the WTO in October 2016, creatively integrating the discussions on investment, trade and development together, as trade and investment are closely interlinked in today's world underlined by in-depth development of global value chains. The initiative focused on developing a framework of rules to ensure transparency and predictability of investment measures; streamline and speed up administrative procedures and requirements; and enhance international cooperation, information sharing, the exchange of best practices, and relations with relevant stakeholders. Building on the positive momentum achieved by the WTO in concluding the TFA, the discussions on investment facilitation have broken the stalemate that the WTO has not been able to discuss investment issues for decades and taken an important step towards the goal of formulating multilateral investment rules in the WTO.

So far, China has made fruitful efforts as one of leading members to facilitate discussions on investment facilitation among WTO members. In April 2017, China coordinated Brazil, Argentina, Korea, Mexico and other developing members to form the 'Friends of Investment Facilitation for Development (FIFD)' to start informal dialogue on investment facilitation in the WTO. This was followed by seventy WTO members including China signing on to a Joint Ministerial Statement on Investment Facilitation for Development calling for 'structured discussions with the aim of developing a multilateral framework on investment facilitation' at the 11th WTO Ministerial Conference in Buenos Aires in December 2017. In 2018, the Structured Discussions focused on the identification of the possible elements of the framework on Investment Facilitation for Development, which were reflected in a 'Checklist of Issues raised by Members'. On 5 November 2019, in the margin of Informal WTO Ministerial Meeting in Shanghai, China hosted a Ministerial Luncheon Meeting on Investment Facilitation for Development to facilitate discussions and exchanges of views. On the same day, ninety-two WTO members issued a new Joint Ministerial Statement on Investment Facilitation for Development. This Statement highlights the link between investment and development and to make sure that any eventual framework considers the needs of developing members and LDCs. As of December 2020, there were 105 WTO Members participating in the negotiation process, comprised of a mix of developed, developing and least developed members, and this number is expected to keep growing.

For China, it is particularly encouraging that many developing members, especially the LDCs, from differently geographic regions including Asia, Africa, Eurasia, Mid-east and Latin America have showed their support for ongoing discussions on investment facilitation. The broad participation of WTO members sends a clear message that the investment facilitation reflects the common interest of the broad WTO membership. It is promising to reach forward-looking and results-oriented outcomes that could reactivate the WTO negotiating function and increase relevance of the WTO in the world economic governance. The success of launching the Initiative on Investment Facilitation also inspires other members to follow suit. Some of the members launched the JSIs on E-commerce, Services Domestic Regulation as well as Micro-, Small- and Medium-Sized Enterprises later on. All of these JSIs are making good progress, injecting momentum for WTO negotiations.

IV China's Basic Stance towards the WTO Reform

China benefited enormously from entering the WTO and is now an important stakeholder in the existing multilateral trading system. China has been an active participant, staunch supporter and major contributor in the multilateral trading system. However, uncertainties in global trade governance are on the rise, and the WTO is facing multiple challenges.

First, the world economy and trade need to pull out of the sluggish situation. The sudden outbreak of COVID-19 accelerated the decline of world trade that was already on the downward trend, and severely disrupted global supply chain, causing widespread negative impacts on the world economy. Second, the new trend of technological revolution has changed the shape and pattern of world economy. With the rise of information technology, digital trade and cross-border e-commerce, new challenges and problems in international trade are constantly emerging. The traditional WTO rules system cannot fully adapt to the new international economic and trade realities and needs to be improved. Third, the WTO has internal institutional problems from its three key dimensions. The Doha negotiation process is stalled, the trade policy review lacks effectiveness and the dispute settlement mechanism has been challenged by certain WTO members, making it difficult to effectively respond to emerging issues and coordinate interests among WTO members.

In the above context, the WTO reform is imperative. Since 2018, major WTO members have put forward a number of proposals on WTO reform. Although they share the same objectives of WTO reform, differences on substances remain. Discussions on WTO reform continue after the outbreak of COVID-19 but have to tackle with increased inward-looking trade policies of certain countries when dealing with the pandemic, which would negatively affect their political will to promote multilateral trade cooperation.

For China, the WTO reform will be a long-term process that will bring all-round influence to itself. On the one hand, participating in the process of WTO reform will be an important strategic practice for China to play a constructive role in the global economic governance under the current complex international situation. Maintaining a strong WTO-centred multilateral trading system is in line with China's economic and trade interests and strategic needs. In turn, a successful WTO reform may provide a favourable external environment for China to stimulate domestic economic transformation, industrial upgrading and technological innovation and enhance China's ability to participate in global economic governance. On the other hand, there is no escaping the fact that the focal issues in the current China–USA trade frictions are gradually evolving into issues that may affect the WTO reform. The demands for 'market orientation' and 'structural reform' put forward by a few developed members, such as the USA, EU and Japan, tried to change trade policy reform into debate of economic system and are clearly beyond the mandate of a trade organization such as the WTO. Such discussions would lead nowhere.

To support the stability and authority of the WTO-centred multilateral trading system, China issued two documents on WTO reform. The first document was issued in December 2018, setting out China's basic principles and suggestions on WTO reform. The second document was formally submitted to the WTO to further elaborate the main concerns of China and specific actions that need to be taken for the WTO.[24] Generally speaking, China is open to any discussion that can strengthen the multilateral trading system and seeks cooperation with both developed and developing members. Since its WTO accession, China has made remarkable economic achievements, but it still faces the similar problems during economic development and shares broad common interests with other developing countries. In addition, the conclusion of Regional Economic Cooperation Partnership and China-EU Comprehensive Investment Agreement (CAI) shows China's determination to further open up and achieve win–win outcome with both developed and developing members.

More specifically, China could promote WTO reform in the following aspects. First, regarding the crucial and urgent issues threatening the existence of the WTO, China proposed to break the impasse of the Appellate Body appointment, tighten disciplines to curb the abuse of national security exception and unilateral trade measures. China together with the EU and other WTO members submitted several proposals to the WTO to address the Appellate Body crisis,[25] and participated in a multi-party interim appeal arrangement (MPIA) to maintain an appeal process in the WTO dispute settlement mechanism. In addition, due to concerns on unilateral measures inconsistent with the WTO rules, China initiated three successive WTO disputes against the different rounds of USA unilateral tariff increases. Second, regarding the operational issues affecting the efficiency of the WTO, China shares common ground with other WTO members in strengthening the compliance of notification obligation and

[24] China's Proposal on WTO Reform. WTO: WT/GC/W/773, 13 May 2019, available at: https://docs.wto.org/dol2fe/Pages/FE_Search/FE_S_S009-DP.aspx?CatalogueIdList=254127&CurrentCatalogueIdIndex=0.

[25] Communication from the European Union, China, Canada, India, Norway, New Zealand, Switzerland, Australia, Republic of Korea, Iceland, Singapore, Mexico, Costa Rica and Montenegro to the General Council. WTO: WT/GC/W/752/Rev.2, available at: https://docs.wto.org/dol2fe/Pages/SS/directdoc.aspx?filename=q:/WT/GC/W752R2.pdf&Open=True; Communication from the European Union, China, India and Montenegro to the General Council. WTO: WT/GC/W/753/Rev.1, available at: https://docs.wto.org/dol2fe/Pages/SS/directdoc.aspx?filename=q:/WT/GC/W753R1.pdf&Open=True.

improving the efficiency of WTO subsidiary bodies. Third, regarding the emerging issues that reflect the twenty-first century business reality, China holds positive attitude towards open plurilateral approach to update the multilateral trade rules and believe that in new areas such as digital economy and artificial intelligence, the WTO members need to fill the gap between the reality and the WTO rule book, so as to bring new impetus for global economic growth and technological progress.

The last but more important, the new demand for global economic governance in the context of COVID-19 should be taken as a major opportunity to improve the WTO system, with China playing an critical role in it. On the one hand, as a leading trading nation, China became the largest exporter of COVID-19 critical medical products in 2020. It exported medical products with a value of US$105 billion, about 2.8 times its exports in 2019 (WTO, 2021). As of early September 2020, China has provided more than 200 countries and regions with more than 320 billion masks, 3.9 billion protective suits and 5.6 billion nucleic acid testing kits and provided more than 100 countries and international organizations with 1.2 billion doses of vaccines (Ministry of Foreign Affairs of the People's Republic of China, 2021a, b). Furthermore, China has taken a series of trade facilitation measures to relieve logistic bottlenecks that have affected trade in medicines, equipment and essential supplies to fight against the pandemic, so as to prevent supply chain disruption and to facilitate the resuming of business operations. For example, China launched an emergency plan which simplified customs procedures, reduced port charges and accelerated inspections and quarantine procedures. The Chinese Customs managed to reduce the release time of relief cargo to 45 minutes and set up online services to guide importers throughout the fast clearance of anti-epidemic supplies. Import materials donated for epidemic prevention and control are exempted from import duties, import value-added tax and consumption tax. Sanitary registration for donated medical items has been suspended. The Chinese Customs can release directly selected medical items, such as vaccines, blood products and reagents, essential to prevent, diagnose or cure COVID-19, according to the certificate issued by competent authorities provided that the health risks can be controlled (UNCTAD, 2020). By utilizing its manufacturing capacities and trade facilitation measures, China did its part in closing global immunization gap especially in developing countries.

On the other hand, China plays an active role in multilateral agenda setting relevant to COVID-19. As of October 2021, China has submitted eleven proposals with other WTO members relevant to COVID-19.[26] Meanwhile, China has committed to making COVID-19 vaccines a global public good and promoting vaccine accessibility and affordability in developing countries. China supports discussions on TRIPS waiver for COVID-19 vaccines in the WTO and would like to facilitate such discussions to enter the text consultation stage. The above positive measures to facilitate anti-pandemic supplies, medical supplies and daily necessities would strengthen the fundamental role of the WTO in upholding trade liberalization during the pandemic and beyond.

V Concluding Remarks

China's accession to the WTO in December 2001 has proven to be one of the most significant economic events both in our lifetime and in modern world history. In bringing China under its umbrella, the WTO took a huge step towards achieving its goal of universal membership and inclusiveness. As a result of China's accession, one of the world's biggest economies is now playing by the same multilaterally agreed rule book just as other major trading nations. This is no small achievement, particularly in terms of strengthening global trade governance and the multilateral trading system. China's successful accession has also inspired many other developing countries to join the WTO.

Upon its WTO accession, China's economy has undergone a systemic transformation and all-round opening up. The past 20 years have proven that by embracing globalization and integrating into world economy, China has successfully become a global manufacturing hub and trade centre. A wide range of Chinese industries, particularly those that were opened up due to China's WTO commitment, have emerged much stronger in global competition and climbed up the value chain. Keeping the same path is therefore a strategic choice for China to enhance its international positioning and avoid falling into the 'middle-income trap' in the next decades.

The less known reason for China's success in speedy development and industrial upgrading after its WTO accession is its proactive participation in global value chains. It is convinced that continuous trade and investment liberalization in the future will improve the business environment, attract foreign investment and help China remain firmly embedded in global value chains. It in turn will greatly reinforce its economic resilience

[26] The WTO website, available at: www.wto.org/english/tratop_e/covid19_e/covid_details_by_country_e.htm?country=CHN.

to withstand various crises and risks and break the ill-founded 'decoupling argument'.

At present, the multilateral trading system is going through the most difficult moment in its more than 70 years of history. Trade protectionism is spreading around the world. The WTO is in a deep crisis, with the vacuum of leadership, stalled multilateral negotiations and paralyzed dispute settlement mechanism. However, an open, non-discriminatory and rules-based multilateral trading system that can keep pace with modern times is indispensable for the growth of both China and the world economy. In a multipolar world, China should promote a new pattern of collective leadership and good co-governance in the WTO. Therefore, China is needed to provide more public goods to WTO members by opening its market and promote win–win multilateral cooperation. China is also expected to stay firm in observing multilateral trade rules so as to gain the trust of the members.

Regarding the ongoing WTO reform, China should actively participate in the process and firmly uphold open, inclusive and non-discriminatory principles, while preventing the multilateral trading system from moving towards protectionism.

In conclusion, while China's huge achievements during 20 years of WTO membership are to be commended, the country must not rest on its successes. Our task now is to find a way to restore multilateral cooperation, keep strengthening the system and deliver new reforms. In an increasingly interdependent and multipolar world economy, it is our shared responsibility to ensure that we bolster global economic cooperation – and that we leave a strong and well-functioning trading system for the future generations.

References

American Chamber of Commerce in China (AmChamChina). (2021). Business Climate Survey, available at: www.amchamchina.org/climate-survey/2021-business-climate-survey/.

The Business Confidence Survey. (2021). European Union Chamber of Commerce in China (European Chamber), available at: www.europeanchamber.com.cn/en/publications-archive/917/Business_Confidence_Survey_2021.

China and the WTO. (2021). Remarks of Alan Wm. Wolff at U.C. Berkeley's Third Annual Conference on Technology, Trade and China. 27 April 2021, available at: www.piie.com/sites/default/files/documents/wolff2021-04-27.pdf.

Li, S. Q., and Tu, X. Q. (2018). 'Impact of Chinese Characteristics on the World Trade Organization: Challenges and Strategies'. *China & World Economy*, 26(2): 107–126.

Mattoo, A. (2003). 'China's Accession to the WTO: The Services Dimension'. *Journal of International Economic Law*, 6(2): 299–339.

Ministry of Commerce of the People's Republic of China. (2018). China's Position Paper on WTO Reform, available at: www.mofcom.gov.cn/article/jiguanzx/201812/20181202817611.shtml.

Ministry of Commerce of the People's Republic of China (MOFCOM). (2021). Available at: http://data.mofcom.gov.cn/article/zxtj/202101/55593.html.

Ministry of Foreign Affairs of the People's Republic of China. (2021a). China Takes Five 'Leads' in Global Fight against COVID-19 (in Chinese), available at: www.mfa.gov.cn/web/gjhdq_676201/gj_676203/yz_676205/1206_677076/xgxw_677082/202109/t20210914_10405406.shtml.

Ministry of Foreign Affairs of the People's Republic of China. (2021b). China Provided 1.2 Billion Doses of COVID-19 Vaccines to More Than 100 Countries and International Organisations (in Chinese), available at: www.gov.cn/xinwen/2021-09/23/content_5638974.htm.

Qin, J. Y. (2010). 'The Challenge of Interpreting "WTO-PLUS" Provisions'. *Journal of World Trade*, 44(1): 127–172.

The State Council Information Office of the People's Republic of China. (2018). White Paper on China and the WTO, available at: www.scio.gov.cn/zfbps/32832/Document/1632345/1632345.htm.

Sun, Z. Y. (2011). China's Experience of 10 Years in the WTO. In Ricardo Meléndez-Ortiz, Christophe Bellmann, and Shuaihua Cheng (eds.), *A Decade in the WTO: Implications for China and Global Trade Governance*. Geneva, Switzerland: ICTSD Programme on Global Economic Policy and Institutions, pp. 11–16.

Total Assets of Foreign Banks in China Totalled 3.48 trillion CNY (in Chinese). (2020). Xinhua Finance, available at: http://bank.xinhua08.com/a/20200924/1956812.shtml.

Total Assets of Foreign Insurance Companies Totalled 1.71 trillion CNY in 2020(in Chinese). (2021). China Economic Net, available at: https://baijiahao.baidu.com/s?id=1695791553619203455&wfr=spider&for=pc.

UNCTAD. (2020). Case Study: China's Trade Facilitation Responses to the COVID-19 Pandemic, available at: https://unctad.org/es/node/2374.

Wolfe, R. (2015). 'First Diagnose, Then Treat: What Ails the Doha Round'? *World Trade Review*, 14(1): 7–28.

The World Bank and Development Research Center of the State Council of the People's Republic of China. (2013). China 2030: Building a Modern, Harmonious, and Creative Society, available at: https://openknowledge.worldbank.org/handle/10986/12925.

WTO. (2021). Trade in Medical Goods in the Context of Tackling COVID-19: Developments in 2020, available at: www.wto.org/english/tratop_e/covid19_e/medical_goods_update_jun21_e.pdf.

Xinhua Finance. (2021). China's Import and Export Volume Hit a Record High in 2020 (in Chinese), available at: https://baijiahao.baidu.com/s?id=1688827908679521010&wfr=spider&for=pc.2021.

2

China's Changing Perspective on the WTO

From Aspiration, Assimilation to Alienation

HENRY GAO

Twenty years after it became a member of the WTO, China's image in popular perception has shifted from the biggest success story of the world trading system to its biggest challenge.[1] In the past few years, tons of research have been conducted on what other WTO members should or could do to deal with the China challenge,[2] but not much attempt has been made to understand the Chinese perspective on its WTO membership. Focusing only on the China challenge without understanding the Chinese perspective is rather problematic as it treats China as a passive object rather than an active subject, despite its significant economic and political clouts in the world trading system today. This chapter fills the research gap by providing the first systemic review of this important yet ignored question, which in my view, would be the key to addressing the China challenge. The chapter argues that the Chinese perspective on the WTO has changed from viewing it as the symbol for its aspiration to integrate into the world economy, to trying to assimilate the Chinese

This research has been supported by the National Research Foundation, Singapore under its Emerging Areas Research Projects (EARP) Funding Initiative. Any opinions, findings and conclusions or recommendations expressed in this material are those of the author(s) and do not reflect the views of the National Research Foundation, Singapore. An earlier version of this paper was published in *World Trade Review*, 21(3), 342–358.

1 See, e.g., Petros C. Mavroidis and André Sapir, 'The WTO at the Crossroads: How to Avoid the China Syndrome', *World Trade Review*, 21(3), 359–366. https://doi.org/10.1017/S147474562200009X.

2 See, e.g., M. Wu (2016), 'The "China, Inc" Challenge to Global Trade Governance', *Harvard International Law Journal* 57(2); J. Hillman (2018) Hearing on US Tools to Address Chinese Market Distortion; P. C. Mavroidis and A. Sapir (2021) *China and WTO: Why Multilateralism Still Matters*; R. L. Howse, 'Official Business: International Trade Law and the Resurgence (or Resilience) of the State as an Economic Actor', 43 *University of Pennsylvania Journal of International Law* 821 (2022); W. Zhou, H. Gao, and X. Bai (2019) 'Building a Market Economy Through WTO-Inspired Reform of State-owned Enterprises in China', *International and Comparative Law Quarterly* 68, 977.

economic system with that of the market-based multilateral trading system, to increasing alienations with the core values of WTO in response to the attacks on its economic system. The paper concludes with lessons drawing from China's changing perspective, especially on how to manage the China challenge in the multilateral trading system.

I The Aspiration: Pre-2001

While China was a founding contracting party to the GATT, it did not participate in the activities of the GATT due to the withdrawal from the GATT by the government of the Republic of China in 1950 and the subsequent Cold War.[3] This did not change even when China resumed its seat in the United Nations in 1971 when the Chinese Ministry of Foreign Trade and Ministry of Foreign Affairs submitted a joint report advising against China's participation in the GATT by calling it "a tool for the imperialists, especially American imperialists to expand foreign trade and grab world markets."[4]

However, China's perspective started to change when it started its economic reform in the late 1970s. In particular, learning from the success stories of other export-oriented economies in East Asia, China tried to boost its trade and investment, and started to realize the key role played by the GATT in the facilitation of international trade. In a joint report submitted to the State Council in 1982,[5] the Ministry of Foreign Economic Relations and Trade (MOFERT), Ministry of Foreign Affairs, State Economic Commission, Ministry of Finance, and General Customs Administration noted that China's foreign trade is rapidly developing with the adoption of the reform and opening up policy, and trade with members of the GATT already constitute 80% of its overall trade.[6] Thus, they suggested China to participate in the GATT and enjoy the MFN tariffs.[7] After learning more about the GATT in the next few years, China

[3] For a detailed discussion of China's history with the GATT and WTO, see H. Gao (2007) 'China's Participation in the WTO: A Lawyer's Perspective', *Singapore Year Book of International Law* 11, 41–74.

[4] Chinese Ministry of Foreign Trade and Ministry of Foreign Affairs, 'Report on the "GATT" Issue [Guanyu "Guanshui ji Maoyi Zongxieding" Wenti de Qingshi]', 30 November 1971, as quoted in G. Shi (2011) *Reader on China's Accession to the World Trade Organization (Four): Negotiation History of China's Accession to the World Trade Organization [Zhongguo Jiaru Shijie Maoyi Zuzhi Zhishi Duben (Si): Zhongguo Jiaru Shijie Maoyi Zuzhi Tanpan Licheng]*, People's Publishing House [Renmin Chubanshe], at 19–21.

[5] *Id.*, at 24–26.

[6] *Id.*, at 24.

[7] *Id.*

formally submitted the application to resume its status as a GATT contracting party on July 10, 1986.[8]

In its Memorandum on China's Foreign Trade Regime submitted in February 1987, China stated that the "objective of the reform is to establish a new system of planned commodity economy of Chinese style."[9] The strange term "planned commodity economy" is essentially just a euphemism for "market economy," disguised in such a way so as to overcome the ideological opposition from Party hardliners. This was officially confirmed in 1992 when the Fourteenth National Congress of the Communist Party adopted a Resolution to make "socialist market economy" the goal of the reform,[10] which was subsequently incorporated into the PRC Constitution in 1993.[11]

As China's reform goal was to establish market economy and the GATT was the pinnacle international institution based on market economy principles, it is no wonder that China looked up to its accession to the GATT/WTO with great enthusiasm. For example, Li Zhongzhou, the first division chief for GATT Affairs at MOFERT who was responsible for China's GATT bid for a long time in the 1980s, summarized nine benefits of China's participation in the GATT, which includes boosting its trade and investment, getting MFN tariffs, enjoying special and differential treatment for developing countries, and participating in various GATT activities such as negotiations and dispute settlement.[12]

China's eagerness as an aspiring convert of the multilateral trading system is also demonstrated by its willingness to move past four major

[8] GATT, *China's Status as A Contracting Party: Communication from the People's Republic of China*, GATT Doc. L/6017 (Oct. 26, 1986).

[9] GATT, *China's Status as a Contracting Party, Memorandum on China's Foreign Trade Regime*, L/6125, 18 February 1987, at 4.

[10] Z. Jian, *Jiakuai Gaige Kaifang he Xiandaihua Jianshe Bufa, Duoqu Youzhongguo Tese Shehui Zhuyi Shiye de Weida Shengli* [*Accelerate Steps of Reform and Opening Up and the Development of Modernization, Seize Greater Success in the Endeavor on Socialism with Chinese Characteristics*], *Report at the Fourteenth National Congress of the China Communist Party*, Oct. 12, 1992, www.gov.cn/test/2007-08/29/content_730511.htm.

[11] Article 15 of the Constitution used to state "[t]he state practices planned economy on the basis of Socialist public ownership." It was amended to "[t]he state practices Socialist market." *Zhonghua Renmin Gongheguo Xianfa Xiuzhengan (1993 Nian)* [*Amendment to the Constitution of the People's Republic of China (2013)*] (adopted by the First Session of the Eighth National People's Congress on Mar. 29, 1993), www.npc.gov.cn/wxzl/wxzl/2000-12/05/content_4585.htm.

[12] Z. Li (1993) 'The Issue of China's Participation in the Multilateral Trading System', www.uvic.ca/research/centres/capi/assets/docs/Zhongzhou_China_Multilateral_Trading.pdf, at 11–12.

political crises during its accession process: the boycott against China in the aftermath of the "June Fourth incident" in 1989; the unilateral release of China's concessions on market access and protocol (including some still under negotiation) by the US in April 1999; the NATO bombing of China's embassy in Yugoslavia in May 1999; and the collision of a US Navy spy plane with a Chinese fighter jet in April 2001. Any of the four crises, if they were to happen today, could easily derail or even terminate the whole negotiation. Yet, China was willing to set them aside and press forward with its accession talk. Indeed, in each case, a deliberate decision was made by China's then top leader to de-escalate the situation and move on, such as Deng Xiaoping's speech affirming the goal of "market economy" in his southern tour in 1992, Jiang Zemin's decision to resume negotiation with the US in August 1999,[13] and his call to President Bush at 2 AM Beijing Time on 12 September 2001, just 5 hours after the first of the 9/11 terrorist attacks, to condemn the attacks and send condolences to American people.[14]

II The Assimilation: 2001–2008

With the same joy as Monk Tang entering the Western Heaven,[15] China finally acceded to the WTO at the Doha Ministerial Conference in November 2001. The accession was celebrated universally across China, with CCTV hosting a "Who Wants to be a Millionaire"-style show testing people's knowledge on WTO issues, various local campaigns to teach WTO to people from all trades including taxi drivers, and a high-level seminar on WTO issues for Provincial Governors and Ministers in February 2002 with an opening speech by President Jiang Zemin. In the speech, Jiang repeatedly emphasized how the accession could help China to act in accordance with internationally accepted rules, build a foreign trade legal system compatible with common international

[13] B. Suo et al. (eds.) (2013) 'Basic Instruments and Selected Documents on the Negotiations for China's Accession to the World Trade Organization [Zhongguo Jiaru Shijie Maoyi Zuzhi Tanpan Wenjian Ziliao Xuanbian]', Beijing: China Commerce and Trade Press [Zhongguo Shangwu Chubanshe]', Bilaterals 3, 1002.

[14] J. Wu (2008), China's Fast Reactions to 911 [Zhongguo dui '911' Shijian de Kuaisu Fanying], Digest of Chinese and Foreign Books [Zhongwai Shuzhai], 6, www.xiaoshuo.online/zhongwaiwz/zwsz2008/zwsz20080614-1.html.

[15] This is the story in Journey to the West, a classic Chinese novel with a romantic account of the story of Xuanzang, a monk from the Tang Dynasty, going to India to study Buddhism at the famed Nalanda monastery.

practices, and use WTO rules to "constrain China's policy and govern the government."[16]

Of course, China's decision to embrace WTO rules was in no way made out of altruism or naiveté. Indeed, Jiang made it quite clear that the US' willingness to let China in was not "a sudden act of kindness."[17] Instead, Jiang highlighted the strategic considerations of the US, that is, "pushing for political liberalization through economic liberalization" and thus "Westernize and divide the Socialist countries."[18] Referring to Clinton's speech on China's PNTR status, which hailed the role of WTO accession in "removing government from vast areas of people's lives"[19] and promoting social and political reform in China, Jiang stressed the need for China to keep a clear mind and strive to achieve its own "strategic intentions."[20]

So what are China's "strategic intentions"? The first is the promotion of China's economic development. Jiang mentioned that he thought "long and hard" about China's accession to the WTO and decided that China must "swim in the sea of international markets" given the increasing competition at the international level.[21] According to him, WTO accession will help China to attract foreign investment, enhance the competitiveness of its industries, participate in international rule-making, and promote the development of the socialist market economy, which are all aligned with China's long-term development goals.[22] The second is to improve China's approach to running its economy. In his speech, Jiang called for a major overhaul of the Chinese government's way to manage the economy upon WTO accession. In particular, he stated that the primary task of the government in managing the economy shall be regulating the market economy order using WTO rules, guiding the proper development of a socialist market economy, and nurturing and strengthening the international competitiveness of the Chinese economy.[23] In other words, China essentially takes the WTO rules as a manual for economic reform, which is why Jiang repeatedly mentioned the need for government officials and

16 Z. Jiang (2006) 'Seize the Initiative amidst Intense International Competition [Zai Jilie de Guoji Jingzheng zhong Zhangwo Zhudong]', in *Selected Works of Jiang Zemin: Volume III [Jiang Zemin Wenxuan: Disan Juan]*. Beijing: People's Press, at 453–454.

17 *Id.*, at 450.

18 *Id.*

19 "Full Text of Clinton's Speech on China Trade Bill", www.iatp.org/sites/default/files/Full_Text_of_Clintons_Speech_on_China_Trade_Bi.htm (accessed 22 January 2022).

20 Jiang, *supra* note 16, at 450.

21 *Id.*, at 450–451.

22 *Id.*, at 451.

23 *Id.*, at 451–453.

Party members to "study WTO rules … in this new exam," and ended his speech by calling all government leaders to "pass the exam, and strive to get good results."[24]

How did China fare on the exam? The main question on the exam is the implementation of its accession commitments, which China passed with flying colors. For example, in China's first transitional review conducted in 2002, Sergio Marchi, then chairman of the WTO General Council, gave China an A+.[25] Similarly, Pascal Lamy also gave China an A+ in 2011.[26]

In addition, China also performed well on the bonus question on learning the rules of the WTO and fully participated in all areas of WTO's work.[27] In WTO negotiations, China has emerged from a Member that struggled to fully understand the content of discussion[28] to a key player.[29] In WTO dispute settlement, China has also risen from a reluctant participant that tried very hard to avoid disputes to one of the most active litigants.

It is worth noting that China's assimilation efforts in the WTO are largely because China deemed it to be in its own benefits. As explained by Shi Guangsheng, China's trade minister at the time of the accession, WTO membership is beneficial to China in three ways:[30] First, it promoted China's own economic development, as shown by China's accelerating GDP growth rate from 2001 to 2007, reversing the trend of declining GDP growth pre-2001; Second, it promoted China's reform and opening up, as shown by China's exponential growth in both exports and FDI; Third, it promoted the development of the socialist market economy in China, as shown by China's improving score in the World Bank's Ease of Doing Business Index.[31]

[24] *Id.*, at 458.

[25] Z. Sun (2011), *Busy years in Geneva [Rineiwa Kongzong Suiyue]*. Beijing: People's Publishing House, at 121.

[26] 'WTO Chief: China Got A+ Performance since Entry', www.chinadaily.com.cn/china/2011-10/19/content_13928704. htm (accessed 22 January 2022).

[27] See H. Gao (2011) 'China's Ascent in Global Trade Governance: From Rule Taker to Rule Shaker, and Maybe Rule Maker?', in Carolyn Deere-Birkbech (ed.) *Making Global Trade Governance Work for Development*. Cambridge: Cambridge University Press, at 156–167.

[28] Sun, *supra* note 25, at 97.

[29] Gao, *supra* note 27, at 175.

[30] G. Shi (2020) 'Working Together for a Better Future Based on Mutual Benefit', in H. Gao and Don Lewis (eds.), *China's Participation in the WTO*. London: Cameron May, at 17–18.

[31] M. Piatkowski, S. Solf, and W. Wei (2020) *China's Doing Business Success*. Washington, DC: World Bank.

III The Awakening: 2008–2012

Right before China's first WTO Ambassador Sun Zhenyu went to Geneva to assume his position in early 2002, he met with former USTR Charlene Barshefsky in Beijing.[32] Barshefsky told Sun that China's accession will change the balance of power in the WTO, but it would be better for China to observe how things were done in the WTO first before joining any group. Taking her advice, China adopted a cautious approach in its first few years in the WTO: while it claimed its position as a developing country for political reasons, its positions on various issues do not always follow the developing country's "party-line." For example, China participated actively in the trade facilitation negotiation even though many developing countries opposed the negotiation. China was also the first developing country to express support for the chairman's texts in agriculture and NAMA negotiations.[33] In the words of Zhang Xiangchen, then Director-General of the Division on WTO Affairs of MOFCOM and later China's WTO Ambassador, China should play "a balancing, bridging and constructive role" between developed and developing countries.[34] This is confirmed by Chinese Premier Wen Jiabao, who stated at the Forum on the 10th Anniversary of China's Accession to the WTO that China was "a responsible country that has actively shouldered international responsibilities commensurate with the level of its development."[35]

While it recognizes that it has special responsibilities as a large developing country, China resents being singled out in the negotiations due to the painful memory of its "century of humiliation" starting from the Opium War. Therefore, when the July 2008 meeting ran into an impasse due to India's refusal to give in on special products and special safeguard mechanisms, China rejected the US request for it to provide additional concessions on special products in agriculture and sectoral negotiations on industrial goods as the same demands were not made to India or Brazil. When the US tried to accuse China of walking back the text despite getting "a seat at the big kids' table"

[32] Sun, *supra* note 25, at 45.

[33] Sun, *supra* note 25, at 187.

[34] '21st Century Business Herald, China's Doha Strategy [Zhongguo de Duoha Celue]', http://finance.sina.com.cn/chanjing/b/20051130/09052159265.shtml (accessed 30 November 2005).

[35] 'China Will Keep Its Door Open Forever', www.mfa.gov.cn/ce/ceus//eng/zgyw/t867816.htm (accessed 22 January 2022).

as it requested.[36] Ambassador Sun gave a diatribe outlining China's contributions to the round in various areas as a retort to the US "finger pointing."[37]

As the July min-ministerial was underway in Geneva, an editorial titled "Elephant in the Room"[38] was published by the *China WTO Tribune* – a journal published by MOFCOM and edited by Zhang Xiangchen, who assumed his new position as the Deputy Permanent Representative of China's WTO mission the month before. In the editorial, Zhang argued that China's low-profile approach did not prevent it from playing a major role in the WTO. Moreover, as the world plunged into the financial crisis in 2008, China's visibility would become even more prominent. In 2009, despite the contraction of world trade by 13%, China became the biggest exporter for the first time in modern history, which led to two major developments:

First, the fact that China emerged not only unscathed but also triumphant from the financial crisis bolstered China's confidence in the so-called Beijing Model, a model of economic growth that relies heavily on government intervention.[39] Moreover, as China was able to avoid the contagious effects of the global crisis by maintaining its restrictions on foreign exchange and capital flows, its incomplete market reform was hailed as a feature rather than a defect of the Chinese system and Chinese leaders started to question the wisdom of more market-oriented reforms. On the other hand, concerned with the continued rise of China, the US announced its "pivot to Asia" and launched negotiations to join the TPP to reinforce both economic ties and strategic relationships in the Asia Pacific.[40]

[36] P. Blustein (2009) *Misadventures of the Most Favored Nations: Clashing Egos, Inflated Ambitions, and the Great Shambles of the World Trade System*. New York: PublicAffairs, at p. 274. See also H. Gao (2015), 'From the Doha Round to the China Round: China's Growing Role in WTO Negotiations', in L. Toohey, and J. Greenacre (eds.), *China in the International Economic Order: New Directions and Changing Paradigms*. Cambridge: Cambridge University Press, pp. 79–97.

[37] Z. Sun, H.E. Ambassador, Permanent Mission P.R.C. to the WTO, Statement at the Informal Trade Negotiations Committee Meeting (11 August 2008), http://wtoandchina.blogspot.com/2008/08/chinas-contributions-in-dda-from.html (last visited 16 October 2021).

[38] X. Zhang (2008) 'Elephant in the Room [Wuzi li de Daxiang]', *China WTO Tribune* 7, 3.

[39] For more on the Beijing Model, see G. Shaffer and H. Gao (2020) 'A New Chinese Economic Order?', *Journal of International Economic Law* 23(3), 607–635, https://doi.org/10.1093/jiel/jgaa013.

[40] I. Fergusson and B. Vaughn (2009) 'The Trans-Pacific Strategic Economic Partnership Agreement', Report for Congress, Congressional Research Service.

Second, China's emergence as the largest exporter, combined with the growth contractions in many countries, resulted in new waves of export restrictions against China even though the textile safeguard mechanism and the product-specific safeguard mechanism in China's Accession Protocol started to expire. With its surge of exports, China tried to ensure the supply of raw materials for its domestic producers by enacting export restrictions on raw materials. Based on its understanding of WTO rules, China regarded such measures to be justified by the general exceptions clause under GATT Art. XX.[41] However, the US and EU sued China in the WTO, and managed to win the case by arguing that China could not invoke the general exceptions clause due to the lack of explicit reference to such provision in China's Accession Protocol. At the DSB meeting adopting the AB report, China criticized the report for creating "a two tier membership, which was neither legally sustainable, nor systemically desirable."[42] Li Zhongzhou was even more explicit in his op-ed in the *China WTO Tribune*, where he blasted the decision as downgrading China to a "second-class citizen."[43] In view of such double standards, China started to question the value of WTO rules, which led to its efforts seeking alternatives.

IV The Alternative: 2013–2015

With the US reaching across the Pacific to assemble its allies in the TPP to contain China and "make sure the United States – and not countries like China – is the one writing this century's rules for the world's economy,"[44] China also started to make its own move. The first piece of the strategy is to form an RTA in response to the TPP, which led to the launch of negotiations on the Regional Comprehensive Economic Partnership (RCEP)

[41] X. Wang (2011) 'Analysis of the Case on Raw Materials Export Restrictions by the US, EU and Mexico [Meiguo, Oumeng, Moxige Suwo Yuancailiao Chukou Xianzhi an Pingxi]', in C. Li (ed.), *Gaming with WTO Rules: China's Ten Years' Experience in WTO Dispute Settlement Practices [Shimao Zuzhi Guize Boyi: Zhongguo Canyu WTO Zhengduan Jiejue de Shinian Falu Shijian]*. Beijing: Commercial Press, at 397–399.

[42] WTO Dispute Settlement Body, Minutes of Meeting, Held in the Centre William Rappard on 22 February 2012, WT/ DSB/M/312, 22 May 2012.

[43] Z. Li (2011) 'Appeal to WTO to Refrain from Treating China as Second Class Citizen [Jihu WTO Moba Zhongguo ru Lingce]', *China WTO Tribune* 9, at 94.

[44] "President Obama: 'Writing the Rules for 21st Century Trade'," February 2015, https://obamawhitehouse.archives.gov/blog/2015/02/18/president-obama-writing-rules-21st-century-trade (accessed 3 November 2021).

in November 2012.[45] China had long advocated for regional economic integration between East and Southeast Asia, but its preferred set-up was ASEAN plus three, that is, China, Japan, and Korea. Japan, on the other hand, prefers to add three more countries, that is, India, Australia, and New Zealand, as counterbalances to China. China's willingness to go with the ASEAN plus six model reveals its urgency following the US accession to the TPP, which could severely disrupt China's supply chains in the region with provisions such as the yarn-forwarding rule that makes it difficult for TPP members to use inputs from non-members in the production process.

Second, in 2013, China announced two major initiatives: the Silk Road Economic Belt, which connects China with Europe through the Eurasian Continent,[46] and the 21st Century Maritime Silk Road, which links China with Southeast Asian countries, Africa, and Europe across the Pacific and Indian oceans.[47] Later combined together as the Belt and Road Initiative, this has since become the centerpiece of President Xi's foreign policy. Spanning sixty-five countries on three continents with a total population of 4.4 billion,[48] the BRI reportedly accounts for 29% of global GDP and 23.4% of global merchandise and services exports.[49] By "linking up the interests of China with those of developing countries in Asia, Africa, and Latin America,"[50] the BRI helps China to build its own supply chain without direct confrontation with the US in the Pacific.

[45] Joint Declaration on the Launch of Negotiations for the Regional Comprehensive Economic Partnership, https://asean.org/wp-content/uploads/2016/10/SEOM-AFPs-Bali-Annex-4-Joint-Declaration-on-the-Launch-of-Negotiations-for-the-RCEP.pdf.

[46] First suggested by President Xi Jinping in a speech titled 'Promote People-to-People Friendship and Create a Better Future' at Kazakhstan's Nazarbayev University on 7 September 2013. See 'President Xi Jinping Delivers Important Speech and Proposes to Build a Silk Road Economic Belt with Central Asian Countries', 7 September 2013, www.mfa.gov. cn/ce/cegy//eng/zgyw/t1076334.htm (last visited 1 June 2020).

[47] First proposed by President Xi in his speech to the People's Representative Council of Indonesia on 2 October 2013. See W. Jiao (2013) 'President Xi Gives Speech to Indonesia's Parliament', *China Daily*, 2 October 2013, www.chinadaily.com.cn/china/2013xiapec/2013-10/02/content_17007915_2.htm (last visited 1 June 2020).

[48] MOFCOM, 'One Belt One Road Initiative: The Proposal and Development [Yidai Yilu Zhanlue de Tichu he Xingcheng]', http://history.mofcom.gov.cn/?special=2ydylzldtc (last visited 1 June 2020).

[49] *Id.* For a detailed review of the Belt and Road Initiative, see G. Shaffer and H. Gao (2020), *supra* note 39, 614–620.

[50] J. Xi, 'Coordinate Two Grand Schemes and Lay a Solid Foundation for the Path of Peaceful Development [Tongchou Liangge Daju, Hangshi zou Heping Fazhan Daolu de Jichu]', speech at the third joint study session of the 18th Politburo of the China Communist Party, 28 January 2013, www.gov.cn/ldhd/2013-01/29/content_2321822.htm (accessed 22 January 2022).

V The Attack: 2016–2020

China's efforts to build the alternatives turned out to be rather prescient, as attacks started to pour in from all fronts in the next few years.

(i) Unilateral Attack

On the unilateral front, the US launched a trade war against China when Trump came into office. In August 2017, President Trump requested the USTR, to 'determine, consistent with Section 302(b) of the Trade Act of 1974 (19 U.S.C. 2412(b)), whether to investigate any of China's laws, policies, practices, or actions that may be unreasonable or discriminatory and that may be harming American intellectual property rights, innovation, or technology development.'[51] On 22 March 2018, the USTR released its Section 301 Report into China's Acts, Policies, and Practices Related to Technology Transfer, Intellectual Property, and Innovation, which suggested '[a] range of tools may be appropriate to address these serious matters including more intensive bilateral engagement, WTO dispute settlement, and/or additional Section 301 investigations.'[52] On the same day, President Trump directed the USTR to raise tariffs against Chinese products, bring WTO cases against China's discriminatory licensing practices, and the Treasury Department to impose investment restrictions on Chinese firms.[53] On 3 April 2018, the USTR published a proposed list of Chinese products subject to an additional tariff of 25%.[54] In total, the list covers about 1,300 separate tariff lines with an estimated worth of roughly $50 billion. In the next one and a half years, the list was expanded several times to cover $550 billion worth of Chinese products.

These tariff measures are clearly in violation of WTO rules such as MFN and tariff bindings. In addition, despite its ultimate finding of

[51] United States Trade Representative (USTR) (2018) 'Findings of the Investigation into China's Acts, Policies, and Practices Related to Technology Transfer, Intellectual Property, and Innovation Under Section 301 of the Trade Act of 1974', 22 March 2018, https://ustr.gov/sites/default/files/Section%20301%20FINAL.PDF (last visited 23 January 2022).

[52] *Id.*

[53] 'Presidential Memorandum on the Actions by the United States Related to the Section 301 Investigation – the White House', https://trumpwhitehouse.archives.gov/presidential-actions/presidential-memorandum-actions-united-states-relatedsection-301-investigation/ (accessed 23 January 2022).

[54] USTR (2018) 'Under Section 301 Action, USTR Releases Proposed Tariff List on Chinese Products', 3 April 2018, https://ustr.gov/about-us/policy-offices/press-office/press-releases/2018/april/under-section-301-action-ustr (last visited 23 January 2022).

consistency on the Section 301 legislation in the *US – Sections 301* case, the WTO Panel also explicitly warned that making a unilateral determination of WTO-inconsistency against another country's trade measures "*before* the adoption of DSB findings" could constitute "a *prima facie* violation of Article 23.2(a) [of the DSU]" (emphases original).[55] Commenting on the US Section 301 investigations in the General Council, China's WTO Ambassador Zhang Xiangchen criticized the US measures for "violat[ing] the most fundamental values and principles of this organization." China filed a dispute against the US the day after the first rounds of tariffs were announced,[56] and brought two successive WTO cases against subsequent rounds of US tariffs.[57]

(ii) Plurilateral Attack

In addition to unilateral actions, the US also started to take a coordinated approach against China with its allies. This started with a joint statement the US issued along with the EU and Japan at the 11th WTO Ministerial Conference in December 2017,[58] where they agreed to "enhance trilateral cooperation in the WTO and in other forums" to address the "critical concerns" on "severe excess capacity in key sectors exacerbated by government-financed and supported capacity expansion, unfair competitive conditions caused by large market-distorting subsidies and state-owned enterprises, forced technology transfer, and local content requirements and preferences." Since then, the trilateral group has intensified its work with several more joint statements, all targeting China's trade practices without explicitly naming it.

In China's view, the other major attack on the plurilateral front is the refusal to recognize China's market economy status. According to Section 15(a)(ii) of China's WTO Accession Protocol, China agreed to be treated as a non-market economy (NME) in antidumping investigations, with the proviso that such provision "shall expire 15 years after the date of accession." China understood this to mean that "China will be recognized as

[55] Panel Report, United States – Sections 301-310 of the Trade Act of 1974, WT/DS152/R, adopted 27 January 2000, DSR 2000:II, p. 815, para. 7.95–7.97.

[56] United States – Tariff Measures on Certain Goods from China, DS543.

[57] US – Tariff Measures on Certain Goods from China II, DS565; US – Tariff Measures on Certain Goods from China III, DS587.

[58] USTR (2017) 'Joint Statement by the United States, European Union and Japan at MC11', 12 December 2017, https://ustr.gov/about-us/policy-offices/press-office/press-releases/2017/december/joint-statement-united-states (last visited 23 January 2022).

a full market economy" on 11 December 2016, as stated by then-Chinese Premier Wen Jiabao to world leaders in 2011.[59] Since its accession, China has been working hard to persuade other WTO members to recognize China's market economy status, both by inserting the provision in its free trade agreements, as well as making direct demands to the governments of other members. As of 2016, more than 80 countries have recognized China's market economy status. In addition to the practical benefit of avoiding discriminatory treatments in the antidumping investigation, the recognition of market economy status is also regarded by China to be of great symbolic value as it marks China's coming of age in the WTO. However, starting from 2011, some foreign lawyers started to argue that the expiration of the clause does not automatically grant China market economy status.[60] In 2016, the EU[61] and the US[62] respectively announced that they would not recognize China's market economy status.[63] In response, China dropped its earlier position which mixed the two issues together and started to separate them by treating market economy status as a political issue and NME methodology as a legal/technical issue. On 11 December 2016, China took the unprecedented move by suing both the EU and the US in the WTO.[64]

At the first panel hearing of the case against the EU in December 2017, Chinese WTO Ambassador Zhang Xiangchen made a rare appearance before the panel.[65] Quoting the Latin maxim "*pacta sunt servanda*"

59 'Premier Wen Jiabao Attends the Opening Plenary Session and Business Dialogue of the World Economic Forum Annual Meeting of New Champions 2011 and Answers Questions', 2011, www.fmprc.gov.cn/mfa_eng/wjdt_665385/zyjh_665391/t859433.shtml (accessed 4 November 2021).

60 B. O'Connor (2011) 'Is China a market economy?', https://voxeu.org/article/china-market-economy (accessed 3 November 2021).

61 'Texts Adopted – China's Market Economy Status – Thursday, 12 May 2016', www.europarl.europa.eu/doceo/document/TA-8-2016-0223_EN.html (accessed 22 January 2022).

62 US Department of Commerce (2017) 'Memorandum on China's Status as a Non-Market Economy Country', 1, 9, A-570-053, 26 October 2017.

63 'China's Market Economy Status' – European Parliament Resolution of 12 May 2016 on China's market economy status, 2016/2677/RSP, European Parliament, www.europarl.europa.eu/sides/getDoc.do?pubRef=-//EP//NONSGML±TA±P8-TA2016-0223±0±DOC±PDF±V0//EN.

64 'China Files WTO Complaint against US, EU over Price Comparison Methodologies' (2016), www.wto.org/english/news_e/news16_e/ds515_516rfc_12dec16_e.htm (visited 15 January 2022). The two cases are United States – Measures Related to Price Comparison Methodologies, DS515 and European Union – Measures Related to Price Comparison Methodologies, DS516.

65 H. Gao (2018) 'Broken Promises Set a Bad Example for China in the WTO', *East Asia Forum*, 9 March 2018, www.eastasiaforum.org/2018/03/09/broken-promises-set-a-bad-example-for-china-in-the-wto/ (accessed 17 March 2022).

("agreements must be kept"), Zhang made clear at the outset that "China brought this matter to dispute settlement with the objective to establish that promises made must be respected, and treaty terms struck must be honoured."[66] In China's 14-page statement, Zhang referred to the word "promise" six times and lambasted the US and EU for breaking their promises on ending China's NME status after 15 years. Zhang also highlighted the high stakes at play, including "the credibility of the dispute settlement mechanism, the integrity of the World Trade Organization, and the membership's faith in the multilateral trading system."[67]

In the end, however, the panel did not side with China. According to a leaked interim report, the panel supported the EU's argument that the expiration of the clause merely shifted the burden of proof and did not terminate the substantive right to apply the NME methodology.[68] In June 2019, China decided to suspend the case[69] and then abandoned the case by letting the authority for the panel lapse in June 2020.[70] While MOFCOM later clarified by stating that the termination of the proceedings in the case does not affect China's rights under the WTO,[71] it did indirectly reflect China's disappointment and despair toward the decision of the panel.

(iii) Multilateral Attack

At the multilateral level, the trilateral initiative spurred a new wave of WTO reform proposals, with key players, led by the US, EU, and Canada, all submitting major proposals. While there are considerable variations

66 'Opening Statement by Ambassador Zhang Xiangchen as a Part of the Oral Statement of China at the First Substantive Meeting of the Panel in the Dispute: European Union – Measures Related to Price Comparison Methodologies (DS516)', at para 2, http://wto.mofcom.gov.cn/article/newsupdates/201712/20171202684583.shtml (accessed 22 January 2022).

67 *Id.*, at para. 16.

68 H. Gao and W. Zhou, 'The End of the WTO and the Last Case?', *East Asia Forum*, 10 July 2019, www.eastasiaforum.org/2019/07/10/the-end-of-the-wto-and-the-last-case/ (accessed 22 January 2022). See also the comment by Geraldo R on 3 July 2019, Jesse Kreier, 'China NME Case Suspended', International Economic Law and Policy Blog, https://ielp.worldtradelaw. net/2019/06/china-nme-case-suspended.html (accessed 17 March 2022).

69 Communication from the Panel, European Union – Measures Related to Price Comparison Methodologies, WT/DS516/3, 17/06/2019.

70 European Union – Measures Related to Price Comparison Methodologies – Lapse of authority for the establishment of the Panel – Note by the Secretariat, WT/DS516/14.

71 'MOFCOM Responds to the Termination of the Litigation Process on the Case against the EU's "Surrogate Country" Approach in Anti-dumping [Shangwubu Huiying Zhongzhi su Oumeng Fanqingxiao "Tidaiguo" Shimao Zhengduanan Susong Chengxu]', 11 July 2020, www.thepaper.cn/newsDetail_forward_8230020 (accessed 7 November 2021).

among these proposals, they mainly focus on three groups of issues, all of which are regarded by China as China-specific:

The first group addresses the need to update the substantive rules of the WTO, such as clarifying the application of the "public body" rule to SOEs, expanding the rules on forced technology transfer, and reducing barriers to digital trade.[72] All of these reflect long-standing concerns over China's trade and economic systems, which have been litigated in the WTO. For example, concerns over China's unique state-led development model that emphasizes the role of state-owned firms in the Chinese economy were litigated in the *US – Anti-Dumping and Countervailing Duties (China)*.[73] Similarly, cases were also brought over China's over-zealous drive to obtain and absorb foreign intellectual property rights, where foreign firms are allegedly asked to trade their technologies for markets.[74] China's censorship regime and its tight control over information and the Internet were also the subjects of both actual and potential WTO litigation.[75] Unhappy with the results of these cases, the West tries to make new rules and tighten the discipline through their reform proposals.

The second group addresses the procedural issue of boosting the efficiency and effectiveness of the WTO's monitoring function, especially the rules relating to compliance with the WTO's notification requirements, such as those under the WTO Agreement on Subsidies and Countervailing Measures.[76] While no WTO Member may claim a perfect record in subsidy notifications, China's compliance seems to be particularly problematic and has been a constant subject of complaint by the USTR ever

[72] See European Commission, 'WTO Modernisation: Introduction to Future EU Proposals', 18 September 2018), at pp. 4–6; 'Communication from Canada, Strengthening and Modernizing the WTO: Discussion Paper', WTO Doc. JOB/GC/201 at 1, 24 September 2018, at p. 5.

[73] Appellate Body Report, *US – Anti-Dumping and Countervailing Duties (China)*, WT/DS379/AB/R, adopted 25 March 2011, paras. 276–359.

[74] See *China – Intellectual Property Rights II*, Request for consultations by the United States, WT/DS542/1, IP/D/38 (26 March 2018); *China – Certain Measures on the Transfer of Technology*, Request for consultations by the European Union, WT/DS549/1, G/L/1244, IP/D/39 (6 June 2018).

[75] Appellate Body Report, *China – Publications and Audiovisual Products*, WT/DS363/AB/R, adopted 19 January 2010, paras. 338–413; see also the potential WTO case when Google pulled out of China, which was discussed in H. Gao (2011), 'Google's China Problem: A Case Study on Trade, Technology and Human Rights Under the GATS', *Asian Journal of WTO & International Health Law and Policy (AJWH)*, 6, 347. For an overview of China's data regulation framework, see H. Gao (2021), 'Data Regulation with Chinese Characteristics', in M. Burri (ed.), *Big Data and Global Trade Law* (Cambridge: Cambridge University Press, 2021) 245–267.

[76] See EU proposal, *supra* note 72, at 9–11; Canada proposal, *supra* note 72, at 2.

since China's accession to the WTO.[77] After much prodding from the US, China finally submitted its first subsidies notification in April 2006, nearly five years behind schedule.[78] However, even that remained incomplete as China did not notify subsidies by subcentral governments, which would eventually take China another ten years to report, with the subsequent notification took another four years.[79] In frustration, the US filed a "counter notification" in October 2011 pursuant to Article 25.10 of the SCM Agreement, and identified more than 200 unreported subsidy measures.[80] To address the problem, the joint proposal by the United States, the European Union, Japan and Canada on strengthening the notification requirements suggested some rather drastic measures, such as naming and shaming the non-compliant Member by designating it as "a Member with notification delay," curtailing its right to intervene in WTO meetings and nominate chairs to WTO bodies, and even levying a 5% fine based on its annual WTO contribution.[81]

The last significant issue is development, another long-standing issue stemming from the call of the US and the EU for greater "differentiation" among WTO members. While they are willing to extend special and differential treatment (S&DT) to smaller developing countries, it is politically difficult for them to extend the same treatment to large developing countries, such as China, a growing economic powerhouse. Among the major economies, the US never granted China preferences under the Generalized System of Preferences (GSP), while Canada and the EU terminated GSP benefits for China in 2014 and 2015 respectively. At the time of writing, only Australia, New Zealand, and Norway continue to provide GSP preferences to China. The EU and Canada, in their proposals, called for the rejection of "blanket flexibilities"[82] for all WTO members, which

[77] USTR (2002) '2002 Report to Congress on China's WTO Compliance' (1 December 2002), https://china.usc.edu/sites/default/files/article/attachments/2002-report-chinas-wto-compliance.pdf (last visited 1 June 2020), at 22–23.

[78] USTR (2018) '2018 Report to Congress on China's WTO Compliance' (February 2019), https://ustr.gov/sites/default/files/2018-USTR-Report-to-Congress-on-China%27s-WTO-Compliance.pdf (last visited 1 June 2020), at 75.

[79] *Id.*

[80] *Id.*, at 76.

[81] General Council and Council for Trade in Goods, 'Procedures to enhance transparency and strengthen notification requirements under WTO Agreements – Communication from Argentina, Australia, Canada, Costa Rica, the European Union, Israel, Japan, New Zealand, the Separate Customs Territory of Taiwan, Penghu, Kinmen and Matsu, and the United States – Revision', JOB/GC/204/Rev.3, JOB/CTG/14/Rev.3 (5 March 2020), at 3–4.

[82] EU Proposal, *supra* note 72, at 6.

are to be replaced by "a needs-driven and evidence-based approach"[83] that "recognizes the need for flexibility for development purposes while acknowledging that not all countries need or should benefit from the same level of flexibility."[84] The US proposal went even further by proposing the automatic termination of S&DT for members who meet one of the following criteria: OECD membership, G20 membership, classification as "high income" by the World Bank, or a share of global goods trade at 0.5% or above.[85] With such a classification system, many WTO members, including China, will be stripped of their developing countries' status.

Commenting on these reform proposals at the Luncheon in Paris Workshop in November 2018, Ambassador Zhang criticized these efforts as trying to "put China in a tailor-made straightjacket of trade rules to constrain China's development...in the name of reform."[86] Drawing an analogy from the attempts by some countries to change the rules of the International Table Tennis Federation to reduce China's "advantages," Zhang pointed out that "[w]inning a game should be done through strengthen and hard work, not by altering the rules."

Another multilateral attack is the persistent blockage of the launch of the selection process for AB members by the US, which effectively shuts down the institution in December 2020. While such an attack ostensibly had nothing to do with China, a close examination of the US criticisms against the AB reveals that many of the complaints relate to the China cases. For example, among the six substantive "interpretive errors" enumerated by the USTR in its Report on the AB,[87] three are directed against the AB's decisions in cases concerning China.[88] These include, for example, the "public body" jurisprudence developed in US – Anti-Dumping and Countervailing Duties (China),[89] the requirement to consider

[83] *Id.*, at 7.

[84] Canada Proposal, *supra* note 72, at 5.

[85] United States, 'Draft General Council Decision – Procedures to strengthen the negotiating function of the WTO – Decision of X Date', WT/GC/W/764, 15 February 2019, at 1–2.

[86] 'On the Reform of the WTO Intervention by H.E. Ambassador Zhang Xiangchen at the Luncheon in Paris Workshop', 2018, http://wto.mofcom.gov.cn/article/meetingsandstatements/201811/20181102808197.shtml (accessed 22 January 2022).

[87] USTR (2020) 'Introduction', Report on the Appellate Body of the World Trade Organization, February 2020, https://ustr.gov/sites/default/files/Report_on_the_Appellate_Body_of_the_World_Trade_Organization.pdf.

[88] For a discussion on the merits of the US complaints, see H. Gao (2019), 'Disruptive Construction or Constructive Destruction? Reflections on the Appellate Body Crisis', in Chang-fa Lo, Junji Nakagawa, and Tsai-yu Lin (eds.), *The Appellate Body of the WTO and Its Reform.*, Singapore: Springer, at 215–238.

[89] USTR, *supra* note 87, at pp. 85–89.

government prices before using out-of-country benchmarks in *US – Countervailing Measures (China)* (21.5),[90] and the ban on "double remedies" through the concurrent application of countervailing duties and antidumping duties in *US – Anti-Dumping and Countervailing Duties (China)*.[91] Thus, it is no wonder that China also regarded the attack on the AB as an indirect attack on China.

VI The Aftermath: Affirmation and Alienation

In response to these attacks, China took a bifurcated approach: First, while many of these measures against China posed challenges to China's foreign trade, the fact that the US abandoning its long-standing position as the champion of the rules-based multilateral trading system left a power vacuum that China was eager to fill by affirming the principles of WTO. Second, by disregarding WTO rules for political conveniences, the US and the EU also set "bad examples"[92] which China quickly picked up. This section explores both themes.

(i) Affirmation

At the World Economic Forum in Davos in January 2017, Chinese President Xi Jinping gave a widely reported speech,[93] in which he called on countries around the world to embrace rather than blame globalization for the world's problems. Using China's WTO accession as an example, he said that China made "a right strategic choice" by "bracing the storm and exploring the new world." Despite "having had [its] fair share of choking in the water and encountered whirlpools and choppy waves," China has "learned how to swim in this process." Moreover, in a veiled reference to the protectionist tendencies of Trump, he called on everyone to "adhere to multilateralism to uphold the authority and efficacy of multilateral institutions," "honor promises and abide by rules," rather than "select or bend rules as he sees fit"

China's pledge as "a steadfast defender of free trade, globalization, and economic openness"[94] did not stop just at words. Instead, China

[90] USTR, *supra* note 87, at pp. 105–109.
[91] USTR, *supra* note 87, at pp. 116–119.
[92] H. Gao *supra* note 65.
[93] 'Xi's Davos Speech: Is China the New Champion for the Liberal International Order?', 24 January 2017, https://thediplomat.com/2017/01/xis-davos-speech-is-china-the-new-champion-for-the-liberal-international-order/ (accessed 22 January 2022).
[94] *Id.*

introduced a variety of measures to further bring down trade and investment barriers in the next few years. For example, in the midst of the trade war with the US, China reduced the tariffs on 1,449 tariff lines, which includes reducing tariffs on cars from 25% to 15%.[95] This is the largest round of tariff reduction in Chinese history, where the tariff lines covered are seven times those of the earlier rounds and covers 70% of consumer products.[96] Similarly, in the area of investment, China converted the market access catalog into a negative listing system in 2017 and has kept reducing the restrictions on foreign investment since.[97] In April 2018, Xi further announced that the whole island of Hainan will be converted into a free trade pilot zone.[98] With an area similar to Taiwan and a population a bit larger than Hong Kong, the Hainan Free Trade Zone (FTZ), if successful, will be the largest FTZ in the whole world and essentially re-create another Hong Kong for China.

At the international level, China also sped up its efforts to promote free trade, with the negotiations on the RCEP with its neighbors and the Comprehensive Agreement on Investment with the EU concluded in November and December 2020 respectively. Both agreements reflect China's view that it needs to seize the "important period of strategic opportunity for development" despite "profound and complex changes" both domestically and internationally,[99] as announced by Xi in his Report at the 19th Party Congress in 2017.[100]

In the WTO, China has also been playing a constructive role by leading the negotiation on certain issues.[101] These include launching offensive negotiations on issues such as investment facilitation, which China has

[95] L. Li (2018) 'Voluntarily Expand Imports to Enrich Consumer's Choices [Zhudong Kuoda Jinkou, Fengfu Xiaofei Xuanze]', *People's Daily*, 2 June 2018, 2.

[96] *Id.*

[97] H. Qiu (2021) '2021 Version of the Negative List on Foreign Investment Further Reduced [2021 Nian Ban Waizi Zhunru Fumian Qingdan zai Suojian]', *People's Daily*, 28 December 2021, http://finance.people.com.cn/n1/2021/1228/c100432318379.html (accessed 23 January 2022).

[98] 'SCIO Briefing on the Progress of Hainan Free Trade Port Policies and Institution', 2021, http://english.scio.gov.cn/pressroom/node_8023584.htm (accessed 23 January 2022).

[99] For discussion on the CAI, see H.S. Gao (2022) 'The EU–China Comprehensive Agreement on Investment: Strategic Opportunity Meets Strategic Autonomy', in M. Chi et al. (eds.), *Asian Yearbook of International Economic Law* (2022), 47–70.

[100] 'Full Text of Xi Jinping's Report at 19th CPC National Congress', 2017, www.chinadaily.com.cn/china/19thcpcnationalcongress/2017-11/04/content_34115212.htm (accessed 23 January 2022).

[101] X. Yi (2021) 'China and WTO Reform [Zhongguo He WTO Gaige]', 28 October 2021, www.ccg.org.cn/archives/66333 (accessed 23 January 2022).

been promoting at the WTO since 2014 as the coordinator of the group "friends of investment facilitation for development."[102] Designed to complement its Belt and Road Initiative, China successfully persuaded seventy WTO members to co-sponsor a Joint Statement on the issue at the 11th Ministerial Conference.[103] On the other hand, China initially took a defensive approach to issues such as e-commerce, due to its unpleasant experience with e-commerce issues in the WTO such as the China-Publications Case,[104] which China lost even though it did not wish to open up the online delivery of audiovisual services; as well as its restrictive data regulation framework domestically.[105] To counter the US initiative for negotiations on e-commerce, China pushed the WTO and World Economic Forum to endorse the "Enabling e-commerce" initiative – the brainchild of the Alibaba-backed eWTP. While this mission was also accomplished,[106] it was eclipsed by the Joint Statement Initiative on E-commerce, which was backed by the US. While it was initially wary of the US initiative, China changed its position and jumped on board when the negotiations on the e-commerce Joint Statement Initiative were officially launched in Davos on January 25, 2019.[107] As explained by Ambassador Zhang,[108] this decision also reflects China's wish to shape the rules in the negotiations, rather than being left out as in the Trade in Services Agreement negotiations. Since then, China has emerged as one of the most active participants with four submissions out of a total of fifty-two substantive submissions so far. In its submissions, China pushed for negotiations on its preferred issues relating to "trade in goods facilitated by the Internet" issues, especially the trade facilitation issues.[109]

102 "Investment Facilitation for Development", https://perma.cc/8LKD-LPCV.

103 *Joint Ministerial Statement on Investment, Facilitation for Development*, WT/MIN(17)/59, 13 December 2017.

104 H. Gao (2021) 'Across the Great Wall: E-Commerce Joint Statement Initiative Negotiation and China', in Shin-yi Peng, Ching-Fu Lin, and T. Streinz (eds.), *Artificial Intelligence and International Economic Law: Disruption, Regulation, and Reconfiguration*. Cambridge: Cambridge University Press.

105 H. Gao (2021) *supra* note 75.

106 'WTO, World Economic Forum and eWTP Launch Joint Public–Private Dialogue to Open up E-commerce for Small Business', WTO, 11 December 2017, https://perma.cc/W97H-SQ5F.

107 B. Baschuk and S. Donnan, 'China to Join Talks on $25 Trillion E-Commerce Market at Last Minute', *Bloomberg*, 25 January 2019, https://perma.cc/273Y-EEHK.

108 X. Ling, 'WTO Members Sign Joint Statement on E-Commerce at Davos [Shimao Zuzhi Chengyuan zai Dawosi Qianshu Dianzi Shangwu Lianhe Shengming]', www.gov.cn/xinwen/2019-01/25/content_5361275.htm (accessed 23 January 2022).

109 H. Gao (2018) 'Digital or Trade? The Contrasting Approaches of China and US to Digital Trade', *Journal of International Economic Law* 21(2), 297–321, https://doi.org/10.1093/jiel/jgy015.

More broadly, China has cleverly used existing rules in the WTO framework to pre-empt attempts by some countries to make China-specific rules. For example, in its November 2018 position paper on WTO reform,[110] China set out three principles, that is, "preserve the core values of the multilateral trading system" such as non-discrimination, "safeguard the development interests of developing members," and "follow the practice of decision-making by consensus." Together, these rules serve to prevent the US and other countries from introducing China-specific rules. More specifically, in its formal proposal on WTO reform issued in May 2019,[111] China also listed several specific issues to be addressed,[112] such as resolving the AB crisis, tightening rules to "curb the abuse of national security exception" as well as "unilateral measures inconsistent with WTO rules," rectifying "the inequity in rules on agriculture," and improving trade remedies rules.

On WTO dispute settlement, China also teamed up with the EU and other members to establish the multi-party interim appeal arrangement (MPIA). In its announcement on the MPIA, MOFCOM emphasized that the MPIA would help to maintain the operation of the WTO dispute settlement mechanism, safeguard the rule-based multilateral trading system, and affirms the confidence and support of the international society in the multilateral trading system.[113] In response to the US criticisms on the MPIA, China further stressed that the arrangement is consistent with WTO rules and made pursuant to Article 25 of the DSU,[114] even though the claim is debatable.[115]

110 MOFCOM (2018) 'China's Position Paper on WTO Reform', 20 December 2018, www.mofcom.gov.cn/article/jiguanzx/ 201812/20181202817611.shtml (accessed 23 January 2022).

111 WTO, General Council, 'China's Proposal on WTO Reform: Communication from China', WT/GC/W/773 (13 May 2019).

112 *Id.*, at 3–5.

113 MOFCOM (2020) 'China, EU and Other WTO Members Decide to Establish Multi-Party Interim Appeal Arbitration Arrangement [Zhongguo Yu Oumeng Deng Shimao Zuzhi Chengyuan Jueding Jianli Duofang Linshi Shangsu Zhongcai Anpai]', 27 March 2020, www.mofcom.gov.cn/article/ae/ai/202003/20200302949253.shtml (accessed 23 January 2022).

114 X. Xia (2020) 'US Obstructing Establishment of Interim Appeal Arbitration Mechanism at the WTO, China's Ministry of Commerce Refutes: US Actions Lacking Basis under WTO Rules [Meiguo Zunao WTO Chengli Linshi Shangsu Zhongcai Jizhi, Shangwubu Bochi: Meifang Xingwei Quefa Shimao Guize Yiju]', *21st Century Business Herald*, 18 June 2020, https://m. 21jingji.com/article/20200618/herald/015b28132bad9647b86d74b19e28a604_zaker.html (accessed 23 January 2022).

115 For a criticism of the MPIA, see H. Gao (2021) 'Finding a Rule-Based Solution to the Appellate Body Crisis: Looking Beyond the Multiparty Interim Appeal Arbitration

(ii) *Alienation*

The day after the US announced 25% additional tariffs on $50 billion worth of Chinese products, MOFCOM retaliated with the same additional tariff on US products of equivalent value.[116] The next one and half years witnessed several more rounds of tit-for-tat retaliations, with the stakes quickly escalating to cover $550 billion worth of Chinese products and $185 billion worth of US goods.[117] Altogether, these additional tariffs cover almost the entire bilateral trade between the two, with only limited exceptions.[118]

By firing its own rounds of additional tariffs, China has also lost its innocence in the trade war. In its announcements, China stated that its retaliatory tariffs were necessary to "respond to the emergency caused by the violation of international obligations by the US, defend China's lawful self-interests', and were justified by 'the relevant laws and regulations such as the Foreign Trade Law of the People's Republic of China and basic principles of international law."[119] No further details were provided by MOFCOM, but the most relevant would appear to be Article 7 of Foreign Trade Law, which states that China may take corresponding measures against any country imposing discriminatory trade measures against China. However, this provision suffers from the same problem as the US Section 301 legislation discussed earlier. With regard to international law principles, Dr. Yang Guohua, a formal senior MOFCOM official, has mentioned the following possibilities[120]: the right of self-defense under

Arrangement', *Journal of International Economic Law* 24(3), 534–550, https://doi.org/10.1093/jiel/jgab031.

116 MOFCOM (2018) 'Notice on the Collection of Additional Tariff on Some Imported Products from the United States [Guanyu dui Yuanchanyu Meiguo de Bufen Jinkou Shangpin Jiazheng Guanshui de Gonggao]', ShangwubuGonggao No. 34, 4 April 2018, www.mofcom.gov.cn/article/b/e/201804/20180402728516.shtml (accessed 23 January 2022).

117 D. Wong and A. Chipman Koty (2020) 'The US–China Trade War: A Timeline', *China Briefing News*, 25 August 2020, www.china-briefing.com/news/the-us-china-trade-war-a-timeline/ (accessed 23 January 2022). For a detailed analysis of the different phases of trade war, see C.P. Bown, 'US–China Trade War: The Guns of August', www.piie.com/blogs/trade-andinvestment-policy-watch/us-china-trade-war-guns-august (accessed 23 January 2022).

118 According to the US government, US import from China in 2018 was only $540 billion with its export to China $120 billion. See United Sates Census Bureau Foreign Trade Division, 'Foreign Trade Data: Trade in Goods with China', www.census.gov/foreign-trade/balance/c5700.html (accessed 23 January 2022).

119 MOFCOM, *supra* note 116.

120 G. Yang (2018) 'International Law behind the Trade War between US and China [Zhongmei Maoyizhan Zhong de Guojifa]', *International Law Review of Wuhan*

Article 51 of the UN Charter, the termination or suspension of a treaty's operation as a consequence of its breach by another party under Article 60 of the VCLT, and necessary measures to safeguard an essential interest against a grave and imminent peril under Article 25 of the Draft Articles on State Responsibility. Most WTO lawyers would not agree, however, that such general principles could be used to justify blatant violations of explicit WTO obligations.

Not only are the additional tariffs inconsistent with WTO rules, but the bilateral Phase One trade deal[121] signed by the US and China on 15 January 2020 is also of dubious legality under WTO law. This is especially the case for Chapter 6 on "Expanding Trade," which essentially set out managed trading regimes under which China agrees to import given quantities of US products, which is also supposed to expand on an annual basis.[122] Such practices have been outlawed by the Agreement on Safeguards, which contains explicit prohibitions on "orderly marketing arrangements or any other similar measures on the export or the import side,"[123] including both "actions taken by a single Member as well as actions under agreements, arrangements and understandings entered into by two or more Members." It is true that such commitments were forced upon China by the US, but China's willingness to go along with such WTO-inconsistent arrangement also made it an accomplice in the crime.

At a broader level, with its blatant violation of WTO rules, such as the attack on the AB, and the imposition of additional tariffs against China and other countries, the US has effectively taught China that WTO rules could be just ignored, especially as it gets in the way. Soon, China started to apply what it learned to other countries, by enacting various trade restrictions on Australia, Canada, and other countries that stepped on its toes.

At the WTO, China also followed in the footsteps of the US in using its power to block consensus liberally, including blocking the appointment of a Taiwan trade official as the next Chair of the Committee on

University [Wuda Guojifa Pinglun], 120, at 135–138, http://ilr.whu.edu.cn/d/file/zxqk/dqml/2018-11-12/75156e95c2e263ec08cb89708dca031c.pdf (last visited 23 January 2022).

121 USTR, 'Economic and Trade Agreement between the Government of the United States of America and the Government of the People's Republic of China', 15 January 2020, https://ustr.gov/countries-regions/china-mongolia-taiwan/peoplesrepublicchina/phase-one-trade-agreement/text (last visited 1 June 2020). For a detailed analysis of the phase 1 deal, see W. Zhou and H. Gao, 'US–China Phase One Deal: A Brief Account – Regulating for Globalization', January 2020, http://regulatingforglobalization.com/2020/01/22/us-china-phase-one-deal-a-brief-account/ (accessed 7 November 2021). 122 Ibid., Art. 6.2.

122 *Id.*, Art. 6.2.

123 *Id.*, Art. 11.1(b).

Government Procurement through Hong Kong in October 2021.[124] When the US won a case against China on safeguard measures on solar panels, China nullified the victory of the US by "appealing into the void."[125] In the discussions on WTO reform, China also took an aggressive position by stating explicitly in its position paper that "the reform should respect members' development models" and it would "opposes special and discriminatory disciplines against state-owned-enterprises in the name of WTO reform,"[126] a point further reiterated in its reform proposal.[127] For China, discussions on its economic model will be regarded as a "trap" that it will stay away from,[128] but it would not shy away from defending the model when it came under attack in the WTO, as shown by Ambassador Zhang's speeches in the WTO on several occasions.[129]

VII Conclusion

As we look back upon China's two decades in the WTO, we can see the shift of China from an eager, serious A+ student to one that grows increasingly alienated from the core values of the multilateral trading system. China is not alone. The US is essentially taking the same approach despite the professed affinity for multilateralism and international law by the new Biden Administration. New US Trade Representative Katherine Tai, for example, has repeatedly stated that she would not lift the WTO-inconsistent Trump-tariffs, but prefer to "retain" them as "leverage" against China.[130]

124 S. Lester (2021), 'At WTO General Council Meeting, US and Other WTO Members Push for Taiwanese Chair of GPA Committee', October 2021, www.chinatrademonitor.com/wto-general-council-us-others-push-taiwanese-chair/ (accessed 7 November 2021).

125 J. Pauwelyn (2019) 'WTO Dispute Settlement Post 2019: What to Expect?', *Journal of International Economic Law* 22(3), 297–321, https://doi.org/10.1093/jiel/jgz024.

126 MOFCOM, *supra* note 110.

127 WTO, *supra* note 111, Section 2.4.2.

128 'On the Reform of the WTO Intervention by H.E. Ambassador Zhang Xiangchen at the Luncheon in Paris Workshop', 20 November 2018, http://wto.mofcom.gov.cn/article/meetingsandstatements/201811/20181102808197.shtml (accessed 23 January 2022).

129 'Statement by H.E. Ambassador Dr ZHANG Xiangchen at the WTO General Council Meeting', 2018, http://wto.mofcom.gov.cn/article/meetingsandstatements/201807/20180702770676.shtml (accessed 7 November 2021); 'Statement by H.E. Ambassador Zhang Xiangchen of China at the General Council Meeting (Item 6 and 7) 13 October 2020', http://wto.mofcom.gov.cn/article/meetingsandstatements/202010/20201003007644.shtml (accessed 7 November 2021).

130 B. Davis and Y. Hayashi, 'New Trade Representative Says US Isn't Ready to Lift China Tariffs –WSJ' www.wsj. com/articles/new-trade-representative-says-u-s-isnt-ready-to-lift-china-tariffs-11616929200 (accessed 23 January 2022).

As the largest trader in the world and the second largest economy, it would be naïve for other countries to assume that they can change China's perspective on the multilateral trading system, let alone its behavior. Instead, to help steer China back toward a more receptive position on WTO, more will need to be done, with the following as starters:

First, the West need to abandon their own double standards. They should stop applying the NME methodology in antidumping investigations against China, despite explicit provisions supported by negotiating history[131] affirming its expiration in 15 years. They should stop applying WTO-inconsistent tariffs while accusing China of violating WTO rules. They should allow China to invoke the exceptions clause to justify its export restrictions on raw materials and rare earth while applying restrictions against Chinese imports on environmental grounds.

Second, in terms of detailed negotiating tactics, I have outlined the following in a policy brief published earlier this year,[132] which are summarized here: making the proposed rules neutral on their face so that they would not be deemed as China-specific or discriminatory against China so as to avoid evoking China's painful memory of the "century of humiliation," which would put China in a defensive mode; instead of holding the negotiations in a one-sided manner with a long list of demands on China, try to make it more balanced by giving China something in return, even if just as a token, so as to give "face" to China; try to understand China's own reform goals and policy movements, so as to gain insights on what China may agree to.

At its latest Trade Policy Review held in October 2021, China announced that it has "fully implemented all of its WTO commitments."[133] While people may debate the validity of such a claim of "full compliance," as I wrote three years ago, "the more important fact is that China acknowledges the legitimacy of the WTO rules and is willing to subject itself to the authority of the WTO. But as the WTO increasingly comes under attack

[131] W. Zhou and D. Peng (2018) 'EU – Price Comparison Methodologies (DS516): Challenging the Non- Market Economy Methodology in Light of the Negotiating History of Article 15 of China's WTO Accession Protocol', UNSW Law Research Paper No. 18-3, *Journal of World Trade* 52(3), https://ssrn.com/abstract=3115861 or http://dx.doi.org/10.2139/ssrn.3115861.

[132] H. Gao, 'Rethinking China Trade Policy: Lessons Learned and Options Ahead', National Foundation for American Policy 2021, https://nfap.com/wp-content/uploads/2021/01/Rethinking-China-Trade-Policy.NFAP-Policy-Brief.January2021-2.pdf.

[133] 'China Has Entirely Fulfilled Its WTO Commitments: Ministry', www.news.cn/english/2021-10/28/c_1310275388.htm (accessed 23 January 2022).

in the West, China will start to doubt the WTO as well. When China escalates its emulation of the West from words to actions, the United States and the European Union might finally remember the warnings from Ambassador Zhang, but it will be too late."[134] Unfortunately, the developments over the past three years have largely confirmed my prediction, with China increasingly following the bad examples set by the West. If there is anything positive coming out of these unfortunate developments, it is the hope that people can finally heed my warning repeated today, before it becomes really too late.

[134] H. Gao *supra* note 65.

PART II

Political and Economic Implications of China's WTO Membership

3

Assessing the Impact of WTO Accession on China's Economic Growth

A Synthetic Control Approach

JING LI, YE LIU, AND YINGGANG ZHOU

I Introduction

Before China joined the World Trade Organization (WTO) in December 2001, annual constant GDP per capita for China in 2010 US Dollars increased by 32% between 1997 and 2001. After the WTO accession, there was an acceleration as the Chinese economy grew 49% between 2002 and 2006. Even more remarkably, the Chinese growth rate remained at 43% between 2007 and 2011 despite the 2007–2009 Great Recession. Behind those numbers is a steady improvement in Chinese living standards.

The goal of this paper is to quantify the treatment effect of WTO entry on Chinese economic growth, an important topic against a backdrop of ongoing US-China trade war and recent debates about whether US government made a mistake by allowing China to join WTO, see for instance the article titled "Was Letting China Into the WTO a Mistake? Why There Were No Better Alternatives" published at *Foreign Affairs* in April 2018. So far the discussion has mainly centered on the negative impact on rising trade deficit from the US viewpoint. This study on the other hand intends to highlight Chinese perspectives on WTO's positive influence on its growth.

This research makes a contribution to the literature by using the synthetic control method (SCM) to provide a quantitative comparative case study contrasting the post-WTO economic growth of China to similar economies. The foremost output of SCM is a weighted average of control economies called synthetic China, which is constructed in such a way that it mimics pre-WTO China to the largest extent. Then the economic growth of synthetic China is compared to real China. The gap or divergence in the GDP trajectories can serve as evidence for the treatment effect.

SCM is suitable for a comparative case study for two reasons. First, country-specific idiosyncratic shocks can be smoothed out through averaging; Chins is compared to not just one country, but a weighted average of several countries. Second, optimal weights for control economies are determined endogenously in a data-driven fashion. We let data reveal the degree to which an economy imitates China. Thus, the concern about cherry-picking results can be alleviated.

In this paper, the treatment or intervention refers to joining WTO. Our identification of the treatment effect stems from the across-country variation in economic growth. More specifically, we contrast the growth trajectory of China to (1) the first group of nine countries that joined WTO at least five years later than China but no later than 2015 (donor pool A), and (2) the second group of twelve economies that joined WTO around the same time as China (donor pool B). The first comparison aims to produce the counterfactual of what would have happened to China's economy in the absence of WTO accession, while the second comparison can shed light on the issue of whether China gains "abnormally" from WTO membership. The second issue is crucial for understanding how WTO accession affects China, but to our best knowledge, it hasn't been investigated empirically in the literature.

The success of SCM hinges on the assumption that the treatment and control units are comparable. That being said, it is challenging to find control groups that are comparable to China given the sheer size of Chinese economy. Using donor pool B adds the difficulty that, while their dates of joining WTO are close to China's, they are not the same. Our solution is to normalize the living standard of each economy in donor pool A by its level in one year prior to China's date of joining WTO; for the country in donor pool B, its living standard is normalized by the level in one year before that country's own joining date. Thanks to the normalization, the outcome variable in this study effectively becomes an index of living standard as opposed to a level, and that index is much more comparable across countries than the level. Accordingly, the treatment effect is estimated as the cross-economy difference in the growth rate of living standard, rather than the difference in levels of living standard.

To rule out the possibility that the observed gap in GDP trajectories is due to chance, we apply SCM to conduct placebo studies (permutation test). For instance, we apply SCM to the year 2000, before the actual date of Chinese WTO accession, and we do not observe a divergence in outcome variables between China and synthetic China. Moreover, we apply SCM to Kazakhstan, an untreated unit in donor pool A. We see patterns in the trajectory of living standards different from what we observed after applying SCM to China in 2001.

There are studies examining other impacts of China's WTO entry (Chen, 2002; Kim, 2002; Shafaeddin, 2004; Tang and Wei, 2009; Bown, 2010). In terms of focusing on the impact on economic growth, Ching et al. (2011) is similar to this study, but the two differ in the following ways: first, this paper uses SCM while Ching et al. (2011) use a panel data evaluation method that assumes the outcome variable is driven by unobserved common factors and economy-specific fixed effects. Second, Ching et al. (2011) do not compare China to economies that joined WTO at times close to China. Given those differences, this study can be seen as a complement to Ching et al. (2011).

II Data and Methodology

For each economy, annual constant GDP per capita in 2010 US Dollars is downloaded from FRED economic data. For expository simplicity, GDP refers to the constant GDP per capita in 2010 US Dollars thereafter. If an economy joins WTO in the last three months of a year, we set the intervention or treatment period to next year. China for example entered WTO in December 2001, so the intervention period is set to 2002.

Donor pool A consists of nine economies that joined WTO at least five years later than China. In other words, those economies were untreated units in 2002 when China was subject to the treatment. The samples for China and economies in donor pool A range from 1997 to 2011, covering five pre-treatment years and ten post-treatment years for China. The beginning and ending dates are determined by data availability for all economies considered in this paper. In our view, five pre-treatment years are sufficient to capture the pre-treatment trend, and ten post-treatment years are sufficient to reveal possible divergence in growth trajectories.

No other economies joined WTO at the same time as China, but some were close. To obtain donor pool B with the proper size, we consider economies joining WTO no earlier than January 1999 and no later than December 2004. For those economies in donor pool B their samples include five pre-treatment years and ten post-treatment years just like China, albeit the treatment date varies across economies. We preclude economies that had already been members of WTO before 1999 or haven't joined WTO since 2016 because a substantial difference in joining-WTO dates signals lack of comparability to China. The name of economies in each donor pool, their dates of joining WTO, and the beginning

Table 3.1 *Summary of donor pool*

	Joining-WTO date	Sample	$\overline{GDP}$	$\overline{NGDP}$
China	December 2001	1997–2011	1,658	87
Donor Pool A				
Kazakhstan	November 2015	1997–2011	4,310	84
Lao	February 2013	1997–2011	647	92
Montenegro	April 2012	1997–2011	5,004	100
Russia	August 2012	1997–2011	6,106	89
Seychelles	April 2015	1997–2011	9,597	100
Tajikistan	March 2013	1997–2011	400	89
Ukraine	May 2008	1997–2011	1,783	89
Vietnam	January 2007	1997–2011	733	91
Yemen	June 2014	1997–2011	1,138	97
Synthetic China A				89
Donor Pool B				
Albania	September 2000	1995–2009	1,834	88
Armenia	February 2003	1998–2012	1,460	83
Cambodia	October 2004	2000–2014	483	88
Croatia	November 2000	1996–2010	9,908	95
Estonia	November 1999	1995–2009	8,490	92
Georgia	June 2000	1995–2009	1,294	87
Jordan	April 2000	1995–2009	2,693	98
Lithuania	May 2001	1996–2010	6,403	92
Moldova	July 2001	1996–2010	1,191	103
Nepal	April 2004	1999–2013	460	97
Oman	November 2000	1996–2010	17,685	95
Taiwan	January 2002	1997–2011	13,818	103
Synthetic China B				87

Note: $\overline{GDP}$ denotes the average GDP in the five pre-treatment years; $\overline{NGDP}$ denotes the average normalized GDP in the pre-treatment years.

and ending dates of the sample are reported in Table 3.1. For instance, Kazakhstan joined WTO in November 2015, fourteen years later than China. So it is in donor pool A, and its sample spans from 1997 to 2011. By contrast, Albania joined WTO in September 2000, only one year earlier than China, so it belongs to donor pool B. Its sample is from 1995 to 2009 (i.e., five years before joining WTO and ten years after).

There is noticeable across-economy heterogeneity in living standards before treatment, as shown by $\overline{GDP}$ in Table 3.1, which denotes the average GDP in five pre-treatment periods. Take donor pool A. China's average GDP (1,658) was more than twice of Vietnam's average GDP (733) between 1997 and 2001, although it was only about one-sixth of Seychelles'. Variations alike can also be seen in donor pool B – China was richer than say, Cambodia and Nepal, but poorer than Croatia and Oman.

Therefore a direct comparison of China to other economies is like comparing apples to oranges. In order to put all economies on equal footing and facilitate apple-to-apple comparison, the outcome variable used for constructing synthetic China is the GDP normalized by its value in one year before treatment. In other words, the normalized GDP is set to 100 in 2001 for China and economies in donor pool A. The same normalization is applied to donor pool B but using the GDP from one year before that particular economy joined WTO. For instance, the GDP of Albania is divided by its value in 1999. Because of the normalization, readers are cautioned that all the subsequent results are expressed in terms of an economy-specific *index* of living standard (the base period is one year before the treatment), or in terms relative to one year prior to the treatment.

The average normalized GDP (NGDP for shorthand) in the pre-treatment periods is denoted by $\overline{NGDP}$ in Table 3.1. It equals 87 for China, meaning that on average the GDP of China between 1997 and 2001 is 87% of its GDP in the year 2001. By comparing $\overline{NGDP}$ to $\overline{GDP}$, we see that the normalized GDP has much smaller variation, and therefore is much more comparable across economies relative to un-normalized GDP. Overall, the enhanced comparability increases the likelihood of constructing a satisfactory synthetic China. Note that even after the normalization, Montenegro, Seychelles, Moldova, and Taiwan differ substantially from China by having $\overline{NGDP}$ greater than or equal to 100.

Next, we use NGDP as the outcome variable and apply the SCM proposed by Abadie and Gardeazabal (2003) to obtain two versions of synthetic China based on donor pool A and donor pool B, respectively. In a nutshell, synthetic China is a weighted average of economies in the control group, and an economy with a growth path similar to China receives a greater weight than an economy with a dissimilar growth path. Put differently, SCM assigns data-driven weights to untreated units and the weights are determined by the predictive power. Mathematically, two nested optimization problems are solved by SCM:

$$W(V) = \text{argmin}_W (A_1 - A_0 W)' V (A_1 - A_0 W), \quad (0 \le w_j \le 1, j = 1, \ldots, J) \qquad (1)$$

$$V^{\text{optimal}} = \text{argmin}_V (B_1 - B_0 W(V))' (B_1 - B_0 W(V)) \qquad (2)$$

where V is a diagonal matrix of weights for predictors; W is a vector of weights for controlled units; A_1 is a vector of predictors for the treated unit in the training set; A_0 is a matrix of values of predictors for controlled units in the training set; B_1 is the vector of outcome variables of the treated unit in the validation set, and B_0 is the matrix of outcome variables of controlled units in the validation set.

Minimizing the quadratic form in (1) is a restricted quadratic programming problem because the weight is bounded between 0 and 1. The results are the optimal weights for controlled units for given V, and the optimal V is obtained by cross-validation (i.e., minimizing the mean squared out-of-sample prediction error in the training set given by $B_1 - B_0W(V)$). Finally, the synthetic control estimate for the treatment effect is given by

$$C_1 - C_0W(V^{\text{optimal}}) \tag{3}$$

where C_1 and C_0 contain values of outcome variables in the post-intervention periods for the treated and controlled units, respectively. The intuition is that the weighted average of post-intervention outcome variables of controlled units $C_0W(V^{\text{optimal}})$ is used to approximate the potential outcome of the treated unit in the absence of treatment. For more details about SCM, see Abadie et al. (2015). We follow Ching et al. (2011) and use lagged values of the outcome variable and their averages as predictors.

III Synthetic China A

To summarize, the synthetic China A is a weighted average of economies in donor pool A and the weight is determined by the extent to which each economy in that group helps predict China's normalized GDP in the validation period of 2000 and 2001. An economy with a greater forecasting power is assigned a greater weight.

Table 3.2 reports the model specification for constructing synthetic China A, and each column represents one specification. The criterion for model selection is RMSPE – the root of mean squared prediction error for the outcome variable in validation periods. A model with the smallest RMSPE is deemed the best one. Panel A of Table 3.2 shows weights for controlled economies while Panel B shows weights for predictors. Those weights are solutions of $W(V^{\text{optimal}})$ and V^{optimal} in (1) and (2).

In Model 1 all economies in donor pool A are included, and predictors are normalized GDPs in 1998 and 1999, and the average normalized GDP of 1997–1999. We see only two economies are assigned nonzero weights – Kazakhstan's weight is 0.585 and Lao's weight is 0.415. The weights for the

Table 3.2 *Model specification for constructing synthetic China A*

	Model 1	Model 2	Model 3	Model 4	Model 5
RMSPE	1.164	.591	1.337	.731	.571
Panel A: Weight for Untreated Unit					
Kazakhstan	.585	.453	0	.51	.482
Lao	.415	.349	.09	.49	.518
Montenegro	0	na	Na	na	Na
Russia	0	.198	.91	0	0
Seychelles	0	na	Na	na	Na
Tajikistan	0	0	0	0	0
Ukraine	0	0	0	0	0
Vietnam	0	0	0	0	0
Yemen	0	0	0	0	0
Panel B: Weight for Predictor					
$NGDP_{1998}$	.304	.366	.112	.221	Na
$NGDP_{1999}$	.298	.430	.888	.751	.980
$\overline{NGDP}_{1997-99}$	.398	.204	Na	na	.020
$NGDP_{1997}$	na	na	Na	.028	Na

Note: Each column represents one specification for SCM. A predictor with overline denotes the sample mean. Those weights are solutions of $W(V^{optimal})$ and $V^{optimal}$ in (1) and (2).

three predictors are 0.304, 0.298 and 0.398, respectively. Note that in terms of average pre-treatment normalized GDP, Kazakhstan, and Lao are not the ones closest to China, see Table 3.1. But Model 1 also uses normalized GDPs in 1998 and 1999 as predictors. Kazakhstan and Lao have pre-treatment NGDP paths that are closest to China, so they dominate in Model 1.

Because Montenegro and Seychelles have unusually high $\overline{NGDP}$ in pre-intervention periods, Model 2 re-estimates Model 1 after dropping those two economies from the donor pool. Now Russia receives a nonzero weight of 0.198. Model 3 removes the average normalized GDP of 1997–1999 from the set of predictors, resulting in a deterioration in fit as RMSPE jumps remarkably from 0.591 in Model 2 to 1.337 in Model 3. Model 4 replaces the average normalized GDP of 1997–1999 with normalized GDP in 1997 as a predictor. It performs worse than Model 2 because in general GDP is trending upward and the 1997 value lags behind the trend more than the average value.

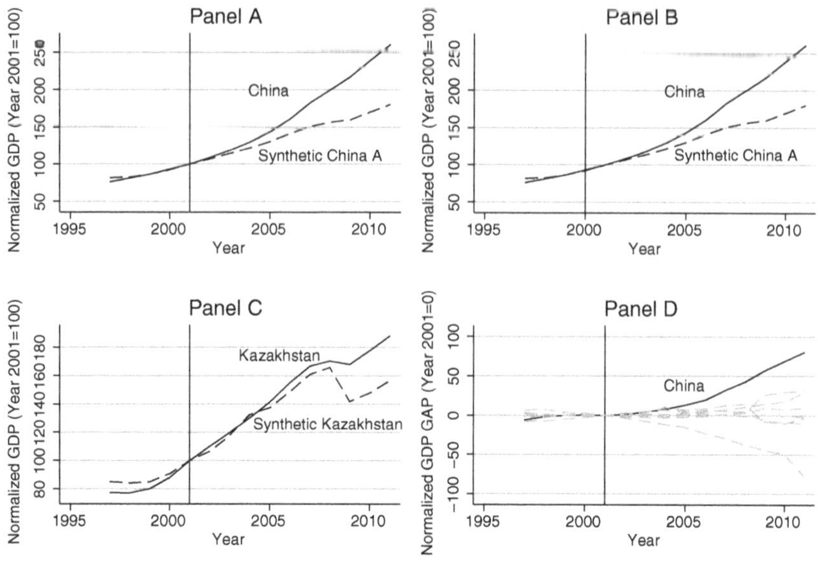

Figure 3.1 Synthetic China A

Note: Panel A compares the trajectory of normalized GDP of China and synthetic China A; Panel B conducts an "in time" placebo; Panel C conducts an "in place" placebo; Panel D contrasts the gap in normalized GDP between China and synthetic China A (solid black line) to gaps between economies in donor pool A and their synthetic counterparts (dashed gray line)

In terms of minimizing RMSPE or obtaining optimal out-of-sample forecasts in validation periods, Model 5 is the best one by having the smallest RMSPE of 0.571. Model 5 uses normalized GDP in 1999 and the average normalized GDP of 1997–1999 as predictors, and is our chosen model for constructing synthetic China A. Ignoring the worst Model 3, we only see a slight change in the weights for Kazakhstan and Lao, so those two weights are robust.

The best way to present the result of SCM is by visualizing its output. Panel A of Figure 3.1 displays the trajectory of the normalized GDP of China (solid line) and synthetic China A (dash line) constructed with Model 5 in Table 3.2. A vertical line is drawn in the year 2001 (the last pre-treatment year) and the normalized GDP is set to 100 in the year 2001. The divergence in the two trajectories after China's WTO accession is obvious and persistent. For instance, in 2006 the normalized GDP was 161 for China but only 141 for synthetic China A. That means relative to the 2001 GDP, China's economy had grown 61% within five years after WTO entry, but synthetic China A had only grown 41%.

Economic growth could be driven by factors other than the WTO accession. That is why the economies embodied in synthetic China A could grow even without the WTO treatment. One benefit of SCM is using synthetic China to control for other factors, and our identification of the treatment effect of WTO accession stems from the *difference* between China and synthetic China. Because the economies in donor pool A were not members of WTO in 2002–2006, the GDP trajectory of synthetic China A *during that period* is able to reveal the counterfactual of what would have happened to China's economy had China not joined WTO. In other words, the 20% *difference* in relative growth between China and synthetic China A provides an SCM estimate of the within-five-year treatment effect on Chinese economic growth of joining WTO.

We provide four pieces of evidence to support that SCM estimate. First, in Panel A there is a tight overlap between the two trajectories before 2001, implying that synthetic China A mimics China reasonably well prior to the treatment and therefore is suitable for generating satisfactory counterfactual. In fact, the average normalized GDP between 1997 and 2001 is 87 for China and 89 for synthetic China A. Those two values being close reflects that China and synthetic China A share a common trend before the treatment. In other words, China and its synthetic counterpart are likely to have similar confounding factors, so a comparison between them is akin to an apple-to-apple comparison.

Second, to rule out the possibility that we observe Panel A just by chance, two placebo experiments are carried out. Panel B of Figure 3.1 illustrates an "in time" placebo experiment by re-estimating Model 5 but using the year 2000 as the intervention period. That is, we pretend China joined WTO in 2000, before the actual date. Panel A would be problematic if Panel B displays a post-treatment gap between the two trajectories that looks similar to Panel A. That is not the case here – instead we see in Panel B a close-to-zero gap immediately after 2000, which indicates no treatment effect. Overall Panel B shows that it is unlikely to observe Panel A due to sampling variability.

Third, Panel C of Figure 3.1 presents an "in place" placebo by conducting the synthetic control analysis in Kazakhstan. That country had not joined WTO until November 2015, so there was no WTO treatment effect on its economy in 2002. Nevertheless, we pretend a WTO treatment occurred in 2002 and set the intervention period accordingly. In Panel C we see no persistent widening gap between the trajectories of Kazakhstan and synthetic Kazakhstan after 2002. That finding is consistent with our expectations and adds support to Panel A.

Finally, Panel D of Figure 3.1 plots the gap in normalized GDP between an economy and its synthetic counterpart after SCM is applied to every economy in donor pool A. The normalized GDP gap of China is represented by a solid black line and gaps of other economies are represented by dashed gray lines. Two facts are noteworthy – first, most dashed gray lines are near zero after 2002, consistent with the fact that those economies are not subject to WTO treatment. Second, the Chinese normalized GDP gap is consistently positive and above all dashed gray lines, indicating that China's relative growth dominates other economies in donor pool A. In short, China's economic growth is indeed positively affected by WTO accession.

IV Synthetic China B

In this section, we examine the issue of whether China's economic growth after WTO accession is "exceptional" compared to economies joining WTO between 1999 and 2004. For each economy in donor pool B, we include five pre-treatment years and ten post-treatment years. The GDP is normalized by dividing the level by one year prior to the treatment. Since the intervention period varies for economies in donor pool B, synthetic China B is a weighted average of normalized GDPs of the controlled economies within ten years after *their own* WTO entries.

The model selection for constructing synthetic China B is presented in Table 3.3, which differs from Table 3.2 in two aspects. First, because all the economies in donor pool B are more comparable to China in terms of having joining-WTO dates close to China, almost all of them receive nonzero weights in Panel A of Table 3.3. Second, the best specification is Model 6 that includes every economy in donor pool B and uses lagged values of normalized GDPs in 1998 and 1999 and average normalized GDP between 1997 and 1999 as predictors. Note that the RMSPE of Model 6 is similar to Model 5 in Table 3.2. Moreover, the average pre-treatment normalized GDPs are 87 and 87 for China and synthetic China B, respectively, a finding that implies that the pre-treatment common trend is captured by the synthetic China B.

Panel A of Figure 3.2 compares the trajectory of normalized GDP of China and synthetic China B. Unlike Panel A in Figure 3.1, we do not see a widening divergence between the two trajectories immediately after WTO accession. This finding is anticipated because donor pool B is unlike donor pool A, and the former supposedly benefits from WTO accession just like China. Actually, the gap between the two trajectories is not

Table 3.3 *Model specification for constructing synthetic China B*

	Model 6	Model 7	Model 8	Model 9	Model 10
RMSPE	.576	625	.601	.589	.625
Panel A: Weight for Untreated Unit					
Albania	.058	.056	.042	.057	.046
Armenia	.432	.428	.449	.434	.436
Cambodia	.064	.088	.076	.065	.073
Croatia	.031	.032	.031	.031	.032
Estonia	.049	.086	.046	.051	.037
Georgia	.223	.18	.206	.218	.232
Jordan	.021	.027	.026	.021	.025
Lithuania	.043	.045	.039	.044	.035
Moldova	.008	na	.013	.008	.015
Nepal	.024	.024	.024	.024	.023
Oman	.031	.035	.033	.031	.032
Taiwan	.017	na	.017	.015	.013
Panel B: Weight for Predictor					
$NGDP_{1998}$	.416	.236	.095	.419	na
$NGDP_{1999}$	.010	.667	.905	.272	.956
$\overline{NGDP}_{1997-99}$	.573	.098	Na	na	.044
$NGDP_{1997}$	na	na	.308	na	na

Note: Each column is one specification using SCM. A predictor with an overline denotes its sample mean. Those weights are solutions of $W(V^{optimal})$ and $V^{optimal}$ in (1) and (2).

noticeable until 2007 – there is a dip in growth for synthetic China B in 2008 thanks to the Great Recession. By contrast, the economic growth of China remained largely unchanged in 2008. According to Panel A, the impact of Great Recession on economies in donor pool B is profound in the sense that there seems no tendency for synthetic China B to return to its pre-recession trajectory.

A closer look at Panel A, especially between 2002 and 2007, illustrates that China actually falls a little behind its synthetic counterpart (i.e., the solid line lies slightly below the dashed line). This is the first indication that China's post-WTO growth is not exceptional, at least in the five-year short term. The second indication of China's average performance before 2007 is provided by Panel B of Figure 3.2, which contrasts the gap in normalized GDP between China and synthetic China B (solid black line) to

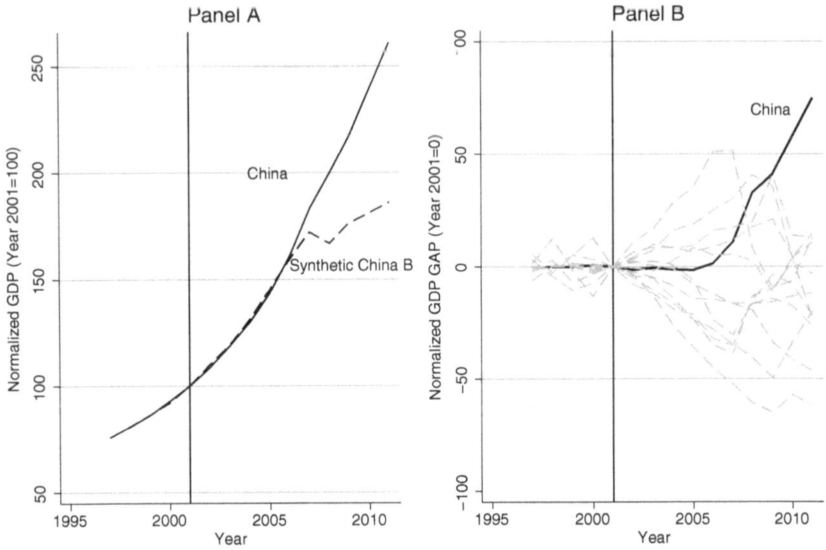

Figure 3.2 Synthetic China B
Note: Panel A compares the trajectory of the normalized GDP of China and synthetic China B; Panel B contrasts the gap in normalized GDP between China and synthetic China B (solid black line) to gaps between economies in donor pool B and their synthetic counterparts (dashed gray line)

gaps between economies in donor pool B and their synthetic counterparts (dashed gray line). In Panel B, China does not stand out in the crowd until around 2007, and this finding is in line with Panel A.

Notice that in Panel B some gray lines are consistently below 0. That means joining WTO is not necessarily associated with accelerated economic growth since there may be other factors neutralizing WTO's treatment effect. One example is that Georgia had the Russo-Georgian War after joining WTO in June 2000. One advantage of SCM is smoothing out country-specific idiosyncratic shock through weighting averaging.

V Comparative Case Study

In order to better understand the heterogeneity in post-WTO economic growth, Figure 3.3 compares the average post-WTO normalized GDP gap between an economy and its synthetic counterpart. First, Panel A shows that China distinguishes itself in comparison to donor pool A between 2002 and 2011. On average China outperforms synthetic China A by 33% during that period, whereas Kazakhstan and Lao outperform their synthetic counterparts only by 11% and 9%. Since Kazakhstan and Lao receive

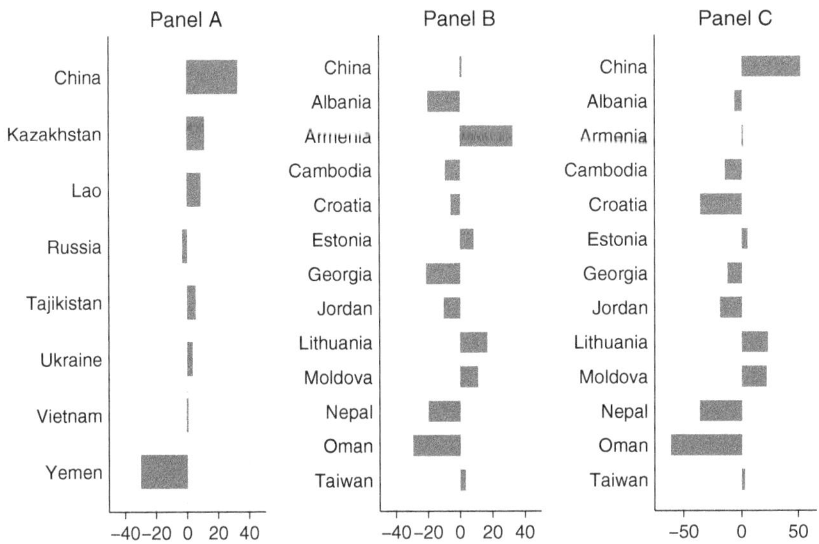

Figure 3.3 Average post-treatment normalized GDP gap
Note: Panel A compares the average 2002–2011 post-WTO normalized GDP gap between China and synthetic China A to gaps between economies in donor pool A and their synthetic counterparts; Panel B compares the average within-five-year post-WTO normalized GDP gap between China and synthetic China B to gaps between economies in donor pool B and their synthetic counterparts; Panel C compares the average within-ten-year post-WTO normalized GDP gap between China and synthetic China B to gaps between economies in donor pool B and their synthetic counterparts

almost equal weights in Model 5 in Table 3.2, the SCM estimate of treatment effect within ten years is about $33\% - 0.5(11\% + 9\%) = 23\%$, three percentage points greater than the estimate of the five-year treatment effect. Note that there is negative economic growth in Yemen during that period, which may partially lead to the Yemeni Crisis beginning with the 2011–2012 revolution.

In light of Panel A in Figure 3.2, we need to separately discuss the short-run and long-run when comparing China to donor pool B. Panel B of Figure 3.3 presents the average normalized GDP gap between each economy and its synthetic counterpart in the short-run (within five years of joining WTO). China on average grows faster than synthetic China B by only 1% during that period, while Armenia, Estonia, Lithuania, Moldova, and Taiwan outperform their synthetic counterparts by 32% 8% 17% 11% and 3%. Those five economies are also the ones having gray lines above China before 2007 in Panel B of Figure 3.2. Given this finding, the post-WTO growth in China is not exceptional.

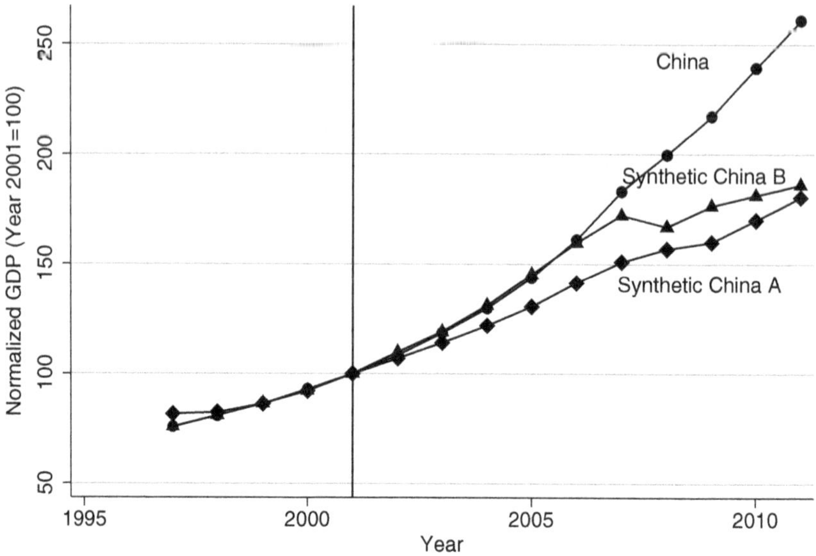

Figure 3.4 China and synthetic China
Note: Comparison of the normalized GDP trajectories of China, synthetic China A, and synthetic China B

We see a remarkable change in Panel C of Figure 3.3, which reports the long-run (within ten years of joining WTO) average gap for China and donor pool B. Now China has the best performance relative to other economies with an average gap of 51% between 2008 and 2011. By contrast, Armenia only outperforms synthetic Armenia by 1% between 2009 and 2012. A general pattern is evident: from Panel B to Panel C, a positive gap becomes less positive whereas a negative gap becomes more negative, largely because of the negative impact from Great Recession. China is an exception thanks to favorable shocks such as the 2008 Beijing Summer Olympics.

Finally, Figure 3.4 puts together the normalized GDP trajectories of China, synthetic China A, and synthetic China B. It is obvious that China outperforms synthetic China A. By contrast, the gap between China and synthetic China B is not noticeable until the 2008–2009 Great Recession.

VI Conclusion and Discussion

The goal of this paper is to estimate the treatment effect of WTO entry on China's economic growth. Our identification strategy is contrasting the growth trajectory of China to economies that either joined the WTO much later than China or around the same time as China. By combining economies in the control groups into synthetic China A and synthetic China B, with weights being determined endogenously by data, we are able to capture the pre-treatment common trend between China and its synthetic counterparts. Moreover, the synthetic control method enables us to control for unobserved confounding factors, and smooth out country-specific idiosyncratic shocks.

China's economy is unique given its sheer size and relatively low living standards before WTO accession. In order to increase the comparability across economies and the likelihood of obtaining a successful synthetic control, we put all economies on equal footing by normalizing each economy's real GDP per capita by the level in one year before joining WTO. When interpreting our results, readers should keep in mind that the outcome variable is an index of living standards that is specific to each economy.

We report a persistent and positive gap between the growth trajectory of China and synthetic China A. More explicitly, relative to the 2001 GDP, China's economy had grown 61% within five years after WTO entry, but synthetic China A had only grown 41% This finding implies that China would have grown much slower in the absence of WTO entry. This positive impact of WTO on China's economy is consistent with the general belief that trade contributes to growth.

The second research question we attempt to answer is whether the post-WTO growth of China is exceptional. Our finding is that within five years after WTO accession, China's growth had been comparable to other economies with similar joining-WTO dates. China's growth hadn't become distinguishable until 2008 when Great Recession affected other economies much more severely than China.

Several factors contribute to China's robust growth after Great Recession. For one thing, from 1997 to 2011 the length of railways in China increased by 41%, the length of the expressway network increased by 1,600%, the number of university graduates increased by 634 and foreign direct investment in China increased by 156%. Furthermore, the 2008 Chinese Economic Stimulus Program implemented by the Chinese government injected into the economy a stimulus package worth four trillion Renminbi or 586 billion US dollars. The 2008 Beijing Summer Olympics also helped the economy tremendously.

To summarize, our study suggests that China did not gain an unusual benefit from the WTO accession. Accelerated post-WTO growth happened in many countries, not just in China. Becoming a WTO member is only one of the factors leading to rapid improvement in Chinese living standards.

References

Abadie, A., Diamond, A. and Hainmueller, J. (2015) 'Comparative politics and the synthetic control method'. *American Journal of Political Science* 59, 495–510.

Abadie, A. and Gardeazabal. J. (2003) 'The economic costs of conflict: A case study of the Basque Country'. *American Economic Review* 93, 112–132.

Bown, C. P. (2010) 'China's WTO entry: Antidumping, safeguards, and dispute settlement'. In R. C. Feenstra and S.-J. Wei (eds.), *China's Growing Role in World Trade* (pp. 281–337). Chicago: University of Chicago Press.

Chen, A. (2002) 'The structure of Chinese industry and the impact from China's WTO entry'. *Comparative Economic Studies* 44, 72–98.

Ching, H. S., Hsiao, C., Wan, S. K. and Wang, T. (2011) 'Economic benefits of globalization: The impact of entry to the WTO on China's growth'. *Pacific Economic Review* 16, 285–301.

Kim, I. (2002) 'Accession into the WTO: External pressure for internal reforms in China'. *Journal of Contemporary China* 11, 433–458.

Shafaeddin, S. M. (2004) 'Is China's accession to WTO threatening exports of developing countries?' *China Economic Review* 15, 109–144.

Tang, M. K. and Wei, S. J. (2009) 'The value of making commitments externally: Evidence from WTO accessions'. *Journal of International Economics* 78, 216–229.

4

Two Decades of TRIPS in China

PETER K. YU

I Introduction

When China became the 143rd member of the World Trade Organization on December 11, 2001, the country had been heavily criticized for more than a decade for providing inadequate protection and enforcement of intellectual property rights (Yu, 2000, 2006a, 2007a). Based on the statistics provided by the World Intellectual Property Organization (WIPO) (2002, p. 8), China at that time ranked just outside the top ten in the world in terms of international applications under the Patent Cooperation Treaty (PCT). With over 1,600 PCT applications, it was right behind Australia and slightly ahead of Finland, Italy, and Israel. Fast forward twenty years. China has now become the world's leader in the same category, overtaking the United States in 2019 and Japan two years before. The country also ranked 12th in the 2021 Global Innovation Index, moving up considerably from 29th when the index was launched in 2007.

Notwithstanding these rather impressive data points, China remains heavily criticized for its lack of intellectual property protection and enforcement and frequently also for its non-compliance with the Agreement on Trade-Related Aspects of Intellectual Property Rights (TRIPS Agreement). In 2011, a decade after China's WTO accession, the US International Trade Commission (2011, p. xiv) released a report, estimating that "firms in the U.S. IP [intellectual property]-intensive economy that conducted business in China in 2009 reported losses of approximately $48.2 billion in sales, royalties, or license fees due to [intellectual property] infringement in China." More recently, the Office of the US Trade Representative (USTR) (2018a, 2018b) released a lengthy report on its Section 301 investigation into Chinese laws, policies, and practices

 This chapter draws on and adapts research that the author conducted for Yu (2013b, 2019b, 2022d).

in the areas of intellectual property, innovation, and technology development, which was quickly followed by a substantial update. Among the identified problems were forced technology transfer, discriminatory licensing restrictions, computer hacking, trade secret theft, and industrial espionage. As if these documents had not made the United States' intellectual property concerns loud and clear, the USTR has placed China on the Priority Watch List in its *Special 301 Report* every year since 2005, after a brief four-year post-accession "honeymoon" (Yu, 2012b, p. 526, fn. 2).

At this critical juncture when we commemorate the 20th anniversary of China's accession to the WTO – which coincidentally is named the "china anniversary" with a small c – it will be instructive to revisit intellectual property developments in China, especially those involving the TRIPS Agreement. This chapter begins by highlighting TRIPS-related developments in the first decade of China's WTO membership. It then discusses the country's "innovative turn" in the mid-2000s and the ramifications of its changing policy positions. The chapter continues to examine the US–China trade war, in particular the second TRIPS complaint that the United States filed against China in March 2018. The chapter concludes with observations about the impact of the TRIPS Agreement on China, China's impact on that agreement, and how the changing Chinese intellectual property landscape has altered the developing countries' coalition dynamics within the WTO.

II The First Decade

In the run-up to the WTO accession, China completely revamped its copyright, patent, and trademark laws while introducing or updating a large volume of laws and regulations in other trade-related areas (Blustein, 2019, p. 73; Yu, 2006a, pp. 906–23, 2013b, pp. 127–9). After 15 years of exhaustive negotiations, China finally became the 143rd member of the international trading body on December 11, 2001. While the United States and its industries were initially patient during the transition, the mid-2000s saw US industries complaining again to the USTR about the lack of intellectual property protection and enforcement in China (Yu, 2006a, pp. 923–5).

Taking advantage of a new-found weapon in the trade arsenal – the mandatory WTO dispute settlement process – the USTR took major steps to prepare for its first TRIPS complaint against China. In anticipation of the highly information-intensive process, the agency solicited information from industries through the Section 301 submission procedures

(Yu, 2006a, pp. 929–31). In addition, the United States signals its willingness to take WTO actions to resolve the trade dispute through a request to China under Article 63.3 of the TRIPS Agreement. Released in October 2005 in collaboration with Japan and Switzerland, that request asked specifically for "clarifications regarding specific cases of IPR [intellectual property right] enforcement that China has identified for the years 2001 through 2004, and other relevant cases" (Yu, 2006a, p. 926). China politely declined this request.

On April 16, 2007, the United States finally filed a complaint against China over the failure to protect and enforce intellectual property rights pursuant to the TRIPS Agreement. This complaint comprised four specific claims: (1) the high thresholds for criminal procedures and penalties in the intellectual property area; (2) the failure of the Chinese customs authorities to properly dispose of infringing goods seized at the border; (3) the denial of copyright protection to works that have not been authorized for publication or dissemination within China; and (4) the unavailability of criminal procedures and penalties for infringing activities that involved either reproduction or distribution, but not both.

Because the Supreme People's Court and the Supreme People's Procuratorate released a joint interpretation shortly before this complaint, the last issue was resolved, and the WTO panel proceeded to address only the first three claims (World Trade Organization, 2009; Yu, 2011c, 2011e). While the panel found that China had violated Articles 9.1 and 41.1 of the TRIPS Agreement when it did not protect the copyright in works that had not been approved for publication (World Trade Organization, 2009, para. 8.1(a)), it rejected the United States' claim on criminal thresholds by noting its failure to provide sufficient evidence to demonstrate what constituted "a commercial scale" in China's marketplace (World Trade Organization, 2009, paras. 7.614, 8.1(c)). With respect to the claim on customs measures, the panel was split. Although it noted that China had exceeded TRIPS requirements by extending border measures to exports in addition to imports (World Trade Organization, 2009, paras. 7.227–8), it also identified inconsistencies between Article 27 of the Regulations on Customs Protection of Intellectual Property Rights (Customs Regulations) and Article 46 of the TRIPS Agreement (World Trade Organization, 2009, para. 8.1(b)).

Following the WTO panel report, China quickly amended both the Copyright Law and the Customs Regulations. For the former, China removed the challenged language in Article 4, which stipulated that "works the publication and/or dissemination of which are prohibited by law shall not be protected by this Law." In its place, China added at the end of the provision a new sentence stating that "[t]he publication and dissemination of works shall be subject to the administration and supervision of the state." For the Customs Regulations, China incorporated verbatim the language in Article 46 of the TRIPS Agreement. The relevant treaty language states that "in regard to counterfeit trademark goods, the simple removal of the trademark unlawfully affixed shall not be sufficient, other than in exceptional cases, to permit release of the goods into the channels of commerce."

In retrospect, the United States' WTO actions took up quite some effort and energy on the part of the USTR while greatly reducing, if not freezing, government-level collaborations for a couple of years. It also kept US businesses in a waiting mode. All of these delays and disruptions would have been worthwhile had the panel report significantly improved intellectual property protection and enforcement in China. Unfortunately, that report did not have such a positive impact.

Although the WTO panel found Article 4 of the Copyright Law to be inconsistent with the TRIPS Agreement, the report gave the United States and its right holders only a paper victory (Yu, 2011c, p. 1098). Publications that were banned for distribution or that had to undergo content review would still have no market access in China despite receiving copyright protection. Likewise, because imports "represented a mere 0.15 percent by value of the infringing goods disposed of or destroyed in China between 2005 and 2007" and Chinese authorities did not auction off any confiscated imports during this period (Yu, 2011c, p. 1091), it is questionable how much benefit the amended Customs Regulations would provide to US rights holders. After the USTR's very limited success with the WTO dispute settlement process in the intellectual property area, US businesses were understandably disillusioned with that process. It was not until the arrival of the Trump Administration that the USTR filed another WTO complaint to push again for intellectual property reforms in China.

III China's Innovative Turn

While China was waiting for the WTO panel to issue its report on the first US–China TRIPS dispute, which was eventually released in January 2009 after some initial delay, the State Council adopted a National Intellectual Property Strategy in June 2008. That strategy "provided a comprehensive plan to improve the creation, utilization, protection, and administration of intellectual property rights" (Yu, 2018a, pp. 1079–85).

Paragraph 7 specifically emphasized the need for the active development of independent or self-controlled intellectual property (*zizhu zhishi chanquan*). Although this term has been frequently translated as indigenous intellectual property – or, in the larger policy context, indigenous innovation – independent intellectual property can be developed through the acquisition of foreign intellectual property assets (Prud'homme, 2012, p. 79; Yu, 2013a, pp. 94–5). There is no requirement that the intellectual property or innovation involved has to be home-grown.

The origin of China's National Intellectual Property Strategy traced back to the mid-2000s when government leaders began to consider major changes to move the economy forward. These leaders were well aware of the need to develop a new overall economic strategy to "avoid what policymakers and commentators have described as the 'middle-income trap' – the proverbial state of development at which a country is stuck after it has attained a certain level of wealth, but has yet to catch up with its more developed counterparts" (Yu, 2016, p. 27).

In February 2006, the State Council released the National Long-term Scientific and Technological Development Program, formally declaring its commitment to turn China into an innovation-based economy within 15 years. Since then, top Chinese leaders increasingly recognized the economic and strategic significance of a well-functioning intellectual property system. As the State Intellectual Property Office recounted in the report entitled *China's Intellectual Property Protection in 2008*:

> During the Ninth Collective Study of the 17th [Chinese Communist Party] Politburo, General Secretary Hu Jintao stressed specifically the importance of sticking to innovation with Chinese characteristics, energetically implementing the strategy of making the country prosperous with science and technology, the strategy of capitalizing on talent to make the country strong, IP strategy, and accelerating the construction of innovative country. When addressing the Party's meeting mobilizing the study and practice of scientific outlook on development, Premier Wen Jiabao said, "One thing necessary to stress is to concretely strengthen IPR protection. In the new era, competition of world science and technology as well as economy is mainly competition of IPRs. Underscoring IP protection is underscoring and inspiring innovation." ... Vice Premier Wang Qishan published an article in his own name entitled China no longer tolerates piracy, infringement on the Chinese version of the *Wall Street Journal* ....

A few months after the adoption of the National Intellectual Property Strategy, China undertook a complete overhaul of its Patent Law – the first revamp of a major intellectual property law following the WTO accession. Known officially as the Third Amendment to the Patent Law, the overhaul allowed China to make substantial adjustments to the patent system based on internal needs, as opposed to external considerations (Guo, 2011, p. 28; Yu, 2016, pp. 27–8). As Guo He (2011, p. 28) recounted, "The impetus for the early amendments [in 1992 and 2000] came from outside, whilst the need for the third amendment originated from within China, that is to say, the majority of the third amendment was to meet the needs of the development of the domestic economy and technology originating in China."

In the next 12 years, China unleashed a flurry of legislative amendments in the intellectual property area. Immediately following the 2008 patent law amendment was the Third Amendment to the Trademark Law, which was adopted in August 2013 and led to a complete overhaul of the Chinese trademark system. Then came the First Amendment to the Law Against Unfair Competition in November 2017. The unfair competition law had not been revised since its adoption in September 1993, and the US government and its supportive business community had widely criticized the old statute for its ineffectiveness and obsolescence. The Trademark Law was again amended in April 2019 – this time addressing issues raised by bad-faith trademark filings. Finally, during the COVID-19 pandemic, China adopted the Fourth Amendment to the Patent Law in October 2020, which focused on changes related to pharmaceuticals and enforcement. The Third Amendment to the Copyright Law was also adopted in November 2020, ushering in a complete overhaul of the Chinese copyright system (Yu, 2022a, 2022c). The last time that system went through a major revamp was in October 2001, two months before China joined the WTO.

Taken together, all of these new laws and related regulations have transformed China into an emerging intellectual property power. Today, China is the world's leader in PCT applications. Based on WIPO statistics, Huawei, OPPO, and BOE ranked among the world's top seven corporate PCT applicants in 2021. Ping An, ZTE, Vivo, and DJI were not far behind in the top 20. In the same year, China also had the world's third-largest volume of international trademark applications under the Madrid Agreement Concerning the International Registration of Marks and its related protocol. In addition, the 2021 Global Innovation Index ranked China 12th in the world, moving up from 14th in the two years before. Given these developments, it is no surprise that the State Council, in its *Outline for Building a Powerful Intellectual Property Nation (2021–2035)*, set bold 2025 targets for the contributions of the Chinese patent and copyright industries to the country's gross domestic product at 13 and 7.5 percent, respectively.

IV Forced Technology Transfer Disputes

China's growing strength in the intellectual property area attracts increased international policy scrutiny. Two days after WIPO announced that China had overtaken Japan to become the country with the world's second-largest volume of PCT applications, the United States filed its second TRIPS complaint against China, drawing evidence from the USTR's then-recently completed Section 301 investigation. The complaint focused specifically on the challenging subject of forced technology transfer (Abbott, 2022; Lee, 2020; Prud'homme and von Zedtwitz, 2019; Prud'homme et al., 2018; Yu, 2022b). It alleged that "China deprive[d] foreign intellectual property rights holders of the ability to protect their intellectual property rights in China as well as freely negotiate market-based terms in licensing and other technology-related contracts" (World Trade Organization, 2018, p. 1). At issue were the inconsistencies between the Regulations on the Administration of the Import and Export of Technologies and the Regulations for the Implementation of the Law on Chinese-Foreign Equity Joint Ventures on the one hand and Articles 3 and 28 of the TRIPS Agreement on the other. Article 3, which provides for national treatment, prevents countries from discriminating against foreign authors and inventors. Article 28, which focuses on patent rights, states explicitly that "[p]atent owners shall … have the right to assign, or transfer by succession, the patent and to conclude licensing contracts."

In November 2018, the WTO established a panel to address this dispute. Although the length and scope of this chapter do not allow for a full analysis of the merits of this complaint, commentators, myself included, have questioned its likelihood of success (Yu, 2022b, pp. 1014–24). After all, China did not force US businesses to form equity joint ventures, although it did impose foreign ownership restrictions in select sectors, such as those involving high-speed rail, new energy vehicles, and other frontier technologies (Lau, 2019, p. 173; Lee, 2020, p. 335; Prud'homme and von Zedtwitz, 2019, p. 7; Prud'homme et al., 2018, p. 164). In the developing world, it is also not uncommon to find countries embracing "market for technology" policies (Lee, 2020, p. 340). In addition, the issues implicated in the WTO complaint, such as indemnification and improvements in patent law, are highly technical. The lack of specific textual language governing these issues suggests that the TRIPS negotiators had not deliberated or reached a consensus on these issues (Yu, 2022b, p. 1014).

Moreover, the technology transfer issues involved in this complaint were at the center of a rather controversial international policy debate in the 1970s and 1980s concerning the restrictive clauses in the transfer-of-technology contracts found in developing countries. This debate, which continues even today (Chapter 22), led to the negotiation of the International Code of Conduct on the Transfer of Technology under the auspices of the UN Conference on Trade and Development (Patel et al., 2001; Yu, 2009, pp. 493–505, 2017a). Although the negotiations ultimately failed, some of the draft language in the Code made its way to the TRIPS Agreement (Roffe, 1998, p. 266; Yu, 2011a, pp. 315–16; Yusuf, 2016, p. 10, fn. 19). For instance, Article 40.1 expressly recognizes that "some licensing practices or conditions pertaining to intellectual property rights which restrain competition may have adverse effects on trade and may impede the transfer and dissemination of technology." Article 40.2 further provides: "Nothing in this Agreement shall prevent Members from specifying in their legislation licensing practices or conditions that may in particular cases constitute an abuse of intellectual property rights having an adverse effect on competition in the relevant market." Although no WTO panel has weighed in on these provisions, the textual language provides China with some strong defenses to the United States' complaint.

Notwithstanding these potential challenges to the US complaint, China adopted a new Foreign Investment Law in March 2019, replacing the Law on Chinese-Foreign Equity Joint Ventures whose implementing regulations were at issue in the WTO complaint. A few days later, the State Council also amended the two regulations implicated in the complaint. It is therefore no surprise that the United States requested the WTO panel to suspend its work in June 2019. A few months later, the two countries signed the United States–China Economic and Trade Agreement. Known widely as the Phase One Agreement, this instrument included over 40 provisions on either intellectual property or technology transfer measures. Because the United States did not request the WTO panel to resume its work within twelve months, the panel's authority lapsed in June 2021.

On June 6, 2018, more than two months after the United States filed the second TRIPS complaint against China, the European Union filed a similar but more extended complaint. *China – Certain Measures on the Transfer of Technology* marked the second TRIPS complaint that the European Union has filed against China, although the first complaint in *China – Measures Affecting Financial Information Services and Foreign Financial Information Suppliers* focused primarily on the General

Agreement on Trade in Services. That earlier complaint merely invoked Article 39.2 of the TRIPS Agreement when addressing the reduced ability of financial information services and suppliers to protect secret and commercially valuable information from unauthorized disclosure, acquisition, or use. At the time of writing, China and the European Union have not yet reached an agreement in relation to the forced technology transfer dispute.

Although the two complaints on forced technology transfer are highly interesting from a trade law standpoint, especially in view of the split outcome in the WTO panel report on the earlier US–China TRIPS dispute, the more recent US complaint should not be viewed in isolation from the ongoing US–China trade war. That war began with the arrival of the Trump Administration in January 2017 and has continued into the Biden Administration. During the 2016 US presidential campaign, candidate Trump repeatedly blamed China for the United States' economic woes. Among his key grievances were trade imbalance, currency manipulation, intellectual property theft, market access restrictions, and unfair trade practices.

To address trade imbalance and to fulfill his campaign promises, the Administration announced its plan to impose trade tariffs on Chinese goods in the area of aerospace, information communication technology, and machinery in March 2018 (Wong and Koty, 2019). The country further imposed tariffs of 25 percent on all steel imports and 10 percent on all aluminum exports, except for those originating in select countries. Slightly more than a week later, China responded with tariffs of between 15 and 25 percent on US goods, including fruits, wine, seamless steel pipes, pork, and recycled aluminum. The next day, the USTR retaliated with a potential 25 percent tariff on a list of over a thousand Chinese products that were worth US$50 billion. China responded the day after with a potential 25 percent tariff on $50 billion worth of US goods, including soybeans, automobiles, and chemicals. With trade actions intensified on both sides in a tit-for-tat fashion (Zeng, 2004, p. 14), the trade war began to take shape.

At the end of the Trump Administration, the total amount for three rounds of trade tariffs that the United States imposed on Chinese goods exceeded $500 billion. The retaliatory tariffs China imposed on US goods also amounted to close to $200 billion. The permissibility of these tariffs, including the WTO panel report on *United States – Tariff Measures on Certain Goods*, is outside the scope of this chapter and will be addressed elsewhere in this volume (Chapters 2 and 16).

V Expected and Intriguing Impacts

Thus far, this chapter has documented the last two decades of TRIPS-based intellectual property developments in China. It is therefore logical to interrogate the impact of the TRIPS Agreement on China. Considering that influences are rarely unidirectional, it will also be instructive to evaluate China's impacts on the TRIPS Agreement and the WTO. This section will identify impacts in both directions, including those that are expected and that have been widely documented in the policy and scholarly literature and those that are more intriguing or, for some, somewhat unexpected. These impacts illustrate the "two-way socialization" described by the editors in their Introduction to this volume.

(i) TRIPS Impact on China

Based on a wide range of amendments to intellectual property laws that China had adopted in the run-up to the WTO accession, including the complete overhauls of its patent, copyright, and trademark laws at the turn of the millennium, there is no question that the WTO and its TRIPS Agreement have had a significant impact on China and its intellectual property regime. To a large extent, the accession-related amendments continued the longstanding history of transplanting foreign intellectual property laws onto Chinese soil (Yu, 2016). From the bilateral commercial treaties that China signed with colonial powers at the turn of the twentieth century, to the intellectual property laws it adopted in the Republican era, the 1980s, and the early 1990s, to the WTO-related amendments it introduced shortly before the WTO accession, all of these laws brought to China intellectual property norms that were established abroad, mostly in the developed world.

The influence of the TRIPS Agreement did not stop at the WTO accession, however. Even though China did not overhaul another major intellectual property law until the country began making an innovative turn in the mid-2000s (Yu, 2018a, pp. 1079–87, 2020a, pp. 599–608), the WTO and its TRIPS Agreement have continued to influence intellectual property reforms in China. There is no better example than the Second Amendment to the Chinese Copyright Law, which was adopted in the wake of the WTO panel report on *China – Measures Affecting the Protection and Enforcement of Intellectual Property Rights*. In response to that report, China also incorporated TRIPS language into its Customs Regulations.

Notwithstanding the TRIPS Agreement's undeniable impacts, many of the intellectual property laws that China adopted since the late 2000s have focused primarily on internal needs, as opposed to compliance with external norms, including those enshrined in the TRIPS Agreement. This change of direction has raised interesting questions about the Agreement's lingering impact. It also invites debates about the relationship between those legal reforms undertaken before and immediately after the WTO accession and those that were introduced more recently, following China's innovative turn.

To the extent that the early reforms have paved the way for later reforms, one could certainly question whether this innovative turn is attributed to the TRIPS Agreement or the WTO. The latter provides developing countries with concessions in other trade sectors, such as agriculture and textiles. Nevertheless, the WTO's "single undertaking" arrangement has made it very difficult, if not impossible, to separate TRIPS contributions from WTO contributions (Yu, 2018b, p. 12).

Moreover, China has been practicing what commentators have described as "selective adaptation" (Yu, 2020b, pp. 207–15) – or taking advantage of what Frederick Abbott (2005, p. 100) and other commentators have referred to as "benign neglect." Since joining the WTO, China has carefully selected international intellectual property norms that align more closely with its needs, interests, conditions, and priorities. Such an approach has also been deployed by other emerging countries. It will be interesting to see whether this approach will present a useful model for other developing countries to effectively adapt to the TRIPS-based international intellectual property regime.

(ii) China's Impact on TRIPS

It has been a longstanding practice for China scholars to focus on the Western impact on China (Cohen, 1984, pp. 12–16) – whether in relation to modern Chinese history, international trade, or Internet communication. Much of the literature examining the TRIPS Agreement in the Chinese context has therefore focused on the TRIPS impact on China. Nevertheless, as much as we should evaluate this impact, we should also explore how China has affected TRIPS developments both within the WTO and outside. Such exploration is particularly important considering that most TRIPS-related research in the run-up to China's accession has fixated on the TRIPS impact on China, not the impact in the opposite direction.

Although China was expected to play an important role in the WTO upon its accession, including at the Council for Trade-Related Aspects of Intellectual Property Rights (TRIPS Council), it did not do so in the first few years in the international trading body. Instead, it kept a rather low profile (Gao, 2007, p. 69; Yu, 2011b, pp. 229–37, 2015, pp. 273–7). There are many reasons for such an approach. Among the oft-cited explanations are the Chinese leaders' priority focus on domestic matters, the country's need to cultivate goodwill from its neighbors, the complications created by changes within the Chinese leadership, the WTO-plus concessions China had made before joining the international trading body and the highly uneven developments within the country (Yu, 2012b, pp. 229–37, 2013b, pp. 129–31).

One of the editors of this volume has advanced a typology using "norm taker," "norm shaker," and "norm maker" to illustrate the different ways China could engage with international trade norms, in particular WTO standards (Gao, 2011). In the intellectual property area, China has been mostly a norm taker, even though it has become increasingly assertive in this area (Yu, 2011b, pp. 258–9, 2019b, pp. 438–9). In the first decade of its WTO membership, the only time China sought to take the role of a norm shaker in the TRIPS arena was when it joined a group of developing countries in July 2006 to co-sponsor a proposal for a new Article 29*bis* of the TRIPS Agreement. Consistent with what later became Article 26 of the 2008 Chinese Patent Law, this amendment sought to create a new obligation to disclose in patent applications the origin of the biological resources and traditional knowledge used in inventions (World Trade Organization, 2006a).

The other time when China advanced an intellectual property-related submission was before the Committee on Technical Barriers to Trade, which was technically outside the TRIPS arena. That paper warned that the inclusion of intellectual property rights into standards might have a "serious impact on the international standards setting efforts and the corresponding implementations" (World Trade Organization, 2006b, para. 13). This submission is historically important because it "marked the first time China made an intellectual property-related submission to a WTO body" (Yu, 2013b, p. 132). More importantly, it foretold the developments that were to emerge more than a decade later. In 2020, Chinese courts began issuing anti-suit injunctions to protect jurisdiction in litigation involving standards-essential patents (Yu et al., 2022, pp. 1578–88). In the past few years, Chinese policymakers have also paid growing attention to international intellectual property disputes involving these patents, due in part to their tremendous importance to future economic and technological development and in part to the fact that a number of Chinese firms, including Huawei and ZTE, are now leading players in the international telecommunications market.

Apart from activities within the TRIPS Council, one may also wonder whether the piracy and counterfeiting problems in China have undermined the performance of the TRIPS Agreement by ignoring or overburdening the WTO dispute settlement process – the fear of many policymakers and commentators for more than two decades (Cass, 2003, p. 45). Interestingly, despite their fears and widespread concerns that China would flout international trade norms, the country has been quite willing to amend its intellectual property laws when the WTO panels have found inconsistencies between those laws and existing WTO norms (Blustein, 2019, p. 6; Yu, 2011a, pp. 336–7, 2011b, pp. 210–11). For instance, after the WTO panel released its report on *China – Measures Affecting the Protection and Enforcement of Intellectual Property Rights*, China quickly implemented the decision by amending the Copyright Law and the Customs Regulations. In the wake of the United States' second TRIPS complaint, China also introduced a new Foreign Investment Law to replace the Law on Chinese-Foreign Equity Joint Ventures while amending the Regulations on the Administration of the Import and Export of Technologies.

Although China's low profile at the WTO and its willingness to amend laws and regulations in response to complaints and panel reports suggest its very limited footprint on the TRIPS Agreement, China has had at least three major impacts. First, its success in economic and technological developments has shown the viability of the TRIPS model (Yu, 2018b, p. 14). Since its inception, policymakers and commentators have heavily criticized the Agreement for ignoring local needs, national interests, technological capabilities, institutional capacities, and public health conditions (Yu, 2007b, p. 828). Many have also characterized the Agreement as "coercive" (Deere, 2009, p. 2; Dinwoodie and Dreyfuss, 2012, pp. 33–4; Yu, 2006b, pp. 373–5). Yet, the success in China has suggested that the TRIPS Agreement can benefit developing countries just as they have provided value to developed countries. The Agreement becomes even more appealing when compared with other new international trade and intellectual property agreements that call for protections and enforcement beyond TRIPS requirements. To some extent, China has made the TRIPS Agreement more acceptable for the developing world.

Second, the limited success that the United States and other developed countries had in using the WTO dispute settlement process to induce more intellectual property reforms in China has caused these countries to look outside the WTO for ways to raise international intellectual property enforcement standards (Yu, 2011d, p. 511). A key US strategy was the negotiation of regional or plurilateral agreements with developed countries and like-minded partners. These negotiations included the Anti-Counterfeiting Trade Agreement (ACTA), the Trans-Pacific Partnership Agreement (which has been incorporated into the Comprehensive and Progressive Agreement for Trans-Pacific Partnership (CPTPP) following the United States' withdrawal), and the United States–Mexico–Canada Agreement. Such negotiations, to a large extent, have slowed down TRIPS-based international intellectual property norm-setting at the WTO.

Third, and related to the first two, China has begun to slowly defend the multilateral intellectual property system, now that it has found TRIPS standards consistent with its national ambitions and local conditions. During the ACTA negotiations, for example, China joined India in mounting a high-profile intervention at the TRIPS Council, registering their concern about the development of TRIPS-plus enforcement standards (Council for Trade-Related Aspects of Intellectual Property Rights, 2010, paras. 248–63; Yu, 2011d, pp. 518–19). China has also advanced similar arguments to counter TRIPS-plus efforts both within the WTO and outside.

(iii) Impact of China's Intellectual Property Developments on the WTO

The last set of impacts concerns how the TRIPS-related intellectual property developments in China affect the WTO, in particular its developing country members. When the country joined the international trading body, it was expected to become a primary leader in the developing world. Although China has remained the so-called "elephant in the room," it has assumed a rather low profile at the TRIPS Council and in the larger international trading body. As a result, it has not been as vocal as other traditional leaders in the developing world, such as Brazil and India.

Nevertheless, because of its fast-evolving economic and technological developments, China has impacted the developing countries' coalition dynamics at the WTO in two ways. First, as noted earlier, because of its innovative turn, China is now taking positions that align more closely with those of developed countries than those of developing countries (Yu, 2016, p. 38, 2017b, p. 726; Chapters 9 and 10). To be certain, China has not given up its leadership role in the developing world. In 2018, the State Council released a white paper entitled *China and the World Trade Organization*, stating that the country "[v]igorously support[s] the integration of developing members into the multilateral trading system." Nevertheless, in the intellectual property area, China is more likely to take middle-of-the-road positions than those embraced by other developing country members.

For instance, during the global pandemic, India and South Africa submitted a proposal to the TRIPS Council, calling for a temporary waiver of Sections 1, 4, 5, and 7 of Part II of the TRIPS Agreement and related enforcement obligations to combat the global pandemic (Yu, 2023a). This waiver has subsequently attracted more than 60 cosponsors from the developing world, including both the African Group and the Least Developed Country Group. Nevertheless, China has only extended support to the proposal but has not assumed cosponsorship (Yu, 2023b) – a position that is quite different from its earlier approach toward the Article 29*bis* proposal on the disclosure requirement. As the Chinese delegation stated at the TRIPS Council when India and South Africa submitted the proposal in October 2020:

> China ... supports the discussions on possible waiver or other emergency measures to respond to the pandemic, which are "targeted, proportional, transparent and temporary,", and which do not create unnecessary barriers to trade or disruption to global supply chains. (Council for Trade-Related Aspects of Intellectual Property Rights, 2021, para. 977)

Indeed, China did not become more assertive until toward the end of the waiver negotiations – when the draft Ministerial Decision proposed for adoption at the Twelfth WTO Ministerial Conference included a requirement that would de facto single out China as the only developing country ineligible for the negotiated arrangement (Yu, 2023b, 2023c).

The second impact concerns plurilateral negotiations. As noted earlier, the intellectual property enforcement problems in China and the United States' lack of success in utilizing the WTO dispute settlement process to address those problems have caused developed countries and their like-minded trading partners to shift the international intellectual property norm-setting activities to plurilateral fora. Such a shift has taken a valuable norm-setting forum away from developing countries, greatly increasing their negotiation costs while creating possibilities for inconsistencies, tensions, or even conflicts across multiple fora (Benvenisti and Downs, 2007, pp. 597–8; Yu, 2012a, pp. 1089–90, 2021, p. 52).

More importantly, China has been at the forefront of these negotiations, assuming a highly influential role. There is no better example than the negotiations for the Regional Comprehensive Economic Partnership (RCEP) (Yu, 2017b, 2019a, pp. 103–05), which culminated in the adoption of the RCEP Agreement in November 2020. Included in this Agreement is an intellectual property chapter that contains 83 provisions, covering a wide variety of intellectual property rights as well as domestic, cross-border, and digital enforcement. In September 2021, China also made a formal request to join the CPTPP (Chapter 12).

China's active role in plurilateral negotiations will certainly undercut its efforts to fight off the developed countries' attempt to establish new international intellectual property norms outside the WTO. Nevertheless, the country seems to have made a conscious choice to negotiate in both multilateral and non-multilateral fora. As Martin Jacques (2009, p. 362) observed more than a decade ago:

> In the long term … China is likely to operate both within and outside the existing international system, seeking to transform that system while at the same time, in effect, sponsoring a new China-centric international system which will exist alongside the present system and probably slowly begin to usurp it.

With considerable human and economic resources, China is certainly in a good position to negotiate on multiple fronts.

VI Conclusion

China joined the WTO in December 2001. In the run-up to its accession, the country amended its intellectual property laws to promote compliance with the TRIPS-based international intellectual property norms. Although the recent decade has seen Chinese intellectual property reforms focusing more on internal needs, as opposed to external considerations, it is hard to overlook the many benefits provided by the TRIPS Agreement. Without these benefits, it is unclear whether China will make its innovative turn in less than a decade following its WTO accession. In return, China's success in making dramatic improvements in both the intellectual property and innovation areas has strengthened the appeal of the TRIPS Agreement, reinforcing its position as the predominant international intellectual property instrument. This chapter has shown that China and the WTO have affected each other in the intellectual property area. Just as the WTO and its TRIPS Agreement have had major impacts on China, the country also has had important impacts on both the TRIPS Agreement and the negotiation dynamics in the international trading body.

References

Abbott, F. M. (2005). 'Toward a new era of objective assessment in the field of TRIPS and variable geometry for the preservation of multilateralism'. *Journal of International Economic Law* 8: 77–100.

Abbott, F. M. (2022). 'Technology governance in a devolved global legal order: Lessons from the China–USA strategic conflict'. In C.-J. Cheng (ed.), *A New Global Economic Order: New Challenges to International Trade Law*. Leiden: Brill Nijhoff, pp. 197–226.

Benvenisti, E., and Downs, G. W. (2007). 'The Empire's new clothes: Political economy and the fragmentation of international law'. *Stanford Law Review* 60: 595–631.

Blustein, P. (2019). *Schism: China, America and the Fracturing of the Global Trading System*. Waterloo: Centre for International Governance Innovation.

Cass, D. Z. (2003). 'China and the "Constitutionalization" of international trade law'. In D. Z. Cass, B. G. Williams, and G. Barker (eds.), *China and the World Trading System: Entering the New Millennium*. Cambridge: Cambridge University Press, pp. 40–52.

Cohen, P. A. (1984). *Discovering History in China: American Historical Writing on the Recent Chinese Past*. New York: Columbia University Press.

Council for Trade-Related Aspects of Intellectual Property Rights. (2010). 'Minutes of meeting: Held in the Centre William Rappard on 8–9 June 2010'. IP/C/M/63. Geneva: Council for Trade-Related Aspects of Intellectual Property Rights.

Council for Trade-Related Aspects of Intellectual Property Rights. (2021). 'Minutes of meeting: Held in the Centre William Rappard on 15–16 October and 10 December 2020'. IP/C/M/96/Add.1. Geneva: Council for Trade-Related Aspects of Intellectual Property Rights.

Deere, C. (2009). *The Implementation Game: The TRIPS Agreement and the Global Politics of Intellectual Property Reform in Developing Countries*. Oxford: Oxford University Press.

Dinwoodie, G. B., and Dreyfuss, R. C. (2012). *A Neofederalist Vision of TRIPS: The Resilience of the International Intellectual Property Regime*. Oxford: Oxford University Press.

Gao, H. (2007). 'China's participation in the WTO: A lawyer's perspective'. *Singapore Year Book of International Law* 11: 41–74.

Gao, H. S. (2011). 'China's ascent in global trade governance: From rule taker to rule shaker and maybe rule maker?'. In C. D. Birkbeck (ed.), *Making Global Trade Governance Work for Development: Perspectives and Priorities from Developing Countries*. Cambridge: Cambridge University Press, pp. 153–80.

Guo, H. (2011). 'Patents'. In R. Kariyawasam (ed.), *Chinese Intellectual Property and Technology Laws*. Cheltenham: Edward Elgar Publishing, pp. 25–45.

Jacques, M. (2009). *When China Rules the World: The End of the Western World and the Birth of a New Global Order*. New York: Penguin Books.

Lau, L. J. (2019). *The China–U.S. Trade War and Future Economic Relations*. Hong Kong: Chinese University Press.

Lee, J.-A. (2020). 'Forced technology transfer in the case of China'. *Boston University Journal of Science and Technology Law* 26: 324–52.

Office of the US Trade Representative. (2018a). *Findings of the Investigation into China's Acts, Policies, and Practices Related to Technology Transfer, Intellectual Property, and Innovation under Section 301 of the Trade Act of 1974*. Washington, DC: Office of the US Trade Representative.

Office of the US Trade Representative. (2018b). *Update Concerning China's Acts, Policies and Practices Related to Technology Transfer, Intellectual Property, and Innovation*. Washington, DC: Office of the US Trade Representative.

Patel, S. J., Roffe, P., and Yusuf, A. (eds.). (2001). *International Technology Transfer: The Origins and Aftermath of the United Nations Negotiations on a Draft Code of Conduct*. The Hague: Kluwer Law International.

Prud'homme, D. (2012). *Dulling the Cutting Edge: How Patent-Related Policies and Practices Hamper Innovation in China*. Shanghai: European Union Chamber of Commerce.

Prud'homme, D., and von Zedtwitz, M. (2019). 'Managing "forced" technology transfer in emerging markets: The case of China'. *Journal of International Management* 25: 100670.

Prud'homme, D., von Zedtwitz, M., Thraen, J. J., and Bader, M. (2018). '"Forced technology transfer" policies: Workings in China and strategic implications'. *Technological Forecasting and Social Change* 134: 150–68.

Roffe, P. (1998). 'Control of anti-competitive practices in contractual licences under the TRIPs Agreement'. In C. M. Correa and A. A. Yusuf (eds.), *Intellectual Property and International Trade: The TRIPS Agreement*, 1st ed. The Hague: Kluwer Law International, pp. 261–96.

US International Trade Commission. (2011). *China: Effects of Intellectual Property Infringement and Indigenous Innovation Policies on the U.S. Economy*. Washington, DC: US International Trade Commission.

Wong, D., and Koty, A. C. (2019). 'The US–China Trade War: A timeline'. www.china-briefing.com/news/the-us-china-trade-war-a-timeline/. Accessed September 6, 2021.

World Intellectual Property Organization. (2002). 'The Patent Cooperation Treaty (PCT) in 2001'. www.wipo.int/export/sites/www/pct/en/activity/pct_2001.pdf. Accessed November 9, 2021.

World Trade Organization. (2006a). 'Doha Work Programme – The Outstanding implementation issue on the relationship between the TRIPS agreement and the convention on biological diversity'. WT/GC/W/564/Rev.2. Geneva: World Trade Organization.

World Trade Organization. (2006b). 'Intellectual Property Right (IPR) issues in standardization'. G/TBT/W/251/Add.1. Geneva: World Trade Organization.

World Trade Organization. (2009). 'China – Measures Affecting the protection and enforcement of intellectual property rights: Report of the panel'. WT/DS362/R. Geneva: World Trade Organization.

World Trade Organization. (2018). 'China – Certain measures concerning the protection of intellectual property rights: Request for consultations by the United States'. WT/DS542/1. Geneva: World Trade Organization.

Yu, P. K. (2000). 'From pirates to partners: Protecting intellectual property in China in the twenty-first century'. *American University Law Review* 50: 131–243.

Yu, P. K. (2006a). 'From pirates to partners (Episode II): Protecting intellectual property in post-WTO China'. *American University Law Review* 55: 901–1000.

Yu, P. K. (2006b). 'TRIPS and its discontents'. *Marquette Intellectual Property Law Review* 10: 369–410.

Yu, P. K. (2007a). 'Intellectual property, economic development, and the China puzzle'. In D. J. Gervais (ed.), *Intellectual Property, Trade and Development: Strategies to Optimize Economic Development in a TRIPS Plus Era*, 1st ed. Oxford: Oxford University Press, pp. 173–220.

Yu, P. K. (2007b). 'The international enclosure movement'. *Indiana Law Journal* 82: 827–907.

Yu, P. K. (2009). 'A tale of two development agendas'. *Ohio Northern University Law Review* 35: 465–73.

Yu, P. K. (2011a). 'Are developing countries playing a better TRIPS game?'. *UCLA Journal of International Law and Foreign Affairs* 16: 311–43.

Yu, P. K. (2011b). 'The Middle Kingdom and the intellectual property world'. *Oregon Review of International Law* 13: 209–62.

Yu, P. K. (2011c). 'The TRIPS enforcement dispute'. *Nebraska Law Review* 89: 1046–131.

Yu, P. K. (2011d). 'TRIPS and its Achilles' Heel'. *Journal of Intellectual Property Law* 18: 479–531.

Yu, P. K. (2011e). 'TRIPS enforcement and developing countries'. *American University International Law Review* 26: 727–82.

Yu, P. K. (2012a). 'Intellectual property and human rights in the nonmultilateral era'. *Florida Law Review* 64: 1045–100.

Yu, P. K. (2012b). 'The rise and decline of the intellectual property powers'. *Campbell Law Review* 34: 525–80.

Yu, P. K. (2013a). 'Five oft-repeated questions about China's recent rise as a patent power'. *Cardozo Law Review de Novo* 2013: 78–114.

Yu, P. K. (2013b). 'The first decade of TRIPS in China'. In K. Zeng and W. Liang (eds.), *China and Global Trade Governance: China's First Decade in the World Trade Organization*. Abingdon: Routledge, pp. 126–43.

Yu, P. K. (2015). 'Sinic trade agreements and China's global intellectual property strategy'. In C. Antons and R. M. Hilty (eds.), *Intellectual Property and Free Trade Agreements in the Asia-Pacific Region*. Heidelberg: Springer, pp. 247–83.

Yu, P. K. (2016). 'The transplant and transformation of intellectual property laws in China'. In N. Lee, N. Bruun, and M. Li (eds.), *Governance of Intellectual Property Rights in China and Europe*. Cheltenham: Edward Elgar Publishing, pp. 20–42.

Yu, P. K. (2017a). 'International technology contracts, restrictive covenants and the UNCTAD Code'. In C. Heath and A. Kamperman Sanders (eds.), *Employees, Trade Secrets and Restrictive Covenants*. Alphen aan den Rijn: Wolters Kluwer, pp. 41–57.

Yu, P. K. (2017b). 'The RCEP and Trans-Pacific intellectual property norms'. *Vanderbilt Journal of Transnational Law* 50: 673–740.

Yu, P. K. (2018a). 'A half-century of scholarship on the Chinese intellectual property system'. *American University Law Review* 67: 1045–1140.

Yu, P. K. (2018b). 'When the Chinese intellectual property system hits 35'. *Queen Mary Journal of Intellectual Property* 8: 3–14.

Yu, P. K. (2019a). 'The RCEP negotiations and Asian intellectual property norm setters'. In K.-C. Liu and J. Chaisse (eds.), *The Future of Asian Trade Deals and IP*. Oxford: Hart Publishing, pp. 85–110.

Yu, P. K. (2019b). 'The rise of China in the international intellectual property regime'. In K. Zeng (ed.), *Handbook on the International Political Economy of China*. Cheltenham: Edward Elgar Publishing, pp. 424–43.

Yu, P. K. (2020a). 'China's innovative turn and the changing pharmaceutical landscape'. *University of the Pacific Law Review* 51: 593–620.

Yu, P. K. (2020b). 'TRIPS and its contents'. *IDEA: The Law Review of the Franklin Pierce Center for Intellectual Property* 60: 149–234.

Yu, P. K. (2021). 'Realigning TRIPS-plus negotiations with UN sustainable development goals'. In O.-A. Rognstad and I. B. Ørstavik (eds.), *Intellectual Property and Sustainable Markets*. Cheltenham: Edward Elgar Publishing, pp. 38–62.

Yu, P. K. (2022a). 'The long and winding road to effective copyright protection in China'. *Pepperdine Law Review* 49: 681–732.

Yu, P. K. (2022b). 'The U.S.-China forced technology transfer dispute'. *Seton Hall Law Review* 52: 1003–52.

Yu, P. K. (2022c). 'Third amendment to the Chinese Copyright Law'. *Journal of the Copyright Society*. 69: 1–21.

Yu, P. K. (2022d). 'US-China Intellectual Property Trade Wars'. K. Zeng and W. Liang (eds.), *Research Handbook on Trade Wars*. Cheltenham: Edward Elgar Publishing, pp. 271–87.

Yu, P. K. (2023a). 'A critical appraisal of the COVID-19 TRIPS waiver'. In T. E. Pihlajarinne, J. Mähönen, and P. Upreti (eds.), *Intellectual Property Rights in the Post Pandemic World: An Integrated Framework of Sustainability, Innovation and Global Justice*. Cheltenham: Edward Elgar Publishing.

Yu, P. K. (2023b). 'China, the TRIPS waiver and the global pandemic response'. In M. Sunder and H. Sun (eds.), *Intellectual Property, COVID-19, and the Next Pandemic: Diagnosing Problems, Developing Cures*. Cambridge: Cambridge University Press.

Yu, P. K. (2023c). 'The COVID-19 TRIPS waiver and the WTO ministerial decision'. In J. Schovsbo (ed.), *IPR in Times of Crisis: Lessons Learned from the COVID-19 Pandemic*. Cheltenham: Edward Elgar Publishing.

Yu, P. K., Contreras, J. L., and Yu, Y. (2022). 'Transplanting anti-suit injunctions'. *American University Law Review* 71: 1537–618.

Yusuf, A. A. (2016). 'TRIPS: Background, principles and general provisions'. In C. M. Correa and A. A. Yusuf (eds.), *Intellectual Property and International Trade: The TRIPS Agreement*, 3rd ed. Alphen aan den Rijn: Wolters Kluwer, pp. 3–25.

Zeng, K. (2004). *Trade Threats, Trade Wars: Bargaining, Retaliation, and American Coercive Diplomacy*. Ann Arbor: University of Michigan Press.

5

The WTO and the Rule of Law in China

GRANT ALDONAS

I Introduction

Jonathan Spence's classic study, *To Change China*, offers a cautionary tale of Western efforts to reshape the Middle Kingdom.[1] Spence recounts the story of a Jesuit missionary, Adam Schall, predicting a solar eclipse in the late summer of 1644 and requesting Chongzhen, the last emperor of the Ming dynasty, to have the Board of Rites test Schall's prediction.

Chongzhen issued the decree, which called for both Schall and the imperial scientific advisers to make their predictions and test them against the actual eclipse. In the event, only Schall accurately predicted its timing and phases. Schall's success led to his being retained by the emperor as an adviser, where Schall integrated himself deeply into Chinese culture.

But Schall's mission to convert the Chinese to Catholicism failed. In the end, China changed Schall and his fellow Jesuits, rather than the Jesuits changing China.

Critics of China's accession to the World Trade Organization ("WTO") suggest a similar fate has befallen the institution. In their view, rather than changing China, the WTO has been "swallowed" whole by what is now the world's largest trading nation.[2] Some go further, accusing proponents of China's accession of "hubris" in assuming China's accession would "inevitably" lead the People's Republic to "embrace democracy and capitalism."[3]

1 Jonathan Spence. *To Change China – Western Advisers in China*. Little Brown & Company (1969).

2 Jacob M. Schlesinger. 'How China Swallowed the WTO'. The Wall Street Journal. November 1, 2017.

3 See, e.g., Ambassador Robert E. Lighthizer. Evaluating China's Role in the World Trade Organization Over the Past Decade. Testimony Before the U.S.-China Economic and Security Review Commission. June 9, 2010. 25–26 ("Lighthizer Testimony").

Those arguments do not withstand serious scrutiny.[4] Concrete commercial considerations, rather than hubris or misguided beliefs, guided the negotiators and the political debate over China's accession.[5] To the extent the reforms China undertook to join WTO expanded the degrees of freedom individual Chinese citizens could exercise, that consequence was incidental to the WTO members' negotiating objectives.[6]

Yet, nearly two decades after its accession, there is little doubt China finds itself in "an increasingly tense standoff with the U.S. and Europe that

[4] The critics' arguments are, in fact, disingenuous. Ambassador Lighthizer's testimony, for example, cites no contemporaneous statement by US policymakers for his claim regarding the hubris of US policymakers. He relies instead on extensive quotations from Francis Fukuyama's 1989 essay, "The End of History?" and an opinion piece penned by Congressman Tom Delay of the US House of Representatives. Id. Fukuyama's piece was written more than a decade before China's WTO accession and focused on the portents of the Soviet Union's collapse, not China. Francis Fukuyama, The End of History, The National Interest (Summer, 1989) 3–18. Fukuyama played no role in either the negotiation of China's accession or the US Congress' passage of legislation granting China "permanent normal trade relations," which allowed US negotiators authority to agree to China's entry into the WTO. Tom Delay's opinion piece, published in 2001 – more than a year after Congress' action – supported renewal of the US president's trade negotiating authority. Delay's piece never mentions China. The Honorable Tom Delay, Economic Expansion Via Trade Promotion, The Washington Times (December 6, 2001).

[5] In testimony before the House Ways and Means Committee on China's accession, former U.S. Trade Representative and principal U.S. negotiator, Ambassador Charlene Barshefsky, attested to the negotiations' focus on commercial concerns. There, she explained, "In a sense, this decision presents us with a simple choice. Last November, after years of negotiation, we reached a bilateral agreement with China on WTO accession which secures broad-ranging, comprehensive, one-way trade concessions on China's part." Testimony of Ambassador Charlene Barshefsky, U.S. Trade Representative (May 3, 2000), Hearing before the committee on Ways and Means, House of Representatives, 106th Cong., 2d Sess., U.S. Government Printing Office (2001); see also Opening Statement of William V. Roth, Jr., Chairman of the Senate Committee on Finance, China's Application for Accession to the World Trade Organization, Hearing Before the Committee on Finance, United States Senate, S. Hrg. 106–286 (Apr. 13, 1999) ("The Finance Committee will have to determine if an agreement meets the specific needs of U.S. manufacturers, farmers, service providers, and workers. This hearing presents an opportunity to examine the agreement as a trade agreement. There will be other opportunities to address the other issues that affect our bilateral relationship with the Chinese. The question before us, however, is whether common standing alone, an agreement on accession is in the United States interest.").

[6] Ambassador Barshefsky expressly rejected those claims in testimony before the Ways and Means Committee of the U.S. House of Representatives, making clear the accession agreement "[was] not a human rights policy," even while acknowledging it represented "a remarkable victory for economic reformers within China and for our own efforts to give the Chinese people more control over their own destiny and more ability to meet and exchange ideas with the outside world." Testimony of Ambassador Charlene Barshefsky. U.S. – China Bilateral Trade Agreement and the Accession of China to the WTO. Hearing before the Committee on Ways and Means, House of Representatives, 106th Cong., 2d Sess. February 16, 2000.

threatens to undermine the WTO's authority as an arbiter of global trade."[7] And, there is one respect in which the critics are right. China has not, in fact, met the expectations of WTO members that agreed to its accession, either with respect to economic reform or progress toward the rule of law.

Having served as the Majority Chief Trade Counsel to U.S. Senate Finance Committee during the final negotiations over the protocol of accession, I can personally attest to the attention given to the economic and legal reforms under way in China at the time. The members of the Finance Committee paid particularly close attention to China's progress toward the rule of law.[8] More generally, the reforms proved instrumental in persuading policy makers to agree to China's accession.[9]

[7] Id.

[8] See, e.g., Statement of Senate Finance Committee Chairman William V. Roth, Jr., on the Administration's Proposal to Grant China Permanent Normal Trade Relations (March 8, 2000) ("China's entry into the World Trade Organization augurs profound changes both in China's economic practices and in its society. It is not just a question of accelerating economic reforms or a departure from socialism. These changes mark a profound departure from centuries of Chinese history. China has essentially conceded the fact that their own prospects are directly linked to an open market economy based on the rule of law. In so doing, the Chinese government is also accepting the basic underpinnings of a society based on the rule of law, something that represents a far more profound change than the economic reforms launched by Deng Xiao Ping two decades ago."), www.finance.senate .gov/chairmans-news/roth-statement-on-the-administrations-proposal-to-grant-china-permanent-normal-trade-relations.

[9] Statements of members of both U.S. political parties in the Senate debate over the passage of legislation granting permanent normal trade relations to China bear that out. See, e.g., Statement of Senator Ted Kennedy (D-MA), 46 Cong. Rec. NO. 111, 106th Cong., 2d Sess. (Sep. 19, 2000) at S8690 ("By integrating China into this global, rules- based system, the international community will have procedures never available in the past to hold the government of China accountable for its actions, and to promote the development of the rule of law in China."); Statement of senator John Kerrey (D-MA), Id. ("The Chinese people will benefit from the spread of the rule of law, from increased governmental transparency, and from the economic."); Statement of Senator John McCain (R-AZ), Id., at S8690-8691. ("The economic reforms initiated by the late Premier Deng Xiao-ping began a process that has benefited millions of ordinary Chinese and has held out the greatest hope for prosperity and, ultimately, political freedom that country has ever known … Opponents of engaging China in trade should be aware that membership in the World Trade Organization carries with it responsibilities that are at variance with Communist Party practice. That is why Martin Lee, chairman of the Democratic Party of Hong Kong, noted that China's participation in the WTO would 'bolster those in China who understand that the country must embrace the rule of law.'"); Statement of Senator Joe Biden (D-DE), Id., at S8717 ("China's growing participation in the international com- munity over the past quarter century has been marked by growing adherence to international norms in the areas of trade, security, and human rights. If you want to know what China looks like when it is isolated, take a look at the so-called Great Leap Forward and the Cultural Revolution."); Statement of Senator Tom Daschle (D-SD), Id., at S8719 ("By agreeing to these terms, China is, in fact, agreeing to

Moving from the U.S. Congress to serve as the Under Secretary of Commerce for International Trade in the George W. Bush administration in 2001, I was part of the U.S. delegation to the WTO ministerial meeting in Doha where China finally acceded to the WTO. As Under Secretary, I became deeply involved in ensuring China's compliance with its WTO obligations.[10] China's progress on economic and legal reform remained a significant part of both the administration's agenda and Congressional oversight throughout my tenure.[11]

Those experiences highlighted for me the difference between China's WTO accession and the Jesuits' experience in Imperial China. The WTO did not seek to change China. Rather, China pursued accession of its own volition, with President Jiang Zemin and Premier Zhu Rongji using WTO accession as "a lever for promoting domestic economic reform."[12] Following in the footsteps of Deng Xiaoping, they aimed to lift the dead hand of Mao's mercurial one-man rule and end the anarchy and economic disarray left behind by the Cultural Revolution.

Leaving the Mao era behind required fundamental changes in the way China operated. In that, Jiang and Zhu succeeded. Their efforts led to a retreat by the state from the market, "a major downsizing and restructuring of state-owned companies … and a significant opening of the economy to external competition, paving the way for China's entry into the World Trade Organization."[13]

live by the rule of law. And while that agreement may be limited – for now – to trade issues, eventually it is likely to be extended to other areas as well – including human rights."); Statement of Senator William Roth (R-DE), Id., at 8720 ("a China fully immersed in the global trade regime, subject to all the rules and sanctions applicable to WTO members, is far likelier to live under the rule of law and to act in ways that comply with global norms.").

10 In that capacity, I served as the Executive Director of the U.S.-China Joint Commission on Commerce and Trade, the main bilateral avenue for raising and resolving concerns with respect to China's compliance. I also served on the congressionally mandated commission responsible for oversight of the U.S.-China trade relationship and China's ability to comply with the WTO rules.

11 See, e.g., 2003 Report to Congress on China's WTO Compliance, Office of the United States Trade Representative (December 11, 2003); Human Rights in China in the Context of the Rule of Law, Hearing Before the Congressional-Executive Commission on China, 107th Cong., 2d Sess. (Feb. 7, 2002). GPO 78-790, U.S. government printing office (2002); Opportunities to Improve U.S. Government Efforts to Ensure China's Compliance with World Trade Organization Commitments, United States General Accounting Office, GAO-05-53 (October 2004) (assessing U.S. executive branch oversight of China's WTO compliance compliance).

12 Nicholas R. Lardy, Issues in China's WTO Accession, The Brookings Institution (May 9, 2001) ("Lardy, Issues in China's WTO Accession").

13 Nicholas R. Lardy, *The State Strikes Back*, Peterson Institute for International Economics (2019) ("Lardy, The State Strikes Back").

Jiang and Zhu's reforms extended to China's legal regime as well. According to Chinese state media, the two leaders viewed WTO accession as a means of "cleaning up of laws, regulations, and policies" and establishing an "impartial, efficient judicial system."[14]

In that, Jiang and Zhu's reforms formed the backdrop of China's efforts to accede to the WTO. Their reforms, including the changes to China's legal regime, played an instrumental role in convincing WTO members to accept the resulting protocol. The reforms shaped WTO members' expectations of the of the benefits that would accrue from China's accession and its agreement to abide by the WTO rules.

Since then, however, Xi Jinping has set China on a fundamentally different course – one that departs sharply from the path Deng Xiaoping charted and reverses many of the reforms Jiang and Zhu introduced. It is fair to describe Xi's approach as retrenchment, both economically and institutionally. Xi's reinflation of the state-owned sector not only diminished the scope for free and open competition in China's market, but it also expanded the scope for "guanxi" – the age-old Chinese use of connections with the powerful to advance one's economic interests and the local favoritism it entails. As has been widely reported, commercial success in Xi's China depends less on price or quality than it does on political access and a willingness to embrace the Communist Party's line.

In parallel, Xi has reneged on Jiang and Zhu's commitment to expanding the reach of the rule of law. Rather than openly abandoning Jiang and Zhu's stated goal, Xi has simply redefined the rule of law to suit his and the Party's purpose.[15] Under the rubric of a "socialist rule of law with Chinese characteristics," Xi has stripped away any pretense of progress toward the rule of law in favor of a vision of unchallengeable central authority demanding obedience from "a law-abiding population."[16]

Xi's expansion of the state-owned sector has had its own ramifications for the reach of the rule of law. Just as economic reform and downsizing the state-owned sector created the need for stronger legal institutions and legal reform to govern relations between enterprises and consumers

[14] Lardy, Issues in China's WTO Accession.

[15] See, e.g., Maya Wang, Xi is Bending Chinese Law to His Will – How a Public Good Became a Tool of Personal Power, Foreign Affairs (Nov. 24, 2021).

[16] Moritz Rudolf, Xi Jinping Thought on the Rule of Law – New Substance in the Conflict of Systems with China, SWP Comment No. 28, Stiftung these Wissenschaft und Politik, German Institute for International and Security Affairs (April, 2021) ("Xi Jinping Thought on the Rule of Law"); see also Sam Crane, Why Xi Jinping's China is Legalist, Not Confucian – The Philosophical Basis of China's "New Era," Los Angeles Review of Books – China Channel (Jun. 29, 2018).

in private markets, re-inflating the state-owned sector has expanded that part of the market that has remained resolutely outside the scope of law in China throughout the reform.[17] Under Xi, the distinction between state-owned and private enterprises has, moreover, become increasingly blurred.[18]

The changes Xi wrought, including his retrogression of the rule of law, have significant implications for China's ability to comply with its WTO obligations. As will be discussed in greater detail below, the WTO represents a contract among its members – one that reflects a balance of advantages achieved through negotiation. The acid test is not in compliance with the "letter of the law" alone. The issue is whether the expectations of the parties with respect to the benefits derived from negotiation have been met.

China, in my view, has failed to satisfy that standard. it would do well to recommit itself both to economic reform and progress toward the rule of law in its own interest as well as in the interests of WTO compliance. The following discussion explains why.

The discussion is divided into two parts. The first puts the Chinese legal system and its progress toward the rule of law in a historical context, including the post-Mao reforms and Xi Jinping's more recent retrenchment. The second part explains why China's progress on economic reform and the rule of law matters in terms of WTO compliance.

II China's Legal Regime and the Impact of Xi's Reforms

China's legal culture derives from two competing traditions – the precepts of Confucius and the "legalist" imperative introduced at the outset of the

[17] As Stanley Lubman explained as early as 1999, "The state sector of the economy, only partially reformed, continues to face difficult obstacles to economic and legal reform. Twenty years after reform began, bargaining rather than rules still determines outcomes in relations between the center and locality and between administrative superiors and inferiors." Stanley Lubman, *Bird in a Cage – Legal Reform in China After Mao*, Stanford University Press (1999) 106; see further Che Luyao, Legal Implications of the Deepened Reform of Chinese State-Owned Enterprises: What Can Be Expected from Recent Reforms?, 8 *Tsinghua China Laura view* 171 (2016). (Noting, in a comment on proposed 2015 reforms, "[s]ince the early stage of economic reform, an unclear separation between entrepreneurial and administrative issues has been often described as a weakness of SOEs" and the weakness will remain in the absence of investing state-owned enterprises with full, legal personality, a move the CCP has resisted in practice.)

[18] See, e.g., Curtis Milhaupt and Wentong Zheng, Beyond Ownership: State Capitalism and the Chinese Firm, 103 *Geo. L. J.* 665 (2015) ("The boundary between public and private enterprises is even more blurred in China, a country with long tradition of state dominance

Qin dynasty.[19] Confucius aimed to create a harmonious society through norms and ritual practices.[20] The norms he advocated were designed to ensure proper conduct, rather than obedience to rules.[21] They wove a web of reciprocal obligations designed to bind the Chinese together in service to their families, their community and, ultimately, the state.[22] Under those circumstances, the ruler could rule by virtue, rather than law and enforcement.[23]

The legalist imperative, associated with the Qin dynasty and the first emperor's adviser, Shang Yang, started from the opposite premise. In the legalists' view, a "well-ordered society [could] be maintained only through a set of formal, publicly promulgated rules." The ruler's duty was to establish and enforce the law "with uniformity, certainty, celerity, and severity."[24] The legalists viewed the law as a system of rewards and punishments designed to control the citizenry.[25]

in the economy, underdeveloped legal institutions, and relatively inchoate conceptions of property rights. In practice, the ownership types of many firms in China are ambiguous.").

19 Peerenboom Long March. There were, of course, other schools of thought and other traditions. One, the syncretic blend of legalism and Daoism advocated by Huang-Lao, called for the "impartial application of publicly promulgated, codified laws," but also sought "to constrain the power of the ruler" by invoking the Way as the ultimate universal authority that even the ruler must obey. Id.

20 Asked how to govern, Confucius famously replied, "Let the ruler be a ruler, the subject be a subject, a father be a father, a son be a son." The Analects. 12.11.

21 As Confucius put it, "[i]f you guide the people with ordinances and statutes and keep them in line with [threats of] punishment, they will try to stay out of trouble but will have no sense of shame. If you guide them with exemplary virtue [de] and keep them in line with the practice of the rites [li], they will have a sense of shame and will know to reform themselves." Confucius. The Analects. 2.3. Penguin Publishing Group. 2014. ("The Analects").

22 Confucius saw reciprocity as virtuous, rather than corrupting. See The Analects. 6.30. ("A humane person wishes to steady himself, and so he helps others to steady themselves. Because he wishes to reach his goal, he helps others to reach theirs.") Confucius believed "li" governs all social relationships, "designat[ing] behavioral norms, and defining one's "moral responsibilities to others." See Xin Ren.

23 The Analects. 2.1. ("To rule by virtue is like the way the North Star rules, standing in its place with all the other stars revolving around it and paying court to it.")

24 Xin Ren. Shang Yang insisted that rule by law is fundamental to governing and that "nothing is more basic for putting an end to crimes than the imposition of heavy penalties." Id. See also The Book of Lord Shang. 17.3. ("[T]o prohibit depravity and to stop transgressions nothing is better than to make punishments heavy. When punishments are heavy and [criminals] are inevitably captured, then the people dare not try [to break the law].").

25 John Delury and Orville Schell. *Wealth and Power: China's Long March to the Twenty-first Century*. Random House Publishing Group. ("Legalism emphasized the law as a way for the state to control its people, including government officials, through strict punishment, and thereby maintain order … in other words, the rule of law had nothing to do with protecting people's rights against the state.") ("Delury & Schell").

Although Confucianism became the organizing principle of succeeding Chinese dynasties beginning with Han's ouster of the Qin,[26] legalism did not disappear.[27] With Confucianism, it continues to shape China's legal culture today. The resulting legal system retains a mixture of the two traditions.[28]

Hu Jintao's notion of a "harmonious society," first put forward in a speech before the Central Party School in February 2005, plainly draws on Confucian thought.[29] Hu called for a society built on the ideas of "democracy, the rule of law, fairness, justice, sincerity, trustworthiness, amity, full vitality, stability, orderliness, and harmony between mankind and nature." With the notable exceptions of democracy and the rule of law, Hu's speech otherwise runs the gamut of traditional Confucian values.

The recent crackdown on the tech sector in China, on the other hand, has the hallmarks of legalism. The means are legalist – the elements of the crackdown include, *inter alia*, "scrutinizing the initial public offerings of major internet companies, proposing broad new rules to limit overseas public listings, and introducing sweeping data security laws" as a means of bringing China's tech sector to heel.[30] The intent is legalist as well – the government aims "to rein in Chinese technology firms and shore up its political power over private enterprises" more generally.[31]

[26] Xin Ren, supra. (Explaining Confucianism became "the dominant official orthodoxy endorsed by generations of imperial rulers," beginning with the Eastern Han Dynasty (A.D. 25-220), when imperial law "under[went] a process of Confucianization as it incorporated the idealistic vision of the Confucian 'superior man' who is motivated by piety and good example, not by fear of the law.")

[27] Peerenboom Long March. ("The Imperial system showed clear signs of both Legalist and Confucian influence. The former was most apparent in the emphasis on codified laws and punishment.... The Legalist concern for constraining the power and discretion of officials is also evident in the large number of regulations governing the behavior of officials.")

[28] Xin Ren, supra. ("the Chinese legal tradition is not limited to the influence of Confucianism but is a combination of both philosophies. Even today's legalization process is the continuation of the long struggle between Legalism-rule by law or "rule under the law"-and Confucianism-rule by man or "rule above the law").

[29] Delury & Schell. ("traditional Chinese thinking esteemed the Confucian adage heweigui ... "[t]here is nothing more precious than harmony").

[30] Josh Bramble. Beijing's Tech Sector Crackdown Sends a Clear Warning to Companies Going Global. Center for Strategic and International Studies. October 4, 2021.

[31] Id. Didi, the Chinese ride-hailing service, offers a paradigmatic example of the crackdown. The firm and other Chinese internet companies "grew big and powerful by learning to thrive in regulatory gray zones." Raymond Zhong; Li Yuan. The Rise and Fall of the World's Ride-Hailing Giant. The New York Times. Aug. 27, 2021. Chinese regulators tolerated Didi's behavior, in part, because of its reputation as "the homegrown hero that stopped Uber's global expansion in its tracks." Id. In early July, 2021, two days after Didi went public in New York, China's internet regulator ordered it to stop signing up new

Beyond Confucian principles and the legalist tradition, the legal regime reflects the advent of the Chinese Communist Party (CCP) and its 1949 victory in China's civil war. Early in Mao's rule, legal developments "followed the Marxist view that law should serve as an ideological instrument of politics."[32] But, even that limited concept of law gave way amidst the anarchy of the Cultural Revolution and Mao's praise of "lawlessness."[33] The Cultural Revolution's cruelty and chaos resulted in "a deep 'crisis of faith' among the people," who "openly questioned the benefits conferred on them by a rigid, aloof, and seemingly insensitive Communist Party."[34]

In response, the post-Mao Chinese leadership invoked the rule of law to mark a departure from Mao's mercurial one-man rule and the institutional and economic disarray that followed the Cultural Revolution he led. As Yuhua Wang of Harvard puts it –

> The post-Mao leadership believed that installing a reliable legal system in which there are constitutional checks on individual power would prevent political disasters such as the Cultural Revolution from happening again. More systematic legal reforms, in which building a professional, efficient, and fair legal system was the essential goal, started in the 1990s as market reforms deepened.[35]

The process of reform began with Deng Xiaoping's speech to the Third Plenum of the Eleventh Central Committee Congress in December 1978.[36]

users while officials examined its cybersecurity practices. Id. As part of the crackdown, China's internet regulator shut off the availability of Didi's apps online. Raymond Zhong. China Orders Didi Off App Stores in an Escalating Crackdown. The New York Times. July 4, 2021. Didi was, along with other internet firms, also the target of an investigation by Chinese authorities for violations of China's anti-monopoly laws. See Raymond Zhong; Peter Eavis. Didi's Regulatory Troubles Might Just Be Getting Started. The New York Times. July 7, 2021.

32 Eric W. Orts, The Rule of Law in China, 34 *Vand. J. Transnatl. L.* 43, 57 (2001) (indicating Chinese jurists "adopted the recommendations of Stalinist legal theorists who believed that 'the Communist Party, as the representative of the ruling proletariat, should enjoy absolute control over the creation of positive law by the organs of the state,'" quoting Perry Keller, Sources of Order in Chinese Law, 42 *Am. J. Comp. L.* 711, 720 (1994).

33 Id. Citing Laszlo Ladany, "Law and Legality" in China: The Testament of a China Watcher 35, 57 (1992) and Albert H.Y. Chen, Toward a Legal Enlightenment – Discussions in Contemporary China on the Rule of Law, 17 *UCLA Pac. Basin L. J.* 125, 126 (Fall 1999–Spring 2000).

34 Richard Baum, *Burying Mao: Chinese Politics in the Age of Deng Xiaoping*, Princeton University Press, Kindle Edition 3 (1994) ("Baum").

35 Yuhua Wang at 10.

36 For an absorbing first-hand account of Deng's historic speech, see You Guangyuan, *Deng Xiaoping Shakes the World – An Eyewitness Account of China's Party Work Conference in the Third Plenum*, Eastbridge Signature Books (2004) 141–148.

The Plenum's response included a mandate to overhaul China's legal system.[37] Peng Zhen, a close associate of Deng Xiaoping installed as chairman of the National People's Congress Legislative Affairs Commission, seized the opportunity of his first public appearance since being purged by Mao in 1966, to "denounce[ ] the legal anarchism spawned by the Gang of Four and strongly asserted the need to restore socialist legality and the rule of law."[38]

That view was reflected in one of the signal pieces of legislation passed by the NPC in 1979 – a new code of criminal procedure that declared "the law is equally applicable to all citizens" and affirmed "no special privilege whatever is permissible before the law."[39] That said, the broad statement of principle was limited by other language reducing the scope of judicial due process and permitting arbitrary government action in a variety of instances.[40]

Further signaling a shift from the Mao era, China adopted an entirely new constitution in 1982 that incorporated basic elements of the rule of law. Article 5 of the constitution provided "No organization or individual may enjoy the privilege of being above the Constitution and the law."[41] Like the 1979 criminal procedure law, however, the protections afforded by Article 5 were limited by caveats tucked elsewhere in the constitution, including a broad escape clause stating the "exercise by citizens … of their freedoms and rights may not infringe upon the interests of the state, of society, and of the collective, or upon the lawful freedoms and rights of other citizens."[42]

China did, nonetheless, introduce a means of challenging agencies' administrative decisions as part of its Administrative Litigation Law ("ALL"), which was enacted in 1989, three years into the negotiations on China's eventual accession to the WTO.[43] In the ensuing decade, Chinese citizens made active use of the new rules to challenge agency action.

[37] Baum at 84.

[38] Id. Despite his comment, Peng would not prove an ardent supporter of legal reform. To the contrary, Peng became leading voice opposing any effort toward democratic reform, including with respect to the rule of law. See generally Merle Goldman, *Sowing the Seeds of Democracy in China – Political Reform in the Deng Xiaoping Era*, Harvard University Press (1994).

[39] Id., at 84–85.

[40] Id., at 85.

[41] Constitution of the People's Republic of China (1982), art. 5.

[42] Baum at 150.

[43] Chris X. Lin. A Quiet Revolution: An Overview of China's Judicial Reform. *Asian-Pacific Law & Policy Journal*. Summer, 2003.

According to Vice-Chief Justice Li Guoguang of the Supreme People's Court, Chinese courts heard nearly 600,000 cases involving judicial review of agency action in that timeframe, with the plaintiff's prevailing in 40 percent of those decisions.[44]

The process of legal reform continued throughout the 1990s as the WTO accession negotiations ground toward their conclusion. In 1996, President Jiang Zemin reinforced the commitment made in Article 5 of the constitution, promising the Party and the state would rule in accordance with the rule of law.[45] Jiang's promise was later codified as part of China's constitution in 1999 as the accession negotiations approached their end.[46]

Premier Zhu Rongji similarly emphasized the need for progress toward the rule of law in statements contemporaneous with the negotiations over China's accession. In remarks during a 1992 high-level inspection tour of Guangdong, Zhu indicated China had yet to "guide[ ] all economic activities onto the path of rule of law," leaving too much room for arbitrary "interference with enterprises."[47] Similarly, in the area of finance, Zhu emphasized in 1995 the need for the impartial application of the law in terms of financial oversight, warning, "If finance doesn't get on track and recognize the rule of law, there won't be any order in the entire national economy."[48]

Thus, just like China's reform of state-owned enterprises and its shift toward a greater reliance on markets to organize economic activity, progress toward the rule was significant, if incomplete. China had created what Professor Randall Peerenboom refers to as a "thin" version of the rule of law.[49]

[44] Id.

[45] Jiang Zemin, Report to the 15th National Congress of the Communist Party of China (1996).

[46] Yuhua Wang, *Tying the Autocrat's Hands – The Rise of the Rule of Law in China, Cambridge Studies in Comparative Politics*, Cambridge University Press, Kindle Edition 17 (2015) ("Yuhua Wang").

[47] Zhu, Rongji, Guangdong's Practice Demonstrates the Success of the Policy of Reform and Opening Up, Remarks During an Inspection Tour of Guangdong After Listening to Reports by the Provincial Party Committee and Provincial Government, September 28, 1992, in Zhu Rongji on the Record 102, 105, Brookings Institution Press, Kindle Edition (2013).

[48] Zhu, Rongji, A Memorable Two Years as Governor of the Central Bank, Remarks During a Discussion with Attendees at an Advanced Seminar on Financial Law Organized by the People's Bank of China, August 28, 1995, in Zhu Rongji on the Record 286, 289, Brookings Institution Press, Kindle Edition (2013).

[49] See Statement of Randy Peerenboom, Professor of Law, University of California Los Angeles Law School What's a Liberal to Do? The Pursuit of Non-liberal Rule of Law in

By the time of the final negotiation of China's protocol of accession late in the 1990s, the direction of both economic and legal reform was evident to China's interlocutors in the WTO and persisted through China's accession in 2001. Jiang and Zhu's successors, President Hu Jintao and Premier Wen Jiabao, continued the reform effort in the years following China's WTO accession.

The continuing overhaul of China's legal regime took a substantial step forward in 2004 with the national people's Congress approval of thirteen amendments to the constitution.[50] Those amendments made general commitments to human rights and private property, although they did not limit the government's ability to repress speech or public protests deemed inimical to national security.[51]

The "partial withdrawal" by the party allowed "the development of a 'rule of law with Chinese characteristics,'" as Jiang had promised.[52] As one commentator notes, "it is no exaggeration to state that, across the span of more than a century, Chinese citizens had not enjoyed such a degree of legal protection and security," despite the caveat that the state might intervene where its "core interests" were at stake.[53]

Reforms in the legal regime led Chinese citizens to make use of the courts to enforce their rights. While they were often disappointed, the outcomes galvanized social protests, which not infrequently led to significant concessions on the government's part.[54] These "mass incidents" led to revised legal and regulatory decisions and further amendments to the law itself.[55]

China, Congressional-Executive Commission on China Roundtable (April 1, 2003). ("Conceptions of rule of law generally come in two varieties. A thin conception stresses the formal or instrumental aspects of rule of law – those features that any legal system allegedly must possess to function effectively as a system of laws, regardless of whether the legal system is part of a democratic or non-democratic society, capitalist or socialist, liberal or theocratic. Although proponents of thin conceptions of rule of law define it in slightly different ways, there is considerable common ground. The key features are that there must be rules for lawmaking and laws must be made in accordance with such rules (including by the courts through precedent) to be valid; laws must be general, public, prospective, relatively clear, consistent, stable, impartially applied and enforced so that the gap between law and practice is relatively small.")

50 Klaus Mühlhahn, *Making China Modern*, Harvard University Press, Kindle Edition 590 (2019).

51 Id.

52 Id.

53 Id.

54 Id., at 590–591.

55 Id.

What that suggests is progress toward the rule of law continued well into the Hu and Wen era in the years immediately following China's accession to the WTO. But the process of reform overall began to slow as conservative forces within the CCP sought to limit further change. That period coincided with the rise of the so-called "princeling generation" (the sons and daughters of the early leaders of the CCP) to leadership positions within the party and the Chinese economy.[56] In addition to jockeying for leadership positions in the Party hierarchy and state-owned enterprises, the princelings, unsurprisingly, resisted reform that diminished their privilege and position.[57]

While styling himself as a reformer, Xi Jinping has proved as resistant to further reform as any of the other princelings. In sharp contrast to Deng, Jiang, and Zhu, Xi pursued retrenchment, rather than reform, with the state playing an increasing, rather than diminishing, role in the economy and the lives of Chinese citizens.[58] Under Xi, China has witnessed greater state intervention in the economy and the consolidation and reinforcement of state-owned enterprises relative to the private sector.[59] In terms of economic policy, the China of today is not the China that joined the WTO two decades ago.

The same holds true in terms of China's legal regime. As noted at the outset, Xi has pursued a vision of "socialist rule of law with Chinese characteristics" fundamentally inconsistent with Jiang Zemin's 1997 vision.[60] Toward that end, the Central Committee of the CCP recently adopted a five-year plan to establish the rule of law in China consistent with "Xi Jinping Thought."[61]

56 See, e.g., Cheng Li, *Rule of the Princelings*, Brookings Institution (February 10, 2013) ("It has been widely noted that large numbers of prominent party leaders and families have used their political power to convert state assets into their own private wealth. The unprecedentedly strong presence of princelings in the new [Politburo Standing Committee] is likely to reinforce public resentment of how power and wealth continue to converge in China. Chinese politics thus seem to be entering a new era characterized by the concentration of princeling power at the top."); David Barboza and Sharon LaFraniere, "Princelings" in China Use Family Ties to Gain Riches, The New York Times (May 17, 2012) (Illustrating "how the Communist Party shares the spoils, allowing the relatives of senior leaders to cash in on one of the biggest economic booms in history").

57 See, e.g., Ian Johnson, Dynasty of Different Order Is Reshaping China, The New York Times (Nov. 13, 2012) (Highlighting instances in which the princeling generation have become obstacles to further economic reform).

58 Lardy, The State Strikes Back.

59 Id.

60 Xi Jinping Thought on the Rule of Law.

61 Id.

The overall theme of the plan reinforces Elizabeth Economy's impression of Xi and China's "neo-Maoist moment."[62] The plan summarizes Xi's thoughts on the rule of law as "[s]trengthening the CPC's centralized and unified leadership, 'scientific legislation', strict law enforcement, fair trials, a law-abiding population."[63] Xi plainly "appreciates the legitimating power of law," regularly promising "law-based governance," even while strengthening the CCP's "absolute" control over the legal regime.[64] Notably absent are concepts like an independent judiciary or the principle of separation of powers, which China's leadership regards as "erroneous western thought."[65]

From the perspective of western legal tradition, Xi's formulation misstates the rule of law, which entails "meaningful restraints on the state and individual members of the ruling elite."[66] To those familiar with China's long legal tradition, the summary will nonetheless sound familiar – it represents rule by law, rather than the rule of law.

With that in mind, we turn to the WTO implications of Xi's "counter-reformation."

III The WTO's Role and the Concept of Nullification and Impairment

At a distance of twenty years, it is easy to forget how significant China's concessions actually were. To join the WTO, China assumed the obligations of more than twenty existing multilateral agreements; reduced tariffs substantially on industrial and agricultural goods; liberalized its service sector significantly; consented to the creation of special safeguard mechanisms for the benefit of industries in other WTO member countries; and

62 Elizabeth Economy, China's Neo-Maoist Moment – How Xi Jinping Is Using China's Past to Accomplish What His Predecessors Could Not, Foreign Affairs (Oct. 1, 2019).

63 Xi Jinping Thought on the Rule of Law.

64 Jamie Horsley, Party Leadership and the Rule of Law in the Xi Jinping Era – What Does an Ascendant Chinese Communist Party Mean for China's Legal Development? Global China, Brookings Institution (September 2019).

65 Id.

66 Randall Peerenboom, *China's Long March toward Rule of Law*. Cambridge University Press, (2002) ("Peerenboom Long March"). See further Randall Peerenboom. A Government of Laws Democracy, Rule of Law, and Administrative Law Reform in China in Zhao Suisheng – Rule of Law vs. Democratization (ed.). *Debating Political Reform in China*. Routledge, (2015). ("In a rule of law state, law is not just a tool to be used by the ruling regime to control the people or promote the interests of the privileged few. Law also binds government leaders and officials. One of the main purposes of rule of law is to limit the arbitrary acts of the government and impose meaningful constraints on the ruling elite.")

undertook systemic reforms designed to promote transparency, predictability, and fairness in commercial dealings.[67]

Critics of China's WTO accession rarely acknowledge the extraordinary effort the Chinese government undertook to ensure compliance with China's protocol of accession and the underlying WTO rules.[68] In addition to the substantive changes to China's legal regime necessary to comply with the WTO rules and China's protocol of accession, China also agreed to make a series of significant systemic reforms that bear directly on its commitment to the rule of law.[69] Those changes, as implemented, imposed limits on the Chinese government as a matter of domestic, as well as international, law.[70]

Just as important, however, China's economic reforms expanded the contestability of its market, and Jiang and Zhu's commitment to expanding the rule of law promised greater certainty of market access, ensuring the bargain reached at the WTO negotiating table, rather than intervention or favoritism by the Chinese government, would determine market outcomes. In the absence of those reforms, China's WTO trading partners

[67] Accession of the People's Republic of China, Decision of 10 November 2001, WTO/L/432, 23 November 2001.

[68] Donald C. Clarke, *China's Legal System and the WTO: Prospects for Compliance*, Washington University Global Studies Law Review (January, 2003) (According to Clarks, the Chinese trade ministry alone had, prior to China's accession, reviewed "over 1400 laws, regulations, and similar documents, including six statutes (of which five were revised), 164 State Council regulations (of which 114 were to be repealed and 25 amended), 887 of its own ministry regulations (of which 459 were to be repealed and 95 amended), 191 bilateral trade agreements, 72 bilateral investment treaties, and 93 tax treaties." Various other ministries and certain commissions of the State Council reviewed "some 2300 laws and regulations, of which 830 were identified as in need of repeal and 325 as in need of revision.") ("Clarke").

[69] The reforms pertinent to the rule of law included publication in official journals of all laws, regulations and other measures affecting commerce, as well as their effective dates and the agencies or authorities responsible for their implementation; procedures for providing notice and comment on proposed legislation and regulations; universal and impartial application of the law at all levels of government; and the availability of judicial review with respect to certain regulatory actions and administrative decisions. Accession of the People's Republic of China, Decision of 10 November 2001, WTO/L/432, 23 November 2001.

[70] The changes introduced in Chinese administrative law to provide independent judicial review of agency determinations under China's anti-dumping and countervailing duty laws offer a concrete example. The scope of review and the decisional rule to be applied by Chinese courts in their review of antidumping and countervailing duty actions broke significant new ground, as did the specific requirement of independent and impartial review, leading some Chinese legal scholars to hail the "rules as China's first step toward real judicial review."

would have asked for stronger explicit guarantees as part of the protocol of accession.

Why does this matter? Is easy to think of the WTO as an institution – the sturdy Centre William Rappard overlooking Lac Leman in Geneva. But, by its nature, WTO represents a contract among the signatories. China's protocol of accession offers a concrete example.

As is true of contracts in domestic law, the WTO agreements contain specific binding commitments, violation of which create legal consequences. But, again like domestic contract law, a cause of action also lies when a WTO member's actions frustrate the purpose of the contract, even though they may not violate a specific WTO rule or trade liberalizing commitment.[71]

In that, the WTO is about expectations – in this instance, the expectations of market access that would reasonably accrue from China's protocol of accession. For that reason, the acid test of China's compliance with its WTO obligations lies not just in its adherence to the letter of WTO law, but whether its policies and practices afford the market access its WTO trading partners reasonably expected would accrue from China's accession. In so far as it relates to the rule of law, China's compliance depends on the extent to which it –

> fosters a broader respect for the rule of law within China, a far lesser role for the state and the Communist Party in the operation of the Chinese economy, and the steady erosion of the system of guanxi – the connections that dominate both China's politics and its commerce.[72]

[71] See, e.g., Uniform Commercial Code § 1-304 – Obligation of Good Faith: "Every contract or duty within the Uniform Commercial Code imposes an obligation of good faith in its performance and enforcement." The UCC defines "good faith" as "honesty in fact and the observance of reasonable commercial standards of fair dealing." UCC § 1-201 (2)); Restatement (Second) of the Law of Contracts § 205 – Duty of Good Faith and Fair Dealing (indicating "[e]very contract imposes upon each party a duty of good faith and fair dealing in its performance and its enforcement," which implies an injunction against practices such as "evasion of the spirit of the bargain" and "willful rendering of imperfect performance"); see also Catherine Pastrikos Kelly, What You Should Know about the Implied Duty of Good Faith and Fair Dealing, Practice Points, American Bar Association (Jul. 26, 2016). ("In general, every contract contains an implied duty of good faith and fair dealing. This duty requires that neither party will do anything that will destroy or injure the right of the other party to receive the benefits of the contract.")

[72] Testimony of the Honorable Grant D. Aldonas, *Ten Years in the WTO: Has China Kept Its Promises?*, Congressional-Executive Commission on China (December 13, 2011) ("Aldonas 2011 Testimony").

Seen in that light, Xi Jinping's retrenchment in economic reform and his pursuit of a "socialist rule of law with Chinese characteristics" has significant implications for China's WTO compliance. Explaining how and why requires an understanding of the concept of nullification and impairment embodied in Article XXIII of the General Agreement on Tariffs and Trade 1994 as interpreted by subsequent dispute settlement panels and the WTO Appellate Body.

The WTO rules allow for two types of claims in dispute settlement. One cause of action lies in clear violations of the rules.[73] The other allows for a claim of "nullification and impairment" when a member's actions frustrate the bargain the parties reached through negotiation regardless of whether the actions violate specific WTO rules or commitments.[74]

In the relevant part, Article XXIII provides –

> 1. If any contracting party should consider that any benefit accruing to it directly or indirectly under this agreement is being nullified or impaired or that the attainment of any objective of the agreement is being impeded as the result of …
>
> b. the application by another contracting party of any measure, whether or not it conflicts with the provisions of this agreement …
>
> the contracting party may, with a view to the satisfactory adjustment of the matter, make written representations or proposals to the other contracting party or parties which it considers to be concerned.[75]

The purpose of Article XXIII:1(b) is "to protect the balance of concessions under GATT by providing a means to redress government actions not otherwise regulated by GATT rules that nonetheless nullify or impair a Member's legitimate expectations of benefits from tariff negotiations."[76] In that, Article XXIII does no more than vindicate the core principle of

[73] In Article 3 of the Understanding on Dispute Settlement concluded as part of the Uruguay Round of multilateral negotiations, WTO members "affirm[ed] their adherence to the principles for the management of disputes heretofore applied under Articles XXII and XXIII of GATT 1947." See Art. 3:1, Understanding on Dispute Settlement. Article XXIII:1 authorizes a WTO member to request consultations and begin the dispute settlement process where it considers that "any benefit accruing to it directly or indirectly" is being "nullified or impaired or that the attainment of any objective of the agreement is being impeded as a result of … (a) the failure of another contracting party to carry out its obligations under this Agreement…." Art. XXIII:1 (a), GATT 1994.

[74] Art. XXIII:1 (b), GATT 1994.

[75] Id.

[76] Japan – Measures Affecting Consumer Photographic Film and Paper, Report of the Panel, para. 1050, WT/DS44/R, World Trade Organization (31 March 1998).

international treaty law – *pacta sunt servanda* – the obligation to implement a treaty in "good faith."[77]

Drawn from to work of the League of Nations on international trade in the 1920s and bilateral trade agreements of the 1930s,[78] the provision of "non-violation nullification and impairment" formed a part of the originally suggested charter of the International Trade Organization and, ultimately, Article XXIII of the GATT 1947.[79] The clause satisfied the recognized need for a "more general provision which would address itself to any other government action that produced an adverse effect on the balance of commercial opportunity."[80]

As explained by Frieder Roessler, former Director of the GATT's Legal Affairs Division, and his colleague at the Advisory Centre on WTO Law, Petina Gappah –

> The possibility of bringing complaints relating to perfectly legal measures was introduced into the GATT because its founders realized that the intended effect of a tariff negotiation could be easily frustrated by measures that the GATT did not regulate ... As the GATT did not contain any substantive commitments on such internal measures, a procedure for the adjustment of tariff concessions following the introduction of such measures was required. The purpose of Article XXIII:1(b) was to provide such a procedure.[81]

Although non-violation nullification impairment disputes have proved rare, the decisions in those cases have featured prominently in GATT and WTO jurisprudence. The first non-violation dispute, a Chilean action raising concerns with respect to Australian subsidies affecting ammonium

77 Art. 26, Vienna Convention on the Law of Treaties (adopted and opened to signature on 23 May 1969; entered into force on 27 January 1980). The Vienna Convention is recognized by non-ratifying parties, such as the United States, as a restatement of customary international law and binding upon them as such.

78 James Durling and Simon Lester, Original Meanings and the Film Dispute: The Drafting History, Textual Evolution, and Application of the Non-Violation Nullification or Impairment Remedy, 32 *Geo. Wash. J. Int'l L. and Econ.* 212 (1999) at 216–219, 225–230.

79 See John Jackson World Trade in the Law of GATT, The Miche Company (1969) 166–171.

80 Robert Hudec, *The GATT Legal System and World Trade Diplomacy*, 2nd ed., Butterworth Legal Publishers (1990) 24 (citing the work of trade experts at the London Monetary and Economic Conference of 1933, League of Nations, Reports Approved by the Conference on 27 July 1933 and Resolutions Adopted by the Bureau and the Exec. Comm. (Official No.: C.435.M. 220. 1933.II. Spec 4) at 30).

81 Frieder Roessler and Petina Gappah, A Re-Appraisal of Non-Violation Complaints Under the WTO Dispute Settlement Procedures, in The World Trade Organization: Legal, Economic and Political Analysis (2005) 1371–1387.

sulfate, arose shortly after the GATT's inception and established the basic elements of a non-violation cause of action.[82]

Australia had granted war-time subsidies to local distributors for the purchase of fertilizers, including sodium nitrate fertilizers exported by Chile. The subsidies remained in force when, in 1947 as part of the negotiations leading to the launch of the GATT, Australia granted a tariff concession to Chile affording Chilean exports duty-free treatment. When Australia subsequently removed the subsidy on Chilean fertilizer, while leaving the subsidy to competing products in place, it created a competitive advantage for suppliers of the competing goods.

The panel report found in favor of Chile, explaining nullification or impairment existed "when the action of the Australian government … resulted in upsetting competitive relationship" between Chile's exports and the competing fertilizers, an action which "could not reasonably have been anticipated but the Chilean government, taking into consideration all pertinent circumstances and the provisions of the General Agreement" at the time it was negotiated.[83]

The panel based its decision on the need to maintain the balance of advantages achieved at the negotiating table.[84] Professor Robert Hudec explained the panel's rationale in the following terms –

> The purpose of the nullification impairment remedy is to preserve the balance of the original exchange of values. If some new commercial disadvantage measure can be foreseen, at the time of negotiations, the country receiving concessions is able to discount the possibility in advance by paying a lesser value for the concessions affected. If that is so, then the actual occurrence of the foreseen disadvantage will not upset the balance, for it will already have been taken into account. Conversely, if the new commercial disadvantage cannot be anticipated, the country receiving the concessions is more likely to pay full value and thus suffer an imbalance when the commercial advantage is later reduced.[85]

Subsequent litigation under both the GATT and WTO followed the same logic. In the EEC – Oilseeds dispute, the United States complained European Economic Community ("EEC") subsidies afforded producers and processors of oilseeds nullified or impaired tariff concessions previously granted American oilseed exports by the EEC as part of the 1960

[82] Australia – Measures Affecting Ammonium Sulfate, GATT/CP. 4/39, GATT BISD II/188 (3 April 1950).
[83] Id.
[84] Id.
[85] Hudec at 163.

Dillon Round of GATT negotiations.[86] The panel endorsed the rule established in the Australian ammonium sulfate dispute, affirming that nullification or impairment resulted when benefits reasonably expected to accrue from previous negotiations were undercut by unforeseen actions or measures of another party.[87] Following up on its earlier decision, the Oilseeds panel also held that complainants in non-violation cases need not demonstrate an actual impact on levels of trade to prove their case, finding "the subsidies concerned had impaired the tariff concessions because they upset the competitive relationship between domestic and imported oilseeds, not because of any effect on trade flows."[88]

The panel report in Japan – Film, the first non-violation complaint under the WTO dispute settlement rules, similarly found nullification and impairment occurred when unforeseen actions by one WTO member designed to "strengthen the competitiveness of certain distribution or industrial sectors through non-financial assistance" undermine benefits reasonably expected to accrue from prior negotiations.[89] The United States had complained that a series of actions by the Japanese government nullified or impaired the benefits of tariff concessions previously granted on black and white and color photographic film and paper.[90] Those actions included the creation of an exclusive distribution sector, restrictions on the growth of large stores, and restrictions on the use of sales promotions.[91] While the panel found the United States failed to satisfy its burden of proof, it emphasized that non-trade measures such as those raised by the United States could nullify or impair benefits the United States reasonably expected to accrue from previous negotiations.[92]

The logic established in the panel decisions cited above applies with equal force to Xi Jinping's retrenchment from economic reform and his abandonment of progress toward the rule of law. China made its initial request to accede to the GATT in 1986, in the midst of Deng Xiaoping's

[86] Panel Report on European Economic Community Payments and Subsidies Paid to Processors and Producers of Oilseeds and Related Animal-Feed Proteins, Jan. 25, 1990, GATT BISD (37th Supp.) (1991).

[87] Id.

[88] Follow-up on the Panel Report on Payments and Subsidies Paid to Processors and Producers of Oilseeds and Related Animal-Feed Proteins, Apr. 30, 1992, GATT BISD (39th Supp.) at 115 (1993).

[89] WTO Report of the Panel on Japan – Measures Affecting Consumer Photographic Film and Paper, WT/DS 44/R (March 31, 1998).

[90] Id.

[91] Id.

[92] Id.

push for economic reform and barely four years after the introduction of China's new constitution in 1982.[93] The negotiations took place against the backdrop of Deng's reforms and those of his successors, Jiang Zemin and Zhu Rongji, including Jiang's pronouncement at the 14th National Congress of the Communist Party identifying a "socialist market economy" as the goal of China's reforms.[94]

The negotiations, furthermore, did not conclude until a decade after significant changes were made in China's legal regime, such as the introduction of judicial review of agency action. Reinforcing those reforms, China agreed in the final protocol of accession to ensure the impartial administration of justice.[95] It agreed, as well, to introduce a judicial review of "all administrative actions relating to the implementation of laws, regulations, judicial decisions and administrative review rulings of general application" under certain aspects of its trade laws and include the opportunity for appeal to the Chinese courts.[96]

With that as context, China's WTO trading partners had reason to expect that China would continue on the path toward economic and legal reform. They could not reasonably have foreseen Xi's resurrection of Mao-like one-man rule or his appeal to a mix of Marx, Mao, and Confucianism in lieu of the rule of law. His consolidation and reinforcement of state-owned enterprises have fundamentally altered the basis of competition in a number of industries relative to the conditions that prevailed at the time of accession. The inability of the government under Xi to curtail government violations of private property rights has made doing business far more uncertain. Xi's actions (or inaction) have made significant parts of the Chinese market less contestable than China's trading partners could

93 The process of requesting accession began with the following missive – China Status as a Contracting Party: Communication from the People's Republic of China, GATT Doc. L/6017 (Oct. 26, 1984).

94 Jiang Zemin, Accelerate Steps of Reform and Opening Up and the Development of Modernization, Seize Greater Success in the Endeavor on Socialism with Chinese Characteristics, Report at the 14th National Congress of the Communist Party, www.gov.cn/test/2007-08/29/content_730511.htm (Oct. 12, 1992).

95 The Protocol on the Accession of the People's Republic of China provides "China shall apply and administer in a uniform, impartial and reasonable manner all its laws, regulations and other measures of the central government as well as local regulations, rules and other measures issued or applied at the sub national level (collectively referred to as 'laws, regulations and other measures') pertaining to or affecting trade in goods, services, trade-related aspects of intellectual property rights ('TRIPS') or the control of foreign exchange." Accession of the People's Republic of China, Decision of 10 November 2001, WTO/L/432, 23 November 2001.

96 Id.

have foreseen at the time of China's accession. And Xi's efforts to erode even the thin version of the rule of law that previously prevailed has cast a pall of uncertainty over access to the Chinese market.

To make the argument more concrete, consider the economic effect of the increasing subsidies that both the national and local governments in China have bestowed on select industries and enterprises during Xi's tenure. Subsidies are usually decried as a benefit to China's exporters that distorts trade and injures industries in the importing country. But those same subsidies are the equivalent of tariffs in terms of the protection they afford local Chinese companies in their home market. The increased subsidies offered under Xi's aegis undercut China's tariff bindings – the most basic commitment China made as a part of its accession.

Xi's abandonment of reform and retrogression in terms of the rule of law can, as a consequence, quite fairly be said to have nullified or impaired China's trading partners' reasonable expectation of market access. Indeed, it is highly likely the WTO membership would have rejected China's request for accession in the absence of the reforms Xi has unwound. At a minimum, China's trading partners would have bargained for more in the way of rules guaranteeing market access, ensuring it is determined by price and quality, rather than guanxi and connections to the Zhongnanhai in Beijing.

China cannot, moreover, claim it failed to appreciate its obligation to maintain the contestability of its market. Not only is the claim of nullification and impairment plainly set out in Article XXIII, but the negotiation of China's protocol of accession took place against the backdrop of high-profile litigation over the issue between the United States and the European Union and the United States and Japan.[97] The legal standard of "reasonable expectations of market access" played a core role in both of those high-profile cases.[98]

In sum, thinking in terms of nullification and impairment casts the question of China's compliance in an entirely different light. The question becomes whether the Chinese market is more contestable today than it was when China acceded to the WTO. Considering the changes President Xi has made to the Chinese economy over the past ten years, the answer is clearly no – Xi's retrenchment on economic and legal reform has led to a far less open and contestable market and less certain market access.

[97] See discussion of EEC – Oilseeds and Japan – Film disputes above.

[98] Id.

IV Conclusion

I am under no illusion that General Secretary Xi or the rest of the current Chinese leadership would currently be inclined to return to the path of reform. But political currents do change. Should Xi and the CCP leadership confront growing demands in China for a new era of reform, the prospect of facing a WTO dispute settlement case that asserted Xi's retrenchment had nullified and impaired the benefits China's trading partners reasonably expected would accrue from China's accession could offer the Chinese leadership a reason to pursue reform once again.

As a matter of trade diplomacy, the wise thing for China's trading partners to do would be to lay the groundwork – developing the legal and economic basis for a claim of non-violation nullification and impairment – to discuss with their Chinese counterparts. As a part of that process, China's trading partners should make clear what their expectations are in terms of solution (i.e., what it would take on China's part to ameliorate the injury caused by its measures or, alternatively, the "compensation" in terms of trade concessions they believe are due).

China's trading partners should make clear their preference for reform, rather than concessions, while recognizing Xi and his generation are unlikely to take that path, at least initially. But China confronts challenges of its own that only economic and legal reform can fundamentally address. The aim of China's trading partners should be to open the door China's leaders must eventually walk through. While making China's own challenges more tractable, returning to the path of reform would go some considerable distance toward addressing the concerns raised by China's trading partners. That alone would serve China's foreign policy interests by removing an already boiling pot from the stove.

6

China's Accession to the WTO and Its Impact on Global Agricultural Trade

JOSEPH W. GLAUBER

I Introduction

China's rapid rise as a leading global exporter of manufacturing goods since its accession to the WTO in 2001 has been the focus of both admiration and, increasingly, concern (Mavroidis and Sapir, 2021). But it is sometimes overlooked that China is also a large importer of goods, particularly agricultural products. Since China's accession to the WTO, China's agricultural exports have increased by 8 per cent annually while imports have risen by almost twice that rate. China has become the world's largest importer of agricultural products and the first or second largest destination for many of the world's top agricultural exporters such as the US, Brazil, Australia, New Zealand, Canada, and Argentina.

Under terms of its accession agreement, China agreed to bind its agricultural tariffs at low levels relative to many other developing (and developed economies). China established tariff rate quotas (TRQs) for a number of commodities and significantly, agreed to liberalize commercial imports by phasing out or limiting the operation of state trading enterprises (STEs).

Many analyses conducted at the time of accession projected increased wheat and maize imports by virtue of the creation of tariff rate quotas and increased imports of meat and dairy products as growth in China's per capita income was projected to result in shifts in diets to include more meat and dairy products (Tuan and Hsin-hui, 2001; USITC, 1999). Those expected gains were a primary reason why US producer groups provided large political support for the passage of Permanent Normal Trade Relations with China in 2000 (Glauber and Lester, 2021).

While food and agricultural disputes have accounted for almost 45 per cent of total disputes brought to the WTO Dispute Settlement Body since 1995 (Bianchi, 2021), agricultural disputes involving China have been relatively rare, particularly over the first 15 years of China's membership in the WTO. Since 2016, however, China's trade and agricultural policies have become an increasing focus of attention in the WTO. Trade wars, first with the United States, and then with Canada and Australia, have disrupted agricultural trade, and have threatened to disrupt the pattern of growth experienced over the past 20 years.

This paper examines the evolution of China's agricultural trade since its accession. It will examine how China's trade has grown over the past 20 years. It will also discuss how agricultural trade policy and domestic support policies have evolved, and how trade disputes have arisen within this context, with particular emphasis on China's experience as complainant and respondent in WTO trade disputes. Lastly, it will conclude with thoughts on the outlook for China's agricultural trade and trade policy.

II Evolution of China's Agricultural Trade

Since 2000, China has gone from being a net exporter of agricultural products,[1] with a positive net trade balance of USD 2.3 billion in 2000, to a larger net importer, with a net deficit of over USD 100 billion in 2020 (Figure 6.1). Exports have grown by over 8 per cent annually over the past 20 years, but imports have skyrocketed, growing by an average of 15 per cent per year.

Despite its large negative trade balance, China was the world's fourth largest exporter of agricultural products in 2020 (behind the EU-27, United States, and Brazil), exporting over USD 57 billion. Annual growth rates for China over the last 20 years were about one-third higher than that of global agricultural export growth (8.2 per cent compared to 6.5 per cent). With the exception of the EU-27 and the US, China's main markets for agricultural products are in East Asia (Hong Kong, Korea, and Japan) and the growing markets of Southeast Asia (Vietnam, Thailand, Malaysia, Indonesia, and the Philippines) (Table 6.1).

The composition of China's agricultural exports has changed over the past 20 years (Figure 6.2). In 2000, almost one third of China's agricultural exports were grain and grain products (14 per cent of total agricultural exports) and meat (17 per cent of total exports). By 2020, those categories had fallen to 3 per cent and 8 per cent respectively, as China became a net importer of those products by the late 2000s. At the time of accession, a number of

[1] Unless otherwise specified we use the definition of agricultural products defined in Annex 1 of the Agreement on Agriculture. This excludes, for example, fish and forestry products. It also includes various degrees of processing for different commodities (WTO, 2003).

Table 6.1 *Top 10 markets for China agricultural exports, various years*

Rank	2000	2010	2020
1	Japan	Japan	Hong Kong
2	Hong Kong	European Union	European Union
3	European Union	Hong Kong	Japan
4	South Korea	United States	Vietnam
5	United States	South Korea	United States
6	Malaysia	Indonesia	South Korea
7	Indonesia	Malaysia	Thailand
8	India	Vietnam	Malaysia
9	Singapore	Russia	Indonesia
10	Taiwan	Thailand	Philippines
Percent of trade accounted for by top 10 markets	82%	73%	74%

Source: United Nations (2021).

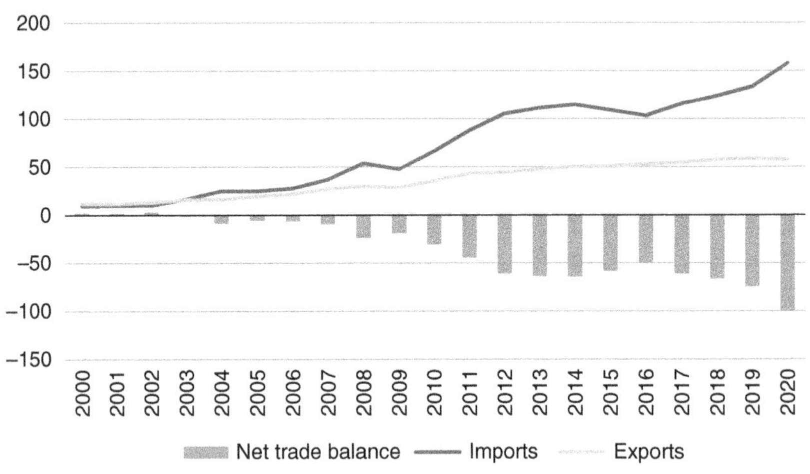

Figure 6.1 China's agricultural trade 2000–2020 (USD billion)
Source: United Nations (2021).

studies (e.g., Colby et al., 2000; Coleman et al., 2003; USITC, 1999) projected that China's exports of fruits and vegetables and processed foods would grow. Indeed, since 2000, exports of fruits and preparations, vegetables and preparations, and food preparations have soared, accounting for 50 per cent of total exports in 2020 compared with 32 per cent in 2000.

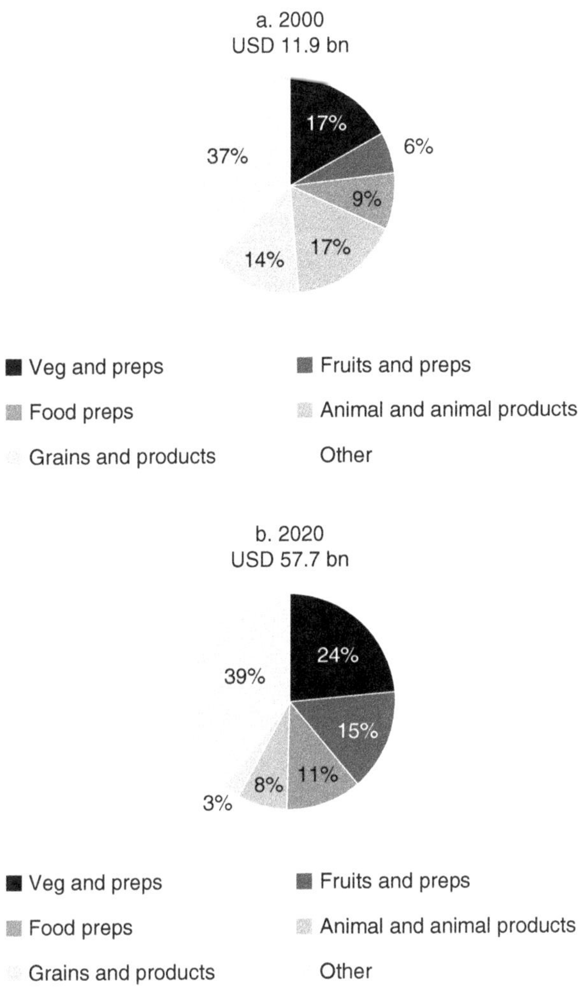

Figure 6.2 China's agricultural exports by product type, 2000 and 2020
Source: United Nations (2021).

In 2020, China was the world's largest importer of agricultural products, importing over USD 157 billion. From 2000 to 2020, China's agricultural imports grew by an annual rate of 14 per cent and over that time, China became a major destination for the largest exporting countries in the world. Table 6.2 shows the 15 top import suppliers to China in 2020 and how China was ranked as the destination for those countries' agricultural exports in 2000 and 2020. Of the 15, only Vietnam counted China

Table 6.2 *Top 15 agricultural import suppliers to China, 2020*

Rank	Exporter	Bilateral agricultural imports in 2020 (USD million)	China's rank as a destination for exporter's agricultural exports	
			2000	2020
1	Brazil	35,271	5	1
2	United States	22,826	7	1
3	European Union	22,148	15	3
4	Australia	8,920	3	1
5	New Zealand	8,531	6	1
6	Thailand	7,383	8	1
7	Canada	6,388	5	2
8	Indonesia	6,090	6	1
9	Argentina	5,986	4	1
10	Ukraine	3,668	27	2
11	Chile	3,361	16	1
12	Malaysia	3,148	4	1
13	Vietnam	2,760	1	1
14	Russia	2,121	7	3
15	India	1,876	17	4

Source: United Nations (2021).

as its top destination in 2000. By 2020, China was the largest or second-largest destination for 12 of the 15 top suppliers.

At the time of China's accession, China was viewed as a large potential market for global feed grain exports (Crook and Colby, 1996; U.S. Department of Agriculture, 1997; Wailes et al., 1998). Lester Brown's 1995 report, *Who Will Feed China? Wake-up Call for a Small Planet* warned that China's rising consumption of animal protein and domestic resource limits would cause rapid growth in import demand and disrupt global grain markets (Brown, 1995).[2] A 1996 study by Crook and Colby reviewed several projections of China's grain imports for various years in the twenty-first century and found a broad range of estimates from 15 million tonnes to over 200 million tonnes (Crook and Colby, 1996).

[2] Similar concerns were voiced during the agricultural price spikes of 2007–2011, when China was accused of buying up foreign cropland in Africa and elsewhere to feed its population – charges that were shown to be grossly exaggerated (Brautigam, 2015).

Table 6.3 *The composition of China's agricultural imports, 2000 and 2020 (USD million)*

Commodity	2000	2020	Annual percent change 2000–2020
Oilseeds, oils and fats	4,071	55,530	14
Grains and preps	841	11,917	14
Meats	732	31,198	20
Dairy products	289	13,323	21
Fruits and veg	548	15,827	18
Cotton	74	3,563	21
Other	3,059	26,415	11
Total	9,614	157,772	15

Source: United Nations (2021).

A 2000 study by the US Department of Agriculture (USDA) concluded that China's accession to the WTO would increase the value of annual US grain exports by about $1 billion (5 per cent) from 2000 to 2009 (Colby et al., 2000). In its analysis of the impacts of China's accession to the United States, the United States International Trade Commission (USITC) concluded that wheat exports to China would increase by $43 million (21 per cent increase) while corn and other feed grains would increase by $66 million (34 per cent) (U.S. International Trade Commission, 1999).[3] By contrast, because of Chinese rice policies aimed at maintaining self-sufficiency, China remained a small, but significant net exporter of rice throughout the 30 years and was not viewed as a growing market for global rice exports (Colby et al., 2000; Tuan and Hsu, 2001; USITC, 1999). The analyses projected small gains in the oilseed sector though it was projected that China would import fewer soybeans and more oilseed products such as soybean oil and soybean meal (Colby et al., 2000). Cotton exports were also projected to grow significantly.[4]

Table 6.3 shows the growth in China's agricultural imports between 2000 and 2020. What is striking is the size of annual growth over most product categories. As predicted, grains and oilseed imports increased over the period but at slightly smaller annual growth rates than the

[3] Impacts assume full implementation relative to the 1998 base year (USITC, 1999).

[4] Neither the USDA nor the USITC studies made projections regarding livestock or dairy products, or fruits and vegetables though the USDA study noted that there would likely be gains in those sectors as well (Colby et al., 2000).

average. The relative importance of oilseeds and products declined marginally relative to other product groups, but they still account for 35 per cent of total agricultural imports in 2020. Meat and dairy product imports increased by over 20 per cent *per year* over the past 20 years and account for 28 per cent of total imports in 2020 compared to just 10 per cent of total imports in 2000. Fruit and vegetable imports increased by over 18 per cent per year and accounted for 10 per cent of total imports in 2020 compared to 6 per cent in 2000.

III Drivers of China's Food Demand

The rapid growth in China's agricultural trade has been driven by several interrelated factors, including population and income growth, urbanization, economic reforms, and trade liberalization, including reforms associated with China's accession to the WTO (Alexandratos and Bruinsma, 2012; FAO, 2017). Table 6.4 presents a number of development indicators for China showing its growth over the past 20 years. While population grew annually by less than 1 per cent per year, real per capita income growth averaged over 8 per cent annually over the past 20 years. The rapid industrialization of the China economy resulted in increased urbanization as job growth stimulated rapid rural-to-urban migration. In 2000, less than 36 per cent of China's population lived in urban areas. By 2020, over 60 per cent lived in urban areas. With rising incomes, per capita food consumption[5] rose from 2,815 kcal/day in 2000 to over 3,200 kcal/day by 2020, while the percent of the population that is undernourished fell to less than 2.5 per cent from 10 per cent over the same period.[6]

Accompanying the significant increases in overall calorie availability have been reductions in the shares of calorie intakes from cereals and roots and tubers and increases in the shares of livestock products, vegetable oils, sugar, and processed foods. Figure 6.3 shows China's per capita meat consumption versus inflation-adjusted per capita GDP drawn from data from 1961 to 2018.[7] As households earn more income, they tend to spend purchase more income, particularly at lower income levels (Popkin, 2014). In China, per capita income reached USD 2000 (in $2015) in the late 1990s, at

[5] Per capita food supply is a proxy measure for per capita consumption and includes both food consumption and food waste (FAO, 2021).

[6] Undernourishment means that a person is not able to acquire enough food to meet the daily minimum dietary energy requirements, over a period of one year (FAO, 2021).

[7] Note that FAO changed its methodology for calculating per capita food consumption (availability) in 2014 (FAO, 2021).

Table 6.4 *Selected China indicators*

Indicator	2000	2005	2010	2015	2020
Population (billions)	1.283	1.322	1.360	1.397	1.425
Rate of urbanization (percent)	35.9%	42.5%	49.2%	55.5%	61.4%
Per capita income (2015 USD)	2,194	3,391	4,712	8,067	10,431
Per capita food supply (Kcal/cap/day)	2,814	2,883	3,044	3,188	3,203
Prevalence of undernourishment (percent)	10.0%	7%	2.8%	<2.5%	<2.5%

Sources: United Nations (2019); World Bank Group (2021); UN Food and Agriculture Organization (2021).

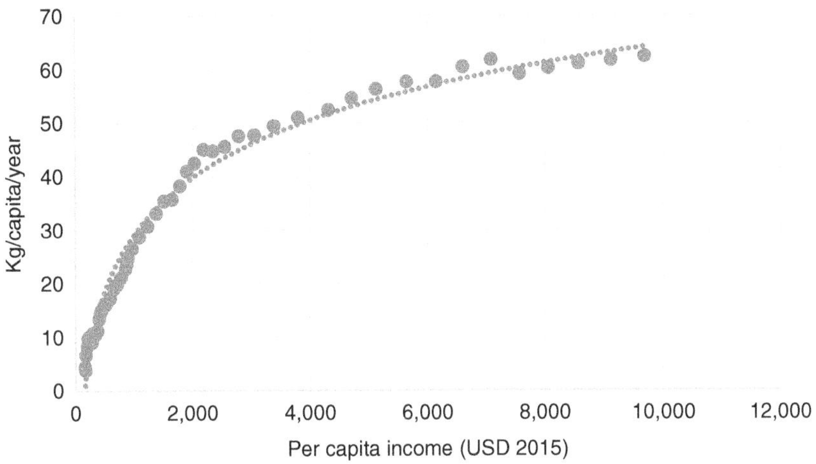

Figure 6.3 China's per capita meat consumption and income, 1961–2018
Source: UN FAO (2021).

which point the rate of growth in consumption began to slow and flatten out. Nonetheless, it was this shift in diets that has propelled (and continues to propel) the growth in imports of dairy, meats, feedstuffs, and fresh fruits and vegetables since 2000.[8]

To meet the increased demand for meat, China's livestock production has increased in numbers and production efficiency (Gale, 2015). Hog and

[8] China imports fresh fruits such as cherries, durians and grapes and vegetables (primarily fresh peppers). It exports largely processed rather than fresh fruits and vegetables.

poultry production has been transformed from "backyard operations," where households kept a few animals for home consumption and occasional sale, to more industrialized production practices, based on confined feed operations and processed feeds for inputs.[9] The growth of factory-style livestock and poultry operations has fueled demand for feedstuffs such as maize and other feed grains and soybean meal. While China grows ample supplies of food-grade soybeans (for tofu and other food products) it imports most of its feed-grade soybeans to be crushed into soybean meal and soybean oil. Feed grain imports have grown in importance as well, particularly since 2010 (Gale, 2015).

The growth in China exports is expected to continue in the future (Alexandratos and Bruinsma, 2012; FAO, 2017; OECD/FAO, 2021; USDA/ERS, 2021). For example, USDA's Economic Research Service (2021) projects that about half of the growth in global soybean consumption over the next 10 years will be in China. It is projected that the growth in China soybean imports over 2021–2030 will account for 80 per cent of the growth in global soybean imports over that period (USDA/ERS, 2021). China is also expected to continue to increase its imports of meat products and is projected to account for 40 per cent of the growth in global pork imports and 49 per cent of the growth in global beef imports over 2021–2030 (USDA/ERS, 2021).

IV China Trade and Agricultural Policies

China supports its agricultural producers through a variety of policy instruments including tariffs and other border measures and direct price and income support measures (WTO, 2021a). On occasion, the government has intervened to restrict exports to maintain lower prices as they did to restrict rice exports during the price spikes of 2007–2008 (Slayton, 2009).

(i) Market Access

Prior to accession, China's imports of agricultural products were largely in the hands of China State Trading Enterprises (STEs). Import quotas were arbitrarily set on an annual and often as-needed basis. With accession, China agreed to bind its tariffs at then-applied levels.[10] As a result, the

[9] Gale (2015) notes that over the period 2006–2010, a renewed push for livestock industry modernization under the 11th Five-Year Plan prompted greater use of manufactured feed.

[10] Agricultural products are, with the exception of some animal products, subject to *ad valorem* applied rates (WTO, 2021a).

Table 6.5 *Average China tariff rates for various agricultural product groups, 2020*

Product group	Average bound tariff	Average applied MFN duty
Animal products	14.9	13.2
Dairy products	12.2	12.3
Fruits, vegetables and plants	14.8	12.2
Coffee, tea	14.9	12.3
Cereals and preparations	23.7	19.5
Oilseeds, fats and oils	11.1	10.9
Sugars and confections	27.4	28.7
Beverages and tobacco	23.2	18.2
Cotton	22.0	22.0
Other agricultural products	12.1	9.3
All agricultural products	15.7	13.8

Source: WTO/ITC/UNCTAD (2021).

difference between applied and bound rates is relatively small compared to many other developing (and developed) countries.[11] In 2020 the average applied MFN duty across all agricultural products was 13.8 per cent (compared with an average bound tariff rate of 15.7 per cent). Table 6.5 shows average bound tariffs and average applied MFN duties across a variety of agricultural product groups (WTO/ITC/UNCTAD, 2021). The oilseed sector has generally lower protection than other sectors. For example, the bound tariff rate on soybeans is 3 per cent. Sectors receiving higher than average protection include beverages and tobacco (average applied MFN duty of 18.2 per cent), cereals and preparations (19.5 per cent), cotton (22.0 per cent), and sugars and confections (28.7 per cent).

China continues to operate tariff rate quotas (TRQs) on a number of tariff lines, which are administered through import licenses (WTO, 2021a). China's accession to the WTO was particularly significant for commodities such as soybeans where quotas were phased out and commercial traders were allowed to import agricultural productions in place of STEs. For grains, cotton, and sugar, TRQs were established and while their operation was partially liberalized to allow commercial traders, STEs

[11] For example, the simple average bound tariff for agricultural goods for India was 113.1 per cent while the simple average MFN applied rate was 34 per cent in 2020 (WTO/ITC/UNCTAD, 2021).

Table 6.6 *Tariff rate quotas on agricultural products and their utilization, 2019–2020*

Product	Out-of-quota rates	In quota rates	Tariff quota quantity	In-quota imports Tonnes		Percent of TRQ allocated to STEs
	Percent		Tonnes	2019	2020	
Wheat (7 lines)			9,636,000	3,487,625	5,151,565	90%
Wheat and meslin (4 lines)	65	1				
Wheat or meslin flour (1 line)	65	6				
Groats and meal of wheat (1 line)	65	9				
Pellets of wheat	65	10				
Corn (5 lines)			7,200,000	4,793,424	7,200,000	60%
Maize (corn) seed (1 line)	20	1				
Maize (corn), other than seed (1 line)	65	1				
Maize (corn) flour (1 line)	40	9				
Groats and meal of corn (1 line)	65	9				
Rolled or flaked corn (1 line)	65	10				
Rice (14 lines)			5,320,000	2,545,726	2,911,467	50%
Rice, other than broken (8 lines)	65	1				
Broken rice (2 lines)	10	1				
Rice flour (2 lines)	40	9				
Meal of rice (2 lines)	10	9				
Sugar (7 lines)	50	15	1,945,000	1,945,000	1,945,000	70%
Cotton (2 lines)	40	1	894,000	894,000	894,000	33%

Source: WTO (2021a, 2021c).

continued to play a significant role. Table 6.6 shows tariff rates (both out-of-quota and in-quota) and the tariff quota quantity for various agricultural products. Generally, fill rates for TRQs have been high for sugar, cotton, and wool. Fill rates for grains, by contrast, were until recently generally low, often below 50 per cent (Glauber and Lester, 2021). In 2016, the United States requested consultations under the WTO dispute settlement understanding (DSU) over China's administration of its TRQs for corn, rice, and wheat. The case is discussed more fully in Section 4. In 2020, the fill rates for corn, wheat, and rice were 100 per cent, 53 per cent, and 55 per cent, respectively, in part due to commitments under the Phase 1 agreement and in part due to strong import demand for cereals.

(ii) Domestic Support

Under the terms of accession to the WTO, China has no domestic support entitlements under Article 6.3 of the Agreement on Agriculture (AoA). In practical terms, support is thus capped at the *de minimis* threshold for trade distorting support set out in Article 6.4 of the AoA and in China's Schedule of Commitments, and equal to 8.5 per cent of the value of production for the commodity receiving support.[12] The *de minimis* threshold is higher than that for developed countries (5 per cent) but less than the *de minimis* threshold for most developing countries (10 per cent). China has access to other support provisions of the AoA including Article 6.5, which exempts production-limiting measures from reduction commitments (the so-called blue box), and Annex 2 of the AoA which exempts measures that are minimally production- and trade-distorting (the so-called Green Box). However, China agreed to forego recourse to Article 6.2 of the AoA which exempts investment aids and certain input subsidies from reduction commitments for developing countries.

At the time of accession, China taxed many of its agricultural producers by offering procurement prices below global market prices and imposing other duties (Gale, 2013). In 2004, authorities began eliminating an agricultural tax on farmers and introduced a broad program of agricultural support that included tax reductions, direct subsidies, price supports, policy loans, expenditure on infrastructure, and intergovernmental transfers (Gale et al., 2005). Price floors for rice and wheat were introduced in 2004–2006 while price supports for corn, soybeans, and rapeseed

[12] Non-product specific support is capped at 8.5 per cent of the total value of China's agricultural production.

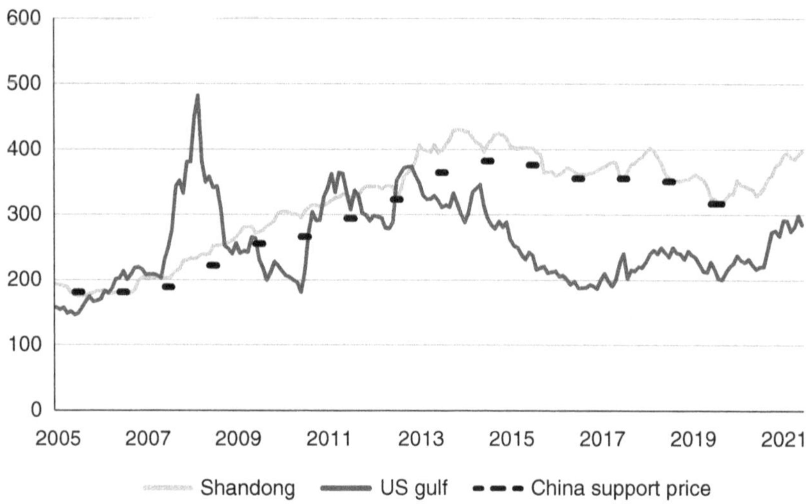

Figure 6.4 Wheat prices (USD/tonne)
Source: Gale (2013) with updates from Gale (2021).

were introduced in 2008. Cotton price support was introduced in 2012 (MacDonald et al., 2015).

Global prices rose in the late 2000s due to several factors including the growth of biofuels (primarily in the US), strong import demand from emerging markets like China, and production shortfalls in Australia (Abbott et al., 2011; Alexandratos and Bruinsma, 2012). As global prices rose from 2005 to 2013, China raised its support prices, but starting in 2013, global supplies recovered and by late 2013, world market prices had fallen and were significantly less than China's domestic prices, as shown in Figure 6.4 for wheat. Domestic grain production was increasingly finding its way into government stockpiles to maintain prices above support levels. While there is a paucity of reliable data on China stocks, available estimates suggest that government stockpiles by the mid-2010s were ample enough to satisfy nearly a year's worth of domestic consumption (Figure 6.5).

Reforms began in 2015 as cotton price supports began to be phased out and in 2016, corn supports were eliminated (MacDonald et al., 2015). Price supports for wheat and rice were maintained but lowered to minimize acquisitions. Stock levels have decreased since then as the government has taken advantage of higher prices to release grain and cotton from their stockpiles.

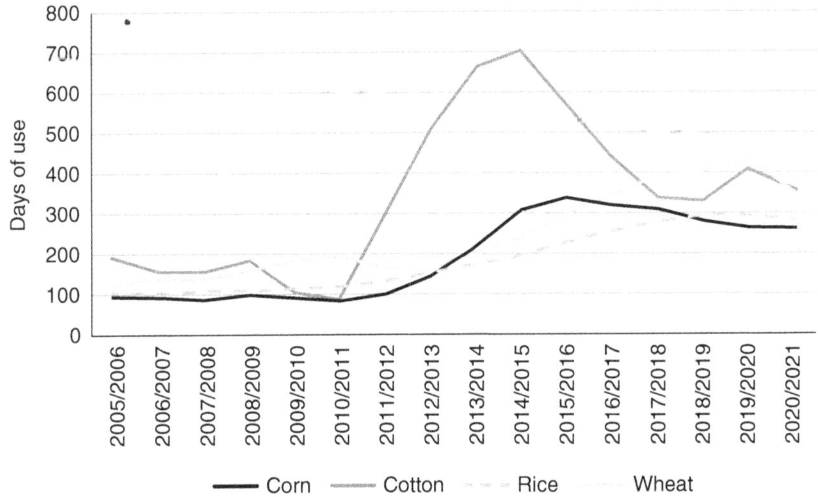

Figure 6.5 China's stocks of corn, cotton, rice, and wheat (measured in days of use)
Source: US Department of Agriculture/Foreign Agricultural Service (2021).

Figure 6.6 shows the evolution of China's producer support as measured by the Organization for Economic Cooperation and Development (OECD) over the period 1993–2020. China's Producer Support Estimate (PSE), measured as a percent of the value of agricultural production, peaked in 2015 and 2016 at just over 16 per cent.[13] Since then, their PSE has fallen relative to production value, reflecting, in part, lower support prices and other reforms, including the growth of its subsidized insurance program (Kenderdine, 2018).

In 2016, the United States requested consultations with China over its support measures for maize (corn), wheat, and rice (Ahn and Orden, 2021). That case is discussed in more detail below.

(iii) Export Subsidies and Restrictions

Exports of cotton, rice, maize, and tobacco are subject to state trading (WTO, 2021a). These products, except for tobacco, are also subject to export quotas and are allocated only to state trading enterprises. Wheat

[13] The PSE represents the value of transfers to producers, unlike support under Amber, Blue, and Green Boxes that measure compliance with WTO commitments. Therefore, the value of support as notified to the WTO is neither compatible nor comparable with the values calculated by the OECD (WTO, 2021a). In China's most recent Trade Policy

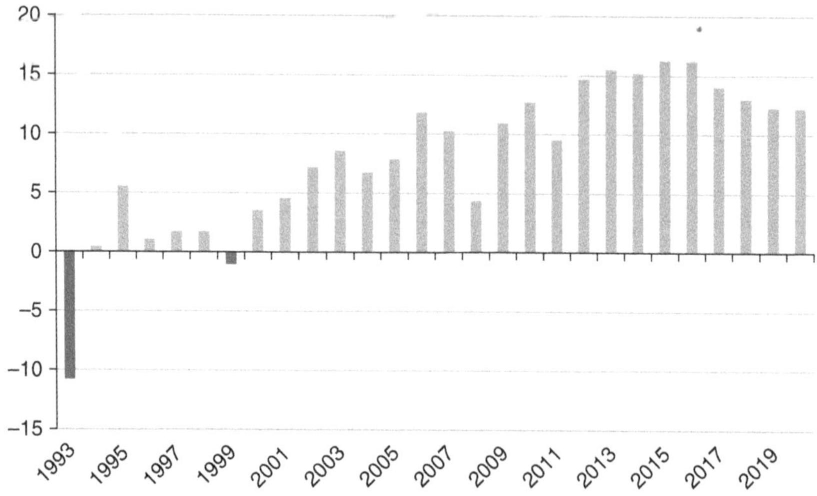

Figure 6.6 China's Producer Support Estimate (PSE) as a percent of the value of agricultural production
Source: OECD (2021).

is also subject to export quotas. As part of its accession, China agreed to forego the use of export subsidies for agricultural products.

In 2008, there was much concern over the use of export taxes by a number of countries, including China, in response to global price spikes in wheat and rice prices. Such actions were seen as beggaring-thy-neighbor policies that exacerbated price volatility (Bouët and Laborde Debucquet, 2012; Martin and Anderson, 2012; Slayton, 2009). Between 1 January and 31 December 2008, China imposed interim export tariffs, ranging from 5% to 25% on 57 tariff lines (HS 8-digit) covering wheat, corn, rice, and soybeans. In China's third Trade Policy Review, Chinese officials maintained that the objective of such measures was to conserve natural resources or to protect the environment (WTO, 2010). On 1 July 2009, some of these export taxes were removed or lowered, including on wheat and rice. Slayton (2009) points out that, unlike other large Asian rice exporters (such as Vietnam and Thailand), China did not prohibit exports during this period.

Review, officials reiterated that "OECD data do not reflect China's official position and that they could not confirm OECD estimates; they do not agree with the methodologies or data source of the estimation." (WTO, 2021a, p. 131).

V China and the WTO

Over the past 20 years, China has become increasingly active in WTO committees dealing with agriculture issues such as the Committee on Agriculture and the Sanitary and Phytosanitary (SPS) Committee. Agricultural disputes involving China, while limited in the first 15 years following China, have increased over the past 5 years as trade wars with some of its large partners have been brought to the WTO Dispute Settlement Body for adjudication.

The WTO's Committee on Agriculture oversees the implementation of the Agriculture Agreement and provides a forum for members to raise and address related questions and concerns. Its key responsibility is to monitor how WTO members are complying with their commitments. Over the first 15 years following accession China was relatively quiet in the Committee on Agriculture, raising only 13 questions about other members' notifications and policies. Over the same period, WTO members raised 231 questions to China. Over 2017–2021, China raised 31 questions to other WTO members compared to 125 questions raised by other members of China's policies and notifications.

Of the 44 questions raised by China, all were directed at developed country members, with 25 being addressed to the United States, 10 to the European Union, and 7 to Japan. Of those questions addressed to China, 141 of the 356 (40 per cent) were by the United States (Table 6.7).

The SPS Committee is the forum where WTO members discuss issues related to the implementation of the SPS Agreement and potential trade concerns. China has been an active member since its accession. As with the Committee on Agriculture, a majority of the questions asked by China have been directed to developed economies such as the US, EU, and Japan. The EU and the United States have accounted for most of the questions directed to China concerning SPS issues (Table 6.8).

Since China acceded to the WTO in 2001, they have been involved with 69 disputes: 22 as a complainant and 47 as a respondent.[14] Surprisingly only 10 have involved agriculture and food products, about 15 per cent. By contrast, Bianchi (2021) estimates that 45 per cent of disputes brought by all Members before the DSB over 1995–2020 involved agricultural or food products.

China was a complainant in three disputes involving food products (Table 6.9). Two of those disputes involved poultry exports to the

[14] China was an interested third party in 190 disputes as of 4 November 2021.

Table 6.7 *Number of questions involving China in the Committee on Agriculture*

Period	Questions posed to other members by China	Questions posed to China by other members
2002–2006	0	35
2007–2011	11	75
2012–2016	2	121
2017–2021	31	125
Total	44	356
Member	Questions posed by China to:	Questions posed to China by:
Australia	1	50
Brazil	0	14
Canada	0	50
EU	10	65
Japan	7	25
Korea	1	0
Pakistan	0	1
Russia	0	7
Taipei	0	2
Thailand	0	8
USA	25	141

Source: WTO (2021b).

Table 6.8 *Number of questions involving China in the SPS Committee*

Period	Questions posed to other members by China	Questions posed to China by other members
2002–2006	17	10
2007–2011	12	10
2012–2016	7	12
2017–2021	9	11
Total	45	43
Member	Questions posed by China to:	Questions posed to China by:
Argentina	0	1
Australia	1	5
Brazil	1	2
Canada	2	4

Member	Questions posed by China to:	Questions posed to China by:
China Taipei	0	1
EU	15	14
India	1	6
Indonesia	1	2
Israel	0	1
Japan	8	2
Mexico	2	3
Norway	0	2
Paraguay	0	1
Philippines	1	0
Russian Federation	0	1
Ukraine	0	1
USA	15	15

Source: WTO (2021d) Sanitary and Phytosanitary Management Information System.

Table 6.9 *Disputes brought by China before the WTO Dispute Settlement Body involving agricultural and food products*

Dispute number	Respondent	Request for consultations	Short title	Most recent action/date
DS392	United States	17/04/2009	US – Poultry (China)	Panel report adopted 23/07/2010
DS422	United States	28/02/2011	US – Shrimp and Diamond Sawblades	Panel report adopted 23/07/2012
DS492	European Union	08/04/2015	EU – Poultry Meat (China)	Panel report adopted 19/09/2017

Source: WTO (2021c).

US (DS392) and the EU (DS492). The third involved shrimp exports to the US (DS422) (Ahn and Messerlin, 2014). All three disputes went to panel determination where the reports were ultimately adopted by the DSB. Despite positive rulings on claims made in the poultry cases against the EU and United States, China's exports remain minimal due to SPS

Table 6.10 *Disputes brought against China before the WTO Dispute Settlement Body involving agricultural and food products*

Dispute number	Complainant	Request for consultations	Short title	Most recent action/date
DS427	United States	20/09/2011	China – Broiler Products	Art. 21.5 report adopted 28/02/2018
DS511	United States	13/09/2016	China – Agricultural Producers	Art. 21.5 request referred to original panel 28/09/2020
DS517	United States	15/12/2016	China – TRQs	Art. 21.5 request referred to original panel 30/08/2021
DS568	Brazil	16/10/2018	China – Certain Measures concerning Imports of Sugar	In consultations
DS589	Canada	09/09/2019	China – Canola Seed (Canada)	Request for panel 17/06/2021
DS598	Australia	16/12/2020	China – AD/ CVD on Barley (Australia)	Panel composed 03/09/2021
DS602	Australia	22/06/2021	China – AD/ CVD on Wine (Australia)	Request for panel 16/09/2021

restrictions in those countries. US imports of shrimp from China were almost USD 340 million in 2018 but have fallen since then to less than USD 56 million in 2020 as a result of anti-dumping actions by the US Department of Commerce.

As of November 4, 2021, there have been seven requests for consultations with China involving food and agricultural products; all but one of those disputes were initiated within the last 5 years (Table 6.10). In 2011, the United States requested consultations with China concerning China's measures imposing anti-dumping and countervailing duties on broiler products from the United States (DS427). The Panel report was adopted in 2013. In 2016, the United States requested a compliance hearing under Article 21.5. That report was adopted in 2018. US chicken product exports to China totaled USD 759 million in 2020.

In 2016, the United States requested consultations with China on the level of subsidies provided to agricultural producers (DS511) and consultations on China's administration of its TRQs (DS517). In *China – Agricultural Producers* (DS511), the issue was China's provision for domestic support, in the form of market price support, in excess of its product-specific *de minimis* level, provided to agricultural producers of wheat, India rice, Japonica rice, and corn in 2012, 2013, 2014, and 2015 (Ahn and Orden, 2021). The Panel sided with the United States on its claim that China's support had exceeded *de minimis* levels for India rice, Japonica rice and wheat and hence was in excess of its commitment level of "nil"[15] under China's Schedule of Concessions on Goods. The Panel report was adopted in 2019, but in 2020, the United States requested a compliance panel under Article 21.5 of the DSU, which has been referred to the original panel for deliberation.

In *China-TRQs* (DS517), the United States requested consultations with China regarding its administration of TRQs for wheat, rice, and corn. A key finding of the Panel was the administration of state-trading-enterprises (STE) and non-STE portions of TRQs was inconsistent with the obligations to administer TRQs on a transparent, predictable, and fair basis, using clearly specified administrative procedures, and in a manner that would not inhibit the filling of each TRQ (Glauber and Lester, 2021; WTO, 2021c). The Panel Report was adopted by the DSB in 2019. In August 2021, the United States requested the DSB to establish a compliance panel under Article 21.5 of the DSU.

Four additional trade disputes involving agricultural products have been brought against China. In *China – Certain Measures affecting Imports of Sugar* (DS568), Brazil requested consultations with China in 2018 concerning (i) a safeguard measure imposed by China on imported sugar, (ii) China's administration of its tariff-rate quota for sugar, and (iii) China's import licensing system for out-of-quota sugar. The European

[15] The Panel concluded that the reform to China's corn policy removed an essential element (the Applied Administrative Price) of the challenged corn measure, thus marking the expiry of this measure in years 2012 through 2015. As such, despite this corn measure being within the Panel's terms of reference, the Panel did not find any reason to make a ruling on this measure (WTO, 2021c, p. 226).

Union, Thailand, and Guatemala have also requested consultations. In *China – Canola Seed (Canada)* (DS589), Canada requested a consultation with China in 2019 concerning two sets of measures allegedly affecting the importation of canola seed (intended for processing and consumption, not for planting) from Canada: (a) measures suspending the importation of canola seed from two Canadian companies; and (b) measures applying enhanced inspections on all imports of Canadian canola seed. In June 2021, Canada requested a Panel to be formed.

Lastly, two disputes have been brought by Australia regarding recent actions taken by China affecting barley and wine imports from Australia. In *China – AD/CVD on Barley (Australia)* (DS598), Australia requested consultations with China in 2020 regarding its use of anti-dumping and countervailing measures against barley imports from Australia. A Panel was formed in September 2021. In *China – AD/CVD on Wine (Australia)* (DS602), Australia requested consultations with China in 2021 with respect to anti-dumping and countervailing measures on bottled wine in containers of 2 liters or less imported from Australia. In September 2021, Australia requested the establishment of a Panel.

Over the next couple of years, China will face Panel decisions on a number of disputes involving agricultural products including two disputes with Australia (barley and wine), one dispute with Canada (canola), and two compliance hearings with the United States (agricultural subsidies and TRQ administration). Zhou (2019) has pointed out how China has had a high rate of compliance with WTO rulings in the past. The current impasse in the Appellate Body means that Panel rulings that are appealed face an uncertain future and this may affect China's compliance with future Panel and compliance rulings.

(i) China's Trade War with the United States

In addition to trade disputes within the WTO, China has also been embroiled in a trade war with the United States (Bown and Irwin, 2019; Bown and Kolb, 2021). In 2018, in response to duties placed on China goods by the United States, China placed counter-retaliatory duties on a number of US agricultural exports, including soybeans. Total US agricultural exports to China fell to $9.1 billion in 2019 and soybean exports fell by almost 75 per cent, to USD 3.1 billion, the lowest level since 2006 (Glauber, 2020). Brazil was a big beneficiary as China sourced most of its soybean imports from them in 2018 and 2019, and while the United States was able to send some of its soybeans to markets that would have normally imported from Brazil, overall, US soybean exports fell by USD 4 billion in 2018 and USD 3 billion in 2019 and US soybean receipts in 2019 fell by 12 per cent from 2017 levels (Adjemian et al., 2021; Carter and Steinbach, 2020).

On January 15, 2020, China and the United States signed The Phase One Economic and Trade Agreement. The agreement included chapters addressing intellectual property protection, technology transfer, trade in food and agricultural products, some new market access in China for financial services, exchange rates and transparency, and a government-to-government enforcement mechanism that could result in unilaterally determined trade sanctions if one side did not live up to the agreement (Bown, 2021a). China agreed to import USD 36.5 billion in US agricultural goods in 2020 and USD 43.6 billion.[16] Actual China agricultural imports from the United States in 2020 totaled USD 23.6 billion, about 64 per cent of the target. Based on import data through November 2021, Bown (2021b) estimates that China is on track to achieve 87 per cent of the targeted level for agriculture for 2021.

In their analysis of the Phase One Agreement, Feenstra and Hong (2021) pointed out the adverse impact of the agreement on other export suppliers to China, particularly Australia, and Canada, followed by Brazil, Indonesia, Malaysia, Thailand, and Vietnam. At the WTO Committee on Agriculture meeting in March 2021, in response to questions concerning trade diversion and deviation from MFN treatment as a result of the Phase One Agreement, China assured Members that:

> *Purchases are based on commercial considerations and market conditions. In 2020, COVID-19 severely hit global economy, trade flow, and transportation. These unexpected factors, among others, could influence the market. China is a large market. We welcome competitive products from all Members. We will continue to import products based on market conditions in line with WTO rules. As the economy recovers, we expect that the demands would increase. China will continue to facilitate trade from all Members based on market conditions and in line with WTO rules.* (WTO, 2021)

Figure 6.7 shows that China's agricultural imports from the United States in 2020 increased by almost 80 per cent over imports from the United States in 2019. The large increase was due to the low level of imports in 2019 due to the trade war. Compared to 2017 – the last year before the trade war started in 2018, imports from the United States in 2020 were up only 1 per cent. Moreover, China showed a very large increase in total agricultural

[16] Chapter 3 of the Phase One agreement also included a number of provisions that addressed more substantive trade issues such as biotechnology approvals, SPS concerns, and TRQ administration (USDA, 2020).

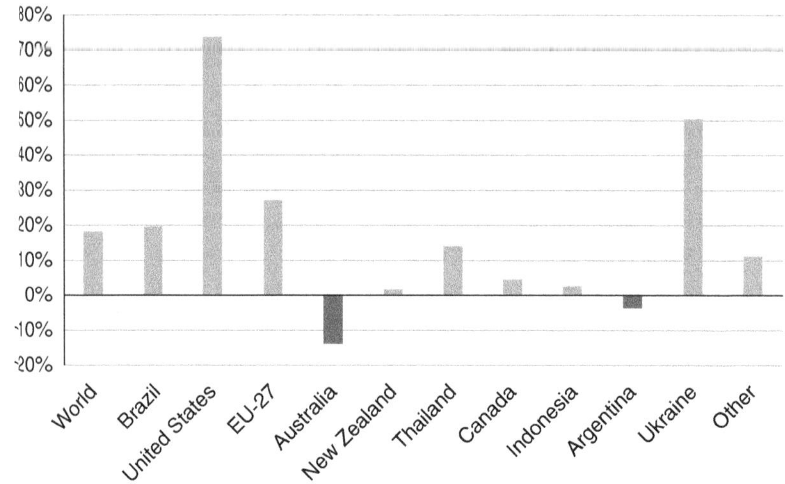

Figure 6.7 China's agricultural imports, change from 2019 to 2020
Source: United Nations, COMTRADE.

imports in 2020, up 18 per cent over 2019 levels. Agricultural imports from most of China's top 10 suppliers showed large gains. Agricultural imports from Brazil, for example, increased by USD 5.8 billion over 2019 levels (up 20 per cent) while agricultural imports from the EU-27 were up USD 4.7 billion (27 per cent). By contrast, agricultural imports from Australia were down due to Chinese restrictions on barley and wine imports. Overall, the data suggest that much of the increase in imports was due to factors other than Phase 1 such as the rapid recovery in hog populations in China in 2020 after herds had been sharply reduced in 2018–2019 due to African Swine Fever (USDA/FAS, 2021).

Chapter 3 of the Phase One agreement also included a number of provisions that addressed more substantive trade issues such as biotechnology approvals, SPS concerns, and TRQ administration (USDA, 2020). Significantly, however, supplemental duties remain on key agricultural products lending uncertainty to what is now a tenuous truce in agricultural trade relations between the two parties.

VI Conclusions

Twenty years after its accession to the WTO, China has become the world's largest agricultural importer and one of the top export destinations for the world's largest agricultural exporters. Population, income growth, and increased urbanization have driven dietary changes and consumption growth that have outpaced domestic production and required China to import an increasingly larger share of its consumption needs. Those trends are projected to increase over the next 10 years, and likely beyond.

Accession to the WTO has been a significant factor in the growth of agricultural trade (both exports and imports). Binding tariffs at relatively low rates provided certainty to exporters and the phase-out of some tariff rate quotas and operation of importing STEs has allowed commercial interests to flourish. Moreover, WTO trade disciplines have arguably shaped China's agricultural policies. China's agricultural support has fallen in recent years, in part due to adverse rulings at the WTO Dispute Settlement Body but also in part due to domestic reforms to correct unsustainable policies that distorted internal market prices.

Recent WTO disputes on agricultural support and TRQ administration point to the challenge of how to support domestic producers and be consistent with WTO trade rules. Further, trade wars with trade partners such as the United States, Australia, and Canada have disrupted trade patterns, not just bilaterally, but because of the size of China's imports, have been disruptive to world trade as well. Worse, they threaten to undermine liberalization trends by raising tariff levels and placing importing decisions back into the hands of STEs and other government entities. A functioning WTO DSB helps ensure compliance with WTO trade rules, but the current impasse over appointing new members of the Appellate Body undermines its function (Bown and Irwin, 2019; Glauber and Xing, 2020; Mavroidis and Sapir, 2021).

Time will tell whether these recent trends will be reversed but growing China food demand will likely keep pressure on the China government to keep markets open to agricultural imports.

References

Abbott, P., C. Hurt, and W. Tyner. 2011. *What's Driving Food Prices in 2011?* Oak Brook, IL: Farm Foundation.

Adjemian, M., A. Smith, and W. He. 2021. 'Estimating the Market Effect of a Trade War: The Case of Soybean Tariffs.' *Food Policy*: 102152. https://doi.org/10.1016/j.foodpol.2021.102152

Ahn, D. and P. Messerlin. 2014. 'United States – Anti-Dumping Measures on Certain Shrimp and Diamond Sawblades from China: Never Ending Zeroing in the WTO?' *World Trade Review* 13 (2): 267–279.

Ahn, D. and D. Orden. 2021. 'China – Domestic Support for Agricultural Producers. One Policy, Multiple Parameters Imply Modest Discipline.' *World Trade Review* 20 (4): 389–404.

Alexandratos, N. and J. Bruinsma. 2012. *World Agriculture towards 2030/2050: The 2012 Revision*. Rome: Food and Agriculture Organization of the United Nations.

Bianchi, E. 2021. 'Food Products, the WTO Dispute Settlement System and Trade Remedies.' in V. Piñeiro, A. Campos, and M. Piñeiro (eds.), *The Road to the WTO Twelfth Ministerial Conference: A Latin American and Caribbean Perspective*. Washington, DC: IICA and IFPRI. https://repositorio.iica.int/handle/11324/19221

Blustein, P. 2009. *Misadventures of the Most Favored Nations*. New York: Public Affairs Books.

Blustein, P. 2019. *Schism: China, America, and the Fracturing of the Global Trading System*. Waterloo, ON: Centre for International Governance Innovation.

Bouët, A. and D. L. Debucquet. 2012. 'Food Crisis and Export Taxation: The Cost of Non-cooperative Trade Policies.' *Review of World Economics/Weltwirtschaftliches Archiv* 148 (1): 209–233. www.jstor.org/stable/41485792

Bouët, A. and D. L. Debucquet. 2018. 'US Trade Wars with Emerging Countries in the 21st Century: Make America and Its Partners Lose Again.' *The World Economy* 41 (9): 2276–2319.

Bown, C. 2021a. *The US-China Trade War and Phase One Agreement*. Washington, DC: Peterson Institute of International Economics. www.piie.com/sites/default/files/documents/wp21-2.pdf

Bown, C. 2021b. *US-China Phase One Tracker: China's Purchases of US Goods*. Washington, DC: Peterson Institute of International Economics. www.piie.com/research/piie-charts/us-china-phase-one-tracker-chinas-purchases-us-goods

Bown, C. and D. Irwin. 2019. 'Trump's Assault on the Global Trading System.' *Foreign Affairs* 98 (September–October): 125–136.

Bown, C. and M. Kolb. 2021. *Trump's Trade War Timeline: An Up-to-Date Guide*. Washington, DC: Peterson Institute for International Economics. www.piie.com/sites/default/files/documents/trump-trade-war-timeline.pdf

Brautigam, D. 2015. *Will Africa Feed China?* New York: Oxford University Press.

Brown, L. R. 1995. *Who Will Feed China?* New York: W.W. Norton & Co.

Carter, C. A. and S. Steinbach. 2020. The Impact of Retaliatory Tariffs on Agricultural and Food Trade. Working Paper 27147, NBER.

Crook, Frederick W. and W. Hunter Colby. 1996. 'The Future of China's Grain Market.' U.S. Department of Agriculture, Economic Research Service Agriculture Information Bulletin Number 730. www.ers.usda.gov/publications/pub-details/?pubid=42115

Colby, W. Hunter, M. J. Price, and F. C. Tuan 2000. 'China's WTO Accession Would Boost U.S. Ag Exports & Farm Income.' *Agricultural Outlook* 269: 11–16.

Coleman, J., J. Fry, and D. Boughner. 2003. 'The Impact of China's Accession to the WTO on U.S. Agricultural Exports.' USITC Office of Industries Working Paper No. ID- 03. US International Trade Commission. Washington.

Feenstra, R., and C. Hong. 2021. 'China's Import Demand for Agricultural Products: The Impact of the Phase One Trade Agreement.' *Review of International Economics*, 1–24. https://doi.org/10.1111/roie.12568

Gale, F. 2013. 'Growth and Evolution in China's Agricultural Support Policies.' U.S. Department of Agriculture, Economic Research Service Economic Research Report Number 153. www.ers.usda.gov/media/1156829/err153.pdf

Gale, F. 2015. 'Development of China's Feed Industry and Demand for Imported Commodities,' FDS-15K-01 US Department of Agriculture, Economic Research Service. www.ers.usda.gov/webdocs/outlooks/36929/55490_fds-15k-01.pdf?v=2510.2

Gale, F. 2021. Personal communication.

Gale, Fred, B. Lohmar, and F. Tuan. 2005. *China's New Farm Subsidies*. WRS-0501, USDA, Economic Research Service. www.ers.usda.gov/publications/wrs0501/

Glauber, J. 2020. 'US Trade Aid Payments and the WTO.' *Applied Economic Perspectives and Policy* 43 (2):586–603.

Glauber, J. and X. Xing. 2020. WTO Dispute Settlement Cases Involving the Agreement on Agriculture, 1995–2019. IFPRI Discussion Paper 1917. Washington, DC: International Food Policy Research Institute (IFPRI).

Glauber J. and S. Lester. 2021. 'China – Tariff Rate Quotas for Certain Agricultural Products: Against the Grain: Can the WTO Open Chinese Markets? A Contaminated Experiment'. *World Trade Review* 20 (4): 405–420. https://doi.org/10.1017/S1474745621000148

Kenderdine, T. 2018. 'Insurance Plus Futures: Agricultural Commodity Price Reform in China'. *Asia & The Pacific Policy Studies* 2 (5): 331–346.

MacDonald, S., F. Gale, and J. Hansen. 2015. 'Cotton Policy in China.' US Department of Agriculture, Economic Research Service CWS-15c-01 Washington, DC. www.ers.usda.gov/webdocs/outlooks/36244/52550_cws-15c-01.pdf?v=9723.7

Martin, W. and K. Anderson. 2012. 'Export Restrictions and Price Insulation during Commodity Price Booms.' *American Journal of Agricultural Economics* 94 (2): 422–427.

Mavroidis, P. and A. Sapir. 2021. *China and the WTO: Why Multilateralism Still Matters*. Princeton, NJ: Princeton University Press.

OECD-FAO. 2021. *OECD–FAO Agricultural Outlook 2021–2030*. Paris: OECD Publishing. Rome: Food and Agriculture Organization of the United Nations.

Organization for Economic Cooperation and Development (OECD). 2021. *Agricultural Policy Monitoring and Evaluation*. www.oecd.org/agriculture/topics/agricultural-policy-monitoring-and-evaluation/

Popkin, B. 2014. 'Nutrition, Agriculture and the Global Food System in Low and Middle Income Countries.' *Food Policy* 47: 91–96.

Slayton, T. 2009. 'Rice Crisis Forensics: How Asian Governments Carelessly Set the World Rice Market on Fire.' CGD Working Paper 163. Washington, DC: Center for Global Development. www.cgdev.org/content/publications/detail/1421260/

Tuan, Francis C. and Hsu Hsin-Hui. 2001. 'U.S.-China Bilateral WTO Agreement and Beyond.' In *China: Agriculture in Transition*. U.S. Department of Agriculture, Economic Research Service.

United Nations, Department of Economic and Social Affairs. 2019. World Population Prospects. https://population.un.org/wpp/

United Nations Food and Agriculture Organization (FAO). 2017. *The Future of Food and Agriculture – Trends and Challenges*. Rome: FAO.

United Nations Food and Agriculture Organization (FAO). 2021. FAOSTAT. FoodBalances. www.fao.org/faostat/en/#data

U.S. Department of Agriculture, Economic Research Service (USDA/ERS). 2021. '2021 International Long-Term Projections to 2030.' www.ers.usda.gov/data-products/international-baseline-data/

U.S. Department of Agriculture, Foreign Agricultural Service. 2021. 'PS&D Online.' https://apps.fas.usda.gov/psdonline/app/index.html#/app/home

U.S. Department of Agriculture, Office of the Chief Economist. 1997. 'Agricultural Baseline Projections to 2005, Reflecting the 1996 Farm Act.' World Agricultural Outlook Board Staff Report WOAB-97-1. www.ers.usda.gov/webdocs/outlooks/98720/waob-97-1.pdf?v=2436.6

U.S. Department of Agriculture (USDA). 2020. China Phase One agreement. www.fas.usda.gov/topics/china-phase-one-agreement

U.S. International Trade Commission. 1999. 'Assessment of the Economic Effects on the United States of China's Accession to the WTO.' Publication 3229.

Wailes, E., C. Fang, and F.C. Tuan. 1998. 'US–China Agricultural Trade: Constraints and Potential.' *Journal of Agricultural and Applied Economics* 30 (1): 113–126.

World Bank Group. 2021. World Development Indicators. https://data.worldbank.org

World Trade Organization (WTO). 2003. *WTO Agreements Series: 3. Agriculture*. Geneva: World Trade Organization Secretariat.

World Trade Organization (WTO). 2010. Trade Policy Review – China. WT/TPR/S/230.

World Trade Organization (WTO). 2021a. Trade Policy Review – China. WT/TPR/S/415.

World Trade Organization (WTO). 2021b. Agriculture Information Management System. https://agims.wto.org/

World Trade Organization (WTO). 2021c. WTO Dispute Settlement: One-Page Case Summaries 1995–2020. www.wto.org/english/res_e/booksp_e/dispu_settl_1995_2020_e.pdf

World Trade Organization (WTO). 2021d. *Sanitary and Phytosanitary Management Information System*. WTO SPS and TBT Platform. https://eping.wto.org/

World Trade Organization, International Trade Centre and UN Conference on Trade and Development (WTO/ITC/UNCTAD). 2021. World Tariff Profiles 2021. Geneva. www.wto.org/english/res_e/booksp_e/tariff_profiles21_e.pdf

Zhou, W. 2019. *China's Implementation of the Rulings of the World Trade Organization*. Oxford: Hart Publishing.

7

China's Use of Export Restrictions and WTO Law

Heading toward "Weaponization" of Exports?

IRYNA BOGDANOVA AND ANQI WANG

I Introduction

In its twenty years of participation in the multilateral trading system, the People's Republic of China (China) has been using various types of export restrictions. Some of these policies were brought to the attention of the WTO dispute settlement system and provoked heated scholarly debates.

However, recent amendments to Chinese laws and regulations represent a major shift: even a shallow analysis is indicative of a new role that China ascribes to the use of unilateral economic sanctions in general and export restraints in particular. These actions were most likely instigated by the US-China trade war, tightening of US export control regulations, economic sanctions against Chinese technology companies, and a looming US-China "technological de-coupling."

Given the recency of this policy shift, it has not been a subject of thorough academic scrutiny yet. Notwithstanding this, its potentially significant implications for both China-US bilateral relations and the multilateral trading system make it worthy of a detailed academic inquiry.

The working hypothesis of this paper is that China's use of export restraints has been traditionally heavily dependent on domestic factors, yet the recent changes signal the shift towards the use of export restrictions as a strategic geopolitical tool, thus reinforcing the role of external factors. To test the accuracy of this assumption, we analyze China's use of export restrictions in the period from 2001 to 2021. In particular, we suggest that three distinct

We express our cordial thanks to Professors Henry Gao and Damian Raess, editors of the volume, for their overall feedback and support. This chapter has immensely benefitted from the comments and discussion following its presentation at the World Trade Forum 2021, for which we are grateful to the participants, especially Professors Peter Van Den Bossche and Weihuan Zhou. We also thank Dr Zaker Ahmad for commenting on an earlier draft. Errors that remain are the authors' own.

phases can be discerned along this period: (i) elimination of export restrictions before and after joining the WTO; (ii) selective use of export restrictions mostly for domestic policy reasons till 2016; (iii) shift towards strategic use of export restrictions as an instrument of geopolitical competition since 2017. The latest stage has evolved as a response to the ongoing trade and technological wars waged by the United States against China and economic sanctions against China and its technology companies, as well as a reflection of China's growing assertiveness in its use of economic coercion.

The paper proceeds in five parts. This introduction sets the stage for a subsequent discussion. The analysis in the following three parts covers the abovementioned three periods of China's use of export restrictions with the identification of the rationales behind their use. Furthermore, the WTO consistency of these export restraints is briefly examined. The last – the fifth part – presents a forward-looking discussion of the recent changes in China's laws and regulations, their expected operation and WTO consistency, as well as their potential to disrupt existing global value chains, in particular in the technology sector.

One more clarification is warranted here. In the WTO context, the term export restriction may encompass various types of measures such as export duties (tariffs) and export taxes, export quotas, export licenses, export prohibitions, and minimum export prices (Marceau, 2016). Our analysis in Parts I and II considers diverse types of export restrictions, while our subsequent inquiry in Part IV examines export prohibitions and non-automatic export licenses, that is, instruments that aim at restricting exports as a part of broader economic coercive efforts.

II Elimination of Export Restrictions before and after Acceding to the WTO

China's economic strategy of gradual opening declared by Deng Xiaoping in 1978 and described as "crossing the river by touching the stones" (Morrison, 2019, p. 5) culminated in China's accession to the WTO in late 2001 and the subsequent comprehensive liberalization.

Before the economic reforms of the late 1970s, China's participation in international trade was controlled by a small number of foreign trade corporations, which held monopolies in diverse categories of goods (Ianchovichina & Martin, 2001). At that time, export volumes were defined by planned levels of imports, that is, imports were financed by export earnings, thus allowing the country to pursue its policy of self-sufficiency (Ianchovichina & Martin, 2001). A drastic increase in the number of foreign trade corporations from twelve national monopolies to many thousands was among the early reforms put in place by the Chinese government (Harrison, 2014). Li and Jiang (2018, p. 576) provide the following numbers: "export trade companies increased from 12 in 1978 to about 1,200 in 1986, reaching a peak of 5,075 in 1988." This and other economic reforms of 1978–1991 aspired to raise the role of exports in the country's economic development (Li & Jiang, 2018).

Later, in the 1990s, as a part of the efforts to liberalize its international trade regime, China significantly reduced categories of products subject to export licensing from 143 categories (48.3% of total exports) in 1992 to 58 categories constituting 9.5% of total exports in 1999 (WTO, 2001b, p. 32). After becoming a WTO Member, China further shortened the list of items subject to export licensing and the WTO Secretariat reported that in 2004 the value of Chinese exports subject to licensing requirement was equal to 4.1% of total exports (WTO, 2006, p. 104).

Thus, in the period leading to the WTO accession, China was pursuing the strategy of export-led growth, and exports were aimed at contributing to the country's economic development. Despite this, various forms of export restrictions were occasionally employed. The process of China's WTO accession demonstrated that other WTO Members had serious concerns in this regard. In particular, WTO Members drew attention to the use of non-automatic export licenses, the use of export restrictions on raw materials and intermediate products such as tungsten ore concentrates, rare earths, and other metals, and restrictions on the export of silk (WTO, 2001b). China confirmed its intention to gradually eliminate these restrictions (WTO, 2001b).

Furthermore, in its Accession Protocol, China agreed to eliminate "all taxes and charges applied to exports" with the exception of the fees "specifically provided for in Annex 6 of this Protocol" or "applied in conformity with the provisions of Article VIII of the GATT 1994" (WTO, 2001a). As a matter of law, export duties (tariffs) are permitted under WTO law unless a WTO Member included relevant commitments in its schedule (Marceau, 2016). Since China explicitly included the relevant commitment in its Accession Protocol, it bound itself and agreed to additional WTO obligations not incumbent on other WTO Members, apart from several recently acceded states. In this regard, the panel in *China – Raw Materials* reiterated that China's Accession Protocol is an integral part of the WTO Agreement and therefore can be enforced in dispute settlement proceedings.

After its accession to the WTO in 2001, China abolished export quotas and export licences on certain categories of goods (WTO, 2006).

III China's Use of Export Restrictions for Domestic Policy Reasons in 2001–2016

According to the TPR Report issued in 2006, China had used export taxes, including interim duties that were defined on an annual basis; tax rebates on exports, some of which were paid at a lower rate and thus constituted an export levy; export prohibitions "to avoid shortages in domestic supply, conserve exhaustible natural resources, or in accordance with international obligations" as well as "to meet industry development requirements"; export quotas, which China believed it can justify under Articles XI, XVII, and XX of the GATT 1994 and Annex 2A2 of its Accession Protocol; automatic and non-automatic export licensing (WTO, 2006). Already in this first TPR Report the WTO Secretariat noted that China was purposefully using export restrictions to subsidize downstream industries: "With regard to its trade policy objectives, China is currently aiming to increase its exports of value added products. To this end, China continues to use trade and other measures, to promote local production in certain sectors, either for export, or as inputs for producers in China. The measures include: export taxes, reduced VAT rebate rates, and export licensing to deter exports of some products" (WTO, 2006, p. 44).

The next TPR Report issued in 2008 emphasized China's increasing use of various types of export restrictions: "the number of tariff lines subject to interim export duties was almost doubled in the last two years, VAT rebate rates on exports of some 2,800 lines (HS 8-digit) were eliminated or lowered in July 2007, and the number of lines subject to export quotas and licensing requirements has increased" (WTO, 2008, p. xi). The subsequent Report of 2010 confirmed that China continued to use various export restrictions (WTO, 2010), while the Report prepared in 2012 documented that export duties were eliminated and interim export duty rates were reduced although the total number of tariff lines subject to export quotas increased, and seasonal special export taxes were adopted (WTO, 2012). The 2014 TPR Report mentioned China's application of diverse export restrictions and underlined that China's position of the leading world exporter of certain products, which are subject to its export taxes, may have an impact on the world price of these products (WTO, 2014). The next TPR Report demonstrated that China eliminated or reduced some export restrictions, while tightening others (WTO, 2016).

The World Bank analysts in their 2011 study identified Chinese export restrictions as one of the four issues of significant concern for other WTO Members (Mattoo & Subramanian, 2011). It comes as no surprise since the economic repercussions of those export restrictions were felt acutely: according to some estimates, a reduction in Chinese export quotas in rare earth resulted in more than a seven-fold increase in world prices (Bond & Trachtman, 2016).

Several WTO Members questioned the compatibility of Chinese export restrictions with its WTO commitments. Table 7.1 presents a short summary of these disputes.

The legal discussions in these disputes revolved around two core issues: first, the application of general exceptions prescribed by Article XX of the GATT 1994 to China's commitment to eliminate export duties enshrined in its Protocol of Accession; and second, the possibility to justify export restrictions inconsistent with Article XI:1 of the GATT 1994 under Articles XI:2(a), XX(b) and XX(g) of the GATT 1994. To be more specific, China claimed that its diverse export restrictions were aimed at the conservation of exhaustible natural resources as well as the prevention of environmental pollution and thus, protection of human life and health,[1] while the WTO Members that initiated these disputes contended that the subsidization of downstream industries[2] and the relocation of foreign firms to China[3] were the main objectives. China, in an attempt to justify its export restrictions as "related to" the conservation of exhaustible natural

[1] In *China – Measures Related to the Exportation of Various Raw Materials*, China argued that the temporary export duties applied to fluorspar are justified pursuant to Article XX(g) of the GATT 1994 and the temporary export duties to non-ferrous metal scrap of zinc, magnesium metal, and manganese metal, and to coke, magnesium metal and manganese metal are justified pursuant to Article XX(b) of the GATT 1994; the export quota applied to refractory-grade bauxite is justified pursuant to Article XI:2(a) of the GATT 1994, or is otherwise justified pursuant to Article XX(g) of the GATT 1994; export quotas applied to coke and silicon carbide are justified pursuant to Article XX(b) of the GATT 1994. In *China – Measures Related to the Exportation of Rare Earths, Tungsten and Molybdenum*, China argued that the export duties on rare earths, tungsten, and molybdenum are justified under Article XX(b) of the GATT 1994 and the 2012 export quotas on rare earths, tungsten, and molybdenum are justified under Article XX(g) of the GATT 1994.

[2] "The export restraints that China imposes on the Raw Materials are part of this industrial policy, which is predicated on advantaging China's domestic producers and industries, but distorts the international economic marketplace and is inconsistent with China's WTO obligations." (Reports of the Panel, China – Measures Related to the Exportation of Various Raw Materials, Addendum.)

[3] "The United States and the European Union argue that, by raising international prices while reducing domestic prices, the export quota creates two markets, resulting in a 'two-tiered' pricing structure and a corresponding incentive for foreign users of rare earths to relocate to China to obtain rare earths at a cheaper price." (Reports of the Panel, China – Measures Related to the Exportation of Rare Earths, Tungsten and Molybdenum, para. 7.441.)

Table 7.1 *WTO disputes, wherein the WTO compatibility of Chinese export restrictions was questioned*

WTO Members that initiated disputes	Types of export restrictions	Raw materials covered	Outcomes of the disputes
The United States (DS394), the European Communities (the European Union, DS395), and Mexico (DS398) initiated disputes in 2009.	Export duties; export quotas; export licensing; and minimum export price requirements; allocation and administration of export quotas, export licences, and minimum export prices, and alleged non-publication of certain measures	Various forms of bauxite, coke, fluorspar, magnesium, manganese, silicon carbide, silicon metal, yellow phosphorous, and zinc	Both the panel and the Appellate Body found that China's use of various forms of export restrictions violates its obligations under China's Accession Protocol and obligations under the GATT 1994 and these breaches could not be justified under Articles XI:2(a), XX(b) and XX(g) of the GATT 1994.
The United States (DS431), the European Union (DS432), and Japan (DS433) initiated disputes in 2012.	Export quotas; export duties; administration and allocation of export quotas, including through export licensing	Rare earths, tungsten, and molybdenum	The panel found that China applied export duties that were inconsistent with its obligations under the Accession Protocol and it could not justify them under Article XX(b) of the GATT 1994. China's export quotas breached Article XI:1 of the GATT 1994 and could not be justified under Article XX(g) of the GATT 1994. China's trading rights restrictions violated its WTO obligations and were not justified. China did not appeal the final conclusions of the panel but appealed some aspects of its reasoning.
The United States (DS508) and the European Union (DS509) initiated disputes in 2016.	Export duties, export quotas, administration, and allocation of export quotas	Various forms of antimony, cobalt, copper, graphite, lead, magnesia, talc, tantalum, and tin; longer list in DS509	Pending disputes (panels established, but not yet composed)

resources, emphasized their "signalling" function,[4] a point to which we will return in the next section.

Discussing the veracity of China's assertion that export restrictions, in particular export quotas, were implemented to conserve natural resources, commentators point out that the efficiency of export restraints in contributing to the declared goal of conserving exhaustible natural resources and reducing pollution could be undermined by the growing domestic consumption (Pothen & Fink, 2015; Bond & Trachtman, 2016).

The WTO rulings in these disputes were vehemently criticized. For example, Qin (2012) contends that the AB in *China – Raw Materials* dispute misinterpreted China's commitments under its Accession Protocol. In particular, she concludes that the correct application of the rules of treaty interpretation enshrined in the VCLT would allow exceptions under Article XX of the GATT 1994 to serve as exceptions to China's additional commitments to eliminate export tariffs (Qin, 2012). Gao (2023) argues in this volume that the flawed legal reasoning followed by the WTO adjudicators not only downgraded China to a "second-class citizen" but also led to China's growing disillusionment with the multilateral trading system. This disillusionment has been strongly reinforced by the recent unilateral, plurilateral, and multilateral attacks carried out by the United States and its allies against China and resulting in what Gao (2023) calls China's "alienation" from the WTO and its core principles. Echoing our assertion that since recently China is more willing to use trade policy as a weapon, Gao (2023) observes that "the US has effectively taught China that WTO rules could be just ignored, especially as it gets in the way."

Economic studies reveal that Chinese export restrictions pursued diverse policy goals. The empirical study by Gourdon, Monjon, and Poncet (2016) analyzed the rationales behind the Chinese fiscal policies aimed at curtailing exports (export taxes and VAT rebates) in the period of 2004–2012. They conclude that these fiscal tools were employed for a number of reasons: to support sophisticated high-technology products, to curb exports of water polluting sectors and air polluting products, to benefit upstream industries and to limit the cost of the application of antidumping measures by trade partners (Gourdon et al., 2016). Another

[4] China argued that its export restrictions, in particular export quotas, sent a signal to the foreign consumers to diversify their sources of supply and to find substitutes ("[...] the Panel should have found that the structure and design of China's export quotas relate to conservation based on its finding that the quotas can send effective conservation signals to foreign users."). (Reports of the Appellate Body, China – Measures Related to the Exportation of Rare Earths, Tungsten and Molybdenum, para. 2.39.)

study by Pothen and Fink (2015) conclude that China's export restrictions on rare earth pursued three main objectives: to create incentives for foreign industries to relocate to China, to conserve exhaustible natural resources and to reduce pollution. Chad Bown (2020) draws a similar conclusion that China's export restrictions provided unfair advantages to Chinese manufacturers and enabled them to use cheap local inputs. In view of this, it is reasonable to assume that Chinese export restrictions, among other things, pursued environmental objectives as well.

Legal scholars echo some of the abovementioned views. For example, Wu (2017) asserted that Chinese policies of curtailing exports of critical minerals pursued multiple economic goals: (i) to entice foreign producers to relocate to China; (ii) to instigate the transfer of foreign technologies that would occur as a result of the relocation of foreign producers combined with investment restrictions, thus requiring foreign producers to partner with Chinese firms; and (iii) to promote a "cluster effect" enabling China to dominate in manufacturing in new industries. Writing in 2017, Mark Wu argued that the Chinese practice of using export restrictions still persists. In his view, China takes advantage of a "free pass" – the lack of retrospective remedies in the WTO dispute settlement system – to bolster its industrial policy through export restrictions (Wu, 2017). In this regard, it should be noted that not only China takes advantage of systemic loopholes in the WTO dispute settlement system but, as Zhou (2023) accurately observes in this volume, other WTO Members also use these systemic constraints and loopholes and do it even more frequently.

In this period, China at least once employed export restrictions as an instrument of economic coercion, when it targeted Japan in 2010 after the accident in the disputed waters near the Senkaku (Diaoyu) islands in the East China Sea (Bradsher, 2010; Tabuchi, 2010; Poh, 2021).

IV Strategic Use of Export Restrictions as an Instrument of Geopolitical Competition

In this section, we analyze China's shift towards the explicit use of export restrictions as a tool of unilateral economic coercion, which contradicts its prior long-standing practice.

(i) China's Attitude towards Unilateral Economic Sanctions (Non-UN Sanctions) and Its Practice

China has traditionally generated strong headwinds against economic coercion in the form of unilateral economic sanctions (non-UN sanctions).[5] In particular, it opposes the recognition of unilateral economic sanctions' legality in international law (Hofer, 2017; Poh, 2021). Although this position may rest on shaky legal ground – international law scholars refuse to acknowledge the existence of the right to be free from economic coercion (Tzanakopoulos, 2015), China's vehement opposition to unilateral sanctions is reflected in its persistent anti-sanctions rhetoric, which depicts Western sanctions as imperialist and interventionist (Poh, 2021). According to some commentators, this rhetoric has a constraining effect on China's use of unilateral economic coercion (Poh, 2021).

Until recently China's use of unilateral economic coercion was of a limited nature and was confined to consumer boycotts silently supported by the government (Kashin et al., 2020). Yet a decade ago, the tide has slowly begun to shift: commentators took note of an increasing Chinese "assertiveness" in deploying not only economic inducements but also unilateral economic sanctions for geopolitical objectives (Glaser, 2012; Reilly, 2013).

Distinctive features that characterize Chinese unilateral sanctions are their unofficial and undocumented application as well as their narrow scope that is, only specific sectors were targeted, while the existing trade and investment patterns were preserved (Poh, 2021). Scholars also point out China's ability to deftly combine instruments of economic coercion with economic inducements and diplomatic negotiations (Harrell et al., 2018).

The literature on China's use of unilateral economic sanctions highlights their signaling function (Poh, 2021). This signaling function is of a dualistic nature: it sends a signal to sanctioned states and other states (Blackwill & Harris, 2016; Poh, 2021), as well as to domestic audiences, thus serving domestic political purposes (Harrell et al., 2018). Concerning the former aspect, Robert Blackwill and Jennifer Harris (2016, p. 120) observe: "[…] China has merely signaled to its neighbors the costs of risking geopolitical daylight between it and them, making those governments less inclined to act in ways that would run counter to China's strategic objectives."

China's growing assertiveness, which has been observed in the past decade, encompasses the use of various forms of restrictions, yet export restrictions have been the least employed ones (Harrell et al., 2018). This

[5] Unilateral economic sanctions are defined as restrictive economic measures imposed by individual states against other states, their bodies, government officials, or legal entities and individuals, without any prior authorization of an international or regional organization, i.e., based on their domestic laws.

hesitation could be explained by the following factors: (i) China's reliance on its exports and its desire to maintain its status as a reliable supplier, hence securing its place in the existing supply chains; (ii) the previous rulings of the WTO adjudicators, wherein Chinese export restrictions were recognized as inconsistent with its obligations under WTO law (Harrell et al., 2018). Notwithstanding this, the recent shift towards a new geo-economic global order characterized by "securitisation of economic policy and economisation of strategic policy" (Roberts et al., 2019) and the "weaponization" of export restrictions by the United States (Fuller, 2021) paved the way for new Chinese laws that establish a framework for using unilateral economic sanctions, including targeted export restrictions. Talking about "weaponization" of export restrictions by the United States, the US export regulations were vastly expanded to prohibit exports of inputs crucial for the integrated circuit industry, in particular design and fabrication of chips, to Huawei and its subsidiaries and thus, undermining company's growth and its capacity to provide competitive 5G equipment (Fuller, 2021). Those US unilateral sanctions crippling Huawei's potential to compete globally reinvigorated the ambitious technonationalist agenda in China – China's attempts to promote self-sufficiency in strategic technologies, which are deeply rooted in the Chinese national development strategy (Feigenbaum, 2017), as well as spurred retaliatory moves (Fuller, 2021).

(ii) Recent Changes in China's Laws and Regulations

Even before the WTO accession, Article 7 of China's Foreign Trade Law allowed retaliation in the form of economic sanctions against any other country if it takes "discriminatory, prohibitive, or restrictive trade measures." The law does not define what measures constitute "discriminatory, prohibitive, or restrictive trade measures"; thus, enabling its ambiguous application. It is noteworthy that similar provisions in the US legislation – Sections 301–310 of the Trade Act of 1974 – were ruled to be inconsistent with WTO obligations (Panel Report, US – Section 301 Trade Act).

Trade and tech wars between the United States and China instigated major revisions to China's laws and regulations. To be more specific, China started to pursue more advanced economic statecraft, emulating Western tools used for this purpose. In May 2019, China announced the creation of the Unreliable Entities List (UEL) and the later adopted regulation defines "unreliable entity" as a foreign legal entity, organization, or an individual that boycotts or cuts off supplies to Chinese entities for non-commercial reasons, takes discriminatory measures against Chinese companies, and, as a result, causes material damage to Chinese companies or related industries and threatens or potentially threatens China's national security (MOFCOM, 2020). According to Article 10 of the relevant regulation, blacklisted entities are subject to import and export restrictions (MOFCOM, 2020). The US commentators have compared this new Chinese regulation with similar US procedures and concluded as follows: "While the list triggers export control action similar to the U.S. Department of Commerce's Entity List, China's justifications for including an entity on the list appear to be much broader" (Sutter, 2020, pp. 2–3).

Attempts to unify previously fragmented export control regimes into a single and comprehensive framework culminated in the enactment of the Export Control Law (ECL) in 2020. This law aims to protect China's national security and to provide a basis for export restrictions that exceed the typical remit of security and defense measures, that is, it gives the Chinese government a toehold to enact retaliatory measures against other states and their entities (PRC Export Control Law, 2020). The ECL (2020) regulates exports of dual-use, military and nuclear items, as well as other goods, technologies, and services related to national security and national interests. The law uses ambiguous language that leaves ample room for further interpretations (Zhu, 2020). Article 48 of the ECL is of importance for our analysis: it stipulates specific rules authorizing reciprocal measures to be taken in response to export controls implemented by other states.

This new statutory power comes at a time when the US Export Controls Act of 2018 introduced major changes to US export control regulations by expanding the scope of technologies subject to export controls to include a new category called "emerging and foundational technologies" (John S. McCain National Defense Authorization Act, 2018). This development has been described by Whang (2019, p. 598) as: "Export control regimes have now been incorporated to also reflect a country's economic policies." In other words, the United States can use export control regulations to implement additional restrictions against China by making exports of "emerging and foundational technologies" subject to such regulations.

Furthermore, in 2019, the US Bureau of Industry and Security (BIS) included Huawei and its non-US subsidiaries in the so-called Entity List, making all exports, re-exports, and in-country transfers subject to a license requirement issued under the presumption of denial (US Department of Commerce, 2019a, 2019b). Later, the BIS further tightened these export restrictions to practically deprive Huawei and any of its affiliated entities from accessing integrated circuits (chips) either produced in the United

States or produced with the use of US technologies or equipment (US Department of Commerce, 2020). In view of this, the powers granted under Article 48 of the ECL seem to carry not only political overtones but also to enable Chinese retaliatory actions.

Commentators have already noted this shift in Chinese policy: "This law [ECL] helps China to align its export control practices with those of the United States, giving it legal grounds to apply similar tactics in their growing technology war" (Zhu, 2020). The US analysts have observed that: "The final language [of the ECL] includes several new provisions that appear aimed at creating a Chinese policy counterweight to the U.S. government's use of export control authorities to restrict the transfer of U.S. dual-use technology to China, including provisions for retaliatory action and extraterritorial jurisdiction" (Sutter, 2020, p. 1).

China issued its first control list under the ECL, which includes encryption technology and data security chips as the first subjects of its new export control regime (Kawate, 2020). According to Article 12 of the ECL, Chinese companies seeking to export products on the control list must obtain prior approval from the export control administrations.

Apart from enacting the ECL, China engaged in international efforts to build a coalition of like-minded states in order to counterweight the US policy of adding "emerging and foundational technologies" to the list of items subject to export control regulations. In particular, China sponsored the UN General Assembly resolution "Promoting International Cooperation on Peaceful Uses in the Context of International Security" that was adopted in December 2021. This resolution not only emphasizes the significance of international cooperation on materials, equipment, and technology for peaceful purposes but also urges all UN Members to lift undue restrictions on the exports of technology to developing countries if it is used for peaceful purposes (UN General Assembly, 2021). Furthermore, in late December 2021, the State Council Information Office of the People's Republic of China issued a white paper on China's export controls, which criticizes abuse of export control regulations by saying: "No country or region should abuse export control measures, gratuitously impose discriminatory restrictions, apply double standards to matters related to non-proliferation, or abuse multilateral mechanisms related to export controls for the purposes of discrimination and exclusion."

This move – China's active engagement in setting new global rules – is not a new development. In this regard, Gao (2011) has already contended that China has emerged as an international rule-maker contrary to its earlier role as a rule-taker.

In April 2021, China's Ministry of Commerce released an updated version of the Guiding Opinion of the Ministry of Commerce on the Establishment of Internal Compliance Mechanism for Export Controls on Exporters of Dual-Use Items (Guidelines). The Guidelines are the latest substantive effort to expand export controls since the ECL was adopted. As an implementing regulation of the ECL, the Guidelines aim to provide companies with the guidance on establishment and enhancement of internal export compliance programs and in such a way promote compliance with the new export control regime (Crowell & Moring, 2021). To this end, companies are encouraged to set up an export control compliance committee and an export control compliance department (Crowell & Moring, 2021).

Another pertinent development in this regard is the second update of the Catalogue of Technologies Prohibited or Restricted from Export (Catalogue) published in August 2020, which resulted in an addition of 23 new items to the export-restricted technologies. The newly added technologies are those related to encryption, cyber defense, metal 3D printing, aero remote sensors, and unmanned aerial vehicles (Catalogue, 2020). These technologies are subject to a license requirement, and they cannot be exported without approval from the Chinese commerce authorities (Yunfeng, 2020). In September 2020, Beijing Commerce Bureau made a public announcement that it would strictly enforce the Catalogue, and if technology falls into the restricted category, it would demand that business operators file an application for approval before they enter into any negotiations for the export of such technology (Cai et al., 2020).

These recent developments attest to the accuracy of our assertion that China modifies its policy and is willing to use its export restrictions as a geopolitical tool.

Two other laws deserve our attention as well. These laws are the Data Security Law and the Anti-foreign Sanctions Law. In June 2021, China adopted its Data Security Law, which enhances the state's authority over the collection, use, and protection of data. Article 26 of the law allows for "equal countermeasures" to be taken if another state enacts any "discriminatory" or "restrictive" investment or trade measure related to data or technology for data development and utilization (Data Security Law, 2021). By enacting this law, Beijing establishes statutory power to retaliate against foreign restrictions on Chinese technology firms.

Furthermore, in June 2021, China passed Anti-foreign Sanctions Law (AFSL). This law empowers competent Chinese authorities to sanction persons and organizations that are directly or indirectly involved in the formulation, decision-making, or implementation of discriminatory restrictive measures directed against China (Anti-foreign Sanctions Law, 2021). According to Articles 4 and 5 of the law, these sanctions may also be extended to spouses and immediate family members of the sanctioned persons and to the managers of the listed organizations (Anti-foreign Sanctions Law, 2021). Article 6 of this law specifies restrictive measures that could be used against sanctioned individuals and organizations, and they include denial of visa issuance, denial of entry, deportation, prohibition or restriction to conduct transactions, to cooperate or engage in other activities with Chinese individuals or organizations, and other necessary measures (Anti-foreign Sanctions Law, 2021). Pursuant to Article 6(3) of the AFSL sanctioned individuals and organizations are prohibited from having any transaction with organizations and individuals on the territory of China, and consequently, Chinese entities and individuals are prevented from engaging in exporting to sanctioned persons and entities (Anti-foreign Sanctions Law, 2021). The AFSL laid the groundwork for China's efforts to expand its retaliatory toolkit, to establish the application of its laws extraterritorially,[6] and to police behavior beyond the Chinese border (Drinhausen & Legarda, 2021).

(iii) Are We Heading towards "Weaponization" of Exports by China?

While in the past Chinese economic sanctions played second fiddle to economic inducements, the recent changes in China's regulatory framework are reflective of its willingness to be more assertive in employing economic coercion. In this regard, Mingjiang Li (2017, p. xxv) observes that "China is gradually becoming more prepared to use its economic power for coercive purposes."

This growing assertiveness is further fuelled by several contributory factors. First, the abovementioned Chinese laws have been introduced against the background of the US-China trade and tech wars and the US efforts to tighten its export controls by empowering the Bureau of Industry and Security to update export control regulations to include "emerging

[6] We came to this conclusion based on Articles 4 and 15, both of which forbid individuals and organizations outside of the territory of China to conduct any activities against China's national security.

and foundational technologies" that are "essential to the national security" (Bown, 2020). Second, China's ambition to become a global leader in innovative technologies is grounded not only in its desire to become technologically self-sufficient but also in its intention to use this leverage against its adversaries. Commentators posit that "China's efforts to move up in the value chain and to master the transformative technologies of the future – from robotics to electric vehicles – may not only protect Beijing from foreign attempts to coerce it but may also give it new export restriction levers to pull to coerce adversaries" (Harrell et al., 2018, p. 17).

This shift contrasts with the previous instances of Chinese economic coercion in one essential element – more open and transparent use of economic coercion – that is achieved through the revision of the existing laws and regulations as well as through the enactment of the new ones. Put it differently, the process of economic sanctions formalization, which has been achieved through the establishment of a formal legal regulatory framework, is a core element in a new China sanctions policy.

V What Are the Broader Implications of China's Shift in Use of Export Restrictions?

These new laws and regulations herald a departure from China's traditional policy of avoiding unilateral economic sanctions. What would these new legislations portend for multinational corporations and existing supply chains? The implications of the new Chinese assertiveness in using economic coercion may be felt acutely by multinational businesses. Lovely and Schott (2021) predict that these new rules would force companies to choose between access to the Chinese market and access to the US market, and this choice may also entail penalties that might be imposed by both sides. Discussing China's new policy Greg Gilligan, chairman of the American Chamber of Commerce in China, has already warned that the recent developments may present "potentially irreconcilable compliance problems" (Bloomberg News, 2021).

Even if China never invokes its new regulations, their existence creates new risks for multinational corporations doing business either in China or with their Chinese counterparts. Furthermore, these new regulations add pressure to the growing US-China trade frictions and may, in the long run, result in the restructuring of the global supply chains. Concerns have been already expressed that the US sanctions against Chinese tech companies would create a risk of a "divided tech world," in particular by undermining trust in the existing global supply chains (Knight, 2019).

If China begins to erect technology transfer controls as a part of its economic coercive strategy, such export restrictions may play a growing role as implements of the tech war between the United States and China. Discussing this possibility, one more peculiarity of Chinese unilateral sanctions should be noted. As a rule, China targets politically and economically sensitive foreign constituencies irrespective of their connection to the sanctionable conduct (Harrell et al., 2018). Thus, from a global perspective, these actions may further bifurcate the global economy and lead to a full-scale "technological de-coupling" (Webster et al., 2020).

The new Chinese laws prescribe the use of the two types of export restrictions as potential sanctions: either a complete prohibition of exports or an export license requirement as a precondition for exports. It is worth observing that export prohibitions (bans) as well as non-automatic export licensing schemes, especially if they are administered in a non-transparent and discriminatory way, run afoul of the WTO commitments (Bogdanova, 2021). To be more specific, export bans on goods are inconsistent with the prohibition of quantitative restrictions enshrined in Article XI:1 of the GATT 1994, which has been interpreted broadly: "[T]he text of Article XI:1 is very broad in scope, providing for a general ban on import or export restrictions or prohibitions 'other than duties, taxes or other charges'" (Panel Report, India – Quantitative Restrictions). Restrictions on the exportation of services may be GATS-incompatible only if a WTO Member has undertaken market access commitments in a specific services sector and under mode 3, which also covers the right to export services to recipients abroad (Bogdanova, 2021). Regarding export license schemes, the panel in *China – Raw Materials* concluded that: "a licence requirement that results in a restriction [...] would be inconsistent with GATT Article XI:1. Such restriction may arise in cases where licensing agencies have unfettered or undefined discretion to reject a licence application." Thus, depending on the administration of export license schemes, such measures might breach an obligation to eliminate quantitative restrictions of Article XI:1 of the GATT 1994.

Wu (2017) has already pointed out that the lack of retrospective remedies in the WTO dispute settlement system ought to be blamed for China's willingness to temporary free-ride and enact export restrictions to the benefit of its domestic downstream industries. The same logic may be used for its strategic export restrictions. Foreign producers, faced with the need to respond to such Chinese policies, could not hold back and thus risk jeopardizing their supply chain and damaging their economic interests. In such circumstances, some companies may decide to relocate to China,[7] while others might restructure their supply chains. This development may further erode the multilateral trading system as well as undermine its credibility for WTO Members and for private businesses.

VI Concluding Remarks

This chapter argues that China is more willing than before to use instruments of economic coercion such as unilateral economic sanctions for its political goals. Several implications flow from this new development. First, it may have a bearing on the existing global supply chains. In particular, the use of various export restrictions, especially those related to novel and emerging technologies, by the two leading tech powerhouses – the United States and China – may result in a de-globalization of the technology supply chains. Second, China's strategic use of export restrictions, especially in the tech industry, may bifurcate the global economy resulting in what has been dubbed a "technological de-coupling" and sapping the potential growth performance of the global economy. This possibility looms large on the horizon. Third, export bans and ambiguous and non-transparent export licensing requirements are incompatible with WTO obligations. However, the duration of the WTO dispute settlement procedures and the lack of retrospective remedies significantly undermine the ability to provide an effective remedy for multinational businesses that operate in a globally interdependent environment, thus further contributing to the erosion of the multilateral trading system and the WTO as an institution.

References

Anti-foreign Sanctions Law of the People's Republic of China. (2021). www.npc.gov.cn/npc/c30834/202106/d4a714d5813c4ad2ac54a5f0f78a5270.shtml

Blackwill, R. D., and Harris, J. M. (2016). *War by Other Means: Geoeconomics and Statecraft*. Cambridge, MA: The Belknap Press of Harvard University Press.

Bloomberg News. (2021). 'How China is trying to fight back against sanctions'. *Bloomberg News*, 29 June (Updated on 28 July).

Bogdanova, I. (2021). 'Targeted economic sanctions and WTO law: Examining the adequacy of the national security exception'. *Legal Issues of Economic Integration*, 48(2): 171–200.

[7] Wu (2017) argued that pressing economic need for essential inputs reinforced by the peculiarities of the WTO dispute settlement system, in particular duration of dispute settlement proceedings and the lack of retrospective remedies, urge foreign producers to respond to such policies, sometimes even by relocating their production.

Bond, E. W., and Trachtman, J. (2016). 'China–rare earths: Export restrictions and the limits of textual interpretation'. *World Trade Review* 15(2): 189–209.

Bown, C. P. (2020). 'Export controls: America's other national security threat'. *Duke Journal of Comparative & International Law* 30(2): 283–308.

Bradsher, K. (2010). 'Amid tension, China blocks vital exports to Japan'. *The New York Times*. www.nytimes.com/2010/09/23/business/global/23rare.html

Cai, R., Zhang. G., Zhang, S., and Li, D. (2020). 'China's export control regulation and its impact on MNCs'. *Zhong Lun*. www.zhonglun.com/Content/2020/09-15/1410340412.html

Catalogue of Technologies Prohibited or Restricted from Export. (2020). www.gov.cn/zhengce/zhengceku/2020-08/29/5538299/files/135c5cdd6baa46a986ac5e51a1a49ac3.pdf

Crowell & Moring. (2021). 'China releases guidelines on how to develop export control compliance programs'. www.crowell.com/NewsEvents/AlertsNewsletters/all/China-Releases-Guidelines-on-How-to-Develop-Export-Control-Compliance-Programs

Data Security Law of the People's Republic of China. (2021). https://digichina.stanford.edu/work/translation-data-security-law-of-the-peoples-republic-of-china/

Drinhausen, K., and Legarda, H. (2021). 'China's Anti-Foreign Sanctions Law: A warning to the world'. *MERICS*. https://merics.org/en/short-analysis/chinas-anti-foreign-sanctions-law-warning-world

Feigenbaum, E. A. (2017). 'The deep roots and long branches of Chinese technonationalism'. Washington: Carnegie Endowment for International Peace. https://carnegieendowment.org/2017/08/12/deep-roots-and-long-branches-of-chinese-technonationalism-pub-72815

Foreign Trade Law of the People's Republic of China. http://tradeinservices.mofcom.gov.cn/article/zhengce/zcwd/201710/2543.html

Fuller, D. B. (2021). 'China's counter-strategy to American export controls in integrated circuits'. *China Leadership Monitor* 67: 1–16.

Gao, H. (2011). 'China's ascent in global trade governance: From rule taker to rule shaker, and maybe rule maker?' In Carolyn Deere-Birkbeck (eds.), *Making Global Trade Governance Work for Development*. Cambridge: Cambridge University Press, pp. 153–180.

Gao, H. (2023). 'China's changing perspective on the WTO: From aspiration, assimilation to alienation'. In Henry Gao, Damian Raess, and Ka Zeng (eds.), *China and the WTO: A Twenty-Year Assessment*. Cambridge: Cambridge University Press.

Glaser, B. S. (2012). 'China's coercive economic diplomacy: A new and worrying trend'. The Center for Strategic and International Studies. www.csis.org/analysis/chinas-coercive-economic-diplomacy-new-and-worrying-trend

Gourdon, J., Monjon, S., and Poncet, S. (2016). 'Trade policy and industrial policy in China: What motivates public authorities to apply restrictions on exports?' *China Economic Review* 40: 105–120.

Harrell, P., Rosenberg, E., and Saravalle, E. (2018). *China's Use of Coercive Economic Measures*. Washington: The Center for a New American Security.

Harrison, A. (2014). 'Trade and industrial policy China in the 1990s to today'. In Shenggen Fan, Ravi Kanbur, Shang-Jin Wei, and Xiaobo Zhang (eds.), *The Oxford Companion to the Economics of China*. Oxford: Oxford University Press.

Hofer, A. (2017). 'The developed/developing divide on unilateral coercive measures: legitimate enforcement or illegitimate intervention?' *Chinese Journal of International Law* 16(2): 175–214.

Ianchovichina, E., and Martin, W. (2001). *Trade Liberalization in China's Accession to the World Trade Organization*. Policy Research Working Paper 2623, Washington: The World Bank.

John S. (2018). McCain National Defense Authorization Act for Fiscal Year 2019, Pub. L. No. 115–232. www.congress.gov/bill/115th-congress/house-bill/5515/text

Kashin, V. B., Piatachkova, A. S., and Krasheninnikova, L. S. (2020). 'Kitayskaya politika v sfere primeneniya ekonomicheskikh sanktsiy: teoriya i praktika (Chinese Economic Sanctions Policy: Theory and Practice)'. *Comparative Politics Russia* 2: 123–138.

Kawate, I. (2020). 'Encryption first target of China's new export restriction law'. *Nikkei Asia*. https://asia.nikkei.com/Economy/Trade/Encryption-first-target-of-China-s-new-export-restriction-law

Knight, W. (2019). 'Trump's feud with Huawei and China could lead to the balkanization of tech'. *MIT Technology Review*. www.technologyreview.com/2019/05/24/239073/trumps-feud-with-huawei-and-china-could-lead-to-the-balkanization-of-tech/

Li, K., and Jiang, W. (2018). 'China's foreign trade: Reform, performance and contribution to economic growth'. In Ross Garnaut, Ligang Song and Cai Fang (eds.), *China's 40 Years of Reform and Development: 1978–2018*. Canberra: Australian National University Press, pp. 575–593.

Li, M., ed. (2017). *China's Economic Statecraft: Co-optation, Cooperation, and Coercion*. Singapore: World Scientific Publishing.

Lovely, M. E., and Schott, J. J. (2021). *Can China Blunt the Impact of New US Economic Sanctions?* Washington: Peterson Institute for International Economics.

Marceau, G. (2016). 'WTO and export restrictions'. *Journal of World Trade* 50(4): 563–586.

Mattoo, A. and Subramanian, A. (2011). *China and the World Trading System*. Policy Research Working Paper 5897, Washington: The World Bank.

MOFCOM. (2020). Order No. 4 of 2020 on provisions on the unreliable entity list. https://perma.cc/B7JS-E4PY

Morrison, W. M. (2019). *China's Economic Rise: History, Trends, Challenges, and Implications for the United States*. Congressional Research Service, RL33534. https://crsreports.congress.gov

People's Republic of China. (2020). 'Export Control Law as passed by Standing Committee of the National People's Congress'. www.npc.gov.cn/englishnpc/c23934/202112/63aff482fece44a591b45810fa2c25c4.shtml

Poh, A. (2021). *Sanctions with Chinese Characteristics: Rhetoric and Restraint in China's Diplomacy*. Amsterdam: Amsterdam University Press.

Pothen, F., and Fink, K. (2015). *A Political Economy of China's Export Restrictions on Rare Earth Elements*. Discussion Paper No. 15-025.

Qin, J. Y. (2012). 'The predicament of China's "WTO-Plus" obligation to eliminate export duties: A commentary on the China–raw materials case'. *Chinese Journal of International Law* 11: 237–246.

Reilly, J. (2013). 'China's economic statecraft: Turning wealth into power'. Lowy Institute. www.lowyinstitute.org/publications/chinas-economic-statecraft-turning-wealth-power.

Reports of the Appellate Body. (2012). China – Measures Related to the Exportation of Various Raw Materials [China – Raw Materials]. WT/DS394/AB/R; WT/DS395/AB/R; WT/DS398/AB/R.

Reports of the Appellate Body. (2014). China – Measures Related to the Exportation of Rare Earths, Tungsten and Molybdenum [China – Rare Earths]. WT/DS431/AB/R, WT/DS432/AB/R, WT/DS433/AB/R.

Report of the Panel. (1999). India – Quantitative Restrictions on Imports of Agricultural, Textile and Industrial Products [India – Quantitative Restrictions]. WT/DS90/R.

Report of the Panel. (2000). United States – Sections 301–310 of the Trade Act 1974 [US – Section 301 Trade Act]. WT/DS152/R.

Reports of the Panel. (2011). China – Measures Related to the Exportation of Various Raw Materials [China – Raw Materials]. WT/DS394/R, WT/DS395/R, WT/DS398/R.

Reports of the Panel. (2014). China – Measures Related to the Exportation of Rare Earths, Tungsten and Molybdenum [China – Rare Earths]. WT/DS431/R, WT/DS432/R, WT/DS433/R.

Roberts, A., Moraes, H. C., and Ferguson, V. (2019). 'Toward a geoeconomic order in international trade and investment'. *Journal of International Economic Law* 22(4): 655–676.

State Council Information Office of the People's Republic of China. (2021). White Paper: China's Export Controls. https://english.www.gov.cn/archive/whitepaper/202112/29/content_WS61cc01b8c6d09c94e48a2df0.html

Sutter, K. M. (2020). 'China issues new export control law and related policies'. Congressional Research Service. https://fas.org/sgp/crs/row/IN11524.pdf

Tabuchi, H. (2010). 'Block on minerals called threat to Japan's economy'. *The New York Times*. www.nytimes.com/2010/09/29/business/global/29rare.html

Tzanakopoulos, A. (2015). 'The right to be free from economic coercion'. *Cambridge International Law Journal* 4(3): 616–633.

UN General Assembly. (2021). Resolution 'Promoting international cooperation on peaceful uses in the context of international security.' UN Doc. A/RES/76/234.

US Department of Commerce. (2020). Press release. *Commerce Department Further Restricts Huawei Access to US Technology and Adds Another 38 Affiliates to the Entity List*. www.commerce.gov/news/press-releases/2020/08/commerce-department-further-restricts-huawei-access-us-technology-and

US Department of Commerce, Bureau of Industry and Security. (2019a). 15 C.F.R. §744 Addition of Entities to the Entity List, Final Rule (16 May 2019).

US Department of Commerce, Bureau of Industry and Security. (2019b) 15 C.F.R. §744 Addition of Certain Entities to the Entity List and Revision of Entries on the Entity List, Final Rule (19 Aug. 2019).

Webster, G., Luo, Y., Sacks, S., Wilson, N., and Coplin, A. (2020). 'Mapping U.S. – China technology decoupling'. Stanford Freeman Spogli Institute for International Studies. https://fsi.stanford.edu/publication/mapping-us–china-technology-decoupling.

Whang, C. (2019). 'Undermining the consensus-building and list-based standards in export controls: What the US export controls act means to the global export control regime'. *Journal of International Economic Law* 22: 579–599.

World Trade Organization. (2001a). *Protocol on the Accession of the People's Republic of China to the World Trade Organization*. WTO Doc. WT/L/432.

World Trade Organization. (2001b). *The Report of the Working Party on the Accession of China*. WTO Doc. WT/MIN(01)/3.

World Trade Organization. (2006). *Trade Policy Review of the People's Republic of China, Report by the Secretariat*. WTO Doc. WT/TPR/S/161.

World Trade Organization. (2008). *Trade Policy Review of the People's Republic of China, Report by the Secretariat*. WTO Doc. WT/TPR/S/199.

World Trade Organization. (2010). *Trade Policy Review of the People's Republic of China, Report by the Secretariat*. WTO Doc. WT/TPR/S/230.

World Trade Organization. (2012). *Trade Policy Review of the People's Republic of China, Report by the Secretariat*. WTO Doc. WT/TPR/S/264.

World Trade Organization. (2014). *Trade Policy Review of the People's Republic of China, Report by the Secretariat*. WTO Doc. WT/TPR/S/300.

World Trade Organization. (2016). *Trade Policy Review of the People's Republic of China, Report by the Secretariat*. WTO Doc. WT/TPR/S/342.

Wu, M. (2017). 'China's export restrictions and the limits of WTO law'. *World Trade Review* 16(4): 673–691.

Yunfeng, J. (2020). 'Revision of the catalogue of technologies prohibited or restricted from export of the PRC'. *China Law Insight*. www.chinalawinsight.com/2020/10/articles/customs-business/revision-of-the-catalogue-of-technologies-prohibited-or-restricted-from-export-of-the-prc/

Zhou, W. (2023). 'The impact of the WTO dispute settlement system on China: Effectiveness, challenges and broader issues'. In Henry Gao, Damian Raess, and Ka Zeng (eds.), *China and the WTO: A Twenty-Year Assessment*. Cambridge: Cambridge University Press.

Zhu, H. (2020). 'Navigating China's new export control law'. *Trade Experettes Blog* www.tradeexperettes.org/blog/articles/navigating-chinas-new-export-control-law

PART III

China and Global Trade Governance

8

Tumult in the Trading System

The China Paradox, Declining US Institutional Power, and the Crisis at the WTO

KRISTEN HOPEWELL

On the twentieth anniversary of China's WTO accession, there has been considerable discussion of the failure of the WTO to transform China in the ways many scholars and policymakers expected. At the time of China's accession, it was widely assumed that China's membership in the trade body – by fueling exports, growth, and economic development – would help to foster greater political and economic liberalization within the country. Instead, however, just the opposite has occurred. Despite an extraordinary boom in China's exports, which has in turn fueled remarkably rapid economic growth and development, after an initial period of relative opening, China has more recently gone in the opposite direction of rising authoritarianism and greater state intervention in the economy (Pearson et al., 2021; Weiss, 2019).

If the conventional wisdom was wrong about the impact of the WTO on China, it has been equally wrong about the impact of China on the WTO. In contrast to prevailing expectations that China would be smoothly incorporated into global trade governance, the rise of China – and the corresponding decline in the relative power of the US – have created serious problems for the functioning of the multilateral trading system. The WTO's core negotiation function has collapsed, as evident in the breakdown of the Doha Round and the repeated failure of subsequent negotiating efforts. Its dispute settlement and enforcement mechanism is in jeopardy amid the US blockage of Appellate Body appointments. The US has abandoned its traditional leadership role in the multilateral trading

This paper draws on Hopewell, Kristen. 2020. *Clash of Powers: US-China Rivalry in Global Trade Governance*. Cambridge: Cambridge University Press.

system, turning away from trade multilateralism in favor of aggressive unilateralism, arbitrarily imposing tariffs on its trading partners, and launching a trade war with China. The rules-based multilateral trading system is now in danger of collapse.

China's rise has precipitated a crisis within the multilateral trading system. Many commentators have blamed the current crisis on the inability of the WTO to adequality address China's model of state-sponsored capitalism (Petersmann, 2019; Wu, 2016). But that framing of the problem is, I argue, potentially misleading. The primary complaints that the US and others have about China's trade policy – such as its use of industrial subsidies, forced technology transfer, intellectual property violations, and so forth – are not unique to China's more heavily state-controlled economy. Instead, these are typical features of the developmental state, commonly deployed by states seeking to catch up with more advanced economies and used by most successful late developers. The more fundamental conflict thus centers on how the multilateral trading system deals with a developing country that is also an economic powerhouse.

The question of how China should be classified and treated under global trade rules has become an acute source of conflict in the trade regime. The *China paradox* – the fact that China is simultaneously both a major economic heavyweight as well as a developing country – has created significant challenges for global trade governance. Developing countries are afforded special status in the multilateral trading system, and allowed greater policy space for state intervention to foster economic growth and development, including "special and differential treatment" in WTO agreements. But extending such status to China has become increasingly controversial as its economic weight has grown. The US and other advanced-industrialized states fiercely object to providing special treatment to a country they view as a major economic powerhouse and competitor. This fundamental conflict over what scope China should be allowed for a developmental state has paralyzed global trade governance and led to a breakdown in rule-making. It was a central factor in the collapse of the Doha Round, and it has remained an acute and persistent source of conflict in subsequent negotiating efforts at the WTO since then (Efstathopoulos, 2016; Hopewell, 2016; Narlikar, 2020; Sinha, 2021; Weinhardt, 2020).

At the same time, the rise of China and other emerging powers has sharply curtailed the US's "institutional power" (Barnett and Duvall, 2005) – the ability to shape global institutions and rules to guide, steer and constrain the actions of others. The US constructed the GATT/WTO, which served as a channel for the projection of American power, and its rules have reflected US primacy. Now, however, the rise of China has significantly constrained the US's power over the core institution and rules governing trade. The US's ability to dominate global trade governance and write the rules of global trade has greatly diminished, leading to an erosion of American support for the multilateral trading system it once created and led.

I Power Shifts and the Global Trade Regime

Upon China's accession to the WTO, the prevailing expectation was that China would be smoothly integrated into the US-led liberal international economic order because China has benefited from the existence of that order and has an interest in maintaining it. It was assumed not only that the multilateral trading system would continue to function effectively but also that the system would in fact be strengthened by the inclusion of China, given its growing importance in international trade and the global economy more broadly. The conventional wisdom – both at the time of China's accession and in the ensuing years of its emergence as a major economic power – has been that China is a supporter of, and would therefore seek to maintain, the international economic order that has facilitated and enabled its rise (Cox, 2012; Nye, 2015; Snyder, 2011; Xiao, 2013). Many have argued that China's objectives are fundamentally status-quo-oriented and system-supporting, and that its rise is accordingly "not threatening to the order's basic arrangements or principles" (Brooks and Wohlforth, 2016: 100; see also Kahler, 2010). In an era of global economic interdependence, the assumption that all states have an interest in maintaining the system has led many to conclude that the US and China will find ways to cooperate and jointly participate in the management of the international economic architecture, and collective action will prevail to preserve an open, liberal trading order (Cox, 2012; Ikenberry, 2011; Nye, 2015; Snyder, 2011; Xiao, 2013).

For many, a key factor in determining whether power shifts will result in conflict or cooperation is whether the US and other established powers adapt to the rise of China and other new powers by integrating them into existing institutions and their decision-making structures – meaning giving China and other emerging powers a seat at the table that reflects their economic weight and allowing them to assume a leadership role in global economic institutions like the WTO (Kahler, 2016; Paul, 2016b; Zangl et al., 2016). Many have argued that the future of global economic governance hinges on the willingness of the US to redistribute authority, make room for rising powers like China, and develop a system of shared leadership that accommodates their demands for greater voice and authority (Drezner, 2007; Ikenberry, 2015; Zakaria, 2008). The liberal international economic order can be maintained, it has been argued, if rising states are welcomed and incorporated into the power structures of its constitutive institutions. Much is therefore believed to rest on the established powers' willingness to make adjustments to accommodate rising powers: China will "actively seek to integrate into an expanded and reorganized liberal international order," provided that the US and other Western states act to reform global institutions to make room for China (Ikenberry, 2011: 344). Incorporating China and other rising powers into multilateral institutions like the WTO has been seen as a means to lock in their support for the global economic order (Drezner, 2007; Zakaria, 2008), while renewing and strengthening multilateralism by making those institutions more inclusive, representative, and legitimate (Vestergaard and Wade, 2015; Warwick Commission, 2008; Zoellick, 2010).

Existing international relations scholarship has thus assumed that if rising powers are supporters of established governance institutions and successfully incorporated into their decision-making structures, then those institutions will continue to function smoothly and effectively (Ikenberry, 2011; Paul, 2016a). However, in the case of the WTO, China was incorporated into the institution and subsequently became part of its core power structure. Moreover, as one of the prime beneficiaries of the liberal global trading order, which has enabled the boom in its exports that has propelled its extraordinarily rapid economic growth and development, China has an interest in maintaining the established trading order (Breslin, 2013; Gao, 2015; Quark, 2013; Scott and Wilkinson, 2013). Yet, China's rise has nonetheless proven profoundly disruptive to the WTO, leading to the breakdown of the institution's core negotiation function. The central cause of this breakdown is an intractable conflict over how China should be treated in the multilateral trading system and what scope it should be allowed for a developmental state.

II The China Paradox

China's rise represents a new bifurcation of economic power and development status in the trading system. Paradoxically, although China is now one of the world's dominant economic powers, it nonetheless remains a developing country. This seeming contradiction between

China's economic might and its level of development has created significant challenges for the WTO.

As the world's second-largest economy and its biggest trader, China has emerged as a core center of global economic activity. It is widely projected that China may soon overtake the US as the world's largest economy. Indeed, measured at purchasing power parity (PPP) rates, China's GDP ($27 trillion) has already surpassed the US ($23 trillion).[1] China has replaced America as the top manufacturer and exporter, with export volumes that now vastly exceed those of the US ($2.5 trillion versus $1.7 trillion). Nearly two-thirds of countries trade more with China than the US (Leng and Rajah, 2019). China has become the largest market for many commodities and consumer goods, home to many of the world's biggest corporations, and a massive source of outward investment, aid, and lending. It is also establishing itself as the dominant player and technological leader across an increasing range of industrial sectors.

Despite its emergence as an economic powerhouse, however, China continues to face significant development challenges. China's per capita income, for example, is only 16% of that of the US (with a per capita GNI of just $10,550 compared to $64,550 in the US).[2] Compared to the world's other advanced economies, China is thus at a significantly lower level of economic development, measured in terms of average incomes. Even if China crosses the World Bank's threshold for a "high-income country" (currently defined as a per capita GNI of $12,695) in coming years, it will still continue to lag far behind the US and other advanced economies. One of China's key overarching goals is to ensure its continued economic development (Gao, 2023), in order to raise its per capita income levels and bring them closer to those in developed countries. It faces immense challenges, however, in trying to do so. These include the challenges of trying to escape the middle-income trap; fostering industrial upgrading to move up the value chain into higher-value-added activities; a rapidly aging population and demographics that are increasingly unfavorable to economic growth; extraordinarily high rates of inequality, especially between rural and urban areas; inadequate social safety nets; relatively low levels of education and human capital, resulting in a massive population of low-skilled, underemployed workers; and rising wages combined with increasing competition from lower-wage countries for low-skilled manufacturing (Rozelle and Hell, 2020). The right to development is recognized

1 IMF Data, 2021.

2 IMF Data, 2021.

by the United Nations as a universal human right,[3] and denying the Chinese population – which includes 600 million people living in poverty on less than $1900 per year (Kuo, 2021) – the right to continued economic development would be a profound injustice.

But given its paradoxical status as both a major economic power and a developing country, the question of how China should be treated under global trade rules has become a major source of controversy (see also Gao, 2023). A core principle of the WTO is that developing countries should be allowed greater scope for state intervention – including tariffs, subsidies, and other trade policy tools – to promote their economic development. This often takes the form of "special and differential treatment" (SDT) providing various flexibilities and exemptions from WTO rules (Weinhardt, 2020). There are no established criteria for determining what constitutes a "developing country" at the WTO. Instead, states are allowed to self-designate as developing countries in order to access SDT (Eagleton-Pierce, 2012). China insists that, as a developing country, it is entitled to SDT. However, for the established economic powers, making largely one-sided concessions in opening their markets without equivalent concessions from China is a non-starter. Instead, the US, EU, and others insist that China must take on greater responsibility commensurate with its role as the world's second-largest economy – meaning undertaking greater commitments to liberalize its market and accept disciplines on its use of subsidies and other trade-distorting policies.

China's rise has thus heightened the tension between two core principles of the multilateral trading system. The first is the principle of reciprocity – that trade negotiations should take place based on a reciprocal exchange of concessions, with participants gaining roughly equivalent benefits or, conversely, incurring roughly equal costs (Brown and Stern, 2012). Closely related to this is the notion of creating universal rules – at least for the world's major trading states – with rights and obligations applying equally to all participants. The principle of reciprocity and universality, however, coexists somewhat uneasily with a second key principle of the trading system – preferential treatment for developing countries. The latter stems from the recognition that equal treatment is not equal for countries at different levels of development. Dating back to Alexander Hamilton's (1790) call for the US to adopt infant industry protections to enable the expansion of its manufacturing sector in the context of British

[3] The US was the sole country to vote against the 1986 *Declaration on the Right to Development* in the UN General Assembly.

industrial supremacy, there has been skepticism about free trade as a path to development and the capacity of developing countries to catch-up with more advanced economies without interventionist trade policy measures such as tariffs and subsidies.

SDT is based on the principle that developing countries should not be expected to engage in a reciprocal exchange of concessions with more advanced economies, or assume the same obligations (Hannah and Scott, 2017). Instead, rather than universal rules applying equally to all countries, countries at lower levels of development should be granted greater flexibility (or "policy space") to protect their domestic markets and promote the development of their exports, firms, and industries, as well as given preferential and non-reciprocal access for their exports to developed country markets (Narlikar, 2020; Singh, 2017). SDT is seen as an important means for the WTO to address the needs of developing countries and aid in fostering global development. While the notion of providing additional policy space to developing countries has never been uncontroversial (Hannah et al., 2017), with the rise of China as a major economic power that is also a developing country, it has now emerged as a central source of conflict within the trading system.

The conflict rests on whether the rules should be universal and concessions reciprocal, or China should have access to SDT in recognition of its status as a developing country, along with continued scope for state intervention to promote its economic development. At the heart of this conflict are competing interests, as well as ideas of fairness. From the perspective of the US and other advanced-industrialized states, fairness means a level playing field undistorted by state intervention, with universal rules applying equally to all and the reciprocal exchange of concessions in multilateral trade negotiations. But from China's perspective, what those states define as a level playing field is, in fact, one that serves to perpetuate their industrial and economic supremacy.

For China, it is considered vital to maintain the policy space needed to engage effectively in industrial policy and foster industrial upgrading, in order to continue its process of economic development and avoid becoming stuck in the middle-income trap. China's development model rests on an active state engaged in supporting the competitiveness of national firms and industries and helping them to move up the value chain into higher value-added activities thereby boosting growth, incomes, and the quality of employment (Lin and Chang, 2009; Stiglitz et al., 2013). An interventionist state remains central to its strategy for continued development, as evident in its Made in China 2025 industrial policy program (Ban and Blyth, 2013;

Hopewell, 2018). China's emphasis on state intervention is backed by the experience of other successful late developers (Chang, 2002).

Indeed, even the US and other advanced-industrialized states relied on state intervention and employed a range of protectionist policies during their own process of economic development (Kupchan, 2014). This included using tariffs and subsidies to foster the growth of infant industries and sequence their integration into the global economy; aggressively adopting technology from more advanced countries; and controlling the inflow of foreign investment to direct it toward the goals of national development (Chang, 2002; Gallagher, 2008; Wade, 2003). Moreover, even from a position of global economic dominance, the US has continued to deviate from the principles of free trade and make use of protectionism when it serves its interests (Block and Keller, 2011; Schrank and Whitford, 2009; Weiss, 2014). From China's perspective, in seeking to preserve the scope for state intervention to promote its industrial development, it is simply seeking to follow in the footsteps of the US and other advanced-industrialized states, while those countries are seeking to "kick away the ladder" by preventing China from using many of the same policy tools that were vital to their own growth and development (Chang, 2002; Stiglitz and Greenwald, 2014).

However, while China remains a developing country and continues to face significant development challenges, it is now an extremely large and immensely powerful force in the global economy and is seen by the US and many other advanced economies as a major competitive threat. The justification for allowing developing countries greater policy space is to enable them to catch up with more advanced economies. But opponents argue that China has gone beyond "catching up" to crushing its established competitors in many industries. Rail equipment – which has been prioritized as a key strategic sector under China's Made in China 2025 program – provides an illustration. After years of receiving subsidized financing to undercut its competitors and facilitate its global expansion, China's state-owned CRRC now dominates the global rail industry, with annual revenues of $34 billion, dwarfing its rivals, Germany's Siemens (with $10 billion in annual revenue), France's Alstom ($9 billion), Canada's Bombardier ($8 billion), and the US's GE ($4 billion) (Hopewell, 2021a). Seeking to better compete with CRRC, Siemens, and Alstom attempted to merge in 2018–19, but the merger was blocked by EU competition authorities, while both Bombardier and GE have been forced to sell off their rail businesses. Access to cheap, subsidized loans similarly facilitated the global expansion of Huawei, which is now the world's largest telecoms equipment company and the global leader in 5G technology (Hopewell, 2021a).

This clash between US demands for reciprocity and universal rules, on the one hand, and China's demands for special and differential treatment as a developing country, on the other, was at the center of the Doha Round breakdown, and it has remained an enduring issue of conflict severely impeding the WTO's negotiation function. But this dispute goes beyond SDT, narrowly defined. It is also more broadly about what commitments China should be expected to assume, how much space China should be allowed for state intervention to promote continued economic growth and development, and whether China should be forced to accept new disciplines or restrictions on its use of industrial policy more broadly.

III Breakdown of the WTO's Negotiation Function

The dispute over how China should be treated under global trade rules has played a central role in the breakdown of the WTO's negotiating function, starting with the collapse of the Doha Round. Extensive SDT for developing countries was a key promise of the Doha "Development" Round. The Ministerial Declaration launching the Round contained references to SDT across virtually all areas of the negotiations. These stated commitments to SDT could have proven little more than empty promises. However, over the course of the round, developing country coalitions, such as the G20 and G33, led by Brazil and India – and backed by the weight of China – transformed developing countries into a far more effective negotiating force than ever before (Hopewell, 2016; Narlikar, 2010). Consequently, developing countries were able to secure substantial SDT in the draft texts of the proposed agreement, including weaker tariff-reduction formulas in agriculture and manufactured goods, as well as substantial flexibilities.

By the latter stages of the round, the prospect of extending such extensive SDT to China in particular had become untenable for the US, provoking protests from Congress as well as business and farm lobby groups. From the US's perspective, it would be making substantial, meaningful concessions in opening its market – including significantly cutting its tariffs and its agricultural subsidies – but see little from China in return (US, 2008). As one US negotiator put it, "we'd be giving everything and getting nothing."[4] The US had become unwilling to extend that kind of

[4] Interview, Geneva, April 2009.

less-than-full-reciprocity to a country that it now sees as a major economic competitor and an emerging hegemonic rival.

The US sought to improve the deal by securing additional liberalization commitments from China in manufacturing and agriculture. It pressed China to participate in "sectorals" (aggressive tariff reduction in specific industrial sectors) in two key areas of US competitiveness – chemicals and industrial machinery. The US also pressed China to agree not to use its special product exemptions in agriculture against specific products of export interest to the US – namely, cotton, wheat, and corn – in order to guarantee the US market access gains in those areas. The US also sought a restrictive operationalization of the special safeguard mechanism (SSM) in agriculture in order to ensure that its market access gains were not eroded.

China proved far less malleable, however, than the US anticipated. From Beijing's perspective, the US's demands were a violation of the implicit bargain struck during China's accession, where in exchange for the deep concessions China was forced to make in opening its market, it was promised that relatively little new liberalization would be required of it during the Doha Round. From China's point of view, the US was now trying to renege on its earlier promises. China also saw the US's demands as a violation of the development mandate of the Round, and the promise that the final agreement would be reached on the basis of "less than full reciprocity" in favor of developing countries. China argued that the US was now unfairly seeking to change the terms of the deal and singling it out for further tariff cuts when its tariffs were already far lower than most other developing counties. As a result, China refused to agree to the sectorals sought by the US in chemicals and industrial machinery, which are key sectors China is trying to foster as part of its industrial upgrading strategy. If it opened those sectors, relinquishing its infant industry protections, Chinese policymakers feared they would be undercut by foreign competition, impeding its continued economic development. Similarly, on agriculture, China is eager to ensure that it retains its ability to use trade policy tools to protect vulnerable (and potentially politically volatile) parts of its population – such as poor, peasant farmers – leading China to refuse to concede to US demands on agriculture, instead insisting on a maximal definition of the SSM and that it retain full use of its special product exemptions.

The Doha negotiations broke down in 2008, ostensibly due to conflict over the design of the SSM. Yet the deeper cause of the Doha breakdown was this fundamental conflict over the US's desire to "rebalance" the deal by securing greater access for its exports to the Chinese market. China stood firm, refusing to give in to the US and rebuffing its demands for additional market opening. In doing so, China showed that had sufficient power to refuse to concede to US demands that it viewed as fundamentally against its own interests. The result has been a stalemate. The Doha Round was officially declared at an impasse in 2011, and the 2015 Nairobi Ministerial Declaration acknowledged that most members now consider the round dead (Scott and Wilkinson, 2020).

The US argues that it is no longer appropriate to treat China and other large emerging economies like other developing countries. To quote a former US Trade Representative, "the size and growth trajectories of the emerging economies combined with the fact that some are now leading producers and exporters in key sectors ... set them apart" (Schwab, 2011). According to the President's 2011 Trade Agenda:

> The remarkable growth of emerging economies like China, India, and Brazil has fundamentally changed the landscape ... [W]e are asking these emerging economies to accept responsibility commensurate with their expanded roles in the global economy. ... Countries with rapidly expanding degrees of global competitiveness and exporting success should be prepared to contribute meaningfully towards trade liberalization.[5]

The US insists that the WTO differentiate among developing countries in determining access to SDT, arguing that many emerging economies have "graduated" from developing country status and need to engage in a more reciprocal exchange of concessions. US officials and industry representatives make it clear that their primary concern is China, whose economic might and perceived geopolitical threat vastly overshadow that of other large emerging economies. The US has refused to accept new obligations unless greater liberalization is required of China and the other large emerging economies (US, 2011). Yet China staunchly maintains that, as a developing country, it is entitled to SDT and has refused to make concessions to appease the US. With the US and China at loggerheads, WTO negotiations have been beset by repeated deadlock.

Since the Doha collapse, the focus of the WTO has shifted from seeking to conclude a broad-based, comprehensive trade round to trying to craft narrower, targeted agreements on specific trade issues, such as agricultural subsidies and fisheries subsidies. Yet the same conflict over how China and other emerging economies should be classified and treated

[5] "2011 trade policy agenda and 2010 annual report of the President of the United States on the Trade Agreements Program," Office of the US Trade Representative, Washington DC, March 2011.

under multilateral trade rules has persisted and continues to impede efforts to construct new and expanded WTO rules (Hopewell, 2019).

This conflict has only grown deeper and more entrenched, with the US stepping up its criticism of allowing China and other large emerging economies to access SDT. Under the Trump administration, the issue became one of the US's chief complaints about the WTO. As a White House memorandum put it, "the WTO continues to rest on an outdated dichotomy between developed and developing countries that has allowed some WTO members to gain unfair advantages in the international trade arena."[6] Indeed, this alleged fundamental "unfairness" of the WTO became a key justification for the US to turn away from trade multilateralism and embrace aggressive unilateralism (in blatant violation of WTO rules) under President Trump.

The Trump administration used various carrots and sticks to pressure several countries – including Brazil, South Korea, Taiwan, and Singapore – to agree to forgo SDT in future WTO agreements. Brazil, for example, agreed to relinquish its claim to SDT in exchange for the US supporting its bid to join the OECD, which Brasilia views as essential for attracting foreign investment (Inside U.S. Trade, 2019). The US also unilaterally revoked access to SDT for many emerging economies under its own national trade laws. In 2020, for instance, the US removed 19 emerging economies, including India, Brazil, and South Africa, from its list of developing countries eligible for SDT under US countervailing duty (CVD) law, which allows certain developing countries to be exempt from countervailing duties if the subsidy level or import volume is below a certain threshold (Fortnam, 2020).

Insisting that WTO agreements should be "reciprocal and mutually advantageous," the US submitted a proposal in 2019 calling for an end to the practice of allowing states to "self-designate" as developing countries to claim SDT, arguing that this is outdated and "has severely damaged the negotiating arm of the WTO by making every negotiation a negotiation about setting high standards for a few, and allowing vast flexibilities for the many."[7] The US proposed that the WTO adopt criteria for SDT, whereby a country would be ineligible for SDT if it is: (1) a member of the

[6] "Memorandum on Reforming Developing-Country Status in the World Trade Organization: Presidential Memorandum for the United States Trade Representative," White House, Washington, DC, July 26, 2019.

[7] "An Undifferentiated WTO: Self-Declared Development Status Risks Institutional Irrelevance." Communication from the US. WTO General Council, February 14, 2019. WT/GC/W/757/Rev.1.

OECD, a club of primarily advanced-industrialized states, or in the process of accession; (2) a member of the G20; (3) considered a "high income" country by the World Bank; or (4) accounts for more than 0.5% of world merchandise trade.[8] These criteria would exclude China from accessing SDT in future WTO negotiations. The US proposal also left open the possibility that additional criteria could be established to exclude countries from SDT in sector-specific negotiations.

The US has enlisted the support of other established powers, such as the EU and Japan. Collectively, as part of the Trilateral Initiative, they have made SDT one of their primary objectives for WTO reform, arguing that: "Overly broad classifications of development, combined with self-designation of development status, inhibits the WTO's ability to negotiate new, trade-expanding agreements and undermines their effectiveness."[9] Together, these states have called on "advanced WTO Members claiming developing country status to undertake full commitments in ongoing and future WTO negotiations."[10] The EU has also echoed the US in calling for criteria for SDT and explicitly singled out China as a country that should be excluded from access to SDT.[11]

For its part, however, China has refused to relinquish its claim to SDT, characterizing SDT as a "fundamental" and "unconditional right" of developing countries that is essential for ensuring "equity and fairness" in the WTO system.[12] In the words of China's Ambassador to the WTO, "we will never give up the institutional right of special and differential treatment granted to developing countries."[13] It has described any attempt to "water down" SDT or differentiate between developing countries as "a certain recipe for intractable deadlock in negotiations."[14]

8 "Draft General Council Decision: Procedures to Strengthen the Negotiating Function of the WTO." Submission by the US. February 15, 2019. WT/GC/W/764.

9 "Joint Statement on Trilateral Meeting of the Trade Ministers of the United States, Japan, and the European Union," New York, September 25, 2018.

10 Ibid.

11 Trade Policy Review, European Commission, Brussels, February 18, 2021, p. 6.

12 "The Continued Relevance of Special and Differential Treatment in Favour of Developing Members to Promote Development and Ensure Inclusiveness." Communication from China, India, South Africa, Venezuela, Laos, Bolivia, Kenya and Cuba. General Council, February 28, 2019. WT/GC/W/765/Rev.1, p. 11. "Statement on Special and Differential Treatment to Promote Development." Co-sponsored by the African Group, Bolivia, Cambodia, China, Cuba, India, Laos, Oman, Pakistan and Venezuela. WT/GC/202/Rev. 1, October 14, 2019.

13 "WTO Reform from the Perspective of Developing Countries," Speech by Ambassador Zhang Xiangchen, WTO Reform Seminar, Pune, India, February 29, 2020.

14 WT/GC/202/Rev. 1.

This conflict over how much policy space China should be allowed under WTO rules has moved beyond SDT to calls from the US and other advanced-industrialized states for reforms of the WTO to reign in China's interventionist state and constrain its scope for developmentalist industrial policy. Under the Trilateral Initiative, the US, EU, and Japan have pushed to create stronger WTO disciplines on industrial subsidies, state-owned enterprises, and forced technology transfer – all of which are targeted at China. The established powers have proposed changes to WTO rules to expand the list of prohibited industrial subsidies and establish rules to address subsidies that cause overcapacity. The Trilateral Group has also proposed shifting the burden of proof by requiring states to demonstrate that their subsidy programs are not distorting trade or contributing to overcapacity, as well as advocating more stringent notification standards for industrial subsidies. They have also called for an expanded definition of "public body," maintaining that the Appellate Body's excessively narrow interpretation of the term has undermined the effectiveness of WTO subsidy rules vis-à-vis China. Not surprisingly, China has rejected the Trilateral Group's proposals, which are specifically intended to restrict the very policies Beijing sees as essential to continuing its process of economic development and industrial upgrading. For China, the reforms proposed by the Trilateral Group are evidence that the established powers are trying to block its rise by denying it the tools necessary to catch up with the world's most advanced economies. Once again, this fundamental dispute over how China should be treated in the trade regime and what scope it should be allowed for a developmental state has resulted in an impasse.

IV The Decline of the American Hegemon's Institutional Power

In international relations theory, it is rising powers that are expected to be the revisionist states – those seeking to change the rules of the system to better reflect their own interests – while the hegemon seeks to defend the existing order and maintain the status quo (Gilpin, 1981; Kirshner, 2009). Yet within the trading system, China is not a revisionist actor, in the sense of an actor seeking to alter the established rules of the game. On the contrary, China is broadly satisfied with the existing system of global trade rules, which has enabled its remarkable economic rise by providing access to global markets, while still allowing considerable scope for its interventionist state policies to facilitate economic development, industrial upgrading, and catch-up (Hopewell, 2016). China thus has no desire to change the rules – in fact, just the opposite, it is eager to maintain the status quo. Instead, if anything, it is the US that has become the "revisionist" state in the global trade regime, dissatisfied with the inability of the WTO system and its existing rules to adequately address China's trading practices. The US has therefore sought to alter the rules to eliminate China's ability to claim special status as a developing country as well as to better discipline its heavy industrial subsidies and other interventionist trade policies, which the US fears are being used to erode its economic dominance. But the US has been unable to force China to capitulate to its demands or accept its desired new rules.

Until now, a distinct and defining aspect of American hegemony has been its dominance of international institutions. Emerging from the Second World War with an overwhelming preponderance of power, the US used its primacy to construct a new and unprecedented institutional order that reflected and reinforced its primacy. The WTO – as "a constitution for the global economy" (Director-General Ruggiero, cited in McMichael, 2004: 166) – was a core pillar of this American hegemonic order, which some have called the "American imperium" (Katzenstein, 2005) or the US's "informal empire" (Panitch and Gindin, 2012; Wood, 2005).

Rule-making power is a crucial aspect of hegemony: a hegemon is powerful enough to maintain the rules of the system and "play the dominant role in constructing new rules" (Keohane and Nye, 2011: 37). For over half a century, the American hegemon dominated the GATT/WTO; it had sufficient power to play the dominant role in writing and enforcing the rules of the global trading system, including driving forward the ongoing process of constructing new rules to govern international commerce. But its rule-making power has now been impeded by China, an emerging challenger that has been unwilling to defer to American hegemony in global trade governance. The US and China are engaged in a struggle over the rules of the game – and specifically whether, and how, the rules will apply to China. China has been able to persistently block the US from achieving its objectives in global trade governance. Despite intense pressure, the US has been unable to force China to undertake greater commitments to liberalize its market in the Doha Round, subsequent post-Doha negotiations, or ongoing WTO reform efforts.

To quote Christopher Layne (2018: 110), "in international politics, who rules makes the rules." In short, China's rise has profoundly disrupted the US's ability to make the rules. Even if the US maintains a preponderance of power in the international system, its capacity to direct and steer global trade governance – which until now has been a defining feature of its hegemony has been severely diminished. In other words, if the US once "ran the system" as John Ikenberry (2015) puts it, that has now been profoundly disrupted: China has proven a significant counterbalance to US power that has substantially weakened American dominance within the WTO.

V Conclusion

It has frequently been assumed that if rising powers are supporters of established governance institutions like the WTO and successfully incorporated into their decision-making structures, then those institutions will continue to function smoothly and effectively. Yet analysis of China's impact on global trade governance refutes this view. As the world's largest exporter, China is a beneficiary and supporter of the established trading order. In addition, China has been integrated into the WTO and incorporated into its core power structure, given a seat at the table that reflects its economic weight. The result, however, has been a direct confrontation between the US and China over the rules of global trade that has paralyzed the institution. The clash between the trading system's two dominant powers has produced a repeated stalemate, which has effectively brought the core negotiating function of the WTO to a halt. This was evident in the breakdown of the Doha Round, and the same fundamental conflict between the US and China has persisted since the Doha collapse and continues to impede the construction of global trade rules, as well as efforts to reform the institution.

This conflict centers on how China should be treated in the trade regime. Under the rules of the WTO, developing countries are generally allowed greater scope for state intervention to foster economic growth and development. Yet while China remains a developing country, it is also now a major economic power. This paradoxical nature of China's position in the global trading system has created serious challenges for global trade governance. China's rise represents a new and unprecedented bifurcation of economic power and development status. Despite its considerable aggregate economic might, in terms of the average standard of living of its population, a vast gulf still separates China from the US and other advanced-industrialized states. From China's perspective, protecting its policy space – including its ability to use interventionist trade measures such as subsidies – is essential to continuing its process of economic development. China's interest in maintaining its scope for continued development has, however, thrown it into direct conflict with the US and other established economic powers. China maintains that, as a developing country, it should be entitled to special and differential treatment, but many states are unwilling to extend such treatment to a major economic competitor and have instead demanded universal rules and reciprocal concessions from China. Moreover, the US and other established powers have also sought to explicitly constrain China's scope to use interventionist trade policies through the creation of stricter WTO rules on industrial subsidies and other trade-distorting measures.

For most of its history, the American hegemon played the dominant role in constructing and enforcing the rules of the trading system. But the US's institutional power – its power over the governing institutions of the trading system and ability to set the rules of global trade – has been severely weakened by contemporary power shifts. US efforts to construct new trade rules in the Doha Round failed due to the rise of China and other emerging powers, who refused to defer to US power or capitulate to its demands. China has similarly blocked US attempts to constrain its policy space through the Trilateral Initiative's proposed reforms. American efforts to use the multilateral trading system to discipline China's trading practices have thus been unsuccessful, while the Appellate Body has increasingly interpreted WTO rules in ways that the US perceives as running counter to its interests. Having lost its previous dominance over the core institution and rules governing global trade, the US has grown increasingly dissatisfied with the workings of the multilateral trading system.

This is an important part of the explanation for the US to turn away from the multilateral trading system, its growing dissatisfaction with the system, and its flagrant rule-breaking. This momentous shift cannot simply be explained by the idiosyncrasies of the Trump administration or the rise of populist anti-trade sentiment that both fueled, and was fueled by, his presidency (cf. Kahler, 2020; Scott and Wilkinson, 2020). These trends both began before and have continued after the Trump administration (Hopewell, 2021b). Explanations centered on domestic politics alone are inadequate to explain the US's changing orientation towards the multilateral trading system. It is also a response to changes in the distribution of power in the international system. The US is responding not only to a decline in its structural power – that is, its relative economic might vis-à-vis a rising China – but also to a significant decline in its institutional power – its ability to dominate global trade governance and write the rules of global trade.

References

Ban, Cornel, and Mark Blyth. 2013. 'The BRICs and the Washington Consensus: An introduction.' *Review of International Political Economy* 20(2):241–55.

Barnett, Michael, and Raymond Duvall. 2005. 'Power in international politics.' *International Organization* 59(Winter):39–75.

Block, Fred, and Matthew R. Keller. 2011. *State of Innovation: The U.S. Government's Role in Technology Development*. Boulder, CO: Paradigm Publishers.

Breslin, Shaun. 2013. 'China and the global order: Signalling threat or friendship?' *International Affairs* 89(3):615–34.

Brooks, Stephen G., and William C. Wohlforth. 2016. 'The once and future superpower.' *Foreign Affairs* 95(3):91–104.

Brown, Andrew G., and Robert M. Stern. 2012. 'Fairness in the Wto trading system.' in *The Oxford Handbook on the World Trade Organization*, edited by A. Narlikar, M. Daunton and R. M. Stern. Oxford: Oxford University Press.

Chang, Ha-Joon. 2002. *Kicking Away the Ladder: Development Strategy in Historical Perspective*. London: Anthem Press.

Cox, Michael. 2012. 'Power shifts, economic change and the decline of the west?' *International Relations* 26(4):369–88.

Drezner, Daniel W. 2007. 'The new world order.' *Foreign Affairs* 86(2).

Eagleton-Pierce, Matthew. 2012. *Symbolic Power in the World Trade Organization*. Oxford: Oxford University Press.

Efstathopoulos, Charalampos. 2016. 'Reformist multipolarity and global trade governance in an era of systemic power redistribution.' *Global Journal of Emerging Market Economies* 8(1):3–21.

Fortnam, Brett. 2020. 'USTR uses new developing country criteria to adjust CVD de minimis rates.' *Inside US Trade Daily Report*.

Gallagher, Kevin P. 2008. 'Understanding developing country resistance to the Doha Round.' *Review of International Political Economy* 15(1):62–85.

Gao, Henry. 2015. 'From the Doha round to the china round.' pp. 79–97 in *China in the International Economic Order: New Directions and Changing Paradigms*, edited by Colin B. Picker, Jonathan Greenacre, and Lisa Toohey. Cambridge: Cambridge University Press.

Gao, Henry. 2023. 'China's changing perspective on the WTO: From aspiration, assimilation to alienation.' in *China and the WTO: A Twenty-Year Assessment*, edited by Henry Gao, Damian Raess, and Ka Zeng. Cambridge: Cambridge University Press.

Gilpin, Robert. 1981. *War and Change in World Politics*. New York: Cambridge University Press.

Hannah, Erin, and James Scott. 2017. 'From Palais de Nations to Centre William Rappard: Raúl Prebisch and UNCTAD as sources of ideas in the GATT/WTO.' pp. 116–34 in *The Global Political Economy of Raúl Prebisch*, edited by Matias E. Margulis. New York: Routledge.

Hannah, Erin, Holly Ryan, and James Scott. 2017. 'Power, knowledge and resistance: Between co-optation and revolution in global trade.' *Review of International Political Economy* 24(5):741–75.

Hopewell, Kristen. 2016. *Breaking the WTO: How Emerging Powers Disrupted the Neoliberal Project*. Stanford: Stanford University Press.

Hopewell, Kristen. 2018. 'What is "Made in China 2025" – and Why is it a threat to Trump's trade goals?' *Washington Post* (May 3).

Hopewell, Kristen. 2019. 'US-China conflict in global trade governance: The new politics of agricultural subsidies at the WTO.' *Review of International Political Economy* 26(2):207–31.

Hopewell, Kristen. 2021a. 'Power transitions and global trade governance: The impact of a rising China on the export credit regime.' *Regulation & Governance* 15(3):634–52.

Hopewell, Kristen. 2021b. 'Trump & trade: The crisis in the multilateral trading system.' *New Political Economy* 26(2):271–82.

Ikenberry, G. John. 2011. *Liberal Leviathan: The Origins, Crisis, and Transformation of the American World Order*. Princeton, NJ: Princeton University Press.

Ikenberry, G. John. 2015. 'The future of liberal world order.' *Japanese Journal of Political Science* 16(03):450–55.

Inside U.S. Trade. 2019. 'U.S. said to follow through on support for Brazil's OECD bid.' *Inside U.S. Trade* (May 24).

Kahler, Miles. 2010. 'Asia and the reform of global governance.' *Asian Economic Policy Review* 5(2):178–93.

Kahler, Miles. 2016. 'The global economic multilaterals: Will eighty years be enough?' *Global Governance* 22(1):1–9.

Kahler, Miles. 2020. 'Cosmopolitans and parochials: Economy, culture and political conflict.' pp. 87–112 in *Cultural Values in Political Economy*, edited by J. P. Singh. Stanford: Stanford University Press.

Katzenstein, Peter J. 2005. *A World of Regions: Asia and Europe in the American Imperium*. Ithaca: Cornell University Press.

Keohane, Robert, and Joseph S. Nye. 2011. *Power and Interdependence*. New York: Longman.

Kirshner, J. 2009. 'Realist political economy: Traditional themes and contemporary challenges.' pp. 36–47 in *Routledge Handbook of International Political Economy*, edited by M. Blyth. New York: Routledge.

Kuo, Lily. 2021. 'China claims to have eliminated poverty, but the figures mask harsh challenges.' *The Washington Post* (February 25).

Kupchan, Charles A. 2014. 'The normative foundations of hegemony and the coming challenge to Pax Americana.' *Security Studies* 23(2):219–57.

Layne, Christopher. 2018. 'The US–Chinese power shift and the end of the Pax Americana.' *International Affairs* 94(1):89–111.

Leng, Alyssa, and Roland Rajah. 2019. 'Chart of the week: Global trade through a US-China lens.' Lowy Interpreter (December 18), www.lowyinstitute.org/the-interpreter/chart-week-global-trade-through-us-china-lens.

Lin, Justin, and Ha-Joon Chang. 2009. 'Should industrial policy in developing countries conform to comparative advantage or Defy it? A debate between Justin Lin and Ha-Joon Chang.' *Development Policy Review* 27(5):483–502.

McMichael, Phillip. 2004. *Development and Social Change: A Global Perspective*. Thousand Oaks, CA: Pine Forge Press.

Narlikar, Amrita. 2010. 'New powers in the club: The challenges of global trade governance.' *International Affairs* 86(3):717–28.

Narlikar, Amrita. 2020. *Poverty Narratives and Power Paradoxes in International Trade Negotiations and Beyond*. Cambridge: Cambridge University Press.

Nye, Joseph. 2015. *Is the American Century Over?* Cambridge: Polity.

Panitch, Leo, and Sam Gindin. 2012. *The Making of Global Capitalism: The Political Economy of American Empire*. New York: Verso.

Paul, T. V. 2016a. *Accommodating Rising Powers: Past, Present, and Future*. Cambridge: Cambridge University Press.

Paul, T. V. 2016b. 'The accommodation of rising powers in world politics.' pp. 3–32 in *Accommodating Rising Powers: Past, Present, and Future*, edited by T. V. Paul. Cambridge: Cambridge University Press.

Pearson, Margaret, Meg Rithmire, and Kellee S. Tsai. 2021. 'Party-state capitalism in China.' *Current History* 120(827):207–13.

Petersmann, Ernst-Ulrich. 2019. 'How should WTO members react to their WTO crises?' *World Trade Review* 18(3):503–25.

Quark, Amy A. 2013. *Global Rivalries: Standards Wars and the Transnational Cotton Trade*. University of Chicago Press.

Rozelle, Scott, and Natalie Hell. 2020. *Invisible China: How the Urban-Rural Divide Threatens China's Rise*. Chicago: University of Chicago Press.

Schrank, Andrew, and Josh Whitford. 2009. 'Industrial policy in the United States: A Neo-Polanyian interpretation.' *Politics & Society* 37(4):521–53.

Schwab, Susan C. 2011. 'After Doha: Why the negotiations are doomed and what we should do about it.' *Foreign Affairs* 90(3):104–17.

Scott, James, and Rorden Wilkinson. 2013. 'China threat? Evidence from the WTO.' *Journal of World Trade* 47(4):761–82.

Scott, James, and Rorden Wilkinson. 2020. 'Reglobalizing trade: Progressive global governance in an age of uncertainty.' *Globalizations* 18(1):55–69.

Singh, J. P. 2017. *Sweet Talk: Paternalism and Collective Action in North-South Trade Relations*. Stanford: Stanford University Press.

Sinha, Aseema. 2021. 'Understanding the "crisis of the institution" in the liberal trade order at the WTO.' *International Affairs* 97(5):1521–40.

Snyder, Quddus Z. 2011. 'Integrating rising powers: Liberal systemic theory and the mechanism of competition.' *Review of International Studies* 39(1):209–31.

Stiglitz, J. E., and Bruce C. Greenwald. 2014. *Creating a Learning Society: A New Approach to Growth, Development, and Social Progress*. New York: Columbia University Press.

Stiglitz, J. E., J. Esteban, and J.Y. Lin. 2013. *The Industrial Policy Revolution I: The Role of Government Beyond Ideology*. New York: Palgrave Macmillan.

US. 2008. 'Senate Committee on Finance Press Release: Finance, Ways and Means Leaders Urge President to Stand Firm on Doha Round.' December 2.

US. 2011. 'The President's 2011 Trade Agenda.' Washington, DC: Office of the US Trade Representative.

Vestergaard, Jakob, and Robert H. Wade. 2015. 'Still in the woods: Gridlock in the IMF and the World Bank puts multilateralism at risk.' *Global Policy* 6(1):1–12.

Wade, Robert H. 2003. 'What strategies are viable for developing countries today? The World Trade Organization and the Shrinking of "Development Space".' *Review of International Political Economy* 10(4):621–44.

Warwick Commission. 2008. *The Multilateral Trade Regime: Which Way Forward?* Coventry, UK: University of Warwick.

Weinhardt, Clara. 2020. 'Emerging powers in the world trading system: Contestation of the developing country status and the reproduction of inequalities.' *Global Society* 34:1–21.

Weiss, Jessica Chen. 2019. 'A world safe for autocracy: China's rise and the future of global politics.' *Foreign Affairs* 98:92.

Weiss, Linda. 2014. *America Inc.? Innovation and Enterprise in the National Security State*. Ithaca: Cornell University Press.

Wood, Ellen Meiksins. 2005. *Empire of Capital*. New York: Verso.

Wu, Mark. 2016. 'The China Inc. Challenge to global trade governance.' *Harvard International Law Journal* 57(2):261–324.

Xiao, Ren. 2013. 'Debating China's rise in China.' in *After Liberalism? The Future of Liberalism in International Relations*, edited by R. Friedman, K. Oskanian, and R. P. Pardo. Basingstoke: Palgrave Macmillan.

Zakaria, Fareed. 2008. *The Post-American World: And the Rise of the Rest*. New York: Norton.

Zangl, Bernhard, Frederick Heußner, Andreas Kruck, and Xenia Lanzendörfer. 2016. 'Imperfect adaptation: How the WTO and the IMF adjust to shifting power distributions among their members.' *Review of International Organizations* 11(2):171–96.

Zoellick, Robert. 2010. 'The end of the third world? Modernizing multilateralism for a multipolar world.' President of the World Bank, Speech at the Woodrow Wilson Centre, April 14.

9

China's Relations with the Global South in the World Trade Organization

CLARA WEINHARDT

I Introduction

When China joined the WTO in 2001, it declared that the recently launched Doha Development Round negotiations need to put the interests of developing countries centre stage. The Chinese representative speaking at the country's first full participation of the General Council Meeting of WTO on 19 December 2001, Mr. Long Yongtu, called for WTO negotiations to facilitate 'the establishment of a new international economic order which is fair, just and reasonable', which would entail 'a balance of interests between developed countries and developing countries, especially conducive to the development of developing countries' (Mfa.gov.cn, 2001). In its 2019 communication on the Chinese reform proposal for the WTO, China reiterated that the '[d]evelopment issue is at the centre of WTO work' (WTO, 2019a, para. 2.4.1). More than twenty years after its accession to the WTO, it is time to (re)assess the role that China has played on development. Has China indeed positioned itself as a development partner in WTO negotiations that sides with the Global South vis-à-vis the Global North, or has its own economic transformation diminished the scope for a shared agenda on development?

Academics that touch upon China's role in the WTO vis-à-vis the Global South are so far divided in their assessment: those that emphasise ideological South-South ties tend to portray China's role as a development partner (Bishop and Zhang, 2020; Muzaka and Bishop, 2015; Vieira, 2012), while scholars that highlight political economy dynamics either see mixed or even competing interests vis-à-vis other developing countries (Hopewell,

The author thanks Henry Gao, Damian Raess, Ka Zeng and the participants in the World Trade Forum 2021 for helpful comments and suggestions. She thanks Kate Tepper for input on bargaining patterns. The interviews conducted for this contribution were funded by the Bremen International Graduate School of Social Sciences. The author acknowledges funding by the German Research Foundation [grant number WE 6012/2-1].

2021; Vickers, 2014, pp. 268–69). This chapter starts with a brief discussion of these conflicting perspectives on China's role vis-à-vis the Global South, followed by an examination of China's negotiating behaviour in the WTO. These patterns in China's negotiation positions are then compared and contrasted with perceptions of China's role by other WTO members.

The chapter reveals that while China seeks to align itself politically with the development agenda of the Global South in its bargaining behaviour in Trade Negotiating Committees, perceptions of its role in the WTO are mixed. As the chapter argues, China's political intention to support a broader development agenda is increasingly undermined by the way in which its larger economic size leads to competition with other developing countries. In particular, China's distinct economic size increasingly puts it in an ambiguous position when joining other developing country members in their demands to strengthen Special and Differential Treatment (S&D).[1] The specific conflict lines that arise reflect in part the increasing heterogeneity of the Global South. Three main patterns emerge: First, developing countries that are non-emerging economically are more likely to see China as a competitor for S&D, as compared to other emerging economies or Least Developed Countries (LDCs). Second, developing countries that share the defensive trade policy orientation of the S&D agenda are more likely to perceive China as a development partner as compared to those with a more liberal orientation. Here, conflict lines vary across negotiation issues. Third, the role China plays vis-à-vis the Global South is shaped by the larger context of their specific trade and investment relationship. China thus plays an increasingly contradictory role in the WTO, acting as a development partner for some and as a competitor for other developing countries – dependent on the negotiating issues at stake.

This chapter makes use of the following types of primary sources. First, it relies on official documentation of the WTO's Trade Negotiations Committee (2001–2019) to assess the negotiation behaviour of China. Second, to reconstruct perceptions of China's role, the chapter draws on a sample of 33 interviews[2] and a survey with 22 officials conducted in Geneva with country representatives at WTO missions, WTO officials, and other trade experts.

[1] S&D grants developing country members special rights such as flexibilities and exemptions regarding trade liberalization negotiated at the WTO.

[2] The interviews were conducted in Geneva in September 2016 with representatives from the Global South and the Global North at WTO missions, WTO headquarters, and other trade experts. The interviews were semi-structured to allow for an inductive exploration of the themes that underpin perceptions of China's role as a development partner or competitor.

II China and the Global South in the WTO: An Overview of the Debate

The existing literature on China's role in the WTO is primarily interested in its participation in global trade governance, as well as the extent to which it challenges or supports the WTO's liberal trade order. Questions about China's relations with the Global South do not take centre stage. The most direct engagement with China's role vis-à-vis the Global South is part of the literature that analyses bargaining coalitions at the WTO (Hopewell, 2017; Narlikar, 2010).

Some scholars emphasise that China has tended to side with developing country coalitions because of its growing self-identification with the so-called Global South. In particular, its shared identity as part of the Global South (Nel, 2010) or the 'power South' (Acharya, 2014, p. 654) leads to 'pro-Southern' negotiating behaviour (Muzaka and Bishop, 2015; Vieira, 2012). The decision in the July 2008 mini-ministerial to side with India rather than the US is, for instance, seen as an expression of South-South solidarity 'when this has required sacrificing a measure of China's national interests, to support the cause of this developing country coalition' (Chin, 2009, p. 143). Johnson and Urpeleinan (2020) find that developing countries – including China – exhibit surprising unity at the WTO, an assessment they base on the statistical analysis of 3.600 paragraphs of negotiation-related text on trade and environmental policy.

Southern unity in bargaining coalitions does not necessarily indicate altruistic motives. Political initiatives in favour of developing countries, and Least Developed Countries in particular, are seen to reflect the country's intention to build soft power by projecting itself as a responsible and benign developing country (Jain, 2014, p. 190). A number of authors mention China's support for LDCs in the WTO (Bhattacharya and Misha, 2015; Jain, 2014), as well as statements of support for the LDCs, the group of African, Caribbean and Pacific countries and the African Group (Jain, 2014, p. 189). China has also put forward four proposals designed to protect and promote the interest of developing countries in WTO dispute settlement (Liu, 2014, p. 127). At the same time, political considerations at times make it difficult for China to demand better market access in developing rather than developed countries, even if economic benefits are involved (Gao, 2011, p. 166).

Yet, other scholars offer a more cautious assessment of China's role as a partner of developing countries in WTO negotiations – regardless of the motives. While they acknowledge ideological South-South ties, they claim that China's economic interests as a major exporter and importer increasingly tend to converge with those of developed countries (Bishop and Zhang, 2020, p. 7; Lim and Wang, 2010, p. 1314). This explains why China has not proactively promoted the interests of developing countries in the bargaining coalitions it joined (Lawrence, 2008, pp. 152–153) and remains a reluctant leader in the WTO (Bishop and Zhang, 2020). As noted by Vickers, 'China's supportive, yet backseat, role in Southern coalitions partly reflects the fact that Beijing actually shared an interest with the US and the EU in seeking greater access to large developing country markets – including Brazil and India – for its manufactured exports' (Vickers, 2014, pp. 268–269). With regard to the G-20 coalition of developing countries, China, for instance, took a backseat to Brazil and India which exerted much stronger leadership (Lim and Wang, 2010, p. 1316). In other cases, China did not even join developing country coalitions. While China endorsed many of the positions of the NAMA-11 coalition, which includes India and Brazil, it did not join the group to champion its concerns (Vickers, 2014, p. 267). Tu (2013, p. 175) similarly concludes that even if China repeatedly claims that development should be at the heart of the Doha round, it is seen as 'not … very active in advocating special and differential treatment' (Tu, 2013, p. 175).

More recently, some scholars argue that China even acts as a competitor to the Global South, given its economic interest has become too far apart from those of the majority of (small) developing countries. Hopewell (2022) prominently claims that in the case of agricultural negotiations, China's insistence on maintaining high levels of domestic support is harmful to other developing countries that seek access to agricultural markets. What matters here is China's tremendous economic growth, which allowed it to become the world's leading provider of agricultural subsidies – estimated at $212 billion in 2016 (Ibid., p. 11). Weinhardt (2020) also finds that, inadvertently, China's contested claims to maintain its developing country status has undermined the principle of special and differential treatment that grants exemptions and flexibilities to developing countries.

There is, however, also a growing recognition of the ambiguous position that China finds itself in between developed and developing countries. China stands out among developing country members of the WTO because of its enormous market size, continuously high growth rates and its role in driving global growth. Despite its tremendous growth trajectory, however, developmental challenges continue to exist, especially in rural China. As a result, Bishop and Zhang's (2020, p. 7) claim that China is caught between its roles as a developing country and a country in the transformation to a 'developed' one. This explains why Chinese policy-makers still adhere to 'a discourse of developmental unity' (Bishop and Zhang, 2020, p. 7) – even if it pursues 'selfish' interests that increasingly cut across North-South lines (Gao, 2015, p. 92). More generally, China's emphasis on its developing country identity is not only an expression of historically grown South-South solidarity, but also considered as important to help forge and maintain relations with the Global South that forms 'the political basis of China's international support' (Pu, 2019, p. 46). These more recent assessments suggest that China's role vis-à-vis the Global South is unlikely to easily fit the binary categories of development partner *or* competitor. What is missing, however, is a systematic assessment that goes beyond specific negotiating issues and contrasts China's negotiation behaviour with perceptions of others.

III China in WTO Negotiations: Eager to Position Itself as a Development Partner

China itself has been eager to position itself as a development partner in WTO negotiations. This becomes apparent both in its political support for the development orientation of the WTO's ongoing negotiating round as well as in the pattern of its submissions to the WTO's Trade Negotiation Committees.

(i) China's Political Support for the Doha Development Agenda

When Doha Development round negotiations were launched in 2001, there was a clear sentiment that development needs to be central for the WTO to succeed. The Doha Ministerial Declaration (WTO, 2001) explicitly stated that '[t]he majority of WTO members are developing countries. We seek to place their needs and interests at the heart of the Work Programme adopted in this Declaration'. It soon became clear, however, that the political will to deliver on this promise was rather limited. Agriculture became the major issue of the Doha Development round. Initially, China took a back seat in developing country coalitions pushing for the conclusion of a development-oriented round. For instance, at the 2003 Ministerial conference in Cancún, India and Brazil were central to the creation of the G-20 coalition that focused on agricultural negotiations. As China became more active in WTO negotiations and joined its core decision-making group in 2008 (Gao, 2015, 2021), it also became more vocal in lending political support to the demands of developing countries in WTO negotiations.

China's support for a 'developmental orientation' of the organisation could be witnessed prominently at the WTO's 10th Ministerial Conference (MC10), held in December 2015 in Nairobi in Kenya. The MC10 stood out as it thought to resolve the deadlock over the continued viability of the Doha Development Agenda as a mandate for the ongoing negotiation round (Wilkinson et al., 2016, p. 247). Major developed country members, and in particular the United States, intended to use the occasion of the MC10 to officially move beyond the Doha Development Round's original mandate, including the Single Undertaking rule.[3] Faced with a deadlock situation since 2008, they emphasised that it was time to move on to negotiate new issues – such as e-commerce (compare Liang and Zeng, 2022, this volume) – relying on new negotiating approaches that were more flexible in excluding highly contested issues from the agenda. However, developing country members fiercely opposed this demand, as they feared that adopting a more flexible negotiating approach would effectively imply dropping those negotiating issues of particular concern to them, especially agriculture. China positioned itself as part of a developing country camp in this conflict. In a joint proposal for the conference's final Ministerial Declaration together with Ecuador, India, Indonesia, South Africa and Venezuela, China clearly reaffirmed the original Doha mandate.[4] As acknowledged by a developed country trade official: '[China] has been pretty clear in all their statements that they want to complete the Doha agenda … they have been pushing hard for commitment to complete the Doha agenda. Many of us are weary of such statements'.[5] The rift between both camps was so substantial that, in a historically unprecedented way, WTO members in the end agreed to disagree.

China's support for the Doha Development Agenda tends to reflect the importance of political ties with the Global South in Chinese foreign policy, rather than shared economic interests. China has always been keen to emphasise that it stands with the developing world, in part because close

[3] This negotiation rule stipulates that the negotiation round can only be concluded as a package, which means that an agreement needs to be reached on all issues that are part of the negotiation mandate.

[4] The submission explicitly 'seeks to reaffirm Members' commitments to respect the mandates under the Doha Development Agenda (DDA) and continue to negotiate the remaining DDA issues after MC10 consistent with the DDA mandates and framework' (Par. 2).

[5] Interview with developed country representative, Geneva, 19 September 2016.

economic relations with the Global South have helped China to increase its political influence (Pu, 2019, p. 46). Positioning China as a developing country member in WTO negotiations has thus not only been used to claim continued access to flexibilities under Special and Differential Treatment (Hopewell, 2021; Weinhardt, 2020), but also to consolidate support from other developing countries (compare Pu, 2019, p. 47). Conversely, China's decision to side with developing countries that defend the original Doha Development Round's mandate does not necessarily reflect its own economic interests. For instance, China has in the meantime joined the WTO negotiations for an e-commerce agreement. Launching these negotiations in January 2019 while the Doha Round had not been concluded yet has been interpreted to go against the original Doha mandate (Abendin and Duan, 2021). Many developing countries that are less competitive than China in the e-commerce sector, for instance in Africa, had criticised the plan to launch these negotiations (Liang and Zeng, 2023, this volume; SAIIA, 2021).

China's attempts to position itself as a development partner extends beyond lending support to the development orientation of WTO talks, and includes political initiatives geared towards capacity-building in the Global South. In 2011, China, for instance, launched the Least-Developed Countries (LDCs) and Accessions Programme. It comprises several round tables, workshops, and South-South dialogue forums, as well as an internship programme for countries that seek to accede to the WTO.[6] China has, moreover, sought to support LDCs that seek to accede to the WTO informally. For instance, when the accession negotiations with Laos ran into difficulties, the Chinese chairperson of the Accession Working Group at the time, Zhang Xiangchen, was reported to have been instrumental in facilitating a mediation process.[7] Moreover, the Chinese Deputy Director-General at the time supported Laos' accession.[8] Drawing on its own experiences of the recent accession negotiations, China has thus been eager to position itself as a development partner of LDCs. Beyond its support for LDCs, China has also put forward four proposals designed to protect and promote the interest of developing countries more generally in WTO dispute settlement (Liu, 2014, p. 127).

[6] The China Programme consists of five pillars: (1) Annual Accession Round Table Meeting; (2) WTO Accession Internship; (3) LDCs' Participation in WTO or WTO-Related Meetings; (4) South-South Dialogue on LDCs And Development and (5) LDCs' Trade Policy Review Follow-up Workshops.

[7] Interview with WTO official, 30 September 2016.

[8] Interview with WTO official, 30 September 2016.

(ii) Chinese Submissions to the WTO's Trade Negotiating Committee: Siding with Developing Countries

China's preference to portray itself as a champion of developing country concerns in the WTO also becomes apparent when analysing the pattern in its submissions to the WTO's Trade Negotiating Committees (TNCs).[9] China prefers submissions with other developing countries, rather than with developed countries. In case of conflicting economic interests, China tends to opt for unilateral submission.

The analysis of China's negotiating behaviour in the WTO's TNCs reveals that if China makes joint submissions, it has a clear preference for submissions together with other developing countries (see Figure 9.1). Out of 36 submissions that China made together with other WTO members, none was made with a group comprised primarily of developed countries or comprised of developed countries only. On the contrary, 30 were submitted with other developing countries only or with groups comprising developing countries as the majority. China only rarely made submissions as part of 'mixed' country groups (6 submissions).

This pattern holds across all ten TNCs (see Table 9.1), and includes committees in which China's economic interests are arguably closer to those of the developed rather than the developing world. This can be for instance seen in the market access negotiations, an area in which its offensive interests in improved market access for non-agricultural goods tend to converge with those of developed country members. However, China only made one related submission to the market access committee as part of the Asia-Pacific Economic Cooperation coalition that includes the United States, Canada, and Japan, which reflected a shared interest in better market access for IT products. This contrasts with the behavior of other emerging economies that more frequently joined developed country members for joint submissions regarding market access for non-agricultural goods.[10]

[9] All Chinese submissions were coded as either 'unilateral,' 'majority developing countries,' 'majority developed countries,' or 'mixed.' The category 'mixed' applies to groups of countries that are composed 50%/50% of developed and developing country, allowing for changes of ±5% (i.e. up to 45%/55% or 55%/45%). All groups with a higher percentage of developing or developed countries are either 'majority developing countries' or 'majority developed countries.' For the classification of countries into developed and developing countries, the chapter relies on membership in the OECD (proxy for developed countries) and membership in the G-77 (proxy for developing countries) or other developing country negotiating groups at the WTO.

[10] India made, for instance, six and Brazil four submissions with a group of countries that included the European Union in the WTO Rules committee (same time period).

Table 9.1 *Overview of China's joint submissions in the Trade Negotiation Committee's sub-groups (2001–2019)*

	Composition of WTO members in joint submissions including China				
	Solely developing countries	Majority developing countries	Mixed (45–55%)	Majority developed countries	Solely developed countries
WTO rules	4	2	0	0	0
Services	3	0	1	0	0
Development	0	0	0	0	0
TRIPS	0	0	0	0	0
General	4	3	0	0	0
Dispute settlement	0	0	0	0	0
Trade facilitation	4	0	2	0	0
Market access	1	1	1	0	0
Agriculture	7	0	2	0	0
Trade and environment	1	0	0	0	0

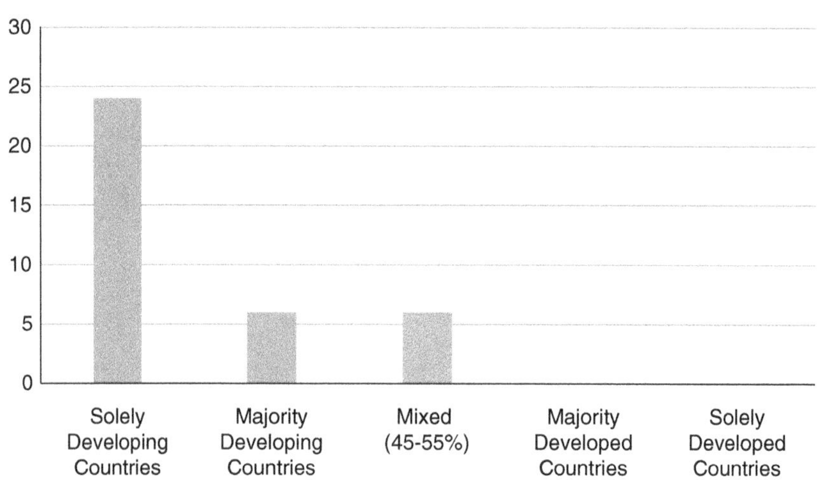

Figure 9.1 Patterns of coalition partners in Chinese submissions in the WTO Trade Negotiating Committee and its sub-groups (2001–2019)

What is notable, however, is that a considerable number of Chinese submissions to the WTO'S TNC did not include other WTO members: 34% of its submissions were unilateral, while 64% were submitted together with other countries. This suggests that China prefers to side with developing countries whenever it is able to find partners on given negotiating issues but does not shy away from defending its own interests unilaterally if necessary.

IV Perceptions of China's Role vis-à-vis the Global South: Mixed Assessments

Despite China's attempts to position itself as a development partner, its role vis-à-vis the Global South has become increasingly ambiguous in the past decade of WTO negotiations. Both its market size and its state-led economy set it apart from other developing country members of the WTO. In terms of its Gross Domestic Product, China has overtaken the United States as the largest economy worldwide in 2017, measured in terms of purchasing power parity. While China's National Bureau of Statistics has been quick to point out that this does not change that China remains 'the world's largest developing country' (SCMP, 2020), its rapidly increasing share in world trade puts the country in a central position in the world economy. In particular, with regard to trade in goods, China has become a leading exporter (16.1% of world exports) and the third largest importer (13.1% of world imports).[11] In contrast to many other developing countries that primarily trade raw materials, 43% of China's global goods trade is in the more valuable category of high-value-added machines and electrical goods.[12] While this does not imply that China does not face development challenges anymore, the tremendous economic transformation of the country in a relatively short period of time sets it apart from other developing country members in the WTO.

While China clearly seeks to position itself as a development partner, its increasingly divergent economic position from other developing country members leads to mixed perceptions of its role. Trade representatives acknowledge both China's desire to position itself as a partner of the developing world, as well as the way in which it may pursue self-interested economic motives. One representative claimed, for instance, that China is 'devoting its attention to the development aspect of the WTO and ensuring that there is special differential treatment for developing countries in the negotiating functions of the WTO' and that 'they are very serious about

[11] Data source: Eurostat, https://ec.europa.eu/eurostat.

[12] WITS database, https://wits.worldbank.org/.

being seen as a leader among developing countries in WTO'.[13] There was, however, also the perception that China defends its own economic interests against the Global South. For instance, regarding the Government Procurement Agreement (GPA), China was allegedly reluctant to grant preferences negotiated as part of GPA to India as a non-participating country.[14] Another trade official complained in an interview that 'China has put its hand where its mouth is'.[15] In particular, regarding negotiations on agriculture, where China has become a major subsidiser itself, developing country officials increasingly perceive conflicts of interest.[16]

The ambiguity that exists about China's role vis-à-vis the Global South also comes across in the result of the survey conducted among trade officials from developed and developing countries based in Geneva. When asked whether trade officials feel that China's negotiating positions in the WTO overlap with the interests of developing countries, the average answer is 4.5 on a scale from 1 to 7, suggesting a slightly positive answer (see Figure 9.2). Yet, variation is rather strong, with answers ranging from 2 to 7. A similar pattern emerges when interviewees were asked whether they feel that Chinese negotiating positions during the Doha round were informed by historical roles that reaffirm the importance of South-South cooperation (see Figure 9.3), with answers varying from 1 to 7, and the average answer being 4.8. In these surveys, developed country representatives tended to have a slightly more favourable view of China's role as a development partner than developing country representatives.

While the sample size (n = 22) is too small to be representative, these findings suggest that there is no uniform perception of China's role vis-à-vis the Global South in the WTO. Some perceive China to act in pro-Southern ways, while others remain sceptical regarding the extent to which Chinese interests overlap with those of other countries in the Global South.

Notably, developed country representatives tended to share these mixed assessments of China's role vis-à-vis the Global South. The semi-structured interviews and the survey revealed that, on the one hand, they tended to perceive China as more clearly in line with the agenda of developing countries. On the other hand, however, some of these officials acknowledged that regarding particular negotiation outcomes, China also defends its own economic interests against the Global South. Examples included China's tough negotiations with South Korea that were crucial for

[13] Interview with developed country representative, Geneva, 15 September 2016.
[14] Interview with developed country official, 30 September 2016.
[15] Interview with former developing country representative, Geneva, 30 September 2016.
[16] Interview with two developing country trade officials, 16 September 2016.

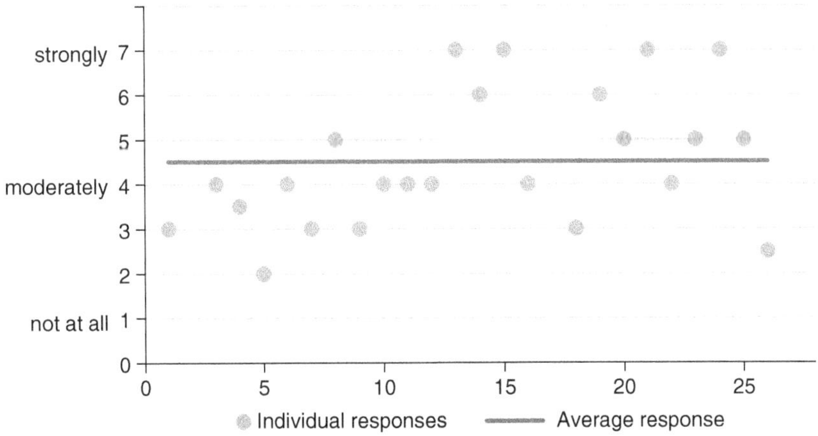

Figure 9.2 To what extent do you feel that China's negotiating positions in the WTO overlap with the interests of developing countries?

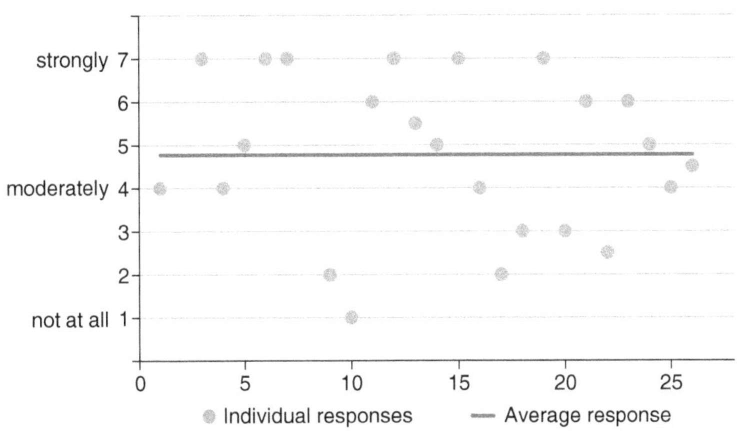

Figure 9.3 To what extent do you feel that Chinese negotiating positions during the Doha round were informed by historical roles that reaffirm the importance of South-South cooperation?

reaching an agreement on the Expansion of the Information Technology Agreement,[17] or China's alleged reluctance to grant preferences negotiated as part of the Government Procurement Agreement to India as a non-participating country.[18] The following section further unpacks the

17 Interview with developed country representative, Geneva, 15 September 2016.
18 Interview with developed country representative, Geneva, 30 September 2016.

patterns that emerge amongst those countries that China seeks to partner with on development issues the Global South.

V Unpacking Mixed Perceptions across the Global South: The Emergence of New Conflict Lines Linked to Special and Differential Treatment

Why do some developing countries perceive China to act as a development partner, while others do not? The explanatory patterns that emerge are linked to the political agenda of S&D for developing countries in the WTO. Three main patterns emerge: First, whether or not China is seen as a partner or competitor in S&D is shaped in part by the political status that developing countries have. In particular, non-emerging developing countries tend to see China as a competitor for these special rights. Conversely, LDCs and other emerging developing country members are more likely to continue to see China as a development partner. Second, however, issue-specific conflict lines are influenced by the extent to which other developing country members share the defensive trade policy orientation of the S&D agenda. Third, political South-South ties – and variation therein – further shape perceptions of China's role vis-à-vis developing countries within the WTO.

(i) China as a Competitor for Special and Differential Treatment: Emergent vs. Non-Emerging Developing Countries

S&D was introduced into the world trading system to counterbalance the demands for trade liberalisation with those for 'equitable socio-economic development' (Lichtenbaum, 2001, 1008). The principle grants special rights such as exemptions from liberalisation commitments or longer transition periods to developing countries, given that they are perceived to be in a disadvantaged position versus developed countries. Whether or not, and how, such a defensive S&D agenda serves the interests of developing countries in the WTO has been and remains hotly contested. Divergent viewpoints reflect different assessments of the causal link between the depths of trade liberalisation commitments and economic development (compare Low, 2021).

Another highly controversial aspect of S&D in the WTO is that regime members can self-declare the status they have. This creates incentives for emerging economies such as China to maintain their political status as developing countries, given the special rights that this status is associated with. For the same reason, the US and other developed countries contest China's political status as a developing country in the WTO, given that they perceive China increasingly as an economic competitor. As a result, the status of emerging economies such as China has become a central issue of conflict and contestation in the WTO (Hopewell, 2020; Weinhardt, 2020; Weinhardt and Schöfer, 2022).

What has received less attention, however, is that other developing country members may also increasingly perceive China as a competitor. Perception is different, however, depending on whether developing countries are themselves considered to be emerging. While China's self-declared status has been at the centre of US calls for reforming S&D, the proposed changes affect other larger developing countries as well. In 2019, the US proposed a set of criteria[19] in the WTO General Council to define and delimit who should have access to S&D (WTO, 2019c). According to this definition, 34 self-declared developing country members of the WTO were to graduate from developing country rights. Larger developing countries that are also considered to be emerging are thus more likely to side with China, as they fear that greater differentiation would also reduce their own access to S&D. Indeed, in response to the US proposal, China, India, South Africa and Venezuela submitted a joint communication at the General Council to defend the existing system of S&D that allows all WTO members to self-declare their status as developing countries (WTO, 2019d).[20] For these countries, China acted as a development partner.

Conversely, developing country members that are not commonly considered to be emerging economically are more likely to see China (and other emerging economies) as unfair competitors for these special rights. The benefits derived from S&D may become smaller for them if they have to be shared with emerging economies such as China. One representative from the Global South for instance complained that: 'Amongst developing countries, there is China, there is India, Brazil, but if they are allowed the sorts of flexibilities that are usually carved out for developing countries, it will put them in stronger economic position than us the developing countries who are their direct competitors in the market' (quoted in Weinhardt, 2020, p. 405). This concern was shared by other

[19] These criteria are either OECD membership (or accession), membership of the Group of 20, classification as "high income" country by the World Bank or accounting for no less than 0.5 per cent of global merchandise trade (imports and exports).

[20] Note that Venezuela is – in contrast to the other three countries – not covered by the criteria proposed by the US for the graduation from the developing country status. Subsequently, a group of 52 developing countries – including India and China – submitted a joint statement at the General Council of the WTO in which they also defended the current system of S&D (WTO, 2019b).

representatives from non-emerging countries in the Global South,[21] with one official claiming that among the negotiation group comprised entirely of developing countries that he was working for, there is 'the sentiment that they do the competition with them [emerging economies such as China] for S&D but are not at the same level of development'.[22]

Lastly, China's support for S&D in its negotiation positions is least controversial when it seeks to strengthen these special rights for the narrow group of LDCs – rather than for itself.[23] An example is China's support for the LDC countries' repeated requests for a prolongation of the TRIPS waiver, which developed countries tended to question. Here, flexibilities are reserved for a clearly defined and narrow group of WTO members – which excludes most developing countries, and most certainly those that are emerging economies.[24] Evidence from the semi-structured interviews suggests that LDC representatives also assess China's political support within the WTO positively. One representative, for instance, mentioned that China urges other developed countries to be more flexible when LDCs negotiate accession to the WTO compared to other countries.[25] The trade official also positively referred to the South-South Dialogue on LDCs and development than China initiated, and that China is granting duty-free and quota-free market access to all LDCs.[26] This indicates that China most unambiguously acts and is perceived as a development partner in negotiating issues where its distinct economic size is less pertinent, such as support for LDCs.

(ii) Issue-Specific Conflict Lines: Defensive or Offensive Trade Policy Orientation?

Perceptions of China's role are, however, not only shaped by the political status of countries from the Global South. Issue-specific conflict lines are central in shaping whether or not China is perceived as a development

[21] Interview with developing country representative, Geneva, 23 September 2016.

[22] Interview with developing country representative, Geneva, 14 September 2016.

[23] Note that in the past decade, there has been a general shift towards S&D limited to LDCs – rather than the more contested S&D provisions accessible for all developing countries (Weinhardt and Schöfer 2022).

[24] Who counts as a LDC is determined by the UN and reviewed regularly, based on a combination of economic and human development criteria. There are currently only 46 countries that qualify as LDCs. The graduation criteria built into the LDC status ensure only marginalised countries that represent around 1% of aggregate exports of WTO members qualify for the status.

[25] Interview with developing country official, Geneva, 22 September 2016.

[26] Ibid.

partner. Given the inherently defensive nature of the S&D agenda on development, developing countries that pursue a liberal, and more offensive, trade policy orientation are more likely to see China as a competitor rather than a development partner. Notably, these conflict lines can vary across negotiating issues, and partly cut across the political conflict lines (see Section V(i)).

An insightful example of how these issue-specific conflict lines play out is WTO negotiations on agriculture, a key aspect of the Doha Development Agenda. The issue of agricultural subsidies has traditionally split WTO members along North-South lines, pitting developing country members that do not have the capacity to subsidies their own agricultural sectors against developed country members as heavy users of domestic support. However, these conflict lines have recently shifted since China itself – facilitated by its economic rise – has become one of the major providers of agricultural subsidies (Hopewell, 2021). With the Nairobi Ministerial Conference in 2015, attention in agricultural negotiations shifted away from questions of market access to a primary focus on domestic support. This brought to the forefront China's support measures for domestic farmers, which China justifies with reference to its status as a developing country and as support to the subsistence of farmers – in contrast to subsidies in the US, the EU, and other developed countries paid to agribusinesses.[27] WTO rules indeed grant China more flexibility regarding specific domestic support levels as compared to developed countries. It holds a so-called *de minimis* threshold that allows for subsidies of up to 8.5% of the value of production, while this level of subsidies for developed country members is 5%.

Whether or not other developing country members of the WTO perceive China's defensive position on domestic support is shaped by the specific constellations of interests at stake. China has consistently been a net importer of foodstuffs over the past two decades. Strong state-permeation continues to characterise the agricultural sector which is deemed largely uncompetitive despite substantial reforms since the 1980s (Weinhardt and ten Brink, 2020, pp. 268–269). Moreover, since the 2008 world food price crisis, the provision of subsidies in agriculture is seen as necessary not only for stability, employment, poverty alleviation, and development (Liang, 2013, p. 213) but also for food security. Together, these features in China's trade profile lead to a defensive stance that China has adopted on international agricultural policy since WTO accession in 2001.

[27] Interview with two developing country trade officials, 16 September 2016.

Whether or not other (emerging) developing countries see China as a development partner in these negotiations depends in part on their specific trade policy orientation. China's defensive stance on domestic support is, for instance, shared by India. The continued prevalence of large-scale subsistence farming in its economy, that is, of small, peasant-based production for domestic, and the need to safeguard rural employment and the livelihoods of peasant farmers lead to a defensive position in agricultural trade. This convergence of defensive interests, as well as their reluctance to graduate from the developing country status, made them development partners in agriculture. In 2017, India and China, for instance, submitted a joint reform proposal on agriculture at the WTO Ministerial Conference in Buenos Aires. Conversely, Brazil – even though also an emerging developing country member – sided with the European Union and tabled a reform proposal that also entailed subsidy cuts by developing country members. This difference in position reflected Brazil's highly liberal trade policy orientation in agriculture, which conflicted with China's defensive stance adopted on domestic support.

Non-emerging developing countries were likely to perceive China's position on domestic support as unfair competition if they were net-agricultural exporters, and hence offensive in policy orientation. More precisely, the trade-distorting effects of Chinese subsidies are of particular concern to developing countries that export agricultural products that receive domestic support. These products include cotton in the case of African countries, soybean in the case of Brazil and other Latin American countries, and rice in the case of Laos, Bangladesh and Vietnam.[28] An official from a non-emerging developing country, for instance, complained that Chinese subsidies negatively affect other developing countries because of the size of its domestic market: 'China says it is using its domestic support only for farmers that produce for the domestic market, but even this affects others. There will be fewer imports.'[29] China's domestic economic policies on agriculture indeed have a crucial effect on the growing South-South flows of agricultural trade (Belesky and Lawrence, 2019, p. 1123). That China has become the world's largest agricultural import market in 2020 (United States Department of Agriculture, 2020) magnifies the trade-distorting effects of its subsidies.

The example of WTO negotiations thus illustrates that China has become a competitor for some developing countries, and remains a

[28] Interview with trade expert, Geneva, 28 September 2016.

[29] Interview with two developing country trade officials, 20 September 2016.

development partner for others. Developing countries that do not share the defensive trade policy orientation of the S&D agenda are likely to hold conflicting interests with China, as it seeks to promote special rights for developing countries – including itself. These conflict lines may partly cut across the political differentiation between emerging and non-emerging developing countries.

(iii) Perceptions of China's Role Are Shaped by Larger Context of South-South Ties

Mixed perceptions of China's role via-a-vis the Global South in part also reflect the ambiguous role that South-South ties play in the WTO context. China's paradoxical situation (see Hopewell, 2022, this volume) – a major economic power, but politically part of the developing country group – may lead to ambiguous assessments. The difficulty of assessing its role stems from weighing the economic implications of individual Chinese negotiating positions that may be detrimental for some developing country members against the broader political support for a 'Southern' agenda that they may stand for, a theme that emerged in several interviews.[30] Developing country officials are, moreover, cautious not to side with the Western trading nations in the conflict over agriculture. While they may share in interest in China reducing its domestic support, conflict lines are more complex: Developed countries are also perceived to be part of the problem. Regarding agricultural subsidies, a developing country official for instance remarked: 'Because if we say, let's support the US in terms of pressing China to reduce its subsidies, the danger is that the US takes advantage of China not doing it and turn around and say, "because they are not willing, we are not willing"'.[31]

Moreover, few developing countries openly portray China as a competitor for S&D. This lack of open criticism of China should not be mistaken for reaffirmation of China's position. The interviews revealed that developing country members often do not dare to speak up against China given its importance as a development partner outside of the WTO context (compare Shaffer and Gao, 2020). One developing country trade representative stated that there is a sentiment that China is not a developing country and therefore should not receive the same treatment as other

[30] Interview with developing country official, skype call, 27 September 2016; interview with two developing country representatives, Geneva, 19 September 2016.

[31] Interview with two developing country trade officials, 16 September 2016.

developing countries under S&D – a call for greater differentiation within the developing country group. Yet, the negotiating group the interviewee worked for would never openly make such as claim, mainly because 'it is political.'[32] A former trade official from Africa similarly argued that: 'The economic relations with China are so that any African country cannot dare to stand up against China. China is the largest export destination of African commodities, China is the biggest donor…. this means that you cannot open your mouth to speak up on differentiation.'[33] The role that China plays vis-à-vis the Global South is thus in part shaped by the larger trade and investment relations it has with other developing countries – and how the rise of China has affected them.

VI Conclusion

Since joining the WTO in 2001, China has become a major economic player in global politics. This chapter has revisited its role vis-à-vis the Global South in multilateral trade policymaking. The scholarly literature tends to portray China either as a development partner, given ideological South-South ties, or as a competitor whose economic interests as a major trading nation increasingly overlap with those of developed country members. This chapter shows that as China transforms economically but continues to seek political alliances with the Global South, its role cuts across that of either a development partner or a competitor.

The chapter has shown that China plays an ambiguous role in the WTO. On the one hand, China continues to lend its support to the broad development agenda of the WTO's ongoing Doha Development Round. Similarly, China's submissions to the WTO's Trade Negotiation Committee are primarily together with other developing country members. On the other hand, the analysis of perceptions of other WTO members reveals that China's attempts to portray itself as a development partner do not always succeed. First, there is no uniform assessment of China's position towards the Global South. Trade representatives disagreed substantively on the importance of South-South ties and the overlap between China's economic interests and those of other developing country members. Second, China's political claims to the developing country status are increasingly seen as a source of competition, especially by other non-emerging developing country members. In this regard, China's role vis-à-vis the Global

[32] Interview with developing country representative, Geneva, 14 September 2016.

[33] Interview with former developing country representative, Geneva, 30 September 2016.

South is similar to those of other emerging economies such as India that are reluctant to graduate from the developing country status. Third, developing countries that share the defensive orientation of the S&D agenda on a given negotiating issue are more likely to see China as a development partner than those with a more offensive, or liberal, policy orientation. This point illustrates that what counts as 'development-oriented' is in part shaped by ideological beliefs about what depths of liberalisation commitments are conducive for economic development. Lastly, China's role is interpreted against the context of China's role as a development partner outside of the WTO, which also differs across countries and regions.

Taken together these findings illustrate how the paradoxical situation of China (Hopewell, 2022, this volume) – as a major economic player that self-identifies as a developing country – leads to ambiguity in its role vis-à-vis the Global South. This finding contrast with one-sided assessments as either 'pro-Southern' or detrimental for other developing countries, and contradict, for instance, Johnson and Urpelainen's (2020, p. 468) conclusion that 'major developing countries do not seem to be abandoning their less prosperous Southern brethren', and in turn 'receiv[e] Southern backing'. Considering the broader context of WTO negotiations, moreover, helps us to contextualise findings about China's role as a competitor for developing countries in specific issues such as agricultural negotiations (Hopewell, 2021): While China's rise does not translate into a strengthened development agenda across the board, old North-South dividing lines do not necessarily disappear. Instead, coalitions within the Global South become more fragmented and complex. The relation between China and the Global South thus develops in parallel to the broader conflict over the future of the WTO (Hoekman et al. 2023 this volume; Hopewell 2020; Muzaka and Bishop, 2015).

References

Abendin, S., & Duan, P. (2021). 'Global E-commerce talks at the WTO: positions on selected issues of the United States, European Union, China, and Japan'. *World Trade Review*, 20(5), 707–24.

Acharya, A. (2014). 'Global International Relations (IR) and regional worlds'. *International Studies Quarterly*, 58(4), 647–59.

Belesky, P., & Lawrence, G. (2019). 'Chinese state capitalism and neomercantilism in the contemporary food regime: contradictions, continuity and change'. *The Journal of Peasant Studies*, 46(6), 1119–41.

Bhattacharya, D., & Misha, F. (2015). 'China and the least developed countries: an enquiry into the trade relationship during the post-WTO accession period'. In W. Luolin (ed.), *China's WTO Accession Reassessed,* Routledge, pp. 496–520.

Bishop, M. L., & Zhang, X. (2020). 'Why is China a reluctant leader of the World Trade Organization?', *New Political Economy* 25(5), 755–72.

Chin, G. (2009). 'Reforming the WTO: China, the Doha round and beyond'. In A. Narlikar and B. Vickers (eds.), *Leadership and Change in the Multilateral Trading System*, Republic of Letters Publishing, pp. 121–48.

Gao, H. (2011). 'China's ascent in global trade governance: from rule taker to rule shaker to maybe rule maker?' In C. Deere-Birkbeck (ed.), *Making Global Trade Governance Work for Development: Perspectives and Priorities from Developing Countries*, Cambridge University Press, pp. 153–80.

Gao, H. (2015). 'China's growing role in WTO negotiations: from the Doha round to the China round'. In L. Toohey, C. Picker and J. Greenacre, (eds.), *China in the International Economic Order: New Directions and Changing Paradigms*, Cambridge University Press, pp. 79–97.

Gao, H. (2021). 'How China took on the United States and Europe at the WTO'. In G. Shaffer (ed.), *Emerging Powers and the World Trading System: The Past and Future of International Economic Law,* Cambridge University Press, pp. 174–221.

Hoekman, B., Tu, X., & Wolfe, R. (2023). 'China and WTO reform'. In H. Gao, D. Raess, and K. Zeng (eds.), *China and the WTO: A Twenty-Year Assessment*, Cambridge University Press, pp. 275–97.

Hopewell, K. (2017). 'The BRICS – merely a fable? Emerging power alliances in global trade governance'. *International Affairs*, 93(6), 1377–96.

Hopewell, K. (2020). *Clash of Powers: US-China Rivalry in Global Trade Governance*, Cambridge University Press.

Hopewell, K. (2022). 'Heroes of the developing world? Emerging powers in WTO agriculture negotiations and dispute settlement'. *The Journal of Peasant Studies*, 49(3), 561–84.

Jain, R. (2014). 'China: enmeshed in or escaping the WTO?' *American Journal of Chinese Studies,* 21(2), 185–204.

Johnson, T., & Urpelainen, J. (2020). 'The more things change, the more they stay the same: developing countries' unity at the nexus of trade and environmental policy'. *The Review of International Organizations,* 15(2), 1–29.

Lawrence, R. Z. (2008). 'China and the multilateral trading system'. In B. Eichengreen, C. Wyplosz, and Y. C. Park (eds.), *China, Asia, and the New World Economy*, Oxford University Press, pp. 145–67.

Liang, W. (2013). 'China, developing countries, and the Doha agricultural negotiations'. In K. Zeng and W. Liang (eds.), *China and Global Trade Governance: China's First Decade in the World Trade Organization*, Routledge, pp. 233–54.

Liang, W., & Zeng, K. (2023), 'China and the BRICS in WTO e-commerce and fisheries negotiations: competition and convergence'. In H. Gao, D. Raess, and K. Zeng (eds.), *China and the WTO: A Twenty-Year Assessment*, Cambridge University Press, pp. 227–251.

Lichtenbaum, P. (2001). 'Special treatment vs. equal participation: striking a balance in the Doha negotiations'. *American University International Law Review*, 17, 1003–44.

Lim, C. L., & Wang, J. (2010). 'China and the Doha development agenda'. *Journal of World Trade*, 44(6), 1309–31.

Liu, H. (2014). 'China's proposing behavior in Global Governance: the cases of the WTO Doha Round negotiation and G-20 process'. *Revista Brasileira de Política Internacional*, 57, 121–37.

Low, P. (2021). 'Special and differential treatment and developing country status: can the two be separated?' In B. Hoekman, X. Tu, and D. Wand (eds.), *Rebooting Multilateral Trade Cooperation: Perspectives from China and Europe*, CEPR Press, pp. 76–103.

Muzaka, V., & Bishop, M. L. (2015). 'Doha stalemate: the end of trade multilateralism?' *Review of International Studies*, 41(2), 383–406.

Mfa.gov.cn. (2001). Speech by Mr. Long Yongtu, Chief Negotiator and Vice-Minister of Foreign Trade and Economic Cooperation of the People's Republic of China, at the General Council Meeting of WTO, Webpage of the permanent missions of the PRC to the UN/Geneva, 19 December 2001, www.mfa.gov.cn/ce/cegv//eng/qtzz/gjzzda/gjzz2001/t85636.htm

Narlikar, A. (2010). 'New powers in the club: the challenges of global trade governance'. *International Affairs*, 86(3), 717–28.

Nel, P. (2010). 'Redistribution and recognition: what emerging regional powers want'. *Review of International Studies*, 36(4), 951–74.

Pu, X. (2019). *Rebranding China: Contested Status Signaling in the Changing Global Order*, Stanford University Press.

SAIIA. (2021). 'The WTO and Africa: the state of play and key priorities going forward', South African Institute of International Affairs Policy Briefing 243. 6 July 2021, [online]. Available at: https://saiia.org.za/research/the-wto-and-africa-the-state-of-play-and-key-priorities-going-forward/

Shaffer, G., & Gao, H. (2020). 'A new Chinese economic order?' *Journal of International Economic Law*, 23(3), 607–35.

South China Morning Post (SCMP). (2020). 'China insists it is a "developing country"; While it overtakes US on buying power, per capita output below average', *South China Morning Post*. 21 May 2020 [online]. Available at: www.scmp.com/economy/china-economy/article/3085501/china-overtakes-us-no-1-buying-power-still-clings-developing [Accessed 22 May 2020].

Tu, X. (2013). 'China's position and role in the Doha round negotiations'. In K. Zeng and W. Liang (eds.), *China and Global Trade Governance: China's First Decade in the World Trade Organization*, Routledge, pp. 167–88.

United States Department of Agriculture. (2020). *China: Evolving Demand in the World's Largest Agricultural Import Market* [online]. International Agricultural Trade Report, US Department of Agriculture. Available at: www.fas.usda.gov/data/china-evolving-demand-world-s-largest-agricultural-import-market [29 September 2020].

Vickers, B. (2014). 'The role of the Brics in the WTO: system-supporters or change agents in multilateral trade?' In A. Narlikar, M. J. Daunton, and R.

M. Stern (eds.), *The Oxford Handbook on the World Trade Organization*, Oxford University Press, pp. 254–74.

Vieira, M. (2012). 'Rising states and distributive justice: reforming international order in the twenty-first century'. *Global Society*, 26(3), 311–29.

Weinhardt, C. (2020). 'Emerging powers in the world trading system: contestation of the developing country status and the reproduction of inequalities'. *Global Society*, 34(3), 388–408.

Weinhardt, C., & Schöfer, T. (2022). 'Differential treatment for developing countries in the WTO: the unmaking of the North–South distinction in a multipolar world'. *Third World Quarterly*, 43(1), 74–93.

Weinhardt, C., & ten Brink, T. (2020). 'Varieties of contestation: China's rise and the liberal trade order: [Contribution to forum: China's rise in a liberal world order in transition]'. *Review of International Political Economy*, 27(2), 258–80.

Wilkinson, R., Hannah, E., & Scott, J. (2016). 'The WTO in Nairobi: the demise of the Doha development agenda and the future of the multilateral trading system'. *Global Policy*, 7(2), 247–55.

WTO. (2001). 'Doha WTO ministerial declaration'. Ministerial Conference, Doha. 20 November 2001. WT/MIN(01)/DEC/1. (2001a). Available at: www.wto.org/english/thewto_e/minist_e/min01_e/mindecl_e.htm

WTO. (2019a). 'China's proposal on WTO reform'. General Council, Communication from China, 13 May 2019. WT/GC/W/773.

WTO. (2019b). 'The continued relevance of special and differential treatment in favour of developing members to promote development and ensure inclusiveness'. General Council, Communication from China, India, South Africa and the Bolivarian Republic of Venezuela, 28 February 2019, WT/GC/W/765/Rev.2.

WTO. (2019c). 'Draft general council decision: procedures to strengthen the negotiating function of the WTO'. General Council, Communication circulated by the US. 15 February 2019, WT/GC/W/764.

WTO. (2019d). The continued relevance of special and differential treatment in favour of developing members to promote development and ensure inclusiveness. General Council, Communication circulated by China, India, South Africa and the Bolivarian Republic of Venezuela. 18 February 2019, WT/GC/W/765.

10

China and the BRICS in WTO E-Commerce and Fisheries Negotiations

Competition and Convergence

WEI LIANG AND KA ZENG

I Introduction

As the guardian of multilateral trade liberalization, the World Trade Organization (WTO) is currently confronted with the deepest crisis since its initial inception. Among other challenges, the rising economic clout of China and the incompatibilities between its model of state capitalism and the rules-based neoliberal economic order have raised important questions about the degree to which China's participation in the WTO may have compromised the effectiveness and credibility of the multilateral trade institution.

Coincidentally, we have also witnessed the growing influence of emerging economies, including India, Brazil, Russia, and South Africa in WTO negotiations in the past two decades. Different from the interactions and policy coordination among the Quad countries consisting of the United States (US), the European Union (EU), Canada, and Japan in past negotiations taking place within the WTO and its predecessor, the General Agreement on Tariffs and Trade (GATT), the BRICS have presented a unique model of "coopetition" featuring both the pursuit of a common development agenda and competing national interests.

What role have China and other BRICS countries played in more recent WTO negotiations? This paper addresses this question through an analysis of the behavior of the BRICS in WTO negotiations on e-commerce and fisheries subsidies. By examining the evolving positions and tactics of this group of countries during various stages of the negotiation process, we illuminate areas where the BRICS have been able to proactively cooperate with one another through coalition building and areas in which they have failed to effectively negotiate as a group due to disparate domestic interests and the absence of a common vision on how (and where) to move forward. The chapter further assesses the extent to which such differences have influenced negotiation outcomes across the key issue areas under consideration.

We choose to focus on the e-commerce and fisheries subsidies negotiations for a couple of reasons. First, e-commerce and fisheries subsidies are two important ongoing WTO negotiations that have important implications for the future legitimacy and credibility of the WTO. Second, these two negotiations represent two different sets of challenges presented to the WTO in the future – making new trade rules to regulate today's global trade practices in the case of e-commerce and developing viable solutions to the challenges of addressing environmental and developmental concerns within the WTO framework in the case of fisheries subsidies. Third, with the rise of China in the past two decades, its trade interests have diverged from that of the majority of the developing countries and in particular those of India and Brazil in important ways.

In the e-commerce negotiations, seeing itself as a potential leader in this new trade issue area, China seeks a driving seat to write new rules to reflect its dominant position in global e-commerce and to safeguard its commercial interests and ability to effectively compete with the US and other developed countries. In contrast, India and Brazil have been less keen to play a proactive role in the e-commerce negotiations as e-commerce is not a top priority in the making of their trade policy. In the fisheries subsidies negotiations, China chose to take a low-profile and ambiguous position. Today China has emerged as the world's largest fisheries subsidizer. Therefore, pressuring China to make deep cuts in its fisheries subsidies, especially those supporting capacity-enhancing activities, in the negotiation is the only way to ensure a meaningful and impactful WTO fisheries subsidies agreement. Although China, India, and Brazil all support the flexibility of special and differential treatment (SDT), the reality is that India and Brazil stand a better chance of receiving the SDT flexibilities they need to keep some policy space in this issue area when China is no longer viewed as a helpful addition to their coalition. Hence a comparison of these two cases will shed light on the effect of the semi-coordination among the BRICS countries on multilateral trade negotiations, WTO reform, and the BRICS' future cooperation in global governance.

Our findings suggest that while North-South conflicts still present a major impediment to WTO negotiations, the nuanced and differentiated interests among the BRICS have further complicated the picture, contributing to the impasses in the WTO negotiations and to the current crisis faced by the WTO in general.[1] Despite its shared identity and common

[1] This pattern is consistent with China's behavior earlier in the history of its engagement with the WTO. See, for example, discussions of China's negotiation behavior in the WTO agricultural and non-agricultural market access (NAMA) negotiations (e.g., Liang, 2013; Wang and Zeng, 2013).

interests with the latter in promoting the development needs of the South, China's specific negotiation interests frequently departed from those of the emerging economies and the majority of the smaller developing countries. More importantly, since the Uruguay round negotiations, the developing countries coalitions led by India and Brazil have increasingly treated China as a liability which impeded them from receiving SDT flexibilities, and this is especially the case as China has continued to insist that it is still a developing country.

Especially, in e-commerce negotiations, China's much more developed domestic e-commerce market means that it is much less concerned than BRICS countries such as India and South Africa about the potential of e-commerce negotiations to undermine the goals of the Doha Development Agenda (DDA). However, while Beijing is more willing to support negotiations designed to facilitate data flows compared to some other BRICs and the least-developing countries (LDCs), its stronger concerns about the need to maintain sovereignty and domestic regulatory control also means that its preferences are far apart from those of the major players such as the US and the EU over issues such as data localization, privacy and personal data, and transfer of source code. China's different negotiation stance vis-à-vis both developed countries and emerging powers, along with the heterogeneity of the preferences among the BRICS countries, thus undercut the possibility that the BRICs could form an effective coalition to assert and advance their interests in the negotiation process.

In the fisheries subsidies negotiations, China continues to seek greater flexibilities granted to developing countries even though it is the largest fishing nation, the largest exporter of fish, and the largest subsidizer. Both India and Brazil's latest proposals have explicitly provided metrics to exclude China from receiving the preferences associated with SDT. The split of interests among both developed countries and developing countries, in addition to the North-South divide, thus complicated and significantly delayed the negotiation process. The new reality seems to be that being the largest subsidizer, China's effort to defend the SDT has de facto weakened the likelihood for other developing countries to receive it. Excluding China from the developing countries' coalition has become a necessity for developing countries to achieve their desired negotiation outcome.

The rest of the chapter is organized as follows. Section II presents an overview of how the differences in the negotiation preferences and positions between China and the rest of the BRICs have shaped the processes of the WTO e-commerce negotiations. Section III turns to a detailed discussion of the fisheries subsidies negotiations. The chapter concludes by comparing the dynamics of the two sets of negotiations and discussing the implications of our findings for the future of global trade governance.

II WTO E-Commerce Negotiations

The drawn-out negotiations over e-commerce highlight sharp conflicts between China and other major powers such as the US and the EU. The substantially different negotiation preferences and approaches among the BRICS further compounded these differences and undermined the group's ability to pursue a common negotiation agenda.

(i) Divergences among the Major Players

Progress toward WTO negotiations over e-commerce has been impeded by significant differences in the negotiation approaches among the US, the EU, and China over highly contentious issues such as data flows, data location, and "privacy invasion by data collectors." Notably, the US position focused on eliminating cross-border restrictions on data, promoting the competitiveness of US digital networks, minimizing regulatory divergences across countries, and reducing the burden of regulatory compliance (US Mission in Geneva, 2019). In line with this goal, the US approach sought to limit the extent to which considerations about consumer protection or privacy regulations may influence the design of global e-commerce rules (Kilic, 2021).

In contrast to the United States and some other developed country governments which place greater emphasis on reining in Big Tech, the EU, with its stronger oversight of the industry and a less developed digital economy (UNCTAD, 2019), puts a stronger emphasis on the protection of data privacy and favors strong disciplines on algorithms and/or source code. In addition, the EU has strong concerns about the lack of coherent rules regarding internet taxation that could effectively tackle tax avoidance by multinational corporations, proposing both a digital services tax and a digital profits tax targeting large technology firms' revenue and profits associated with activities in EU member states in 2018. The US strongly opposes such unilateral proposals on the grounds that they potentially violate tax treaties and other agreements.

China's approach toward e-commerce negotiations diverges from those of the US and EU in a few important respects. While many of China's proposals favor measures that would facilitate digital trade and protect consumer interests, its proposals have also emphasized security exception and content review, raising concerns about whether it would be willing to accept the main demands of the US and other Western countries regarding the free flow of information across borders, prohibition on localization requirements, the protection of privacy and personal data, and the forced transfer of source code (Gao, 2020; Hufbauer and Lu, 2019).

Overall, while the US and other industrialized countries aim to reach an ambitious high-standard WTO agreement, China has placed considerable emphasis on the development dimension of e-commerce, insisting that developing countries should receive SDT in WTO negotiations, including e-commerce negotiations. Not surprisingly, the US strongly opposed China's self-identified developing county status on the ground that it can be invoked by Beijing to exempt itself from certain obligations, potentially leading to the abuse of SDT for developing countries in the WTO system.

(ii) Dissension among the BRICS Countries

The divide between developed and developing countries was further compounded by the divergent negotiation preferences and approaches among the latter, notably among the BRICS countries. India, for example, was highly critical of moves to craft rules on e-commerce before the conclusion of the DDA trade negotiations. Along with many least developed and developing countries, India emphasized that in view of its nascent e-commerce policy and ongoing "digital transformation," the promulgation of data regulation laws and digital industrialization plans should take precedence over the negotiation of rules governing digital trade. India additionally "highlighted the importance of policy space in terms of ownership, use, and flows of data in rapidly growing sectors such as cloud computing and data storage" (UNCTAD, 2020: 15). Due to such concerns, India and South Africa have chosen to stay outside of WTO e-commerce negotiations.

In contrast to India and South Africa which have taken an uncompromising stance on the issue, Brazil and Russia have adopted a more proactive approach toward the joint statement initiative (JSI) negotiations. As both countries have relatively large e-commerce markets and relatively well-developed regulatory frameworks for e-commerce (Thorstensen et al., 2019), they are less concerned about the potential adverse developmental impact of e-commerce negotiations and have been actively involved in efforts to submit proposals and to create small working groups to encourage regulatory cooperation and facilitate the free flow of data. The BRICS countries' divergent interests in e-commerce therefore have accentuated the heterogeneity of WTO members' negotiation positions and exacerbated the difficulties of reaching an agreement among the participating members.

(iii) The Run-Up to the 2017 11th Ministerial Conference (MC 11)

While earlier e-commerce negotiations have generated some positive results (Ismail, 2020), it was not until 2016 that negotiations once again gained momentum. According to Gao (2020: 6), China was initially reluctant to support the launch of the negotiations, insisting that it was not ready for the negotiation of new rules on e-commerce and that the negotiations should, at least initially, focus on trade facilitation and transparency measures and exclude new market access commitments (WTO, 2017a). Unlike either developed countries which sought to make digital commerce a high priority in the WTO agenda or LDCs and most developing countries calling for the negotiation of the unresolved DDA issues, China took a middle approach that supports more focused negotiations on e-commerce, while at the same time prioritizing developing country issues. While generally favoring the development of new rules to facilitate e-commerce, China simultaneously opposed those prohibiting data controls (Macleod, 2017). Together with countries such as Argentina, Chile, Colombia, Costa Rica, Kenya, Mexico, Nigeria, Pakistan, Sri Lanka, and Uruguay, China formed the group of the Friends of E-commerce for Development to emphasize the development dimension of e-commerce issues (Darsinouei, 2017).

In the run-up to MC 11, a group of countries sought to pursue multilateral negotiations by converting the work program into negotiation mode with a new ministerial declaration. BRICS countries such as Russia, along with other proponents of the proposal, called for the establishment of a "Working Party" at the Buenos Aires meeting to engage in preparatory work for future international rule-making on e-commerce issues (WTO, 2017d). They further supported "the continuation of the current practice of not imposing customs duties on electronic transmissions" until the next sessions which would be held in 2019 (UNCTAD, 2020). This group of countries issued statements and proposals on potential issues for discussion, including data flows, data protection, market access, infrastructure development, and trade facilitation.

Brazil has also been actively making submissions, putting forward a proposal with Argentina and Paraguay on electronic signatures in December 2016 (JOB/GC/115) and another one with Argentina on e-commerce and copyright in March 2017 (JOB/GC/113/Rev.1) (WTO, 2016, 2017e). The

2016 submission on e-signature details the definition, legal effects, and liability associated with electronic documents and electronic signatures (WTO, 2016). The 2017 submission in turn underscores the importance of the principle of transparency as it relates to digital trade. It further highlights the need to uphold the principle that "exceptions and limitations available in physical formats should also be made available in the digital environment" (WTO, 2017e).

However, the proposal to create a new working group encountered strong resistance from many developing and least-developed countries. For example, along with the African Group, Uganda, which represented the interests of LDCs, and several other members, India raised serious concerns about the underlying motives of the negotiations, arguing that the proposals may potentially undermine the 1998 work program and jeopardize the "development space" for industrialization provided by the DDA (Lemma, 2017). India argued that it would like to see the continuation of the 1998 e-commerce work program that provided an exploratory and non-negotiating mandate, criticizing proposals to establish a Working Group at Buenos Aires as efforts aimed at imposing a "top-down" instead of a "bottom-up" approach (Kanth, 2017). India further linked the extension of the two-year moratorium for not imposing customs duties on e-commerce transactions with the moratorium on TRIPS non-violation and situation complaints.

South Africa joined India in this effort, promising to fight ferociously against the proposals. Along with the African group, it strongly resisted efforts to change the current structure of institutional arrangements of the Work Program, raising questions about whether the commitments negotiated under the Uruguay Round should be applied post hoc to emerging technologies, services, and business models (Kanth, 2017). Viewing e-commerce negotiations as reflecting divergent views among members regarding the technological neutrality of the General Agreement on Trade in Services and whether products delivered electronically should be considered as goods or services or both, the African Group pointed out that the negotiation of new multilateral e-commerce rules would be unlikely to deliver concrete results before these issues could be resolved. Rwanda echoed this view, suggesting that the establishment of a Working Group would not undo these divergences and that more time should be given to put the Work Programme to work before changes are made to its underlying structure (Kanth, 2017).

In short, India and South Africa, along with other developing countries and LDCs, were strongly concerned about the digital divide that prevents them from fully participating in e-commerce activities, focusing instead on "enabling issues" that will allow them to overcome the barriers they face in relation to their better participation in e-commerce. They therefore opposed e-commerce negotiations and called for focusing the negotiations on the unresolved DDA issues and continuing the discussions about e-commerce within the current mandate of the Electronic Commerce Work Programme.

As a result of divergent negotiation approaches, Member countries dropped the idea of beginning multilateral negotiations on e-commerce early into MC11 (WTO, 2017c). Instead, 43 WTO member countries issued the JSI 2017 indicating an intention to undertake "exploratory work" in preparation for future plurilateral negotiations on the issue (WTO, 2017b). The JSI 2017 received a mixed reception among WTO members. In particular, there remained concerns that it might run counter to some core WTO principles, that the new issues lacked specific negotiating mandates, and that they were not prepared to take on commitments in these new areas (Kanth, 2017).

(iv) The Second E-Commerce Joint Statement Initiative and the Road to MC12

While key players in the first JSI have continued negotiations following MC11 and issued three trilateral statements after 2018, the divergent negotiation approaches among member states were again reflected in the negotiations leading up to the conclusion of the second Joint Statement of January 25, 2019, in Davos and afterward. While the number of cosponsors had increased to 76 members by the time of the second JSI talks and more members have been invited to join the process, there existed widespread recognition among negotiation parties of the different challenges faced by developing countries and LDCs (WTO, 2019a, 2019b).

As one of the first parties to submit an initial discussion paper, the US position represented an extension and, in some respects, enhancement of the commitments it made in the Trans-Pacific Partnership, which subsequently have been refined in the Digital Trade chapter in the US-Mexico-Canada Agreement. As such, it included strong commitments to the protection of cross-border data flows and prohibitions on data localization mandates and signaled a strong commitment to the protection of proprietary information (Fefer, 2020: 19–20).

At this time, China had come around and made a "last-minute" decision to join the second JSI in order to revitalize the rules-based multilateral trading system, promote developing country interests in global value chain integration, and influence the process of rule-making for e-commerce and cyberspace (Gao, 2020; WTO, 2019b). However, despite its participation, China insisted that the negotiations should "set a reasonable level of ambition" and "uphold the development dimension" considering "the difficulties and challenges faced by developing Members" (WTO, 2019b: 1–2). It has also sought to maintain a delicate "balance between international rule-making and the sovereign right to regulate" and continued to insist on "cyber sovereignty," as reflected in its adoption of a series of cybersecurity laws, internet censorship, and data localization requirements.

The EU took a somewhat different approach from both the US and China in its proposal. While the EU position was similar to that of the US on issues such as the protection of cross-border data flows and the prohibition of localization requirements, it also put a stronger emphasis on the protection of data privacy in a way that reflects the EU's domestic policy priorities, potentially undercutting its commitment to cross-border data flows (Fefer, 2020).

The proposals submitted by other countries sought to bridge the differences between the US and Chinese proposals. However, progress toward the conclusion of an agreement continued to be stymied by the heterogenous negotiation positions of the participating parties on issues such as the implications of e-commerce negotiations for domestic regulatory sovereignty, the continuation of the moratorium on duties on electronic transmissions, and consumer protection and security.

In its submission, Russia emphasized that "future discussions should cover all aspects of e-commerce without splitting topics on e-commerce for separate discussions" and proposed a work structure to examine gaps in existing WTO agreements as they pertain to e-commerce "as a first step to understanding the potential gains of a future agreement" (ICTSD, 2018). The Brazilian communication in turn emphasized the importance of development as a core dimension in e-commerce negotiations and called on participating countries to adopt a flexible approach and engage in a closer examination of the opportunities and challenges faced by developing countries as well as their specific needs regarding e-commerce development (WTO, 2018). Other issues that have gained some prominence in the Brazilian submission included improved market access commitments for e-commerce trade in goods and services and electronic authentication methods and access to online payment solutions (WTO, 2018).

Notably, India and South Africa have continued to remain outside of the negotiations of an e-commerce agreement. Both countries have reiterated their position that plurilateral negotiations on e-commerce trade may limit their ability to protect or promote domestic industrial development or to raise tariffs on digital products, preferring instead to preserve their policy autonomy and flexibility. In contrast to the position of most of the negotiation parties, both have also been pushing for the discontinuation of the e-commerce moratorium which they fear may constrain their ability to generate the much-needed revenue and produce globally competitive internet companies.

On June 4, 2019, the two countries issued a communique requesting that the WTO revisit the moratorium renewal ("India, SA ask WTO to Review Moratorium on E-Commerce Custom Duties," 2019). In March 2020, India and South Africa tabled a joint submission regarding the moratorium, once again highlighting developing countries' concerns about the importance of retaining the necessary space for digital development ("India Not Participating in Plurilateral Discussions on E-Commerce at WTO," 2021). In December 2020, they circulated a communication (WT/GC/W/812) cautioning against the narrow focus on the "development of legally binding rules" which could risk the "further marginalization of developing countries in global trade" (WTO, 2020b). The communication additionally encouraged the members to structure the discussions on the moratorium around the themes outlined in a proposal (WT/GC/W/747) that the two countries submitted in 2018.[2]

A group of members composed of both developed and developing countries, including Australia, China, Colombia, and Switzerland, subsequently carried out the structured discussions and circulated a communication calling for a "more holistic approach" towards the negotiations that would take into consideration their impact on consumers and the competitiveness of different sectors of the economy (WTO, 2020c). At a General Council meeting in March 2021, India and South Africa further submitted a communication for discussion challenging the "legal status of Joint Statement Initiatives and their negotiated outcomes" (WTO, 2021a, 2021b, 2021c). The paper raised questions not only about current WTO practices for modifying existing agreements and for including plurilateral agreements but also about whether discussions of digital trade rules should take place within or outside of the WTO institutional structure (Stewart, 2021).

Overall, while the number of participants in the JSI has grown to include 86 WTO members (WTO, 2020a), progress remained slow due to

[2] The proposal was circulated at the request of India and South Africa on July 13, 2018, and was titled "Moratorium on Customs Duties on Electronic Transmissions: Need for a Re-think."

opposition and the lack of participation from India, South Africa, LDCs, and members from Africa, the Caribbean, and the Pacific regions. While a draft consolidated text was circulated among participants in December 2020 and negotiations have subsequently proceeded under the leadership of Australia, Japan, and Singapore, no agreement has yet been reached on key issues of concern to the participants. With MC12 being postponed to November 2021 due to the ongoing pandemic, it remains unclear whether any negotiation breakthroughs could be achieved at the conference.

III WTO Fisheries Subsidies Negotiations

This section turns to an analysis of the fisheries subsidies negotiations, showing how this set of negotiations demonstrates a somewhat similar, though not entirely identical, pattern to that observed for e-commerce negotiations.

Sustainable and equitable fisheries are essential for alleviating poverty, providing nutrition, and protecting marine biodiversity. The WTO is in the final stages of negotiating an agreement to prohibit harmful fisheries subsidies, which is the United Nations Sustainable Development Goal (SDG) 14.6 (UN, 2015). The prolonged fisheries subsidies negotiation represents a top priority on the WTO agenda today and is crucial for keeping the WTO relevant as the global trade governance organization. As stated by the WTO Director General (DG) Okonjo-Iweala (2021), "I think everyone agrees with me that if there is anything that would demonstrate that the WTO is back and capable of having positive results, it is a good outcome early enough this year to these fisheries subsidies negotiations." However, despite their presumed importance, the negotiations have missed a few scheduled deadlines, from June 2020 to July 2021, due to the logjam of several contentious issues that have set key negotiation parties apart.

Subsidies refer to financial transfers from public entities to benefit private actors (WTO SCM agreement). The WTO provides general disciplines on categorizing and addressing trade-distorting subsidies through the Agreement on Subsidies and Countervailing Measures (SCM agreement). Fisheries subsidies are broadly classified as beneficial (e.g., management), ambiguous (e.g., infrastructure), and "harmful" (e.g., fuel and vessels subsidies). Fisheries subsidies have expanded significantly in recent decades among many WTO member states. Public entities around the world have provided $35.4 billion in fisheries subsidies in 2018. Among them, capacity-enhancing subsidies constituted 52.7 percent of total subsidies, at over $22.2 billion (Sumaila et al., 2019), followed by beneficial and ambiguous subsidies, each accounting for about 29.9 percent and 7.1 percent of total subsidies, respectively (Wong, 2021). The effects of harmful fisheries subsidies are well-publicized and widely agreed upon. When subsidies are tied either directly or indirectly to capacity enhancement, they will cause overcapacity (i.e., the existence of more fishing power than needed to take the maximum sustainable yield), which will further lead to overfishing with growing economic waste and declining fish stocks.

Harmful fisheries subsidies have put developing countries in a more disadvantaged position in global trade. The top-five subsidizing nations, China, the EU, the US, South Korea, and Japan, provide four times as much subsidies as all the low-income countries combined (Sumaila et al., 2019). Countries high on the UN Human Development Index (HDI) provide roughly 87 percent of total subsidies and China, the EU, and the US are the top three on the list. Among the low HDI countries, Indonesia, Vietnam, Morocco, Senegal, and India are the main subsidizers. Fisheries subsidies have further caused inequity between large- and small-scale fisheries (SSF) within nations. SSF constitutes 90 percent of global fisheries employment yet only received 16 percent of total fisheries subsidies (Schuhbauer et al., 2020). Concluding the fisheries subsidies negotiations will therefore offer a unique opportunity for the WTO to effectively address development and environmental challenges through trade liberalization.

(i) Overview of Negotiation Preferences and Approaches

This section provides an overview of the divergent positions of the main parties participating in the fisheries subsidy negotiations, highlighting the distinct interests of China vis-à-vis both developed and developing countries.

1 Can Fish Save the WTO?

International organizations and global environmental non-governmental organizations started to raise concerns about the economic and environmental impact of fisheries subsidies in the 1990s. The UN Food and Agriculture Organization has sought to raise concerns and issued reports documenting the detrimental effects of overfishing motivated by fisheries subsidies provided by countries around the world (Schrank, 2003). During the agenda-setting discussions leading up to the DDA, a small group of countries, including the US, Australia, Chile, Ecuador, Iceland, New Zealand, Peru, and the Philippines, known as the "Friends of Fish," pressed for the inclusion of fisheries subsidies reduction into the DDA agenda as the existing SCM did not adequately cover the additional negative impact of fisheries subsidies on environmental concerns (Jones, 2010). This group of WTO Members initially pursued the issue of fisheries subsidies in the WTO Committee on Trade and Environment which has the power only to make recommendations. At the Doha Ministerial Conference, they were able to put forth a mandate highlighted in the Doha Ministerial Declaration to clarify and strengthen WTO disciplines on fisheries subsidies. Since then, negotiations on fisheries subsidies have been taking place in the WTO Negotiating Group on Rules, which is under the authority of the WTO Trade Negotiations Committee. The goal of the negotiation was clarified in the 2005 Hong Kong Declaration, which called for both the prohibition of harmful subsidies and the granting of appropriate and effective SDT to developing members as an integral part of the negotiations taking into account the importance of the fisheries sector for development, poverty reduction, and concerns over livelihoods and food security. A first set of rules was subsequently drafted in November 2007, but member states could not agree upon the specific terms of SDT and the scope of prohibited subsidies (Wong, 2021). The 2008 draft text of a WTO agreement on fisheries agreement, prepared by the chair of the Negotiating Group on Rules, proposed prohibiting a wide range of "harmful subsidies" while recognizing the need for flexibility in the application of subsidies disciplines to small-scale, labor-intensive fishing in developing countries (Hoekman et al., 2009). But the fisheries subsidies negotiations have been deadlocked since the failure of the last major push to conclude the Doha round in July 2008. The chairman of the rules negotiations group, in particular, wrote in his report that "there is too little convergence on even the technical issues, and indeed virtually none on the core substantive issues" in fisheries subsidies (WTO, 2011). While the fisheries subsidies negotiations have regained momentum since 2015, this was partly due to the adoption of the UN sustainable development goals, with goal 14.6 specifically aiming to prohibit subsidies contributing to overfishing and illegal, unreported, and unregulated (IUU) fishing, and partly because of the member states' drive to conduct sectoral negotiations to continue some of the Doha trade liberalization agenda.

With the hope to revive WTO negotiations and to pull the organization out of the crisis, member states instilled a new sense of urgency during the 11th Ministerial Conference in 2017 to set a timetable to conclude the negotiations by the end of 2020. That deadline, and a later deadline of July 2021 and December 2021, have all been missed due to persistent disagreements over several contentious issues. Member states have been negotiating on the basis of a draft consolidated text introduced in June 2020 and later updated in May 2021 and November 2021 by the chair of the negotiations (WTO, 2021a, 2021b, 2021c). Another deadline was set to finish the negotiations before the 12th Ministerial Conference, which was scheduled to be held on November 30, 2021, but had to be rescheduled due to the Covid-19 pandemic. Finally, the WTO Agreement on Fisheries Subsidies was adopted at the 12th Ministerial Conference (MC12) on 17 June 17, 2022. It marks the successful conclusion of this marathon talk. This agreement is the first broad, binding, multilateral agreement on ocean sustainability and the second agreement reached since the inception of the WTO. In the meantime, the WTO members also recognize that they failed to agree on some of the most contentious issues such as developing disciplines on subsidies contributing to overcapacity and overfishing, and the provision of special and differential treatment associated to them. Therefore, they committed to continue the second wave of fisheries subsidies negotiation and set a new target to complete negotiations by the 13th Ministerial Conference (MC13) in February 2024.

(ii) Divergences among the Major Players in the Fisheries Subsidies Negotiations

The agenda-setting of the fisheries subsidies negotiations has evolved over time. It began with a vague and broad goal to create disciplines to negotiate the subsidies issue in the area of fisheries and later developed more concrete agenda issues agreed upon by WTO members. By 2021, the main agenda items included the following (WTO, 2021a, 2021b, 2021c):

- prohibit certain forms of fisheries subsidies which contribute to overcapacity and overfishing (e.g., subsidies for building or upgrading vessels, fuel subsidies, price support for fish caught);
- eliminate subsidies that contribute to IUU fishing;
- curb subsidies to fishing where stocks are overfished; and
- recognize the need for appropriate and effective special and differential treatment for developing and least-developed countries (delayed implementation of provisions and aid for technical assistance/capacity building)

While much progress has been made in the negotiations leading to the latest version of the November 8, 2021, revised text, there still exist key areas of disagreement. First, although WTO members have a consensus that SDT as an important WTO principle should apply to the fisheries subsidies negotiations, developed and developing countries have disagreed on what flexibility should be granted. Developing countries, especially China, prefer to have broader SDT provisions and keep some permanent exceptions. In contrast, developed countries argue that flexibilities should not only be more limited and targeted to the specific needs of the developing countries but should also be phased out over time (Wong, 2021). Second, developing countries are concerned that the draft text, which includes provisions exempting the cut of fisheries subsidies that aim to maintain or promote sustainability, will disproportionately benefit large and developed subsidizers such as the EU and the US.

In addition to differences in commercial interests, the norm of environmental protection and sustainability has become another major concern that has set many member states apart. In the early years of the negotiations, the "Friends of Fish" group led by the US emphasized the importance of prohibiting harmful fisheries subsidies (WTO, 2002a), while the "Friends of Fishers" group that relied heavily on fishing, such as Korea, Taiwan, and Japan, argued against discussing fishing subsidies separately from the general SCM agreement. In the early years of the negotiations, they argued that fisheries subsidies were not significant and did not have any negative impact on stock depletion (WTO, 2002b). In addition, developing countries tended to hold a very defensive position in the early stages of the negotiations, calling for SDT and broad exemptions given to the small-scale "artisanal" nature of their fisheries sector (WTO, 2004).

After receiving multiple proposals from the member states between 2002 and 2007, the chair of the WTO rules negotiation put together the first-ever chair's draft text on introducing disciplines in fisheries subsidies (TN/RL/W/213). The November 2007 draft text on fisheries subsidies largely reflected the growing consensus that fisheries subsidies should not be continued. To ensure that SDT was included in the text, Article III contained provisions that proposed exempting developing country members from most of the prohibited subsidies in Article I, provided that all fisheries activities receiving these subsidies are conducted within the territorial waters of the member *and* with non-mechanized net retrieval.

In contrast to most other GATT/WTO negotiations, the divergent interests of the member states cannot simply be categorized as a North-South divide. With different views on the commercial, environmental, and developmental dimensions of global fishing, developed member states were highly divided on the approaches, structure, and scope of the fisheries subsidies rules-making. As illustrated above, the "Friends of Fish" Group members led by the US have urged for an extensive prohibition of fisheries subsidies. The "Friends of Fisher" group members, including Japan, South Korea, Taiwan, the EU, and Norway, in contrast, have a strong interest in keeping some types of fisheries subsidies. Insisting that not all fisheries subsidies cause overfishing and overcapacity, they have argued that prohibition should be limited to those "harmful subsidies."

The lack of leadership from the EU and the US and coordination among the traditional Quad countries were obvious in the last few years' WTO negotiations. Although the WTO DG has placed great confidence in the revised text of the agreement as the basis to conclude the negotiations, the recent remark made by USTR Tai suggests that the US does not consider it "enough meaningful" as it does not yet contain the elements required for reaching conclusion (Wong, 2021). Specifically, the US advocates for adding or revising additional issues. First, in May 2021, driven by the explicit emphasis of the Biden administration on pursuing a "worker-centric" trade policy, the United States submitted a proposal urging WTO Members to address the global problem of the use of forced labor on fishing vessels. The proposal came in too late to be included in the June 30 draft text of the agreement. Second, the US has highlighted the importance of addressing some members' self-identified developing country status and, in particular, China's entitlement to continue to enjoy the SDT granted to developing countries (Wong, 2021). Furthermore, the internal divisions among the developed countries camp have not only made the convergence of existing proposals difficult but have also made it more difficult for them to collectively pressure China and other large developing countries to commit to more "meaningful and impactful" subsidies reduction concessions.

(iii) BRICS in WTO Fisheries Subsidies Negotiations

On July 21, 2021, the Chair of the Negotiation Group on Rules, Ambassador Santiago Wills of Colombia, introduced a revised draft text which recognized that Article 5.5 (SDT) in the overcapacity and overfishing pillar is the "most commonly identified area of concern for many delegations" and reflects fundamental differences in views on the purpose and the applications of SDT (IISD, 2021a). On this most thorny issue in the fisheries subsidies negotiation (Hopewell, 2021), the BRICS countries' positions have subtly evolved. It should be noted that the Chinese central government did not subsidize the fisheries sector until 2006 because China's distance water fisheries were very limited due to the lack of capital and technology to build, manage and operate the large-size fishing fleet. Consequently, during the early stage of the negotiations, China shared similar interests with other large developing countries, especially India, Brazil, Indonesia, and South Africa in defending the preferences enjoyed by developing countries through SDT and in creating a mandate for developed countries to cut subsidies due to their historical responsibilities. In emphasizing the right to development, the need to support subsistence fishing, and the historical impact of developed countries' enduring subsidies on overfishing, they strongly promoted SDT in a way that would leave developing countries with virtually no obligations to cut subsidies other than not subsidizing illegal fishing (Hopewell, 2021). As a marginal player, China chose to present its proposal with other large emerging economies, such as India, Brazil, Mexico, and Indonesia. For instance, in a joint 2008 submission, India, Indonesia, and China advocated for SDT provision expansion to allow developing countries to continue their fisheries subsidies beyond subsistence fishing to address livelihood and employment issues (Submission by India, Indonesia and China, 2008). In another joint submission with Brazil, Mexico, Ecuador, and Venezuela, China insisted on developing countries' right to continue to subsidize fishing activities in the high sea (Communication from Brazil, China, Ecuador, Mexico and Venezuela, 2009).

Since the 2010s, China's fisheries sector has achieved extraordinary expansion in terms of output, size, and level of sophistication. The country has emerged as a fisheries superpower, with the largest capture amount, as well as the largest aquaculture producer and largest exporter (Hu, 2019). However, while some slow changes have been taking place domestically, both in terms of the norms on sustainability, and the policy rationale to better support fishers through less trade-distorting and environmentally detrimental subsidies, China was still not ready to sharply reduce its fisheries subsidies, especially on fuel subsidies of the distant-water fisheries. There are two domestic reasons that have prevented China from adopting needed policy changes. First, China has a growing demand for fish that simply cannot be met by fisheries in its Exclusive Economic Zones (EEZs). Second, high-sea fishing is an integral part of China's maritime Silk Road initiative to expand its commercial footprint beyond the Pacific Ocean.

China's growing prominence as a fisheries producer and subsidizer and its continued reluctance to scale back its subsidies has increasingly set its negotiation preferences apart from those of other large developing countries. Noticeably, many developing countries, including emerging powers like India and Brazil, have begun to realize that keeping China within the coalition no longer provided them with greater leverage and might instead potentially weaken their negotiation position, especially on the issue of SDT. Consequently, the focus of the rest of the BRIC countries has shifted from working together to defend the rights of developing countries to singling out China in order to ensure the SDT enjoyed by themselves. For example, India and Brazil have tacitly distanced themselves from China even though they have tried to maintain solidarity on the surface. They collectively issued a statement after the BRICS summit held in India early in 2021 to vaguely support the conclusion of the fisheries subsidies negotiations before MC12 but did not present any concrete steps to do so (BRICS, 2021).

Furthermore, while the BRICS all seemed to support granting SDT treatment to developing and least-developed countries, they held conflicting views about how to ensure that SDT would be honored. As repeatedly argued by India's Commerce and Industry Minister Piyush Goyal, India's concerns were that irrational subsidies and overfishing by many countries were hurting Indian fishermen and their livelihoods (Financial Express, 2021). To bring the right balance to the draft text, it is therefore essential that big subsidies providers who offer massive state funding for distant-water fishing that lower the cost of fuel and vessel construction – such as Japan, Spain, China, South Korea the US, among others – assume greater responsibility for reducing their subsidies and fishing capacities in accordance with the principles of "polluter pays." India's emphasis on seeking SDT flexibility is driven by the fact that its subsidies to fishers are mostly in the form of support for the motorization of fishing boats, fuel rebates, and infrastructure support, all falling under the targeted subsidies included in the Chair's draft text (Sen, 2018). To circumvent the broad prohibition, India proposed that developing countries with gross annual national incomes below $5,000 should be exempted from the need to take on commitments for fisheries subsidies cuts. India's matrix to define the eligibility criteria has *de facto* excluded China from the rank of developing countries.

India further suggested that nations engaged in fishing in areas beyond their EEZs should end subsidies for 25 years to control overfishing. These subsidies to distant-water fishing fleets have contributed to overfishing according to an open letter to the WTO written by scientists in Marine Science (Bruder, 2021). India also proposed to ensure the transparency of subsidies reporting, which again targeted China due to its history of the lack of transparency and repeated refusals to report fully and accurately its domestic subsidies to the WTO in a timely manner. For example, on domestic support for fisheries during 2015–2017, the type of support that

China submitted to the WTO only concerned transfer payments, while there were indications that the fuel subsidies provided for the world's largest fishing fleet constituted the biggest fisheries subsidies program (Mallory, 2016). On this particular issue of subsidy notification, China lost a dispute brought by the US against China's agricultural subsidies in 2019.

Brazil introduced its revised proposal on October 20, 2020, to reduce and limit WTO members' fisheries subsidies based on the size of its fisheries subsidies. The proposal would increase the amount of a subsidy program shielded from cuts from $15 million to $25 million. Members falling under the smallest subsidies bracket, who can also demonstrate small catch volumes and short fishing distances, would have the possibility to add an additional $5 million, increasing their total cap to $30 million. Similarly, this proposal excluded China from enjoying the SDT given the size of its subsidies and its focus on high-sea fishing. Brazil's proposal stated that big subsidizers who delay their notification would receive a penalty (IISD, 2020). Leivas Leite of the Brazilian mission to the WTO specifically indicated that Brazil is not in favor of "blanket" exemptions for all developing country members, especially because some of the world's largest fishing fleets are from developing countries. "We cannot have overly broad exemptions. We want something that is time-bound, geographically-bound, and needs-based" (WTO Public Forum, 2021).

In contrast to its high-profile role in the e-commerce negotiations, China has been largely quiet in the fisheries subsidies negotiations. During the negotiations spanning 20 years, it has largely held an ambiguous stance. China submitted its first WTO proposal on fisheries subsidies on June 20, 2002 (TN/RL/W/9) and its latest proposal on June 4, 2019 (TN/RL/GEN/199). China supports disciplines that would prohibit fisheries subsidies that contribute to overcapacity and overfishing and eliminate subsidies that contribute to IUU fishing, while "recognizing that appropriate and effective SDT for developing country Members and least developed country Members should be an integral part of the negotiations" (WTO, 2019). Throughout the negotiations, China has persistently called for SDT flexibilities for developing and least-developed countries. In the 2019 proposal, China urged member states to call for a cap-based approach to reduce rather than prohibit subsidies that contribute to overfishing and overcapacity. China sought a limited phase-out of subsidies to IUU fishing, instead of a total phase-out of subsidies.

Overall, it seems that both India and Brazil have developed a strategy to "decouple" away from China to emphasize the need to continue to support low-income fishers' livelihood. Both countries have also made it clear that the best strategy to achieve this goal is to keep a distance from China. With China being the largest subsidizer and the main target of the fisheries subsidies negotiations, it has become unwise for them to continue to build coalitions with China on seeking SDT flexibilities.

Consequently, while many believe that fisheries subsidies negotiations represent a low-hanging fruit for WTO members – as there exists a consensus on the need to take actions to curb fisheries subsidies to liberalize trade, promote development, and protect the ocean – the agreement reached at the MC12 is a 'shallow' agreement that covers only a small subset of the issues negotiated over the past decade. The agreement was reached mainly because the WTO needs an agreement to prove its relevancy. WTO members have agreed to prohibit subsidies for fishing vessels or operators that engage in IUU fishing, as well as prohibit subsidies that support fishing of overfished. Members also agreed to ban subsidies for fishing and fishing-related activities on the high seas (international waters). Though it is an important first step, the agreement lacks the substance needed in order to effectively address the negative social, economic and environmental impacts brought by fisheries subsidies adopted by major fishing countries. Among them, the most important type of subsidies that have been omitted from this agreement include subsidies that support overcapacity and overfishing. Negotiations to expand the agreement to include more comprehensive rules will continue in the coming years.

IV Conclusion

This chapter examines the role of China, along with the rest of the BRICS countries, in the WTO e-commerce and fisheries subsidies negotiations. The analysis suggests that despite China's self-proclaimed developing country status, the fact that it is now one of the most competitive players in global e-commerce and the largest subsidizer in the fisheries sector has made it increasingly difficult for China to continue to align its negotiation position with other BRICS countries. Over time, the dynamics of WTO negotiations have been transformed. The North-South divide under the GATT, which later evolved into a three-tiered structure of developed, emerging powers and the rest of the developing countries during the early years of the Doha negotiations, has given away to a more complex matrix of interest-based and issue-specific coalition building which is no longer bound by the developed/developing division in today's WTO negotiations. Due to its sheer size and unique domestic political and economic system, China has increasingly been singled out in the negotiations due to the difficulties for it to align with either developed or developing countries.

In the e-commerce negotiations, the refusal by India and South Africa to join the talks has constrained the ability of the BRICS to form an effective coalition. While Brazil and Russia were more favorably disposed toward e-commerce negotiations, their specific concerns and approaches were also sufficiently different from those of China which placed greater emphasis on maintaining domestic regulatory sovereignty and control, further limiting the group's ability to act as a coherent bloc to advance the member countries' otherwise shared interests in promoting the development agenda. In the fisheries subsidies negotiation, China's insistence on being treated as a developing country and enjoying SDT despite it is the largest subsidizer has thwarted the willingness of the developed countries to provide flexibilities and policy spaces to developing countries as a whole. As a response, India and Brazil, together with a group of smaller developing countries, have strategically adopted negotiation positions to quietly distance themselves from China.

November 2021 marks the 20th anniversary of the BRIC acronym coined by Jim O'Neill of Goldman Sachs to capture the economic potential of the four emerging economies and the important implications of their rapid economic growth for global governance (O'Neill, 2021). Recently, Goldman Sachs released another report making the recommendation of separating China from the broader Emerging Markets indexes due to China's overweight and what the authors refer to as "idiosyncratic factors" like geopolitics (Lewis, 2021). While this recommendation pertains mostly to portfolio investment, it can inspire us to revisit the role played by China in the Doha negotiations. The two cases presented above clearly suggest that it is outdated and no longer accurately reflects today's reality if we continue to focus on emerging powers as a separate grouping in the multilateral trade negotiations, as we did a decade ago (Liang, 2013; Vickers, 2012). Rather, it might be more illuminating and helpful if we exclude China from the emerging power grouping and make it a separate category.

In recent years, scholars have analyzed the impact of China's WTO participation on the crisis the WTO is facing today (Wu, 2016). Some (e.g., Hopewell, 2019) have also identified the US-China conflict as the key obstacle to forging agreement in the WTO agricultural subsidies negotiations (Hopewell, 2019). Our paper sheds light along the same lines by emphasizing China's isolated position as an emerging trend taking place in the two ongoing negotiations detailed above. Regardless of China's preferences, it is a shared understanding among the rest of the BRICS countries and the larger group of developing countries that it is no longer in their best interests to keep China in their coalition. China indeed might do more harm than good in helping to defend its fundamental interests of securing the

SDT guarantee within the WTO framework. Additionally, it seems that developed and developing countries are reaching a consensus that the size of China's subsidies and other protectionist trade policies will hurt developing countries' interests more than ever. Taken together, these dynamics have contributed to reinforcing concerns that the rise of China may have exacerbated the difficulty of multilateral economic cooperation and deepened the crisis faced by the WTO regime, raising questions about the degree to which the multilateral trading system centered on the WTO can effectively accommodate the rise of a large non-market economy such as China.

References

BRICS (2021). Statement for BRICS Cooperation on the Multilateral Trading System. https://brics2021.gov.in/brics/public/uploads/docpdf/getdocu-43.pdf

Bruder, Madeleine (2021). 'WTO's Fisheries-Subsidies Curbs Need Balance'. World News Era. November 5. https://worldnewsera.com/news/finance/wtos-fisheries-subsidies-curbs-need-balance/

Communication from Brazil, China, Ecuador, Mexico and Venezuela (2009). TN/RL/W/241/Rev.1, October 16. www.google.com/url?sa=i&rct=j&q=&esrc=s&source=web&cd=&cad=rja&uact=8&ved=0CDYQw7AJahcKEwjI79nIjLL-AhUAAAAAHQAAAAAQAg&url=https%3A%2F%2Fdocsonline.wto.org%2Fdol2fe%2FPages%2FSS%2FDirectDoc.aspx%3Ffilename%3Dt%253A%252Ftn%252Frl%252Fw243.doc%26&psig=AOvVaw10n5rSQxZMAg4s2hHAbCM2&ust=1681861512870443

Darsinouei, Amir Ebrahimi (2017). *Understanding E-Commerce Issues in Trade Agreements: A Development Perspective Towards MC11 and Beyond.* Geneva: CUTS International.

Fefer, Rachel (2020). *Internet Regimes and WTO E-Commerce Negotiations.* Washington, DC: Congressional Research Service Report, January 28.

Gao, Henry S. (2020). 'Across the Great Wall: E-Commerce Joint Statement Initiative Negotiation and China'. In Shin-yi Peng, Ching-Fu Lin, and Thomas Streinz (eds.), *Artificial Intelligence and International Economic Law.* New York: Cambridge University Press, pp. 295–318.

Hoekman, Bernard, Will Martin, and Aaditya Matto (2009). Conclude Doha, It Matters! World Bank Policy Research Working Paper 5135.

Hopewell, Kristen (2019). 'US-China Conflict in Global Trade Governance: The New Politics of Agricultural Subsidies at the WTO'. *Review of International Political Economy* 26 (2), 207–31.

Hopewell, Kristen (2021). *Clash of Power: US-China Rivalry in Global Trade Governance.* New York: Cambridge University Press.

Hu, Weinian (2019). China as a WTO Developing Member, Is It a Problem? CEPS Insights Report, No 2019/16, November. www.ceps.eu/wp-content/uploads/2019/11/PI2019_16_WH_China-as-a-WTO-developing-member.pdf

Hufbauer, Gary Clyde, and Zhiyao (Lucy) Lu (2019). *Global E-Commerce Talks Stumble on Data Issues, Privacy, and More.* Policy Brief 19-14. Washington, DC: Peterson Institute for International Economics.

International Centre for Trade and Sustainable Development (2018). 'WTO Members Submit Proposals Aimed at Advancing Exploratory E-Commerce Work'. *Bridges* 22 (13). www.tralac.org/news/article/12964-wto-members-submit-proposals-aimed-at-advancing-exploratory-e-commerce-work.html

IISD (2020). WTO Negotiating Group Hears Brazil's Proposal on Fisheries Subsidies. November 4. https://sdg.iisd.org/news/wto-negotiating-group-hears-brazils-proposal-on-fisheries-subsidies/

IISD (2021a). Fisheries Talks Chair Presents Revised Text Ahead of July Ministerial. July 8. https://sdg.iisd.org/news/fisheries-talks-chair-presents-revised-text-ahead-of-july-ministerial/

"India Not Participating in Plurilateral Discussions on E-Commerce at WTO." (2021) *Economic Times*, March 19.

"India, SA Ask WTO to Review Moratorium on E-Commerce Customs Duties." (2019) *Business Standards*, June 4.

Ismail, Yasmin (2020). *E-Commerce in the World Trade Organization: History and Latest Developments in the Negotiations under the Joint Statement.* Geneva: International Institute for Sustainable Development and CUTS International.

Jones, Vivian C. (2010). *Trade Remedy and WTO Rules Negotiation.* Congressional Research Service. June 7. https://nationalaglawcenter.org/wp-content/uploads/assets/crs/R40606.pdf

Kanth, Ravi (2017). South Countries Shoot Down Proposals for E-Commerce. Third World Network Info Service on WTO and Trade Issues (Oct. 17/15), October 2019. www.twn.my/title2/wto.info/2017/ti171015.htm. Accessed on October 2, 2019.

Kilic, Burcu (2021). *Digital Trade Rules: Big Tech's End Run Around Domestic Regulations.* Brussels, Belgium: Heinrich-Böll-Stiftung European Union, May 19.

Lemma, Alberto (2017). E-Commerce: The Implications of Current WTO Negotiations for Economic Transformation for Developing Countries. Supporting Economic Transformation, Overseas Development Institute. https://set.odi.org/wp-content/uploads/2017/12/SET-WTO-Negotiations-E-Commerce.pdf

Lewis, Leo (2021). 'The Case for Splitting China Out of the EM Index Preponderance of Chinese Stocks Deprives Investors of Broader Exposure'. *Financial Times.* October 30. www.google.com/url?sa=i&rct=j&q=&esrc=s&source=web&cd=&cad=rja&uact=8&ved=0CDYQw7AJahcKEwigkavFk7L-AhUAAAAAHQAAAAAQAg&url=https%3A%2F%2Fwww.ft.com%2Fcontent%2Faa4c31be-4615-4219-afec-75bab99e29e2&psig=AOvVaw2eML_O96BRrWBVd5mkYsfL&ust=1681863397218237

Liang, Wei (2013). 'China, Developing Countries, and the Doha Agricultural Negotiations'. In Ka Zeng and Wei Liang (eds.), *China and Global Trade Governance.* London: Routledge, pp. 211–32.

Macleod, Jamie (2017). E-Commerce and the WTO: A Developmental Agenda? Global Economic Governance (GEG) Africa Discussion Paper, December.

Mallory, T. G. (2016). 'Fisheries Subsidies in China: Quantitative and Qualitative Assessment of Policy Coherence and Effectiveness'. *Marine Policy* 68 (5800), 74–82.

Okonjo-Iweala, N. (2021). Negotiating Group on Rules – Fisheries Subsidies: Plenary Meeting at the Level of Heads of Delegation, April 12. www.wto.org/english/news_e/spno_e/spno6_e.htm

O'Neill, Jim (2021). BRIC at Twenty. Project Syndicate. January 13. www.google.com/url?sa=i&rct=j&q=&esrc=s&source=web&cd=&cad=rja&uact=8&ved=0CDYQw7AJahcKEwjYpL33k7L-AhUAAAAAHQAAAAAQAg&url=https%3A%2F%2Fwww.project-syndicate.org%2Fcommentary%2Fbrics-first-two-decades-and-today-by-jim-o-neill-2021-01&psig=AOvVaw3cv0rt0MU_WGttEILCXlBa&ust=1681863501711604

Schrank, William E. (2003). Introducing Fisheries Subsidies 437. FAO Fisheries, Technical Paper No. 437.

Schuhbauer, Anna, Ratana Chuenpagdee, William W. L. Cheung, Krista Greer, and U. Rashid Sumaila (2020). How Subsidies Affect the Economic Viability of Small-Scale Fisheries *Marine Policy* 82, 114–121.

Sen, Amiti (2018). WTO: India, China Call for Flexibility in Proposed Pact on Fisheries Subsidies, The Hindu BusinessLine, September 19. www.thehindubusinessline.com/economy/india-makes-strong-case-at-wto-for-continuing-fisheries-subsidies/article28596286.ece

Stewart, Terence P. (2021). Will India and South Africa (and Others) Prevent Future Relevance of the WTO? Current Thoughts on Trade, February 20.

Submission by India, Indonesia and China. TN/RL/GEN/155/Rev.1, May 19, 2018. https://docs.wto.org/dol2fe/Pages/FE_Search/FE_S_S009-DP.aspx?language=E&CatalogueIdList=81869,87711,88342,87457,92202,85265,91350,85257,82506,84232&CurrentCatalogueIdIndex=6&FullTextHash=&HasEnglishRecord=True&HasFrenchRecord=True&HasSpanishRecord=True

Thorstensen Vera, Fernanda Mascarenhas, and Giulia de Paola (2019). E-Commerce in Brazil: Where We Are in Terms of Regulatory Practices. CCGI – No 15, Working Paper Series. https://bibliotecadigital.fgv.br/dspace/bitstream/handle/10438/28007/TD%20510%20-%20CCGI_15.pdf?sequence=1&isAllowed=y

Umaila, U. Rashid, et al. (2019). 'Updated Estimates and Analysis of Global Fisheries Subsidies'. *Marine Policy* 109 (2019), 103695.

UN (2015). *Transforming Our World: The 2030 Agenda for Sustainable Development*. New York: United Nations.

United Nations Conference on Trade and Investment (UNCTAD) (2020). What Is at Stake for Developing Countries in Trade Negotiations on E-Commerce? The Case of the Joint Statement Initiative. United Nations: UNCTAD/DITC/TNCD/2020/5. https://unctad.org/publication/what-stake-developing-countries-trade-negotiations-e-commerce

U.S. Mission Geneva (2019). U.S. Statement at the Meeting of the WTO Joint Statement Initiative on E-Commerce. March 6, https://geneva.usmission.gov/2019/03/06/u-s-statement-at-the-meeting-of-the-wto-joint-statement-initiative-on-e-commerce/

Vickers, Brendan (2012). 'The Role of the BRICS in the WTO: System-Supporters or Change Agents in Multilateral Trade'? In Amrita Narlikar, Martin Daunton, and Robert M. Stern (eds.), *The Oxford Handbook on The World Trade Organization*. New York: Oxford University Press, pp. 254–74.

Wang, Xiaodong, and Ka Zeng (2013). 'China and the Doha Round Nonagricultural Market Access (NAMA) Negotiations'. In Ka Zeng and Wei Liang (eds.), *China and Global Trade Governance*. London: Routledge, pp. 189–210.
Wong, Liana (2021). WTO Fisheries Subsidies Negotiations. Congressional Research Service. In Focus, September 16.
WTO (2002a). World Trade Organization, Negotiating Group on Rules, The Doha Mandate to Address Fisheries Subsidies, TN/RL/W/3, April 24, 2002.
WTO (2002b). Negotiating Group on Rules, Japan's Basic Position on the Fisheries Subsidies Issue, July2, TN/RL/W/11.
WTO (2004). Negotiating Group on Rules, UNEP Workshop on Fisheries Subsidies and Sustainable Fisheries Management: Summary of the Chairs, See TN/RL/W/161, Geneva, April 26.
WTO (2011). Communication from the Chairman. TN/R/W/254, April 21.
WTO (2016). Work Programme on Electronic Commerce: Electronic Signatures, Communication from Argentina, Brazil and Paraguay, December 21.
WTO (2017a). E-Commerce Elements for MC 11: Communication from China. JOB/GC/142, October 19.
WTO (2017b). Joint Statement on Electronic Commerce. WT/MIN(17)/59.
WTO (2017c). MC 11 Press Briefing, December 12.
WTO (2017d). Work Programme on E-Commerce: Communication from the Russian Federation, October 5.
WTO (2017e). Electronic Commerce and Copyright: Revision. March 7.
WTO (2018). Exploratory Work on Electronic Commerce: Non-paper from Brazil.
WTO (2019a). Joint Statement on Electronic Commerce, WT/L/1056, January 25.
WTO (2019b). Joint Statement on Electronic Commerce: Communication from China. Geneva, WTO: INF/ECOM/19, April 24.
WTO (2020a). Joint Statement Initiative on E-commerce: Co-conveners' Update, www.wto.org/english/news_e/news20_e/ecom_14dec20_e.pdf.
WTO (2020b). Work Programme on Electronic Commerce: Reinvigorating the Work under the 1998 Work Programme on Electronic Commerce: Communication from South Africa and India (WT/GC/W/812).
WTO (2020c). Broadening and Deepening the Discussions on the Moratorium on Imposing Customs Duties on Electronic Transmissions (WT/GC/W/799/Rev.1, 29), June.
WTO (2021a). The Legal Status of 'Joint Statement Initiatives' and Their Negotiated Outcomes.
WTO (2021b) General Council, March 1–2, WT/GC/W/819.
WTO (2021c). Chair Introduces Revised Fishing Subsidies Text to Facilitate 15 July Ministerial Meeting. www.wto.org/english/news_e/news21_e/fish_30jun21_e.htm
WTO Public Forum (2021). A WTO Fisheries Subsidies Deal: What It Means and Why It Matters. Session 35. September 29. www.wto.org/english/forums_e/public_forum21_e/pf21_programme_e.htm
"WTO's Fisheries-Subsidies Curbs Need Balance" (2021). The Financial Express, November 5.
Wu, Mark (2016). 'The "China, Inc." Challenge to Global Trade Governance'. *Harvard International Law Journal* 57 (2), 261–324.

11

The Impact of the WTO Dispute Settlement System on China

Effectiveness, Challenges and Broader Issues

WEIHUAN ZHOU

I Introduction

Since China joined the World Trade Organization (WTO) in 2001, its role in the WTO's dispute settlement system (DSS) has developed significantly over the past twenty years. As widely observed, this period has witnessed China becoming an increasingly experienced and influential player, that is from a 'rule taker' (2001–2005) to a 'rule shaker' (2006–2009) and then a 'rule maker' since 2010 (Gao, 2011; Mercurio and Tyagi, 2012; Toohey, 2011). This observation is supported not only by China's active engagement in pushing for the appointment of new Appellate Body (AB) members so as to restore a functional DSS and its agreement to and use of the Multi-Party Interim Appeal Arbitration Arrangement (MPIA) to maintain a temporary appellate review mechanism. This observation is also supported by the number of disputes in which China has been involved. By 1 October 2021, China had been a complainant in 22 cases, a respondent in 47 cases and a third party in 190 cases, making it one of the most active players in the DSS: see Figure 11.1. While many factors may be employed to explain China's behaviour and evolving practices (Ji and Huang, 2010; Wang and Zhou, 2022), a major one has to do with its growing capacity and expertise in WTO law and dispute settlement (Shaffer and Gao, 2018).

This chapter is not intended to examine all the disputes in which China has participated. Instead, it focuses on select disputes involving China as a respondent, with an aim to critically analyse the impact of the DSS on China's economic reforms and policymaking. This analysis necessarily involves a consideration of the overall pattern of development in China's strategies and behaviours in these disputes and more specifically, the factors behind China's approaches to implementing unfavourable WTO

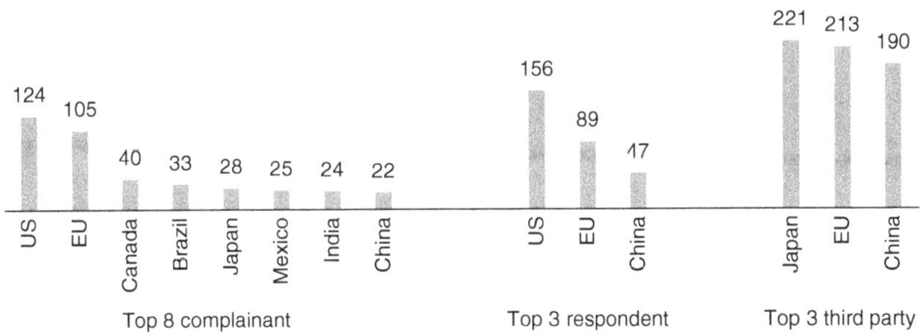

Figure 11.1 Top users of the WTO dispute settlement system

rulings. Section II discusses the effectiveness of the DSS, arguing that the system has been largely effective in leading not only to changes to a range of WTO-illegal policy instruments but also gradual and systematic adjustments of certain complex regulatory regimes in China. Despite China's impressive record of implementing WTO rulings, its approaches have revealed three challenges for the DSS in relation to temporary breaches, repetitive breaches and post-compliance regulatory developments, which are discussed in Section III. These challenges, however, concern systemic constraints or loopholes in the system which can be utilised by all WTO Members. Section IV extends beyond the DSS to consider the broader issues relating to overwhelming criticisms about China's failure to adhere to the spirit of WTO law and the WTO's failure to push China to change its state-led economic model and transition to a full-fledged market economy. Section V sets forth some concluding remarks.

II Effectiveness

The efficacy of WTO rules would be significantly weakened without an effective mechanism that enforces the rules. The DSS, in serving this key function, has long been praised as 'the jewel in the crown' of the multilateral trading system. Since commencing its operation in 1995, the DSS has managed over 600 disputes, which demonstrates WTO Members' continued belief in the utility of the system. Despite the United States (US)'s criticisms of the AB, it sees the value of the DSS in resolving trade disputes (USTR, 2021) and continues to resort to the system for that purpose.

When it comes to the implementation of WTO rulings, there is evidence to show that the DSS is largely effective in inducing compliance in most cases (Davey, 2014; WTO, 2017a). Yet, the impact of the system on China remains controversial. The US, under the Trump administration, vehemently criticised the WTO for being 'incapable of fundamentally changing [China's] trade regime that broadly conflicts with the fundamental underpinnings of the WTO system' (USTR, 2020a, p. 14). This perception of the WTO's ineffectiveness was a key driver of the US's recourse to unilateral actions that provoked the US-China trade war. The Biden administration has maintained this position. In a recent speech, United States Trade Representative (USTR) Katherine Tai criticised 'China's lack of adherence to global trading rules' and failure to make 'meaningful reforms to address the concerns' about 'its state-centered economic system', and reiterated the need for the US to use all tools at its disposal including by creating new ones 'to defend American economic interests from harmful policies and practices' (CSIS, 2021). These concerns are shared by other major WTO Members particularly the European Union (EU) (European Commission, 2021).

There is little doubt that the current WTO rules and the DSS have their limits, some of which will be considered in Section III. However, these limits have largely resulted from the way in which the rules and the DSS are designed by WTO Members and hence can only be addressed through their collective efforts via negotiations. In other words, many perceived problems in the multilateral trading system that may have caused its lack of effectiveness are not specific to China. Thus, an assessment of the effect of the DSS on China must be undertaken objectively in light of these systemic constraints or loopholes that can be utilised by all Members.

Against this backdrop, I briefly discuss China's compliance with adverse WTO rulings and the impact of the DSS on China's economic reform and policymaking. As noted above, China has been a respondent in 47 disputes involving a total of 34 matters. Among the 34 cases, 27 have been completed either through a mutually agreed solution (15 cases) or China's implementation of WTO rulings (12 cases). As regards the other seven cases, six remain in the litigation process and one has lapsed as the panel's work was suspended for more than 12 months under Article 12.12 of the *Understanding on Rules and Procedures Governing the Settlement of Disputes* (WTO, 2018a). One may also divide these disputes into non-trade-remedy cases and trade remedy cases. The latter can be brought by the countries subject to antidumping (AD) and/or countervailing duties (CVD) only. Among the 27 completed cases, the US was the sole or joint complainant in 16 out of the 20 non-trade-remedy cases. Table 11.1 provides a summary of the completed cases, the major measures and

Table 11.1 *Completed WTO disputes involving China as a respondent 2001–2021*[1]

Short title (DS No.)	Complainant(s)	Measures (industries/goods/ entities)	Status of compliance
Settled disputes (15 cases)			
1. *China – VAT on Integrated Circuits* (DS309)	US	Discriminatory value-added tax (VAT) rebates (integrated circuits producers and design services providers)	Implemented by abolishing the VAT rebates
2. *China – Taxes* (DS358, 359)	US, Mexico	Tax preferences (foreign-invested enterprises)	Implemented by abolishing the tax preferences
3. *China – Financial Information Services* (DS372, 373, 378)	US, EC, Canada	Market access restriction and discrimination (financial information services providers)	Implemented by removing the restriction and discrimination
4. *China – Grants, Loans and Other Incentives* (DS387, 388, 390)	US, Mexico, Guatemala	Export subsidies (all kinds of Chinese merchandise recognised as 'famous brands')	Implemented by abolishing the subsidies and export performance requirements
5. *China – Fasteners* (DS407)	EU	AD (fasteners)	Implemented by re-investigation. Dec 2009 – ongoing (2nd sunset review commenced in Jun 2021)
6. *China – Wind Power Equipment* (DS419)	US	Subsidies based on local content requirements (wind power equipment)	Implemented by removing the subsidies

Table 11.1 (*cont.*)

Short title (DS No.)	Complainant(s)	Measures (industries/goods/ entities)	Status of compliance
7. *China – Autos and Auto Parts* (DS450)	US	Export subsidies (auto and auto parts)	Settled as part of DS489
8. *China – Apparel and Textile Products* (DS451)	Mexico	Subsidies (apparel and textile, cotton and chemical fibres)	Diplomatic solution, without detailed information on the revision of relevant policies
9. *China – Demonstration* Bases (DS489)	US	Export subsidies (7 industries and many sub-sectors)	Implemented by abolishing the subsidies and export performance requirements
10. *China – Aircraft* (DS501)	US	Discriminatory VAT exemptions (aircraft)	Implemented by terminating the VAT exemptions
11. *China – Raw Materials II* (US) (DS508)	US	Export duties (raw materials)	Implemented by removing the duties
12. *China – Raw Materials II* (EU) (DS509)	EU	Export duties and restraints (raw materials)	Implemented by removing the duties and restraints
13. *China – Intellectual Property Rights II* (DS542)	US	IPR protection and technology transfer	Implemented by revising the relevant law and regulations as well as agreeing to detailed obligations under the US–China Phase One Deal

Table 11.1 (*cont.*)

Short title (DS No.)	Complainant(s)	Measures (industries/goods/ entities)	Status of compliance
14. *China – Transfer of Technology* (DS549)	EU	IPR protection and technology transfer	Implemented by revising the relevant law and regulations as well as agreeing to detailed obligations under the EU–China Comprehensive Agreement on Investment
15. *China – Imports of Sugar* (DS568)	Brazil	Safeguard measure on sugar	Diplomatic solution, without detailed information about the revision of relevant measures
Litigated disputes (12 cases)			
16. *China – Auto Parts* (DS339, 340, 342)	EC, US, Canada	Discriminatory internal charges (auto parts)	Implemented by revising the relevant policies and regulations
17. *China – Intellectual Property Rights* (DS362)	US	Inadequate IPR protection (copyright of content goods and trademark regarding confiscated imported goods)	Implemented by revising the relevant law and regulations
18. *China – Publications and Audiovisual Products* (DS363)	US	Trading rights and distribution services (cultural sector)	Partially implemented by revising the relevant regulations except for those relating to films. (Mutually agreed compensation on film)

Table 11.1 (*cont.*)

Short title (DS No.)	Complainant(s)	Measures (industries/goods/ entities)	Status of compliance
19. *China – Raw Materials* (DS394, 395, 398)	EC, US, Mexico	Export duties and restrictions (raw materials)	Implemented by removing WTO-illegal duties and restraints
20. *China – Electronic Payment Services* (DS413)	US	Market access restriction and discrimination (electronic payment services)	Implemented by revising the relevant regulations
21. *China – GOES* (DS414)	US	AD and CVD (grain oriented flat-rolled electrical steel)	Implemented by re-investigation. Apr 2010–Apr 2015
22. *China – X-Ray Equipment* (DS425)	EU	AD (X-Ray Equipment)	Implemented by re-investigation. Jan 2011–Feb 2014
23. *China – Broiler Products* (DS427)	US	AD and CVD (broiler)	Implemented by re-investigation. Aug/Sep 2010 (CVD/ AD) – Feb 2018
24. *China – Rare Earths* (DS431, 432, 433)	US, EU, Japan	Export duties and restrictions (rare earths)	Implemented by removing WTO-illegal duties and restraints
25. *China – Autos (US)* (DS440)	US	AD and CVD (autos)	Implemented by terminating the duties. Dec 2011–Dec 2013
26. *China – HP-SSST* (DS454, 460)	Japan, EU	AD (high-performance stainless steel seamless tubes)	Implemented by re-investigation
27. *China – Cellulose Pulp* (DS483)	Canada	AD (cellulose pulp)	Implemented by re-investigation

[1] This table is based on Wang, Chenxi and Weihuan Zhou, (2022) 'A Political Anatomy of China's Compliance in WTO Disputes', *Journal of Contemporary China* 1, 3–4 (online).

goods/industries involved, and the status of compliance. For trade remedy cases (highlighted in grey), it further shows the period between the imposition and the termination of the duties.

This section considers the non-trade-remedy cases while the trade remedy cases will be examined in Section III as they create some unique challenges for enforcement. As discussed in detail elsewhere, in all the completed non-trade-remedy cases China maintained an impressive record of compliance, more favourable than those of the other key players in the system (Zhou, 2019). This record is strong evidence of the effective influence of the DSS on China, which has caused not only changes to specific policy instruments but also systematic adjustments of China's complex regulatory regime in an incremental manner. More specifically, these disputes pushed China to repeal or modify laws, regulations and other policy instruments which led to the application of:

(1) **discriminatory internal taxes** including VAT rebates in the integrated circuits (IC) industry (WTO, 2005), VAT exemptions in the aircraft industry (Zhou, 2019, p. 35) and internal charges in the auto parts sector (WTO, 2009, p. 21);
(2) **subsidies** in a variety of forms at both national and local levels which were primarily aimed at fostering China's industrial policies in select sectors such as wind towers (USTR, 2012, p. 51), auto and auto parts, textiles, agriculture, medical products, light industry, special chemical engineering, new materials, and hardware and building materials (USTR, 2015, 2016; WTO, 2016a) or more broadly at promoting exports of famous brands of Chinese merchandise in all sectors (USTR, 2009) or attracting foreign investment (WTO, 2008a);
(3) **export duties and restrictions** on a range of raw materials and rare earths (WTO, 2013a 2015, p. 18);
(4) **restrictions on the right to import** reading materials, audio-visual products, sound recordings and films for theatrical release in the cultural industries and **restrictions on the supply of distribution services**, that is the right of foreign-invested enterprises to engage in the wholesaling and retailing, of these cultural goods (WTO, 2012a);
(5) **certain restrictions on market access for and discriminatory requirements on foreign services suppliers** in the financial information services sector (WTO, 2008b) and the electronic payment services sector (WTO, 2013b); and
(6) **inadequate protection of intellectual property rights (IPRs)** including copyright and related rights for goods containing prohibited

content and trademarks in relation to goods confiscated by Chinese customs due to IPR infringements (WTO, 2010).

It is true that China's compliance in these disputes was confined to strictly addressing the findings of inconsistencies by WTO tribunals. Nevertheless, this issue concerns the limitation of WTO rulings in general that has been used by other Members. China's approaches to implementation have shown its growing sophistication in the DSS with full comprehension of the limits of WTO rulings and how to implement the rulings in a narrow but adequate fashion.

However, even such 'narrow' implementation has required some significant changes to China's economic policies, showing the broad and systemic impact that the DSS can have on domestic policymaking. The most notable example is the *China – Publications and Audiovisual Products* case, which was also the most difficult to implement due to the sensitivity of the cultural sector in China and the need for coordinated efforts by multiple departments or ministries of the State Council to revise a range of jointly published measures. China abolished or revised all WTO-inconsistent measures (other than two measures applied to films) to lift restrictions on the right to import the cultural goods involved. This was a significant step toward the dismantling of China's state monopoly of trading rights in the cultural sector which was long regarded by the Chinese government as being essential for maintaining a rigorous censorship system to safeguard fundamental social values and political interests (Shi and Chen, 2011). While China was not required to reduce the rigour of its censorship, the WTO rulings effectively pushed China to disentangle trading rights from censorship so that all entities are entitled to engage in the importation of the relevant goods. Although China failed to liberalise the right to import films apparently due to the resistance of the state entities involved (Zhang and Li, 2014, p. 159), it entered into a memorandum of understanding with the US granting more market access to US films, a step toward further liberalisation of the market (WTO, 2012b). Notably, this was China's only major failure of compliance in all the completed disputes.

Another example concerns China's application of export duties and restrictions on raw materials and rare earths. While these measures were initially imposed to drive up world prices of these goods and hence increase China's earnings from export sales (Lardy, 2002, p. 47), at the time of the dispute they had become part of China's policy prescriptions to safeguard the security of exhaustible natural resources and sustainable development

(Information Office of the State Council, 2012). Thus, this dispute raised some fundamental and sensitive issues relating to states' economic sovereignty over natural resources and prerogative rights to prevent the depletion of these resources and protect the environment. Moreover, while export duties are generally allowed under the WTO and are widely used by Members for various regulatory goals, China is obliged to eliminate all such taxes and charges (subject to limited exceptions) under Section 11.3 of the *Protocol on the Accession of China* (Accession Protocol). Moreover, China has no recourse to the general exceptions to WTO rules (such as protection of exhaustible natural resources and the environment) to justify a deviation from this obligation, as the AB held in the two relevant disputes. Despite the strategic importance of China's regulatory goals and the (unreasonable) rigidity of the WTO rulings, China removed all the WTO-illegal measures.

The final example concerns the disputes in which China took a tremendous effort to eliminate a wide range of subsidies applied across many industries at both national and local levels, as noted above. China's implementation speaks against the widespread concerns about the potential difficulties of challenging Chinese subsidies due to a lack of transparency. On the contrary, most Chinese industrial subsidies take the typical forms contemplated in the WTO *Agreement on Subsidies and Countervailing Measures* (ASCM), and it is possible for WTO Members to use the existing rules and the DSS to push China to remove or reduce these subsidies that harm their interests (Zhou and Fang, 2021). In addition, one must consider the numerous AD and CVD actions against Chinese exports, which are frequently used to address the Chinese government's intervention in the market including through subsidies (Nedumpara and Zhou, 2018). Here, while there is a longstanding and ongoing debate about the AB's 'authority-based' test for determining whether a granting entity constitutes a 'public body', this test did not prevent investigating authorities from finding Chinese state banks, state-owned enterprises (SOEs) and state-invested enterprises (SIEs) as public bodies (Appellate Body Report, 2011, 2019). In addition, China's WTO-plus obligations under Section 15(b) of the Accession Protocol provide wide latitude for authorities to apply countervailing measures to address the negative effects of Chinese subsidies (Zhou and Fang, 2021).

The above analysis is not to suggest that China's decisions to settle some of the disputes or implement unfavourable WTO rulings were detrimental to its own interest. In all the disputes, China's strategy was driven by a mix of factors including consideration of reputational cost and legal capacity and resources *vis-à-vis* the feasibility and complexity of litigation and compliance (Ji and Huang, 2010; Yang, 2015). More importantly, it also involved careful assessments of the economic and political impact of implementation, particularly whether the termination of the contested measures served China's economic and strategic goals. For instance, the removal of the discriminatory VAT rebates in the IC industry, the subsidies to manufacturers of wind power equipment and the discriminatory internal charges in the auto parts sector was consistent with China's reform strategies and industrial policies and had insignificant impacts on the domestic industries involved (ICTSD, 2011; Ngangjoh-Hodu and Zhang, 2016; Zhou, 2019, pp. 49–50). The liberalisation of trading rights and distribution services in the cultural sector was consistent with China's progressive liberalisation of the sector and its effort to liberalise trading rights more generally and did not undermine its censorship regime. The elimination of the export taxes and restrictions on raw materials and rare earths was aligned with China's industry reform strategies (Wang, 2018) and did not prevent China from pursuing conservation and environmental goals. Accordingly, one may argue that at the core of China's approaches to WTO compliance has been the use of the DSS as an external lever to facilitate domestic economic reforms while at the same time, limiting the impacts of the WTO rulings on its pursuit of chosen policy objectives. This approach will remain essential for discussions of China's engagement in the DSS including responses to adverse rulings in future disputes.

III Challenges

Despite China's record of implementing WTO rulings, its approaches and subsequent regulatory activities have revealed some systemic issues in the DSS. Below, I consider three major challenges and explain why they are not China-specific: (1) temporary breaches, (2) repetitive breaches and (3) post-compliance developments. The issue of temporary breaches is mainly associated with the lengthy process of WTO litigation, which provides room for a defaulting Member to use the process to buy time for WTO-illegal measures. The lack of retrospective remedies under the DSS further incentivises such practices (Wu, 2017). The other two issues are an extension of temporary breaches also based on the abuse of the dispute settlement process. However, they involve some additional features. Repetitive breaches involve the application of the same policy instruments or practices which were found to be WTO-inconsistent in past disputes. Repetitive breaches are possible because WTO rulings in a dispute are generally constrained by the facts, claims and evidence in that particular case and are 'not binding precedents for other disputes between the same parties on other matters or different parties on the same matter, even though the same questions of WTO law might arise' (WTO, 2003). The issue of post-compliance developments concerns the introduction of new measures in similar or different forms as those adjudicated in past disputes for existing or new policy objectives. This issue not only shows the limitation of the DSS in general but also raises the question of how WTO Members balance the pursuit of domestic policy objectives with the observance of WTO rules more broadly.

All the litigated non-trade-remedy disputes, displayed in Table 11.1, took three or more years between the commencement of consultations and implementation. The *China – Publications and Audiovisual Products* case took five years due to the sensitivity and complexity of compliance as discussed above. Given the clear breach of China's WTO accession commitments, one may argue that China deliberately chose to maintain the restrictions on trading rights in the cultural sector and used the dispute settlement process to buy time for its sectoral reforms.

Another example is the *China – Auto Parts* case which took around 3.5 years. This period of temporary breach provided extra time for China's auto parts industry to further restructure and grow under the protection of discriminatory internal charges. When China terminated the measures, its auto industry had already become the world's second-largest in terms of production volume (Tang, 2009). This case can also be used to illustrate the issue of post-compliance developments. In light of its upgraded industrial policies for technological advancement and global competitiveness, China has resorted to other measures to advance the auto industry, with the new energy vehicles (NEVs) sector being the most notable example. To promote innovation and the production capability of NEVs, China has been providing massive subsidies and other supportive measures at both national and local levels (Fang and Zhou, 2022). While the DSS was effective in pushing China to remove a wide range of subsidies including in the auto industry (see Section II), China's compliance in a specific dispute does not preclude it from introducing similar measures afterwards. Given China's approaches to compliance, it is likely to continue to prioritise domestic policy objectives over the observance of WTO rules, and when necessary, pursue the objectives through WTO-incompatible means.

The *China – Raw Materials* and *China – Rare Earths* disputes offer an illustration of repetitive breaches. In both disputes, what China was required to change or remove were temporary instruments, that is export tariffs and quotas, which are typically updated and issued on an annual basis. The involvement of such temporary measures not only made it easy for China to implement but also provided room for China to reintroduce these measures. In 2016, merely one year after China's implementation, the US and the EU challenged the same measures at the WTO as China maintained export restrictions on a range of raw materials that were not covered in the previous disputes. Although China quickly removed these measures (USTR, 2017, p. 31, 2018a, p. 35), it would be possible for a Member to use the proceedings to prolong the life of WTO-unlawful measures in such circumstances. The high similarity of the past and new measures and the products involved not only makes repetitive breaches more problematic than post-compliance developments but also raises the question of how the DSS may be reformed to simplify the adjudication process and facilitate a quicker resolution of disputes of this kind.

The above challenges are not China-specific and apply to all WTO Members. There are many examples. A well-known one is the US's practice of 'zeroing' in AD actions despite a series of WTO rulings against it (Prusa and Rubini, 2013). Another is the protracted WTO proceedings concerning the US's and the EU's subsidisation of their own national champions in the aviation sector (Crivelli and Rubini, 2020; Reuters, 2020). More generally, the facts that the US and the EU are the top two respondents in the DSS as well as the largest targets in compliance proceedings and retaliation requests (Reich, 2017) suggest that these more sophisticated players have used the systemic constraints and loopholes in the DSS even more frequently. As Krikorian has observed:

> the US government has acted in its own self-interest and thwarted the potential impact of the dispute settlement mechanism either by effectively ignoring its decisions or by implementing them in such a way as to minimise their overall effect. (Krikorian, 2012, p. 81)

Thus, China's approaches to WTO compliance demonstrate that it has merely become a similarly sophisticated player.

As flagged above, trade remedy cases have presented some distinctive features and challenges. China's approach to compliance has routinely involved the initiation of a re-investigation, an approach adopted in the *Interim Rules on the Implementation of the Rulings of the World Trade Organization on Trade Remedy Disputes* published by China's Ministry of Commerce (MOFCOM) in 2013. Since the MOFCOM's decisions to modify or terminate an existing measure rely on re-investigations, such an investigation does not cause a suspension of the measure and may result in a decision to maintain it. Where a re-investigation leads to the continuation of an existing measure (at the original or a modified rate), compliance would only be achieved if the re-investigation had sufficiently addressed the substantive and/or procedural deficiencies in the original investigation. Given the technicality and complexity of these issues, it would be considerably more difficult to ascertain the adequacy of compliance in trade remedy cases than in non-trade-remedy cases without resorting to compliance proceedings. Thus, re-investigation may well be (ab)used to trigger compliance proceedings and hence prolong the life of AD/CVD measures. As shown in Table 11.1, most of the trade remedy disputes have seen Chinese AD/CVD duties staying in place for years close to or until the time for sunset reviews, with a few even extended for extra time after such a review. Such practices not only offer a perfect illustration of temporary breaches but also raises the issue of repetitive breaches given the similarities of the substantive and procedural issues in MOFCOM's investigations that were challenged in these disputes (Zhou, 2019, pp. 158–78). As a WTO decision is binding on the parties to that specific dispute only, it does not prevent the MOFCOM from repeating the same or similar practices in subsequent investigations. Again, such temporary and repetitive breaches are not specific to China. Since 1995, a majority of WTO disputes have focused on trade remedies (WTO, 2017b). Yet, the effect of the DSS on inducing compliance in trade remedy disputes has been rather limited. The core cause of the limitation is that WTO's findings of violations often concern the application of domestic trade remedy legislation in individual investigations (i.e., an 'as applied' breach) rather than the legislation *per se* (i.e., an 'as such' breach). Piecemeal attacks tend to be ineffective at ensuring meaningful compliance or systemic changes in a Member's regulatory regime and practices (Mitchell and Prusa, 2016). Given the rampant (ab) use of trade remedies particularly AD worldwide, it is unlikely that China will retreat from its current practices. In recent years, we have seen China's AD actions continuing to flourish and MOFCOM's growing sophistication in reproducing the practices of the US, the EU and Australia to retaliate against their treatment of China as a non-market economy (NME) in AD actions (Zhou and Qu, 2022).

IV Broader Issues

Beyond the specific challenges for the DSS, the broader question is whether China has fulfilled its WTO obligations. As noted in Section

II, the overwhelming criticism has focused on China's failure to adhere to the spirit of the world trade rules and the ineffectiveness of the WTO to compel China to change its state-led economic model and become a full-fledged market economy. In the WTO's latest Trade Policy Review of China in October 2021, the US, the EU, the United Kingdom and Australia reiterated these fundamental concerns (Lester, 2021). In contrast, China stated that it is committed to 'developing new systems for an open economy', to 'creating a market-oriented, law-based, and internationalized business environment'and to 'comprehensively deepening reform, fully leverag[ing] the decisive role of the market in allocating resources and giv[ing] better play to the role of government to ensure better alignment between an efficient market and a well-functioning government'. Its goal is to carry on the over four decades of economic reform and opening up 'towards fully building a modern socialist country' (WTO, 2021). The interesting questions here are 'do China's WTO commitments require a fundamental change to its economic model and a transition to a Western-type market economy?', and 'if this was indeed the expectation of some WTO Members during China's WTO accession negotiations, did these Members manage to incorporate relevant commitments in China's accession instruments that reflect such expectation?' These questions cannot be fully addressed in this chapter. But some general observations are provided below.

On the one hand, let's consider Section 15(a) of China's Accession Protocol which sets out a special AD rule allowing WTO Members to treat China as an NME in AD investigations. This special rule is subject to an expiry date contemplated in Section 15(d), that is, fifteen years after China's entry into the WTO until 11 December 2016. The US and the EU continued to apply the special rule after the expiry date arguing that Section 15(d) does not terminate their right to use the special rule but merely causes a shift of the burden of proof from China/Chinese producers to investigating authorities. China challenged the practices of the US and the EU in two separate disputes immediately after the expiry date (WTO, 2016b, 2016c). China did not proceed with the case against the US and eventually suspended the case against the EU so that there were no published WTO rulings. Setting aside the highly complex technical issues, the US contended that China was expected to transition to a full market economy or that the special AD rule will continue to apply (USTR, 2017). For China, however, the US's contention 'is beyond the imagination of those ... who actually participated in the negotiations' as there was a clear agreement that the special rule shall exist for fifteen years only (MOFCOM, 2017). My assessment, based on detailed research of the limited negotiating record between the US and China (which was key to China's WTO accession negotiations), is that China regarded the special AD rule as discriminatory and initially rejected it. Due to the US's insistence, the two sides reached a compromise that the special rule must be subject to an expiration timeframe. This eventually led to the inclusion of the sunset clause envisaged in Section 15(d). In other words, the compromise reached was that while China accepted the special rule, the US agreed that it would remain applicable for fifteen years only (Zhou and Peng, 2018). Thus, this compromise was not based on or conditional upon whether China transitions into a full-fledged market economy but was merely intended to enable WTO Members to apply a discriminatory method to facilitate AD actions against China for an agreed period of time.

On the other hand, there are some very broad commitments made by China that may be considered as a promise to transition to a full market economy. Two of the most telling examples are paragraph 46 of the *Report of the Working Party on the Accession of China* and Section 9.1 of the Accession Protocol. While the former provides that all Chinese SOEs and SIEs should 'make purchases and sales based solely on commercial considerations', the latter requires China to 'allow prices for traded goods and services in every sector to be determined by market forces'. One may argue that the expectation of WTO Members that China becomes a full market economy may have been embodied in such broad obligations, although even these obligations do not entail a commitment by China to fundamentally change its economic model. In any event, these obligations provide considerable room for WTO Members to challenge the Chinese government's intervention (including via SOEs) in the market, thereby addressing the associated market distortions or unfair trade practices (Zhou et al., 2019). Since these China-specific rules have never been utilised, what is needed is perhaps not additional disciplines on China but more use of the existing rules. However, if more rules are desirable, then WTO Members will need to ensure these rules incorporate clearer commitments from China that reflect their expectation.

Compared with the controversies above, the lack of transparency in the Chinese economic and political system is almost a consensus among governments and other stakeholders and commentators. This issue has persistently made it difficult for WTO Members to understand and monitor China's trade practices. For example, the WTO Secretariat Report on the latest Trade Policy Review of China noted that the information on China's industrial subsidies remains strikingly inadequate particularly due to the involvement of SOEs even though China claimed to have made a full notification of subsidies in 2019 (WTO, 2021a, p. 16, 2021b, pp. 76–77). The issue of non-transparency has also made it difficult in assessing China's compliance with WTO rulings. For instance, while China formally removed the restrictions on trading rights in the cultural sector, it remains unclear how such rights are granted (or denied) in practice and whether applications for becoming an eligible import entity are assessed objectively based on the statutory criteria rather than by discretion.

The issue of 'forcing technology transfer' offers another good example. Upon WTO accession, China promised that 'approval for importation, the right of importation or investment by national and sub national authorities' will not be conditional upon the transfer of technology under Section 7(3) of the Accession Protocol. Despite this promise, the US and the EU took a series of actions to stop China from practices of 'forcing technology transfer'. They each challenged the relevant laws and practices at the WTO (see Table 11.1), and the US also conducted a meticulous assessment of Chinese practices in its Section 301 investigations (USTR, 2018b). Subsequently, the US-China Phase One Trade deal included more detailed disciplines on this issue (USTR, 2020b), and China introduced a provision in its new Foreign Investment Law 2020 to prohibit 'all administrative organs and their employees … [from] forcing technology transfer through administrative means'. Despite these efforts, it will remain difficult to monitor how these commitments and laws are implemented in practice without enhanced transparency in China's foreign investment review regime (Zhou et al., 2020).

Finally, it is worth pointing out that the combination of state influence in commercial activities and the lack of transparency does pose some systemic and existential challenges for the world trading system. In the recent trade tensions between Australia and China, for instance, China was reported to have restricted the importation of Australian coal through informal instructions of the Chinese government to state-owned importers without a formal measure or decision of the relevant authorities (Tan, 2020). Such practices not only make it hard for WTO Members to challenge Chinese measures but also raise the broader issues of whether China's economic model is compatible with the world trading system and whether the WTO is adequate to cope with China. At the same time, such practices are detrimental to China's own long-term interest as they would only undercut China's credibility in the international community and reinforce the long-standing concerns about its regulatory and political regime.

V Concluding Remarks

China's entry into the WTO is a momentous event in the eight decades of evolution of the multilateral trading system. The impact of the WTO on China is undeniably phenomenal given China's sweeping WTO commitments and unprecedented economic reforms. In its twenty years of WTO membership, China has also maintained an impressive record of compliance with adverse WTO rulings despite the persistent and increasingly acute criticisms about its economic and political model. This record shows that the DSS can have a positive influence on China. While China's compliance has also demonstrated some systemic constraints or loopholes in the system, these are not China-specific and can be utilised by all WTO Members. The absence of a functioning AB, however, has greatly affected the efficacy of the DSS and may cause irreparable damage to the credibility and integrity of the entire multilateral trading system. Following US's and the EU's abuse of their right of appeal to block unfavourable panel rulings in several disputes, China also 'appealed into the void' in one of the latest cases after the panel found in favour of the US's imposition of safeguards measures on certain Chinese crystalline silicon photovoltaic products (WTO, 2021c). If the DSS remains so dysfunctional and other major players continue to abuse the system, then China will be increasingly disincentivised to comply with WTO rulings or to seek to comply with its WTO obligations in domestic policymaking. Over time, countries that are keen to push China to further economic reforms will lose an important policy option (i.e., multilateral disciplines) while other approaches (i.e., unilateral measures) have proven less effective or even counter-productive in dealing with the rising global superpower.

References

Appellate Body Report. (2011). United States – Definitive Anti-Dumping and Countervailing Duties on Certain Products from China, WT/DS379/AB/R (adopted 25 March 2011).

Appellate Body Report. (2019). United States – Countervailing Duty Measures on Certain Products from China – Resources to Article 21.5 of the DSU by China, WT/DS437/AB/RW (adopted 15 August 2019).

Center for Strategic & International Studies (CSIS). (2021). 'A Conversation with Ambassador Katherine Tai, U.S. Trade Representative' (4 October 2021), available at.

Crivelli, Pramila and Rubini, Luca. (2020). '"Flying High in a Plane" appellate body report, European Communities and certain member states – measures affecting trade in large civil aircraft', *World Trade Review* 19(2):316.

Davey, Williams. (2014). 'The WTO and rules-based dispute settlement: historical evolution, operational success, and future challenges'. *Journal of International Economic Law* 17(3):679.

European Commission. (2021). 'Trade Policy review – an open, sustainable and assertive trade policy', COM(2021)66 Final (18 February 2021), available at: https://ec.europa.eu/commission/presscorner/detail/en/qanda_21_645.

Fang, Meng and Zhou, Weihuan. (2022). 'Greening the road: China's low-carbon energy transition and international trade regulation', *Leiden Journal of International Law* 35(2):357.

Gao, Henry (2011). 'China's ascent in global trade governance: From rule taker to rule shaker, and maybe rule maker?' In Carolyn Deere-Birkbeck (ed.), *Making Global Trade Governance Work for Development*. Cambridge: Cambridge University Press, pp. 153–80.

Information Office of the State Council. (2012). 《中国的稀土状况与政策》 [Situations and Policies of China's Rare Earth Industry] (20 June 2012), available at: www.gov.cn/zhengce/2012-06/20/content_2618561.htm.

International Centre for Trade and Sustainable Development (ICTSD). (2011). 'US Proclaims Victory in Wind Power Case; China Ends Challenged Subsidies' (ICTSD, 13 June 2011), available at: https://ictsd.iisd.org/bridges-news/bridges/news/us-proclaims-victory-in-wind-power-case-china-ends-challenged-subsidies.

Ji, Wenhua and Huang, Cui. (2010). 'China's path to the center stage of WTO dispute settlement: challenges and responses', *Global Trade and Customs Journal* 5(9):365.

Ji, Wenhua and Huang, Cui. (2011). 'China's experience in dealing with WTO dispute Settlement: a Chinese perspective', *Journal of World Trade* 45(1):1.

Krikorian, Jacqueline. (2012). *International Trade Law and Domestic Policy*. Vancouver: UBC Press.

Lardy, Nicholas. (2002). *Integrating China into the Global Economy*. Washington DC: The Brookings Institution.

Lester, Simon. (2021). 'Statements by Governments at China's WTO Trade Policy Review', *China Trade Monitor* (21 October 2021), available at: www.chinatrademonitor.com/statements-by-governments-at-chinas-wto-trade-policy-review/.

Mercurio, Bryan and Tyagi, Mitali. (2012). 'China's evolving role in WTO dispute settlement: acceptance, consolidation and activation'. In C Herrmann & J P Terhechte (eds.), *European Yearbook of International Economic Law*, vol. 3. Berlin: Springer, pp. 89–123.

Ministry of Commerce of China (MOFCOM). (2017). *European Union – Measures Related to Price Comparison Methodologies* (DS516), Opening Statement by Ambassador Zhang Xiangchen as a part of the Oral Statement of China at the First Substantive Meeting of the Panel in the Dispute (6 December 2017), available at: http://images.mofcom.gov.cn/wto2/201712/20171213174424357.pdf.

Mitchell, Andrew and Prusa, Thomas. (2016). '*China – Autos*: Haven't We Danced this Dance Before?', *World Trade Review* 15(2): 303.

Nedumpara, James and Zhou, Weihuan. (2018). *Non-Market Economies in the Global Trading System: The Special Case of China*. Singapore: Springer.

Ngangjoh-Hodu, Yenkong and Zhang, Qi. (2016). *The Political Economy of WTO Implementation and China's Approach to Litigation in the WTO*. Cheltenham: Edward Elgar Publishing.

Prusa, Thomas and Rubini, Luca. (2013). '*United States – use of zeroing in anti-dumping measures involving products from Korea*: It's déjà vu all over again', *World Trade Review* 12(2):409.

Reich, Arie, 'The effectiveness of the WTO dispute settlement system: a statistical analysis', EUI Working Papers Law 2017/11.

Reuters. (2020). 'Timeline: highlights of the 16-year airbus, Boeing trade war', *Reuters* (15 February 2020), available at: www.reuters.com/article/usa-trade-eu-chronology-timeline-idUSKBN26Y2O3.

Shaffer, Gregory and Gao, Henry. (2018). 'China's rise: how it took on the U.S. at the WTO', *University of Illinois Law Review* (1): 115.

Shi, Jingxia and Chen, Weidong. (2011). 'The "Specificity" of Cultural Products versus the "Generality" of Trade Obligations: Reflecting on "China – Publications and Audiovisual Products"', *Journal of World Trade* 45(1):159.

Tan, Su-Lin. (2020). 'China-Australia Relations: Canberra "Very Concerned" over Reports of "Discriminatory" Coal Ban', *South China Morning Post* (16 December 2020), available at: www.scmp.com/economy/china-economy/article/3114066/china-australia-relations-canberra-very-concerned-over.

Tang, Rachel. (2009). The Rise of China's Auto Industry and Its Impact on the US Motor Vehicle Industry (Congressional Research Service, 16 November 2009), available at: https://sgp.fas.org/crs/row/R40924.pdf.

Toohey, Lisa. (2011). 'China and the World Trade Organization: the first decade', *International and Comparative Law Quarterly* 60(3):788.

USTR (2009). 'United States Wins End to China's 'Famous Brand' Subsidies after Challenge at WTO; Agreement Levels Playing Field for American Workers in Every Manufacturing Sector' (Press Release, 18 December 2009) available at: https://ustr.gov/about-us/policy-offices/press-office/press-releases/2009/december/united-states-wins-end-china%E2%80%99s-%E2%80%9Cfamous-brand%E2%80%9D-sub.

USTR (2012). 2012 Report to Congress on China's WTO Compliance (December 2012), available at: https://ustr.gov/sites/default/files/uploads/2012%20Report%20to%20Congress%20-%20Dec%2021%20Final.pdf.

USTR (2015). 'United States Launches Challenge to Extensive Chinese Export Subsidy Program', (Press Release, 2 February 2015), available at: https://ustr.gov/about-us/policy-offices/press-office/press-releases/2015/february/united-states-launches-challenge.

USTR (2016). 'Chinese Export Subsidies Under the "Demonstration Bases-Common Service Platform" Program Terminated Thanks to U.S.-China Agreement', (Press Release, 4 April 2016), available at: https://ustr.gov/about-us/policy-offices/press-office/press-releases/2016/april/chinese-export-subsidies-under.

USTR (2017). European Union – Measures Related to Price Comparison Methodologies (DS516), Third Party Submission of the United States of America (21 November 2017), available at: https://ustr.gov/sites/default/files/enforcement/WTO/US.Legal.Interp.Doc.fin.%28public%29.pdf.
USTR (2018a). 2017 Report to Congress on China's WTO Compliance (January 2018), available at: https://ustr.gov/sites/default/files/files/Press/Reports/China%202017%20WTO%20Report.pdf.
USTR (2018b). Findings of the Investigation into China's Acts, Policies and Practices Related to Technology Transfer, Intellectual Property, and Innovation Under Section 301 of the Trade Act of 1974 (22 March 2018), available at: https://ustr.gov/sites/default/files/Section%20301%20FINAL.PDF.
USTR (2019). 2018 Report to Congress on China's WTO Compliance (February 2019), available at: https://ustr.gov/sites/default/files/2018-USTR-Report-to-Congress-on-China%27s-WTO-Compliance.pdf.
USTR (2020a). 2019 Report to Congress on China's WTO Compliance (March 2020), available at: https://ustr.gov/sites/default/files/2019_Report_on_China%E2%80%99s_WTO_Compliance.pdf.
USTR (2020b). Economic and Trade Agreement Between the Government of the United States of America and the Government of the People's Republic of China (15 January 2020), available at: https://ustr.gov/sites/default/files/files/agreements/phase%20one%20agreement/Economic_And_Trade_Agreement_Between_The_United_States_And_China_Text.pdf.
USTR (2021). 'Ambassador Katherine Tai's Remarks as Prepared for Delivery on the World Trade Organization' (14 October 2021), available at: https://ustr.gov/about-us/policy-offices/press-office/speeches-and-remarks/2021/october/ambassador-katherine-tais-remarks-prepared-delivery-world-trade-organization.
Wang, Chenxi. (2018). 'WTO Rare earths case's influence on China's domestic regulatory changes', *Journal of World Trade* 52(2):307.
Wang, Chenxi and Weihuan Zhou. (2022). 'A political anatomy of China's compliance in WTO disputes', *Journal of Contemporary China* 1–17 (online).
Wu, Mark. (2017). 'China's export restrictions and the limits of WTO law', *World Trade Review* 16(4):673.
WTO (2003). 'Dispute Settlement System Training Module – Legal effect of panel and appellate body reports and DSB recommendations and rulings' (July 2003), available at: www.wto.org/english/tratop_e/dispu_e/disp_settlement_cbt_e/c7s1p1_e.htm.
WTO (2005). China – Value-Added Tax on Integrated Circuits, Notification of Mutually Agreed Solution, WT/DS309/8 (6 October 2005).
WTO (2008a). China – Certain Measures Granting Refunds, Reductions or Exemptions from Taxes and Other Payments, Communication from China and the United States, WT/DS358/14 (4 January 2008).
WTO (2008b). China – Measures Affecting Financial Information Services and Foreign Financial Information Suppliers, Joint Communication from China and the United States, WT/DS373/4 (9 December 2008).
WTO (2009). DSB Minutes of Meeting, WT/DSB/M/273 (6 November 2009).

WTO (2010). China – Measures Affecting the Protection and Enforcement of Intellectual Property Rights, Status Report of China, WT/DS362/14/Add 2 (9 March 2010).

WTO (2012a). China – Measures Affecting Trading Rights and Distribution Services for certain Publications and Audiovisual Entertainment Products, Status Report by China – Addendum, WT/DS363/17/Add 14 (13 March 2012).

WTO (2012b). China – Measures Affecting Trading Rights and Distribution Services for Certain Publications and Audiovisual Entertainment Products, Joint Communication from China and the United States, WT/DS363/19 (11 May 2012).

WTO (2013a). China – Measures Related to the Exportation of Various Raw Materials, Status Report by China, WT/DS394/19/Add 1, WT/DS395/18/Add 1, WT/DS398/17/Add 1 (18 January 2013).

WTO (2013b). *China – Certain Measures Affecting Electronic Payment Services*, Status Report by China, WT/DS413/9/Add 1 (12 July 2013).

WTO (2015). DSB Minutes of Meeting, WT/DSB/M/361 (13 July 2015).

WTO (2016a). China – Measures Related to Demonstration Bases and Common Service Platforms Programmes, Communication from China and the United States, WT/DS489/7 (19 April 2016).

WTO (2016b). United States – Measures Related to Price Comparison Methodologies (DS515), available at: www.wto.org/english/tratop_e/dispu_e/cases_e/ds515_e.htm.

WTO (2016c). European Union – Measures Related to Price Comparison Methodologies (DS516), available at: www.wto.org/english/tratop_e/dispu_e/cases_e/ds516_e.htm.

WTO (2017a). 'Eleventh WTO Ministerial Conference Briefing Notes – Dispute Settlement', available at: www.wto.org/english/thewto_e/minist_e/mc11_e/briefing_notes_e/bfdispu_e.htm.

WTO (2017b). Annual Report 2017 (Geneva: World Trade Organization, 2017), available at: www.wto.org/english/res_e/booksp_e/anrep_e/anrep17_e.pdf.

WTO (2021a). 'Trade Policy Review – Report by China', WT/TPR/G/415 (15 September 2021).

WTO (2021b). 'Trade Policy Review – Report by the Secretariat', WT/TPR/S/415 (15 September 2021).

WTO (2021c). United States – Safeguard Measure on Imports of Crystalline Silicon Photovoltaic Products (DS562), available at: www.wto.org/english/tratop_e/dispu_e/cases_e/ds562_e.htm.

Yang, Guohua. (2015). 'China in the WTO dispute settlement', *Journal of World Trade* 49(1):1.

Zhang, Xiaowen and Li, Xiaoling. (2014). 'The politics of compliance with adverse WTO dispute settlement rulings in China', *Journal of Contemporary China* 23(85):143.

Zhou, Weihuan. (2019). *China's Implementation of the Rulings of the World Trade Organization*. Oxford and Portland, Oregon: Hart Publishing.

Zhou, Weihuan and Fang, Meng. (2021). 'Subsidizing technology competition: China's evolving practices and international trade regulation', *Washington International Law Journal* 30(3):470.

Zhou, Weihuan and Peng, Delei. (2018). 'EU – Price Comparison Methodologies (DS516): challenging the non-market economy methodology in light of the negotiating history of Article 15 of China's WTO Accession Protocol', *Journal of World Trade* 52(3):505.

Zhou, Weihuan and Qu, Xiaomeng. (2022). 'Confronting the 'Non-Market Economy' treatment: the evolving WTO jurisprudence on anti-dumping and China's recent practices', *Journal of International Dispute Settlement* 13(3):510.

Zhou, Weihuan, Gao, Henry and Bai, Xue. (2019). 'Building a market economy through WTO-inspired reform of state-owned enterprises in China', *International & Comparative Law Quarterly* 68(4):977.

Zhou, Weihuan, Jiang, Huiqin and Kong, Qingjiang. (2020). 'Technology transfer under China's foreign investment regime: does the WTO provide a solution?', *Journal of World Trade* 54(3):455.

12

China and WTO Reform

BERNARD HOEKMAN, XINQUAN TU, AND ROBERT WOLFE

I Introduction

The holy trinity of the World Trade Organization (WTO) is broken. *Negotiations* on new rules depend on confidence that existing rules will be *implemented*, which requires notifications for robust committee review and *dispute settlement* when clarification is needed, which sometimes should lead to new negotiations rather than authoritative adjudication. When negotiations are blocked, however, some Members are tempted to take unilateral measures to address their problems and/or to pursue bilateral solutions. Most Members want WTO reform, even if they have different aspects in mind. This is reflected in the outcome of the 12th WTO Ministerial conference held in Geneva in June 2022, which instructs the WTO General Council and its subsidiary bodies to develop proposals on how to improve all functions of the organization for consideration.[1]

In this paper, we focus on how China understands WTO reform, and how the other two leading powers see the China problem in the WTO. China, the EU, and the U.S. are the world's largest traders, and many of the tensions in the trading system arise in the relations among them. We discuss elements of the WTO reform agenda through the lens of positions that have been taken by the three major trading powers. In an original survey of the expert trade policy community conducted in June 2020, hereafter referred to as Survey, we found that respondents from the EU and the U.S. are broadly aligned on the WTO reform agenda, while respondents from China often diverge in the priorities accorded to these subjects (Hoekman and Wolfe, 2021; see also Fiorini et al., 2021). Our aim is to shed some light on areas of alignment, or absence of alignment, across these three players on the main subjects associated with reform debates.

We are grateful to a reviewer, Henry Gao, Damian Raess, Ka Zeng and participants in the World Trade Forum 2021 for helpful comments and suggestions.

[1] See www.wto.org/english/thewto_e/minist_e/mc12_e/documents_e.htm.

Our premise is that rising trade conflicts between major players are a signal of both political and economic tensions; absent reform the organization will be less able to assist major Members to attenuate economic conflicts. In turn, agreement among the three major trade powers is necessary to resolve the problems of the WTO. The rules must be seen to support the generalized gains from open trade and global production, not an attempt to isolate or reform China's economic (or political) system. At the same time, China should accept that it has a leading role to play in the regime. As is well known, the WTO has been struggling, reflecting differences in priorities across the membership, an erosion in mutual trust, and working practices that have impeded efforts to agree on changes to the rulebook. Consequently, most new rulemaking has been occurring in preferential trade agreements (PTAs), not the WTO, with high-income countries increasingly focused on attempts to negotiate deeper agreements that include rulemaking in areas that go beyond the WTO.

We begin in Section II with a brief discussion of the global challenges that ought to be on the WTO agenda and why China is central in making progress in addressing them through international cooperation. Section III discusses key dimensions of "fixing the machine" – reforming working practices and mechanisms to provide transparency, support deliberation, and resolve disputes, while Section IV does the same on issues related to the reform of negotiation modalities, the recent return to new rulemaking among groups of WTO Members on a plurilateral basis, and the way that differences in economic development levels are reflected in the WTO. We do not discuss all these areas in depth but refer the reader to the recent literature on this subject.[2] Throughout, we consider the positions that China has taken, as well as those of the EU and the US. In Section V we reflect on the potential implications of China's application to join the Comprehensive and Progressive Agreement on Trans-Pacific Partnership (CPTPP) for the prospects for WTO reform. What matters for the trading system is that the decision to apply signals a willingness by China to engage on many issues that should be – and in part are – on the table in the WTO. Section VI concludes.

II Substantive Policy Challenges for the WTO Membership

Rapid growth in global trade in recent decades was associated with a sustained rise in the production of manufactured products in

[2] Recent research on WTO reform includes Evenett and Baldwin (2020), Liu (2019), Hoekman et al. (2021).

emerging economies, notably China, often as part of – intermediated by – global value chains (GVCs). The resulting rebalancing of global output and incomes gave rise to adjustment pressures in the United States and other OECD countries. These in turn fostered perceptions that China's export success reflected the use of policies that unfairly advantaged Chinese firms. This became a factor in the "backlash against globalization" observed in many high-income countries. Such adjustment pressures will continue to rise as the world economy, driven by technological and organizational innovations, shifts towards services activities and trade come to involve more e-commerce and cross-border digital transactions. Changes in technology, and efforts to address climate change, will impact segments of the labor force that have previously benefitted from or been relatively sheltered from, internationalization.

Global trade governance has not kept up with ongoing changes in the structure of the world economy and shifts in the composition of cross-border flows. Competition between governments to stimulate domestic economic activity through "make it here" policies is growing. Such national policies may give rise to negative cross-border spillovers, either by design or inadvertently. Policies may be designed to limit the ability of foreign firms to sell goods and services and constrain the ability of firms to utilize new technologies. Addressing the associated cross-border policy spillovers calls for international cooperation.

Theory, supported by extensive evidence, suggests that addressing cross-border policy spillovers, whether pecuniary or non-pecuniary, is a major motivation for the negotiation of trade agreements, along with a political economy (commitment) incentive for cooperation. Although global trade was relatively robust in the past decade, implying weaker incentives to engage in multilateral trade agreements than is sometimes supposed by observers, the rising prevalence of trade conflicts associated with the adoption of unilateral protectionist trade policies in major economies suggests there should be a strong basis for such cooperation. However, geopolitics and serious internal political constraints confronting trade policymakers ("worker centricity" in the US; conditioning trade on "values" in the EU; resistance to external pressure in China) raise the question of whether trade agreements are feasible even if policy spillovers are significant.

Alleged international competitive spillovers of subsidies play a major role in the trade tensions between the U.S., EU, and China (Mavroidis and Sapir, 2021). Subsidies can help to address market failures and therefore might have a good economic development rationale despite giving rise to potential negative cross border competitive spillovers. As discussed at greater length in Hoekman and Nelson (2020), this is not simply a China issue. Subsidies of one type or another constitute the great majority of trade interventions imposed since 2009 (Evenett and Fritz, 2021), and the difficulties of crafting appropriate disciplines go back to the original GATT negotiations of 1947. The WTO prohibits export subsidies and has mechanisms through which Members can countervail subsidized imports and challenge the adverse effects of subsidies through dispute settlement procedures. Subsidies are a central focus of two ongoing negotiations, on domestic support in agriculture and support for fishers. China not only supports disciplines that prohibit fisheries subsidies that contribute to overcapacity and overfishing and eliminate subsidies that contribute to illegal and unregulated fishing but also notes the importance of "recognizing that appropriate and effective special and differential treatment for developing country Members and least developed country Members should be an integral part of the negotiations" (WTO, 2019d).

The tensions among China, the EU, and the US are particularly acute with respect to industrial subsidies. Rather than engage in discussions at the WTO, the US pursued unilateral action (see Hillman, 2023), as well as a trilateral process with the EU and Japan to address "concern with the non-market-oriented policies of third countries and [...] actions being taken and possible measures that could be undertaken in the near future." In a May 2018 statement Trilateral ministers endorsed a joint scoping paper defining the basis for the development of stronger rules on industrial subsidies contributing to excess production capacity in sectors such as semiconductors, steel, aluminum, and others, and on state-owned enterprises (SOEs) (USTR, 2018). A subsequent series of Trilateral meetings has made little progress. In an implicit response, Vice Minister Wang, in a press conference on the WTO Trade Policy Review of China in 2021 said that China was open to starting negotiations on subsidies within the framework of WTO reform, mentioning three specific ideas: first, agricultural subsidies must be discussed at the same time as industrial subsidies to ensure fair competition in both important areas; second, tightening trade relief disciplines such as countervailing and anti-dumping should be discussed to solve the current abuse of trade relief measures; third, it should discuss the issue of restoring non-litigable subsidies, which is needed to leave policy space for members to cope with challenges such as climate change (China, 2021).

To give another example of an area where the three powers diverge, the global regime for data flows is highly fragmented, ranging from essential laissez-faire approaches in some countries (with the US being on this end of the spectrum), to more tightly regulated environments in others, whether motivated by protection of privacy and citizen rights, perceived security imperatives or concerns about market power and abuse of dominant positions by lead firms. The EU and China are both on the more regulated end of the spectrum, with the EU maintaining a conditional flow regime and China imposing tight restrictions in specific areas, for example, on the location of computing facilities (Ferracane and Li, 2021) Trade agreements are beginning to include specific obligations on cross-border data flows, and some jurisdictions are establishing "equivalence regimes" that determine whether foreign providers will be treated in the same way as domestic firms when it comes to access and processing of data. The consequences of the potential for the resultant creation of "data blocs" for global wellbeing – and global trade – are still poorly understood, whether from the point of view of individual consumers interacting with websites or social media or from the point of view of companies looking to leverage digital technologies to boost productivity or expand markets.[3]

The technological developments generating structural transformation and national policies that are both causes and responses to shifts in global trade shares call for revisiting and updating international trade rules. Realizing this potential requires WTO reforms. To a significant extent, achieving such reform depends on China.

(i) *Why China Is Central to "WTO Reform"*

Although WTO reform pressures in part reflect increasing dissatisfaction with the operation of the organization by many WTO members, especially its negotiation function leading to an inability to adapt to a changing global economy, a major trigger for the rising prominence of calls and

[3] Data flows and digital regulation more broadly are particularly important for firms that rely on data as a core part of their business, e.g., platform companies and providers of 'software as a service'. See, e.g., Ferracane and van der Marel (2019).

proposals for WTO reform is the impact of China on the trading system. Progress in the WTO will require recognition by all three major players that China must now play a leadership role commensurate with its weight in the world economy. China has indicated it will accept reforms that make the WTO better for all Members, but not ones that challenge its identity as a developing country, that deny it scope for how it organizes its economy, and that fail to recognize its status as a major power (Gao, 2021; Liu, 2019; Tan, 2021). In a submission to the General Council (WTO, 2019b) China indicated that it supports WTO reform if core values of the multilateral trading system such as non-discrimination and openness, safeguards for the development interests of developing Members, and decision-making by consensus are preserved.

The U.S. has repeatedly expressed its serious concerns with China's non-market-oriented economy and associated policies and practices "that have resulted in damage to the world trading system and lead to severe overcapacity, create unfair competitive conditions for workers and businesses, hinder the development and use of innovative technologies, and undermine the proper functioning of international trade" (WTO, 2020a).[4] This theme was echoed in the inaugural joint statement of the U.S.-EU Trade and Technology Council on September 29, 2021. Chinese scholars recognize this U.S. view, which they contrast first with "the vast number of developing members represented by China who adhere to the basic purposes and principles of the WTO," and second with the compromise position of such major economies as Europe, Canada, and Japan (Liu, 2019).

China made clear in its submission on WTO reform (WTO, 2019b) that it sees the U.S. as the problem, with proposals on breaking the impasse of the appointment process of Appellate Body members, tightening disciplines to curb the abuse of national security exceptions; and tightening disciplines on unilateral measures that are inconsistent with WTO rules. China's suggestions on improving trade remedies disciplines target areas where developed countries could be said to have abused the existing rules, for example on price comparison in anti-dumping proceedings, subsidy identification, and calculation of benefits conferred. Chinese officials consistently make the obvious and valid point that the market is not given free rein in OECD countries. These Chinese views are fair but are also a deflection from the core issue: coming to a shared understanding of the role China must play in the system.

[4] See also Hopewell (2023), Chapter 8 in this volume.

III Fixing the Machine

As discussed at greater length in Hoekman et al. (2021) and Hoekman and Wolfe (2021), WTO reform spans two sets of issues: (i) improving working practices and the operation of the institution ("fixing the machine"); and (ii) overcoming obstacles that impede the negotiation of new trade policy disciplines. This section discusses the first set of issues; the next section turns to the second challenge.

(i) Improving Transparency

Transparency of actor behavior and expectations is a core requirement of international regimes. This objective requires high-quality information (Wolfe, 2018). The WTO agreements have dozens of formal notification obligations; compliance varies by the committee and by Member.

Inadequate notification of trade policies is an old issue, but its inclusion on the "WTO reform" agenda only began at the 2017 Ministerial Conference when Robert Lighthizer, then the United States Trade Representative, said that "it is impossible to negotiate new rules when many of the current ones are not being followed" (USTR, 2017). The U.S. tabled a detailed proposal that reviewed how compliance with notification obligations under the Trade in Goods agreements is unsatisfactory. The U.S. proposal included punishment for Members who are behind in their notifications (WTO, 2017). Although not explicit, the target was clearly China.

Whether and to what extent China is not fulfilling its WTO notification obligations is an open question. In a 2021 self-report for the TPR, it said (WTO, 2021c, 4.24) that it "has fully fulfilled its obligations of notification under all WTO agreements." In its report for the TPR, the Secretariat observed (WTO, 2021d, 2.22) that "some notifications, including those on state trading enterprises and domestic support, remain outstanding." During the TPRB meeting to review the reports, most questions posed by members had to do with notifications and transparency. Whatever the facts of the matter, threats to identify the Chinese ambassador as a "Member with notification delay" when offered the floor in the General Council as in a U.S.-led proposal (WTO, 2021a) will not enhance WTO transparency. China, along with most developing countries, will never join a consensus on the wording suggested in this proposal. But Chinese respondents in the Survey expressed stronger preferences than the other two for improving transparency. China does recognize the notification problem (WTO, 2019b) and is willing to engage in discussion of improvements, starting naturally with developed countries leading by example (Li and Tu, 2020, p. 859).

The periodic monitoring reports prepared by the Secretariat ought to be able to provide information that supplements notifications. The reports aim to enhance the transparency of trade policy developments, consistent with the mandate of the Trade Policy Review Mechanism to aid in understanding Members' trade policy but not to assess compliance with formal obligations. The reports therefore do not cover "subsidies," which are defined for legal purposes in Article 1.1 of the ASCM, but they should in principle cover the full extent of the "general economic support" provided by governments. They do not. Central to coverage of general economic support, which goes beyond formal notifications, are responses to periodic questionnaires issued by the WTO Director-General (DG). The overall response is weak, and the response on general economic support is dismal. In the 2020 report, 67 WTO Members and one Observer volunteered information on 638 COVID-19-related general economic support measures. The EU did so; the U.S. and China did not. The U.S. is less cooperative than China or the EU with the trade monitoring exercise, neither responding to the DG's questionnaire nor verifying information the Secretariat found in other places (WTO, 2020b, Appendix 1). The Global Trade Alert makes a valuable contribution to closing the transparency gap on subsidies provided by the big three (Evenett and Fritz, 2021), but they should do more themselves.

(ii) Improving the Operation of WTO Deliberative Bodies

In the short term, agreement on binding rules on contested policies is unlikely to be possible simply because the major players are far apart in their understanding of the sources and magnitude of the problems that call for cooperation. What is needed first and foremost is engagement in processes to collect and share information, policy dialogue, and peer review. This applies to a range of policy areas, including subsidies and SOEs. WTO members do not necessarily know enough about SOEs, not just in China but more broadly, to be sure whether and where SOEs create a systemic problem, and hence what ought to be done. A necessary condition for cooperation is a common understanding of the extent and spillover effects of contested practices (Evenett and Fritz, 2021). As noted by Hoekman and Nelson (2020), calling for work programs to do so may be criticized as kicking the can down the road. It is not. WTO members simply do not have enough information to develop a common understanding of where new rules are needed and the form they should take.

WTO committees and councils are the first deliberative bodies for discussing emerging issues and addressing trade concerns without recourse to the dispute settlement system. Or at least they should be (Wolfe, 2020). The most effective WTO bodies in addressing trade concerns are the Technical Barriers to Trade Committee and the Sanitary and Phytosanitary Measures Committee. Members raise "specific trade concerns" (STCs) to seek clarification, including of already adopted measures, and discussion can lead to modification or even withdrawal of a measure that has adverse consequences for trading partners. Discussion of trade concerns is increasing in other bodies. Since 1995, close to 6000 questions (much like an STC) have been raised in connection with individual notifications under the Committee on Agriculture (CoA) review process. Between mid-October 2014 and mid-October 2019, 1,158 issues and concerns were raised in 129 formal meetings of 17 WTO committees and councils, other than SPS, TBT, and CoA (WTO, 2020b). These numbers dwarf the number of formal disputes.

A handful of large traders make the most frequent use of procedures to raise trade concerns, notably the U.S. and the EU. China is now number 5 on the list of users and is the target of more trade concerns that any country after India (WTO, 2020b). Still, the procedures could be more extensively used, and participation could be enhanced. One of the reasons for improving the discussion of STCs is to avoid escalation to the dispute settlement system, but Chinese respondents to the Survey get considerably less utility than respondents in the U.S. and the EU from using WTO bodies to defuse potential disputes by raising STCs. One suggestion for improvement is to establish guidelines for all WTO bodies. Tabled by the EU and supported by 19 other Members, including China, this proposal aims to make better use of the possibility offered by WTO Council and committee meetings to discuss and resolve concerns with trade-related measures by equipping them with horizontal procedural guidelines (WTO, 2021b).

The proposal encourages the submission of written questions and answers, which would enhance transparency for other Members, or firms, having the same concern. Although the U.S. was cool to the proposal for obscure reasons, it made a similar proposal in the SCM Committee for ensuring timely written responses to questions posed by Members on the subsidy programs of other Members (WTO, 2020d). China has resisted every time the item comes up, including in an October 2021 meeting, arguing that the ASCM does not require members to submit responses to such questions in writing, nor to provide them within a specific time period. In its view, setting deadlines as proposed by the U.S. would impose substantial new notification obligations on WTO members and cause difficulties for developing countries.

Policy dialogue in WTO bodies is important to consider what works well under agreements, what is not working, and what should be next on the agenda. Committees also need to hear from stakeholders who use their agreements, including regulators, other international organizations, and the private sector. Chinese and U.S. respondents to the Survey get more utility than EU respondents from greater engagement with stakeholders in WTO bodies. One instrument for such engagement is meetings that are sponsored by or associated with a WTO body in some way, but that are not part of its formal meetings and thus permit (in principle) participation by stakeholders. The WTO held over 100 such "thematic sessions" from 2017 through 2019 (Wolfe, 2021). China was relatively well represented, with 9 Geneva-based Chinese government officials and 15 capital-based officials speaking in thematic sessions during the 2017–19 period, along with 7 business and 2 academic participants.

(iii) Dispute Settlement and the Appellate Body Crisis

A vital dimension of the "value proposition" offered by the WTO is independent, third-party adjudication of trade disputes reflected in the principle of de-politicized conflict resolution. An effective dispute settlement mechanism is critical for existing WTO agreements to remain meaningful, and for the negotiation of new agreements. The different pillars of the WTO are interdependent. Resolving the Appellate Body crisis and bolstering the dispute settlement function is critical for the continued relevance of the WTO.

The U.S. seems to believe that WTO adjudication is not the best way to resolve its concerns with Chinese practices. Although China lost many of the dispute settlement cases brought against it, Appellate Body rulings on key matters such as what constitutes a public body under the ASCM fuelled U.S. frustration (Ahn, 2021). The Appellate Body ceased operations in December 2019 because of the U.S. refusal to agree to appoint new Appellate Body members and/or re-appoint incumbents. Resolution of the crisis requires reform of how the system works. U.S. concerns are long-standing, and the U.S. is not alone in at least some of its concerns (Fiorini et al., 2020). By the end of 2020, sixteen appeals were pending before the dysfunctional Appellate Body and only five new cases had been filed, the lowest for any of the WTO's 25 years. If appeal "into the void" remains possible, issued panel reports will have no legal value, unless the disputing parties forego their right to appeal, and accept the panel report as the final word in their dispute. The interim Multi-Party Interim Appeal Arbitration Arrangement (MPIA), which includes the EU and China, provides a short-term alternative but is not a solution (Hoekman and Mavroidis, 2020).

We speculate that China values a functioning system that provides some protection from the U.S., or at least some recourse if the U.S. does act unilaterally. Chinese scholars see the dispute settlement system as the first option to reconcile the relationship between China and its trading partners, hence wishing to be seen as a responsible player China is motivated to comply with dispute settlement rulings (Li and Tu, 2018, 121). China is much closer to the EU position than to the U.S. Having invested considerable effort in developing trade law expertise in government and academia, China became a sophisticated user of dispute settlement to push back on U.S. and EU use of trade remedy law (Shaffer and Gao, 2018). In addition to joining the MPIA it is a cosponsor of the proposal led by Mexico to re-start the Appellate Body appointments process–blocked by the U.S. at over 50 meetings of the DSB–and it has joined a proposal an Appellate Body reform with over 40 other Members.

Survey respondents from all three trade powers are of the view that re-establishing an operational dispute resolution system is a top priority, although Chinese respondents to the Survey get more utility than the EU and U.S. respondents from making the Appellate Body operational again and from considering reforms to dispute settlement processes more broadly. The U.S. would see no point in any kind of WTO reform that did not address this problem. Equally, the U.S. would see no point in any new agreements aimed at Chinese practices if dispute settlement remains slow and ineffective.

IV Negotiation Obstacles: Consensus and Special and Differential Treatment

The accession of China at the 2001 Doha ministerial occurred in tandem with the launch of the ill-fated Doha Round at the same ministerial. The backward-looking Doha Round agenda prioritizing tariffs on manufacturing and agricultural support policies became increasingly disconnected from twenty-first-century priorities as the negotiations dragged on eventually becoming deadlocked. One result was that policies affecting the digital economy, cross-border data flows, and foreign investment, among others, were neglected because a consensus could not be achieved to address issues that were not part of the Doha agenda.

With the Doha Round dead, in 2017 many countries decided to shift gears and move away from negotiations including all WTO Members and the working practice of consensus decision-making by launching so-called "joint statement initiatives" (JSIs), meaning simply talks inside the WTO among a subset of Members whose eventual outcome would make use of WTO transparency and dispute settlement procedures. The 2017 JSIs addressed e-commerce, domestic regulation of services (successfully concluded in December 2021, with 67 WTO members, including China, joining), investment facilitation, and measures to enhance the ability of micro and small, and medium enterprises (MSMEs) to capture trade opportunities. Subsequently, additional issues became the subject of discussion among groups among subsets of WTO members. Ministerial statements in December 2021 addressed three new areas where groups of Members have decided to pursue discussions.[5]

These joint initiatives include a broad cross-section of members. But that does not mean that negotiations to establish new plurilateral agreements have been endorsed by all Members. Tu and Wolfe (2021) discuss the opposition to the JSIs led by India and South Africa. Unlike some other developing countries, Chinese officials are not opposed to the principle of pursuing plurilateral agreements in the WTO (Li and Tu, 2020).[6] In its country report for its 2021 trade policy review, China stressed its active participation in the JSIs (WTO, 2021c). China

[5] These Ministerial statements addressed (i) Trade and Environmental Sustainability (WT/MIN(21)/6/Rev.2); (ii) Plastics Pollution and Environmentally Sustainable Plastics Trade (WT/MIN(21)/8/Rev.2); and (iii) Fossil Fuel Subsidies (WT/MIN(21)/9/Rev.1).

[6] China joined the Information Technology Agreement and is in the process of acceding to the Government Procurement Agreement. China also participated in the Environmental Goods Agreement, though with a narrower list of goods than some other participants had wished, and had wanted to participate in the now moribund Trade in Services Agreement (TiSA) negotiations but had been rebuffed (Hoekman and Shi, 2021).

has taken a leadership role in the JSI on investment facilitation, acting as a co-sponsor and actively encouraging participation by developing countries.

The move to plurilateral is only a partial solution to the difficulty of concluding negotiations by consensus. Each negotiation can only be concluded if a critical mass of Members participates, whatever the legal form of an outcome. Plurilateral approaches therefore are not a panacea, but they offer a mechanism for large trade powers to cooperate without engaging in negotiations with all WTO members (Hoekman and Sabel, 2021). An EU paper on WTO reform (EU, 2021) contains an implicit warning: if no effective formula is found to integrate plurilateral agreements in the WTO, there would be no other option than developing such rules outside the WTO framework, which could fragment the system. The warning applies to India, South Africa, and to anybody tempted by their analysis, but it also applies to the three major powers. Plurilateral negotiations can break the dead hand of the single undertaking, but the risk of free riding by any of the three major powers means that each of China, the EU, and the U.S. will be needed to reach a critical mass deal.

V Special and Differential Treatment: A Central Negotiation Obstacle

The prospects for agreement to be possible between the EU, U.S., and China will depend importantly on whether emerging economies insist on being accorded special and differential treatment and more generally on whether and how such agreements address development differences.

In May and November 2019, the U.S. submitted a proposal for a decision on "Procedures to Strengthen the Negotiating Function of the WTO" with criteria for assessing which countries will not avail themselves of SDT in WTO negotiations (WTO, 2019c). The U.S. asked for this item to be placed on the agenda of one General Council meeting after another in 2019 and 2020, with some support from other Members but unrelenting opposition from China and most developing countries. At the July 2020 meeting of the General Council the representative of China, echoing the introduction and much of the argumentation of an earlier submission on SDT by China and others (WTO, 2019a) said that in an international organization with developed and developing Members, non-reciprocity was a means and a principle to realize equity. He argued that the reclassification of WTO members was not a way out. Rather than revisiting the current practice of self-designation of developing country status, he suggested those in a position to do so be encouraged to make a greater contribution to the best of their capabilities, which China was willing to do (WTO, 2020c).

During the October 2021 Trade Policy Review Body (TPRB) meeting on the report on China, Australia, echoing comments made by many others, including the EU and the U.S., encouraged China to play a more constructive leadership role in the WTO, including by relinquishing its access to special and differential treatment. Minister of Commerce Wang Wentao, who led the Chinese delegation, said that "In keeping with the principle of balanced rights and obligations, China is willing to approach special and differential treatment with pragmatism and make more contribution within the WTO that is commensurate with its capacity." In a subsequent press conference in Beijing on the results of the review (China, 2021) Vice Minister of Commerce Wang Shouwen's lengthy response to a question on SDT noted that "The report of the nineteenth National Congress of the Communist Party of China pointed out that China's international status as the largest developing country in the world has not changed. China's international status as a developing country has not changed." This line comes right from the top. President Xi Jinping told Davos in January 2021 that WTO reform must protect the development rights and policy space of developing members (WTO, 2021c). Chinese officials will not give up the principle soon, regardless of what happens in practice.

The debate about the links between levels of development and the depth of policy commitments can be sterile. Low (2021) discusses ways to break the link between what a country calls itself and what access to SDT should be available. He stresses that most aspects of SDT require cooperative action of one kind or another from others besides the SDT recipients – the scope to invoke unilateral "flexibilities" in implementing WTO rules is limited. Nobody thinks China should expect SDT for any new market access commitments or any other provision where special treatment would be offered by another member.

In the Survey, resolving differences in SDT was not a huge priority for any of the three. A possible reason is a recognition that these three major traders will need to negotiate rules that apply equally to each of them, with specific commitments and exceptions, agreed on an issue-specific basis. Doing so need not require China to abandon the principle of identifying itself as a developing country, nor does it need to abandon support for other members who may need SDT more.

VI Prospects for WTO Reform: China's CPTPP Application

One of the questions about whether China can contribute to real WTO reform is how willing the country is to undertake new liberalization and regulatory policy commitments. Its leadership role in the Regional Comprehensive Economic Partnership (RCEP) might be an indicator, although RCEP is a relatively shallow agreement. More significantly, China has been paying close attention to TPP/CPTPP ever since the U.S. decided to join and reframe this initiative in 2009. At the time, China was greatly concerned about the intentions of the U.S. and the possible impact of the TPP on China's position in the Asia-Pacific. One of China's responses was to support and participate in RCEP.

The subsequent developments are well known. The TPP talks concluded successfully in 2016 with a draft text that was agreed upon by the United States. Despite this, President Obama never submitted the TPP to Congress for ratification, and President Trump withdrew the U.S. from the TPP on the first day of his presidency in January 2017. Japan then succeeded in transforming the TPP minus the U.S. into the CPTPP with 11 members later in 2017. In parallel, China and 14 other countries continued the RCEP negotiations, successfully concluding them at the end of 2020. To the surprise of many foreign observers, a few days after the conclusion of RCEP, President Xi Jinping announced that China was positively considering applying to join the CPTPP. There was no open opposition to joining CPTPP in academic debates, although there was some suspicion and concern about the feasibility of doing so. Premier Li Keqiang repeatedly claimed that China was open to it. In September 2021, the Chinese government formally submitted the application.

The application was not a big surprise for Chinese observers. There have been numerous discussions and much research on TPP/CPTPP in China since 2015. Many scholars are very excited about the text of TPP/CPTPP and believe that the text represents the most advanced and ambitious efforts of further international economic integration. Given that implementation of the third plenum reform agenda[7] fell far below expectations, many argue that China needs foreign pressure to break through the obstacles in sensitive areas such as SOE reform and data regulation.

Many foreign observers doubt China's intentions in applying to the CPTPP. The assumption is that China could not accept the high requirements of CPTPP given its poor performance in reform and opening-up

[7] See, e.g., Rosen (2014).

in recent years; they think that the application is just a gesture to the world but that China is not prepared to comply with the rules of CPTPP. A counterargument can be based on what China agreed to in the 2020 Comprehensive Agreement on Investment with the EU. Although ratification of this agreement has been stalled due to political factors and the CAI may never be implemented, what matters is that China accepted a range of provisions on matters that also will be on the table in the CPTPP, including trade and sustainable development, that is, non-trade issues, and disciplines on SOEs (see, e.g., Kurtz and Gong, 2021). It is not reasonable to argue that China is not serious about CPTPP because reforms have been slow. Foreign observers often overestimate the ability of the Chinese government to enforce its policies throughout a huge country. There are countless bureaucratic obstacles to reform in the Chinese system. The central government needs international institutions to enhance the legitimacy and enforceability of its intentions–we know that WTO accession 20 years ago was used by reformers in China for just this purpose.

The application to CPTPP sends a strong signal to the world that China is willing to accept high-standard international rules, as long as the rules are widely considered legitimate and beneficial by other trading partners and Chinese society. Ironically, the rules included in the CPTPP were designed in part by the U.S. with the aim to establish a set of disciplines in which China would not have a voice. Adding to the irony is that the American government decided it was not willing to adopt the disciplines itself, a position that continues to be taken by the Biden Administration at the time of writing. The U.S. accuses China of disrupting the current rules-based international system but China's application to the CPTPP is regarded inside China as a strong riposte.

China is very aware of the political challenges associated with joining CPTPP. China's relations with CPTPP members Japan, Canada, and Australia are complicated and have deteriorated in recent years. But the negotiations will not be easy. China considers Japan to be a caretaker of U.S. interests, highly influenced by the latter. Economic considerations may dominate other concerns, as RCEP shows. Although Australia and Japan have problems with China, they ratified the RCEP agreement quickly.

CPTPP rules on technical issues such as SOEs, data flows, or labor standards are not always clear-cut and subject to the interpretation of members. If some members do not have the political will to let China in or feel pressured by the U.S. to resist a country termed its only peer competitor, they could adopt interpretations of CPTPP provisions that make it more difficult for China. China is more comfortable with possibly making some difficult concessions in CPTPP because a smaller membership means less pressure on China. While the CPTPP chapters on SOEs, data flows, and labor standards are difficult for China, neither the US nor the EU is CPTPP member. China is not naïve about the negotiation process, but China believes that participation will offer a great opportunity to both incumbent and future members. Accession to CPTPP would establish a basis for engagement with the other two major traders.

China's participation in CPTPP will surely affect China's position on WTO reforms, depending on the progress of China's negotiation to join CPTPP. The CPTPP goes further than the WTO on many issues, including in areas such as environmental regulation, labor standards, competition policy, investment liberalization, cross-border data flows, and SOEs. The CPTPP offers China a way to engage in these issues in a smaller group without offending other WTO Members. If the CPTPP process is successful, it would provide a basis on which China would be more comfortable engaging in WTO negotiations on new issues, including on a plurilateral basis through JSIs. An implication may be that patience will be required before it becomes clear what China is willing to commit to in terms of new rules on substantive policy areas.

VII Implications for Future Cooperation on WTO Reform

WTO members face many problems that call for cooperation. Prominent items include ensuring a consistent response to global public health crises, resolution of conflicts regarding the use of industrial-cum-tax-subsidy policies, regulation of data privacy and cross-border data flows, and the appropriate role of trade policy in reducing the carbon intensity of economic activity. Revisiting the terms of engagement with China is a necessary condition for revitalizing the WTO as a forum to address these matters and to sustain an open world economy.

The challenge for China is to defend the existing international rules and its rights under them, while meanwhile exploring the possibilities of creating or supporting forms of cooperation that sustain its economic development. China's support for WTO reform and its application to the CPTPP are intended for that purpose. Reflecting on the priorities of respondents to the Survey (Hoekman and Wolfe, 2021) suggests that compromise will be needed all around on the design of a negotiating agenda or set of issues to be considered. Respondents from all three powers place great weight on resolving the dispute settlement crisis, with China-based respondents indicating that this is a particularly urgent priority. The Survey reveals a striking degree of correlation among respondents from all three major trade powers on assigning a high priority to the cluster of transparency-related issues. They are far apart in negotiating stronger rules on industrial subsidies, clarifying the role of trade policy in tackling climate change, and promoting sustainable development goals (SDGs).

In 2021, Chinese authorities, the media, and academic institutions held a series of events to commemorate the 20th anniversary of China's WTO accession. The general tone was very positive. However, the emphasis was on China's contribution to the WTO and the world rather than on the benefits accruing to China from its WTO membership. China has given up hope that the United States will relax its efforts to suppress China's development. It is widely believed by the Chinese that the US has determined to decouple with China as much as possible. Although the US repeatedly argues that China has been disrupting the rules-based international system, China believes it is the US that has intentionally violated the rules established in the WTO because the outcome of trade liberalization in China and WTO membership has been beneficial to China by making the economy more and more competitive. The view in China is that the US has neither the appetite nor the capability to support further liberalization – as reflected in the Biden Administration's disinterest in new trade agreements. The worry is that the US – the incumbent hegemon – now regrets having provided an international public good and is seeking to deprive China of its rights through calls for WTO reform that are code for relaxing existing rules to facilitate the imposition of import restrictions and measures to restrain China's exports and outward investment.

Chinese officials in Geneva profess support for WTO reform but demand respect and non-discrimination. China does not accept being asked to do things that OECD countries do not ask of themselves. As discussed above, China also insists on the formal status of a "developing country" (Gao, 2021). But China is a very large economy, a very large trader, and is more prosperous than many other developing countries. China cannot expect to be granted the type of special and differential treatment that WTO members are ready to accord to low-income developing countries in any new agreements. What is needed is a political accommodation that ensures continued acceptance of the principle accompanied by a pragmatic acknowledgment that reciprocity will apply among the three major trade powers in new negotiations.[8]

Nothing will happen in the WTO unless China, the EU, and the U.S. want it to, but they will need to find ways to work together consistently, much as the old Quad did in bridging gaps between the EU and the U.S. during the Uruguay Round. The effort would be worthwhile since the best place to work out the major differences between China and the other two is the WTO, especially since neither is likely to engage with CPTPP any time soon. Clearly, all three have no difficulty with participating in plurilateral negotiations, but we argue that they should be working together on governance principles that would make a wider group of Members feel comfortable with such negotiations (Hoekman and Sabel, 2021; Tu and Wolfe, 2021). They should also be considering how best to manage open plurilateral negotiations outside the WTO including the development of open standards for new technologies in ways consistent with the TBT agreement (Lee-Makiyama, 2021). Compromise among the three ought to be possible.[9]

While the single undertaking is dead, package deals are a negotiation reality. WTO ministerials need an agenda proposing a set of agreements that can attract a broad consensus. Without a forcing device, and if the results of each negotiation underway cannot stand on their own, how can they be knit together? The major powers have asymmetric interests with respect to any given trading partner. They also tend to have asymmetric interests in any one issue. IF the three must be part of a deal to get critical mass, and IF they have asymmetric interests, THEN they need a package of critical mass deals to reach an agreement on any one of them.

[8] A step in this direction was taken at the 12th Ministerial conference of the WTO in June 2022. One outcome was a Ministerial decision on the TRIPS Agreement to the effect that developing countries may authorise the use of patented technologies to produce COVID-19 vaccines and supply these to other developing nations without the consent of rights holders (WT/MIN(22)/30). This decision includes a footnote encouraging developing countries with vaccine manufacturing capacity to commit not to avail themselves of this option. China did so, illustrating that developing country status in the WTO need not preclude differentiation in the application of rules.

[9] We refrain from offering specific policy proposals that could form the basis of negotiations as our aim in this chapter was not to provide policy prescriptions, but to consider how the three major powers see WTO reform. Specific reform proposals can be found in the contributions to Evenett and Baldwin (2020), Hoekman et al. (2021) and Hoekman and Mavroidis (2021b). Hoekman and Mavroidis (2020, 2021a) argue that reform of dispute settlement must go beyond the role of the Appellate Body and span the first stage panel process. Wolfe (2020) suggests greater use of WTO committees to defuse and address potential disputes, building on the experience in WTO bodies dealing with product standards in which WTO members can table "specific trade concerns" raised by applied or proposed standards in a WTO member.

When we look at the pattern of current initiatives, it is striking that at least one of the three is a supporter of one. Can trade offs be found whereby all three could assemble a package that they and others could support? While China co-sponsored the Informal Dialogue on Plastics Pollution, unlike the U.S. and EU, the EU is the only one of the three to sponsor the proposed statement on fossil fuel subsidies. China has joined the Trade and Environmental Sustainability Structured Discussions, as have the U.S. and the EU. China was a cosponsor (the U.S. was not) of an Ottawa Group proposal (WT0, 2021e) for a non-binding General Council declaration on the trade policy response to the COVID-19 pandemic that sought to ensure access to essential goods, including therapeutics and vaccines, by avoiding unnecessary restrictions and enhancing transparency. The EU cosponsored a U.S. proposal aimed to improve notifications, but China did not. China cosponsored an EU proposal on improving the work of committees, but the U.S. did not. Compromise on dispute settlement, the other big element of fixing the machine will be harder, but updating the WTO rule book, the other part of what is meant by "WTO reform," will not be enough for the major powers if all WTO can do is make progress on old issues. The WTO already has many new issues on its agenda, but its rulebook must expand to cover other emerging issues.

Is China ready? Its application to join CPTPP suggests a willingness to engage based on extensive preparatory work, but China's contribution to WTO reform depends on engagement with the other two major powers. The initiation of discussions in the CPTPP context suggests negotiations on substantive policy matters between China, the EU, and the US may need to wait until the CPTPP-related talks have progressed. Meanwhile a greater focus on deliberative processes in the WTO and prioritizing those elements of WTO reform that center on fixing the machine appear to offer greater scope for the big three to work together in preparing the ground for negotiating new agreements that span all three. Whether such agreements will be feasible remains an open question, as success is premised not only on China but on the willingness of the United States to consider and accept new disciplines. The CPTPP experience suggests this is by no means a given.

References

Ahn, Dukgeun (2021) 'Why reform is needed: WTO "Public Body" Jurisprudence.' *Global Policy*, 12(S3): 61–70.

China (2021) Record of the Press Conference on the Eighth WTO Trade Policy Review, State Council Information Office, October 28, 2021. Link in Chinese

Evenett, Simon and Richard Baldwin (eds.) (2020) *Revitalising Multilateralism: Pragmatic ideas for the new WTO Director-General*. London: CEPR Press.

Evenett, Simon J. and Johannes Fritz (2021) *Subsidies and Market Access: Towards an Inventory of Corporate Subsidies by China, the European Union and the United States*. London: CEPR Press.

Ferracane, M. and M. Li (2021) 'What kinds of rules are needed to support digital trade?' in In B. Hoekman, X. Tu and D. Wang (eds.), *Rebooting Multilateral Trade Cooperation: Perspectives from China and Europe*. London: CEPR Press.

Ferracane, M. and E. van der Marel (2019) Patterns of Trade Restrictiveness in Online Platforms: A First Look, ECIPE DTE Working Paper Series No. 2, Brussels: ECIPE.

Fiorini, Matteo, Bernard Hoekman, Petros Mavroidis, Maarja Saluste and Robert Wolfe (2020) 'WTO dispute settlement and the appellate body crisis: insider perceptions and members' revealed preferences.' *Journal of World Trade*, 54(5): 667–98.

Fiorini, Matteo, Bernard Hoekman, Petros C. Mavroidis, Douglas Nelson and Robert Wolfe (2021) 'Stakeholder preferences and priorities for the next WTO Director General.' *Global Policy*, 12(S3): 13–22.

Gao, Henry (2021) 'WTO reform: a china round?' *Proceedings of the ASIL Annual Meeting*, 114: 23–32.

Hillman, Jennifer (2023) China's Entry into the WTO – A Mistake by the United States?, In H. Gao, D. Raess, and K. Zeng (eds.), *China and the WTO: A Twenty-Year Assessment*. New York: Cambridge University Press, pp. 400–26.

Hoekman, Bernard and Petros C. Mavroidis (2020) 'To AB or not to AB? Dispute settlement in WTO reform.' *Journal of International Economic Law*, 23(3): 1–20.

Hoekman, Bernard and Petros C. Mavroidis (2021a) 'Preventing the bad from getting worse: is it the end of the World (Trade Organization) as we know it?' *European Journal of International Law*, 32(3): 743–70.

Hoekman, Bernard and Petros C. Mavroidis (2021b) 'WTO reform: back to the past to build for the future.' *Global Policy*, 12(S3): 5–12.

Hoekman, Bernard and Douglas Nelson (2020) 'Rethinking international subsidy rules.' *The World Economy*, 43(12): 3104–32.

Hoekman, Bernard and Charles Sabel (2021) 'Plurilateral cooperation as an alternative to trade agreements: innovating one domain at a time.' *Global Policy*, 12(S3): 49–60.

Hoekman, B. and J. Shi (2021). 'Updating the general agreement on trade in services.' In B. Hoekman, X. Tu and D. Wang (eds.), *Rebooting Multilateral Trade Cooperation: Perspectives from China and Europe*. London: CEPR.

Hoekman, Bernard and Robert Wolfe (2021) 'Reforming the World Trade Organization: practitioner perspectives from China, the EU, and the US.' *China & World Economy*, 29(4): 1–34.

Hoekman, Bernard, Xinquan Tu and Dong Wang (eds.) (2021) *Rebooting Multilateral Trade Cooperation: Perspectives from China and Europe*. London: CEPR Press.

Hopewell, Kristen (2023) Tumult in the Trading System: The China Paradox, Declining US Institutional Power, and the Crisis at the WTO, In H. Gao, D. Raess, and K. Zeng (eds.), *China and the WTO: A Twenty-Year Assessment.* New York: Cambridge University Press, pp. 183–203.

Kurtz, J. and B. Gong (2021) 'The EU–China comprehensive agreement on investment: a model for investment coverage in the World Trade Organization?' In B. Hoekman, X. Tu and D. Wang (eds.), *Rebooting Multilateral Trade Cooperation: Perspectives from China and Europe.* London: CEPR Press.

Lee-Makiyama, Hosuk (2021) Careless Advocacy on 5G RAN. European Centre for International Political Economy.

Li, Siqi and Tu, Xinquan (2018) 'Impact of Chinese characteristics on the World Trade Organization: challenges and strategies.' *China & World Economy,* 26(2): 107–26.

Li, Siqi and Tu, Xinquan (2020) 'Reforming WTO subsidy rules: past experiences and prospects.' *Journal of World Trade,* 54(6): 853–88.

Liu, Jingdong (2019) Research on the necessity of the WTO reform and the design of reform issues. 9 J. WTO & China 3 (Institute of World Economics and Politics, Chinese Academy of Social Sciences).

Low, Patrick (2021) 'Special and differential treatment and developing country status: can the two be separated?.' In B. Hoekman, X. Tu and D. Wang (eds.), *Rebooting Multilateral Trade Cooperation: Perspectives from China and Europe.* London: CEPR Press, pp. 75–102.

Mavroidis, Petros C. and André Sapir (2021) *China and the WTO: Why Multilateralism Still Matters.* Princeton: Princeton University Press.

Rosen, Dan (2014) *Avoiding the Blind Alley: China's Economic Overhaul and Its Global Implications.* New York: The Asia Society.

Shaffer, Gregory and Henry Gao (2018) 'China's rise: how it took on the U.S. At the WTO.' *University of Illinois Law Review,* 2018(1): 115–84.

Tu, Xinquan and Robert Wolfe (2021) 'Reviving the negotiation function of the WTO: why the onus falls on the three major powers.' In B. Hoekman, X. Tu and D. Wang (eds.), *Rebooting Multilateral Trade Cooperation: Perspectives from China and Europe.* London: CEPR Press, pp. 29–43.

Tan, Yeling (2021) 'How the WTO changed China: the mixed legacy of economic engagement.' *Foreign Affairs* 100:2 (March/April). At www.foreignaffairs .com/articles/china/2021-02-16/how-wto-changed-china

USTR (2017) Opening Plenary Statement of USTR Robert Lighthizer at the WTO Ministerial Conference, United States Trade Representative, December 11.

USTR (2018) Joint Statement on Trilateral Meeting of the Trade Ministers of the United States, Japan, and the European Union, 31 May. https:// ustr.gov/about-us/policy-offices/press-office/press-releases/2018/may/ joint-statement-trilateral-meeting.

Wolfe, Robert (2018) Is World Trade Organization Information Good Enough? How a Systematic Reflection by Members on Transparency Could Promote Institutional Learning, Bertelsmann Stiftung.

Wolfe, Robert (2020) 'Reforming WTO conflict management: why and how to improve the use of "specific trade concerns".' *Journal of International Economic Law*, 23(4): 817–39.

Wolfe, Robert (2021) 'Informal learning and WTO renewal using thematic sessions to create more opportunities for dialogue.' *Global Policy* 12(S3): 30–40.

WTO (2017) Procedures to Enhance Transparency and Strengthen Notification Requirements under WTO Agreements: Communication from the United States, JOB/GC/148, JOB/CTG/10, 30 October.

WTO (2019a) The Continued Relevance of Special and Differential Treatment in Favour of Developing Members to Promote Development and Ensure Inclusiveness: Communication from China, India, South Africa and the Bolivarian Republic of Venezuela, General Council, WT/GC/W/765, 18 February.

WTO (2019b) China's Proposal on WTO Reform, General Council, Communication from China WT/GC/W/773, 13 May.

WTO (2019c) Draft General Council Decision: Procedures to Strengthen the Negotiating Function of the WTO, Communication from the United States, 15 February.

WTO (2019d) A CAP-Based Approach to Address Certain Fisheries Subsidies That Contribute to Overcapacity and Overfishing: Communication from China, Negotiating Group on Rules, TN/RL/GEN/199, 4 June.

WTO (2020a) The Importance of Market-Oriented Conditions to the World Trading System: Draft General Council Decision, Communication from the United States WT/GC/W/796, 20 February.

WTO (2020b) Overview of Developments in the International Trading Environment: Annual Report by the Director-General (Mid-October 2019 to Mid-October 2020), WT/TPR/OV/23, 30 November.

WTO (2020c) Minutes of Meeting Held in the Centre William Rappard and in Virtual Format on 22–23 and 31 July 2020, WT/GC/M/186, 28 September.

WTO (2020d) Proposed Procedure for Submission of Questions and Answers under Articles 25.8 and 25.9: Proposal from the United States, G/SCM/W/557/Rev.4, 26 October.

WTO (2021a) Procedures to Enhance Transparency and Improve Compliance with Notification Requirements under WTO Agreements, JOB/GC/204/Rev.6, 14 September.

WTO (2021b) Procedural Guidelines for WTO Councils and Committees Addressing Trade Concerns: Draft General Council Decision, WT/GC/W/777/Rev.6, 15 July.

WTO (2021c) Trade Policy Review: Report by China, WT/TPR/G/415, 15 September.

WTO (2021d) Trade Policy Review: Report by the Secretariat – China, WT/TPR/S/415, 15 September.

WTO (2021e) COVID-19 and Beyond: Trade and Health, WT/GC/W/823/Rev.2, 28 October.

PART IV

Responses of China's Trading Partners

13

The Politics of Preferential Trade Liberalization with China

DAMIAN RAESS

This chapter investigates citizens' attitudes toward preferential trade liberalization with China using original survey data in an advanced economy. I focus on Switzerland as an empirical case due to data availability and the fact that the landlocked, continental European country is one of the few advanced democracies to have concluded a preferential trade agreement (PTA) with China. I consider the Sino-Swiss PTA as an instance of a North-South PTA between countries with significant differences in factor endowments and social standards, and I will assess individual attitudes in North-South trade relations against the benchmark of North-North preferential trading among similar countries, using the case of the bilateral agreements between Switzerland and the European Union (EU).

I am interested in whether the impact of the distributive effects of international trade on preferences over PTAs is conditional upon the type of trade (North-South vs. North-North). Moreover, I am interested in whether the belief that 'deep' economic integration requires the strengthening of compensatory welfare policies – the 'embedded liberalism' compromise redux (Ruggie, 1982) – mitigates the uneven distributional effects of North-South vs. North-North preferential trade liberalization among the losers of international trade. Relatedly, I ask what type of compensation policies – belief in passive and protective labor market policies or actual social investment policies – increases support for North-South PTAs among the losers of trade. Lastly, given that North-South trade has strong distributional consequences and raises issues of social standards in developing countries, I focus on the role of individuals' ideological (i.e., partisan) self-identification on PTA preferences.

The argument is fourfold. First, the losers from international trade in advanced economies (i.e., low-educated, low-skilled, low-status, and poor

The author would like to thank Simon Evenett and Patrick Wagner for helpful comments as well as Peter Hug for guidance on the analysis of the various votes in the Swiss Parliament on the Sino-Swiss trade agreement.

individuals) will less strongly support North-South PTAs, such as PTAs with China, than they do North-North PTAs, such as PTAs with the EU. Second, the belief that compensation policies legitimize deep integration among losers will more strongly increase their support for North-South than for North-North PTAs. Third, compared to social investment policies (i.e., training), belief in compensatory welfare and protective labor market policies more strongly increases support for North-South PTAs among globalization losers. Finally, North-South PTAs, in particular preferential liberalization involving a developing country with low social and human rights standards such as China, will drive a stronger wedge between left- and right-leaning individuals than North-North PTAs. The empirical analysis corroborates these expectations.

The chapter makes three contributions to the literature in international political economy. Firstly, while scholars have extensively examined individual preferences over free trade, we know relatively little about attitudes toward PTAs. This is among the first studies that investigates the determinants of mass attitudes toward preferential trade liberalization with China, and among the first that places such analysis in a more general context by theorizing about individual preferences over North-South versus North-North PTAs (though see Chiang et al. 2013). Secondly, most studies focus on mega-regional or hypothetical PTAs, and find that political factors such as sympathy/antipathy toward particular countries or security concerns outweigh explanations based on the income effects of trade (Spilker et al., 2018; DiGiuseppe and Kleinberg, 2019; see also Naoi and Urata, 2013; Jungherr et al., 2018; Dür, 2019). Focusing on the more common bilateral PTAs and on real PTAs, I find that respondent characteristics related to the distributional effects of trade liberalization, such as education, skills, financial situation, and social status, strongly explain public attitudes toward trade agreements. Lastly, the findings have noteworthy implications for the backlash against globalization. National-populist reactions to the China shock are a big part of the globalization backlash (Autor et al., 2013; Feigenbaum and Hall, 2015; Colantone and Stanig, 2018b). The results provide strong evidence for the role of domestic compensation policies in the form of passive/protective labor market policies in increasing support for trade liberalization with China among globalization losers.

The chapter is organized as follows. The first section identifies blind spots in the literature that the study begins to fill. The second introduces the argument. The third and fourth sections present the empirical analysis. The fifth provides a discussion while the final section concludes.

I Literature

Over the past twenty years, research on individual preferences over free trade has fast grown in number and sophistication, with seemingly no end in sight. One prominent line of inquiry and debate has been whether economic self-interest explains trade policy preferences (e.g., Scheve and Slaughter, 2001; Mayda and Rodrik, 2005; Mansfield and Mutz, 2009). A second, and related line of inquiry has been whether compensatory welfare policies help legitimize trade openness (e.g., Hays et al., 2005; Ehrlich and Hearn, 2014). These studies have largely focused on individual preferences over free trade (or protectionism) in general. Jungherr et al. (2018) interrogate whether individual-level preferences for the general principle of free trade and for specific trade agreements are similar. Using public opinion data from Germany, the authors show that while the standard economic and non-economic models perform well in explaining public opinion on trade, contextual factors unrelated to trade are more useful in explaining support for the Transatlantic Trade and Investment Partnership (TTIP).

In fact, we know little about the determinants of citizens' support for and opposition to PTAs in democracies (Baccini, 2019: 82). The few studies on 'real-world' PTAs tend to focus on atypical PTAs, namely the mega-regional trade agreements, which, due to their sheer scope and geopolitical considerations, may introduce some bias in the literature's research findings. For example, Naoi and Urata (2013) examine individual attitudes toward the Trans-Pacific Partnership Agreement (TPP) in Japan and find that partisanship rather than economic self-interest is the most relevant determinant of TPP support. Jungherr et al. (2018) find that postures toward transatlantic cooperation and predispositions toward the role of interest groups in politics as well as toward domestic market regulation correlate with support for TTIP. Dür (2019) demonstrates that the argument that the TTIP would allow foreign firms to sue domestic governments had a large negative effect on public opinion, while the promise of job creation hardly mattered. Rankin (2004) shows that national identity rather than economic interest explains American and Canadian opinion on the North American Free Trade Agreement.

Experimental studies probing preferences for hypothetical PTAs also conclude about the primacy of non-economic over economic factors. DiGiuseppe and Kleinberg (2019) investigate the role of security considerations. Focusing on American respondents, they find that PTAs involving political rivals and those promising diminished international influence reduce support for PTAs, and that security concerns diminish the degree to which information about the projected economic effects influences individuals' preferences for PTAs. Spilker et al. (2018) study individual attitudes toward PTAs in Costa Rica, Nicaragua, and Vietnam. They show that sympathy/antipathy toward particular countries matters more than economic considerations. Finally, in his study on mass support for potential PTA partners in Canada, India, and the US, Tuxhorn (2019) finds limited support for economic preferences derived from the factor endowment trade model.

II The Argument

North-South trade is based on differences in the factor endowments of countries (Heckscher-Ohlin model). Rich countries have a comparative advantage in the production of goods that make intensive use of capital and skilled labor, their abundant factors. Conversely, poor countries, being well endowed in (semi- and) unskilled labor, will specialize production in goods that make intensive use of low-skilled labor. North-South trade is predominantly inter-industry trade, a type of trade that has sharp distributional consequences. According to Stolper-Samuelson, under the assumption of costless inter-sectoral mobility of production factors, trade benefits the owners of the abundant factors and harms the owners of the scarce factors. In rich countries, the losers are the semi- and low-skilled workers, whereas the winners are capital owners and high-skilled workers. Opposition to trade in advanced countries should therefore be concentrated among low-skilled workers (and unions representing them), particularly opposition to trade liberalization with developing countries richly endowed with unskilled (manual) labor, such as China.

By contrast, North-North trade is predominantly intra-industry trade, driven by customer preferences for differentiated goods. Compared to inter-industry trade, adjustment costs are likely lower as jobs lost due to customers shifting to foreign suppliers may be offset to a large degree by the job-enhancing expansion in foreign demand for similar, differentiated goods produced domestically. A typical example is the case of the Frenchman buying a VW car and the German buying a Renault, whereas prior to trading they bought domestically produced cars. In short, North-North trade has less strong distributional effects than North-South trade and should therefore be less strongly opposed by the losers of international trade in rich countries. Hence:

Hypothesis 1: Among the losers of trade in advanced economies (i.e., low-educated, low-skilled, low-status, and poor individuals), the level of support is lower for North-South PTAs, in particular preferential trade liberalization with China, than for North-North PTAs.

The post-war compromise of "embedded liberalism" was premised on the idea that domestic welfare compensation helps legitimize an open economy (Ruggie, 1982). Governments committed to free trade provided insurance and other transfers to compensate those who lost economically from increased trade. Historical-comparative analysis has demonstrated an association between economic openness and welfare spending in advanced economies (Cameron, 1978; Rodrik, 1998), at least up until the 1990s (Busemeyer, 2009).

Research has corroborated the microfoundations of the 'compensation' thesis. For a sample of thirteen advanced economies, Hays et al. (2005) show that individuals employed in import-competing sectors strongly oppose trade, while unemployment insurance and active labor market programs moderate their opposition. Similarly, using a survey experiment in the United States (US), Ehrlich and Hearn (2014) show that knowledge of the Trade Adjustment Assistance (TAA) program, introduced to the experimental group as a federal program providing expanded unemployment insurance and job retraining opportunities to workers who lose their jobs, results in higher support for free trade among low-income individuals. Based on Swiss survey data, Walter (2010) finds that globalization losers, in particular low-skilled workers, are more likely to experience economic insecurity, demand welfare compensation, and vote for social-democratic parties.

While actual compensatory policies or the belief that compensation buys support for globalization should increase the losers' support for (preferential) trade liberalization, I expect this effect to be stronger in the North-South than in the North-North trade context. North-South trade and trade agreements have strong labor market effects (Hakobyan and McLaren, 2016), stronger than North-North trade. Trade integration with low-wage countries is thus more likely to generate demands for compensation (Burgoon, 2001), and, conversely, compensatory policies are more likely to increase support for North-South than for North-North PTAs and trade.

It is well established that trade with China has strongly affected labor markets in advanced economies. Autor et al. (2013) report negative effects of Chinese import competition on employment levels and wages in local labor markets in the US, but also higher social transfer payments (see also Autor et al., 2016). Thewissen and Van Vliet (2019) generalize the finding of depressing employment effects in sectors facing Chinese imports to eighteen OECD countries while showing that low-skilled workers endure most adjustment costs as production work by these workers is substituted by Chinese exports. Since preferential trade liberalization tends to be associated with more trade flows among trading partners, losers in advanced economies should be particularly prone to oppose PTAs with China, and belief that compensation enables openness should reduce such opposition.

Hypothesis 2: Among the losers of trade in advanced economies, the belief that increased government compensation (i.e., the strengthening of employment protection, unemployment insurance, and the protection of working hours) enables 'deep' economic integration more strongly increases support for North-South PTAs, in particular preferential trade liberalization with China, than for North-North PTAs.

Compensation measures take various forms. Perhaps the most obvious government policies to offset job losses due to increased imports are income support measures. In cross-sectional analysis, the generosity of unemployment benefits correlates with support for free trade (Hays et al., 2005). In the US, the losers of international trade are more inclined to support trade-related unemployment insurance than the winners (Ehrlich, 2010).

Globalization is a source of job insecurity (Rodrik, 1998; Scheve and Slaughter, 2004). The losers report higher levels of fear of losing their jobs (Walter, 2010). Rules that make it costly for employers to fire their workers may prevent job losses and therefore reduce actual or perceived economic insecurity associated with trade openness. Employment protection regulation and unemployment insurance may thus be substitutes in how they increase support for trade liberalization among globalization losers. Alternatively, because wages tend to be sticky due to income policies or collective agreements, labor market adjustments to increased trade competition might occur through longer working hours at a given wage level. European labor markets facing rising Chinese imports might be particularly susceptible to responding in this way. Europeans typically work short hours (while caring about work-life balance issues) whereas the Chinese work long hours, not least because many of them have a preference for working overtime hours to increase their income. Rules and regulations protecting standard working hours in advanced economies might thus also condition attitudes towards (preferential) trade liberalization. In short, not just compensatory welfare institutions but also protective labor market policies ought to moderate the losers' opposition to trade, particularly North-South trade and PTAs.

What about social investment policies such as occupational training? The evidence is mixed. In the cross-national context, Hays et al. (2005) show that spending on active labor market programs is associated with higher individual support for trade, while Hays (2009) finds that it does not increase support for trade among those employed in tradeable sectors. The results are also inconclusive as to whether participation in TAA training programs improves the employment outcomes of participants (Decker and Corson, 1995; Reynolds and Palatucci, 2012). Regarding training, while it might upgrade skills, help career advancement, and/or sustain wage increases, it does not necessarily reduce the risk of job losses due to increased trade competition. With job retraining programs, meanwhile, individuals run the risk of social downgrading, as they might be required to accept employment at lower skill levels. Finally, government spending on active labor market policies remains a small fraction of total social spending in advanced economies. In short, we have the basis for the third hypothesis.

Hypothesis 3: Among the losers of trade in advanced economies, the belief that increased compensatory welfare and protective labor market policies enables 'deep' economic integration more strongly increases the support for North-South PTAs, in particular preferential trade liberalization with China, than social investment policies (i.e., training).

Partisanship matters for trade policy with right-wing parties and individuals being more supportive of free trade than their left-wing counterparts are (Scheve and Slaughter, 2001; Milner and Judkins, 2004). North-South trade integration is likely to raise concerns about poor labor and human rights and low environmental protection in developing countries, opening up a cleavage between left parties that are critical of North-South PTAs and right parties that are supportive. PTAs with China are a case in point, given the extensive violations of fundamental labor rights in China. Moreover, Beijing objects to the inclusion of far-reaching labor provisions in its PTAs, which explains why PTAs signed by China include rather shallow provisions (LABPTA dataset; Raess and Sari, 2018, 2021). This constitutes a major obstacle to the conclusion of bilateral trade agreements between China and the big trading powers. In those circumstances, existing labor-related level playing field rules in Chinese trade agreements are unlikely to increase support for trade liberalization with China in advanced economies, because they do not provide the kind of ex-ante reassurance mechanism or the fair trade norms that help legitimize trade openness (Bastiaens and Postnikov, 2020).

Left-oriented parties and individuals should be particularly concerned, given their stance on labor and human rights issues. Hence the final hypothesis:

Hypothesis 4: In advanced economies, the effect of partisanship – with left-leaning individuals being less supportive than right-leaning individuals – is stronger for North-South PTAs, in particular preferential trade liberalization with China, than for North-North PTAs.

III Data

I use representative data from Swiss individuals to test my arguments. I use an original dataset combining data from the 2015 wave of the Measurement and Observation of Social Attitudes in Switzerland survey (MOSAiCH; Ernst Stähli et al., 2015) and from my topical module on Switzerland's foreign economic relations, which, after a nationally competitive bid, was included in the MOSAiCH survey. While the former provided data on most independent and control variables, the latter provided the survey questions for the dependent variables and a few key independent and control variables.

While the selection of the Swiss case is data related, it is well suited to examine public attitudes toward trade cooperation with China. Switzerland's leading trade partner in Asia and its third largest partner worldwide is China. Importantly, Switzerland is one of the few advanced economies, and the first major European country, to have signed a PTA with China.[1] The Sino-Swiss PTA was concluded in July 2013, after only two years of negotiations, and came into force on July 1, 2014. The Swiss proponents hailed the deal as their most important agreement since the 1972 PTA with the EU (Dadush et al., 2020). While Switzerland was keen to gain preferential market access to the Chinese market before its main competitors (i.e., EU member states, but also the US), "China saw Switzerland as a gateway into Europe and viewed the trade agreement as an important test case, one that might soften the EU's traditional reluctance to negotiate with China" (Dadush et al., 2020). Given the salience of the Sino-Swiss trade deal and the timing of the data collection (the survey was administered between February and July 2015), choices made by survey respondents are likely

[1] China signed PTAs with New Zealand (2008), Singapore (2008), Iceland (2013), Australia (2015), and South Korea (2015).

to accurately capture choices they would make in real-world situations (Hainmueller et al., 2015).[2]

The selection of the EU as the benchmark against which to compare China in terms of attitudes toward trade cooperation is equally fitting. The EU is by far Switzerland's largest trading partner. Bilateral treaties govern the economic relations between Switzerland and the EU. The 1972 PTA created a free trade zone for industrial products. After the Swiss people voted against joining the European Economic Area in 1992, the government proposed bilateral negotiations (Linder, 2011). The Bilaterals I (1999) cover agreements in seven areas (free movement of persons, technical barriers to trade, public procurement, agriculture, research, civil aviation, and overland transport), the Bilaterals II (2004) in nine (processed agricultural products, statistics, pensions, education/vocational training, environment, media, fight against fraud, taxation of savings, and Schengen/Dublin on internal security). So-called 'flanking measures' were adopted in June 2004 in connection with the effective introduction of the free movement of persons. These measures aim to prevent the undercutting of wages and social conditions. They include the reinforcement of collectively agreed on minimum wages, the facilitation of extension clauses (making it easier to declare collective labor agreements generally binding), and the hiring of labor inspectors. In the face of opposition from the national-conservative party, the government, and the business community needed the trade unions' support to win the referendum, which they did with a comfortable majority of two-thirds (Linder, 2011; Oesch, 2011).

Switzerland has historically enjoyed good political relations with both China and the EU. The Swiss government was one of the first Western countries to recognize the People's Republic of China on January 17, 1950. It has maintained broad-based bilateral relations with Beijing since the 1980s, including a high-level annual human rights dialogue since 1991. Geographic, cultural, and economic reasons explain Switzerland's good relations with its European neighbors.

In a comparative perspective, Switzerland is a coordinated market economy, although it has hybrid features not least due to liberal labor market institutions (Hall and Soskice, 2001; Mach and Trampusch, 2011). The Swiss tend to work long hours, collective bargaining

[2] While the Swiss citizens did not vote in a referendum on the Sino-Swiss PTA, they did approve the Indonesia-EFTA trade agreement in 2021.

coverage is moderate, the protection of employment is low, while unemployment benefits are relatively generous (Emmenegger, 2011; Scruggs et al., 2017).

(i) Dependent Variables

Pro-EU PTA is an ordinal variable measuring respondents' opinions on "The bilateral agreements with the EU have reinforced the exchanges of goods and services between Switzerland and the EU. To what extent are you favorable to this policy led by the Confederation?" Answers are recorded on a 5-point scale, as follows: 1 = "very unfavorable"; 2 = "somewhat unfavorable"; 3 = "neither/nor"; 4 = "somewhat favorable"; and 5 = "very favorable." Higher values thus indicate greater support for preferential trade liberalization between Switzerland and the EU. The responses by individuals who expressed no opinion or who did not answer were coded as missing.

Pro-CN PTA measures attitudes towards bilateral trade liberalization between Switzerland and China. Survey respondents were asked their opinion on the following question: "In 2013, Switzerland signed a trade agreement with China, reinforcing the exchanges of goods and services. To what extent are you favorable to this policy led by the Confederation?" Answers are recorded on the same 5-point scale, while "don't knows" and "no responses" were treated as missing values.

Pro-PTA, the main dependent variable in the statistical analysis, is generated by stacking the data, specifically by stacking the variables *Pro-EU PTA* and *Pro-CN PTA*. I created a dummy variable labeled *China PTA*, which takes a score of 1 for all observations of the variable *Pro-CN PTA* (0 otherwise; that is, 0 if the observations pertain to the variable *Pro-EU PTA*). I interacted this dummy with the variables for globalization losers to test Hypothesis 1 and, in a triple interaction model, I interacted these interaction terms with variables measuring compensatory welfare and labor market policies to test Hypotheses 2 and 3.

(ii) Independent Variables

1 Losers of International Trade

I considered four groups of losers in advanced economies, defined by their level of education, their skills, their financial situation, and their (self-declared) social status. Operationalizing the losers of international trade by way of individuals' educational attainment and skill profile is commonplace in the literature. Considering (subjective) measures of individuals' finances and social status is less common though no less important as globalization has led to stagnating or eroding incomes for some workers and, if not outright downward social mobility, the perception of declining (relative) social status.

Low education equals 1 if the respondent has completed less than twelve years of full-time schooling. According to this measure, low-educated individuals are high-school dropouts. *Manual workers* are individuals whose job involves primarily physical work such as building, making, carrying, caring, etc. Individuals in the following major groups of the International Standard Classification of Occupations (ISCO-8) are considered manual workers: clerical support workers (group #4), services and sales workers (#5), skilled agricultural, forestry, and fishery workers (#6), craft and related trades workers (#7), plant and machine operators and assemblers (#8), elementary occupations (#9), and armed forces occupations (#0).[3]

Poor financial situation gets a score of 1 if individuals answer "bad" or "very bad" to the survey question "How do you rate your current financial situation?" (0 otherwise). Finally, *Low status* equals 1 if individuals self-identify as belonging to groups that tend to be toward the bottom of society (i.e., on the reverted 1–10 scale, individuals who place themselves on the scores 6–10). It should be noted that the bivariate correlations between these variables are moderate at best.[4]

2 Compensatory Welfare and Labor Market Institutions

In the drop-off questionnaire, I asked respondents if they believe that government compensatory policies help legitimize deep economic integration. The survey question probes individual opinions regarding various compensatory welfare and protective labor market policies, as follows (English translation): "Would you be more in favor of strengthening foreign investment in Switzerland and trade in goods and services with other countries, if the Swiss government took measures to (1) discourage companies from laying off their employees? (2) protect the weekly working time? (3) strengthen the right to unemployment?" The questions are framed as support for moving beyond existing levels of compensation and openness, which is why earlier I referred to belief in the 'embedded

[3] Non-manual workers comprise managers (#1), professionals (#2), and technicians and associate professionals (#3).

[4] The highest correlation, at .30, is between low education and manual workers.

liberalism' compromise *redux*. *Pro-globalization compensation* (or simply *compensation*), a dummy, equals 1 if respondents say they would be "probably more" or "more" in support (scores of 3 and 4 on the 4-point scale) for each of the policies (0 otherwise). While I aggregated the measures for presentational reasons, I consider disaggregated results in the discussion section.

The measure of social investment policies is actual training. Upskilling through training might thwart trade-related job losses. *Training* is a dummy that equals 1 if the individual received any training that allowed him or her to improve skills in the past 12 months.

3 Individuals' Party Orientation

Included as a control, *Right ideology* measures self-placement on the ideological left-right scale (0–10). Right-wing individuals prefer free markets and should therefore be supportive of PTAs. In the model that tests the variegated effect of partisanship on North-South vs. North-North PTAs (Hypothesis 4), I use a trichotomous variable where Left equals the low scores (0–3), Centre the middle (4–6), and Right the high (7–10).

(iii) Control Variables

The baseline model controls for socio-demographic determinants of trade policy. *Female* is a dummy that equals 1 if respondents are women. If anything, women are more protectionist than men (Mansfield et al., 2015). *Age*, measured in years, captures inter-generational differences in attitudes toward trade due for instance to socialization processes. Previous studies have included the effect of rural-urban residence in models of trade policy preferences (Mayda and Rodrik, 2005; Mansfield and Mutz, 2009). *Urban residence* is a categorical variable with five residential types, ranging from a farm or house in the countryside to a big city. Urban residence should positively correlate with support for PTAs.

Next, I include controls for pre-existing cultural and ideological dispositions. *Swiss-German* is a dummy that equals 1 if the survey was administered in Swiss-German or Romansh (0 if French or Italian). It captures differences in trade opinions and stereotypes of trading partners that may be rooted in different Swiss cultures (and/or related sub-national ideologies of political economy) as well as differences that may exist in the phrasing of the survey questions in each national language. As Swiss-German citizens more strongly embrace economic liberalism than their French-Swiss or Swiss-Italian counterparts, being

Swiss German should positively correlate with Pro-PTA attitudes. *Nationalism* is measured as opinions on the item "open borders and the intermingling of populations endanger important characteristics of Swiss culture," with higher values on the 5-point scale indicating stronger nationalist sentiment. Nationalism should negatively correlate with Pro-PTA attitudes. *Trust in the EU* is an ordinal variable measuring respondents' trust in the EU. Individuals who trust the supranational institution should generally be more supportive of PTAs, particularly PTAs with the EU. As mentioned above, I include a measure of individuals' party orientation.

I also control for alternative explanations derived from competing trade theories. *Foreign business share* is the respondent's answer, measured on a 4-point scale, to the question "How much does your company or employer export its production or engage in economic activities abroad?" Capturing within sector firm heterogeneity (Melitz, 2003), foreign business share ought to positively correlate with Pro-PTA attitudes. *Mobility* is a dummy that takes the value of 1 if respondents have ever moved to improve their employment prospects. Mobility influences attitudes toward trade policy (Mansfield et al., 2015; Owen, 2013: 729). Specifically, it should be positively associated with support for preferential trade liberalization. Moreover, individuals as consumers may have different preferences over trade than they do as producers of goods and services (Baker, 2005). *Trade lowers prices* records opinions on "one must open the borders to trade so that prices fall," measured on a 5-point scale. Individuals who believe that trade openness lowers consumer prices are likely to be more supportive of PTAs.

Finally, *Media exposure* measures the frequency with which respondents use the media (including television, newspapers, radio, and the internet) to obtain political news or information (measured on a 7-point scale). As a proxy for cognitive capacity, we expect individuals who regularly use media to be more favorable toward PTA.

The baseline models include ten industry dummies that control the respondents' sector of employment. Industry characteristics, such as export orientation or import competition, correlate with industry-level preferences over trade policy. I restrict the sample to the working-age population in order to include only individuals directly affected by the distributional effects of trade. The models are estimated using an ordered probit estimator, with robust standard errors clustered by industry. Using ordered logistic models instead does not change the results. Descriptive statistics for all the variables are shown in Appendix Table A1.

IV Results

Figure 13.1 shows the average scores in favor of North-North vs. North-South PTAs among globalization losers. As can be seen in Panels A-D, the level of support is consistently higher for the PTA with the EU than for the PTA with China, providing initial support for Hypothesis 1.

Figure 13.2 displays the difference in support for North-North vs. North-South PTAs for low-status workers as a function of believing in pro-globalization compensation (Panels A and B) and of being recently trained (Panels C and D). The graphs show that belief in compensation more strongly increases support for trade liberalization with China (+14.8%, from 2.98 to 3.42) than with the EU (+7.7%, from 3.66 to 3.94), whereas training does not seem to affect support for PTAs with either the EU or China. This provides initial support for Hypotheses 2 and 3.

Figure 13.3, finally, shows the average support for North-North vs. North-South trade liberalization among left-, centre- and right-leaning

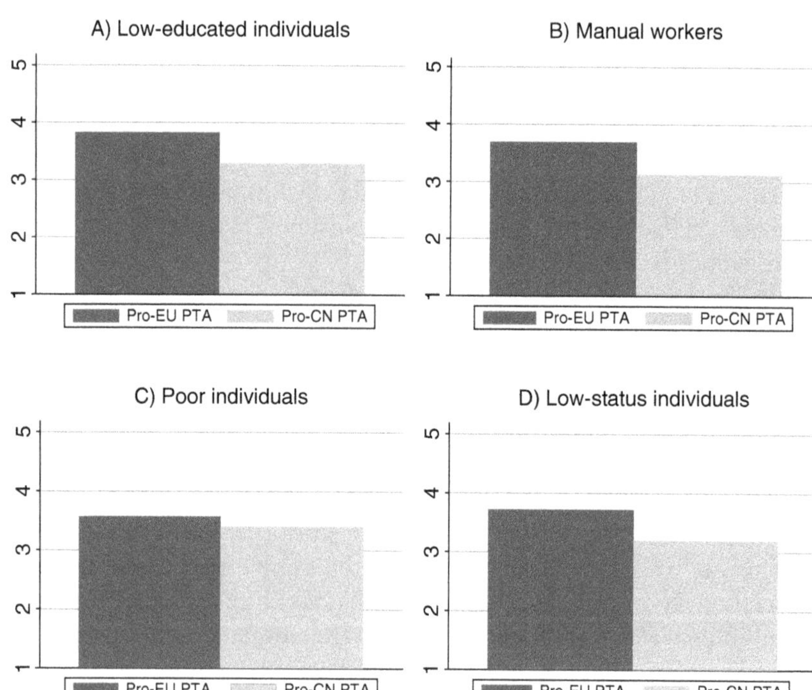

Figure 13.1 Globalization losers and support for EU PTA vs. China PTA.

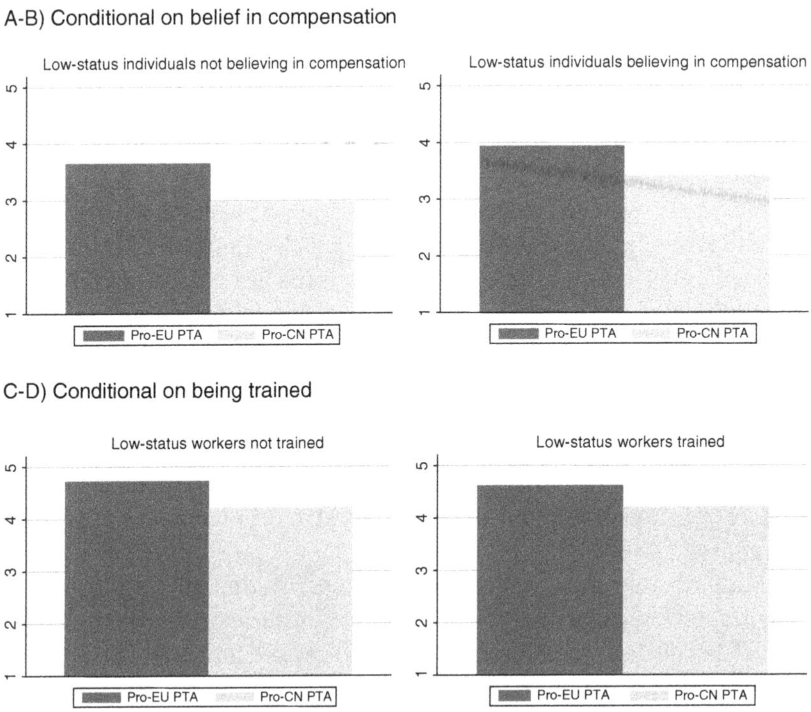

Figure 13.2 Support for EU PTA vs. China PTA among low-status individuals.

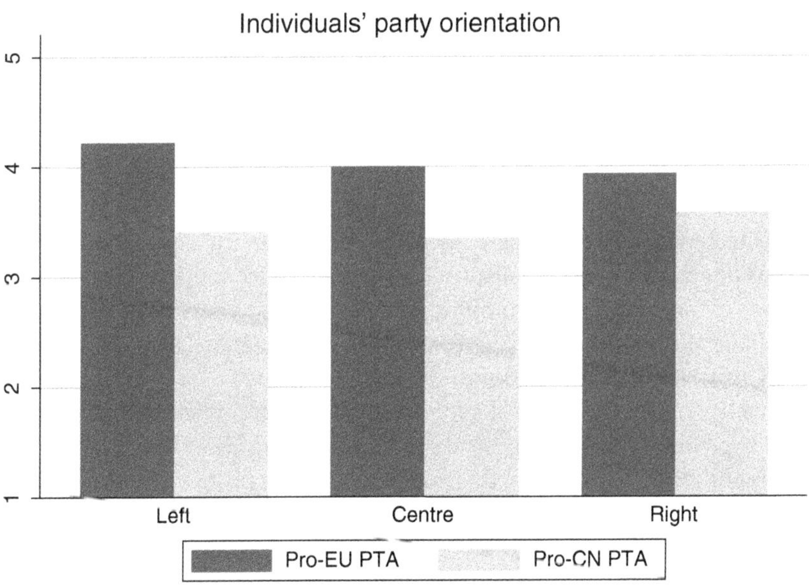

Figure 13.3 Partisan orientation and support for EU PTA vs. China PTA

individuals. Left-wing individuals hold more negative views of preferential trade with China than their right-wing counterparts do, while the same does not hold for preferential trade with the EU, suggesting first evidence for Hypothesis 4.

Table 13.1 shows the multivariate regression results for the interaction models involving one of the measures of globalization losers at the time and the China PTA dummy with *Pro-PTA* as the dependent variable. The statistically significant controls perform as expected, raising our confidence in the model specification. Female respondents and individuals expressing nationalist sentiment are less likely to support PTAs. By contrast, individuals living in urban centers (likely due to their more cosmopolitan worldviews), those trusting in the supranational body of the EU, those working in a firm doing business abroad, those who believe trade is good for consumers, and those more exposed to the media are more likely to support PTAs.

The main results show a consistent pattern across the various measures of globalization losers. First, the coefficients for globalization losers are all negative and statistically significant. In the presence of the interaction terms, these coefficients indicate the difference in support for EU PTA between globalization losers and winners. In line with the factor model of international trade, we find that low-educated individuals, manual workers, poor individuals and low-status individuals are less supportive of preferential trade liberalization with the EU than their respective counterparts are. Second, the coefficients for *China's PTA* are negative and highly significant, indicating that on average individuals are less supportive of the PTA with China compared to the PTA with the EU. Third, the coefficients for the interaction terms are positive and, in two cases out of four, statistically significant. This indicates that the gap in support between globalization losers and winners tends to be narrower for the PTA with China than for the PTA with the EU. While this finding runs against the predictions from international trade theory, it may hide a more complex pattern whereby compensatory policies condition the relationships between being a globalization loser and support for North-North vs. North-South PTAs (see below).

In any event, is the level of support for PTAs among globalization losers lower for PTA with China than for PTA with the EU, as suggested by Hypothesis 1? Answering this question requires post-estimation analysis. Based on Model 4, keeping all other variables are their mean values, low-status workers are approximately 50 per cent less likely to be very favorable (score of 5) to a PTA with China than a PTA with the EU. The corresponding figures for low-skilled individuals, manual workers, and

Table 13.1 *Globalization losers and support for North-North vs. North-South PTAs*

	(1)	(2)	(3)	(4)
	DV = Pro-PTA			
Low education	−0.294*** (0.082)			
Manual worker		−0.527*** (0.078)		
Poor financial situation			−0.390** (0.186)	
Low status				−0.295** (0.141)
China PTA	−0.803*** (0.100)	−0.808*** (0.081)	−0.734*** (0.054)	−0.763*** (0.073)
Low edu*China PTA	0.165 (0.118)			
Manual*China PTA		0.206* (0.113)		
Poor*China PTA			0.613*** (0.162)	
Low stat*China PTA				0.211 (0.150)
Female	−0.423*** (0.074)	−0.392*** (0.087)	−0.415*** (0.081)	−0.407*** (0.087)
Age	0.006* (0.003)	0.004 (0.003)	0.005 (0.003)	0.005* (0.003)
Urban residence	0.099** (0.044)	0.098** (0.050)	0.114** (0.050)	0.121** (0.051)
Swiss-German	0.216** (0.109)	0.181 (0.111)	0.194* (0.118)	0.178 (0.115)
Right ideology	0.036 (0.026)	0.029 (0.024)	0.038 (0.028)	0.033 (0.025)
Nationalism	−0.282*** (0.042)	−0.272*** (0.041)	−0.292*** (0.041)	0.288*** (0.042)
Trust in the EU	0.124** (0.053)	0.110** (0.048)	0.130** (0.053)	0.115** (0.056)
Foreign business share	0.150* (0.081)	0.146** (0.072)	0.170** (0.074)	0.176** (0.078)
Mobility	0.072 (0.077)	0.074 (0.083)	0.110 (0.073)	0.092 (0.076)

Table 13.1 (*cont.*)

	(1)	(2)	(3)	(4)
		DV = Pro-PTA		
Trade lowers prices	0.219***	0.226***	0.214***	0.214***
	(0.038)	(0.038)	(0.037)	(0.035)
Media exposure	0.062**	0.052*	0.073***	0.067**
	(0.028)	(0.028)	(0.026)	(0.028)
Observations	980	978	980	972
Pseudo R-squared	0.130	0.139	0.129	0.130

Robust standard errors in parentheses; ***$p < 0.01$, **$p < 0.05$, *$p < 0.1$.

poor individuals are 53, 54, and 13 per cent, respectively. In short, the empirical analysis corroborates Hypothesis 1.

Table 13.2 shows the results for the triple interaction models with belief in compensation as one of the constituent terms. With one exception, the coefficients for the measures of globalization losers remain negative and statistically significant, and so do the coefficients for PTA with China. Interestingly, the coefficients of the interaction terms globalization losers*China PTA are now negative (with one exception) and statistically insignificant, which is more in line with trade theory. The interpretation of this (double) interaction is that the gap in support between globalization losers and winners who do not believe in compensation tends to increase as one moves from PTA with the EU to PTA with China, although the effect is not statistically significant. The triple interactions are with one exception as expected positive and highly significant, suggesting that the narrowing gap in support between losers and winners tends to be reduced more strongly for PTA with China than PTA with the EU as one moves from non-belief to belief in compensation.

Post-estimation analysis reveals the magnitude of the hypothesized effects. Based on Model 8, low-status individuals are about 65 per cent more likely to strongly support (score of 5) PTA with China when they believe in compensation than when they do not. By contrast, they are about 5 per cent less likely to strongly support PTA with the EU when they believe in compensatory policies than when they do not. For manual workers (Model 6), the corresponding (rounded) figures are +30 and +3 per cent, respectively, while for poor individuals (Model 7) they are

Table 13.2 *The conditional effect of compensatory welfare policies on support for North-North vs. North-South PTAs*

	(5)	(6)	(7)	(8)
	DV = Pro-PTA			
Low edu*China PTA*Compensation.	−0.096 (0.294)			
Manual*China PTA*Compensation.		0.567*** (0.182)		
Poor*China PTA*Compensation.			1.366** (0.648)	
Low stat*China PTA*Compensation.				0.849*** (0.215)
Low education	−0.554*** (0.145)			
Manual worker		−0.520*** (0.163)		
Poor financial situation			0.388 (0.741)	
Low status				−0.321* (0.165)
China PTA	−0.793*** (0.117)	−0.629*** (0.083)	−0.655*** (0.071)	−0.608*** (0.099)
Low education*China PTA	0.215 (0.150)			
Manual*China PTA		−0.116 (0.186)		
Poor*China PTA			−0.184 (0.530)	
Low stat*China PTA				−0.214 (0.206)
Compensation	−0.298 (0.189)	0.015 (0.154)	0.032 (0.104)	−0.012 (0.127)
Low education*Compensation	0.498** (0.225)			
Manual*Compensation		0.017 (0.253)		
Poor*Compensation			−0.952 (0.813)	
Low stat*Compensation				−0.046 (0.220)

Table 13.2 (*cont.*)

	(5)	(6)	(7)	(8)
	DV = Pro-PTA			
China PTA*Compensation	−0.124	−0.422***	−0.270*	−0.429**
	(0.281)	(0.143)	(0.158)	(0.172)
Female	−0.424***	−0.389***	−0.421***	−0.405***
	(0.078)	(0.094)	(0.083)	(0.094)
Age	0.003	0.001	0.003	0.003
	(0.003)	(0.003)	(0.004)	(0.003)
Urban residence	0.130**	0.127**	0.140**	0.151**
	(0.053)	(0.058)	(0.057)	(0.061)
Swiss-German	0.156	0.130	0.159	0.129
	(0.103)	(0.107)	(0.104)	(0.104)
Right ideology	0.036*	0.036*	0.041*	0.030
	(0.022)	(0.020)	(0.023)	(0.019)
Nationalism	−0.282***	−0.284***	−0.304***	−0.293***
	(0.050)	(0.049)	(0.048)	(0.052)
Trust in the EU	0.122*	0.122**	0.136**	0.123*
	(0.067)	(0.059)	(0.065)	(0.070)
Foreign business share	0.106	0.107	0.133	0.128
	(0.105)	(0.097)	(0.102)	(0.107)
Mobility	0.084	0.086	0.111	0.102
	(0.078)	(0.091)	(0.084)	(0.081)
Trade lowers prices	0.207***	0.199***	0.196***	0.192***
	(0.039)	(0.036)	(0.040)	(0.038)
Media exposure	0.051*	0.054*	0.062**	0.058**
	(0.030)	(0.030)	(0.026)	(0.029)
Observations	837	837	837	831
Pseudo *R*-squared	0.143	0.149	0.140	0.146

Robust standard errors in parentheses; $^{***}p < 0.01$, $^{**}p < 0.05$, $^{*}p < 0.1$.

+20 and −55 per cent. Only in the case of low-educated individuals do we observe that belief in compensation less strongly increases support for PTAs with China than with the EU (−3 and +20 per cent, respectively).[5] Overall, these findings provide support for Hypothesis 2.

[5] When support for PTAs is measured with a score of 4 ("somewhat favorable"), there is no difference in how belief in compensation changes support for PTA with China compared to PTA with the EU among low-educated individuals (−1 per cent in both cases).

In Table 13.3, we replace our measure of compensatory welfare and labor market policies with our measure of social investment policy. The results show that none of the double interaction terms of interest (globalization losers*training) and none of the triple interaction terms are statistically significant. This suggests that training does not condition the support for North-South PTAs (or North-North PTAs for that matter) among globalization losers. The main results from Tables 13.2 and 13.3 lend support for Hypothesis 3.

Finally, Table 13.4 shows the results for the effect of individuals' partisan orientation. In this model, left-wing orientation is the reference (and thus omitted) category. While the coefficients for Centre and Right are negative, only the latter is (weakly) statistically significant. In the presence of the interaction term, this means that the support for PTA with the EU tends to be lower among right-wing than among left-wing individuals. This finding comports with the national-conservative Swiss People's Party's opposition to and the Socialist Party's support for the bilateral agreements. The interaction terms *Centre*China PTA* and *Right*China PTA* are positive and statistically significant, as expected. Taken together, we observe 'traditional' partisan effects on individual support for North-South PTAs but not for North-North PTAs, providing support for Hypothesis 4. Indeed, based on Model 13, the predicted probabilities of respondents having a score of 5 ("very favorable") on the dependent variable indicate that left individuals are 10 per cent more likely to support PTA with the EU than individuals who self-identify as centrists, while centrists are 8 per cent more likely to support PTA with the EU than right individuals. By contrast, right-wing individuals are 70 per cent more likely to support PTA with China than centrists, who in turn are about 15 per cent more likely to support PTA with China compared to left-wing individuals.

(i) Robustness Checks

I ran supplementary models to assess the robustness of the results.[6] First, I used an alternate operationalization of the dependent variable. By collapsing the categories 1="very unfavorable" and 2="somewhat unfavorable," on the one hand, and 4="somewhat favorable" and 5="very favorable," on the other hand, I obtained a trichotomous variable. The main results hold up.

[6] Results available upon request.

Table 13.3 *The conditional effect of social investment policies on support for North-North vs. North-South PTAs*

	(9)	(10)	(11)	(12)
	DV = Pro-PTA			
Low edu*China PTA*Training	−0.269 (0.504)			
Manual*China PTA*Training		0.127 (0.351)		
Poor*China PTA*Training			0.140 (0.603)	
Low stat*China PTA*Training				0.240 (0.229)
Low education	−0.422** (0.207)			
Manual worker		−0.567*** (0.147)		
Poor financial situation			−0.942 (0.919)	
Low status				−0.220 (0.238)
China PTA	−1.113*** (0.307)	−0.949*** (0.174)	−0.814*** (0.080)	−0.858*** (0.095)
Low education*China PTA	0.426 (0.386)			
Manual*China PTA		0.187 (0.298)		
Poor*China PTA			0.113 (0.482)	
Low stat*China PTA				0.141 (0.217)
Compensation				
Training	−0.236 (0.183)	−0.167* (0.101)	−0.116 (0.083)	−0.114 (0.092)
Low education*Training	0.108 (0.286)			
Manual*Training		−0.067 (0.208)		
Poor*Training			0.543 (1.060)	

Table 13.3 (*cont.*)

	(9)	(10)	(11)	(12)
		DV = Pro-PTA		
Low stat*Training				−0.158
				(0.225)
China PTA*Training	0.395	0.200	0.166	0.141**
	(0.285)	(0.134)	(0.104)	(0.063)
Female	−0.424***	−0.389***	−0.416***	−0.416***
	(0.081)	(0.083)	(0.093)	(0.087)
Age	0.006***	0.004**	0.006***	0.006***
	(0.002)	(0.002)	(0.002)	(0.002)
Urban residence	0.089*	0.092*	0.111*	0.116*
	(0.054)	(0.056)	(0.060)	(0.063)
Swiss-German	0.307**	0.278*	0.260*	0.271*
	(0.152)	(0.148)	(0.156)	(0.153)
Right ideology	0.016	0.007	0.017	0.014
	(0.038)	(0.033)	(0.039)	(0.036)
Nationalism	−0.279***	−0.267***	−0.291***	−0.288***
	(0.041)	(0.044)	(0.046)	(0.041)
Trust in the EU	0.105**	0.098**	0.118**	0.112**
	(0.054)	(0.047)	(0.049)	(0.049)
Foreign business share	0.181*	0.180**	0.208**	0.198**
	(0.104)	(0.089)	(0.096)	(0.101)
Mobility	0.039	0.036	0.097	0.058
	(0.108)	(0.113)	(0.106)	(0.105)
Trade lowers prices	0.241***	0.248***	0.233***	0.235***
	(0.038)	(0.037)	(0.038)	(0.040)
Media exposure	0.067*	0.056*	0.077**	0.069**
	(0.036)	(0.030)	(0.032)	(0.033)
Observations	830	828	830	823
Pseudo R-squared	0.136	0.146	0.134	0.135

Robust standard errors in parentheses; $^{***}p < 0.01$, $^{**}p < 0.05$, $^{*}p < 0.1$.

Second, I tested for omitted variable bias by including additional controls. The survey question on attitudes toward PTA with the EU is framed in relation to deepening trade liberalization within the context of the Swiss-European bilateral agreements. As explained above, the bilateral agreements consist of a series of sectoral agreements among which the agreement on the free movement of people together with the flanking

Table 13.4 *Individuals' partisan preferences and support for North-North vs North-South PTAs*

	(13)
	DV = Pro-PTA
Centre	−0.120
	(0.103)
Right	−0.215*
	(0.129)
China PTA	−1.038***
	(0.081)
Centre*China PTA	0.212*
	(0.114)
Right*China PTA	0.747***
	(0.137)
Low education	−0.140*
	(0.081)
Manual worker	−0.400***
	(0.098)
Poor financial situation	−0.017
	(0.191)
Low status	−0.070
	(0.124)
Female	−0.393***
	(0.085)
Age	0.004
	(0.003)
Urban residence	0.094*
	(0.050)
Swiss-German	0.182
	(0.123)
Nationalism	−0.271***
	(0.044)
Trust in the EU	0.105**
	(0.051)
Foreign business share	0.140*
	(0.078)
Mobility	0.039
	(0.094)
Trade lowers prices	0.233***
	(0.037)

Table 13.4 (*cont.*)

	(13)
	DV = Pro-PTA
Media exposure	0.036
	(0.029)
Observations	970
Pseudo R-squared	0.147

Robust standard errors in parentheses;
$^{***}p < 0.01$, $^{**}p < 0.05$, $^{*}p < 0.1$.

measures features prominently. Therefore, I added a control measuring respondents' opinion on "the free movement of people with the EU has had positive effects for Switzerland."[7] Moreover, I included a measure of self-assessment of economic knowledge (i.e., understanding of international economic relations). Finally, I controlled for a sector's comparative advantage (i.e., net exports as a share of sector production), to capture the distributional effects as per the sector model of international trade, as well as attitudes toward incoming FDI from the respective countries (EU and China).[8] If I introduce these variables individually or jointly in the baseline model, the results are very similar.[9]

V Discussion

Perhaps the most interesting finding is that domestic compensation strongly increases globalization losers' support for PTAs with China in advanced economies. What compensation policies drive the overall result? Breaking down the aggregate compensation measure in its parts, I find that all three components condition globalization losers' support for the Sino-Swiss PTA.[10] The analysis shows that the literature's finding that generous

7 Alternatively, I included a variable measuring Swiss individuals' Pro-EU membership attitude.

8 Both variables are measured distinctively in relation to the EU and to China to match the survey questions about PTAs with the EU and China, respectively. I stack the variables prior to introducing them in the models.

9 Note that the coefficient for *Right* in Table 13.4 turns insignificant when I control for individuals' attitudes toward the free movement of people.

10 Results available upon request.

unemployment insurance increases support for free trade among losers travels to preferential trade liberalization, particularly in the North South configuration. Not surprisingly perhaps, the strengthening of employment protection has a similar effect. This might hold particularly in countries, such as Switzerland, with low levels of employment protection. The conditional effect of policies aimed at protecting weekly standard hours is more surprising. Arguably, the economies of China and Switzerland are complementary, dampening the fear of job losses. Nonetheless, actual or perceived increased competition in North-South trade might lead to (the fear of) an intensification of work to keep labor costs down. Concerns about work-life balance issues, which are prevalent across advanced economies and particularly in Europe, might explain this result.

Do individuals' partisan preferences over the Sino-Swiss PTA bear any resemblance with how political parties positioned themselves in relation to it? The ratification of the trade agreement exposed a classical left-right cleavage. The Swiss National Council (lower house of Parliament) ratified the agreement in December 2013, despite misgivings by the Socialist Party and the Green Party.[11] The left parties remained concerned about labor rights, the environment, and human rights. Even though the PTA included labor and environmental provisions, they were considered weak. While the agreement made scant and only indirect references to human rights, the substantive labor commitments only referenced the 1998 ILO Declaration on Fundamental Principles and Rights at Work, not the eight ILO fundamental Conventions themselves as is custom in the PTAs signed by the European Free Trade Association (EFTA) – of which Switzerland is a member – since 2011.[12] The Socialists (and the

11 The deal was adopted with a comfortable majority: 120 Members of Parliament (MPs) voted "yes," 46 "no," and 16 abstained. Two Socialist MPs voted "yes," 36 "no," and 6 abstained. Among the Green MPs, 4 voted "yes," 8 voted "no," and 2 abstained. For details on the voting behavior of individual MPs and by party affiliation, see www.parlament.ch/poly/Abstimmung/49/out/vote_49_9739.pdf. The Council of States (higher house) ratified the deal in March 2014 with 25 "yes," 3 "no" and 11 abstentions. Among those who voted against were two Green and one Socialist MPs, and among those who abstained were 7 Socialist MPs (as well as 2 Christian Democrat and 2 Green Liberal MPs). For details, see: www.parlament.ch/poly/AbstimmungSR/49/out/Abstimmung_49_146.pdf.

12 Weaker labor provisions in the Sino-Swiss PTA compared to the EFTA template also include the absence of binding commitments over non-derogation of domestic labor laws and over the requirement to prepare a labor impact assessment. However, China also made some labor concessions to Switzerland, if compared to what it had agreed with New Zealand in 2008, such as a binding commitment to effectively enforce its domestic labor laws and the possibility to have political consultations to resolve any disputes over labor-related commitments (Raess and Sari, 2018, 2021).

labor unions) in particular bemoaned the weak monitoring mechanism (Pedrina and Doka, 2014). They brought forward three motions in the National Council to strengthen the scope and stringency of the labor and human rights commitments as well as the means for the effective monitoring and implementation of the commitments. Large majorities defeated the motions in December 2013.[13] In short, in line with theoretical expectations, non-trade issues such as labor and human rights drove a wedge between left and centre-right parties, and the positions these parties took over the China-Switzerland PTA appear to have affected the preferences of their members and sympathizers.

It is plausible to argue that Swiss citizens have greater sympathy for their neighboring European countries compared to geographically remote and culturally distinct China. This might explain the observed lower level of support for the PTA with China than the PTA with the EU among globalization losers (Hypothesis 1). However, this explanation cannot account for why belief in compensatory policies among the losers tends to more strongly increase support for the former compared to the latter. This finding suggests that it is trade's distributional effects rather than (or as well as) sympathy/antipathy toward particular countries that drive the results for Hypothesis 1.

VI Conclusion

Standard economic models and the 'compensation' hypothesis have considerable explanatory power when it comes to explaining citizens' attitudes toward trade agreements, particularly preferential trade liberalization with China. The main findings are as follows. First, the losers of international trade are more supportive of PTAs with the EU (North-North PTA) than of PTAs with China (North-South PTA). Second, belief in compensation by losers leads to a larger increase in their support for PTA with China than for PTA with the EU. Third, the increase in support for PTA with China among globalization losers is driven by compensatory welfare and protective labor market institutions, not by social investment policies. Finally, reflecting left parties' concerns about poor human and labor rights, left-leaning voters are lukewarm at best to strike

[13] For voting on the Sommaruga, the Friedl and the Fehr minority motions, see www.parlament.ch/poly/Abstimmung/49/out/vote_49_9735.pdf; www.parlament.ch/poly/Abstimmung/49/out/vote_49_9737.pdf; and www.parlament.ch/poly/Abstimmung/49/out/vote_49_9738.pdf.

North-South PTAs, particularly PTAs with China, unless strong human and/or labor rights provisions accompany them, yielding a partisan effect in North-South PTAs, less so in North-North PTAs.

As twenty-first-century globalization is globalization under Chinese influence, not least due to China's accession to the WTO in 2001, which strongly increased its trade integration into the world economy, policies to compensate the losers are of paramount importance to sustain the process of global economic integration with Chinese characteristics. The evidence presented in this study on the role of domestic compensatory policies is consistent with the rise of national-populist and protectionist electoral responses to China shock in countries such as the US and the United Kingdom with small welfare states and flexible labor markets or trade-related compensation programs that are unresponsive to changing market conditions (Colantone and Stanig, 2018a, 2018b; Kim and Pelc, 2021; see also Hays, 2009; Feigenbaum and Hall, 2015; Che et al., 2016). The core finding is a reminder that in more socially embedded forms of capitalism, demands for more compensation remain popular and are likely the best bulwark against mounting protectionism and nationalism against the background of increased Chinese competition. Clearly, to preempt the collapse of preferential trade liberalization in the North-South context, particularly trade liberalization with China, it is essential to compensate the losers.

APPENDIX

Table A1 *Summary statistics*

	N	Mean	Std. dev.	Min	Median	Max
Pro-PTA	1,266	3.674	1.013	1	4	5
Pro-EU PTA	643	3.947	0.907	1	4	5
Pro-CN PTA	623	3.392	1.040	1	3	5
China PTA	1,884	0.5	0.500	0	0.5	1
Low-education	1,874	0.615	0.487	0	1	1
Manual worker	1,872	0.470	0.499	0	0	1
Poor financial situation	1,872	0.088	0.283	0	0	1
Low status	1,822	0.337	0.473	0	0	1
Pro-globalization compensation	1,084	0.535	0.499	0	1	1

Table A1 (*cont.*)

	N	Mean	Std. dev.	Min	Median	Max
Training	1,568	0.534	0.499	0	1	1
Female	1,884	0.519	0.500	0	1	1
Age	1,884	42.50	12.97	19	43	65
Urban residence	1,884	2.676	1.069	1	2	5
Swiss-German	1,884	0.713	0.452	0	1	1
Right ideology	1,692	5.139	1.955	0	5	10
Nationalism	1,832	2.947	1.058	1	3	5
Trust in the EU	1,810	2.088	0.750	1	2	4
Foreign business share	1,246	1.454	0.744	1	1	4
Mobility	1,882	0.242	0.429	0	0	1
Trade lowers prices	1,766	3.190	0.988	1	3	5
Media exposure	1,882	5.548	1.716	1	6	7

The industry dummies are: (1) agriculture; (2) manufacturing; (3) utilities; (4) construction; (5) retail and repair; (6) transport and communication; (7) hotel and restaurant; (8) financial sector, real estate; (9) industrial services; (10) government sector; (11) other services.

References

Autor, D. H., Dorn, D. and Hanson, G. H. (2013). 'The China syndrome: Local labor market effects of import competition in the United States'. *American Economic Review* 103(6): 2121–68.

Autor, D. H., Dorn, D. and Hanson, G. H. (2016). 'The China shock: Learning from labor-market adjustment to large changes in trade'. *Annual Review of Economics* 8: 205–40.

Baccini, L. (2019). 'The economics and politics of preferential trade agreements'. *Annual Review of Political Science* 22: 75–92.

Baker, A. (2005). 'Who wants to globalize? Consumer tastes and labor markets in a theory of trade policy beliefs'. *American Journal of Political Science* 49: 924–38.

Bastiaens, I. and Postnikov, E. (2020). 'Social standards in trade agreements and free trade preferences: An empirical investigation'. *The Review of International Organizations* 15(4): 793–816.

Burgoon, B. (2001). 'Globalization and welfare compensation: Disentangling the ties that bind'. *International Organization* 55(3): 509–51.

Busemeyer, M. R. (2009). 'From myth to reality: Globalization and public spending in OECD countries revisited'. *European Journal of Political Research* 48(4): 455–572.

Cameron, D. (1978). 'The expansion of the public economy: A comparative analysis'. *American Political Science Review* 72(4): 1243–61.

Che, Y., Lu, Y., Pierce, J. R., Schott, P. K. and Tao, Z. (2016). Does Trade Liberalization with China Influence U.S. Elections? NBER Working Paper No. 22178.

Chiang, C.-F., Liu, J.-T. and Wen, T.-W. (2013). 'Individual preferences for trade partners in Taiwan'. *Economics & Politics* 25(1): 91–109.

Colantone, I. and Stanig, P. (2018a). 'Global competition and Brexit'. *American Political Science Review* 112(2): 201–18.

Colantone, I. and Stanig, P. (2018b). 'The trade origins of economic nationalism: Import competition and voting behavior in western Europe'. *American Journal of Political Science* 62: 936–53.

Dadush, U., Domínguez-Jiménez, M. and Bruegel (2020). What can the EU learn from the China-Switzerland free trade agreement? (March 3). Available at: www.bruegel.org/2020/03/bern-after-reading-lessons-from-the-sino-swiss-trade-deal/#:~:text=China%20and%20Switzerland%20signed%20a,the%20deal%20in%20both%20nations. Accessed: 22 Feb. 2022.

Decker, P. T. and Corson, W. (1995). 'International trade and worker displacement: Evaluation of the trade adjustment assistance program'. *ILR Review* 48(4): 758–74.

DiGiuseppe, M. and Kleinberg, K. B. (2019). 'Economics, security, and individual-level preferences for trade agreements'. *International Interactions* 45(2): 289–315.

Dür, A. (2019). 'How interest groups influence public opinion: Arguments matter more than the sources'. *European Journal of Political Research* 58: 514–35.

Ehrlich, S. D. (2010). 'Who supports compensation? Individual preferences for trade-related unemployment insurance'. *Business and Politics* 12(1): 1–22.

Ehrlich, S. D. and Hearn, E. (2014). 'Does compensating the losers increase support for trade? An experimental test of the embedded liberalism thesis'. *Foreign Policy Analysis* 10(2): 149–64.

Emmenegger, P. (2011). 'Ever more liberal? The regulation of job security and working time in Switzerland'. In C. Trampusch, and A. Mach (eds.), *Switzerland in Europe: Continuity and Change in the Swiss Political Economy* (pp. 124–43). Abingdon, Oxon: Routledge.

Ernst Stähli, M., Joye, D., Sapin, M., Pollien, A., Ochsner, M., Nisple, K. and van den Hende, A. (2015). MOSAiCH-ISSP: Enquête sur le sens du travail et la citoyenneté – 2015 (Dataset) [MOSAiCH-ISSP : Meaning of work and citizenship survey (Dataset)]. FORS – Centre de compétences suisse en sciences sociales, Lausanne. Distributed by FORS, Lausanne.

Feigenbaum, J. J. and Hall, A. B. (2015). 'How legislators respond to localized economic shocks: Evidence from chinese import competition'. *The Journal of Politics* 77(4): 1012–30.

Hainmueller, J., Hangartner, D. and Yamamoto T. (2015). 'Validating vignette and conjoint survey experiments against real-world behavior'. *Proceedings of the National Academy of Science* 112(8): 2395–400.

Hakobyan, S. and McLaren, J. (2016). 'Looking for local labor market effects of NAFTA'. *The Review of Economics and Statistics* 98(4): 728–41.

Hall, P. and Soskice, D. (eds.), (2001). *Varieties of Capitalism: The Institutional Foundations of Comparative Advantage*. Oxford: Oxford University Press.

Hays, J. C. (2009). *Globalization and the New Politics of Embedded Liberalism*. Oxford: Oxford University Press.

Hays, J. C., Ehrlich, S. D. and Peinhardt, C. (2005). 'Government spending and public support for trade in the OECD: An empirical test of the embedded liberalism thesis'. *International Organization* 59: 473–94.

Jungherr, A., Mader, M., Schoen, H. and Wuttke, A. (2018). 'Context-driven attitude formation: The difference between supporting free trade in the abstract and supporting specific agreements'. *Review of International Political Economy* 25(2): 215–42.

Kim, S. E. and Pelc, K. (2021). 'How responsive it trade adjustment assistance?' *Political Science Research and Methods* 9(4): 889–98.

Linder, W. (2011). 'Europe and Switzerland: Europeanization without EU membership'. In C. Trampusch and A. Mach (eds.), *Switzerland in Europe: Continuity and Change in the Swiss Political Economy* (pp. 43–59). Abingdon, Oxon: Routledge.

Mach, A. and Trampusch, C. (2011). 'The Swiss political economy in comparative perspective'. In C. Trampusch and A. Mach (eds.), *Switzerland in Europe: Continuity and Change in the Swiss Political Economy* (pp. 11–26). Abingdon, Oxon: Routledge.

Mansfield, E. and Mutz, D. (2009). 'Support for free trade: Self-interest, sociotropic-politics, and out-group anxiety'. *International Organization* 63, 425–57.

Mansfield, E. D., Mutz, D. C. and Silver, L. R. (2015). 'Men, women, trade, and free markets'. *International Studies Quarterly* 59(2): 303–15.

Mayda, A. M. and Rodrik, D. (2005). 'Why are some people (and countries) more protectionist than others?' *European Economic Review* 49: 1393–430.

Melitz, M. J. (2003). 'The impact of trade on intra-industry reallocations and aggregate industry productivity'. *Econometrica* 71(6): 1695–725.

Milner, H. V. and Judkins, B. (2004). 'Partisanship, trade policy, and globalization: Is there a left-right divide on trade policy?' *International Studies Quarterly* 48(1): 95–119.

Naoi, M. and Urata, S. (2013). 'Free trade agreements and domestic politics: The case of the trans-pacific partnership agreement'. *Asian Economic Policy Review* 8: 326–49.

Oesch, D. (2011). 'Swiss trade unions and industrial relations after 1990: A history of decline and renewal'. In C. Trampusch and A. Mach (eds.), *Switzerland in Europe: Continuity and Change in the Swiss Political Economy* (pp. 82–102). Abingdon, Oxon: Routledge.

Owen, E. (2013). 'Unionization and restrictions on foreign direct investment'. *International Interactions* 39(5): 723–47.

Pedrina, V. and Doka, Z. (2014). Switzerland-China Free Trade Agreement and Labour Rights. Global Labour Column, Number 186 (October).

Raess, D. and Sari, S. (2018). 'Labor Provisions in Trade Agreements (LABPTA): Introducing a New Dataset'. *Global Policy* 9(4): 451–66.

Raess, D. and Sari, S. (2021). Labor Provisions in Trade Agreements (LABPTA) Codebook and Coding, 1990–2015. [Data Collection]. Colchester, Essex: UK Data Service. http://doi.org/10.5255/UKDA-SN-855014. Available at https://reshare.ukdataservice.ac.uk/855014/

Rankin, D. M. (2004). 'Borderline interest or identity? American and Canadian opinion on the North American Free Trade Agreement'. *Comparative Politics* 36(3): 331–51.

Reynolds, K. M. and Palatucci, J. S. (2012). 'Does trade adjustment assistance make a difference?' *Contemporary Economic Policy* 30(1): 43–59.

Rodrik, D. (1998). 'Why do more open economies have bigger governments?' *Journal of Political Economy* 106(5): 997–1032.

Ruggie, J. G. (1982). 'International regimes, transactions, and change: Embedded liberalism in the postwar economic order'. *International Organization* 36(2): 379–415.

Scheve, K. and Slaughter, M. J. (2001). 'What determines individual trade-policy preferences?' *Journal of International Economics*, 54, 267–92.

Scheve, K. and Slaughter, M. J. (2004). 'Economic Insecurity and the Globalization of Production'. *American Journal of Political Science* 48(4): 662–74.

Scruggs, L., Detlef, J. and Kuitto, K. (2017). Comparative Welfare Entitlements Data Set 2, Version 2017–09. Available at: http://cwed2.org/

Spilker, G., Bernauer, T. and Umaña, V. (2018). 'What kinds of trade liberalization agreements do people in developing countries want?' *International Interactions* 44(3): 510–36.

Thewissen, S. and Van Vliet, O. (2019). 'Competing with the dragon: Employment effects of chinese trade competition in 17 Sectors across 18 OECD Countries'. *Political Science Research and Methods* 7(2): 215–32.

Tuxhorn, K.-L. (2019). 'Mass support for free trade agreements and factor endowment'. *International Journal* 74(4): 537–58.

Walter, S. (2010). 'Globalization and the welfare state: Testing the microfoundations of the compensation hypothesis'. *International Studies Quarterly* 54: 403–26.

14

Trade as a Foreign Policy Issue

A Bilateral Micro Perspective

TANJA SCHWEINBERGER AND THOMAS SATTLER

I Introduction

The unilateral increase of tariffs on a range of Chinese goods by the former U.S. Trump administration in 2018 fundamentally threatens open-economy politics. By initiating a trade war with China, the U.S. elevation of tariffs has had important political, as well as economic, repercussions (Fajgelbaum et al., 2020; Brutger et al., 2023). The unilateral tariff increase also scathes the multilateral trading system as the U.S. prioritized aggressive protectionism rather than abiding by WTO principles. For instance, the WTO dispute settlement mechanism advocates principles of reciprocity. This procedure helps to ensure that countries only punish others if the latter previously violated WTO rules. This rules-based framework seeks to "mitigate the imbalances between stronger and weaker players by having their disputes settled on the basis of rules rather than having power determine the outcome" (WTO, 2021). Since reciprocity is one of the most promising strategies to induce cooperative behavior (Axelrod, 1984; Keohane, 1986), it is institutionalized in this pivotal liberal international institution.

The tenacity of this American non-cooperative trade policy initiative towards China is striking. Whilst the former Trump administration levied taxes on goods also from a number of European countries, the tariffs towards China still remain in place under the new Biden administration

Previous versions of this paper were presented at the Political Science Research Seminar at the University of Geneva, the WTI Bern, the Conference on the Political Economy of International Organizations (PEIO) in February 2019, the Annual Meeting of the European Political Science Association (EPSA) in June 2019, the Annual Meeting of the American Political Science Association in August 2019 and the World Trade Forum 2021. We thank the participants for their comments. The authors acknowledge financial support from the Swiss National Science Foundation, grant no. 182371.

(The Economist, 2021). The continuation of these non-cooperative trade policies is remarkable, as the current and former administrations' political orientation is different in nearly all policy areas. These developments suggest that China is different from other trading partners. In contrast to European and other trading partners, China is increasingly challenging U.S. power and is considered a political adversary (Nguyen et al., 2021; Schweinberger, 2021; Smeltz and Kafura, 2021). Trading relations with China are currently much more discussed than any other commercial relations between other countries.

Although the perception of China as a trading partner appears distinct, the current literature does not sufficiently account for this potential variation in perceptions across trading partners. Understanding such perceptions within public opinion is important for cooperation because the mass public can serve as a watchdog of international cooperative principles, as long as voters themselves support these principles (Milner and Tingley, 2013; Christenson and Kriner, 2019). This domestic constraint is relaxed if voters evaluate trade policy through a nationalist lens and value international cooperation less, for example, because they increasingly associate international economic relations with concerns of international political competition, as is the case with China. In the worst case, violations of international cooperative principles have their roots in the public itself when nationalist leaders hope to win votes by disregarding these principles.

We, therefore, examine how the mass publics in three large trading nations, the U.S., Germany, and Australia, value reciprocity as a key cooperative principle in international trade towards different trading partners. Thereby, we study to what extent political considerations – as opposed to purely economic concerns – constitute a source of deviations from cooperative trade attitudes. The International Relations (IR) literature has long emphasized that political and economic relations are intertwined, especially in an international system with changing power relations (e.g., Baldwin, 1985; Gilpin, 2001; Gowa and Mansfield, 2004). Following this literature, it is plausible that voters mingle political perceptions and international economic attitudes more than most trade literature (Kleinberg and Fordham, 2010), commonly based on an open-economy politics framework, suggests. The more trade is regarded as a security externality (Gowa and Mansfield, 1993), the more intricate security and economics become.

Such an analysis requires examining trade attitudes bilaterally, rather than unilaterally. We thereby depart from the dominant approach to examine citizens' trade preferences unilaterally, that is without consideration of the behavior of the trading partner and its political relations with the home country of citizens (Scheve and Slaughter, 2001). Even though some research suggests that the actions of the other actor need to be taken seriously for investment cooperation support (Jensen and Lindstädt, 2013; Chilton et al., 2020; Feng et al., 2021; Raess, 2021), trade attitudes are traditionally conceptualized as general and thus the possibility of attitudes varying across trade partners has not received sufficient attention.[1] Unilateral trade attitudes therefore represent the views towards economic openness per se, but do not capture how reciprocal attitudes and political perceptions vary across actual country pairs, for example between the U.S. and China.

Whilst commonly assumed that Western trade attitudes specifically towards China differ from attitudes towards other countries, most of the literature does not directly test this. Importantly, studying such attitudes requires a benchmark. That is, attitudes towards trading with China need to be regarded in comparison to trade views with other countries. The recently emerging trade wars and the politics, as well as public debates surrounding them, illustrate how urgent such a bilateral analysis of trade attitudes is. After all, such events essentially represent a series of bilateral, uncooperative trade policy interactions among selected explicitly named countries, most prominently China. Our study therefore adopts a bilateral approach that enables us to describe how trade attitudes vary depending on specific other countries. Reducing citizens' trade attitudes solely to trade in general is hence inadequate to the extent that citizens evaluate trade relations through a foreign policy lens, as an important part of the previous IR literature suggests.

The results from our survey experiments show that reciprocity continues to play an important role in all three examined countries, especially towards traditional allies, such as Canada, Germany, or Japan. Strikingly, however, a significant share of unconditional, non-cooperative attitudes exists towards non-allies such as China and Russia. Interestingly, Russia is perceived more negatively than China in most cases. Variations in these responses are best explained by perceptions of the other country as political adversary and political ideology of the respondent. Whilst citizens consistently support an increase in trade barriers in response to a protectionist initiative by the other country, at the same time, individuals make significant distinctions between countries that they perceive as political allies, such as Canada, Germany, and Japan, and

[1] Spilker et al. (2016) also look at the effect of the other trading partner more closely.

those that they perceive as political adversaries, such as China and Russia. Support for decreasing trade barriers in response to a free-trade initiative by a trading partner is significantly lower for political adversaries than for political allies.

These findings suggest that citizens view trade policy not only as a means to maximize income but also as a foreign policy instrument that can be used to pursue national political goals in the international arena (Baldwin, 1985). International politics, thus, is an important source of trade attitudes in addition to personal material interests (e.g., Margalit, 2011; Jensen et al., 2017). This is consistent with attitudes towards other foreign economic policies, such as bailouts in the Eurozone (Bechtel et al., 2014) or regulation of foreign investment (Chilton et al., 2020; Raess, 2021). The findings also confirm that sociotropic considerations, such as ideology and national or group-specific distributional concerns, play an important role in evaluations of foreign economic policy (Mansfield and Mutz, 2009; Kleinberg and Fordham, 2010; Mutz and Kim, 2017; Nguyen and Bernauer, 2019; cf. Schaffer and Spilker, 2019).

Finally, the results imply that cooperation within the Western bloc finds broad societal support despite current frictions among Western countries over trade policy. Although attitudes towards adversaries like Russia are more severe than towards China, non-cooperative attitudes towards the most important trading nations are consequential. Precisely when examining Chinese-U.S. economic relations, therefore, these concerns for international political competition need to be taken into account (Kirshner, 2014). To the extent that the growing anti-globalization sentiment is rooted in these international political considerations, a revival of solutions proposed by embedded liberalism, that is the moderation of the distributional consequences of openness through compensatory measures (Hays et al., 2005; Nooruddin and Rudra, 2014), is not sufficient to reinvigorate trade cooperation with China. Instead, the threat to trade cooperation and the multilateral trading system is more fundamental than often assumed.

II A Bilateral Approach to Trade Attitudes

The most striking development in modern U.S. trade policy corresponds to its escalation of commercial relations with China. The former U.S. president, Donald Trump, commenced a trade war by unilaterally raising tariffs on Chinese goods in 2018. As tariffs soared, tariffs on Chinese goods were increased up to 21% and still remain high at approximately

19% as of January 2021 (Bown, 2021). These tariffs, in combination with the retaliatory tariffs emanating in response from China, have severe economic and political consequences (Fajgelbaum et al., 2020; Brutger et al., 2023). Strikingly, whilst the trade confrontation with European powers seems to have diminished, the tariffs targeting China continue to be upheld under the new Biden administration (The Economist, 2021).

More broadly, the U.S. opting for unilateral tariff increases represents an affront to established norms of the multilateral trading system embodied by the WTO. By not selecting the WTO dispute settlement mechanism, the U.S. openly disregarded the institution and its principles. The WTO and its rules are based on openness and reciprocity seeking to mitigate the effects of power in the international trading system (WTO, 2021). Reciprocity is defined by Keohane (1986) as "exchanges [...] in which the actions of each party are contingent on the prior actions of the others in such a way that good is returned for good, and bad for bad." (p. 8) has significantly shaped the creation of WTO rules. The institutionalization of reciprocity allows cooperation in trade to arise even in an anarchical international context. The initiation of the trade war against China is notable because the U.S. is commonly seen as a defender of such international institutions and principles and condemns such unilateral policy moves.

This shift and endurance of hostility in trade politics towards China are accompanied by the impression that trade cooperation with China is distinct from trade relations with other countries. Given China's sheer economic size and trade activity, trade with China is discussed more than with other countries. Cooperation with China represents a case of North-South trade cooperation involving a developing country with lower social and human rights standards (Raess, 2023). As China matters both as the largest domestic market and exporter nation, the redistributive consequences of trade with China are salient. Commonly referred to as "China shocks," economists focus on losses due to import competition resulting in unemployment, as well as lower wages and income (Autor et al., 2013; Acemoglu et al., 2016; Bisbee, 2021).

The importance of international rivalry with China, however, extends beyond these individual economic considerations. China has risen economically due to its reform and opening policies in the 1980s and thus challenges U.S. power primacy (Naughton, 2007). As discussed in an earlier chapter in this edited volume, China's rise as a developing country has diminished US's "institutional power" (Hopewell, 2023). More recently, the U.S. public has begun to increasingly perceive China as a political adversary, rather than an ally (Smeltz and Kafura, 2021). This shift has the potential to throttle important advances in economic cooperation, as political alliances have positive effects on long-term economic interactions and economic exchange (Gowa and Mansfield, 1993, 2004). The salience of adversarial views of other countries, especially China, is thus crucial for the support of trade. These power considerations are inextricably connected and directly threaten principles of economic openness and reciprocity.

Political analyses of international economic relations have highlighted the importance of power and relative gains for trading relations (Viner, 1948; Gilpin, 1987; Grieco, 1988). Economic cooperation often produces unequal gains even if both countries benefit from it in absolute terms. For instance, trade can lead to more efficiency gains, a higher long-term growth rate, or a greater strengthening of critical industries in some countries rather than others. The sensitivity to such unequal, relative gains is particularly high when the possibility exists that the two states will engage in a political conflict in the future (Powell, 1991). If unequal gains from trade can be turned into a military advantage, then these concerns constitute a constraint that inhibits cooperation. Accordingly, some studies find that who the other country is does indeed matter for foreign economic policy attitudes of the mass public (Herrmann et al., 2001; Spilker et al., 2016; Carnegie and Gaikwad, 2022). Such qualms are likely to expand as the rise of China succeeds past decades of uncontested U.S. hegemony and changes the international distribution of power (Kirshner, 2014).

Against this backdrop, how and to what extent does individual support for trade cooperation differ across countries? Whilst current events suggest that attitudes towards trade with China differ from trading with countries, the current trade attitudes literature does not systematically test this notion. Instead, the focus of the literature lies on gauging such attitudes unilaterally, that is economic openness in general, as opposed to trade policy towards specific countries. By commonly relying on questions such as "Do you think the U.S. government should try to encourage or discourage international trade?" or "[…] Do you support or oppose placing new limits on imports?", the literature largely does not distinguish between attitudes across countries (e.g., Scheve and Slaughter, 2001; Mayda and Rodrik, 2005; Hainmueller and Hiscox, 2006; Mansfield and Mutz, 2009; Baccini et al., 2017; Owen and Johnston, 2017). Even though material and non-material factors have been explored, the literature has omitted conceptualizing trade attitudes as heterogeneous, that is also depending on the other country and geopolitical ties.

In contrast, our analysis adopts a bilateral approach that takes into account the behavior and characteristics of a particular trading partner. This approach is useful because many trade policy initiatives involve specific country groups or pairs, for example, in the form of preferential trade (Manger, 2009; Mansfield and Milner, 2012; Dür et al., 2014; Spilker et al., 2016). Even more importantly, recent reversals in trade openness and threats to launch a trade war occur on a bilateral basis when one country directly targets another country, as exemplified by the ongoing trade war between the U.S. and China. Changes in international openness today, thus, are often the result of bilateral decisions, in which the political relations between individual states matter much more. Equally, in public debates surrounding such policy interactions, the potential trading partner country is highly salient. Citizens also take into account the prior behavior and characteristics of other countries when evaluating their own government's foreign economic policy (Spilker et al., 2016; Chilton et al., 2020; Feng et al., 2021; Raess, 2021; Schweinberger, 2021).

The bilateral approach is ideal for studying whether principles of reciprocity or geopolitical alliances matter more for trade attitudes. On the one hand, it is plausible that principles of reciprocity, as institutionalized in the WTO, apply to any potential trading partner, including China, as reciprocity has been discovered to be one of the few cross-cultural norms (Simmel, 1950; Gouldner, 1960; Bowles and Gintis, 2011; Gächter et al., 2017). Correspondingly, the IR literature also promotes the institutionalization of reciprocity to achieve cooperation.[2] On the other hand, attitudes are likely to vary depending on the trading partner. Especially when studying trade attitudes towards China a benchmark is needed, so that Chinese bilateral cooperative and non-cooperative attitudes can be analyzed in relative terms to bilateral attitudes towards other countries considered as political allies and adversaries. By just studying views towards China in isolation, the basis for comparison is unclear. We are therefore especially interested in exploring support for trade cooperation reciprocity with explicitly named countries, such as China.

[2] Trade politics represents a classic cooperation problem in IR, in which actors have an incentive to defect from a cooperative strategy for short-term gains. Specifically, governments have an incentive to raise tariffs or other trade barriers to protect domestic jobs against competition from abroad. When both governments follow such a protectionist strategy, this then not only hurts consumers in both countries because prices increase. But it also prevents the growth of jobs in the export industry due to a lack of export opportunities (Gilligan, 1997; Dür, 2010). With the exception of workers in the protected import-competing sector, this makes citizens in both countries worse off compared to a situation with free trade.

This discussion yields the following hypotheses we test. First, as a default, we expect views to follow principles of reciprocity. In this view, China as a trading partner is not perceived differently than other countries, as individuals response to the same policy initiative reciprocally regardless of the trading partner, that is a non-cooperative initiative from China, is met with the same response as towards Canada. Second, the competing hypothesis expects variation across trading partners to prevail, that is cooperation will be supported differently depending on the trading partner. Third, this variation is likely to correspond to varying perceptions of political alliances. For instance, more U.S. voters should perceive Canada as an ally compared to China. hose voters who consider a trading partner as an ally (adversary) should also be more (less) likely to support a cooperative, reciprocal response. As a result, the average response to a Canadian trade policy initiative should be more cooperative than the average response to a Chinese trade policy initiative.

H1: Individuals, on average, respond to a cooperative policy initiative with a cooperative policy response and to a non-cooperative policy initiative with a non-cooperative policy response.

H2A: Bilateral trade support varies as the average response to a trade policy initiative by another country differs across countries.

H2B: Citizens perceiving the other country as an ally are more likely to support cooperative responses. Citizens perceiving the other country as an adversary are more likely to support non-cooperative responses.

III Bilateral Trade Attitudes in Three Countries

(i) Research Design

We use a survey experimental design to test these claims. This approach lends itself to effectively examine what difference it makes when the object of study is systematically changed in some way. In our case, on the one hand, the trading partner changes so that we can examine whether there are differences across trading partner countries so that we can test what difference it makes when the trading partner is China or Canada. On the other hand, the foreign economic policy initiative varies.

In our study, we follow a factorial design and include vignette treatments varying the policy characteristics. In our case, this means that cooperative and non-cooperative foreign economic policy initiatives, that is tariff decreases and increases, from different countries are proposed to the respondent. The respondent is then asked which policy their own government should pursue in response to the initiative of the other country. This study allows us to examine to what extent respondents in different countries deviate from cooperative reciprocal principles and how the preferred response varies by the trading partner.

The survey experiments were conducted in three different countries: the U.S., Australia, and Germany.[3] We selected this diverse set of countries to examine to what extent respondents in countries that play different roles in the international political and economic system respond differently. All the countries represent important trading nations, but the international political concerns and political relations with other countries vary. Correspondingly, current political rhetoric varies considerably between these countries, particularly in the context of the trade war (Carnegie and Carson, 2019; Schweinberger, 2021). The U.S., for instance, is the global hegemon, even if its hegemony is currently in decline. Australia is a major regional power in the Asia and Pacific area. Moreover, Germany is a European power that is not necessarily a political challenger, however, it is a leading export power.

For our analysis, we conducted experiments embedded in population surveys in August 2018. The surveys were conducted by *respondi*, a survey company that uses different country-specific online access panels. Respondents were selected from these access panels based on quotas on age and gender. The samples were restricted to voting-age nationals under 70. For each country, the sample size is around 1,100 (valid responses).[4]

After reading a brief introduction to this section of the survey, respondents are presented with a policy initiative from different countries.[5] These policy choices include either an increase, a decrease, or no changes in tariffs on imports from the home country of the respondent. Respondents are randomly assigned to one policy initiative per trading partner. The policy initiative, thus, is the treatment that a respondent receives.

[3] A pilot was conducted in February 2018.

[4] Australia: $n = 1{,}084$, Germany: $n = 1{,}093$, USA: $n = 1{,}104$.

[5] All respondents receive the following introduction: "In the following, we ask for your opinion on trading relations with the U.S. and a number of countries. The scenarios that you will see describe possible trade policies by different trading partners of the U.S. The U.S. government can respond to these policies by the other countries in three possible ways: (A) It can keep tariffs on imports from the other country as they are. (B) It can increase tariffs on imports from the other country, which may protect domestic jobs, but may also raise consumer prices. (C) It can decrease tariffs on imports from the other country, which may reduce consumer prices, but also may expose domestic jobs to increased competition."

Additionally, we vary who the trading partner is. We deliberately adopt this bilateral approach because we expect these attitudes to be heterogeneous also across trading partner countries depending on the political alliance. Although this treatment may lead to confounding, we still believe that mentioning concretely who the trading partner is enhances the validity and reliability of our design as we precisely seek to assess what difference China makes. In the real world, trade is with another country that is not abstract. Public debates about trade politics often address the trade partner country and its attributes. So, we seek to understand if attitudes towards trading with China are distinct, or perhaps comparable with commercial exchange evaluations with another political adversary like Russia.

In our experiments, all respondents see a policy initiative from five countries. The sequence, in which the countries were presented, was randomized. For the U.S., we selected Canada, Japan, and Germany as traditional allies. Whilst Canada presents a traditional and proximate ally, Germany is also an important U.S. ally on the European continent. Japan is also a U.S. ally, even though in the 1980s similar accusations were directed towards it as towards China nowadays. For Australia and Germany, the U.S., the UK, and Japan are included in our analysis as allies. For all countries, China and Russia were selected as countries that represent non-allies. Naturally, China differs as a trading partner from these other countries not just in terms of rivalry and power considerations but also with regard to redistributional trade consequences (Hopewell, 2023; Raess, 2023). Whilst we cannot fully control for these different considerations when referring to China, we address this question by asking respondents to place the mentioned countries on an ally-adversary scale, which varies from 0 (adversary) to 10 (ally) before we conduct the experiment (cf. below on the additional variables we collect in the survey).

The outcome variable is the preferred policy response by the respondent. We ask all respondents to choose one out of three possible policy responses by their own government, or to select the option "Don't know." Including this option is important as some citizens may not be knowledgeable about trade policy (Rho and Tomz, 2017). These policy responses include either an increase, a decrease, or no changes in tariffs on imports from the trading partner. Together with the policy initiative of the other country, this policy response indicates the preference for a reciprocal or inverse strategy, that is conditionally cooperative/uncooperative or unconditionally cooperative/uncooperative policy response towards other countries. An example of the exact formulation of the vignette for the U.S. can be found in Table 14.1.

Table 14.1 *Overview of the experiment for U.S.–Chinese trade policy*

Vignette 1: cooperative initiative	Suppose China **strongly decreases** its tariffs on goods produced in the U.S. that are exported to China. Which of the following policies do you think should the U.S. government pursue when it comes to trading with China?
Vignette 2: no policy initiative	Suppose China **does not change** its tariffs on goods produced in the U.S. that are exported to China. Which of the following policies do you think should the U.S. government pursue when it comes to trading with China?
Vignette 3: non-cooperative initiative	Suppose China **strongly increases** its tariffs on goods produced in the U.S. that are exported to China. Which of the following policies do you think should the U.S. government pursue when it comes to trading with China?

We additionally collect the following variables. First, we ask respondents to place the mentioned countries on an ally-adversary scale, which varies from 0 (adversary) to 10 (ally) (cf. Appendix Figures 14.4a–c). Also, we measure the degree of nationalism with the commonly used battery by Rankin (2001). These questions were asked before the experiment together with other common social demographics such as ideology, age, gender, region of origin, and income (in a randomized order). To tap respondents' level of skill and education, we request them to tick the highest obtained degree.

To address whether variations in bilateral economic threats are driving the responses, we also account for the competitiveness of the employment sector as a covariate. We rely on Acemoglu et al. (2016) and the standard SITC codes to categorize the different sectors to examine whether respondents "win" or "lose" from trade with the other country. With Balassa's (1977) Revealed Comparative Advantage, we can calculate whether the sector of employment (broken down to the SITC code level) has a comparative advantage with regard to the other country.[6] This bilateral approach takes into account that economic threats vary depending on the respondents' and the potential trading partner country's economies.

[6] Data obtained from the Comtrade database of the World Bank, which provides data from 2016 for bilateral trade data on the SITC code level. If the value was higher than 1, the industry was coded as competitive. If the value was lower than 1, the industry was coded as non-competitive (with regard to the other country).

(ii) Findings

Figures 14.1a–c show the responses for all the treatments in the U.S., Australia, and Germany. The figures clearly show that reciprocal behavior is rather common in all three countries and towards almost all trading partners. The overall pattern is largely symmetric, that is the distribution of the responses changes strongly with the policy initiative of the other country as expected. Moreover, the reciprocal response to tariff increases by the other country is especially pronounced in the U.S. and Australia, particularly when China or Russia is the country that pursues this non-cooperative policy. Most respondents are conditionally cooperative and uncooperative, depending on the behavior of the other country. The overall responses, thus, are reciprocal, whilst negative reciprocity is more

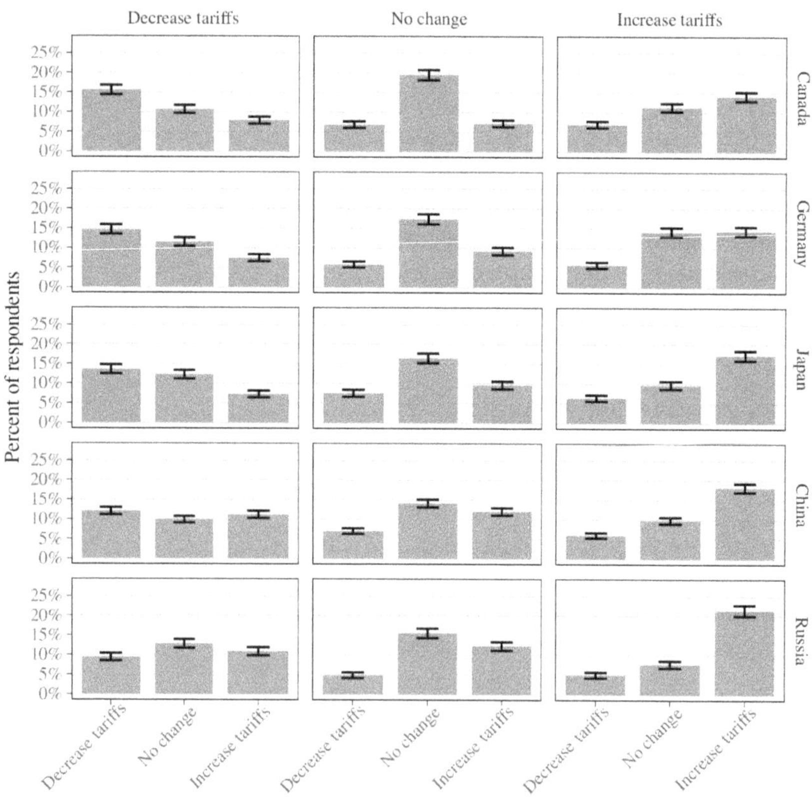

Figure 14.1a U.S. responses to different countries

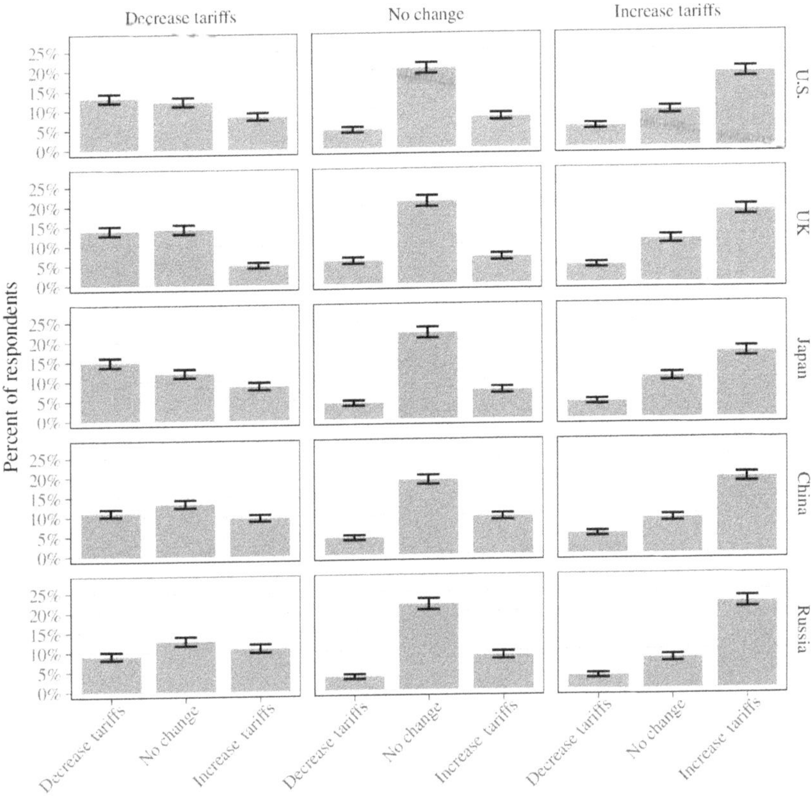

Figure 14.1b Australian responses to different countries

pronounced than positive reciprocity. This largely supports H1, which suggests that responses are reciprocal on average.

Nonetheless, at the same time, the figures also clearly show that a substantial number of respondents are unconditionally uncooperative. As the left columns of Figures 14.1a–c show, a cooperative initiative does not result in a reciprocal effect on the policy response attitudes of a significant share of respondents. The same is true for the situation in which the other country proposes no change, as the middle columns of the same figures show. Among the three countries that we examine, German respondents, on average, are the most reciprocal, while U.S. respondents are the least reciprocal. For the U.S. and Australia, we see that the "Decrease" and "Increase" scenarios are not symmetric in their

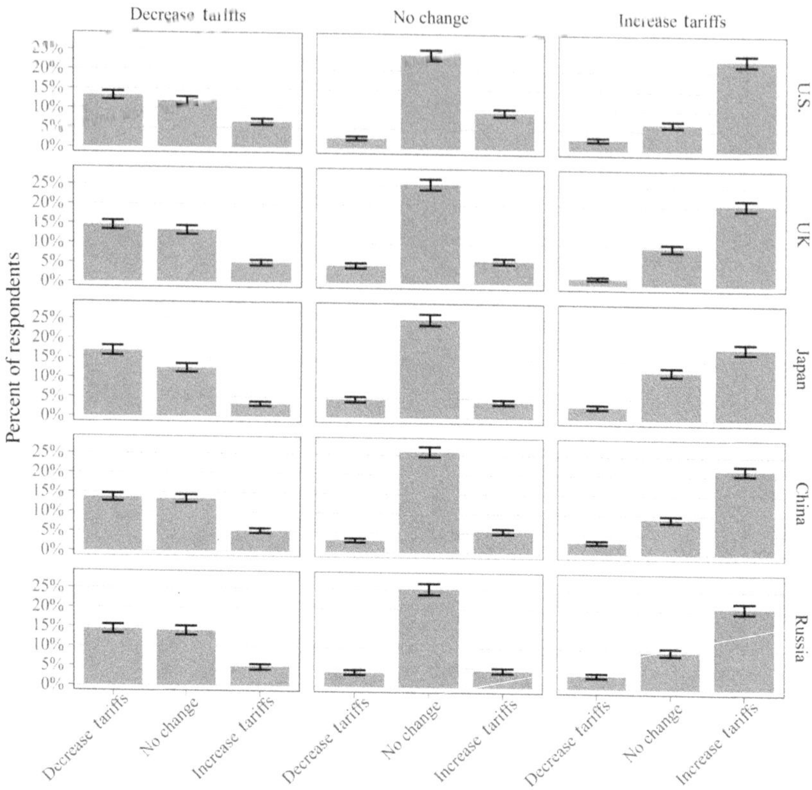

Figure 14.1c German responses to different countries

response distribution, particularly towards Russia and China. Instead, the share of respondents who prefer no change or an increase in tariffs after these two countries proposed to decrease tariffs is quite large. And it is considerably larger than for the other three countries that we examine. Notably, however, attitudes towards Russia are overall more negative than towards China.

We further examine the divergent responses for different trading partners in Figures 14.2a–c. These figures show the differences in the average responses across trading partners and treatments for the three countries. In other words, Figure 14.2a shows how the average responses of U.S. citizens to the same policy initiative, for example, "decrease," differ across countries in the left column of Figure 14.1a. Since for the

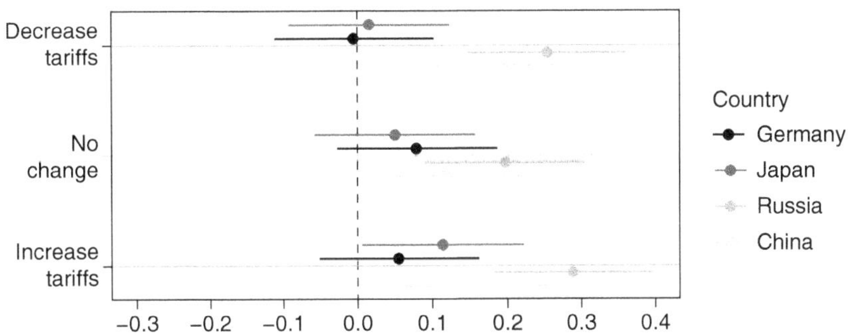

Figure 14.2a Differences U.S. responses Treatment*Partner

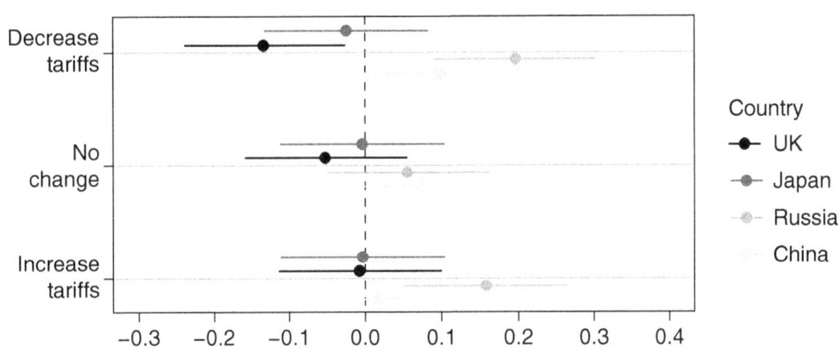

Figure 14.2b Differences Australian responses Treatment*Partner

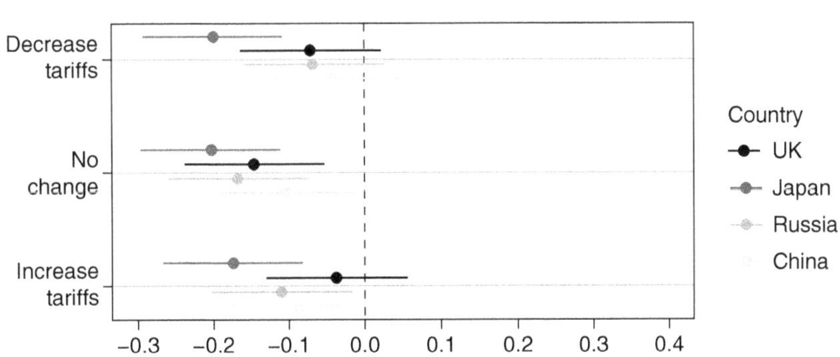

Figure 14.2c Differences German responses Treatment*Partner

U.S., Canada is the reference category, Figure 14.2a shows how the estimated responses for Germany, Japan, Russia, and China differ from the response to Canada.

The figures confirm that respondents react very differently to different trading partners and therefore hold heterogeneous views. For the U.S., respondents largely respond in the same way to policy initiatives from Germany and Japan as they do to initiatives from Canada. But they respond very differently to policy initiatives from Russia and China.

Whatever these two countries propose, U.S. respondents on average react much more uncooperatively to these initiatives than to the same initiative by the other three countries. The results are similar for Australia, although some details differ. Again, Australian respondents react more uncooperatively to cooperative initiatives by China and Russia, compared to their response to a U.S. initiative (baseline). They respond more cooperatively toward cooperative initiatives from the UK. For no policy changes and tariff increases, they respond similarly across countries, except for Russia. As for U.S. respondents, Russia is perceived as more adversarial than China (cf. Appendix Figure 14.4b). In comparison, German citizens react differently. Generally, they respond less cooperatively to all countries than to Japan. The strong, noncooperative behavior towards the U.S. can be explained by the current frictions in trade policy between the EU and the U.S. Contemporary political rhetoric and media reporting about other countries may shape individuals' perceptions. Nonetheless, the size of this non-cooperative response is surprising. The UK is also punished more compared to Japan, but primarily when it threatens to increase tariffs. This could be explained by the tensions surrounding Brexit. Clearly, German respondents are the most cooperative towards Japan.

When examining the interaction between policy initiative and alliance perception of the trading partner in Figures 14.3a–c, we find that the responses vary systematically according to the perceived political relationship with the other country. In all three country samples, individuals prefer raising tariffs on goods from an adversary. Although for the decrease scenario, the difference between allies and adversaries does not have a statistically significant effect on U.S. predicted responses, all other effects are heterogeneous according to the relation with the trade partner. This evidence further supports H2b.

We also examine how a number of covariates help to explain variation in preferred policy responses among respondents. The results are in the Appendix in Tables 14.2a, 14.2b, and 14.2c. We find that the perception of

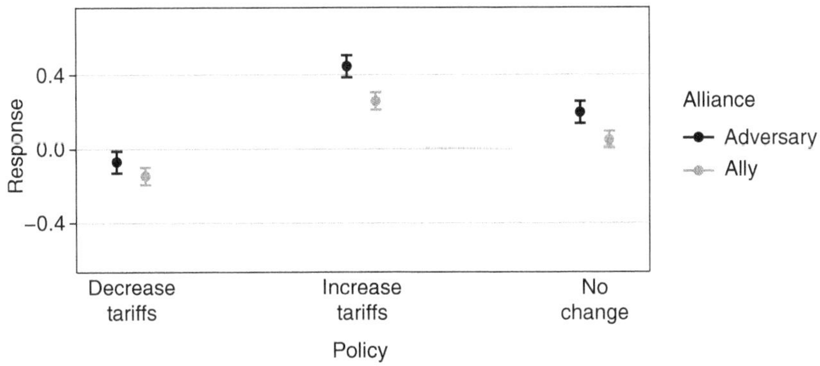

Figure 14.3a U.S. predicted responses to Policy*Alliance

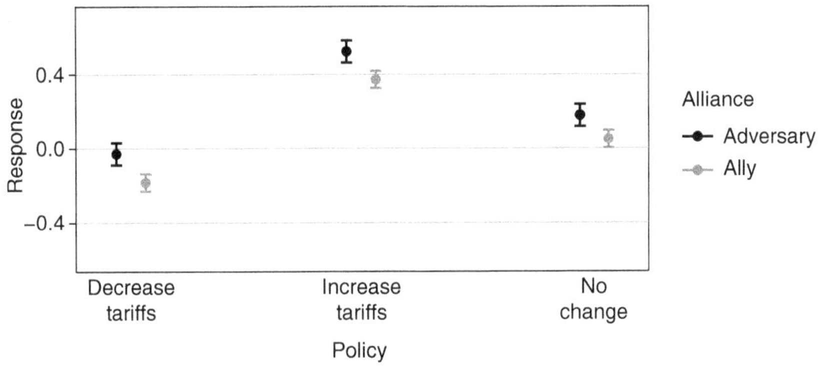

Figure 14.3b Australian predicted responses to Policy*Alliance

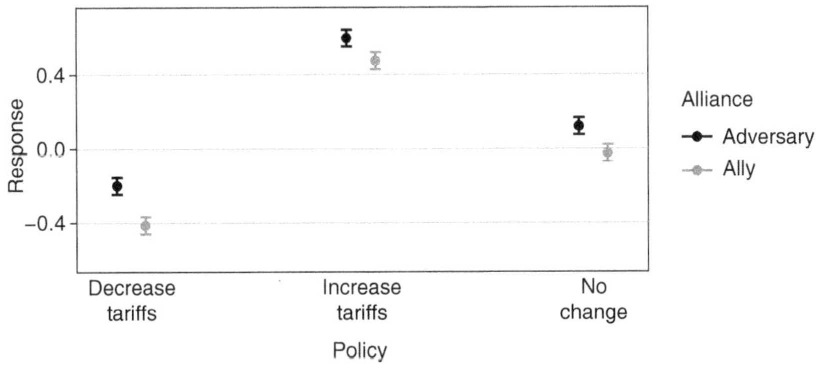

Figure 14.3c German predicted responses to Policy*Alliance

the other country as an ally or adversary plays an important role.[7] In all countries, the ally-adversary variable has the expected impact: if an individual perceives the other country as an ally, then this person is less likely to prefer an increase in tariffs towards the other country. In the U.S., this is the case for Canada and Russia. For Australia and Germany, this effect is even stronger and statistically significant for even more trading partners, although the exact effects vary. Russia is generally perceived as more adversarial than China (cf. Appendix Figures 14.4a–c).[8]

Overall, our results show that reciprocity matters in all three countries for average responses to the trade policies of the respective five trading partners. This supports Hypothesis 1. Nonetheless, a substantial share of unconditionally uncooperative attitudes exist, especially towards non-allies, like China. Respondents differ in the policy responses they select by supporting cooperation with some countries but not with others. This is consistent with Hypothesis 2a. Deviations from cooperative reciprocity are best explained by political perceptions. Reciprocity accordingly appears to be more relevant when confronted with a political ally rather than an adversary. This supports Hypothesis 2b.

IV Conclusion

This study analyzes to what extent the mass publics in the U.S., Australia, and Germany deviate from the principle of reciprocity when facing different political adversaries and allies as trading partners. Whilst we find that citizens in all three countries generally support the principles of reciprocity in trading relations, significant variations across trading partners prevail. There is strong support for commensurate retaliation to protectionist initiatives, towards all countries. However, support for a reduction of trade barriers in response to a free-trade initiative is more difficult to sustain among political adversaries than allies.

Hence, whilst reciprocity is supported on average, we observe important deviations from this baseline. These deviations can be explained through variations in the political perceptions of the trading partner. Particularly for the cooperative policy response, we find that depending on whether the other country is perceived as an ally or adversary matters.

[7] Ally-adversary perception was coded from −5 (strong adversary) to 5 (strong ally) in response to the question: To what extent do you view the following countries as political allies or adversaries?

[8] In nearly all models, education and the competitiveness of the sector of employment do not have a statistically significant influence on the response.

Whilst the direction of causality can also be reversed, that is that the policy initiative shapes how the foreign country is perceived, the main finding of this chapter supports the assumption that perceptions of trading partners are crucial for trade cooperation policy support. Thereby, the results affirm the view of differing security externalities and expected duration of future interaction between allies or adversaries when confronted with a political adversary. Trade and foreign policy issues, therefore, are more strongly intertwined than the existing trade policy literature assumes.

Our bilateral approach, thus, yields interesting new insights into trade politics in the contemporary world economy. By shifting the attention away from the conventional approach to conceptualizing trade attitudes as general, our paper reveals that international political concerns play a much greater role in trade attitudes than previously assumed. This is particularly important as the overarching context of the international trading system has become more susceptible to bilateral considerations. Bilateral trade policy interactions manifest themselves within the WTO Disputes Settlement Mechanism, through the spread of preferential trade agreements, and with the rise of trade wars during the past years. When trade relations become increasingly bilateral, reciprocity and cooperation in trade relations are more appealing with certain countries than with others, depending on the political and economic relations with the other country (Hopewell, 2023; Raess, 2023). Our findings suggest that the sources for these uncooperative attitudes relate to international political competition. Clearly, trade policy is not just seen as a means to maximize income, but also as a foreign policy instrument that is subordinated to political goals.

These results pose a challenge to the stability of the international liberal order. First, the political constraint that nationalist leaders face is relaxed if voters increasingly mix international political and economic issues. During the uncontested U.S. hegemony of the past decades, these international political concerns may have increasingly moved into the background (Cooper, 2000). But owing to shifts in international power and the rise of China, the increasing politicization of trade issues in the wake of rising populism and economic nationalism might have gained renewed importance (Nguyen et al., 2021). Second, and like other existing research, we show that individuals do not solely base their attitudes on their personal economic well-being. This underlines the difficulties of upholding cooperation in international trading relations if international political concerns are eminent. This poses a crucial obstacle to upholding open-economy politics in the long run and ultimately challenges the functioning of liberal international institutions, like the WTO.

Ally Perception

Respondents were asked the following questions (Figures 14.4a–c and Tables 14.2a–c):

[Australian and US version] “To what extent do you consider the following countries as political allies or adversaries of Australia/the U.S.?”[German version] “Inwieweit betrachten Sie die folgenden Länder als politische Verbündete oder Gegner?”

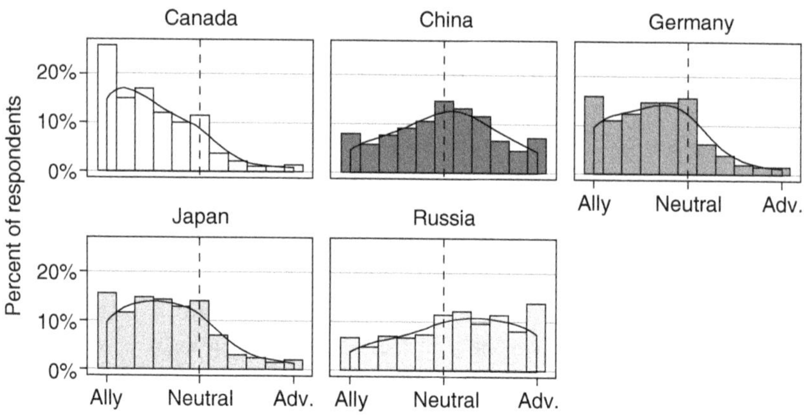

Figure 14.4a Ally-Adversary perception of U.S. citizens

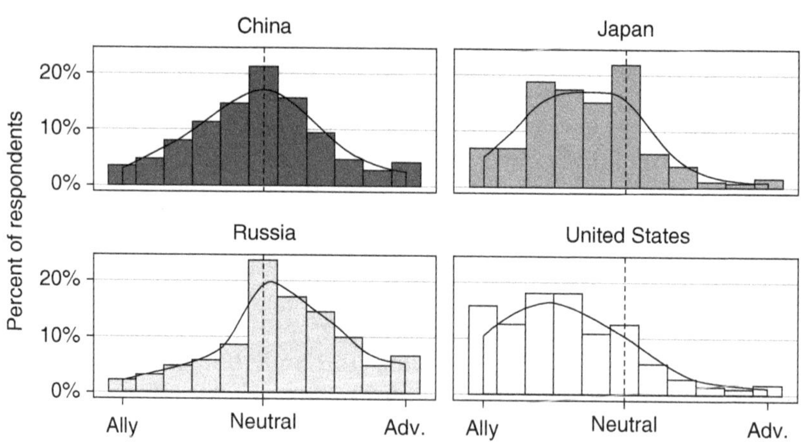

Figure 14.4b Ally-Adversary perception of Australian citizens

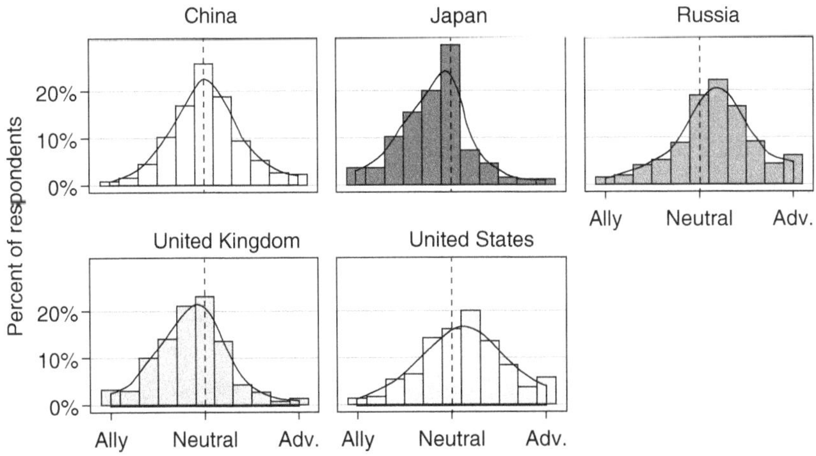

Figure 14.4c Ally-Adversary perception of German citizens

Table 14.2a *Covariates for U.S. responses*

	Canada	Germany	Japan	China	Russia
Treatments					
Decrease Tariffs	−0.239***	−0.333***	−0.253***	−0.156**	−0.163***
	(0.058)	(0.059)	(0.061)	(0.063)	(0.060)
Increase Tariffs	0.210***	0.127**	0.265***	0.199***	0.260***
	(0.059)	(0.059)	(0.061)	(0.063)	(0.059)
Covariates					
Ally Perception	−0.031***	−0.010	−0.016	−0.021**	−0.010
	(0.011)	(0.010)	(0.011)	(0.009)	(0.009)
Ideology	0.059***	0.049***	0.043***	0.053***	−0.004
	(0.009)	(0.009)	(0.009)	(0.010)	(0.010)
Education	0.027	0.019	0.009	0.041*	0.049**
	(0.022)	(0.022)	(0.023)	(0.024)	(0.022)
RCA	−0.064	−0.245**	−0.088	0.087*	−0.049
	(0.468)	(0.119)	(0.071)	(0.052)	(0.030)
Age	−0.003*	−0.001	−0.002	0.003	0.007***
	(0.002)	(0.002)	(0.002)	(0.002)	(0.002)
Female	−0.036	0.024	0.029	−0.039	−0.056
	(0.049)	(0.049)	(0.051)	(0.051)	(0.049)
Constant	0.113	0.274*	0.181	−0.294*	−0.195
	(0.049)	(0.166)	(0.160)	(0.157)	(0.129)
Observations	919	897	889	912	902
Adjusted R^2	0.110	0.098	0.094	0.070	0.079

Note: $^{*}p < 0.1$; $^{**}p < 0.05$; $^{***}p < 0.01$.

Table 14.2b *Covariates for Australian responses*

	US	UK	Japan	China	Russia
Treatments					
Decrease Tariffs	−0.247***	−0.305***	−0.256***	−0.153**	−0.121**
	(0.061)	(0.057)	(0.058)	(0.060)	(0.058)
Increase Tariffs	0.295***	0.401***	0.298***	0.281***	0.395***
	(0.061)	(0.057)	(0.060)	(0.059)	(0.058)
Covariates					
Ally Perception	−0.032***		−0.057***	−0.052***	−0.039***
	(0.011)		(0.012)	(0.011)	(0.011)
Ideology	−0.016	−0.0001	0.030***	0.025**	0.010
	(0.012)	(0.011)	(0.011)	(0.012)	(0.012)
Education	−0.013	0.014	−0.001	−0.028	−0.005
	(0.019)	(0.018)	(0.019)	(0.019)	(0.019)
RCA	−0.002	0.007	0.048	0.010	0.006
	(0.009)	(0.030)	(0.042)	(0.032)	(0.029)
Age	0.001	0.002	0.0001	0.00005	0.001
	(0.002)	(0.002)	(0.002)	(0.002)	(0.002)
Female	0.093*	−0.007	0.057	0.095*	0.056
	(0.050)	(0.048)	(0.049)	(0.049)	(0.048)
Constant	0.160	−0.096	0.089	0.182	0.065
	(0.138)	(0.130)	(0.140)	(0.137)	(0.129)
Observations	846	841	833	854	823
Adjusted R^2	0.100	0.149	0.122	0.094	0.111

Note: *$p < 0.1$; **$p < 0.05$; ***$p < 0.01$; ally perception for UK was not available.

Table 14.2c *Covariates for German responses*

	US	UK	Japan	China	Russia
Treatments					
Decrease Tariffs	−0.398***	−0.323***	−0.323***	−0.361***	−0.311***
	(0.051)	(0.048)	(0.048)	(0.050)	(0.050)
Increase Tariffs	0.450***	0.553***	0.553***	0.445***	0.481***
	(0.051)	(0.049)	(0.049)	(0.049)	(0.050)
Covariates					
Ally Perception	−0.054***	−0.051***	−0.051***	−0.060***	−0.060***
	(0.009)	(0.010)	(0.010)	(0.011)	(0.009)

Table 14.2c (*cont.*)

	US	UK	Japan	China	Russia
Ideology	0.005	−0.009	−0.009	0.012	0.0003
	(0.011)	(0.010)	(0.010)	(0.010)	(0.010)
Education	−0.070***	−0.034	−0.034	0.005	−0.032
	(0.021)	(0.021)	(0.021)	(0.021)	(0.021)
RCA	0.050	0.045	0.045	0.013	0.108
	(0.102)	(0.110)	(0.110)	(0.067)	(0.147)
Age	−0.002	−0.003*	−0.003*	−0.001	−0.004***
	(0.002)	(0.001)	(0.001)	(0.002)	(0.002)
Female	0.022	0.048	0.048	0.097**	0.042
	(0.042)	(0.041)	(0.041)	(0.041)	(0.042)
Constant	0.490***	0.263	0.263	0.046	0.183
	(0.171)	(0.169)	(0.169)	(0.154)	(0.199)
Observations	940	931	931	914	905
Adjusted R^2	0.242	0.275	0.275	0.243	0.257

Note: $^*p < 0.1$; $^{**}p < 0.05$; $^{***}p < 0.01$.

References

Acemoglu, Daron, David Autor, David Dorn, Gordon H Hanson and Brendan Price. 2016. 'Import competition and the great US employment sag of the 2000s.' *Journal of Labor Economics* 34(S1):141–98.

Autor, David, David Dorn and Gordon H. Hanson. 2013. 'The China syndrome: local labor market effects of import competition in the US.' *American Economic Review* 103(6):2121–68.

Axelrod, Robert. 1984. *The Evolution of Cooperation*. vol. 5145. Basic Books (AZ).

Baccini, Leonardo, Pablo M. Pinto and Stephen Weymouth. 2017. 'The distributional consequences of preferential trade liberalization: firm-level evidence.' *International Organization* 71(2):373–95.

Balassa, Bela. 1977. '"Revealed" comparative advantage revisited: an analysis of relative export shares of the industrial countries, 1953–1971.' *The Manchester School* 45(4):327–44.

Baldwin, David Allen. 1985. *Economic Statecraft*. Princeton, NJ: Princeton University Press.

Bechtel, Michael M., Jens Hainmueller and Yotam Margalit. 2014. 'Preferences for international redistribution: the divide over the eurozone bailouts.' *American Journal of Political Science* 58(4):835–56.

Bisbee, James. 2021. 'The China shock for political science: describing the limits of causal identification.' Working Paper.

Bowles, Samuel and Herbert Gintis. 2011. *A Cooperative Species: Human Reciprocity and Its Evolution*. Princeton: Princeton University Press.

Bown, Chad P. 2021. 'The US–China trade war and phase one agreement.' *Journal of Policy Modeling* 43 (4): 805–43.

Brutger, Ryan, Stephen Chaudoin and Max Kagan. 2023. 'Trade War or election interference?'. *Review of International Organizations* 18: 1–25.

Carnegie, Allison and Austin Carson. 2019. 'Reckless rhetoric? Compliance pessimism and international order in the age of trump.' *The Journal of Politics* 81(2):739–46.

Carnegie, Allison and Nikhar Gaikwad. 2022. 'Public opinion on geopolitics and trade: theory and evidence.' *World Politics* 74 (2): 167–204.

Chilton, Adam S., Helen V. Milner and Dustin Tingley. 2020. 'Reciprocity and public opposition to foreign direct investment.' *British Journal of Political Science* 50 (1): 129–53.

Christenson, Dino P. and Douglas L. Kriner. 2019. 'Does public opinion constrain presidential unilateralism?' *American Political Science Review* 113(4):1071–77.

Cooper, Robert. 2000. *The Post-modern State and the World Order*. London: Demos.

Dür, Andreas. 2010. *Protection for Exporters: Power and Discrimination in Transatlantic Trade Relations, 1930–2010*. Ithaca, NY: Cornell University Press.

Dür, Andreas, Leonardo Baccini and Manfred Elsig. 2014. 'The design of international trade agreements: Introducing a new database.' *Review of International Organizations* 9(3):353–75.

The Economist. 2021. 'Joe Biden is determined that China should not displace America.' 17 July. Available at: www.economist.com/briefing/2021/07/17/joe-biden-is-determined-that-china-should-not-displace-america?utm_medium=cpc.adword.pd&utm_source=google&ppccampaignID=18151738051&ppcadID=&utm_campaign=a.22brand_pmax&utm_content=conversion.direct-response.anonymous&gclid=CjwKCAjw__ihBhADEiwAXEazJukDC_nJc41sSSCT3YoyMvacSZkFjpIXZ2y8vd72vXN21PMJwDqcMBoCKCEQAvD_BwE&gclsrc=aw.ds.

Fajgelbaum, Pablo D., Pinelopi K. Goldberg, Patrick J. Kennedy and Amit K. Khandelwal. 2020. 'The return to protectionism.' *The Quarterly Journal of Economics* 135(1):1–55.

Feng, Yilang, Andrew Kerner and Jane L. Sumner. 2021. 'Quitting globalization: trade-related job losses, nationalism, and resistance to FDI in the United States.' *Political Science Research and Methods* 9(2):292–311.

Gächter, Simon, Felix Kölle and Simone Quercia. 2017. 'Reciprocity and the tragedies of maintaining and providing the commons.' *Nature Human Behaviour* 1(9):650.

Gilligan, Michael J. 1997. *Empowering Exporters: Reciprocity, Delegation, and Collective Action in American Trade Policy*. Ann Arbor: University of Michigan Press.

Gilpin, Robert. 1987. *The Political Economy of International Relations*. Princeton, NJ: Princeton University Press.

Gilpin, Robert. 2001. *Global Political Economy.* Princeton, NJ: Princeton University Press.

Gouldner, Alvin W. 1960. 'The norm of reciprocity: a preliminary statement.' *American Sociological Review* 25 (2): 161–78.

Gowa, Joanne and Edward D. Mansfield. 1993. 'Power politics and international trade.' *American Political Science Review* 87(2):408–20.

Gowa, Joanne and Edward D. Mansfield. 2004. 'Alliances, imperfect markets, and major-power trade.' *International Organization* 58(4):775–805.

Grieco, Joseph M. 1988. 'Anarchy and the limits of cooperation: a realist critique of the newest liberal institutionalism.' *International Organization* 42(3):485–507.

Hainmueller, Jens and Michael J. Hiscox. 2006. 'Learning to love globalization: education and individual attitudes toward international trade.' *International Organization* 60(2):469–98.

Hays, Jude C., Sean D. Ehrlich and Clint Peinhardt. 2005. 'Government spending and public support for trade in the OECD: an empirical test of the embedded liberalism thesis.' *International Organization* 59(2):473–94.

Herrmann, Richard K., Philip E. Tetlock and Matthew N. Diascro. 2001. 'How Americans think about trade: reconciling conflicts among money, power, and principles.' *International Studies Quarterly* 45(2):191–218.

Hopewell, Kristen. 2023. 'Tumult in the trading system: the China paradox, declining US institutional power, and the crisis at the WTO.' In Gao, Henry, Raess, Damian and Zeng, Ka. (Eds.). *China and the WTO: A Twenty-Year Assessment.* Cambridge: Cambridge University Press.

Jensen, Nathan M. and René Lindstädt. 2013. Globalization with whom: context-dependent foreign direct investment preferences. Technical report Working Paper. Available at: www.natemjensen.com/wp-content/uploads/2014/09/Globalization_with_Whom_-Working-Paper.pdf

Jensen, J. Bradford, Dennis P. Quinn and Stephen Weymouth. 2017. 'Winners and losers in international trade: the effects on US Presidential voting.' *International Organization* 71(3): 423–57.

Keohane, Robert O. 1986. 'Reciprocity in international relations.' *International Organization* 40(1):1–27.

Kirshner, Jonathan. 2014. *American Power after the Financial Crisis.* Ithaca, NY: Cornell University Press.

Kleinberg, Katja B. and Benjamin O. Fordham. 2010. 'Trade and foreign policy attitudes.' *Journal of Conflict Resolution* 54(5):687–714.

Manger, Mark. 2009. *Investing in Protection: The Politics of Preferential Trade Agreements between North and South.* Cambridge: Cambridge University Press.

Mansfield, Edward D. and Diana C. Mutz. 2009. 'Support for free trade: self-interest, sociotropic politics, and out-group anxiety.' *International Organization* 63(3):425–57.

Mansfield, Edward D. and Helen V. Milner. 2012. *Votes, Vetoes, and the Political Economy of International Trade Agreements.* Princeton, NJ: Princeton University Press.

Margalit, Yotam. 2011. 'Costly jobs: trade-related layoffs, government compensation, and voting in US elections.' *American Political Science Review* 105(1):166–88.

Mayda, Anna Maria and Dani Rodrik. 2005. 'Why are some people (and countries) more protectionist than others?' *European Economic Review* 49(6):1393–430.

Milner, Helen V. and Dustin Tingley. 2013. 'Public opinion and foreign aid: a review essay.' *International Interactions* 39(3):389–401.

Mutz, Diana C. and Eunji Kim. 2017. 'The impact of in-group favoritism on trade preferences.' *International Organization* 71(4):827–50.

Naughton, Barry. 2007. *The Chinese Economy: Transitions and Growth*. Cambridge, MA: The MIT Press.

Nguyen, Quynh and Thomas Bernauer. 2019. 'Does social trust affect public support for international trade? Insights from an experiment in Vietnam.' *Political Studies* 67(2):440–58.

Nguyen, Quynh, Thomas Sattler and Tanja Schweinberger. 2021. 'Power Transitions and International Economic Cooperation: Experimental Evidence from ParallelSurveys in China and the U.S.'

Nooruddin, Irfan and Nita Rudra. 2014. 'Are developing countries really defying the embedded liberalism compact?' *World Politics* 66(4):603–40.

Owen, Erica and Noel P. Johnston. 2017. 'Occupation and the political economy of trade: job routineness, offshorability, and protectionist sentiment.' *International Organization* 71 (4): 665–99.

Powell, Robert. 1991. 'Absolute and relative gains in international relations theory.' *American Political Science Review* 85(4):1303–20.

Raess, Damian. 2021. 'The demand-side politics of China's global buying spree: managers' attitudes toward Chinese inward FDI flows in comparative perspective.' *Review of International Political Economy* 28(6):1555–81. https://doi.org/10.1080/09692290.2020.1778503

Raess, Damian. 2023. The Politics of Preferential Trade Liberalization with China. In Gao, Henry, Raess, Damian and Zeng, Ka. (Eds.). *China and the WTO: A Twenty-Year Assessment*. Cambridge: Cambridge University Press.

Rankin, David M. 2001. 'Identities, interests, and imports.' *Political Behavior* 23(4):351–76.

Rho, Sungmin and Michael Tomz. 2017. 'Why don't trade preferences reflect economic self-interest?' *International Organization* 71(S1):S85–S108.

Schaffer, Lena Maria and Gabriele Spilker. 2019. 'Self-interest versus sociotropic considerations: an information-based perspective to understanding individuals' trade preferences.' *Review of International Political Economy* 26 (6): 1266–92.

Scheve, Kenneth F. and Matthew J. Slaughter. 2001. 'What determines individual trade-policy preferences?' *Journal of International Economics* 54(2):267–92.

Schweinberger, Tanja. 2021. 'How promise-breaking in trade rhetoric shapes attitudes towards bilateral U.S.-China Trade Cooperation.' *Business and Politics* 24(4):463–90.

Simmel, Georg. 1950. *The Sociology of Georg Simmel*. New York: The Free Press.

Smeltz, Dina and Craig Kafura. 2021. 'For First Time, Half of Americans Favor Defending Taiwan If China Invades.' Chicago Council on Global Affairs. Available at: https://globalaffairs.org/sites/default/files/2021-08/2021%20Taiwan%20Brief.pdf

Spilker, Gabriele, Thomas Bernauer and Victor Umaña. 2016. 'Selecting partner countries for preferential trade agreements: experimental evidence from Costa Rica, Nicaragua, and Vietnam.' *International Studies Quarterly* 60(4):706–18.

Viner, Jacob. 1948. 'Power versus plenty as objectives of foreign policy in the seventeenth and eighteenth centuries.' *World Politics* 1(1):1–29.

WTO. 2021. 'Importance of the WTO dispute settlement system'. www.wto.org.

15

The Post-Accession Treatment of Chinese Goods Exports by WTO Members

SIMON J. EVENETT

I Introduction

Twenty years on China's accession to the World Trade Organization (WTO) is rightly regarded as a significant milestone in global economic governance. Much analysis has been devoted to the effects of China's accession on the economies, politics, and trade negotiating stance of its trading partners as evidenced, for example, by the literature on the so-called China Shock. In contrast, apart from papers analysing the impact of U.S. import tariff hikes on Chinese exports imposed by the Trump Administration, there is considerably less analysis on how China's interests have been affected by policy intervention taken by its trading partners since 2001. This chapter seeks to go some way to remedy that deficit.

The often-expressed concern is that Chinese manufactured exports – supported by Chinese government policies – have caused dislocation and disruption in trading partners. In this chapter the perspective is reversed by asking: how much Chinese exports were at risk from unilateral trade policy actions taken by other governments? The goal is to elaborate the factual base, to offer a tentative assessment and, then, to cautiously draw out implications for policy and future research.

The systemic importance of this analysis is that it sheds light on the extent to which Chinese membership of the WTO protected its goods exports from excessive trade discrimination. Excessive is meant here in relative terms – that is, relative to other trading partners. In turn, this raises the possibility that over time the benefits that China enjoyed from its WTO membership may have been clawed back by trading partners.

I thank Apolline Duclaux and Fernando Martin Espejo for their support in preparing the charts for this chapter. Comments on this analysis are welcome and can be sent to simon.evenett@sgept.org.

Put starkly, if China's exporters have faced extensive and growing trade discrimination aboard since 2001, has China's membership of the WTO become a depreciating asset? It is not inconceivable that answers to that question influence Chinese government calculations concerning its future development strategy, in particular the shift away from export-led growth towards a so-called dual circulation strategy. Related policy-relevant questions include: has the trade discrimination faced by Chinese exports influenced Chinese assessments of the wisdom of decoupling from Western economies? And has foreign trade discrimination influenced Chinese incentives to engage in cooperative behaviour in the multilateral trading system?

The approach taken in this chapter is relentlessly empirical. Such an approach does not deny that there may be valuable theoretical and legal perspectives on the foreign treatment of Chinese commercial interests since its accession to the WTO in 2001. Yet, there is value in putting the facts on the table. That is, in documenting what unilateral trade policy actions confront Chinese exports, how long those policy interventions have lasted, and the scale of the market access at risk or, in the case of foreign trade reforms, opportunities. At some point, arguments based on first principles ought to be confronted with the factual record.

The evidence presented in this chapter is relevant to assessments of the impact of China's WTO accession on its own economy and society and on its trading partners, not least because post-accession trade discrimination by the latter is likely to have reduced the net benefit of the former joining the WTO. To date, however, such assessments have tended to emphasise effects related to educational outcomes, the environment, labour markets, trade, and policy uncertainty (Chen et al., 2020; Dai et al., 2021; Garred, 2018; Imbruno, 2019; Kim and Xin, 2021; Lin and Long, 2020).

This chapter is not the first to assess the impact of foreign trade discrimination on China, as the growing literature on the Sino-U.S. trade war can attest. High profile papers in this regard include Amiti et al. (2019, 2020) and Fajgelbaum et al. (2020). That such trade tensions have been linked in extant literature to the economic, political, and social consequences of China's accession to the WTO brings the discussion back to the animating theme of this volume. Assessments of the overseas impact of China's growing exports, in particular of manufactured goods, include Autor et al. (2016, 2019), Autor et al. (2020), Bloom et al. (2019), Dustmann (2021), and Pierce and Schott (2016). While this paper focuses on policy interventions taken by China's trading partners, it is important not to lose sight of the factors that may have driven the implementation of those foreign unilateral acts in the first place.

The rest of this chapter is organised as follows. The next section briefly describes the rise of China as a trading powerhouse since its accession to the WTO in 2001. Given the sustained growth of China's exports and the size of those exports at present, it is unsurprising that there has been a reaction from trading partners. One part of that reaction has been to bring cases against China under the WTO's Dispute Settlement Understanding and, in the interests of completeness, pertinent statistics in this regard are reported.

The third section of the chapter gets to the heart of the matter and reports on the frequency, form, and scale of trade implicated by the unilateral commercial policy acts of China's trading partners. Given the best data available refers to policy intervention taken since the onset of the Global Financial Crisis, the emphasis is on developments since that systemic episode.

The final section of the paper discusses how best to assess or interpret the empirical findings presented earlier. The case is made for a relative assessment as opposed to an absolute assessment of the degree of Chinese goods export exposure to foreign trade discrimination. Four implications for policy and future research are drawn from that relative assessment.

II China's Emergence as a Trading Powerhouse and Push Back from Trading Partners

Since its accession to the WTO, China has become an exporting and importing powerhouse, especially in relation to manufacturing goods. Figure 15.1 shows that China's share of world exports and world imports now exceeds 10%. The growth in China's manufacturing trade is even more impressive. Before its accession China's manufacturing exports accounted for less than 3% of the world total; now nearly one-sixth of world manufacturing exports originate in China. China's share of world manufacturing imports has risen three-fold and reflects extensive sourcing of parts and components from abroad.[1]

[1] Although the focus of this chapter is on China's manufacturing trade, China is also a significant importer of agricultural commodities and fuel and mining products. According to the latest WTO *World Trade Profiles*, the former accounted for 9.6% of total Chinese imports in 2019 and the latter for 27.9%. In contrast, 92.9% of total Chinese exports were manufacturing goods. Chinese service sector imports and exports are approximately one-eighth of the size of its goods trade and, consequently, are not the focus of this analysis.

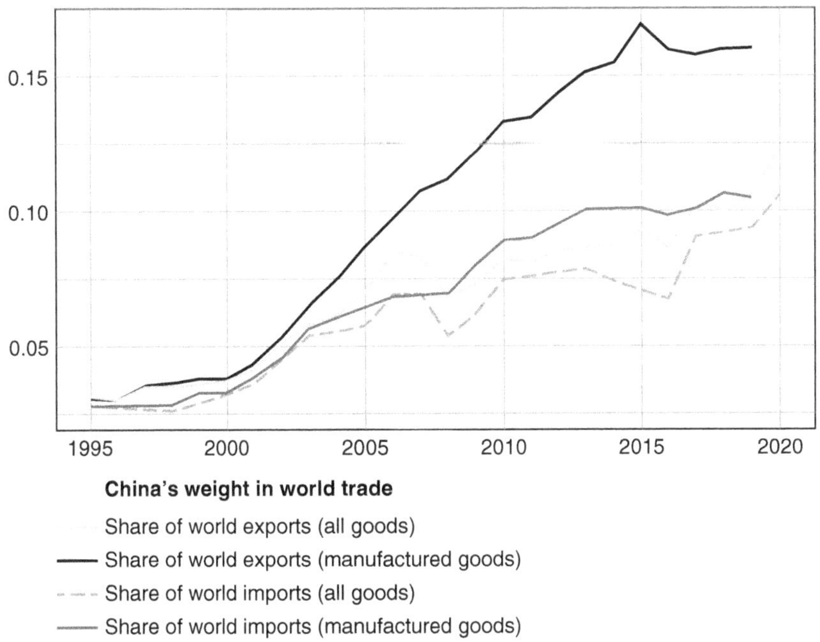

Figure 15.1 China has become an exporting and importing powerhouse

The upshot of these manufacturing trade dynamics is that China has earned sizeable trade surpluses (see Figure 15.2). Those surpluses peaked before the Global Financial Crisis at around 7.5% of current GDP and subsequently have halved. At no time since China's accession to the WTO has it run a trade deficit.

The findings in Figures 15.1 and 15.2 shed some light on why Chinese manufactured goods became a lightening rod for criticism of Chinese government policy. First, for some such unusually high rates of export growth were considered unlikely to have been due to competition on the merits and, on this logic, must have been supported by government policy. Second, while China's trading partners benefited from greater variety and lower prices, the quantum of Chinese manufacturing exports that was absorbed by trading partners after its WTO accession has been linked to disruption to local labour markets, plant closures, reduced profits, and the like. Third, some policymakers associate large trade surpluses with unfair or malign commercial and macroeconomic policies. Under these circumstances, it is unsurprising that Chinese manufacturing exports became a target for foreign trade discrimination.

Figure 15.2 China has consistently generated trade surpluses this century

Having written this, immediate resort to trade discrimination was not the only option available to foreign governments. WTO members could avail themselves of the Dispute Settlement Understanding, bringing cases against Chinese policies considered to be in violation of multilateral trade rules. Many governments did just that. As Figure 15.3 shows, since the middle of the last decade between two to six new cases were typically brought against China every year.

The European Union and the United States initiated a significant number of WTO dispute settlement cases against Chinese policies, see Figure 15.4 which identifies the eight nations that have brought the largest number of cases. It is noteworthy that the governments of countries on the East Asian land mass do not feature in the top eight most litigious nations.

The contention that resort to WTO dispute settlement did not induce China to accelerate broad-based market reforms may have ultimately accelerated the resort to unilateral measures against Chinese manufacturing exports. Perhaps the most obvious manifestation of the latter was the *de facto* revocation of China's Most Favoured Nation status by the Trump Administration. But were these high-profile measures, taken more than fifteen years after China joined the WTO, the only relevant acts of foreign trade discrimination? Could the accumulation over time of less

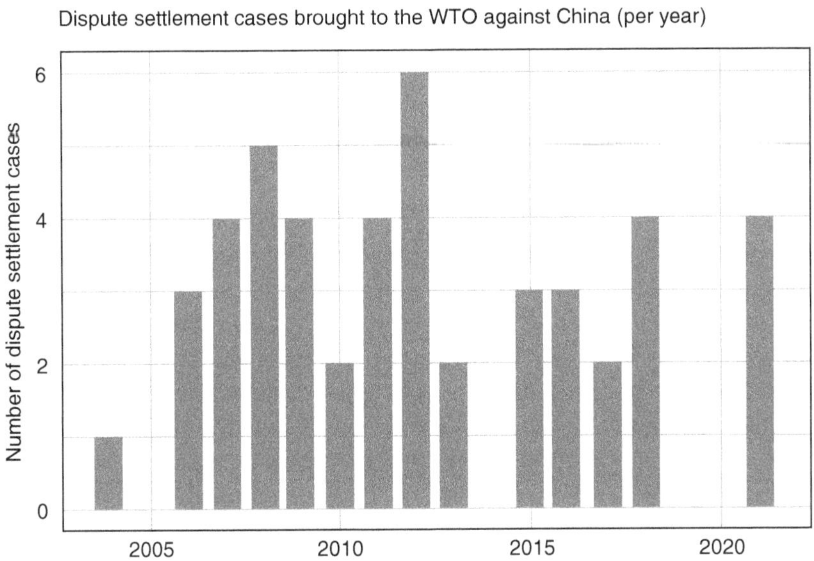

Figure 15.3 A steady stream of WTO dispute settlement cases have been brought against China

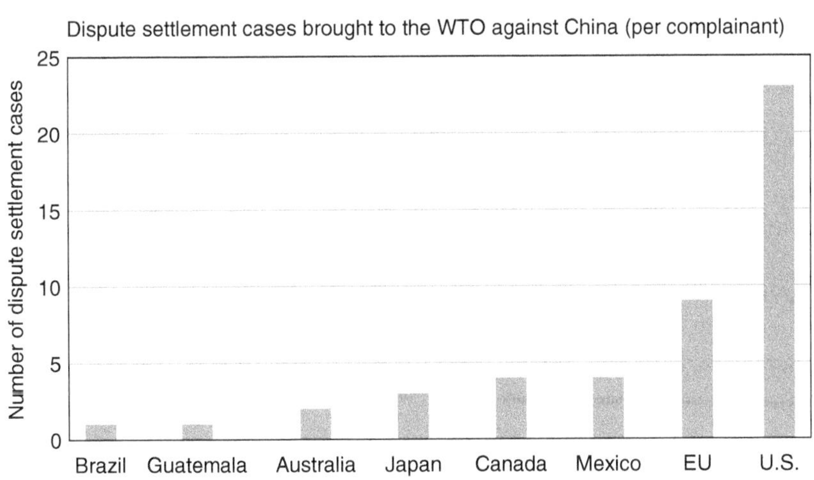

Figure 15.4 By a large margin, the United States has brought the most dispute settlement cases against China

salient discrimination against Chinese goods cover more of that nation's exports? This question and others are answered in the two remaining sections of this chapter.

III Unilateral Trade Policy Responses by China's Trading Partners

Although much tends to be written about trade policy developments in regional and multilateral fora, the focus of this paper is on unilateral trade policy actions taken by governments that implicate Chinese goods exports. This focus is justified on the grounds, as previous research has shown, that for more than a decade the majority of global goods trade has been covered[2] by discriminatory unilateral acts taken since the onset of the Global Financial Crisis of 2008 and 2009 (Evenett, 2019).

Put simply, while multilateral trade processes have stalled, unilateral trade policy is where the action is. Such is the accumulation over time of unilateral acts in force – both liberalising and trade distorting – that any credible assessment of the treatment of Chinese exports after its WTO accession needs to take account of them.

The challenge for analysts is that official sources of trade policy information provide only a fraction of the information required. For sure, not all is lost. The WTO secretariat maintains a comprehensive database of anti-dumping and countervailing duty investigations and this will be referred to below. Beyond that, however, matters deteriorate quickly. The WTO's Trade Monitoring Database (TMDB) does include entries where China is an affected trading partner for goods measures – but not for service sector policy interventions and policy measures affecting the protection of intellectual property rights. UNCTAD's TRAINS database on non-tariff measures contains some valuable information but is widely regarded as incomplete.

For these reasons the principal data source used in this chapter is the Global Trade Alert database.[3] This database includes information on 61 different types of policy intervention whose implementation *can* affect the relative treatment of domestic firms vis-à-vis foreign rivals.[4] These policy

[2] International trade economists use the phrase "covered" in this context to be trade potentially affected by. A trade coverage ratio for a nation's goods exports, therefore, is the share of its aggregate goods exports that are in products and are sold to markets where they face a certain, specified policy instrument.

[3] In the interest of transparency, please note that the author created this database in 2009.

[4] For an overview of the contents and methodology of the GTA database see Evenett and Fritz (2021). For an account of the conceptual foundations of the GTA database and its contemporary relevance see Evenett (2019).

interventions include traditional border barriers (except those associated with Technical Barriers to Trade and Sanitary and Phytosanitary Standards), behind-the-border measures that affect imports (such as government procurement measures), subsidies to import-competing firms, and policy interventions affecting exports, foreign direct investment, labour migration (not refugees), data flows, and intellectual property.

Policy interventions announced or implemented since November 2008 (the month when G20 Leaders first stated they would eschew protectionism) are in scope as the GTA is concerned These policy interventions are at all levels of government in any nation. As of this writing, the GTA database contains reports on over 43,000 distinct policy interventions.

The GTA database includes 13,563 unilateral policy interventions[5] by foreign governments that implicate the commercial interests of China. Of that total, 12,651 policy interventions relate to trade in goods.[6] This contrasts with the 1,397 entries in the WTO's TMDB that list China as an affected trading partner. Three-quarters of the total number of policy interventions affecting Chinese trade in goods in the GTA database were still in force on 24 March 2022.[7]

Of the 12,651 total mentioned in the last paragraph, 9,416 policy interventions by foreign governments tilted the commercial playing field away from Chinese goods exporters. Over three thousand subsidies to import-competing firms have been issued by foreign governments in markets where Chinese firms export. Export measures by foreign governments (both restrictions and state-furnished incentives) that worsen the competitive conditions faced by Chinese exporters have occurred just under two thousand times. Chinese goods exporters have faced 1,631 import tariff increases and have been investigated for dumping, subsidisation, or for causing serious injury a total of 1,231 times since 1 November 2008.

On the other side of the ledger, Chinese firms have benefited from import tariff cuts implemented by trading partners on 2,005 occasions.

[5] In the GTA database joint acts by members of a customs union, such as the European Union, count as unilateral acts. Reciprocal trade policy acts – such as the creation of a free trade agreement – are not treated as unilateral acts. The focus in this paper on unilateral trade policy acts affecting Chinese commercial interests should not be taken as implying that the trade diversion caused by the creation of regional trade agreements that exclude China are irrelevant.

[6] To put this 12,651 total in perspective, it is worth noting that China is fifth most affected trading partner in the GTA database. Germany is affected most often, followed by France, Italy, and the United Kingdom. The United States is the sixth most affected nation, its goods exports being affected a total of 12,573 times.

[7] This amounts to 9,533 policy interventions.

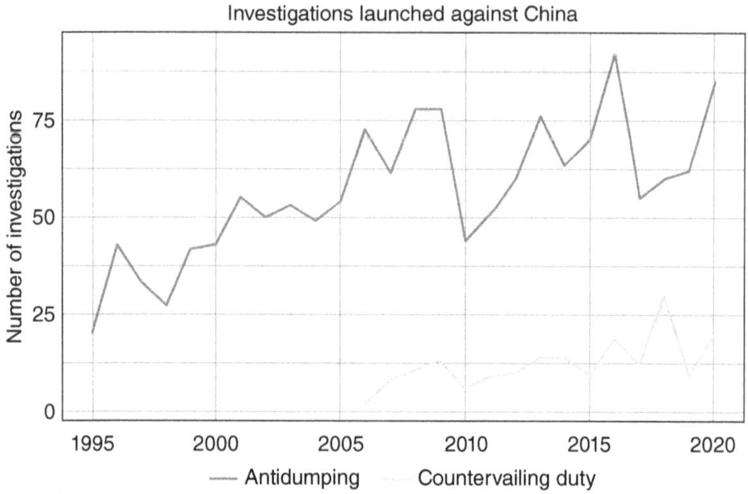

Figure 15.5 Over time a growing number of dumping and countervailing duty investigations have been initiated on products exported from China

Overall, though, for every implemented foreign unilateral act that benefited Chinese exporters since 1 November 2008 there are three that have harmed them. Still, while such counts are informative, the quantum of trade covered reveals more about the exports at risk from foreign trade discrimination. Much of the remainder of this section is devoted to reporting trade coverage calculations based on the policy interventions recorded in the GTA database.[8]

One drawback to using the GTA data is that it starts reporting on policy intervention seven years after China joined the WTO. Quite reasonably, some may want to see if foreign trade discrimination against Chinese exports changed after China joined the WTO. The only known time series of sufficient length relates to antidumping and countervailing duty actions and is collected by the WTO. Figure 15.5 reports the number of such investigations into Chinese exports launched each year from 1995 to 2020.

[8] For unilateral policy intervention affecting trade in goods, where reliable information is available the GTA conservatively assigned six-digit Harmonised System product codes. With those HS codes, the UN COMTRADE database can be used to identify trading partners where the affected level of commerce exceeds $1 million (a *de minimis* threshold). So as to avoid problems of endogeneity, the global trade flow matrix for the year before a policy intervention comes into force was used to identify affected trading partners. The identification of affected trading partners in this manner has been automated so as to reduce human error.

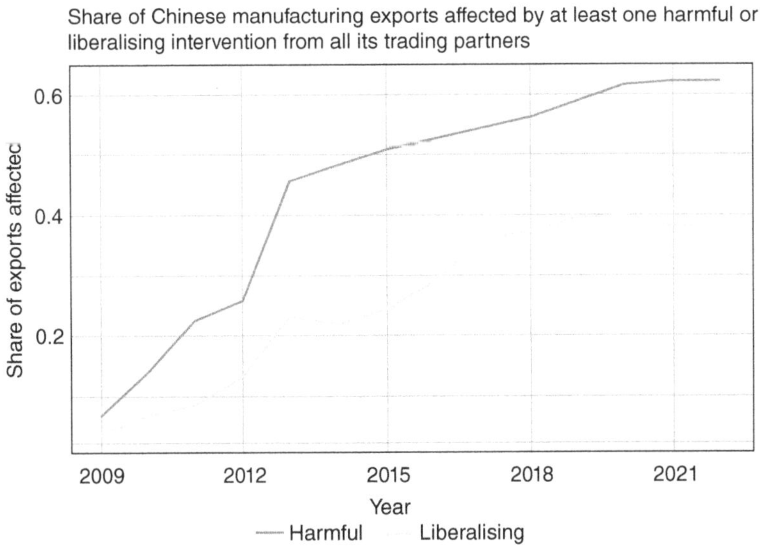

Figure 15.6 The growing shares of Chinese manufactured exports facing unilateral measures in trading partners

Before China joined the WTO approximately 30–35 antidumping investigations into Chinese goods exports were launched each year. After accession, that number has progressively risen and in some years the total number of new investigations exceeded 75. The number of investigations fell sharply in 2010, potentially as a result of the Global Financial Crisis. Similar dynamics, but starting from a much lower base from 2005, can be found with respect to countervailing duty investigations of Chinese exports.

To put the findings in Figure 15.5 in context, it may be useful to compare the growth in the annual totals in that figure with the growth of total Chinese manufacturing exports (as revealed in Figure 15.3). It should be evident that the latter grew faster than the former, implying the propensity to launch dumping and subsidy investigations into Chinese manufactured exports has fallen over time. Put differently, the annual totals of new investigations did not grow in line with the growth of Chinese manufacturing exports.

Turning now to the foreign trade discrimination and trade reform faced by Chinese exporters of manufactures found in the GTA database, Figure 15.6 reports the shares of overall exports where market access gains (potentially from WTO accession) are at risk from subsequent trade discrimination and the shares potentially benefiting from foreign trade liberalisation. The former shares always exceeded the latter and the margin grew sharply from 2013 on.

By the time the COVID-19 pandemic hit, over 60% of Chinese manufacturing exports faced one or more policy-induced competitive disadvantages in overseas markets. The calculations reported in Figure 15.6 take account of the duration that a foreign trade barrier is in force and, when a measure lapses, it no longer counts towards the total in subsequent years.[9] As a result, there is no inherent reason why these export exposure shares must rise over time – still they tend to. Having written that, a plateau was reached in 2019 in Chinese export exposure to foreign trade discrimination, although it should be noted that the estimated share for this and subsequent years may be revised upward as more foreign trade measures are documented by the Global Trade Alert team.[10]

The share of Chinese exports of products in foreign markets where trade reforms were introduced also rises until 2019 when it plateaus at around 0.4. Any comprehensive assessment of the impact of unilateral policy choice by trading partners on Chinese exports ought to take account of the fact these reforms, although it is an open question as to whether China might have benefited from some of these reforms had she not joined the WTO.

Any particular trade route that Chinese manufacturers operate in could be affected by multiple unilateral trade actions by trading partners. One might plausibly assume that the more such harmful (liberalising) actions along a trade route the greater the likely size of the adverse (beneficial) effects on Chinese exports. To examine this matter, the share of Chinese manufacturing exports facing three or more harmful unilateral foreign measures is reported for each year from 2009 to 2022 in Figure 15.7. Likewise, the share faces three or more unilateral trade reforms. The gap between the shares facing multiple harmful and liberalising measures widens, with the latter share never exceeding 0.15. Meanwhile, by 2020 the former exceeded 0.4.[11] This reinforces the finding that the weight of

[9] Moreover, if a measure lapses X days into any given year then only the share (X/365) of the value of the covered trade flow counts towards the shares reported in this and subsequent figures.

[10] Some reporting lags are inevitable, not least because certain governments are slow at publishing information about policy interventions that harm the commercial interests of trading partners.

[11] That this share falls in 2021 and 2022 is likely to be in large part due to reporting lags. Recall, that in Figure 15.7 only trade routes where there are three or more unilateral foreign acts in effect count. Failure to report one act could involve a trade route dropping out of this calculation. Having written this, there is no fall off in the share of exports facing three or more liberalising measures, which raises the possibility that this share may get revised up over time.

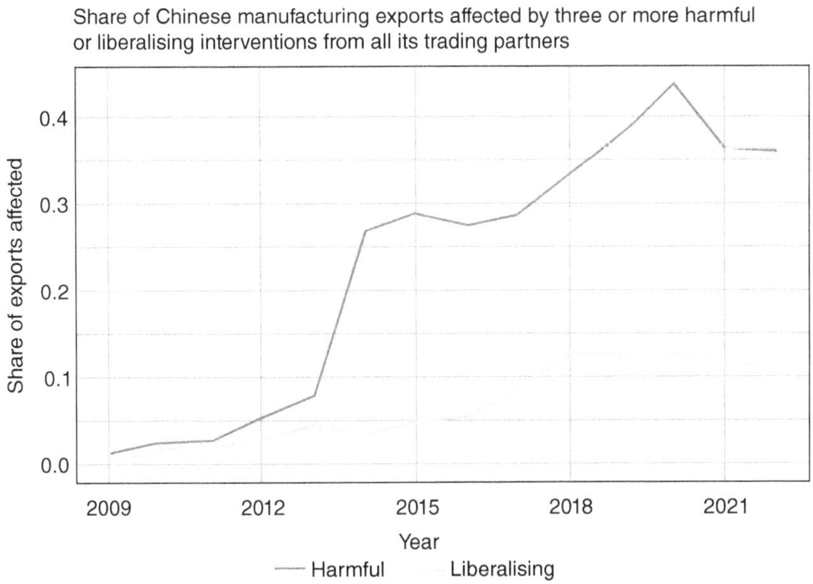

Figure 15.7 Thirty percent of Chinese manufactured exports face three or more trade-related hurdles in foreign markets

foreign unilateral action was to disadvantage Chinese manufacturing exports after its accession to the WTO.

In principle, resorting to discrimination against Chinese manufacturing exports can differ across China's trading partners. To investigate this matter, the equivalent of Figure 15.6 was produced for unilateral actions (both harmful to Chinese interests and beneficial) by the United States, by the European Union,[12] and by the other countries in the East Asia and Pacific (EAP) region.[13] The results can be found in Figures 15.8–15.10 respectively.

There are several noteworthy findings. First, while almost all Chinese manufacturing exports now face policy-induced hurdles in the American market, the share was rising and had reached 0.74 in 2016, that is, before President Trump took office. As is evident from the relevant figure, the share of Chinese exports facing worse market access conditions in the

[12] For the purposes of this chapter and the results reported herein, the European Union is taken to include the 27 remaining Member States even though the United Kingdom finally exited later in the period under examination.

[13] The definition of the East Asia and Pacific region employed here is that of the World Bank's.

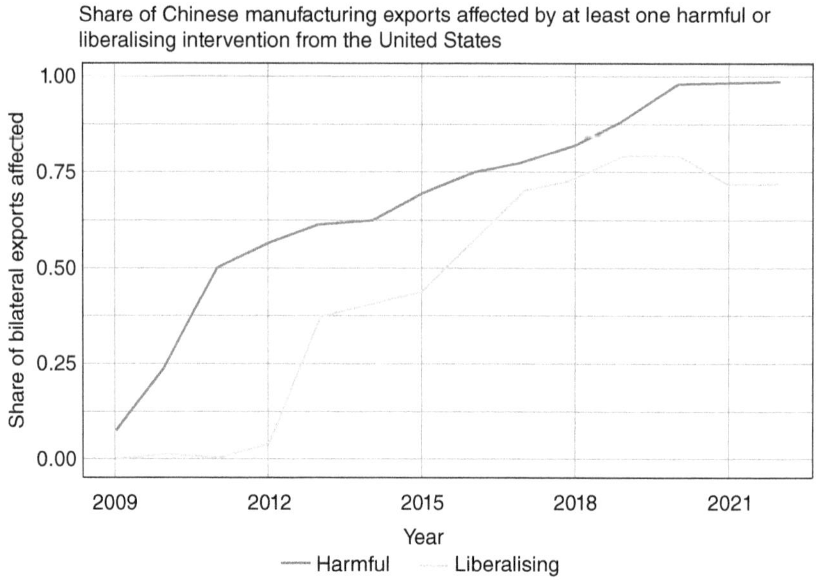

Figure 15.8 Large shares of Chinese exports faced hurdles in the U.S. market before President Trump took office

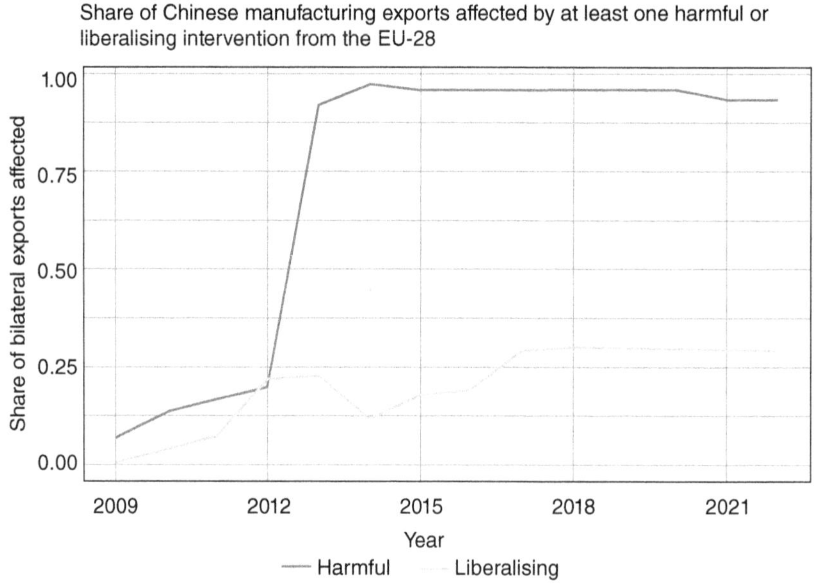

Figure 15.9 Market access impairment in the EU is longstanding

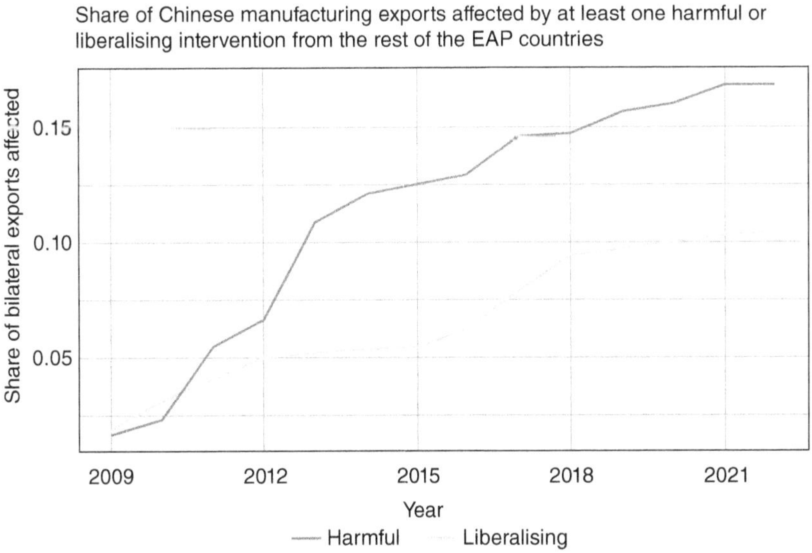

Figure 15.10 The hurdles erected to Chinese exports in its own region cover proportionally less trade than those erected in the EU and the U.S.

United States deteriorated sharply during the two terms of the Obama presidency (see Figure 15.8).

Second, American public bodies have undertaken enough trade reforms in the products that China exports to the United States that the share of Chinese exports facing improved market conditions is significant. It is, of course, possible that a particular product shipped to the American market faces both unilaterally imposed trade hurdles as well as reforms.

Third, the withdrawal of China from the EU's Generalised System of Preferences (GSP) and the extensive award of free CO_2 trading permits[14] to EU firms in import-competing sectors account for the very high shares of Chinese exports facing harmful unilateral acts in the European Union (as shown in Figure 15.9). Ever since 2013 over 90% of Chinese manufacturing exports faced one or more unilateral policy-induced hurdles to competing in the European Union market. In contrast, at no point between 2009 and 2021 does 30% or more of Chinese manufacturing exports benefit from policy-induced market access improvements in the European Union.

[14] Such awards are subsidies are they constitute a transfer of state resources to commercial operators.

Fourth, the shares of Chinese exports facing harmful unilateral acts in the East Asia and Pacific region are smaller than the comparable shares found in the United States and the European Union (compare the upper lines in Figures 15.8–15.10). Similar findings arise also with respect to exposure to liberalising measures implemented in the region and this may reflect the fact that China has signed regional trade agreements with many neighbouring countries.

That the United States chose to target Chinese exports with higher tariffs begs the question of whether other governments have done so and how much Chinese manufacturing exports were at stake. To address this matter, those market access-impairing unilateral trade measures where China was the *sole* affected exporter were identified in the Global Trade Alert database. Refer to these measures as those that "target" Chinese exports.

The shares of Chinese manufacturing exports facing targeted harmful measures in each year from 2009 to 2022 were calculated and contrasted to the shares of Chinese manufacturing exports facing targeted or non-targeted unilateral harmful measures. By construction, the latter share exceeds the former share in any given year; the gap between them reveals the extent to which Chinese exports face untargeted foreign trade discrimination.[15] The comparison is presented graphically in Figure 15.11.

The share of Chinese manufacturing exports that are targeted by foreign governments for discrimination grows slowly over time but jumps twice; the first time with the exclusion of China from the EU's GSP regime and the second time with the Trump Administration's four rounds of tariff hikes issued under Section 301 of the Trade Act of 1974, as amended. By the time the COVID-19 pandemic hit, approximately 42% of Chinese manufacturing exports were singled out for worse treatment by its trading partners.

To conclude, evidence was marshalled in this section that demonstrates that the treatment of Chinese exports by trading partners evolved markedly after China's accession to the WTO. The goal here has been to report the variation over time, across trading partners, and along other meaningful dimensions in Chinese export exposure to better and worse market access conditions abroad. Rather than focus exclusively on high-profile episodes, such as the Sino-U.S. trade war, the approach taken here also

[15] Untargeted trade discrimination could be a policy intervention that disadvantages all imports; that is, the national treatment principle is broken but the Most Favoured Nation principle is not.

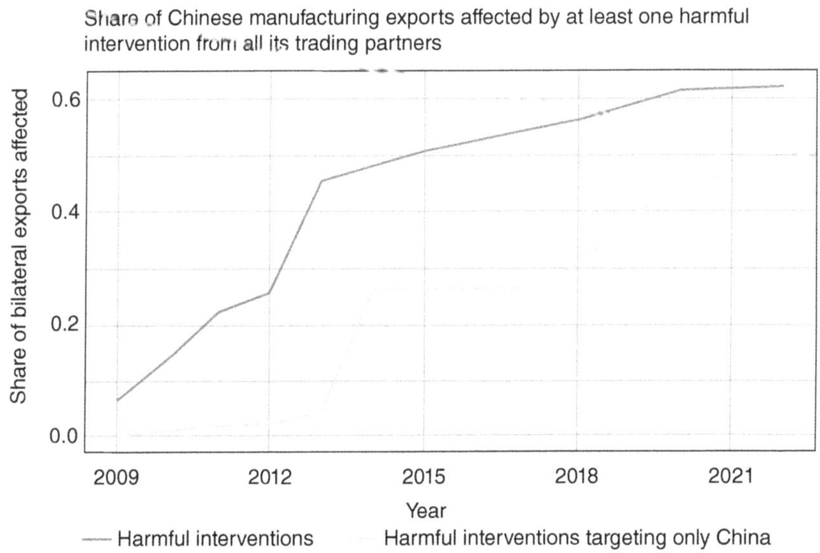

Figure 15.11 Targeting Chinese exports has become more common during the past decade

includes less salience unilateral trade policy acts by China's trading partners and therefore presents a more comprehensive picture of the global commercial policy landscape facing Chinese exporters.

IV Assessment and Policy Implications

How should analysts and policymakers interpret the scale – reported in the last section – of Chinese goods exports facing foreign trade distortions implemented since China joined the WTO reported? What do these findings imply about the degree of protection afforded by WTO rules to one of the world's major trading powers?

Care is needed in interpreting the empirical findings presented here. After all, they demonstrate that significant shares of Chinese goods exports were exposed to foreign trade distortions. They are silent on the effect of those trade distortions, a topic that should be taken up in subsequent research. Still, the former finding is of interest as, plausibly, it is a necessary condition for finding adverse effects.

On reflection, employing an absolute standard to judge the documented levels of export exposure is not sensible. There are reasons why a WTO member's goods exports can legitimately be exposed to discrimination by foreign governments. The WTO rule book is not complete nor is it uncontested (the policy domain of subsidies being a case in point). Furthermore, certain types of trade policy discrimination are allowed under multilateral trade rules. Surely, no one with a basic understanding of the WTO agreements would reasonably expect that any member of that organisation is guaranteed that its exports be completely protected from foreign discrimination. Zero export exposure is not the right benchmark.

Moreover, growing absolute levels of export exposure to foreign trade distortions is not necessarily evidence of violations of WTO rules. Even so, this may offer little comfort to officials having to explain why their nation's exporters face deteriorating market access conditions in trading partners. Just because discrimination is perfectly legal under WTO rules does not mean it cannot alter the political economy of support for multilateralism in the affected trading partner. Seen through this particular lens, the rising shares of Chinese export exposure to foreign discrimination reported earlier might cast a shadow over support in some Chinese quarters for its membership in the WTO.

Perhaps a better way to assess the findings of this paper is to employ a relative criterion. That is, to ask if the exposure of China's goods exports to foreign trade distortions found here is larger than other WTO members. In terms of the figures discussed earlier, one might ask what Figures 15.6 and 15.7 look like for other WTO members or groups of those members.

Before exploring this line of inquiry further one might consider two hypotheses. First, that Chinese export exposure to foreign trade discrimination be lower than smaller and less influential WTO members on account of Beijing's growing clout in world affairs. Second, that the fast pace of China's export growth since its WTO accession made it a lightning rod for foreign trade discrimination and so the opposite outcome would be expected.

To add empirical flesh to this comparison, the exposure of Chinese goods exports to foreign trade discrimination that discourages imports was compared over the same timeframe with that the aggregate for every other nation. The focus on market access impairment from policy interventions affecting domestic conditions of competition in the implementing jurisdiction is deliberate. This design choice excludes state-provided export incentives from the calculations. China has implemented several changes in such export incentives since the onset of the Global Financial Crisis and to include them in the calculations would have increased the estimated export exposure to foreign trade distortions of other nations. In turn, this would inappropriately skew the comparison in favour of finding that China's goods were better protected by its WTO membership.

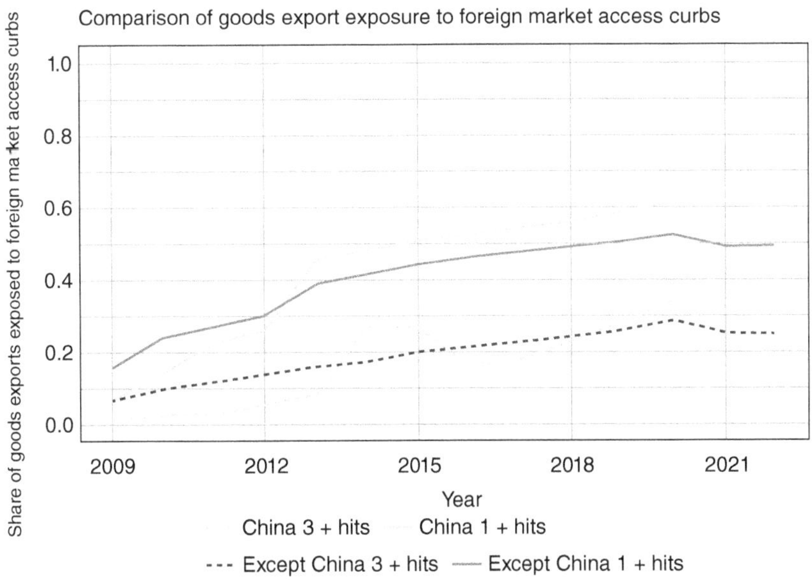

Figure 15.12 Chinese goods exports are more exposed to market access curbs in trading partners than exports from other nations

Figure 15.12 reports the changes over time in Chinese and in non-Chinese export exposure to policy interventions by trading partners that discourage importation.[16] Recall those policies include subsidies to import-competing firms, other behind-the-border policies (such as local sourcing incentives and requirements in government procurement policies) as well as import restrictions including import-related non-tariff barriers.

A comparison is provided between the annual exposure to any trade distortion abroad (represented in Figure 15.12 by line one or more trade distortions) and the annual exposure of exports to three or more foreign trade distortions. Exposure to three or more trade distortions could be thought of as being associated with exposure to greater trade discrimination abroad.

As far as the overall exposure to foreign trade distortions is concerned, since 2013 the share of Chinese goods exports exposed has been greater than for other nations. By 2021 such export exposure for China was more than 10 percentage points higher than for non-Chinese exporters.

16 The non-Chinese export exposure is calculated in terms of absolute export exposure and is not some unweighted average of export exposure of countries other than China.

Similarly, from 2019 Chinese export exposure to three or more trade distortions exceeded that of other nations; with the gap reaching at least five percentage points by 2021. Overall, then, it is difficult to argue that WTO rules have shielded Chinese goods exporters from foreign trade distortions. Put differently, existing multilateral trade rules have not prevented WTO members from taking steps that once added up discriminated against more Chinese exports than the goods exports of other WTO members.

In assessing the policy implications of this relative finding and others in this chapter, four thoughts come to mind. First, China's growing clout – economic and otherwise – does not appear to have spared it from high absolute and relative levels of foreign trade discrimination. Although the finding of lower levels of Chinese export exposure to trade discrimination in the Asia-Pacific region suggests a nuanced clout-based argument might still apply. Further research might usefully investigate whether the carrots and sticks that China deployed had a greater effect in the Asia-Pacific region. The Belt and Road Initiative comes to mind.

Second, that overall exposure to foreign trade discrimination has risen for China and for other nations is a source of concern. It begs the question as to whether and why multilateral trade cooperation has broken down. As argued earlier, any breakdown cannot be solely pinned on the trade wars of the Trump Administration – the rot set in years before. The extent to which China's accession to the WTO influenced observed levels of multilateral trade cooperation could be further researched. What needs to be explained is the gradual breakdown of cooperation (as manifested by greater shares of trade exposed to discrimination), not just the rhetorical fireworks of the past five or six years.

Third, that there is so much export exposure to foreign trade discrimination strongly suggests that either multilateral trade rules afford governments lots of policy space to influence trade flows or that violations of those rules are now widespread. This is important as many analysts and trade diplomats still cling to the notion that existing multilateral trade rules are a first-order constraint on governmental room for manoeuvre. One hypothesis worth further exploration is that existing WTO rules channel the impulse to favour local firms away from certain policy instruments towards others – rather than reducing the pressures to discriminate in the first place.

Fourth, since policy space is alive and kicking and has been deployed extensively to discriminate against Chinese goods exports, then surely ex-post assessments of China's WTO accession ought to take into account the degree to which the benefits of accession have been eroded since 2001, in particular, since the onset of the Global Financial Crisis.

If future research were to establish that a significant share of those benefits was subsequently eroded on account of foreign trade discrimination then, other things being equal, this should moderate expectations of China's willingness to take on additional future multilateral trade obligations in the absence of meaningful binding commitments by other WTO members to temper their resort to discrimination. As far as the potential for progress at the WTO is concerned, one implication of this line of argument is that the next twenty years of Chinese WTO membership is increasingly likely to be an "all or nothing" proposition.

References

Amiti, M., Redding, S., and Weinstein, D. (2019). 'The impact of the 2018 tariffs on prices and welfare'. *Journal of Economic Perspectives*, 33, 187–210.

Amiti, M., Redding, S., and Weinstein, D. (2020). 'Who's paying for the US tariffs? A longer-term perspective.' *American Economic Association Papers and Proceedings*, 110, 541–46.

Autor, D., Dorn, D., and Hanson, G. (2016). 'The China shock: learning from labor market adjustment to large changes in trade'. *Annual Review of Economics*, 8, 205–40.

Autor, D., Dorn, D., and Hanson, G. (2019). 'When work disappears: manufacturing decline and the falling marriage market value of young men'. *American Economic Review: Insights*, 1, 161–78.

Autor, D., Dorn, D., Hanson, G., and Majlesi, K. (2020). 'Importing political polarization? The electoral consequences of rising trade exposure'. *American Economic Review*, 110, 3139–83.

Bloom, N., Handley, K., Kurman, A., and Luck, P. (2019). 'The impact of Chinese trade on U.S. employment: the good, the bad, and the debatable'. Mimeo, Stanford University. https://nbloom.people.stanford.edu/sites/g/files/sbiybj4746/f/bhkl_posted_draft.pdf

Chen, S., Lin, F., Yao, X., and Zhang, P. (2020). 'WTO accession, trade expansion, and air pollution: evidence from China's county-level panel data'. *Review of International Economics*, 28(4), 1020–45. https://onlinelibrary.wiley.com/doi/full/10.1111/roie.12480

Dai, M., Huang, W., and Zhang, Y. (2021). 'How do households adjust to tariff liberalization? Evidence from China's WTO accession'. *Journal of Development Economics*, 150, 102628. www.sciencedirect.com/science/article/pii/S0304387821000055

Dustmann, C. (2021). *Trade, Labor Markets, and the China Shock: What Can Be Learned from the German Experience?* London: Mimeo University College. https://ideas.repec.org/p/crm/wpaper/2112.html

Evenett, S. (2019). 'Protectionism, state discrimination, and international business since the onset of the global financial crisis'. *Journal of International Business Policy*, 2, 9–36.

Evenett, S., and Fritz, J. (2021). 'The GTA handbook.' Obtainable at www.globaltradealert.org/data_extraction

Fajgelbaum, P., Goldberg, P., Kennedy, P., and Khandelwal, A. (2020). 'The return to protectionism'. *The Quarterly Journal of Economics*, 135, 1–55

Garred, J. (2018). 'The persistence of trade policy in China after WTO accession'. *Journal of International Economics*, 114, 130–42. www.sciencedirect.com/science/article/pii/S002219961830120X

Imbruno, M. (2019). 'Importing under trade policy uncertainty: evidence from China'. *Journal of Comparative Economics*, 47(4), 806–26. www.sciencedirect.com/science/article/pii/S0147596719300617?via%3Dihub

Kim, M., and Xin, D. (2021). 'Export spillover from foreign direct investment in China during pre-and post-WTO accession'. *Journal of Asian Economics*, 75, 101337. www.sciencedirect.com/science/article/pii/S104900782100066X

Lin, F., & Long, C. X. (2020). 'The impact of globalization on youth education: empirical evidence from China's WTO accession'. *Journal of Economic Behavior & Organization*, 178, 820–39. www.sciencedirect.com/science/article/pii/S0167268120302948

Pierce, J., and Schott, P. (2016). 'The surprisingly swift decline of US manufacturing employment'. *American Economic Review*, 106 (7), 1632–62.

16

Small Steps toward the Next Phase of U.S.-China Trade Relations

SIMON LESTER AND HUAN ZHU

I Introduction

The Trump administration's four years in power were tumultuous and confrontational for trade policy in general, and for U.S.-China trade relations in particular. Trump's trade policy legacy presents a challenge for the Biden administration. While the Biden trade leadership may want to focus on other policy areas, it cannot avoid making some difficult choices on China trade policy: It will either have to pick a new direction or stay the course.

Staying the course would mean keeping the Trump administration's policies mostly intact. The key aspects of these policies are the Section 301 investigation and tariffs; the Phase One agreement; and the questions about China's role in the WTO. Biden administration officials might not have followed the same approach to these issues if they had been in power in 2017, but having inherited these policies in 2021, they may be difficult to undo.

U.S. Trade Representative Katherine Tai has begun to lay out her vision for a U.S. trade policy as it relates to China. We are still in the early stages, with more words than actions so far. But Tai's words do tell us a bit about where things might go. This paper examines the general guidance and specific details Tai has offered, in an effort to understand the direction of U.S. policy in this area.

The paper begins by reviewing Tai's account of the recent history of U.S.-China trade relations. It then turns to the Trump administration's actions and the Phase One agreement, including its flawed enforcement mechanism; and finally, it examines the Biden administration's apparent decision to stick with the Phase One agreement as the framework of its policy rather than break from it in a significant way.

The paper also considers some broader themes that may inform the Biden administration's approach to trade relations with China. While there are many criticisms that can be offered of the Biden administration's words and actions so far, the role of economic realities and domestic politics helps explain why the Biden administration has adopted the approach that it has. The small steps it has taken will eventually lead somewhere bigger, but for the time being they may be all there is.

II Alternative Versions of the History of U.S.-China Trade Relations

In a major speech at the think tank CSIS in early October of 2021 (Tai, 2021), U.S. Trade Representative Katherine Tai said that she would "lay out the starting point of our administration's strategic vision for realigning our trade policies towards China to defend the interests of America's workers, businesses, farmers, and producers and strengthen our middle class." In the process of doing so, Tai began by "reflect[ing] on how the U.S.-China trade relationship has evolved in recent decades and how we got to where we are today."

In Tai's version of events, "[f]rom the late 1970s to mid-1980s, China went from the world's 11th-largest economy to the eighth largest," with U.S. exports to China increasing "approximately fourfold, while imports grew 14 times in less than 10 years." This economic growth, she said, "set the stage for China's efforts to join the WTO." This created "an important challenge," which was "how to integrate a state-led economy into a trade institution created by those dedicated to open market-oriented principles."

Over the next decade and a half, Tai explained, "the United States pursued a dual-track approach with Beijing." One track involved "annual high-level dialogues between U.S. and Chinese officials over three successive presidential administrations," while the other track "focused on dispute settlement cases at the WTO." But both approaches, she argued, came up short, with "meaningful reforms by China remain[ing] elusive."

In recent years, she said, "China's leaders have doubled down on their state-centric economic model." Facing a "reality that neither the dialogue nor the enforcement tracks were producing meaningful changes," the Trump administration "decided to use a different paradigm – unilateral U.S. pressure – to try to change Beijing's practices." This led to "substantial U.S. tariffs on imports from China, and retaliation by China," and then later to the phase-one agreement.

There is some truth to Tai's version of history, but it also leaves out some key details, as described by Lester and Zhu (2020). China's WTO accession was mainly negotiated during the Clinton era, but the first president to have to deal with China as a WTO member was George W. Bush.

China's economy had already been growing quickly in the pre-WTO era, and its rise continued after entry into the WTO. The continued high growth and the shift to the production of more sophisticated industrial products put Chinese companies in competition with American companies to a degree not seen before. The Bush administration faced a difficult decision on how to respond.

Trade journalist Paul Blustein (2019) describes the Bush administration's trade policy response as "sluggish," and says: "It is reasonable to wonder why a more forceful approach wasn't taken." He offers the following explanations for why more was not done about Chinese trade practices that violated the letter or spirit of WTO rules: optimism that China would continue moving toward freer markets on its own; fear of a U.S.-China trade war; U.S. companies were making money in China and wanted to avoid disruptions, and thus did not complain much; the administration needed Chinese support on its "anti-terrorism" policies; and finally, the global financial crisis weakened the ability of the Bush administration to make demands.

In terms of actions not taken, Blustein focuses on the Bush administration's rejection of domestic industry complaints under Section 421, which provides for the possibility of a product-specific "safeguard" tariff/quota on Chinese imports. But there is also the option of filing WTO complaints, which the administration was slow to pursue at first, although the complaints picked up in later years: one complaint in 2004, one in 2006, three in 2007, and two in 2008. According to U.S. trade officials from this era, there was a sense initially that China deserved a chance to settle in at the WTO before complaints were brought.[1] By 2005, it was clear that complaints were needed. However, U.S. companies were not pressing the U.S. Trade Representative (USTR) to bring claims, and without the evidence they could provide, the cases were unlikely to be successful. As a result, cases emerged slowly.

The Bush administration also found a diplomatic way to pursue these issues, with an approach called the Strategic Economic Dialogue and the Senior Dialogue. This led to some minor successes, but when the financial crisis hit in 2008, the administration became consumed with domestic issues and was not in a position to make demands of China.

President Obama then took office in the middle of that financial crisis, and his initial focus was on domestic policy. Eventually, he turned to trade and foreign policy, and Asia and China were a big part of that. Obama's "pivot to Asia" involved giving greater prominence to the Pacific region, with the Trans-Pacific Partnership (TPP) as a key element. The TPP had

[1] Authors' conversations with U.S. trade officials.

several goals, but one of them was to respond to China's rise.[2] While Obama and others in his administration spoke mostly of "writing the rules" of trade in the region, many commentators emphasized that the TPP would "contain" China. As law professor Daniel Chow (2016) put it: "The U.S. led the TPP negotiations and deliberately excluded China from the negotiations. This ploy by the U.S. was a calculated effort to contain China and to shift power in trade in the Asia-Pacific from China to the U.S." But as is well known, the Obama administration could not get the TPP through Congress, and President Trump formally withdrew the United States from the pact, whose other members have now gone ahead with a modified version of it.

In addition to the TPP as a way to address concerns with China, the Obama administration imposed tariffs on Chinese tires under Section 421.[3] It was also a frequent user of the WTO dispute settlement mechanism: during his eight years in office, his administration brought 14 complaints against China.

At the same time, the Obama administration also tried to engage with China through negotiations. It continued the bilateral negotiating approach started by the Bush administration, replacing the Strategic Economic Dialogue and Senior Dialogue with the U.S.-China Strategic and Economic Dialogue. The Obama administration also carried out a bilateral investment treaty negotiation with China, but the talks were never completed.

Thus, Tai's version of history is not so much wrong as it is incomplete. Many of the wounds U.S. politicians feel in relation to trade with China are self-inflicted. If the U.S. government had not been distracted by the War on Terror or domestic crises, it might have made more progress in its efforts with China.[4] And if the TPP's domestic political strategy had been

[2] President Obama himself explained how he saw TPP as targeting China:

"[The TPP] would give us a leg up on our economic competitors, including China. As we speak, China is negotiating a trade deal that would carve up some of the fastest-growing markets in the world at our expense, putting American jobs, business and goods at risk.… America should write the rules. America should call the shots. Other countries should play by the rules that America and our partners set, not the other way around.… The United States, not China, should write them." Obama (2016).

[3] Proclamation To Address Market Disruption from Imports of Certain Passenger Vehicle and Light Truck Tires from the People's Republic of China, 11 September 2009, https://obamawhitehouse.archives.gov/the-press-office/proclamation-address-market-disruption-imports-certain-passenger-vehicle-and-light-.

[4] Former Bush administration State Department official Even Feigenbaum has written that, prior to 9/11, it looked as though China would be the top priority on the U.S. foreign policy

better conceived, the United States might have been able to use it as a tool to address concerns with China. Furthermore, the United States decided, for various reasons, not to use the tools that it did have, including a broader range of WTO complaints that made use of the various WTO-plus provisions in China's accession protocol, as described in Zhou et al. (2019).

III Trump's Trade War and Phase One Agreement

Trump and his trade team accused many U.S. trading partners of unfair practices and used a variety of U.S. statutes to do it. Section 301 became the vehicle for the tariff war with China, with an investigation by the U.S. Trade Representative's Office under Section 301 providing the factual and legal basis of the U.S. actions against China.

Section 301 provides a mechanism for the U.S. government to take action against a wide range of broadly defined behavior by foreign governments, including an "act, policy, or practice" of a foreign country that "violates, or is inconsistent with, the provisions of, or otherwise denies benefits to the United States under, any trade agreement," or "is unjustifiable and burdens or restricts United States commerce."[5] In this case, the focus of the investigation was on China's laws and policies related to intellectual property, technology transfer, and innovation. The Section 301 investigation was launched in August 2017, soon after Trump took office.

After eight months of a USTR investigation, hearings, and comments from interested parties, USTR reached the following conclusions in March of 2018: China pressures foreign companies to transfer technology to Chinese partners; certain Chinese licensing regulations discriminate against U.S. firms; China directs foreign investment in order to acquire U.S. technology and intellectual property; and China conducts and supports intrusions into U.S. companies' computer networks.[6] A range

agenda. After the attacks, however, much of the attention shifted to the Middle East, and the focus shifted away from China. See, e.g., Simon Lester, "The Place of China in U.S. Foreign Policy After 9/11 and China's WTO Accession," International Economic Law and Policy Blog, 29 August 2021, https://ielp.worldtradelaw.net/2021/08/the-place-of-china-in-us-foreign-policy-after-911-wto-accession.html.

5 Trade Act of 1974, PL 93–618, https://legcounsel.house.gov/Comps/93-618.pdf.

6 Findings of the Investigation into China's Acts, Policies and Practices related to Technology Transfer, Intellectual Property, and Innovation under Section 301 of the Trade Act of 1974, Executive Summary, 22 March, 2018, https://ustr.gov/sites/default/files/enforcement/301Investigations/301%20Draft%20Exec%20Summary%203.22.ustrfinal.pdf.

of tools would be used to address these issues, including filing a WTO complaint for one issue as well as imposing tariffs on Chinese imports immediately.[7] According to USTR, certain issues were not covered by WTO rules, so unilateral tariff action was the only possibility.[8]

The resulting tariff war began in July 2018. After many months of tariff escalation, today both countries face steep tariffs on the goods they trade with each other. According to Bown (2021a), China's average tariffs applied to U.S. exports have risen from 8.0 per cent in January 2018 to 20.7 per cent by January 2021. This is more than triple the average 6.1 per cent tariff rate applied to other countries after China unilaterally cut its tariffs in recent years. On the other side, the average U.S. tariff on Chinese goods has soared from 3.1 per cent in 2017 to 19.3 per cent in 2021. As a result, 66.4 per cent of Chinese imports are subject to additional U.S. tariffs, and 58.3 per cent of U.S. goods face retaliatory tariffs from China.

This tariff war provided the background for the trade negotiations that ultimately led to the Phase One agreement, which was signed on January 15, 2020, and took effect on February 14, 2020. Under this agreement, China made a number of commitments, the most high profile of which was to substantially increase imports from the United States of agricultural products, industrial products, natural resources, and services. As of October 2021, however, China was on track to come up nearly 40% short of the US goods it promised to buy over 2020–21, according to Bown (2021b). This outcome is not surprising, as the purchase targets were set at a level that many people considered to be unrealistic, and on top of that the pandemic undermined trade flows in general.

[7] "… we concluded that, in fact, China does have a policy of forced technology transfer; of requiring licensing at less than economic value; of state capitalism, wherein they go in and buy technology in the United States in non-economic ways; and then, finally, of cyber theft… The result of this has been that the President has analyzed it – we have a 200-page study which we will put out – and he has concluded that we should put in place tariffs on appropriate products – we can explain later how we concluded what products they are; that we would put investment restrictions on China with respect to high technology; and that we'll file a WTO case. Because one of the actions here does involve a WTO violation." Remarks by President Trump at Signing of a Presidential Memorandum Targeting China's Economic Aggression, 22 March 2018, https://trumpwhitehouse.archives.gov/briefings-statements/remarks-president-trump-signing-presidential-memorandum-targeting-chinas-economic-aggression/.

[8] "While the WTO agreements do include a dispute settlement mechanism, this mechanism is not designed to address a situation in which a WTO member has opted for a state-led trade regime that prevails over market forces and pursues policies guided by mercantilism rather than global economic cooperation." U.S. Trade Representative, 2017 USTR Report on China's WTO Compliance, January 2018, https://ustr.gov/sites/default/files/files/Press/Reports/China%202017%20WTO%20Report.pdf.

China also took on other obligations in the Phase One deal, including in relation to intellectual property protection, forced technology transfer, and regulatory trade barriers for various U.S. goods and services. While China has addressed many of these obligations in its recent legislative and regulatory actions, the implementation of these rules in China is still a bit uncertain. However, enforcement of these obligations will be difficult due to the flaws in the agreement's dispute resolution provisions.

IV The Flawed Phase One Enforcement Mechanism

The problem with enforcing the structural obligations under the Phase One agreement is that its dispute resolution section does not have the traditional neutral adjudication mechanism found in most trade agreements. Trade enforcement typically works as follows. If one government thinks another is not complying with the obligations in a trade agreement, the complaining government can raise its concerns through a request for consultations. If the consultations do not resolve the issue, the complaining government can ask for a neutral panel of experts to consider whether the other government's actions violate the terms of the agreement. That panel will issue a ruling on the legal question of whether the respondent government is in compliance.

The WTO has the most advanced version of this process, with 606 complaints since it was established in 1995, and hundreds of panel reports and appellate reports reviewing those complaints. During her CSIS speech, Tai noted that over the years, the United States "brought 27 cases against China … . We secured victories in every case that was decided." (Currently, the United States has blocked appointments to the WTO's Appellate Body, which has caused significant problems for the functioning of WTO dispute settlement.) Bilateral and regional trade agreements have their own version of panels, without appellate review.

The neutral adjudication provided through this kind of process helps with the enforcement of these agreements. One government's view that another is in violation is not seen as objective: It is simply the position of that government, rather than an impartial conclusion. An unbiased adjudicator, by contrast, has the credibility to determine whether a violation exists in a way that can be persuasive to all parties. This process helps bring the rule of law to international trade disputes.

In contrast, the Phase One agreement does not have the typical neutral adjudication mechanism, but rather has a mechanism under which either side can determine on its own if the other is not in compliance, and can then – after a consultations process – take what it considers to be the appropriate action in response (most likely, this will take the form of tariffs).[9]

The Trump administration may have seen this as a tough enforcement mechanism because it would be a quick way for the United States to impose tariffs. The problem is, if China believes it is in compliance, but the United States does not, these unilateral tariffs are unlikely to induce China to take any action to come into compliance. That is especially true in a situation like the current one when significant tariffs are already in place. By contrast, if there were a ruling by a neutral adjudicator that China is not in compliance, China might take some action. It has done so in response to WTO rulings, and it might do so in the context of Phase One disputes as well.

[9] The key provision reads as follows:

> 1. Appeal. Where one Party (the "Complaining Party") believes that the other Party (the "Party Complained Against") is not acting in accordance with this Agreement, the Complaining Party may submit an appeal ("Appeal") to the Bilateral Evaluation and Dispute Resolution Office of the Party Complained Against. …
>
> …
>
> 4.
>
> …
>
> (b) If the concerns of the Complaining Party are not resolved at a meeting between the United States Trade Representative and the designated Vice Premier of the People's Republic of China, the Parties shall engage in expedited consultations on the response to the damages or losses incurred by the Complaining Party. If the Parties reach consensus on a response, the response shall be implemented. If the Parties do not reach consensus on a response, the Complaining Party may resort to taking action based on facts provided during the consultations, including by suspending an obligation under this Agreement or by adopting a remedial measure in a proportionate way that it considers appropriate with the purpose of preventing the escalation of the situation and maintaining the normal bilateral trade relationship. The Party Complained Against can initiate an urgent meeting between the United States Trade Representative and the designated Vice Premier of the People's Republic of China before the effective date of the action to be taken by the Complaining Party. If the Party Complained Against considers that the action by the Complaining Party pursuant to this subparagraph was taken in good faith, the Party Complained Against may not adopt a counter-response, or otherwise challenge such action. If the Party Complained Against considers that the action of the Complaining Party was taken in bad faith, the remedy is to withdraw from this Agreement by providing written notice of withdrawal to the Complaining Party.

Economic and Trade Agreement between the Government of the United States and the Government of the People's Republic of China, Article 7.4.

https://ustr.gov/sites/default/files/files/agreements/phase%20one%20agreement/Economic_And_Trade_Agreement_Between_The_United_States_And_China_Text.pdf.

V The Biden Administration's Decision to Stick with Phase One

Nevertheless, despite these flaws, the Biden administration has made clear that it sees the Phase One deal as the framework for governing the U.S.-China trade relationship. While Biden administration officials have been critical of the Trump administration's approach to China,[10] they are sticking with its set of rules in this area. As Tai put it, "I think that the structure, the architecture of this [Phase One] agreement, is where we have to start, … ." But how exactly she plans to use it is a bit unclear.

In her CSIS speech, she emphasized that the Biden administration would take enforcement actions under Phase One (Tai, 2021). She said that "we will discuss with China its performance under the phase-one agreement. China made commitments that benefit certain American industries, including agriculture, that we must enforce." She did not, however, provide much in the way of details of the specific areas of enforcement, which makes it difficult to evaluate the likelihood of success here. When pressed after the speech, Tai did not seem willing to offer any clarity.

In thinking about what actions they might take, it is useful to examine the different categories of obligations in the Phase One agreement. Broadly speaking, they can be grouped into two categories: Purchase commitments for specific products, and substantive obligations related to structural issues in the Chinese economy. In response to questions, senior administration officials indicated that both kinds of obligations are on the table for enforcement: "We intend to raise all elements of Phase One with China where we think they have not lived up to their commitments. We're not going to shy away from that, we want to make sure that we're discussing kind of the full breadth of obligations there. The engagement with China will determine which ones become the focal

[10] Senior administration officials have stated that "our objective is not to … double down on the previous administration's flawed strategy," and that "[t]he decision to be more deliberative and bring long term thinking into our approach was critical, and a sharp departure from the last administration." More specifically, they noted that "our objection to the previous administration's approach was that it did not build on our strengths and did not really use our leverage to good effect," including failing to "mak[e] the investments at home that we needed to be able to outcompete China" and to "align[] with our allies and partners rather than being at odds with them." The previous administration's approach was "really at times chaotic, including hurting select sectors of the American economy and really not targeted at the primary concerns that we have with China's larger structural policies." One particular point they emphasized was that "[w]e're putting an end to the previous administration's approach of fighting with our allies and weakening the alliances we've long had." October 3 White House Briefing attended by authors.

point of discussions, … ." Given the problems noted earlier with regard to purchase commitments, however, it is not clear how China's failure to comply could be addressed, and thus what the value of these commitments really is.

The bigger compliance concern is the structural rules, such as on forced technology transfer, for which there are detailed provisions in the agreement and genuine concerns about China's practices. If these obligations could be enforced, the Phase One agreement could provide an important means of achieving greater liberalization in the Chinese economy. As noted above, however, the problem with enforcing these kinds of rules under the agreement is that its dispute resolution section does not have the traditional neutral adjudication mechanism found in most trade agreements.

Nevertheless, the Biden administration appears to want to give the Phase One deal's dispute provisions a try. There is no history of using this sort of mechanism to enforce trade agreements, but the Biden administration seems to be indicating that they will test it out.

If this is their plan, it could be helpful if the administration were transparent about its actions. The agreement itself does not offer guarantees of transparency (which is an additional problem with the approach to dispute resolution taken here). However, the Biden administration could push for more of the details related to its complaints about Chinese trade practices to be made public. For example, if the administration files a "Request for Information" under Article 7.3, it could make that document publicly available. The situation relating to an "Appeal" made in writing under Article 7.4, paragraph 1 is more complicated. This provision states that "[t]he Appeal and any information and matters related to it are confidential and shall not be shared beyond the Bilateral Evaluation and Dispute Resolution Office, absent the agreement of the Parties." While the default approach to these appeals is confidentiality, there is the possibility of transparency if the parties agree. The United States has traditionally pushed for more transparency in trade disputes and could follow the same approach here.

Beyond pure enforcement measures, Tai indicated that the Biden administration had broader concerns about China's policies that require engagement but did not specify how she would approach them: "we continue to have serious concerns with China's state-centered and non-market trade practices that were not addressed in the Phase One deal. As we work to enforce the terms of Phase One, we will raise these broader policy concerns with Beijing. And we will use the full range of tools we have, and develop new tools as needed, to defend American economic interests from harmful policies and practices." She later said: "we will also directly engage with China on its industrial policies."

This direct engagement could come in a number of forms: Another Section 301 investigation (which although confrontational could in theory lead to negotiations), which has been rumored in the area of subsidies; trilateral work as has been taking place with Japan and the EU; at the WTO; or new bilateral talks, whether classified as Phase Two or not. This last possibility could even be carried out through Phase One agreement mechanisms. Article 7.2 of the Phase One agreement talks about "high-level engagement" and in this context refers to "arrangements for future work between the Parties." It is not clear whether this formal structure could or should be used here. Ideally, there would be some transparency in the discussions taking place in this context, but the agreement does not provide for that and the public may not get much of a sense of what is happening.

It is worth noting that whatever this engagement is, it will probably not be identified as "Phase Two" of the U.S.-China trade agreement, as Tai seemed opposed to using that terminology.[11] The name of the next stage is not particularly important though.

A few days after Tai's speech at CSIS, she had a call with Chinese Vice Premier Liu He. Very few concrete details were released publicly, but the USTR readout of the call indicates that the two sides "reviewed implementation of the U.S.-China Economic and Trade Agreement and agreed that the two sides would consult on certain outstanding issues," and that "Ambassador Tai emphasized U.S. concerns relating to China's state-led, non-market policies and practices that harm American workers, farmers and businesses." Press reports contain details of Biden administration officials briefing reporters on the call, which repeat many of the points made during the speech: "The main principle is that China needs to live up to its commitments, and we are going to engage with them to make that point,"

[11] Tai had the following exchange after her CSIS speech:

> Q: " … It sounds like you're not going to do phase two …. What happens after phase one as far as purchasing is concerned? …
>
> Tai: "So I'm going to take a little bit of a detour and just express my own personal disinclination for the term "phase-one agreement." The actual name of the agreement is the U.S.-China Trade and Economic Agreement, I believe. But it's kind of a mouthful, so phase one it is.
>
> I'm not quite sure. You'll have to ask my predecessor and the previous administration in setting this up as phase one what they were thinking about as a phase two. So, you know, there's an expectations issue there." (Tai, 2021)

one official said. "And it's up to China to demonstrate whether they're willing to do that"[12]; "We recognise that Beijing is increasingly explicit that it is doubling down on its authoritarian state-centric approach and is resistant to addressing our structural concerns. … Therefore our primary focus will continue to be on building resilience and competitiveness, diversifying markets, and limiting the impact of Beijing's harmful practices."[13] The United States would base future engagement with China on "how China responds to tonight's call," and the call is "a test of whether or not this type of engagement will help to secure the outcomes that we're looking for, and we're going in with the hopes that China will respond positively."[14]

VI The Initial Reaction in China to Tai's Statements on U.S.-China Trade Relations

The early reaction from Chinese officials, scholars, and media was both muted and mixed. The statements by Tai and other officials did not set out a clear new path for U.S. policy here, but the absence of a confrontational tone was probably a relief for people in China.

When asked about Tai's remarks at an October 8 press conference, the spokesperson for China's Ministry of Foreign Affairs provided only very general thoughts on these issues.[15] The Chinese ambassador

[12] Owen Churchill and Frank Tang, "US 'tests' to see if direct engagement with China helps address trade concerns," South China Morning Post, 9 October 2021, www.scmp.com/news/china/diplomacy/article/3151752/us-trade-representative-katherine-tai-and-chinese-vice-premier.

[13] David Lawder, Michael Martina, Engen Tham, "China presses U.S. to cancel tariffs in test of bilateral engagement," Reuters, 9 October 2021, www.reuters.com/business/us-trade-chief-talks-chinese-counterpart-test-bilateral-engagement-2021-10-09/.

[14] *Id.*

[15] "In principle, I'd like to stress that China-US economic and trade relations are essentially mutually-beneficial. There is no winner in a trade war. Issues in bilateral economic and trade relations should be properly dealt with in the spirit of mutual respect and equal-footed consultation. We hope the US will work together with China for the sound and steady development of the bilateral economic and trade ties. The formation and development of global industrial and supply chains is the result of both market law and choices of the business community. Artificial industrial 'transfer' and 'decoupling' runs counter to the law of the economy and objective reality. It cannot solve domestic problems and will only seriously undermine the stability and security of global industrial and supply chains. Cooperation and dialogue instead of decoupling or confrontation is the strong aspiration of various sectors in both China and the US, including the business community. The US should heed these calls and do more things conducive to the sound and steady development of China-US economic and trade ties."

www.fmprc.gov.cn/mfa_eng/xwfw_665399/s2510_665401/2511_665403/t1913254.shtml.

to the United States offered more in-depth comments. He noted that Ambassador Tai mentioned that the United States is now seeking to "recouple" with China, which, he said, "has some positivity in it," as "[t]he two sides can sit down and sort out the areas of 'decoupling' and how to get them 'recoupled.'" More generally, he suggested that "the two countries' trade frictions over the past few years have once again proved that China and the US both stand to gain from cooperation and lose from confrontation," and "[t]here is no winner in a trade war or tariff war." While "[i]t is ... normal for us to have economic competition and trade frictions ... [t]he key is how to deal with them." What China advocates is that "we should pursue solutions acceptable to both sides through communication and consultation, based on the principles of mutual respect and mutual benefit."[16]

In the media, the state-run Global Times, by contrast, published a commentary in which it noted that Tai presented "a tough attitude towards China," and responded with the following statement[17]: "if the US intends to shake China's foundations, prevent China from formulating plans to develop its technological innovation capacity, and change China's national policies conducive to promoting competitiveness, China will never permit it. ... The China-US trade war has lasted for more than three and a half years. Instead of being weakened, China's economy has taken a step forward in comparison with the scale of the US. The Chinese people are more confident and their stamina continues to increase. We are clearly aware that all this is the basis for the US to consider using non-trade war coercive methods to discuss issues with China." A Xinhua opinion piece emphasized the importance of U.S.-China cooperation: "Both nations as well as the whole world will benefit from China-US cooperation, and both countries and the world will suffer from China-US confrontation. It is hoped that the United States will change its course, respect the principles of market economy and international trade rules, and meet China halfway, so as to promote the healthy and stable development of China-US economic and trade relations, and further benefit the people of the two countries and around the world."[18]

[16] Ambassador Qin Gang on "Recoupling" of Chinese and US Economies, 9 October, 2021, www.mfa.gov.cn/ce/ceus//eng/zmgxss/t1913353.htm.

[17] Global Times, "Time for US to seek non-trade war means to consult and solve issues with China," 5 October 2021, www.globaltimes.cn/page/202110/1235648.shtml.

[18] Xinhua, "Remembering the lessons from the past, the US economic and trade policy towards China is set to change course," 5 October 2021, www.news.cn/world/2021-10/05/c_1127931377.htm.

Scholarly reaction to the speech was mixed. Some Chinese scholars reacted somewhat positively to Tai's statements. "Unlike his predecessor Donald Trump's aggressiveness, the Biden administration aims to maintain negotiations while mounting trade restrictions. In a way, it accords with the stance of China, which seeks to solve disputes through dialogue," Huo Jianguo, former president of the research institute of the Ministry of Commerce, told the Global Times. However, it is unlikely that China-US trade relations will go back to the pre-trade war period, Huo warned. "The US should drop its confrontational mentality toward China and facilitate competitive cooperation via dialogue and negotiations," Huo added.[19]

Tu Xinquan, Dean of the China Institute for WTO Studies at the University of International Business and Economics, also expressed positive views on the Biden administration's statement at a CSIS event. "I think, generally speaking, my impression is, it's positive, her remarks and statements, especially if she does not support decoupling. I think it's a very great concern for China. And she used the word like durable coexistence, and recouple. These words, kind of new, but basically I think they are positive for the US-China trade relationship."[20]

In resolving the differences between the two nations, Tu noted that "bilateral conversations and dialogues are important" but "international rules are even more important, because the two [powerful economies] have the capability to hurt each other." Hence, "if we can have the same set of rules, we follow the same set of rules, then it would be easier to deal with conflicts between each other."

Wang Yong, Director of the Center for International Political Economy at Peking University, also praised Ambassador Tai at the same event for "recognize[ing] the value of the US-China commercial relations," and that "she's very right in trying to come back to the dialogue with the Chinese counterparts to settle the differences of interests and positions." When commenting on China's enforcement under the Phase One Agreement – in particular, the purchase commitments – Wang said that "it's very important to recognize … all these factors, including the impact of pandemic and rising cost of cargo …unfortunately, influence the implementations of the Phase One agreement." Wang also called for both sides to "de-politicize or de-securitize the trade," which is "very important."

[19] Global Times, "China-US trade tensions may linger," 7 October 2021, www.globaltimes.cn/page/202110/1235729.shtml.

[20] CSIS, "Chinese Views on the Biden Administration's China Trade Policy," 5 October 2021, www.csis.org/events/chinese-views-biden-administrations-china-trade-policy.

At the same time, some Chinese scholars were more cautious towards the view that this is a turning point in U.S.-China relations. Zhao Dingxin, professor at the Department of Sociology at the University of Chicago and Zhejiang University, stated in a recent article (Zhao, 2021) that "China, as the world's second-largest economy that has a vast territory, huge population, military strength, and a cultural and political system that is very different from the United States and the West, will inevitably bear the brunt of the United States' destructive spillover effects" and the key to China's handling of China-US relations is to avoid falling into the "scapegoat trap" which means China becoming the scapegoat for U.S. domestic problems.

In general, Chinese government officials and Chinese scholars are probably waiting to see what the new Biden administration policy looks like in practice before developing strong views. Tai's speech left a lot of questions unanswered, making it hard to know how the upcoming months and years of the U.S.-China trade relationship will unfold.

VII Broader Themes Guiding the U.S.-China Relationship

Beyond the specific details of the Biden administration's recent statements, there are several important themes lurking in the background that can help inform the issue of the future of U.S.-China trade relations: The calls for "decoupling" of the U.S. and Chinese economies; the role of the state in the economy, in both countries and in the Phase One agreement itself; and the internal political debates in the Democratic party on trade.

(i) Decoupling vs. Recoupling

There has been a great deal of recent talk among foreign policy and trade policy commentators about "decoupling" of the U.S. and Chinese economies. The Biden administration does not appear sympathetic to the idea of decoupling, with Commerce Secretary Gina Raimondo seeming skeptical of it,[21] and Katherine Tai in her CSIS speech characterizing it as not "a realistic outcome."[22] For Tai, the issue is, "what are the goals we're looking

21 Simon Lester, "Gina Raimondo Comments on U.S.-China Trade Competition, Cooperation, and Decoupling," China Trade Monitor, 24 September 2021, www.chinatrademonitor.com/gina-raimondo-on-u-s-china-trade-competition-and-cooperation/.

22 "I know there's a lot of talk about decoupling. I think at the end of the day I still don't have, necessarily, good understanding of what everybody means, if we've got a common definition of decoupling. I think that the concern, maybe the question is whether or not the United States and China need to stop trading with each other. I don't think that's a

for in a kind of re-coupling?" And "[h]ow can we have a trade relationship with China where we are occupying strong and robust positions within the supply chain and that there is a trade that's happening as opposed to a dependency?" In a subsequent interview, she made clear that the United States and China are not, in her view, in a "Cold War."[23]

For Tai, then, the issue seems to be how the United States and China can have an economic relationship that works for both sides politically and economically. The economic concerns are about the impact of trading with China on U.S. workers and companies. The political concerns are more about national security and geopolitical power. The Biden administration does not seem to have an answer to these questions at this point, but that is the goal it is trying to achieve.

(ii) *The Role of the State in the Economy*

In her CSIS speech, Tai referred to China's "industrial policies" and its "state-centered and non-market trade practices" as problems that needed to be addressed. However, it cannot be ignored that at this same moment, within U.S. politics and policy, there are many calls for industrial policy and a greater role for the state in the U.S. economy, and the Biden administration seems eager to move the economy in this direction. From Buy American policies to reconfiguring supply chains to calls for "economic resilience," the Biden administration at times seems to be emulating the same Chinese policies it is criticizing, although to be fair the degree of state involvement in the economy is less.

Along the same lines, at the same time the United States is asking China to be less state-oriented in its approach to the economy, the Phase One agreement adopts a very state-centered vision itself in the form of its purchase commitments. Tai was asked specifically about the purchase commitments but did not acknowledge the contradiction here.[24]

realistic outcome in terms of our global economy. I think that the issue perhaps is, what are the goals we're looking for in a kind of re-coupling? How can we have a trade relationship with China where we are occupying strong and robust positions within the supply chain and that there is a trade that's happening as opposed to a dependency?"

23 "US is not in a 'Cold War' with China, US trade representative tells FRANCE 24," 6 October 2021, www.youtube.com/watch?v=JRU459KNORY

> Tai: "we've had a lot of questions about whether or not we are headed towards a Cold War, whether or not we are in a cold war, and I think that ..." Q: "the answer is yes?" Tai: "the answer is no, and that's why we must engage ..."

24 Q: "I wanted to ask about the phase one ... agreement from January – from 2020. It sounds like, from what you described, that it may not be your first choice, but given where we've

Part of the problem the Biden administration may be having in formulating a way forward on its China trade policy is the dilemma over what economic policy it wants for itself. In the past, the United States has pushed hard at the WTO on issues related to non-market economies.[25] The Biden administration has already picked up on that idea in its work with the EU on the Trade and Technology Council,[26] but some of its own actions could undermine its efforts in this regard if it becomes difficult to distinguish U.S. policy from Chinese policy. For example, there are calls in the United States for significant subsidies to the semiconductor industry. Efforts by the Biden administration to challenge Chinese industrial subsidies will come across as hypocritical if the United States is doing the same thing.

(iii) Democrats' Infighting on Trade

Traditionally, one of the primary goals of U.S. trade policy was "market access," that is, opening up foreign markets to allow more sales of U.S. goods and services. While the idea of imports may have been controversial, exports were seen as universally positive. However, the battle within the Democratic party on trade has called even this view into question.

come from you're comfortable enough with employing the strategy or approached of managed trade that you're not about to abandon it. So I was curious your thoughts about sort of conceptually managed trade, so governments setting targets and trying to achieve them."

> ...
>
> Tai: "I guess managed trade is one way you could describe the purchase commitments. What are my views on it? I'm a tremendously practical person. There are commitments that have been made. That means that there are commitments that we have to seek follow through on. I think that when you talk about managed trade, just to break it down, it is a different model for managing a trade relationship than the model that we've pursued before which was ... let's seek market access, and then ... let the chips fall where they may. I guess what I would say is ... channeling my inner pragmatism, this is the arrangement that we have now, it is an arrangement that has evolved out of a frustration with the previous model. And so the question that I bring to this issue that you've presented is not, ideologically, how do I feel about it, but what is actually going to present results, and what is actually going to be effective, and I think that this conversation around the purchase commitments that we're preparing to have is going to be directly informative to determining how effective this is at this point in time for the challenges that we have in this relationship." (Tai, 2021)

[25] Simon Lester, "The Debate Over China and Market-Orientation at the WTO," China Trade Monitor, 14 July 2021, www.chinatrademonitor.com/the-debate-over-china-and-market-orientation-at-the-wto/.

[26] Simon Lester, "U.S.-EU Trade and Technology Council Statement Discusses Cooperation on Non-Market Economies," China Trade Monitor, 29 September 2021, www.chinatrademonitor.com/us-eu-trade-tech-council-cooperation-non-market-economies/.

After her CSIS speech, Tai was asked about this issue very directly: "Is increasing market access to China one of your goals? And if so, what sectors are you targeting?" Tai's response was vague and non-committal, and seemed to cast the past focus on market access in a negative light.[27] But if market access is being pushed aside, what exactly is U.S. trade policy about? Tai and others in the administration have continuously emphasized "workers," but that does not say much. Any policy, including lower tariffs, can be marketed as something good for workers. What exactly does the Biden administration have in mind here? Without a clearer picture of the broader trade policy they are advocating, it may be difficult for them to come up with a coherent China trade policy. And it may also be that no such policy is forthcoming any time soon, as domestic policy and other foreign policy issues take precedence on the administration's agenda.

VIII Conclusions

With all the emphasis on bilateral trade relations, one might ask, where is the multilateral, that is, the WTO, in all of this? Tai was asked directly at the CSIS event "What role does the WTO play in all this?," and seemed skeptical of its ability to help with U.S. claims about China.[28] It remains to be seen how the Biden administration relates to the WTO in general, and how China's role there continues to progress, but for now, the WTO's role in the U.S.-China trade conflict may be limited.

In terms of the bilateral side of things, at this point in time, it appears that the Biden administration is willing to just put the ball in China's court and see how it reacts. This may mean that the status quo stays in place for a while. As much as that prospect aggravates many U.S. business groups

[27] "I think that part of the story of the U.S.-China trade relationship over these recent few decades has been about this thirst on the part of our business sector in particular for increased market access to China. In business sector I include our agriculture sector, obviously. You know, I think along the traditional lines of the way we've thought about trade and how benefits come from trade, it has been very focused on securing market access. I think that what we've seen is our traditional approach to trade has run into a lot of realities that are today causing us to open our eyes and think about, is what we're looking for more liberalized trade and just more trade or are we looking for smarter and more resilient trade?" (Tai, 2021).

[28] She said, "we focused very heavily on the WTO, certainly in the first 15 years of China's membership at the WTO, and I think that as much as we will continue to invest and commit and try to innovate in terms of being a member at the WTO and seeking to bring reform to the WTO that we also need to be agile and to be open-minded and to think outside of the box with respect to how we can be more effective in addressing the concerns that we really have been struggling to address with China on trade." (Tai, 2021)

and trade policy experts, it does not seem to bother the Biden administration. In part, that may be due to their reluctance to adopt a new policy that will bring criticism from different sides (the progressive left and the nationalist right). They may not like the current deal, but they are not eager to negotiate a new one. There is still plenty to do on the domestic policy agenda, and they can withstand criticism from pro-trade moderates in the meantime. As a result, although the administration has taken tentative first steps on China trade issues, it may end up standing still for a while.

References

Blustein, Paul (2019) 'The untold story of how George W. Bush Lost China.' Foreign Policy (October 2), https://foreignpolicy.com/2019/10/04/the-untold-story-of-how-george-w-bush-lost-china/

Bown, Chad (2021a) 'The US-China trade war and phase one agreement,' February 2021, www.piie.com/sites/default/files/documents/wp21-2.pdf

Bown, Chad (2021b) 'NEW: With only 3 months of purchase commitments left to go under President Trump's phase one agreement, China remains on pace to come up nearly 40% short of US goods it promised to buy over 2020–21,' https://twitter.com/ChadBown/status/1453417067114385408

Chow, Daniel C. K. (2016) 'How the United States uses the trans-pacific partnership to contain China in international trade.' *Chicago Journal of International Law* 17 (2): 370–402.

Lester, Simon and Huan Zhu (2020) 'The U.S.-China trade war: Is there an end in sight?' *Cato Journal*. www.cato.org/cato-journal/winter-2020/us-china-trade-war-there-end-sight

Obama, Barack (2016) 'President Obama: The TPP would let America, not China, lead the way on global trade.' Washington Post (May 2), www.washingtonpost.com/opinions/president-obama-the-tpp-would-let-america-not-china-lead-the-way-on-global-trade/2016/05/02/680540e4-0fd0-11e6-93ae-50921721165d_story.html

Tai, Katherine (2021) 'A conversation with Ambassador Katherine Tai, U.S. Trade Representative,' CSIS, October 4, 2021, www.csis.org/analysis/conversation-ambassador-katherine-tai-us-trade-representative

Zhao, Dingxin (2021) "'Creative destruction' and 'back trap' – The nature of the United States and China's response." *Beijing Cultural Review* (5), https://user.observersnews.com/main/content?id=608072&s=fwtjgzwz

Zhou, Weihuan, Henry S. Gao, and Xue Bai (2019) 'China's SOE reform: Using WTO rules to build a market economy.' *International and Comparative Law Quarterly*, 68(4), 977–1022.

17

China's Entry into the WTO

A Mistake by the United States?

JENNIFER HILLMAN

> ...it seems clear that the United States erred in supporting China's entry into the WTO on terms that have proven to be ineffective in securing China's embrace of an open, market-oriented trade regime
>
> 2017 USTR Report to Congress on China's WTO Compliance

I Introduction

On December 11, 2001, China was admitted to the World Trade Organization (WTO), the culmination of an American-supported process that opened China to global investment and helped make it the workshop of the world. Since then, the halls of Washington D.C. have been wracked by debates over how to understand – and manage – China's entrance onto the global stage.

By delineating the drivers of U.S. decision-making in the lead-up to China's accession to the WTO and cataloging actions taken in the years immediately following, this chapter hopes to offer a partial explanation of how and why the United States has grown skeptical of the rules-based trading system's ability to address concerns with China, despite serving for decades as its chief architect and as a key proponent of China's entry into the WTO. The chapter highlights the wide range of issues that many politicians thought could be addressed as part of China's accession processes, contrasting those views with the reality of what was both achievable and included in China's protocol to join a trade organization with a particular and circumscribed set of rules. While it would be misguided to attribute the current state of the international trading system solely to the choices

Jennifer Hillman is grateful for the extensive research and writing support she received from Alex Tippett, research assistant at CFR, and the research assistance of CFR intern Seara Grundhoefer.

of U.S. policymakers or the actions of China, U.S. decisions, particularly the decision to prevent new judges from being appointed to the Appellate Body and the decision to pursue unilateral tariffs on Chinese exports to the United States, have clearly had a major impact. These choices, once unimaginable, are best understood as part of Washington's reaction to China's rise along with perceived failures by the WTO.

(i) *Shifting Views of Engagement with Trade and China*

The old China consensus was built on a broad understanding of the benefits of engagement, an optimism about liberalization in China, a desire to avoid Sino-American confrontation as well as a belief that Chinese-American economic ties would provide material and, in some cases, domestic political benefits, for key U.S. stakeholders. These interests and beliefs were the basis of U.S.-China policy and ensured relative stability from administration to administration. It was under the auspices of this coalition that the pre-requisite for China's admission to the WTO – "permanent normal trading relations" between China and the United States – was established. Now, however, a growing conviction that the People's Republic of China (PRC) poses a fundamental threat to the United States' hegemonic role, as well as economic losses and growing income inequality associated with trade with China, has undermined support for the expansive trade policy the United States once regularly pursued.

Policymakers on both sides of the aisle have also become skeptical of the material benefits offered by engagement. Rather than opening markets to U.S. firms, a more cynical view that sees globalization and trade as hollowing out the U.S. manufacturing base and the middle class is increasingly common.[1] As China has moved up the global value chain and become a direct competitor in sectors previously thought to be U.S. strongholds like advanced computing and telecommunications, China's economic might and state-led practices have begun to pose a direct threat to the United States' defense industrial base and other influential elements within the U.S. political system.[2] Both parties have endorsed and continue to explore industrial policies that would have once been taboo.

[1] For a Republican example of this mindset, see: "Made in China 2025 and the Future of American Industry", *U.S. Senate Committee on Small Business and Entrepreneurship*, 2019. For a Democratic example see: E. Warren, "A Plan for Economic Patriotism", 2019.

[2] E.S. Medeiros, "The Changing Fundamentals of US-China Relations", *The Washington Quarterly*, 41 (2019), 93–119.

At the same time, the political benefits of opposing a liberal trade policy have grown. Republican Party leaders, a traditional stronghold of free trade sentiment have, in recent years, grown more skeptical both of China and open trade policies more generally. The Democratic Party, long divided on trade, has been faced with the need to compete for blue-collar voters distributed in strategically important states and has grown skeptical that trade can deliver the broad-based growth imagined by members of the Clinton administration, who championed China's accession to the WTO.[3] Those within the Democratic Party who see an open trade agenda as essential to both economic growth and successful competition with China have become more self-conscious of the political liabilities associated with trade and have tempered their aspirations accordingly.[4]

Washington's evolution has deep implications for the future of the WTO. Born in an era of American self-confidence, military dominance, and liberalizing ambition, the WTO is perceived in some quarters to be ill-suited for the current moment. In the face of a growing Chinese-American contest, the WTO's challenge is to avoid being trampled or sidelined while still working to preserve the multilateral, rules-based trading regime. This can only be accomplished if the WTO reorients itself to become a venue where competitors are able to come together to address pressing global problems like climate change, global health, income inequality, digital commerce, and the implications of significant non-market economy actors as members of the WTO.

(ii) Policy of Engagement

From at least the end of the Cold War to the late 2010s, the United States pursued a strategy of "engagement" towards China.[5] Under the auspices

[3] Trade issues became uncomfortable for Republican policymakers by the early 2000s. See: D.A. Irwin, *Clashing Over Commerce* (University of Chicago Press, 2017), p. 679. Donald Trump's political campaign heavily undercut support for free trade among the Republican base, though this support began to rebound midway through his term. See: B. Jones, "Americans Are Generally Positive about Free Trade Agreements, More Critical of Tariff Increases", *Pew Research Center*, 2018, www.pewresearch.org/fact-tank/2018/05/10/americans-are-generally-positive-about-free-trade-agreements-more-critical-of-tariff-increases/. L. Silver, K. Devlin, C. Huang, "Most Americans Support Tough Stance toward China On Human Rights, Economic Issues", *Pew Research Center*, 2021, www.pewresearch.org/global/2021/03/04/most-americans-support-tough-stance-toward-china-on-human-rights-economic-issues/.

[4] See: S. Ahmed and R. Engel, editors, "Making U.S. Foreign Policy Work Better for the Middle Class", *Carnegie Endowment for International Peace*, 2020, 15–17, and 22–23. https://carnegieendowment.org/2020/09/23/making-u.s.-foreign-policy-work-better-for-middle-class-pub-82728.ClkX3QTaP0G28MhKT3Ue/Exmv0yhh22d

[5] The periodization of "engagement" is a subject of debate. David Lampton, for instance, dates the policy back to 1971, while Alastair Ian Johnston sees it as originating in Bill

of this strategy, the United States attempted to expand economic and political ties between the two countries. While trade normalization is the most prominent element of this strategy, it also included military-to-military dialogues, educational and scientific contacts, and collaboration in multilateral fora.

As a strategy, engagement was broadly intended as a way of managing the rise of China. The architects of engagement sought to accomplish a wide variety of goals, ranging from increased Sino-American collaboration on non-proliferation and environmental issues to accelerated economic growth in the United States.[6] Among these goals were the political and economic liberalization of China. By approaching China with an open hand, U.S. officials believed they would be better positioned to accomplish these goals. The engagement was thought to produce comity and trust between the two powers, empower less confrontational elements within the regime, and set the groundwork for liberalization.

In recent years, the policy of engagement has been reconsidered.[7] This shift has been substantially the result of China's growing geopolitical power, increasingly assertive behavior on the international stage, and a turn toward a more state-centric, Chinese Communist Party (CCP) controlled economy. The engagement was explicitly intended to prevent a Sino-American confrontation. Today, there is a sense that some sort of Chinese-American competition is inevitable and, perhaps concerningly, may even be desirable. China's pivot away from market reform has also undercut one of the primary rationalizations for engagement. Unlike their predecessors, policymakers in the United States are increasingly skeptical that reformist elements in China can change China's economic path or that U.S. actions can empower the reformists. Finally, domestic dynamics have made open trade writ large increasingly toxic and trade with China an especially hot-button issue.

As the U.S. policy towards a more assertive China has come under increased scrutiny, attitudes toward the WTO have shifted. Initial

Clinton's pivot to a more conciliatory China policy in the mid-1990s following an initial attempt to aggressively link trade openness to progress on humanitarian issues.

D.M. Lampton, "The China Fantasy", *The China Quarterly*, 191 (2007), 745–49. A.I. Johnston, "The Failures of the 'Failure of Engagement' with China", *The Washington Quarterly*, 42 (2019), 99–114.

6 A.I. Johnston, "The Failures of the 'Failure of Engagement' with China", *The Washington Quarterly*, 42 (2019), 99–114.

7 See: W. Jisi et al., "Did America Get China Wrong? The Engagement Debate", *Foreign Affairs*, July/August, published on June 14, 2018, www.foreignaffairs.com/articles/china/2018-06-14/did-america-get-china-wrong.C1kX3QTaP0G28MhKT3Ue/Exmv0yhh22d

optimism about the power of the WTO to discipline and mold China has been replaced by frustration with the WTO's apparent inability to confront Chinese abuses. That frustration has itself contributed to a lack of support for the WTO as an institution, particularly for its dispute settlement system and its Appellate Body.

II Implications of the Debate over Granting China "Permanent Normal Trade Relations" Status

As noted below, the process for China joining the WTO involved both the negotiation of China's WTO Protocol of Accession (Protocol) and its accompanying Working Party Report (Report) and legislation in the United States to grant China "permanent normal trade relations" (PNTR) to replace the annual review of whether Chinese goods could enter the United States under "Most Favored Nation" (MFN) rates of duty. PNTR was necessary to meet the prerequisite required of the United States to "immediately and unconditionally" grant Chinese goods the same tariffs and trade treatment as goods from all other WTO members – called MFN everywhere but the United States, where the term "normal trade relations" is used instead.[8]

(i) Expansive View of the Role of the WTO Accession Process

China's accession to the WTO was negotiated under the Clinton Administration, taking as their point of departure President Clinton's view that China could play a positive role in advancing environmental standards, fighting transnational crime, bolstering the international trading system, contributing to an arms control regime, and promoting stability in East Asia.[9] While "political pluralism" and "free markets" in China were stated goals of the Clinton administration, these long-term objectives were part of a larger agenda that included pressing short-term concerns like the burgeoning North Korean nuclear program and the desire

[8] GATT Article I: "any advantage, favor, privilege or immunity granted by any contracting party to any product originating in or destined for any other country shall be accorded immediately and unconditionally to the like product originating in or destined for the territories of all other contracting parties."

[9] W.J. Clinton, "Remarks by the President in Address of China and the National Interest", Voice of America, Washington DC, *The White House*, October 24, 1997, https://clintonwhitehouse4.archives.gov/WH/New/html/19971024-3863.html.C1kX3QTaP0G28MhKT3Ue/Exmv0yhh22d

to diffuse tensions over Taiwan. PNTR was viewed internally by advocates, as Ambassador Charlene Barshefsky later recounted, as "the one chance the U.S. and China had to create an enduring foundation for the relationship."[10] The logic was that "if we treated China as an enemy, we were guaranteeing an enemy in the future. If we treated China as a friend, we could not guarantee friendship, but we could at least keep open the possibility of more benign outcomes."[11]

For the Clinton team, the benefits of engagement were not theoretical. They had seen how deeper ties could help diffuse both bilateral and regional stressors. The U.S. Trade Representative at the time, Mickey Kantor, would later argue that trade ties helped the two countries manage the 1995 Taiwan Strait Crisis, commenting that he was "convinced that the trade relationship was a strong connecting bond between the U.S. and China at a time when we needed it, particularly in late '95 and early '96."[12] According to former Secretary of Defense William Perry, the threat posed by North Korea, "provided a pretty strong incentive to see if we could go out and re-establish a reasonable relationship with [China]," which had previously provided useful intelligence about North Korean ambitions.[13]

The Clinton administration also saw their ability to encourage and support reformers within the Chinese regime as essential to accomplishing their varied goals. The contention was the boost to Chinese economic growth contributed by PNTR would "bolster the confidence of Chinese leadership in ways that reduce their fear about political reform."[14]

10 C. Barshefsky Interview, *William J. Clinton Presidential History Project*, Miller Center, University of Virginia, 2005, https://millercenter.org/the-presidency/presidential-oral-histories/charlene-barshefsky-oral-history.ClkX3QTaP0G28MhKT3Ue/Exmv0yhh22d

11 J.S. Nye, Jr., "Should China Be 'Contained'?", *Project Syndicate*, 2011, www.project-syndicate.org/commentary/should-china-be--contained.ClkX3QTaP0G28MhKT3Ue/Exmv0yhh22d

12 M. Kantor Interview, *William J. Clinton Presidential History Project*, Miller Center, University of Virginia, 2002, https://millercenter.org/the-presidency/presidential-oral-histories/michael-mickey-kantor-oral-history.ClkX3QTaP0G28MhKT3Ue/Exmv0yhh22d

13 Quoted in: Y.E. Yang, "Leaders' Conceptual Complexity and Foreign Policy Change: Comparing the Bill Clinton and George W. Bush Foreign Policies toward China", *The Chinese Journal of International Politics*, 3 (2010), 415–46.

W.I. Cohen, *America's Response to China: A History of Sino-American Relations*, (Columbia University Press, 2019), p. 245.

14 See: Memorandum Kenneth Lieberthal, Senior Director for Asia on Clinton's National Security Council, outlining the national security rationale for PNTR. S. Berger, Remarks to the East Asia Institute at Columbia University on China, New York, NY, 2000, https://clinton.presidentiallibraries.us/items/show/11241

Enabling "reformers" within China could allow the United States to pursue a wide range of priorities by creating a China that was "more cooperative on such crucial issues as nonproliferation, regional security, peacekeeping, human rights, and arms control."[15] Rejecting PNTR, however, would empower elements within China "who want to tighten the internal clamps, invest more heavily in the military-industrial complex, and hunker down for the 'inevitable struggle' with America bilaterally, regionally, and globally." The "worst case" scenario was a "US-China confrontation across Asia."

The United States' ability to tip the scales in China's domestic political debates was a core assumption of the engagement strategy. President Clinton suggested that refusing to engage with China "would encourage the Chinese to become hostile," while National Security Sandy Berger argued that U.S. aggressive U.S. policies would "fuel the very inward-looking forces that trample human rights."[16] While the administration was also clear that China would ultimately choose its own destiny, there was a sense that the right set of U.S. actions could enable the rise of reformers who would be amicable to the United States and the international system.

(ii) The PNTR Vote

In the summer of 2000, nearly 18 months before China would formally join the WTO, came the Congress' big moment to weigh in on U.S.-China trade policy. In the end, the vote was not particularly close, especially in the Senate, with the House voting in favor of granting PNTR to China in May 2000, 237–197; and the Senate following in September 2000, approving by a vote of 83–15.[17] But the vote came only after fierce debate before a skeptical Congress. While technically the Congress had been acting on China policy through its annual decision to waive freedom-of-emigration requirements (called Jackson-Vanik provisions) that would have the effect of taking away China's Normal Trade Relations (NTR) status, the reality was that while the House of Representatives voted to deny NTR to China in 1990, 1991 and 1992, there was no agreement

15 Ibid.

16 S. Berger, "Remarks by Samuel R. Berger: Building a New Consensus on China", Council on Foreign Relations, New York, NY, 1997, https://clinton.presidentiallibraries.us/items/show/9678. W.J. Clinton, "Remarks by the President in Address on China and the National Interest", 1997, https://clintonwhitehouse4.archives.gov/WH/New/html/19971024-3863.html

17 U.S.-China Relations Act of 2000 (H.R. 4444).

from the Senate, and neither legislative body took any action to change China's status after 1992.[18] As a result, China had effectively been receiving NTR treatment and access to the U.S. market on terms comparable to other WTO members since 1980. But the lead-up to the 2000 vote to grant China NTR status on a permanent basis underscored deep divisions and concerns over the future economic relationship between the United States and China.

The Clinton Administration put on a full-court press, with most of the cabinet weighing in to support a vote in favor of shifting U.S. policy from one in which China's access to the U.S. market had to be, at least technically, reviewed each year, with the possibility that it's "most favored nation/normal trade relations" status could be removed at any time. In urging Congress to pass PNTR legislation, President Clinton noted that supporting China's entry to the WTO was in the United States' broader national interest because it represented "the most significant opportunity we have had to create positive change in China since the 1970s."[19] He made clear, however, that it would also advance U.S. economic interests, describing the U.S. agreement as "the equivalent of a one-way street. It requires China to open its markets – with a fifth of the world's population, potentially the biggest markets in the world – to both our products and services in unprecedented new ways. All we do is to agree to maintain the present access which China enjoys."[20]

President Clinton described the outcome of the affirmative vote in the House as "a historic step toward continued prosperity in America, reform in China, and peace in the world" and for "an America that will be more prosperous and more secure; for a China that is more open to our products and more respectful of the rule of law at home and abroad."[21]

18 "Termination of the Application of Title IV of the Trade Act of 1974 with Respect to the People's Republic of China", *Senate Finance Committee*, S. Rept. 106–305, 106th Congress, 2000, www.congress.gov/congressional-report/106th-congress/senate-report/305/1?s=2&r=9

19 W.J. Clinton, Speech on China Trade Bill, Paul H. Nitze School of Advanced International Studies of the Johns Hopkins University, 2000, www.iatp.org/sites/default/files/Full_Text_of_Clintons_Speech_on_China_Trade_Bi.htm.C1kX3QTaP0G28MhKT3Ue/Exmv0yhh22d

20 W.J. Clinton, Speech on China Trade Bill, 2000, www.iatp.org/sites/default/files/Full_Text_of_Clintons_Speech_on_China_Trade_Bi.htm.C1kX3QTaP0G28MhKT3Ue/Exmv0yhh22d

21 W.J. Clinton, "Remarks by the President on Passage of Permanent Normal Trade Relations with China", *The White House*, 2000, https://1997-2001.state.gov/regions/eap/000524_clinton_china.html.C1kX3QTaP0G28MhKT3Ue/Exmv0yhh22d

At the same time, Clinton recognized that nothing about the trajectory of China or the U.S.-China relationship was guaranteed – but represented a chance for the U.S. and China to build a better and different future in the Asia Pacific community.

The American business community for its part believed that the normalization of trade relations with China would offer an economic windfall. The business community had long been advocates of increased trade with China. Their lobbying – supported by the Chinese government – helped reverse Clinton's initial China policy, which had linked trade access to progress on human rights.[22] As Warren Christopher, Clinton's Secretary of State and an advocate for the linkage policy, later put it, "the business community had convinced the president that trade for America was a higher value, or perhaps to put it more charitably, that nothing would be accomplished in the field of human rights by denial of trade, and so that became the basic policy."[23]

Advocates argued that PNTR would promote U.S. security and economic interests and have little downside. Then-Senator Joe Biden, for instance, argued that it would "help promote stability across the Taiwan Straits," encourage China to reform its economic system, and "enhance their respect for the rule of law," while offering the United States "one-way" trade concessions.[24] Those supporting PNTR for China focused on the economic gains and the chance to support economic reforms in China, with even Federal Reserve Chairman Alan Greenspan declaring PNTR would "create new opportunities for American businesses and farmers." Critics, on the other hand, focused on China's poor human rights record, its continued threats to Taiwan, its contribution to nuclear proliferation, its violation of environmental standards for development, and its labor abuses.

The Clinton administration explicitly pushed PNTR as a way of accelerating Chinese marketization and democratization, suggesting that it

[22] H. Hung, "The Periphery in the Making of Globalization: The China Lobby and the Reversal of Clinton's China Trade Policy, 1933–1994", *Review of International Political Economy*, 4 (2021) 1004–27.

[23] W. Christopher and S. Talbott Interview, *William J. Clinton Presidential History Project*, Miller Center, University of Virginia, 2002, https://millercenter.org/the-presidency/presidential-oral-histories/warren-christopher-and-strobe-talbott-oral-history.C1kX3QTaP0G28MhKT3Ue/Exmv0yhh22d

[24] "Giving Permanent Normal Trade Relations Status to Communist China: National Security and Diplomatic, Human Rights, Labor, Trade, and Economic Implications", Committee on Foreign Relations, S. Hrg. 106–744, 106th Congress, 2000, www.govinfo.gov/content/pkg/CHRG-106shrg67840/html/CHRG-106shrg67840.htm

would "strengthen reformers" who were "trying to move policy in the right direction."[25] The deal was seen as a potential boon to U.S. exporters, something that excited many Congressional supporters, while USTR Charlene Barshefsky indicated that the administration had "no reason to expect any substantial increases in Chinese imports at all."[26]

(iii) *The Reality of China's Accession Commitments*

While the arguments in the United States for granting China PNTR status in order to pave the way for its entry into the WTO may have focused on a broad range of geostrategic, political, national security, human rights, and economic issues, along with the empowerment of the reformists in China, the negotiations in Geneva were limited to trade issues and to the trading rules that China was signing up to.

When the accession negotiations were ultimately concluded and China joined the WTO in December 2001,[27] it did so only after making a substantial number of commitments and changes to its domestic economic laws, including:

- Major reductions in Chinese tariffs. Average tariffs on industrial products were reduced to 9.4% by 2005; elimination of all tariffs on high-technology products; auto tariffs fell from 80–100% to 25% by 2006; agriculture tariffs fell to an average of 17.5% by 2004.
- Elimination of import quotas and licensing requirements by 2005.
- Granting import and distribution rights to foreign corporations, which allowed them to set up wholly owned distribution, sales (including retail), shipping, and service networks over a three-year phase-in period.
- Financial services and telecommunications – ending the outright ban on any foreign ownership but leaving a number of restrictions and limitations on foreign ownership in place.

[25] G. Sperling, "PNTR and the Prospects for a More Open China", Remarks to the Committee for Economic Development, Washington, DC, 2000, https://clintonwhitehouse4.archives.gov/textonly/WH/EOP/nec/html/PunkeChinaSpeech2.html.C1kX3QTaP0G28MhKT3Ue/Exmv0yhh22d

[26] "The Administration's Proposal for Permanent Normal Trade Relations with China", Committee on Agriculture, S. Hrg. 106–52, 106th Congress, 2000, http://commdocs.house.gov/committees/ag/hag10652.000/hag10652_0f.htm

[27] For a thorough analysis of the negotiations and process of China's accession to the WTO, see: P. Blustein, *Schism: China, America and the Fracturing of the Global Trading System* (Centre for International Governance Innovation, 2019).

- Other services – increased market access for professional services, including accounting, consulting, engineering, medical, and information technology, while maintaining numerous restrictions and limitations.
- Commitment to implement and enforce international standards on the protection of intellectual property; provision for increased access and distribution rights for a specified number of motion pictures, music, and software.

The WTO-Director General at the time, Supachai Panitchpadi, described China's accession agreement as signaling "China's willingness to play by international trade rules and to bring its often opaque and cumbersome government apparatus into harmony with a world order that demands clarity and fairness."[28]

The USTR report to Congress in 2004 summed up the process and the outcome:

> The United States and other WTO members negotiated with China for 15 years over the specific terms pursuant to which China would enter the WTO. As a result of those negotiations, China agreed to extensive, far-reaching, and often complex commitments to change its trade regime, at all levels of government. China committed to implement a set of sweeping reforms that required it to lower trade barriers in virtually every sector of the economy, provide national treatment and improved market access to goods and services imported from the United States and other WTO members, and protect intellectual property rights (IPR). China also agreed to special rules regarding subsidies and the operation of state-owned enterprises, in light of the state's large role in China's economy. In accepting China as a fellow WTO member, the United States also secured a number of significant concessions from China that protect U.S. interests during China's WTO implementation stage. Implementation should be substantially completed – if China fully adheres to the agreed schedule – by December 11, 2007. By contrast, the United States did not make any specific new concessions to China, other than simply to agree to accord China the same treatment it accords the other 146 members of the WTO.[29]

None of these commitments, however, directly addressed the broader issues and aspirations for change within China that were an integral part

[28] S. Panitchpakdi and M.L. Clifford, *China and the WTO: Changing China, Changing World Trade* (Wiley, 2002).

[29] "2004 Report to Congress on China's WTO Compliance", *United States Trade Representative*, 2004, p. 3, https://ustr.gov/archive/assets/Document_Library/Reports_Publications/2004/asset_upload_file281_6986.pdf

of the debate over the passage of PNTR. For example, none of them spoke to issues such as nuclear proliferation or human rights that had been critical points underlying support for PNTR.

III Special Scrutiny for China

The level of concern in some quarters about granting China PNTR and paving the way for its entry into the WTO can be seen in two unusual provisions that were included in the PNTR legislation: (1) the establishment of the U.S.-China Economic and Security Review Commission ("China Commission") and (2) the statutory requirement that USTR report to Congress every year on China's compliance with its WTO obligations. No other country has similar provisions or undergoes the level of scrutiny that China does.

(i) The China Economic and Security Review Commission

The China Commission was created with the legislative mandate to monitor, investigate, and submit to Congress an annual report on the national security implications of the bilateral trade and economic relationship between the United States and China, and to provide recommendations, where appropriate, to Congress for legislative and administrative action. Even the title of the Commission with its joint focus on security and economics reflects the desire to use PNTR and China's accession to the WTO as leverage over security and geostrategic issues as well as trade and economic matters. From its inception, the Commission was skeptical that China would live up to its WTO commitments without constant and extraordinary vigilance from the U.S. In its very first (2002) report issued less than one year after China's accession, the Commission recommended that: (1) the U.S. shore up its toolbox by renewing the "Super 301" law that identifies priority practices and priority countries for trade liberalization, (2) commence WTO litigation over non-compliance with intellectual property rights, (3) engage in a more intensive examination of WTO compliance, and (4) consider a national security-based case to protect the U.S. steel industry.

The Commission also focused early attention on one of the major issues upsetting the balance of concessions reached through China's WTO accession – currency manipulation. Starting in the early 2000s and continuing for at least a decade thereafter, China kept the exchange rate of its currency pegged at artificially low levels.[30] Such currency manipulation made Chinese exports to the world cheap but exports to China more expensive. The Commission noted that "China's currency manipulation acts as a subsidy for Chinese exports to the United States and a tax on imports from the United States, and serves as an incentive for U.S. and foreign firms to move production to China."[31] The Commission noted in 2005 that most economists believe that the Chinese renminbi (RMB) is undervalued by 15–40 per cent.[32] China's ability to manipulate its currency by buying dollars and other foreign currency in China at a fixed rate contributed to an excessive reliance on export-led growth that deepened distortions in the Chinese economy and in its trading relationships.

By the mid-2000s, the China Commission's reports were sounding the alarm about the "profound differences between the open-market approach of the United States and the managed trade principles and predatory practices observed by the Chinese government."[33] It began using a "responsible stakeholder" index to assess whether China not only observes international norms but works to strengthen them, finding that China was far from meeting that standard.[34] Following Chinese President Xi Jinping's first state visit to the United States in 2015, the Commission reports cataloged long and growing lists of grievances the United States has against Chinese behavior, with currency manipulation, forced technology transfer, intellectual property theft, and excessive use of state subsidies often topping the list.[35] The most recent (2020) report concludes:

[30] *Currency Conflict and Trade Policy*, C. Fred Bergsten and Joseph E. Gagnon, Peterson Institute for International Economics, June 2017.

[31] 2005 Report to Congress of the U.S.-China Economic and Security Review Commission, p. 4.

[32] Ibid.

[33] 2006 Report to Congress of the U.S.-China Economic and Security Review Commission, p. 2, 2006.

[34] Ibid.

[35] 2015 report: "The grievances include the alleged theft by Chinese hackers of personal records of 22 million people, including U.S. government employees, their families, and friends; state-sponsored cyber espionage against U.S. companies to steal trade secrets and pass them to Chinese competitors; an unprecedented island-building campaign in disputed waters of the South China Sea; and a series of new laws restricting access by foreign companies to China's market or demanding technology transfers in return for such access."

2015 Report to Congress of the U.S.-China Economic and Security Review Commission, *U.S.-China Economic and Security Review Commission*, 2015. 2020 report: "Over the years, we have tracked the People's Republic of China's (PRC) accountability to its global commitments, including those made in its accession to the World Trade Organization. Two decades later, the Chinese Communist Party (CCP) selectively adheres to its global

> The CCP has launched determined and systematic efforts to hollow out global governance institutions, suppress internal opposition, subjugate free peoples in Hong Kong and around China's periphery, dominate global economic resources, and project military power. These efforts threaten vital interests of the United States and the security and vitality of an increasing number of countries around the globe. A clear understanding of the CCP's adversarial national security and economic ambitions is essential as U.S. and allied leaders develop the policies and programs that will define the conditions of global freedom and shape our future.[36]

(ii) Annual USTR Reports on China's WTO Compliance

To attempt to hold China to its WTO commitments, the United States used a multi-tracked approach. One track involved a series of annual high-level bilateral talks between U.S. and Chinese officials over three successive presidential administrations. These talks, initially called the Joint Commission on Commerce and Trade (JCCT, started in 2004), the Strategic Economic Dialogue, begun in 2006, and the Strategic and Economic Dialogue (S&ED) begun in 2009, were intended to push China towards complying with and internalizing WTO rules and norms and making other market-oriented changes. The second track involved WTO disputes to challenge China's compliance with its WTO obligations.

Both tracks for holding China to its WTO commitments have been cataloged over the past 20 years in the annual report that USTR is required to submit to Congress under the mandate included in the legislation granting China PNTR status. The initial report, submitted in 2002, reflects considerable optimism, noting the significant progress China made in implementing its WTO commitments, including "reviewing more than 2,500 trade-related laws and regulations, repealing 830 of them, and amending 325 more."[37] The report also acknowledges the considerable resources devoted to restructuring the various trade-related government ministries and agencies and to the education and training of central and

economic, trade, and political obligations and has abandoned any concern for international opinion. Now the CCP envisions itself atop a new hierarchical global order in which the world acquiesces to China's worldview while supplying it with markets, capital, resources, and talent." "2020 Report to Congress of the U.S.-China Economic and Security Review Commission", *U.S.-China Economic and Security Review Commission*, 2020.

36 "2020 Report to Congress of the U.S.-China Economic and Security Review Commission", *U.S.-China Economic and Security Review Commission*, 2020.

37 "2002 Report to Congress on China's WTO Compliance", *United States Trade Representative*, 2002, https://china.usc.edu/sites/default/files/article/attachments/2002-report-chinas-wto-compliance.pdf

local government officials. It also emphasized the commitments that the U.S. thought it had obtained regarding China's transition to a market economy: "For much of the past two decades, China had been gradually transitioning toward a market economy from what in the late 1970s was a strict command economy. In acceding to the WTO, China was required by the United States and other WTO members to agree to accelerate this process of market reform in order to comply with WTO requirements."[38]

At the same time, the USTR Report raised early concerns over transparency, agriculture, intellectual property rights, and services. Just two years later, the 2004 report was even more hopeful, quoting two trade associations' view that "China is now substantially in compliance with its WTO obligations – a marked improvement over last year."[39] The report also noted continued areas of concern, including intellectual property rights, services, agriculture, industrial policies, and transparency. It added that the work of one of the many high-level dialogue groups – the Joint Commission on Commerce and Trade (JCCT) – was "highly constructive."

Over the next number of years, these annual reports continued to report on bilateral dialogues and WTO disputes, coming to the general conclusion that the intensive dialogues with China generated positive outcomes on a number of contentious issues, while U.S. use of WTO dispute settlement continued to generate favorable settlements and favorable WTO dispute settlement decisions. The reports also continued to note ongoing problem areas, including principally intellectual property rights, industrial policies, trading rights, agriculture, and services, including distribution services. Increasingly the reports focused on the Chinese government's interventionist policies and practices and the large role of state-owned enterprises and other national champions in China's economy, which generated significant trade distortions giving rise to trade frictions. The final Obama Administration report (2016) noted the major expansion in U.S. goods and services exports to China but concluded that "despite these positive results, the overall picture currently presented by China's WTO membership remains complex."[40]

[38] Ibid.

[39] "2004 Report to Congress on China's WTO Compliance", *United States Trade Representative*, p. 4, https://ustr.gov/archive/assets/Document_Library/Reports_Publications/2004/asset_upload_file281_6986.pdf

[40] "2016 Report to Congress on China's WTO Compliance", *United States Trade Representative*, 2017, p. 2, https://ustr.gov/sites/default/files/2016-China-Report-to-Congress.pdf

Once the Trump Administration took office, however, the tone and underlying message changed to one of failure. The view shifted, noting that "China largely remains a state-led economy today, and the United States and other trading partners continue to encounter serious problems with China's trade regime. Meanwhile, China has used the imprimatur of WTO membership to become a dominant player in international trade." The report concluded: "Given these facts, it seems clear that the United States erred in supporting China's entry into the WTO on terms that have proven to be ineffective in securing China's embrace of an open, market-oriented trade regime."[41]

IV Failure to Use the WTO and China Accession Tools

Critical to gaining support for bringing China into the WTO were the tools built into China's protocol of accession and the WTO rules themselves that many in the United States believed would both protect the American market from any downside risks and hold China to account for its commitments.

Key among the provisions designed to guard against harm to domestic economies around the world were:

(a) a selective safeguard provision lasting 12 years permitting countries to impose safeguards (tariffs or quotas or other restraints) if they found that an increase in imports from China alone was causing disruption to their domestic producers of comparable products,[42]
(b) a right to apply for non-market economy status when calculating anti-dumping duty rates to imports from China, at least for a period of 15 years[43];

41 "2017 Report to Congress on China's WTO Compliance", *United States Trade Representative*, 2018, p. 2, https://ustr.gov/sites/default/files/files/Press/Reports/China%202017%20WTO%20Report.pdf

42 Section 16 of China's Protocol of Accession. See: *Accession of the People's Republic of China*, WTO Doc. WT/L/432, 2001.

43 Because of the ambiguous wording of Section 15 of China's Protocol relating to the non-market economy calculation of anti-dumping margins, doubt remained over what the situation was at the end of the 15-year period after China's accession. While China initially challenged the EU's continued use of a non-market economy methodology for determining antidumping margins, at the request of China, the dispute was allowed to lapse without a published report from the panel. See: *European Union – Measures Related to Price Comparison Methodologies*, WTO Doc. WT/DS516/13, 2016.

(c) a provision making it easier to apply countervailing duties to subsidized imports from China if distorted market conditions in China present "special difficulties" to countries in identifying and measuring subsidies;[44] and

(d) a provision lasting until December 31, 2008, limiting China's textile and apparel exports to amounts no greater than 7.5% (6% for wool products) above the amount entered in the previous year if Chinese imports were impeding the orderly development of trade.[45]

(i) Failures to Guard Domestic Markets

Among the most highly touted of the provisions designed to guard against any potential harm from China was a product-specific, selective safeguard provision that allowed WTO members to impose safeguards (which normally can only be applied to imports from all sources) on imports from China alone.[46] The provision included a lower threshold for its application than traditional safeguard measures which require a showing that imports have caused "serious injury" to a domestic industry producing comparable goods. Here, the standard permitted the application of a China-only safeguard if Chinese imports were causing "market disruption." In addition, a clause in this new safeguard allowed a second country to justify its own imposition of a new import restriction after a first country has implemented a China safeguard on the basis of a "trade deflection" threat alone, without having to carry out its own injury investigation. In the United States, the common answer to Congressional concerns over a potential flood in imports from China was the existence of this special safeguard and the ease in its application. The process to implement it called upon the independent U.S. International Trade Commission (USITC) to investigate all claims of market disruption and to report to the President any affirmative findings, along with recommendations for actions to be taken to address the market disruption caused by Chinese imports.[47]

[44] Section 15(b) of China's Protocol of Accession. See: *Accession of the People's Republic of China*, WTO Doc. WT/L/432, 2001. H. Gao, "Rethinking China Trade Policy: Lessons Learned and Options Ahead", *National Foundation for American Policy*, 2021, https://nfap.com/wp-content/uploads/2021/01/Rethinking-China-Trade-Policy.NFAP-Policy-Brief.January-2021-2.pdf.C1kX3QTaP0G28MhKT3Ue/Exmv0yhh22d

[45] Paragraph 242 of the Working Party Report. See: *Report of the Working Party on the Accession of China*, WTO Doc. WT/ACC/CHN/49, 2001.

[46] Section 16 of China's Protocol of Accession: Transitional Product-Specific Safeguard Mechanism. See: *Accession of the People's Republic of China*, WTO Doc. WT/L/432, 2001.

[47] Section 421 of the Trade Act of 1974, 19 U.S.C.§ 2451.

The President was given the authority to accept, modify or reject the USITC's recommendations.[48]

In the 12 years that the China-specific safeguard provision was in effect and despite the substantial increase in imports from China in a wide variety of products, the United States imposed a China-specific safeguard only once.[49] Part of the reluctance stemmed from decisions made by the Bush administration not to impose safeguards despite a recommendation from the USITC in five cases to do so.[50] Failure to obtain a remedy despite proving market disruption may have deterred potential complainants while concerns over WTO decisions striking down global safeguards may have contributed to reticence in applying for safeguard relief. The one China-specific safeguard that was imposed – on passenger vehicles and light truck tires – came eight years after China's accession to the WTO. It was also the first such safeguard challenged by China, with the WTO's Appellate Body upholding the United States' determination to apply safeguard measures to Chinese tires.[51]

Antidumping (AD) (selling goods in foreign markets for less than prices at home) and countervailing duties (CVD) (offsets for government subsidies), however, were more commonly deployed. From 2001 to 2020, WTO members have reported imposing 917 AD measures against Chinese imports, approximately 30% of the total reported, and 129 CVDs against Chinese imports, approximately 46% of the total actions.[52] For U.S. industries, the primary tool to respond to increased imports from China, particularly in the 2000s, was anti-dumping duties, with the use of the "non-market economy methodology" permitted under Section 15(b) of China's protocol of accession to calculate the amount of those duties. As of September 2021, the United States has 142 AD orders in place on various goods from China, far more than the number of AD measures against imports from any other country.[53]

48 19 U.S.C. § 2451(k).

49 "Certain Passenger Vehicle and Light Truck Tires from China", *U.S. International Trade Commission*, Investigation No. TA-421-7, 2009, www.usitc.gov/publications/safeguards/pub4085.pdf

50 "U.S.-China Trade: The United States Has Not Restricted Imports under the China Safeguard", *U.S. Government Accountability Office*, 2005, www.gao.gov/products/gao-05-1056

51 *United States – Measures Affecting Imports of Certain Passenger Vehicle and Light Truck Tyres from China*, WTO Doc. WT/DS399, 2009.

52 "Subsidies and Countervailing Measures", *World Trade Organization*, www.wto.org/english/tratop_e/scm_e/scm_e.htm

53 "Antidumping and Countervailing Duty Orders in Place", United States International Trade Commission, www.usitc.gov/trade_remedy/documents/orders.xls

Prior to 2007, the United States did not apply its CVD law to countries considered to be nonmarket economies (NMEs) based in part on a conclusion by the Department of Commerce (Commerce) that it could not determine where government action began or ended and therefore could not specifically identify subsidies. In 1986, the US Court of Appeals for the Federal Circuit in *Georgetown Steel Corp. v. United States* upheld this interpretation of the CVD statute as reasonable. In 2006, Commerce changed its position, accepting a petition seeking a CVD on imports of coated free-sheet paper from China. Commerce distinguished the current Chinese economy from the Soviet-style economies at issue in *Georgetown Steel* and found that the imported Chinese paper was subsidized. Numerous CVD cases followed, with 80 CVD orders now in place against imports from China. But the rest of the world has been less willing to use this tool, perhaps in part because it involves a direct challenge to the practices of the Chinese government and the CCP compared to anti-dumping cases, which focus on the behavior of individual companies. Even less clear is how willing countries are to use the "special difficulties" tool provided in Paragraph 15 to overcome evidentiary hurdles in proving the existence of a subsidy.

The textile-specific growth limit was similarly far less utilized than might have been expected, given China's dominant position as a supplier of textiles and clothing. In the United States, the use of such safeguards became bogged down in protracted legal battles over the application when there was only a threat of market disruption.[54]

The world's failure to use these tools – at least not early and often enough – was part of what allowed China's relatively unchecked rise in exports to the world.[55] In the United States, China's rise was documented and labeled in a 2016 article titled "The China Shock: Learning from Labor-Market Adjustment in Large Change in Trade," by David Autor from MIT, David Dorn (University of Zurich) and Gordon Hanson (UC-San Diego).[56] The article noted that China's economic size, speed of growth,

[54] "U.S.-China Trade: Textile Safeguard Procedures Should Be Improved", *U.S. Government Accountability Office*, 2005, www.gao.gov/products/gao-05-296

[55] As noted by Paul Blustein, it was not just the US that suffered. Studies show labor market harms in Spain, Norway, Turkey and the U.K. Brazilian textile and clothing workers demanded increased tariffs to respond to a large influx of Chinese clothing. Honduran and other Central American apparel industry workers also experienced layoffs and additional hardships after losing out to competition from China. *See*: P. Blustein, *Schism: China, America and the Fracturing of the Global Trading System* (Centre for International Governance Innovation, 2019).

[56] D.H. Autor, D. Dorn, and G.H. Hanson, "The China Shock: Learning from Labor-Market Adjustment to Large Changes in Trade", *Annual Review of Economics*, 8 (2016), 205–40.

and import penetration were all of an order of magnitude different from previous waves of imports from Japan or Mexico or others. Imports from China grew from 1.0 per cent of the US GDP in 2000 when China's accession to the WTO was being negotiated to 2.6 per cent of GDP ten years later. The impact on communities where goods competing directly with Chinese imports (such as furniture, toys, electronics, jewelry, shoes, and clothing) were particularly profound, due in part to the lack of sufficient safety nets or trade adjustment assistance and in part due to the unexpected immobility of labor.

While the U.S. imposed 199 anti-dumping and countervailing tariffs, primarily targeting raw and semi-processed imports with some cases addressing finished goods like furniture and tires, the wave of imports appeared to simply overwhelm many companies, leading to a conclusion that the trade rules were not up the task of coping with the China shock and to the parallel determination that it was a mistake for the United States to have allowed China to enter the WTO on the terms that it did.[57]

(ii) Failure to Hold China to Its Commitments on Transparency, Market Economy Orientation, Rule of Law, and More

A critical aspect of its advocacy for PNTR and China's accession to the WTO was the assertion that China's conduct would be "monitored by more than 130 other WTO Members with a common interest in seeing China's market opened."[58] "Unlike our bilateral agreements," the Clinton administration argued, "we will not be alone in our enforcement efforts if China fails to live up to its commitments."[59]

The most significant commitments for which compliance was sought involved those that required China to open up its market under numerous specific commitments with respect to trade in goods, agriculture, and

[57] "2017 Report to Congress on China's WTO Compliance", *United States Trade Representative*, 2018, https://ustr.gov/sites/default/files/files/Press/Reports/China%20 2017%20WTO%20Report.pdf; and

R.E. Lighthizer Testimony, "Evaluating China's Role in the World Trade Organization Over the Past Decade", *U.S.-China Economic and Security Review Commission*, 2010, www .uscc.gov/sites/default/files/6.9.10Lighthizer.pdf

[58] China PNTR Speech in Shakopee, MN and Akron, OH, *Clinton Digital Library*, 2000, https://clinton.presidentiallibraries.us/items/show/12215

[59] "China PNTR Q&A", *Clinton Digital Library*, 2000, https://clinton.presidentiallibraries .us/items/show/11229

particular services commitments;[60] various commitments with respect to the rule of law and transparency in the Chinese system,[61] intellectual property rights requirements,[62] and numerous commitments intended to keep China on the path toward becoming a fully market-oriented economy.[63]

For the first few years following China's 2001 accession to the WTO, most WTO members took a "wait and see" approach. For its part, the United States filed 23 different cases against specific Chinese practices, with its first case filed in 2004, winning all that was completed, settling eight of them through mutual agreement, with three still pending.[64]

[60] For example, Section 5 of China's Protocol of Accession establishes the right to trade all goods other than a short list throughout the customs territory of China, Section 7 provides for the elimination of non-tariff measures and Section 12 commits China to opening its market to agriculture imports on a specific schedule. See: *Accession of the People's Republic of China*, WTO Doc. WT/L/432, 2001.

[61] For example, Section 2 of China's Protocol of Accession requires China to apply its laws constituently throughout the country and stated that the only Chinese laws or regulations pertaining to trade in goods, services, intellectual property rights or foreign exchange controls that could be enforced are those that published and readily available to the United States and other WTO members. In addition, China committed to put in place an independent judicial review process for all actions pertaining to its laws and decisions impacting trade or intellectual property rights. See: *Accession of the People's Republic of China*, WTO Doc. WT/L/432, 2001.

[62] As a coalition representing, among others, the Motion Picture Association of America and the Software and Information Industry Association, wrote: "We are convinced from our own experience that inclusion of China within the framework of multilateral rules and obligations embodied in the WTO is the single best instrument we have to ensure continuing improvement in China's protection of intellectual property." R.A. Kapp, "PNTR Trade Status for China: Ten Key Considerations", *The United States-China Business Council*, 2000, https://clinton.presidentiallibraries.us/items/show/11248

[63] For example, Section 9 of China's Protocol of Accession states that, with certain specified exceptions, China "shall low prices for traded goods and services in every sector to be determined by market forces," while Section 6 requires China to refrain from influencing the purchase and sale decision of its state trade enterprises. See: *Accession of the People's Republic of China*, WTO Doc. WT/L/432, 2001.

[64] *China – Value-Added Tax on Integrated Circuits*, WTO Doc. WT/DS309, 2004; *China – Auto Parts*, WTO Doc. WT/DS340, 2006; *China – Taxes*, WTO Doc. WT/DS358, 2007; *China – Intellectual Property Rights*, WTO Doc. WT/DS362, 2007; *China – Publications and Audiovisual Entertainment Products*, WTO Doc. WT/DS363, 2007; *China – Measures Affecting Financial Services and Foreign Financial Suppliers*, WTO Doc. WT/DS373, 2008; *China – Grants, Loans, and Other Incentives*, WTO Doc. WT/DS387, 2008; *China – Raw Materials*, WTO Doc. WT/DS394, 2009; *China – Electronic Payment Services*, WTO Doc. WT/DS413, 2010; *China – GOES*, WTO Doc. WT/DS414, 2010; *China – Measures Concerning Wind Power Equipment*, WTO Doc. WT/DS419, 2010; *China – Broiler Products*, WTO Doc. WT/DS427, 2011; *China – Rare Earths*, WTO Doc. WT/DS431, 2012; *China – Autos (US)*, WTO Doc. WT/DS427, 2012; *China – Certain Measures Affecting the Automobile and Automobile Parts Industries*, WTO Doc. WT/DS450, 2012; *China – Demonstration Bases*, WTO Doc WT/DS498, 2015; *China – Tax Measures Concerning*

The entire rest of the world combined brought a comparable number of cases, with many countries appearing reluctant, particularly early on, to challenge China for fear of retaliation or for lack of evidence from China's opaque system. However, each of these cases was somewhat narrowly focused on individual measures or particular sectors. None spoke to the bigger, more systemic issues that are at the heart of U.S. concerns with China or to China's failure to fulfill its notification and transparency requirements.

What might have been a better approach would have been a "big, bold, coalition-based case" that would have represented an "opportunity to bring together enough of the trading interests in the world to put sufficient pressure on China to make it clear that fundamental reform is required if China is to remain a member in good standing in the WTO."[65] Just such a case was recommended by the U.S.-China Economic and Security Commission, based in part on the author's testimony to the Commission.[66]

In my construction, the case could include claims to address China's: (1) coercion of technology transfers in light of China's commitment that it would not condition investments on the transfer of technology,[67] (2) restrictions on the right of foreign companies to license their technology (or choose not to license it) under the conditions and terms that they would like in violation of China national treatment and MFN commitments;[68] (3) direction of outbound investment to obtain cutting-edge

Certain Domestically Produced Aircraft, WTO Doc. WT/DS501, 2015; *China – Raw Materials II (US)*, WTO Doc. WT/DS508, 2016; *China – Agricultural Producers*, WTO Doc. WT/DS511, 2016;

China – TRQs, WTO Doc. DS/517, 2016; *China – Subsidies to Producers of Primary Aluminium*, WTO Doc. WT/DS519, 2017; *China – Intellectual Property Rights II*, WTO Doc. WT/DS542, 2018; *China – Additional Duties*, WTO Doc. WT/DS558, 2018.

65 Testimony of J. Hillman, "The Best Way to Address China's Unfair Policies and Practices is Through a Big, Bold Multilateral Case at the WTO", *U.S.-China Economic and Security Review Commission*, 2018, www.uscc.gov/sites/default/files/Hillman%20Testimony%20US%20China%20Comm%20w%20Appendix%20A.pdf.C1kX3QTaP0G28MhKT3Ue/Exmv0yhh22d

66 "2018 Report to Congress of the U.S.-China Economic and Security Review Commission", *U.S.-China Economic and Security Review Commission*, 2018, www.uscc.gov/sites/default/files/2019-09/2018%20Annual%20Report%20to%20Congress.pdf

67 Section 7.3 of China's Protocol of Accession. See: *Accession of the People's Republic of China*, WTO Doc. WT/L/432, 2001.

68 Paragraph 256, Working Party Report, one of the legally binding paragraphs of China's Working Party report. See: *Report of the Working Party on the Accession of China*, WTO Doc. WT/ACC/CHN/49, 2001.

technology in service of China's industrial policy, in violation of China's commitment to treat foreigners on a reciprocity basis;[69] (4) investment restrictions that preclude or unreasonably delay market entry for foreign companies in violation of China's commitment not to condition investments on performance requirements or technology transfer,[70] (5) use of export taxes to restrict or encourage certain exports over others, in violation of China's commitment not to charge such export taxes other than on a specific list of products,[71] (6) services restrictions that are inconsistent with China's GATS schedules, (7) restrictions on agriculture imports under non-transparent and non-science based sanitary and phytosanitary measures, (8) lack of transparency and access to China's laws, regulations and rules on timely basis, (9) failure to establish independent judicial review of trade-related administrative decisions,[72] and (10) failure to meet the reasonable expectations of WTO members that China's economy would become a market-oriented one.[73]

The last claim that I suggested is the one designed to get at the heart of the United States' concern – that China's U-turn away from market orientation to an ever more state-controlled economy violates the spirit, if not always the letter, of the WTO.

(iii) China's Turn Away from Market-Oriented Reforms

The overarching Marrakesh Agreement establishing the WTO declares that the organization was designed as a world trading system "based upon open, market-oriented policies." China, for example, expressly declared as part of its accession commitments that "that all state-owned and state-invested enterprises would make purchases and sales based

[69] Paragraph 256 of China's Working Party Report (one of the paragraphs that is legally binding). See: *Report of the Working Party on the Accession of China*, WTO Doc. WT/ACC/CHN/49, 2001.

[70] Section 7.3 of China's Protocol of Accession. See: *Accession of the People's Republic of China*, WTO Doc. WT/L/432, 2001. China's basic national treatment commitment is underscored in Paragraph 18 of the Working Party report (one of the legally binding paragraphs): "The representative of China further confirmed that China would provide the same treatment to Chinese enterprises, including foreign-funded enterprises, and foreign enterprises and individuals in China. See: See: *Report of the Working Party on the Accession of China*, WTO Doc. WT/ACC/CHN/49, 2001.

[71] Section 11.3 of China's Protocol of Accession. See: *Accession of the People's Republic of China*, WTO Doc. WT/L/432, 2001.

[72] Section 2(D) Judicial Review, China's protocol of Accession. See: *Accession of the People's Republic of China*, WTO Doc. WT/L/432, 2001.

[73] This last claim would be a "non-violation" claim under Article XXIII of the GATT.

solely on commercial considerations, e.g., price, quality, marketability and availability ..."[74]

As a result, the United States and all other WTO members had legitimate expectations that China would increasingly behave as a market economy – that it would achieve a discernable separation between its government and its private sector, that private property rights and an understanding of who controls and makes decisions in major enterprises would be clear, that subsidies would be curtailed, that theft of IP rights would be punished and diminished in amount, that SOEs would make purchases based on commercial considerations, that the Communist Party would not, by fiat, occupy critical seats within major "private" enterprises and that standards and regulations would be published for all to see.

But starting in the mid-2000s, China began what has now become a complete U-turn back to becoming a state and Communist Party dominated economy.[75] While parts of the economy appear to have a thriving private sector, intervention by the government and the CCP has become far more pervasive. Institutions were established giving Beijing tighter control over China's large and fast-growing SOEs (overseen by the State-owned Assets Supervision and Administration Commission (SASAC)) and its banks (influenced via Central Huijin Investment). The overlapping ways in which China's economy is unique and state driven results in a phenomenon dubbed "China, Inc." that is hard to reach with WTO rules.[76] Concerns about the direction of China's economy greatly intensified with the rise of Xi Jinping as China's leader in 2012 and the release of the Made in China 2025 plan designed to create Chinese self-sufficiency in a range of critical technology sectors.

These concerns were succinctly summarized in the statement made by the then U.S. Ambassador to the WTO, Dennis Shea, in a May 8, 2018 statement to the WTO General Council:

> China ... is consistently acting in ways that undermine the global system of open and fair trade. Market access barriers too numerous to mention; forced technology transfers; intellectual property theft on an

[74] Paragraph 46 of the Working Party Report (legally binding paragraph). See: *Report of the Working Party on the Accession of China*, WTO Doc. WT/ACC/CHN/49, 2001.

[75] N. Lardy, *The State Strikes Back: The End of Economic Reform in China?* PIIE, January 2019, www.piie.com/bookstore/state-strikes-back-end-economic-reform-chinaClkX3QTaP0G28MhKT3Ue/Exmv0yhh22d

[76] M. Wu, "The 'China, Inc.' Challenge to Global Trade Governance", *Harvard International Law Journal*, 57 (2016), https://harvardilj.org/wp-content/uploads/sites/15/HLI210_crop.pdf.ClkX3QTaP0G28MhKT3Ue/Exmv0yhh22d

> unprecedented scale; indigenous innovation policies and the Made in China 2025 program; discriminatory use of technical standards; massive government subsidies that have led to chronic overcapacity in key industrial sectors; and a highly restrictive foreign investment regime.[77]

It is this collective failure by China that underlies the trade friction between the United States and China.

The concerns over the market orientation of China's economy are shared by many other WTO members. When the G-20 trade ministers met in September 2020, for example, much of the discussion centered on strengthening the WTO, beginning with a reaffirmation of commitment to the objectives and principles in the Marrakesh Agreement. But when it came to affirming that "market-oriented policies" is a principle of the WTO, China objected. It is this fundamental split that has led some leading trade scholars to conclude that "the world is now presented with two conflicting economic systems: (1) a Western-led, market-driven, model based on the rule of law and (2) an authoritarian state-driven model championed by China," and that the solution is to "establish a 'compact' among like-minded developed market economies to agree to new common approaches to counter unfair non-market practices; address critical twenty-first-century economic issues such as the digital economy, climate change and the environment, and labor; and improve economic ties in industries that are key to innovation, economic growth, and national security."[78]

V Conclusion: Implications of the Failures and Where We Go from Here

The failure of China's accession to the WTO to meet the very large and arguably unrealistic expectations across the economic, trade, geopolitical, and national security arenas likely portends a permanent shift in the U.S. approach to China. The initial vision of the Clinton administration was that the WTO could serve as the backstop to the Sino-American trade relationship – a facially neutral arbiter that could help enforce the liberal trade rules that Washington preferred. It was created and nurtured in an

[77] Statement as delivered by D. Shea, Deputy U.S. Trade Representative and U.S. permanent Representative to the WTO, WTO General Council, Geneva, 2018, https://geneva.usmission.gov/2018/05/08/ambassador-dennis-sheas-statement-at-the-wto-general-council/.C1kX3QTaP0G28MhKT3Ue/Exmv0yhh22d

[78] W. Reinsch and J. Caporal, "Toward a New Global Trade Framework", *Center for Strategic and International Studies Trade Commission on Affirming American Leadership*, 2021.

era where U.S. strategists saw trade with China and the rest of the world as a largely unambiguous good, capable of advancing both their strategic and domestic political ambitions. For the reasons noted above, that view has fundamentally changed.

This new reality means, at a minimum, that the U.S. will need to rely on a far wider array of tools than simply the WTO and its dispute settlement process to address its concerns.[79] It also means that reforms at the WTO will need to be deeper and more directed at addressing the fundamental schism between market-oriented economies and state-controlled ones.

A fulsome explanation of what the U.S. should do outside of the WTO is beyond the scope of this paper, but it should include at a minimum renewed attention to the work of the U.S.-EU-Japan trilateral cooperative process aimed at developing new rules on subsidies and tech transfer and greater reliance on the deep transatlantic alliance with Europe, the recently reinvigorated Quadrilateral Security Dialogue (Australia, India, Japan, and the United States) and alternative forums such as the G-7, the G-20, and the OECD to develop a more coordinated approach to the China trade challenge. Also included should be an exploration of the U.S. rejoining the Trans-Pacific Partnership (now the Comprehensive and Progressive Agreement for Trans-Pacific Partnership (CP-TPP)) in order to ensure that the United States has a seat at the table while the trade architecture in Asia is put in place and reassure our trading partners that the United States remains committed to the region. The U.S. must also follow through on the Biden administration's Build Back Better plan to shore up American competitiveness and supply chain resilience, particularly in key sectors and technologies. It must also rely on both bilateral and plurilateral dialogues to address the many geostrategic and national security concerns raised by a more assertive China.

At the WTO, the United States needs to lead the effort to fix the WTO. The WTO is in desperate need of reform and revitalization, but that will not happen absent U.S. leadership and commitment. Reforming the WTO would also allow it to be a more effective tool among many that the United States will need to address its China concerns. The reforms need to focus on the structural flaws at the WTO, including the imbalance between its dispute settlement, negotiating, and executive functions and

[79] M. Wu, "Managing the China Trade Challenge: Confronting the Limits of the WTO", Working Paper for *The Penn Project on the Future of US-China Relations*, 2020, https://cpb-us-w2.wpmucdn.com/web.sas.upenn.edu/dist/b/732/files/2020/10/Mark-Wu_Limits-of-WTO_Final.pdf.C1kX3QTaP0G28MhKT3Ue/Exmv0yhh22d

the unsustainable bifurcation between developed and developing countries that China has exploited despite its immense economic heft and the power of its trade. The reforms will also need to focus on the gaps in the substantive rules, starting with new disciplines on the transfer of technology, the classification of State-Owned Enterprises (SOEs), and the rules on subsidies. Additional efforts should also be made to bring into the WTO the e-commerce and digital trade provisions from the USMCA or the CP-TPP.

While it is clear that the WTO should not and cannot serve as the only forum for working out America's concerns with the rise of China, the WTO cannot and should not be abandoned. It should be fixed in its own right as the premier forum for bringing together the world's trading nations to negotiate and enforce rules, exchange information, disseminate best practices, and provide transparency with respect to trading practices and measures. In so doing, the WTO can begin what will be a long process of developing rules or norms to address concerns over China's industrial policies, its non-tariff barriers, and its abuse of intellectual property and technology rights.

In the end, the United States expected too much of the WTO and the WTO delivered too little. Righting that balance will require a stronger, more responsive, and more inclusive WTO and a more robust tool kit to address the national security and geostrategic concerns that the WTO was never going to be in a position to resolve.

PART V

China and Investment Governance

18

A Comparison of Inbound and Outbound Investment Regulatory Regimes in China

Focus on Environmental Protection

MATTHEW S. ERIE AND JINGJING ZHANG

I Introduction

China is no longer only a major destination of foreign direct investment (FDI) but is one of the highest exporters of overseas direct investment (ODI) in the world. The two different legal and regulatory regimes for FDI and ODI are often conceptualized separately with the former being more advanced than the latter. The conventional explanation for this difference is that the former has simply had more time to develop, given that China opened to FDI in the 1980s, and it was not until the late 1990s that Chinese enterprises began investing abroad. We stake out a different position on the relationship between the FDI and ODI regimes. Rather than treat them as isolates, we juxtapose them (Bath, 2011) while recognizing that they are organized through different principles.

In accordance with a line of literature that conceptualizes domestic and foreign-related Chinese governance holistically (Foot, 2013; Ferchen, 2016; Shue, 2018; Erie, 2021), we compare the FDI and ODI regimes, finding that, at a general level, whereas the former has transitioned from restrictive to lenient, the latter has evolved in the opposite direction, from lenient to restrictive. The different trajectories cannot be explained solely in terms of the time lag in their respective development. While the primary reasons for change are domestic, we argue that one reason why the FDI regime is more advanced is because of the influence of the WTO accession of 2001. Whereas the FDI regime has become more streamlined, efficient, and coordinated, partly as a result of the WTO accession package, the ODI regime, which has not yet benefited from an analogous multilateral framework, remains bureaucratic, suboptimal, and disaggregated.

Our analysis is based on a data set of hundreds of normative documents that comprise the FDI and ODI regulatory regimes. For the most part, we have focused on normative documents issued by the People's Republic of China (PRC) government that pertain to FDI or ODI governance to provide a more granular view than a focus on the level of China's international investment agreements (Berger, this volume; Chi, this volume). For a number of reasons, including the breadth of documents that comprise these regimes and also our shared interest in China's impact on the environment, we focus on the specific example of the regulation of the environmental impact of FDI and ODI. Environmental concerns are closely related to a host of problems that have emerged in recent years as the most pressing problems for international trade and investment law, including technology transfer, climate change mitigation and adaptation, the protection of biodiversity, and pandemics (Cottier, this volume). Our particular focus is on how the FDI and ODI regimes have disparately affected environmental impact in China and developing countries, respectively. We find that the environmental and social impact of Chinese ODI is inadequately regulated resulting in potential harm to Chinese investors and impacted communities in host states alike in the course of Chinese-financed projects overseas. The remainder of this chapter is organized as follows: in Part II, we provide a snapshot of China's capital inflows and outflows; in Part III, we provide an historical overview of China's regulation of FDI, finding a general transition from restricting FDI to encouraging it; in Part IV, we provide a similar historical appraisal of China's regulation of ODI finding that the general trend works in the opposite direction; in Part V, we juxtapose the two regimes' treatment of environmental impact; and in Part VI, we provide a brief discussion of implications, including for understanding the relationship between China's domestic legal reform, outward-facing legal obligations, and the role of regulators in coordinating the foregoing.

II Trends in Chinese Capital Import and Export

As a preliminary matter, we recognize that FDI and ODI serve different purposes and do not assume that they should necessarily function in the same way; in fact, our comparison is meant to shed light on the different types of priorities a state may have in reforming the respective regimes. In considering the priorities that underlie the regimes, it is clear there are differences. For example, whereas FDI rules are designed to attract capital and technology, ODI rules aim to assist Chinese companies to obtain resources and to transfer excess capacity in manufacturing. There are some shared underpinning principles, however, even if they assume different levels of importance in the two regimes. These include both national security and the encouragement and protection of investment.[1] So while there are clearly different reasons for the capital flows, there is also some overlap.

The overlap also applies to the regulators who determine capital inflows and outflows as they are essentially one and the same; despite this commonality, the regimes have evolved in quite different directions. The regulators include *inter alia* the Ministry of Foreign Trade and Economic Cooperation and its successor the Ministry of Commerce (MOFCOM), the National Development and Reform Commission (NDRC), the Ministry of Finance, the Ministry of Foreign Affairs, the State Administration for Industry and Commerce, the State Administration of Foreign Exchange, and the People's Bank of China. It is important to note, however, that economists, political scientists, and other social scientists who study China have consistently shown that regulators in China do not act with one mind, but rather, may exhibit significant inter-agency competition (Lieberthal, 1992; Mertha, 2008; Jones and Hameiri, 2021; Tan, 2021). Moreover, in the face of these agency problems, scholars have argued that the WTO accession presented China with an opportunity to circumvent entrenched discoordination problems and to marshal resources across the ministries, departments, and related administrative divisions (Kim, 2002; Qin, 2007). Indeed, the WTO accession was an exercise in institutional learning and problem-solving that required an unprecedented level of coordinated action (Hsieh, 2010; Ji and Huang, 2011; Shaffer and Gao, 2017). Yet while regulators underwent a steep learning curve to reform the FDI regime in light of the WTO accession package, there was no comparative multilateral framework for China's ODI regime and thus the same reformers have not undergone a similar process of coordinated learning. In the following sections, we take the FDI and ODI regimes in turn.

[1] 中华人民共和国国家安全法 [National Security Law of the PRC], promulgated by the National People's Congress (NPC) on July 1, 2015, and effective on July 1, 2015, art.59, https://perma.cc/LEW8-EH33. Cf. 企业境外投资管理办法 [Measures for the Administration of Overseas Investment by Enterprises], No. 11, promulgated by the National Development and Reform Commission (NDRC) on March 1, 2018, (hereinafter, "Overseas Investment Measures") art. 5, https://perma.cc/PY7A-YYED. 中华人民共和国外商投资法 [Foreign Investment Law of the PRC], promulgated by the NPC on March 15, 2019 and effective Jan. 1, 2020) [hereinafter, "Foreign Investment Law"], art 3. Cf. Overseas Investment Measures, art. 1, https://perma.cc/R2J4-8HFU.

III China's Regulation of FDI

At a general level, China's regulation of FDI has gone from more restrictive to more lenient, and, while there are a number of factors that contributed to this shift and most of which are domestic in nature, we argue that one reason for this change is the requirements imposed on China through the WTO accession package, a multilateral framework that has no corollary in terms of China's regime for regulating ODI. More specifically, China's approach to regulating FDI was caused by its "opening and reform" policy and the country's willingness to engage with global capital. China's commitments to joining the WTO, including making China a market economy and opening the domestic market to foreign investors, should be seen in this broader context.

We construct a basic chronology of the evolution of China's FDI regime. We find that China's evolving FDI framework coincides with China's national development plans as it transitioned from a command-control economy to one that increasingly integrated market principles without total privatization. This timeline can be broken down into five general phases: phase one (1979–1991), the establishment of a basic regulatory foundation for economic liberalization; phase two (1992–1999), an increased emphasis on economic efficiency causes legislative reform; phase three (2000–2008), the period of the WTO accession during which the government sought to internationalize by balancing economic efficiency with economic fairness; phase four (2009–2014) during which the government sought to balance internationalization with national security concerns; and phase five (2015-present) which is marked by not only efficiency and national security concerns but also greater openness and quality of cross-border business. In what follows, we trace China's gradualist approach to investment reform with particular reference to the pivotal phase three during which China's accession to the WTO shifted its FDI regime toward greater liberalization, yet one responsive to China's specific political economy.

(i) Phase One (1979–1991): The Establishment of a Regulatory Foundation for Economic Liberalization

The first phase of building a house amenable to foreign investment began in 1979 and lasted until the early 1990s. At this early stage in modern China's development, the PRC government sought to incentivize FDI to inject capital into the forces of production, specifically those in light industry, agriculture, and heavy industry. The landmark event of the Third Plenary Session of the Eleventh Central Committee of the Chinese Communist Party (CCP) explicitly promoted legislation for foreign investment. Subsequently, the Sino-Foreign Equity Joint Ventures Law was promulgated in 1979 as the first legislation of the "socialist market economy" (*shehuizhuyi shichang jingji*). Three years later, the 1982 PRC Constitution gave legal recognition to foreign businesses and foreign-invested enterprises.[2]

In this phase, China's regulation of FDI is particularly strict and shows the following characteristics. First, regulators restricted access to foreign capital. The legislation establishes categories for investment (e.g., encouraged, permitted, restricted, prohibited), only some of which were slowly relaxed over time. Moreover, the regulations provide for approval and management of a number of areas, including the capital ratio of the parties involved,[3] and approvals for foreign-invested enterprise contracts and articles of association,[4] among other restrictions.[5] Second, regulators further exercised strict approval for foreign investment. Foreign-invested projects were, for the most part, discouraged, and the approval authority was concentrated at the level of the central government. The process for approval was cumbersome.[6] Third, foreign investment was not granted national treatment. Moreover, there were a number of restrictions placed on the purchase of raw materials as well as on the import and export of products,[7] and,

2 中华人民共和国宪法 (1982年)[1982 PRC Constitution], promulgated by the NPC on Dec. 4, 1982 and effective Dec. 4, 1982, art. 18, https://perma.cc/TK9K-WNMY.

3 关于中外合资经营企业注册资本与投资总额比例的暂行规定 [Interim Previsions on the Ratio of Registered Capital to Total Investment of Sino-Foreign Joint Ventures], issued by the State Administration of Industry and Commerce on March 1, 1987, https://perma.cc/D7N7-75XC.

4 关于严格审核举办中外合资经营企业中方法人资格的通知 [Notice on Strictly Examining the Legal Person Qualifications of the Establishment of Sino-Foreign Joint Ventures], issued by the Ministry of Foreign Economic Relations and Commerce on Sept. 21, 1987, https://perma.cc/DHD8-75UA.

5 中外合资经营企业合营各方出资的若干规定 [Several Provisions on the Capital Contribution of the Parties in a Sino-Foreign Equity Joint Venture], issued by the Ministry of Foreign Trade and Economic Cooperation and the State Administration for Industry and Commerce on Jan. 1, 1988, https://perma.cc/6VV9-JL42.

6 外国（地区）企业在中国境内从事生产经营活动登记管理办法 [Measures for the Registration and Administration of Foreign (Regional) Enterprises Engaged in Production and Business Activities in China], issued by the State Administration for Industry and Commerce on Aug. 15, 1992, https://perma.cc/YX43-YAH4.

7 关于中外合资经营企业外汇收支平衡问题的规定 [Regulations Concerning the Balance of Foreign Exchange Income and Expenditure by Sino-Foreign Joint Equity Ventures], issued by the State Council on Feb. 1, 1986, https://perma.cc/3B5Z-9PPM.

lastly, foreign exchange.[8] Fourth, both the methods to encourage foreign investment and the ultimate destinations were limited. As for methods, the main approach was to provide preferential income tax treatment for foreign-invested enterprises.[9] In terms of the permissible destinations for investment, the PRC government at this stage encouraged foreign investment only in designated locations.[10] In summary, the first phase is one of tight restrictions on amounts, methods, industries, and destinations of foreign investment.

(ii) Phase Two (1992–1999): Economic Efficiency Spurs Legislative Reform

In the second phase, some of the investment rules became more consolidated around the need to increase efficiency which, in turn, generated the need for legislative and regulatory reform. This phase is characterized by a number of features. First, the system for foreign investors to access Chinese markets became more regularized.[11] Whereas the categories for foreign investment were ill-defined in the first phase, in this phase, they became clearer under the Catalogue for the Guidance of Foreign Investment Industries, specifically, its categories of "encouraged," "permitted," "restricted," and "prohibited." Second, the authorities simplified the foreign investment approval system.[12] Third, foreign investments began to receive national treatment, in certain circumstances. Some foreign-invested enterprises even received "super-national treatment"

[8] 中华人民共和国外汇管理暂行条例 [Interim Regulations of the PRC on the Administration of Foreign Exchange], issued by the State Council on March 1, 1981, https://perma.cc/W6US-KFHC.

[9] 关于对中外合资，合作项目征收税问题的通知 [Announcement on Taxation of Joint Ventures and Cooperative Operations with Chinese and Foreign Investment], issued by the State Council on Sept. 21, 1982, https://perma.cc/Y6Y6-GW8E.

[10] 关于经济特区和沿海十四个港口城市减征、免征企业所得税和工商统一税的暂行规定 [Interim Provisions on the Reduction and Exemption of Corporate Income Tax and Consolidated Industrial and Commercial Tax in Special Economic Zones and 14 Coastal Port Cities], issued by the State Council on Dec. 1, 1984, https://perma.cc/X4SC-ZDAF.

[11] 指导外商投资方向暂行规定 [Interim Provisions on Guiding the Direction of Foreign Investment], issued by the NDRC, National Economic and Trade Commission and the Ministry of Civil Affairs on June 20, 1995, https://perma.cc/K7RH-5MG2.

[12] 关于扩大内地省、自治区、计划单列市和国务院有关部门等单位吸收外商直接投资项目审批权限的通知 [Notice on Expanding the Examination and Approval Authority of Inland Provinces, Autonomous Regions, Cities with Separate Plans, and Relevant Departments of the State Council to Absorb Foreign Direct Investment Projects, promulgated by the State Council on Aug. 22, 1996, https://perma.cc/53ZG-X9QR.

(*chaoguo minteyu*). For instance, the PRC Foreign-Invested Enterprise and Foreign Enterprise Income Tax Law grants foreign-invested enterprises the "two exemptions and three reductions" tax preference, and further stipulates that local governments can exempt or reduce local income tax.[13] Fourth, authorities expanded both the scope of foreign investment and the permissible destinations. An example of the former is the inclusion of "build-operate-transfer" projects within the investment regime[14] and the latter widened the type of destinations for foreign investment to include inland areas (Guojia tongji ju, 2002). In short, the second phase began greater liberalization but this process would not fully gain momentum until the WTO accession.

(iii) *Phase Three (2000–2008): Internationalization through WTO Accession*

In advance of its accession to the WTO in 2001, China began to reform its legislative and regulatory framework for FDI on a large scale in conformance with WTO expectations, and in particular, sought to meet the goals of both efficiency and economic fairness. The package agreement of the WTO had a significant influence on the reform of Chinese legislation, that is, the overall alignment of Chinese law with international norms, even if there was regulatory discoordination between different levels of government administration (Tan, 2000). According to the internal documents of the Working Party on the Accession of China, by November 9, 2000, the PRC government revised some 36 laws and regulations and 120 administrative rules for purposes of WTO compliance, including such statutes as the Contract Law of the PRC, Law of the PRC on Chinese-Foreign Equity Joint Ventures, and Law of the PRC on Chinese-Foreign Contractual Joint Ventures (Working Party on the Accession of China, 2000).

The changes to the investment regime were extensive. First, foreign investment access was expanded across industries, methods, and destinations. The Catalogue for the Guidance of Foreign Investment Industries

13 中华人民共和国外商投资企业和外国企业所得税法 [PRC Foreign-Invested Enterprises and Foreign Enterprises Income Tax Law], promulgated by the President of the PRC on Apr. 9, 1991 and effective on July 1, 1991, arts. 8 and 9, https://perma.cc/5PFE-NBUX.

14 关于以BOT方式吸引外商投资有关问题的通知 [Circular Concerning Integrating Investment by Means of BOT], issued by the Ministry of Foreign Trade and Economic Cooperation on Jan. 16, 1995, https://perma.cc/TR3F-RCGF.

was revised three times during this period to narrow the restricted and prohibited categories. Concurrently, separate policies were formulated for many industries to further expand opportunities for foreign investment, including in the financial, transportation, real estate, and entertainment industries.[15] Second, legislative reform began focusing on fair value. In 2004, the State Council promulgated the "Decision on the Reform of the Investment System" which stated that a fair and orderly competitive market environment promotes both investment efficiency and overall social progress.[16] Based on this direction, reforms were initiated in a number of areas. For instance, the 2007 Corporate Income Tax Law unified the income tax of domestic and foreign companies and abolished the "super national treatment" of some foreign-invested companies.[17] Additionally, the Anti-Monopoly Law provided a basis for regulating foreign monopolies and mergers and acquisitions.[18] Third, during this period, China's policy orientation shifted from "encouraging foreign investment" to "relying on foreign investment." This trend is illustrated in the use of foreign capital to reorganize SOEs and foreign mergers and acquisitions.[19]

(iv) Phase Four (2009–2014): Balancing Internationalization and National Security

The WTO accession continued to have transformative effects on the Chinese regulatory regime for FDI well beyond the third phase, and while efficiency continued to drive much of the reform, this requirement was balanced with additional concerns, including national security. The 2008 financial crisis increased international pressure on China to adapt its regulatory structure to resist exogenous shocks while continuing to

15 中华人民共和国外资金融机构管理条例 [Regulations of the PRC on the Administration of Foreign-Funded Financial Institutions], issued by the State Council on Dec. 1, 2001 and effective Feb. 1, 2002, https://perma.cc/MSF7-CBQA.

16 关于投资体制改革的决定 ([2004] 20 hao) [Decision on the Reform of the Investment System], issued by the State Council in 2004 (no. 20), https://perma.cc/8UMB-LFD4.

17 中华人民共和国企业所得税法 [PRC Corporate Income Tax Law], promulgated by the NPC on March 16, 2007, https://perma.cc/XXB5-9NL2.

18 中华人民共和国反垄断法 [PRC Anti-Monopoly Law], promulgated by the NPC on Aug. 30, 2007 and effective Aug. 1, 2008, https://perma.cc/XM2N-K4S6.

19 利用外资改组国有企业暂行规定 [Interim Provisions on the Reorganization of State-Owned Enterprises with Foreign Capital], jointly issued by State Economic and Trade Commission, Ministry of Finance, State Administration for Industry and Commerce, and State Administration of Foreign Exchange on the on Jan. 1, 2003, https://perma.cc/FXL9-EN39.

benefit from FDI. Hence, on the one hand, foreign investment regulations maintained the goal of pursuing efficiency.[20] As part of this process, the approval system was further simplified to delegate approval to lower-level administrative levels.[21]

On the other hand, whereas the WTO era ushered in the notion of "reliance" on foreign investment, the worldwide financial meltdown of 2008 tempered this view. National security and economic sovereignty became important counter-weights to foreign investment dependence. Consequently, the Catalogue for the Guidance of Foreign Investment Industries was revised successively to incorporate national security, and a raft of regulations was issued to introduce greater oversight into the system of mergers and acquisitions.

(v) *Phase Five (2015-present): Embracing "Quality" FDI*

In the most recent phase, the government has sought to increase openness to FDI while also improving the overall quality of FDI. In 2015, the Central Committee of the CCP and the State Council jointly issued the "Certain Opinions on Building a New System of Open Economy" which required that while China should expand market access in the service industry and further open up manufacturing, it should improve the quality of foreign investment.[22] This latter requirement led to adding a negative list to pre-access national treatment.

The NPC promulgated the Foreign Investment Law in 2019 which introduced major changes to unify the regimes for regulating domestic and foreign investment.[23] Specifically, the Foreign Investment Law abolished the trinity of WFOEs, equity JVs, and cooperative JVs. In their place, the new law permits investment from Chinese or foreign parties without the target company needing to change its legal form. Henceforth, corporate form and governance are determined by the Chinese company law, which

20 关于进一步做好利用外资工作的若干意见 [Certain Opinions on Optimizing the Utilization of Foreign Capital], issued by the State Council on Apr. 6, 2010, https://perma.cc/L8MA-K88K.

21 关于做好外商投资项目下方核准权限工作的通知 [Notice on Optimizing the Decentralization of the Approval Authority for Foreign-Invested Projects], issued by the NDRC on May 4, 2010, https://perma.cc/R6A6-5382.

22 关于建构开放性经济新体制的若干意见 Guanyu jiangou kaifang xing jingji xin tizhi de ruogan yijian [Certain Opinions on Building a New System of Open Economy], jointly issued by the Central Committee of the CCP and the State Council on May 5, 2015, https://perma.cc/82CW-LPLG.

23 *See* Foreign Investment Law *above* note 1.

relaxed some of the requirements foreign investors faced under the previous arrangement. Another purpose of the Foreign Investment Law was to further establish the national security review system for foreign investment. The most recent phase has also seen an encouragement of "quality" investment, particularly in the fields of science and technology. For example, the Foreign Investment Law encourages technical cooperation and includes the protection of IP rights.[24]

In summary, this brief chronology of the reform of the legislative and regulatory framework for FDI shows how it has shifted over time from one that was initially restrictive to one that encouraged low-level foreign investment, without a screening mechanism, to the current phase that encourages quality investment, albeit with a screening mechanism in place. These changes over time reflect the general priorities of national development. Specifically, the PRC government viewed the WTO accession as a catalyst for creating a system that was more conducive to attracting FDI. Yet this need has been counter-balanced, over time, with the priority on safeguarding national security.

IV China's Regulation of ODI

Compared with China's legal and regulatory system for governing FDI, which has evolved from more restrictive to more lenient, the legal and regulatory system for ODI has shifted from one of greater lenience to more regulatory control. By control, we mean regulatory tightening; the control does not mean prohibition. Further, control in this sense is a response to a variety of chronic investment failures from speculative investing in luxury sectors in developed economies to high-risk investments in low-income states. In assessing the underlying principles of the ODI regime, one difference with the FDI regime is that the former prioritizes mitigating risks that could harm the national interest.[25] Chinese investors have incurred losses as a result of failed investments, and especially when the investments are state-owned, they potentially endanger state interests abroad.

In addition, poorly governed Chinese investments also generated negative externalities for host states. Whereas foreign investors in

[24] *See* Foreign Investment Law *above* note 1, art. 22(2).

[25] 国家发展改革委关于发布境外投资敏感行业目录(2018年版)的通知 (2018 Edition) [Notice of the National Development and Reform Commission on Issuing the Catalogue of Sensitive Industries for Overseas Investment] No. 251, promulgated Jan. 31, 2018 and effective March 1, 2018, https://perma.cc/PA5Z-7J6L.

China must comply with Chinese environmental and social governance laws, the Chinese ODI regime does not have the corresponding safeguards. The lack of such compliance measures has caused human rights and environmental harm in a number of countries, particularly those with nascent legal systems. We argue the reason for the ODI regime's change from lenient to strict is that, unlike the case of FDI, there was no external-facing process, such as the WTO accession, which reformed domestic priorities in line with international ones, specifically to balance home and host state interests in the course of cross-border capital outflows.

Many of the regulators for ODI are the same for FDI. Specifically, the administrative management of ODI is led mainly by the NDRC and MOFCOM. These entities often issue joint rules, including departmental regulations and other normative documents. However, additional departments may also participate in the drafting and issuance of these rules, including the Foreign Exchange Administration, People's Bank of China, State-Owned Assets Supervision and Administration Commission (SASAC), Ministry of Finance, and Ministry of Foreign Affairs. One result of this pattern of multiple departments and administrators shaping the regulatory environment is inconsistency in rule design and enforcement as well as asymmetrical powers between departments. Likewise, given that each department issues rules within its purview (and sometimes jointly), there is no unified law regulating ODI. Moreover, policies that follow from scattered regulations and multiple and overlapping authorities lack clarity, stability, and rigor. In short, there was no WTO-centralizing force which could realign the authorities and coordinate their normative effects.

The current regulatory system for ODI can be divided into two historical phases. Phase one (1999–2015) was the formative period of China's "going out" (*zouchuqu*) strategy and phase two (2015–present) features the "Belt and Road Initiative" (BRI). The phases show, at a general level, a shift from a more permissive and decentralized regime that encouraged ODI to one that is characterized by a more restrictive "encouragement catalogue and negative list" (*guli mulu fumian qingdan*).

(i) Phase One (1999–2015): The Formative Period of China's "Going Out" Strategy

After the Asian financial crisis of 1997, the Chinese government implemented a strategy to expand exports. The "going out" strategy entered the national development plan in the Tenth Five-Year Plan for National Economic and Social Development, issued in 2000.[26] Six years later, the State Council adopted the Opinions on Encouraging and Regulating Foreign Investment and Cooperation among Chinese Enterprises.[27] During this period, the government promoted dual-direction development, namely, that of "going out" and also "attracting in [FDI]" ([张建平] and [刘恒], 2019).

The regulatory framework for ODI during this period was formulated chiefly by the NDRC and MOFCOM, reflecting their status as the leading twin ministries. The overall trend of the regulation was a process of gradual simplification for the administrative procedure for ODI. The NDRC's regulations for ODI underwent two important changes. The first change occurred in 2004, under the Interim Measures for the Administration of Approval of Overseas Investment Projects, which reflected a shift from an audit to an approval (filing) system for Chinese enterprises engaged in ODI.[28] Subsequent normative documents further refined this system, including distinguishing those enterprises that rely on government funding as well as identifying approval systems for "special" or "sensitive" projects.[29] The second change occurred in 2014 when the NDRC established a "filing-based and approval-based" project management system, replacing the earlier 2004 decree. This regulation further specified two categories of "sensitive" projects, based on investment destination and industry, which required approval by the NDRC regardless of the investment amount.[30] The NDRC's regulatory changes in 2004 and 2014 are roughly mirrored by those of MOFCOM which

[26] 关于制定国民经济和社会发展第十个五年计划的建议 [The Formulation of Proposals for the Tenth Five-Year Plan for the National Economy and Social Development], issued by the Central Committee of the CCP on Oct. 11, 2000, https://perma.cc/Z8GD-DEMX.

[27] 关于鼓励和规范我国企业对外投资合作的意见 [Opinions on Encouraging and Regulating Foreign Investment and Cooperation among Chinese Enterprises], issued by the State Council on Oct. 25, 2006, https://perma.cc/Z7FS-PBNH.

[28] 境外投资项目核准暂行管理办法 (21 号令) [Interim Measures for the Administration of Approval of Overseas Investment Projects (Decree No. 21)], issued by the NDRC on Oct. 9, 2004, www.ndrc.gov.cn/xxgk/zcfb/fzggwl/200510/t20051010_960640.html?code=&state=123.

[29] 关于做好境外投资项目下放核准权限工作的通知 [Notice on Optimizing Decentralization of the Approval Authority in Overseas Investment Projects], issued by the NDRC on Feb. 14, 2011 (hereinafter, "Notice on Optimizing Decentralization"), https://perma.cc/QYU3-99RR.

[30] 境外投资项目核准和备案管理办法 (9 号令) [Administrative Measures for the Approval and Filing of Overseas Investment Projects) (Decree No. 9)], issued by the NDRC on Apr. 8, 2014 (hereinafter, "Decree No. 9"), https://perma.cc/T73A-4YXW.

also decentralized the approval authority and simplified the approval process for ODI.[31] In short, this early phase is characterized by a generally lenient approach to approval for ODI projects.

(ii) Phase Two (2015-Present): The BRI

In March 2015, three Chinese government ministries jointly issued the "Vision and Actions on Jointly Building Silk Road Economic Belt and the Twenty-First Century Maritime Silk Road" (hereinafter, "Vision and Actions"), inaugurating the BRI.[32] Since then, China's ODI administration and sectoral legislation have been closely tied to the BRI. The promotion of the BRI led to a peak in Chinese ODI and equity investment in 2016, an increase of 44 per cent from the year before (Bank, 2021). However, massive Chinese ODI in real estate, luxury hotels, sports and entertainment, and related industries not only failed to drive domestic economic development but also led to capital outflows not tied to state-led strategies, ultimately triggering the Chinese government's concerns about financial security and the safety of state-owned assets.

Subsequent normative documents built upon the Vision and Actions which is mainly an agenda-framing document. Specifically, guidance from the ministries adjusted the "filing and approval" regulatory approach to one based on "encouraging development" alongside a negative list.[33] In particular, ODI was divided into the following categories: encouraged, restricted, and prohibited. NDRC decrees for their part defined eight categories of ODI, abolished the previous reporting system, and narrowed the scope of projects that can be approved.[34] These decrees also introduced a post-event reporting system that specifies that a report must be submitted within five days of a material adverse circumstance in

31 *See e.g.*, 境外投资管理办法(令第五号) [Measures for the Administration of Overseas Investment) (Decree No. 5)], issued by MOFCOM on March 16, 2009, https://perma.cc/733Z-ZJ9M.

32 Vision and Actions on Jointly Building Silk Road Economic Belt and the Twenty-First Century Maritime Silk Road, issued by the NDRC, Ministry of Foreign Affairs, and MOFCOM in March 2015, https://perma.cc/Q37M-RYZN.

33 关于进一步引导和规范境外投资方向指导意见的通知 (国办发(2017)74 号) [Notice of Guiding Opinions Regarding Further Guidance and Regulation of the Direction of Overseas Investment (State Council issued (2017) No. 74), issued by the General Office of the State Council, MOFCOM, NDRC, and Ministry of Foreign Affairs on Aug. 4, 2017, https://perma.cc/C8EW-RVPW.

34 *See above* Overseas Investment Measures note 1.

an investment project (e.g., significant causalities among expatriates, significant loss of assets abroad, or damage to the diplomatic relations with the host state).[35] The NDRC further formulated the Catalogue of Sensitive Sectors for Overseas Investment in 2018 which requires approval.[36] The NDRC has, during this phase, consolidated its authority over ODI, and requires that overseas investment by domestic entities, whether financial or non-financial, direct or indirect, be uniformly included in the scope of filing and approval by the NDRC.

MOFCOM also assumed greater authority over ODI under the new direction of this second phase. MOFCOM, together with other ministries, jointly issued new measures for the filing and approval of ODI projects.[37] These measures standardized the management of ODI by requiring a summary report of approval, supervision during and after the project, and a model for ODI that was characterized by "encouraging development plus negative list."[38] The summary report of approval must include *inter alia* information pertaining to any outbound investment and merger and acquisition, the progress of ODI projects, any problems encountered including compliance issues with local law and regulations, the protection of the environment, and the protection of employees' rights.[39] Additionally, any adverse event or security incident (including security accidents, terrorist attacks, and kidnappings, social security mass incidents, major negative public opinion reports, etc.) must be reported to the relevant competent department which then informs MOFCOM.[40]

Is it significant that the NDRC was not an issuing department for the measures led by MOFCOM? While the regulatory regime for FDI also demonstrates elements of inter-agency competition, the discoordination is greater in the ODI regime. The reason for this is not just the comparatively short period of evolution for the ODI regime but also that there

[35] Id.

[36] 境外投资铭感行业目录 [Catalogue of Sensitive Sectors for Overseas Investment], issued by the NDRC in Jan. 2018, https://perma.cc/V7US-6KST.

[37] 对外投资备案（核准）报告暂行办法 (商合发 [2018] 24 号) [Interim Measures for Foreign Investment Filing (Approval) Reports (issued by MOFCOM and cooperating ministries [2018] no. 24)], issued by MOFCOM, PBC, SASAC, China Banking Regulatory Commission (CRBC), China Securities Regulatory Commission (CSRC), China Insurance Regulatory Commission (CIRC), and Foreign Exchange Bureau (FEB), on Jan. 25, 2018, https://perma.cc/3ZNP-FNE2.

[38] Id.

[39] Id.

[40] Id.

was no external pressure put on the various departments and ministries to achieve greater coordination as was the case with the WTO accession. In the next section, we examine the extent to which the two regimes have integrated concerns about environmental impact.

V A Focus on Environmental Impact

China's regulation of the environmental impact of FDI is much more developed than its environmental regulation of ODI, and while this difference can be explained, in part, by the long history of FDI in China, we argue that because regulation of the environmental impact of FDI grew out of a policy environment wherein China was integrating its national development plan into the global economy through multilateralism, this framework has led to a more robust result than regulation of the environmental impact of ODI. In this section, we briefly review the regulation of the environmental impact of FDI and then the regulation of the environmental impact of ODI to contrast the two regimes. We find that whereas the former suffers from a number of shortcomings, it nonetheless has gained some degree of traction in shaping foreign-invested enterprises conducting business in China. In contrast, the regime for ODI features far more severe "bugs," including a fundamental structural flaw: the limited jurisdiction of the Ministry of Ecology and Environment (MEE).

(i) Regulation of the Environmental Impact of FDI

Whereas the regulation of the environmental impact of FDI has had a long gestation period, China's trade obligations have further incentivized environmental considerations in the course of planning foreign-invested projects. In the early period of the "opening and reform," regulations often did not explicitly state whether they applied to FDI as the operative concept at the time was territoriality, that is, as long as a project was undertaken within the PRC – regardless of the source of the capital (domestic or foreign) – then the environmental rules applied.[41] The 1995 Catalogue for Guidance of Foreign Investment Industries further provided more detailed provisions for defining pollution-intensive industries and categories them accordingly (Zeng and Eastin, 2011, 58).

[41] *See e.g.*, 建设项目环境保护管理条例 [Regulations on the Environmental Protection Management of Construction Projects], issued by the State Council on Nov. 29, 1998, art. 2, https://perma.cc/QLX4-CBLA.

Consistent with phase three identified above (2000–2008), during the accession period, China adopted a number of laws including the Environmental Impact Assessment Law (hereinafter, "EIA Law"), passed in 2002, which further regulated FDI.[42] The EIA Law was notable, in particular, for encouraging the public to participate in EIA.[43] Scholars have criticized the EIA Law for poor implementation, however, and have noted the disconnection between the EIA Law and China's trade regime (Zhao, 2007, 80). In fact, progress made in China's domestic environmental governance since the EIA Law was passed has been chiefly due to domestic reasons, namely, the severity of industrial pollution, the growth of political will and pressure from political leadership, and the emergence of China's environmental movement (Economy, 2004, 62–75; Mertha, 2008, 6–12; Stern, 2013, 25–27).

While reforms, especially those across legal domains such as environmental protection and trade, do not unfold in a unilinear manner, in recent years, the EIA system has become much more stringent through streamlined administration, delegation of powers, and improved service (Yang, 2020, 890–891). The reform of the EIA occurred hand-in-hand with the establishment of the MEE, which replaced the Ministry of Environmental Protection, in 2018. The MEE differs from its predecessors in that it consolidates powers that were previously scattered throughout a number of different regulatory bodies (Yang, 2020, 890). The consolidation of authority under the MEE has been part of an increasing effort to refine the regulation of the environmental impact of investment (Karplus et al., 2021, 315–316), and, yet, as we argue below, there is still room for improvement.

(ii) Regulation of the Environmental Impact of ODI

China's ODI regime is designed with the objectives of serving the BRI and safeguarding the safety of state-owned assets and their financial security. The environmental and social impact of offshore projects has not been a core concern of the Chinese government. As such, there is no legislation with enforcement effect to screen the environmental and social impact of overseas investment projects. Institutionally, the MEE, the main

[42] 中华人民共和国环境影响评价法 [PRC Environmental Impact Assessment Law], promulgated by the NPC on Oct. 28, 2002, and as amended Dec. 29, 2018, https://perma.cc/BG7Q-GPRC.

[43] Id., art. 5.

administrative agency in charge of environmental affairs in China, also does not have the mandate to regulate overseas projects.

There is no doubt that, rhetorically, there is a degree of BRI greenwashing. The Vision and Actions, for example, state the need to "highlight the concept of ecological civilization in investment and trade, strengthen cooperation on ecological environment, biodiversity, and climate change, and build a green Silk Road."[44] Accordingly, the MEE, either alone or jointly with other ministries, has issued a number of policies related to the environmental protection of overseas investments. However, common features of these policies are they are voluntary, not legally binding, and as such, lack enforceability (Boer, 2019; Coenen et al., 2020). Examples of these normative documents include the following: the CBRC's Green Credit Guidelines of 2012,[45] the Environmental Protection Guidelines for Foreign Investment and Cooperation of 2013,[46] the Guiding Opinions on Promoting the Construction of the Green "BRI" of 2017,[47] the "BRI" Ecological and Environmental Protection Plan of 2017,[48] the Guidelines for Green Development of Foreign Investment Cooperation of 2021,[49] and the Ecological and Environmental Protection Guidelines for Overseas Investment Cooperation Construction Projects of 2022.[50]

In summary, while these guidelines and codes of conduct signal an awareness for including environmental impact in ODI planning, they mostly fall short in affecting corporate governance. It should be noted

[44] *See above* note 32.

[45] 关于印发绿色信贷指导的通知 (CBRC (2012) 4 号) (Notice on the Issuance of Green Credit Guidelines (CRBC (2012) No. 4)), issued by the CBRC on Jan. 29, 2012, https://perma.cc/8JBH-HXXE.

[46] 对外投资合作环境保护指南 (商合发 [2013] 74 号) [Environmental Protection Guidelines for Foreign Investment and Cooperation (MOFCOM and cooperating ministries issued [2013] No. 74)], jointly issued by MOFCOM and MEE on Feb. 18, 2013, https://perma.cc/7NST-6VYY.

[47] 关于推进绿色"一带一路"建设的指导意见 [Guiding Opinions on Promoting the Construction of the Green "BRI"], jointly issued by MEE, Ministry of Foreign Affairs, NDRC, MOFCOM on May 8, 2017, https://perma.cc/XW88-BU2V.

[48] "一带一路" 生态环境保护合作规划 [The "BRI" Ecological and Environmental Protection Plan], jointly issued by MEE on May 15, 2017, https://perma.cc/DEY3-52JF.

[49] 对外投资合作绿色发展工作指引 [Guidelines for Green Development of Foreign Investment Cooperation], jointly issued by MOFCOM and MEE on July 16, 2021, https://perma.cc/T8ZW-GEK2.

[50] 对外投资合作建设项目生态环境保护指南 [the Ecological and Environmental Protection Guidelines for Overseas Investment Cooperation Construction Projects], jointly issued by the MEE and MOFCOM on Jan. 5, 2022, https://perma.cc/9UY7-H59Q.

that not only Chinese ministries but also private organizations including chambers of commerce have also issued such soft law sources. For example, the China Chamber of Commerce of Metals, Minerals & Chemicals Importers & Exporters has developed industry guidelines related to environmental protection for ODI in the mining industry.[51] The "Green Investment Principles [for the BRI]" which was jointly issued by the Green Finance Committee and the City of London Corporations' Green Finance Initiative in 2018.[52] Whereas some 37 financial institutions have signed on as of 2020, it is wholly voluntary. Strikingly, the Supreme People's Court (SPC) has cited the Green Investment Principles in its own opinions, reflecting that the SPC has no national legislation to cite or enforce and instead must cite industry guidelines.[53]

In contrast, among the legally binding regulations on overseas investment, there are few provisions for environmental and social impact assessment requirements. One exception is transboundary water resource development and use projects which are classified as sensitive by both the NDRC and MOFCOM, requiring approval rather than filing.[54] It is likely that the reason why transboundary water resource projects are listed as sensitive is the Myitsone Dam project in Myanmar. The Myitsone project, the world's fifteenth largest hydropower plant, in which the China Power Investment Group began investing in 2006, was halted by the Myanmar government in 2011 due to opposition from the local population (Bian, 2018, 236–237). However, neither the NDRC nor MOFCOM requires environmental impact assessments for sensitive projects. Transboundary water resource projects are required to be registered for the purpose of protecting the security of Chinese overseas investment and risk mitigation, rather than on the basis of environmental impact considerations.

Lastly and related, in terms of both legislation and enforcing institutions, Chinese authorities are limited to governing environmental issues only within the PRC and not in the course of overseas projects. Both the

51 中国对外矿业投资社会责任指引 [China's Social Responsibility Guidelines for Foreign Mining Investments], issued by the China Chamber of Commerce of Metals, Minerals & Chemicals Importers & Exporters in 2017, https://perma.cc/AS9E-A9VZ.

52 Green Investment Principles, https://perma.cc/9Z8X-JVC4.

53 关于人民法院进一步为"一带一路"建设提供司法服务和保障的意见 (法发 (2019) 29 号) [Opinion on Providing Judicial Services and Guarantees for the BRI (SPC issued (2019) No. 29)], issued by the SPC on Dec. 27, 2019, art. 11, https://perma.cc/RBE3-N7XC.

54 *See e.g.*, Notice on Optimizing Decentralization *above* note 29.

Environmental Protection Law and the EIA Law apply to matters only within the PRC.[55] Likewise, whereas both the NDRC and MOFCOM have responsibilities for regulating overseas investment projects,[56] the MEE has no such responsibility and thus no authority to regulate environmental concerns in projects abroad. Thus, there are hard limits placed on both the reach of regulators and the legislative basis upon which regulators, namely, the MEE, could govern the environmental impact of ODI. The overall picture is that China is an outlier in a growing trend of states' regulation of their overseas investments in terms of their impacts on host states' environments and social governance, including human rights.[57]

VI Implications

Comparing the reform trajectories of the FDI and ODI regimes has a number of implications for the study of Chinese domestic legal reform, its outward-facing legal obligations, and the role of regulators in coordinating the foregoing. Scholars have shown how the WTO accession process required Chinese regulators, policy makers, and academics to harmonize the WTO obligations with China's national development plans (Gao, 2021; Shaffer, 2021). One result is a degree of coordination between ministries, departments, and administrative units that otherwise may not exist. The ODI regime presents in many ways the counterfactual: there was no similar multilateral framework through which the Chinese regulators learned to balance the needs of China's national development with its obligations to host states. The result is discoordination and inefficiency that affects Chinese investors and host state alike.

This discoordination has specifically affected projects under the mantle of the BRI. As Min Ye (2020) has shown, the BRI was itself, in part, a response to state fragmentation. When Xi Jinping announced the BRI

[55] 中华人民共和国环境保护法 [Environmental Protection Law of the PRC], promulgated by the NPC on Apr. 24, 2014 and effective Jan. 1, 2015; art. 3, https://perma.cc/7JS4-Q3N7; EIA Law *above* note 42, art 3.

[56] 国务院机构改革方案 [State Council Institutional Reform Plan], issued by the Two Sessions of the NPC and CPPCC on March 17, 2018, https://perma.cc/QH72-N9H2.

[57] *See e.g.*, the US Magnitsky Act (2012), the UK Modern Slavery Act (2015), the French Corporate Duty of Vigilance Law (2017), the German Supply Chain Due Diligence Act (effective 2023), the UK Due Diligence Bill proposal, Canada's proposed Corporate Respect for Human Rights and the Environment, and other European supply chain and due diligence laws.

in 2013, it was a "whole-of-government and whole-of-society" call to implement projects that would support the BRI. Yet nearly a decade into the BRI, it is clear that inter-agency coordination has not been attained through internal efforts alone (Hale et al., 2020). To date, there has been no external framework through which BRI-related investment can undergo the type of institutional learning curve which Chinese regulators experienced through the WTO accession. Famously, proposals to conclude a multilateral investment treaty within the Organization for Economic Cooperation and Development (OECD) failed in 1998 due to civil society groups' opposition (Joseph, 2013, 843).[58] China's investment strategy remains reliant on piecemeal bilateral investment treaties, many of which are dated (Chaisse and Kirkwood, 2020). Inter- and intra-sectoral learning among enterprises remains nascent, compliance with local law remains a perennial problem, and, as a result, disputes arise that are addressed through international commercial arbitration, political intervention, or, increasingly, host state courts (Erie, 2021).

Perhaps ironically given the history of the failed OECD multilateral investment treaty, it is, in many cases, civil society groups in host states that are the source of Chinese enterprises' learning about local law, including the environmental and social impact of investment through protest and litigation (see e.g., Reporters, 2017; Zhongguo lüfahui [China Greenification Society], 2019). Certainly, much of the responsibility for protecting the environment of host states falls on local regulators, and not Chinese ones, given that most Chinese investors incorporate companies under local law. Yet for the BRI-like projects to truly promote sustainable development, Chinese regulators, and, specifically, the MEE, can also provide greater guidance for outbound investment, but only if an enforceable ODI law granted them such authority. Indeed, the Fourteenth Five-Year Plan (2021–2025) states the government will "promote ODI legislation."[59] Although it lacks details, it is hoped that the legislation would regulate highly polluted and carbon-intensive ODI projects and grant the MEE authority to screen the environmental,

[58] There are, of course, other examples, such as the Final Act of the UN Conference on Trade and Employment, the Havana Charter for an International Trade Organization, November 21, 1947 E/CONF/278; the failed 1948 effort of the International Chamber of Commerce, and others (Miles, 2013, 82).

[59] 中华人民共和国国民经济和社会发展第十四个五年规划和2035年远景目标纲要 [The Fourteenth Five-Year Plan for National Economic and Social Responsibility of the PRC and the Outline of Long-Term Goals for 2035], issued by the Two Sessions of the NPC and CPPCC on March 13, 2021, https://perma.cc/M4PT-XYEY.

climate, and social impact of ODI projects in order to assure China's climate pledge of carbon neutrality by 2060. While we applaud the inclusion of this ODI law in the future plan, along with communities in host states, we look forward to its practical implementation.

References

[张建平], Zhang Jianping, and Liu Heng [刘恒]. 2019. "Gaige kaifang 40 nian: "yinjinlai" yu "zouchuqu" [40 Years of Opening and Reform: "Attracting In" and "Going Out"." Xian [Pioneer]. Accessed November 5. www.qstheory.cn/llqikan/2019-03/09/c_1124213820.htm.

Bank, The World. 2021. 'Foreign direct investment, net outflows (BoP, current US$) – China.' Accessed November 5 2021. https://data.worldbank.org/indicator/BM.KLT.DINV.CD.WD?end=2019&locations=CN&start=1979&view=chart.

Bath, Vivienne. 2011. 'The quandary for Chinese regulators: controlling the flow of investment into and out of China.' In Vivienne Bath and Luke Nottage (eds.), *Foreign Investment and Dispute Resolution Law and Practice in Asia*, pp. 68–89. New York: Routledge.

Berger, Axel. This volume. 'China's international investment agreement policy; From rule-taker to rule-maker.' In Henry Gao, Damian Raess and Ka Zeng (eds.), *China and the WTO: A Twenty-Year Assessment*. Cambridge: Cambridge University Press.

Bian, Yongmin. 2018. 'The role of environmental impact assessment in the governance of the Nu-Salween River: a comparative study of the Chinese and Myanmar Approaches.' In Yun Zhao (ed.), *International Governance and the Rule of Law in China Under the Belt and Road Initiative*, pp. 218–42. Cambridge: Cambridge University Press.

Boer, Ben. 2019. 'Greening China's belt and road: challenges for environmental law.' *Sydney Law School Research Paper*.

Chaisse, Julien, and Jamieson Kirkwood. 2020. 'Chinese puzzle: anatomy of the (invisible) belt and road investment treaty.' *Journal of International Economic Law* 23 (1):245–69.

Chi, Manjiao. This volume. 'China and investor-state dispute settlement: experiences and prospects.' In Henry Gao, Damian Raess and Ka Zeng (eds.), *China and the WTO: A Twenty-Year Assessment*. Cambridge: Cambridge University Press.

Coenen, Johanna, Simon Bager, Patrick Meyfroidt, Jens Newig, and Edward Challies. 2020. 'Environmental governance of China's belt and road initiative.' *Environmental Policy and Governance* 31(1):3–17.

Cottier, Thomas. This volume. 'Technology diffusion in the triangle of China, the West and developing countries: the contribution of common concern of humankind.' In Henry Gao, Damian Raess and Ka Zeng (eds.), *China and the WTO: A Twenty-Year Assessment*. Cambridge: Cambridge University Press.

Economy, Elizabeth. 2004. *The River Runs Black: The Environmental Challenge to China's Future*. Ithaca: Cornell University Press.

Erie, Matthew S. 2021. 'Chinese law and development.' *Harvard International Law Journal* 62: 51–115.

Ferchen, Matt. 2016. *China, Economic Development, and Global Security: Bridging the Gap*. Beijing: Carnegie-Tsinghua Center for Global Policy.

Foot, Rosemary, ed. 2013. *China Across the Divide: The Domestic and Global in Politics and Society*. Oxford: Oxford University Press.

Gao, Henry. 2021. 'WTO reform and China: defining or defiling the multilateral trading system?' *Harvard International Law Journal* 62:1–39.

Guojia tongji ju, [National Bureau of Statistics]. 2002. "Zhi'er: Duiwai kaifang mai xiang xin jieduan [Second: Opening to the outside world is entering a new stage]." National Bureau of Statistics. Accessed Oct. 26. www.stats.gov.cn/ztjc/ztfx/yjsld/200209/t20020929_36047.html.

Hale, Thomas, Chuyu Liu, and Johannese Urpelainen. 2020. Belt and road decision-making in China and recipient countries: how and to what extent does sustainability matter? ISEP, BSG, ClimateWorks Foundation.

Hsieh, Pasha L. 2010. 'China's development of international economic law and WTO legal capacity building.' *Journal of International Economic Law* 13 (4):997–1036.

Ji, Wenhua, and Cui Huang. 2011. 'China's experience in dealing with WTO dispute settlement: a Chinese perspective.' *Journal of World Trade* 45(1):1–37.

Jones, Lee, and Shahar Hameiri. 2021. *Fractured China: How State Transformation Is Shaping China's Rise*. Cambridge: Cambridge University Press.

Joseph, Sarah. 2013. 'Trade law and investment law.' In Dinah Shelton (ed.), *The Oxford Handbook of International Human Rights Law*, pp. 841–70. Oxford: Oxford University Press.

Karplus, Valerie J., Junjie Zhang, and Jinhua Zhao. 2021. 'Navigating and evaluating the labyrinth of environmental regulation in China.' *Review of Environmental Economics and Policy* 15(2):300–22.

Kim, Icksoo. 2002. 'Accession into the WTO: external pressure for internal reforms in China.' *Journal of Contemporary China* 11(32):433–59.

Lieberthal, Kenneth. 1992. 'The fragmented authoritarianism model and its limitations.' In K. Lieberthal and David M. Lampton (eds.), *Bureaucracy, Politics, and Decision Making in Post-Mao China*, pp. 1–30. Berkeley: University of California Press.

Mertha, Andrew. 2008. *China's Water Warriors: Citizen Action and Policy Change*. Ithaca: Cornell University Press.

Miles, Kate. 2013. *The Origins of International Investment Law: Empire, Environment and the Safeguarding of Capital*. Cambridge: Cambridge University Press.

Qin, Julia Ya. 2007. 'Trade, investment and beyond: the impact of WTO Accession on China's legal system.' *The China Quarterly* 191:720–41.

Reporters, FMT. 2017. 'Environmental groups call for moratorium on ECRL.' *Free Malaysia Today*. Accessed July 30, 2018.

Shaffer, Gregory. 2021. *Emerging Powers and the World Trading System: The Past and Future of International Economic Law*. Cambridge: Cambridge University Press.
Shaffer, Gregory, and Henry S. Gao. 2017. 'China's rise: how it took on the U.S. at the WTO.' *University of Illinois Law Review* 1:115–84.
Shue, Vivienne. 2018. 'Party-State, nation, empire: rethinking the Grammar of Chinese governance.' *Journal of Chinese Governance* 3(1):268–91.
Stern, Rachel E. 2013. *Environmental Litigation in China: A Study in Political Ambivalence*. Cambridge: Cambridge University Press.
Tan, Yeling. 2000. '"Disaggregating "China, Inc.": The Hierarchical Politics of WTO Entry.' *Comparative Political Studies* 53(13):2118–52.
Tan, Yeling. 2021. *Disaggregating China, Inc.: State Strategies in the Liberal Economic Order*. Ithaca: Cornell University Press.
Working Party on the Accession of China. 2000. WT/ACC/CHN/40.
Yang, Yang. 2020. 'Reformed environmental impact assessment in China: an evaluation of its effectiveness.' *Journal of Environmental Protection* 11:889–908.
Ye, Min. 2020. *The Belt Road and Beyond: State-Mobilized Globalization in China: 1998–2018*. Cambridge: Cambridge University Press.
Zeng, Ka, and Joshua Eastin. 2011. *Greening China: The Benefits of Trade and Foreign Direct Investment*. Ann Arbor: University of Michigan Press.
Zhao, Yuhong. 2007. 'Trade and environment: challenges after China's WTO accession.' *Columbia Journal of Environmental Law* 32:41–97.
Zhongguo lüfahui [China Greenification Society]. 2019. 'Xuke bei che, huanjing shehui yingxiang youdai chongxin [The permission has been removed, environmental society influenced the pending renewal].' Accessed June 28. https://tieba.baidu.com/p/6176945416?red_tag=3251675562.

19

China's International Investment Agreement Policy

From Rule-Taker to Rule-Maker?

AXEL BERGER

I Introduction

There has been a long-standing debate whether China will assimilate into the global economic governance system built and shaped by Western countries, or whether it will challenge the system and impose its own rules on other countries. However, despite China's phenomenal economic and political rise, it is still an open question as to whether and how China will reshape the current global economic governance system. In this respect, G. John Ikenberry pointedly asked already more than ten years ago: "*Will China overthrow the existing order or become part of it?*" (Ikenberry, 2008). This question refers to the debate between realists and liberal institutionalists about the effects of the power transition from Organization for Economic Co-operation and Development (OECD) member countries to emerging economies. From a realist perspective, one would expect that China will try to establish its own rules and organizations to better pursue its interests, thus challenging the current order set up by OECD countries. In contrast, Ikenberry argues from a liberal institutionalist perspective that it is more likely that China and other emerging economies will remain part of the current order, which he describes as "*hard to overturn and easy to join*" (Ikenberry, 2008). According to this perspective, China's policies and approaches will converge with the established rules of the game.

Another useful conceptualization of China's role in global economic governance in general and the international investment system in particular distinguished three possible roles it can pursue: rule-taker, rule-maker, or rule-breaker (Chin, 2014; Wang, 2017). While the two first categories would be in line with liberal institutionalist perspectives, the third one would be in line with the view that China challenges the existing status quo. Broadly speaking, we can observe all three positions being adopted in the ongoing transformation of the international investment regime (Bonnitcha et al., 2017). Some countries, in particular capital-exporting countries such as the US and the EU, are developing new model international investment agreements (IIAs) to better balance investor protection and host state regulatory space. Brazil, on the other hand, developed its own distinctive model of Cooperation and Facilitation Investment Agreements (CFIA) (Badin and Morosini, 2017). They clearly assume the role of a rule-maker. Other countries follow these new rules and templates and assume the role of rule-takers. And then there are countries such as Venezuela, South Africa, or India that exit important segments of the international investment regime through the termination of IIAs or the exit from the World Bank's International Centre for Settlement of Investment Disputes (ICSID).

This contribution will investigate whether China assumes the role of a rule-taker, acts as a rule-maker, or even breaks with the system. This question has been investigated in other realms of global economic governance, such as world trade or international monetary relations (Chin, 2014; Gao, 2011), but investigations in the area of global investment governance are scarce. This lack of research is especially worrying in light of the upheavals of the global investment governance system that is facing a deep legitimacy crisis (Waibel, 2010). Given its significant FDI flows and economic as well as political clout, a better understanding of China's ideas for and potential role in the reform of global investment governance is important.

The next section will divide China's international investment policy into four distinct generations of IIA arguing that China has not made attempts to break up the existing system. Rather China acted as a rule-taker by broadly accepting the templates of its treaty partners while sticking to a number of defensive lines. The next two sections will investigate China's current international investment policy-making. Section III analyses the outcomes of the China-EU Comprehensive Agreement on Investment (CAI). I will argue that China accepted the template proposed by its negotiation partner although not to the full extent. Section IV shows that China is one of the key drivers of the development of an alternative set of multilateral rules on investment facilitation under negotiation at the WTO. In this section, I will argue that China has been a key promoter lending diplomatic support to move the investment facilitation agenda forward but did not appear as the main rule-maker. Section V will conclude.

II Four Generations of Chinese Investment Treaties

China started to embrace IIAs as a tool of economic diplomacy and the promotion of foreign direct investment (FDI) right after its decision to open up in the late 1970s and early 1980s. This section will distinguish between four generations of Chinese IIAs.[1]

Since the early 1980s, China had signed a total of 150 bilateral investment treaties (BITs), of which 13 have been terminated upon the entry into force of a newly negotiated treaty. Only the treaty signed in 1994 with Indonesia has been unilaterally terminated in 2015. Five BITs negotiated in the 1980s and 1990s have been amended by a protocol in order to update their provisions. With a total of 114 treaties that are legally in force, China has the second-largest BIT network in the world, behind Germany with 129 BITs.[2] China also includes BIT-like investment chapters in its preferential trade agreements (Berger, 2013). Since 2006, China has negotiated several preferential trade and investment agreements (PTIAs) with substantive investment provisions.

Figure 19.1 shows the development of Chinese IIAs signed since the early 1980s. During the 1980s, the growth of Chinese IIAs was rather slow with only a few treaties signed per year on average. Most of these treaties have been signed with European and Asian capital exporters. From the early 1990s onwards, China entered into an almost two-decade-long period of heightened treaty-making activity. In contrast to the 1980s, China signed most of its IIAs with developing countries during the 1990s. This trend to sign IIAs mainly with developing countries continued in the 2000s. During these years, China updated or amended a number of older treaties that it had signed with West European countries in the 1980s. Since the late 2000s, the number of newly negotiated treaties has declined substantially and China started to include more comprehensive investment rules in its PTIAs. Both trends are in line with the overall trends in the global investment regime.

To understand China's motivations and preferences, it is important to focus both on the design of China's IIAs and the characteristics of the partner countries. Based on these two characteristics it is possible to distinguish four phases of Chinese IIA policy-making (Berger, 2015).

In the first two phases during the 1980s and 1990s, China negotiated IIAs that included the standard provisions of the so-called "European"

[1] This section is based in part on Berger (2019).

[2] See UNCTAD's Investment Policy Hub at http://investmentpolicyhub.unctad.org/, last accessed 7 on November 2021.

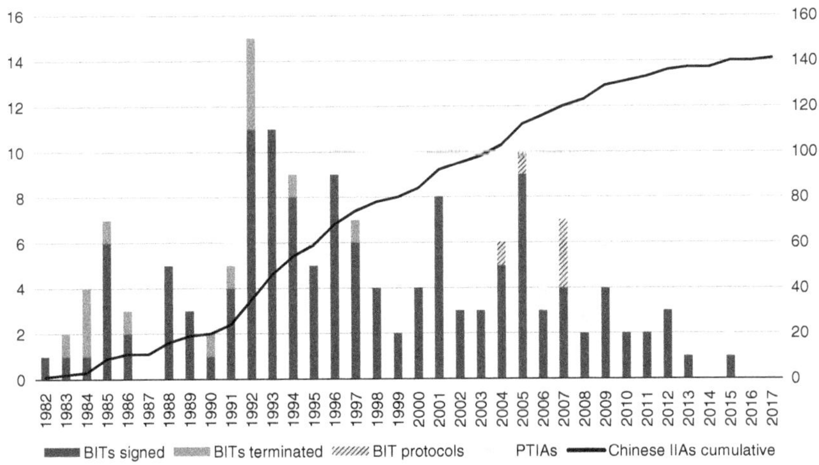

Figure 19.1 Chinese IIAs signed per year and cumulatively, 1982–2017

investment treaty template such as fair and equitable treatment (FET), most-favored-nation (MFN), and clauses on expropriation. The notable feature of these early Chinese treaties was the restriction of the scope of investor-state dispute settlement (ISDS) provisions to claims regarding the amount of compensation in the case of expropriation. With regard to substantive provisions, China permitted the transfer of funds only in accordance with national law and was reluctant to include national treatment clauses. China's approach in the 1980s can be interpreted as cautious learning from the investment treaty templates proposed by developed countries. As a result, the design of the IIAs China signed in the 1980s was specific to the partner country. While most of the key provisions remained largely unchanged, it is apparent that China's treaty practice became much more coherent in the 1990s, which is a sign that it has started to use its own treaty template during negotiations.

Despite these slight differences in design, Chinese IIA negotiations in the 1980s and 1990s can best be distinguished according to the respective partner countries. The first generation of Chinese investment treaties was negotiated in the 1980s mainly with capital-exporting countries from Europe and Asia. The focus of China's second-generation IIAs during the 1990s shifted to developing countries. This marked difference indicates that different political economy motivations explain the negotiation of Chinese treaties in the 1980s and the 1990s, respectively.

From the late 1990s onwards, China changed its legal practice by including comprehensive ISDS provisions and, depending on the partner country, broader national treatment provisions (Berger, 2011). The first treaty of this third generation was the BIT signed in 1997 with South Africa, which included for the first time a comprehensive ISDS provision. This shift in China's treaty-making practice received high attention among legal scholars (e.g., Cai, 2006; Gallagher and Shan, 2009; Schill, 2007; Shen, 2010). While comprehensive ISDS provisions were included in almost all subsequent Chinese IIAs,[3] China's approach towards granting national treatment to foreign investors was a more tailored one (Berger, 2011). Although China included national treatment provisions in almost all treaties signed in the third phase of its international investment policy, the exact wording of the national treatment clauses depended on the partner country: Chinese treaties signed with developing countries granted national treatment only subject to national law, limiting national treatment to a best-effort clause. In contrast, Chinese IIAs with developed countries featured national treatment clauses that were only restricted by the inclusion of an exemption for existing non-conforming measures and included a standstill commitment with regard to the adoption of new discriminatory measures. Interestingly, while the national law restriction in Chinese treaties signed with developing countries was a reciprocal provision, meaning that both contracting parties are allowed to discriminate against foreign investors in line with their respective national laws, the exemption of non-conforming measures in treaties with developed countries only applied to China. As a result, China was able to discriminate against foreign investors from the respective partner country in line with the legal framework in place at the entry into force of the treaty while Chinese investors enjoy full national treatment offered by the partner country (Berger, 2011).

In the fourth-generation IIAs that were signed in the late 2000s, China limited the scope of a number of treaty provisions in line with the global trend to rebalance investment treaties. This rebalancing was the result of a learning process about the effects of the increasing number of ISDS proceedings and at times the extensive interpretations of core substantive provisions like FET and indirect expropriation clauses by arbitration tribunals (Berger, 2013). Because of this international trend of rebalancing, China started to negotiate treaties with countries that base their IIAs on the more extensive and nuanced North American model.

[3] Please see Chi's chapter in this book for an analysis of ISDS cases involving China.

It is, however, puzzling to observe that while China was introducing balanced provisions in a number of treaties signed in the previous years, it was at the same time continuing to negotiate investment treaties that completely lacked balanced provisions. These treaties that were in line with the traditional European model were signed not only with European countries like Switzerland and Malta but also with many developing countries. Given the fact that MFN clauses can be used by investors to import more extensive treatment standards from other treaties their host state has signed with third countries (Schill, 2009), the continuation of the signing of traditional IIAs contradicts the attempts to limit the scope of similar provisions in more balanced treaties signed with other countries. It has therefore become clear that China did not follow a coherent approach with regard to the rebalancing of investment treaties.

The notable aspect of the shift towards more balanced IIAs was that China followed a step-by-step approach towards the rebalancing of core IIA provisions and that this process is interlinked with the negotiation of investment rules in the context of preferential trade agreements in contrast to standalone investment treaties (Berger, 2013). The PTIA signed in 2008 with New Zealand was the first Chinese treaty that included a broader range of balanced provisions such as an FET clause subject to customary international law and general exception clauses. China's adoption of these novel features, however, varied from treaty to treaty. Later treaties, such as the investment treaty with Canada, include a broad range of more balanced substantive and procedural provisions.

The analysis of this section makes clear that throughout the 1980s, 1990s, and 2000s, China negotiated on the basis of the European model. The evolution of the contents of China's IIAs during this time – and especially the policy shift towards more legalized and liberalized investment rules at the turn of the millennium – indicates that China's IIA policy has been converging towards the IIA policies adopted by most capital exporters, in particular from Western Europe. Since the late 2000s, China's IIA policy has become (at least partially) "NAFTA-ized," as China has adopted a number of provisions that were invented by North American Free Trade Agreement (NAFTA) countries as a response to a number of ISDS cases. Besides concluding IIAs with the NAFTA countries Mexico (in 2008) and Canada (in 2012), China has negotiated with a number of countries that have been influenced by the NAFTA approach. In other words, innovative IIA policy models have diffused to China and to a large extent – although not completely, as argued above – substituted the European model as China's main treaty template. This assessment is supported by the most recent decision of China to accept the model IIA text of the US and the EU as the basis for investment treaty negotiations (see next chapter).

Thus, despite the large number of IIAs and the growing role as an FDI host and source country, China has not used its new important role as a global economic powerhouse and major source and destination of FDI flows to redefine the rules of the game in the international investment regime. In fact, China has been swimming with the tide of international investment rule-making, aligning its policies with the approaches of OECD countries.

III Towards a Fifth Generation? The China-EU Comprehensive Agreement on Investment

A fifth generation of Chinese IIAs appeared on the horizon when Beijing entered into investment treaty negotiations with the US in 2008 and with Europe in 2013. It seemed that China was willing to give up on the last line of defense in comparison to US and EU-style IIAs and to commit to investment liberalization. In July 2013, China agreed to negotiate with the US on the basis of the US model treaty which includes the general commitment to open up its markets and schedule exceptions according to a negative list approach, that is only those sectors or measures are exempted that are explicitly recorded. As a result, China changed its regulatory system for foreign investments from a catalog approach, which divides sectors into encouraged, permitted, restricted, and prohibited categories, to a negative list approach that was first tested in a limited number of special free trade zones. In January 2020 a new Foreign Investment Law, which was in the making since 2015, entered into force and applies the negative list approach to the Chinese economy as a whole. Despite these changes to China's regulatory system for inward FDI, the China-US investment treaty negotiations have petered out during the Trump administration. Instead, the Trump administration focused on the Phase One Trade Deal with China that covered investment to a limited extent only, for example by liberalizing market access for US financial services or by regulating forced technology transfers.

The commitment to adopt the US model as a template for a China-US investment agreement is also of high relevance for the negotiations between China and the EU. The CAI should not only update the existing 25 investment protection agreements between individual EU member states and China but also extend their coverage to the market access of European investors in China. The decision to negotiate a so-called "Comprehensive

Agreement on Investment" between China and the EU dates back to the 15th China-EU Summit in February 2012. The 16th China-EU Summit in November 2013 agreed on the official launch of the negotiations that started with a first round of talks in January 2014. After a staggering 35 rounds of negotiations, China and the EU agreed in principle on the CAI on December 30, 2020. The fate of the CAI, however, is uncertain in light of the recent worsening of diplomatic relations between China and the EU. As a result of the EU's decision to impose sanctions on four Chinese officials over human rights abuses against the Muslim Uyghur minority in the Xinjiang region, China imposed sanctions on several European politicians and individuals. In turn, the European Parliament decided to freeze the ratification process of the CAI. These recent developments make it unlikely that the CAI will enter into force in the near future.

A key milestone in the negotiations was the agreement between China and the EU in January 2016 that the CAI should be ambitious and comprehensive, meaning that the envisaged treaty should go beyond the scope of the existing BITs between China and the member states.[4] This important decision shows that the EU aimed at an agreement with China that should at least be on par with the BIT under negotiation between China and the US that intended to cover both pre-establishment and post-establishment investment protection. In addition to post-establishment protection provisions that should be updated in order to create a better balance between investor protection and host states' right to regulate, the CAI would also address issues of market access and the right of establishment. Furthermore, the CAI should improve the regulatory environment such as transparency, licensing, and authorization procedures. In addition, the agreement should include environmental and labor provisions.[5] Last but not the least, the ISDS provisions of the old 25 BITs signed between China and EU member states, from the perspective of the EU, should be replaced by the EU's new investment court system. In sum, the negotiating agenda between China and the EU was highly complex and comprehensive and in a number of key issues, such as market access, sustainability issues, and dispute settlement, China's interests diverge substantially from those of the EU (Li et al., 2019).

[4] European Commission, 'EU and China Agree on Scope of the Future Investment Deal', 15 January 2016, http://trade.ec.europa.eu/doclib/press/index.cfm?id=1435, last accessed on 7 November 2021.

[5] European Commission, 'EU and China Agree on Scope of the Future Investment Deal', 15 January 2016, http://trade.ec.europa.eu/doclib/press/index.cfm?id=1435, last accessed on 7 November 2021.

From an EU perspective, the main objective of a China-EU CAI was to improve and guarantee access of European investors to the Chinese market thus achieving reciprocity in light of the market access European countries already grant to Chinese investors. Technically speaking, the CAI should include national and most-favored-nation treatment provisions that apply to the pre-establishment and post-establishment phases. The actual liberalization should take place on the basis of a negative list approach. Apart from these modalities, there is the important question of how extensive the negative list should be. While China implemented a negative list approach domestically, it appears to be in favor of a cautious and circumscribed approach in contrast to the EU that favors an ambitious opening up of the Chinese market for foreign investors (Bickenbach and Liu, 2015). The CAI should, in addition, include restrictions on the use of performance requirements and include transparency obligations with regard to the operation of SOEs.

The difficult ratification process of the CAI notwithstanding, the agreement text provides insight into the current negotiation strategies and substantive preferences of China. The CAI is a peculiar investment agreement, one that mainly seems to address those issues that are of importance to the EU. In view of the fact that Europe is already open to Chinese investors – additional market opening is thus expected from China – EU preferences are mostly centered around issues of market access, the regulatory environment, and sustainable development. These are the issues that are at the core of the CAI text that includes three main chapters.[6] The first substantive section focuses on investment liberalization where both parties commit to national and most-favored-nation treatment in the pre-establishment phase subject to reservations on non-conforming measures. China commits to opening up its markets in some sectors, including electric cars, private hospitals in Tier-1 cities, cloud services, and computer reservation systems.[7] Despite this rather limited additional market access, it seems that most market access commitments of China in the CAI merely lock in those reforms that China has already undertaken unilaterally (Poulsen, 2021). Arguably, preventing the revocation of economic reforms in China is an important achievement in and by itself. Securing market access and locking-in reforms may be important outcomes, but they are unlikely to substantially increase two-way investment flows.

[6] See https://trade.ec.europa.eu/doclib/press/index.cfm?id=2237, last accessed on 7 November 2021.

[7] See https://trade.ec.europa.eu/doclib/docs/2021/march/tradoc_159480.pdf, last accessed on 7 November 2021.

The second substantive section deals with the regulatory environment for foreign investments. This section of the CAI includes provisions that prohibit forced technology transfers and joint venture requirements. These provisions of the CAI appear more comprehensive than what China agreed to in its WTO accession protocol or in the Phase One Trade Deal with the US.[8] In addition to technology transfer requirements imposed by the state, China and the EU also commit not to "directly or indirectly require, force, pressure or otherwise interfere with the transfer or licensing of technology between natural persons and enterprises". Furthermore, the CAI includes a number of level-playing-field provisions that may improve the transparency of subsidies, enhance procedural transparency, predictability, and fairness of regulatory and administrative procedures, and regulate the operations of state-owned enterprises.

The third main section of the CAI includes provisions on sustainable development. While sustainable development sections are a common feature of EU trade agreements, the CAI is China's first agreement with such a comprehensive section. As the CAI offers the EU much less leverage compared to a fully fledged free trade agreement (FTA), the inclusion of such a comprehensive section on sustainable development is a success. But the obligations under this section are mainly based on the parties' existing commitments under other international environmental and labor treaties. Moreover, the wording of several key provisions characterizes such obligations as "best-effort" in nature (Berger and Chi, 2021).

The outcomes of the CAI do not address all the initial negotiation objectives of the EU. The CAI does not include sections on investment protection and investment dispute settlement. The EU's insistence to replace ISDS with an Investment Court System, as well as the ongoing multilateral discussions on reform of ISDS, could explain this omission. While the parties will continue negotiating the sections on investment protection and ISDS and "endeavour" to conclude them within two years after the signature of the CAI, the 25 BITs with outdated ISDS rules between EU members and China remain in force and could possibly lead to unwanted ISDS claims for the time being. The CAI is thus stuck halfway in the development of China-EU bilateral investment relations.

[8] See Simon Lester, "Forced technology transfer provisions in the CAI and the US-China Phase One deal", in IELP Blog, Jan. 24, 2021, available online at: https://ielp.worldtradelaw.net/2021/01/forced-technology-transfer-provisions-in-the-cai-and-the-us-china-phase-1-deal.html, accessed 24 January 2022.

While it addresses important issues of market access, regulatory cooperation, and sustainable development, it does not replace the old BITs, nor contribute to the overall reform of the international investment regime. Both parties agreed to use the next two years to remedy this omission (Berger and Chi, 2021).

The CAI negotiation process reveals that China is willing to negotiate on the basis of treaty templates put forward by its partner countries. The key sections on market access, regulatory frameworks, and sustainable development are clearly revealing the preferences of the EU rather than China. In the case of the CAI, the section on market access offers the best insight into China's negotiation strategy. China agreed to negotiate on the basis of the negative list approach favored by the US and Europe and initiated a domestic reform program that introduced this new regulatory approach first in a handful of pilot free trade zones before scaling it up to the entire economy and enshrining the principle in a new foreign investment law. The question, however, remains how extensive China's commitment to opening up its markets is. The outcomes of the CAI suggest that China is mainly agreeing to lock in existing unilateral reforms and only to a limited extent to additional market access. While China can still be described as a rule-taker, adopting the templates of its treaty partners, this assessment needs to be marked with an Asterix as China accepts only those treaty commitments that are clearly in line with its domestic preferences.

IV Thinking Outside the Box: From Investment Protection to Facilitation

Traditional models of international investment governance, in particular rules on investment protection, liberalization, and ISDS enshrined in IIAs, are increasingly criticized as one-sided, illegitimate, and ineffective. One important alternative avenue countries, and in particular developing countries, have pursued in recent years is the negotiation of investment facilitation agreements. Investment facilitation can be understood as a set of practical measures concerned with improving the transparency and predictability of investment frameworks, streamlining procedures related to foreign investors, and enhancing coordination and cooperation between stakeholders, such as the host- and home-country governments, foreign investors, domestic corporations, and societal actors. The main forum for negotiations on investment facilitation is the WTO where over 100

Members are negotiating an Investment Facilitation for Development (IFD) Agreement.[9] Furthermore, investment facilitation is becoming an integral part of regional as well as bilateral agreements or non-binding protocols (Schacherer, 2021).

China played an influential role in advancing the international agenda on investment facilitation. The concept was proposed by a group of experts in 2015 (Sauvant and Hamdani, 2015) and practiced by Brazil since 2015 in the so-called Cooperation and Facilitation Investment Agreements (CFIA) (Badin and Morosini, 2017). China played a critical role in placing the idea of investment facilitation at the center of the reform debate on international investment governance during the Chinese G20 presidency in 2016 (Sauvant, 2019). Discussions on investment facilitation were initiated during the Chinese G20 presidency and trade ministers welcomed "efforts to promote and facilitate international investment to boost economic growth and sustainable development".[10] Furthermore, the G20 encouraged international organizations such as "UNCTAD, the World Bank, the OECD and the WTO to advance this work within their respective mandates and work programmes, which could be useful for future consideration by the G20".[11] Discussions within the G20 were continued during the German G20 presidency within the Trade and Investment Working Group. The German chair put forward a non-binding investment facilitation package which reaffirmed the Guiding Principles for Global Investment Policymaking adopted at the G20 Hangzhou Summit in 2016 and which stated that investment policy frameworks should be transparent, efficient, predictable, and consistent (Berger and Evenett, 2018). China was one of the G20 Members that promoted the package to lay the foundation for the initiation of talks on investment facilitation under the auspices of the WTO. While the investment facilitation packages were blocked by the US, South Africa, and India, a group of developing countries, led by China and Brazil nevertheless succeeded in launching so-called structured discussions on investment facilitation for development at the WTO 11th Ministerial conference in December 2017.

9 A summary of the WTO Investment Facilitation for Development negotiations is available online at: https://docs.wto.org/dol2fe/Pages/FE_Search/FE_S_S006.aspx?Language=English&SourcePage=FE_B_009&Context=Script&DataSource=Cat&Query=%40Symbol%3dINF%2fIFD%2f&languageUIChanged=true#, accessed 24 January 2022.

10 See online: www.g20.utoronto.ca/2016/160710-trade.pdf, last accessed on 3 November 2021.

11 Ibid.

China is a key promoter of investment facilitation negotiations in the WTO. China submitted a proposal that suggests three elements of a framework for investment facilitation including measures to increase transparency, and enhance the efficiency of administrative procedures and options for responding to developing and least-developed members' needs.[12] At the same time, China joined a group of emerging and developing country members, the so-called "Friends of Investment Facilitation for Development" (FIFD), to propose an informal WTO dialogue on investment facilitation for development.[13] As the coordinator, China is the leading member of the FIFD group. At the 11th Ministerial Conference of the WTO in Buenos Aires, Argentina, China was among a group of 70 WTO members that signed a Joint Ministerial Statement calling for the start of Structured Discussions with the aim of developing a multilateral framework on investment facilitation. A second Ministerial Statement on investment facilitation was submitted by 98 WTO members during a trade ministers' conference hosted by China in Shanghai.[14]

China participated actively in the structured discussions and negotiations on investment facilitation in the WTO. It submitted another proposal on the entry and temporary stay of business persons for investment purposes. Its role, however, should be characterized more as a facilitator of the negotiation process rather than as a rule-maker similar to the role Brazil played which not only invented the model for bilateral CFIAs but also submitted the first comprehensive agreement text in the WTO negotiations[15] and influenced its regional partners' position on investment facilitation (Perez-Aznar and Choer Moraes, 2017). China's role was nevertheless important to help the concept of investment facilitation, as an

[12] Possible Elements of Investment Facilitation: Communication from China, JOB/GC/123, 26 April 2017, available at: https://docs.wto.org/dol2fe/Pages/FE_Search/FE_S_S009-DP.aspx?CatalogueIdList=236954,236782,236668,236429,236189,236149,235960,235961,235962,235526&CurrentCatalogueIdIndex=7, last accessed on 5 November 2021.

[13] Proposal for a WTO Informal Dialogue on Investment Facilitation for Development: Joint Communication from the Friends of Investment Facilitation for Development, JOB/GC/122, 21 April 2017, available at: https://docs.wto.org/dol2fe/Pages/FE_Search/FE_S_S009-DP.aspx?CatalogueIdList=236954,236782,236668,236429,236189,236149,235960,235961,235962,235526&CurrentCatalogueIdIndex=6, accessed 5.11.2021.

[14] Joint Ministerial Statement on Investment Facilitation for Development, WT/L/1072/Rev.1, 22 November 2019, available at: https://docs.wto.org/dol2fe/Pages/SS/directdoc.aspx?filename=q:/WT/L/1072R1.pdf, last accessed on 5 November 2021.

[15] JOB/GC/169, 1 February 2018, available at: www.tralac.org/images/docs/12699/wto-general-council-structured-discussions-on-investment-facilitation-communication-from-brazil-february-2018.pdf, last accessed on 5 November 2019.

alternative to traditional approaches of investment protection and ISDS, achieve a breakthrough at the multilateral level given its role as a G20 chair, as a host of important trade ministers' meetings or the coordinator of the FIFD group.

V Conclusion

This article assesses China's role in the global investment regime asking whether it can be characterized as a rule-taker, a rule-maker, or rather as a rule-breaker. China has signed a total of 150 BITs since the early 1980s and is an active participant in multilateral fora such as the negotiations towards an IFD Agreement in the WTO. Despite this active involvement in the global investment regime and its significant economic and political clout, China seems to continue to pursue the role of a rule-taker. This passive role is visible in the contents of Chinese IIAs negotiated over four decades and does not seem to be contingent on the partner countries. The most recent and significant agreement negotiated by China, the CAI signed in principle with the EU, seems to be following a template that largely reflects the preferences of its partner. China, however, does not adopt the templates of its treaty partners unchecked. On the contrary, China seems to have a number of defensive positions, for example, comprehensive liberalization commitments, that characterize its treaty-making practice.

In addition to the negotiation of IIAs, China is also an active negotiation party in multilateral fora such as the WTO negotiations on investment facilitation. China did submit a limited number of proposals, which, however, are less comprehensive than those of other negotiating parties such as Brazil or the EU. Despite these proposals, China's role in the IFD Agreement negotiations should be characterized not as a thought leader but as a key promoter of dialogue and negotiations. China used its chairmanship of the G20 in 2016 and hosted a trade ministers meeting in 2019 to promote discussions on investment facilitation. China, furthermore, is part of an informal group of WTO Members, the so-called Friends of Investment Facilitation for Development that assumes an important role to move the investment facilitation agenda in the WTO forward.

What are the implications of this assessment of China as being (still) a rule-taker? First, given its active participation in global investment policy-making, it is not acting as a rule-breaker and pursues its interest within the existing global investment governance system. To paraphrase the words of Ikenberry quoted in the introduction, China gradually becomes a part of the existing system and is not likely to attempt to overthrow it. Second, if an international agenda aligns with its interests, such as in the area of investment facilitation, China can be a very powerful promoter of international dialogue and negotiations. Thirdly, although China is willing to negotiate on its partner countries' treaty templates, it does not indiscriminately accept all provisions and commitments put on the negotiation table by its partners. On the contrary, the changes in the design of Chinese IIAs seem to be conditioned by policy developments within China, as underlined by the CAI. While China seems to be comfortable with lock-in unilateral reforms, it does not seem to accept treaty provisions that would imply additional economic policy reforms at home. At least in this sense, China's investment policy-making is not that different from that of other economic powers such as the US and the EU.

References

Badin, M.S., Morosini, F. (2017). 'Navigating between resistance and conformity with the global investment regime: the new Brazilian agreements on cooperation and facilitation of investment., In Badin, M.S., Morosini, F. (eds.), *Reconceptualizing International Investment Law from the Global South*. Cambridge: Cambridge University Press, pp. 188–217.

Berger, A. (2011). 'The politics of china's investment treaty-making-programm.' In Broude, T., Busch, M.L., Porges, A. (eds.), *The Politics of International Economic Law*. Cambridge: Cambridge University Press, pp. 162–185.

Berger, A. (2013). 'Investment rules in Chinese PTIAs – a partial "NAFTA-ization.' In Hofmann, R., Schill, S., Tams, C. (eds.), *Preferential Trade and Investment Agreements: From Recalibration to Reintegration*. Baden-Baden: Nomos, pp. 297–333.

Berger, A. (2015). 'Hesitant embrace: China's recent approach to international investment rule-making.' *The Journal of World Investment & Trade* 16, 843–868. https://doi.org/ 10.1163/22119000-01606003

Berger, A. (2019). 'The political economy of Chinese investment treaties.' In Zeng, K. (Ed.), *Handbook on the International Political Economy of China*. Cheltenham: Edward Elgar, pp. 151–168.

Berger, A., Chi, M. (2021). The EU-china comprehensive agreement on investment: stuck half-way? Columbia FDI Perspectives Np. 299, March 8, 2021.

Berger, A., Evenett, S.J. (2018). 'The trump-induced G20 stress test on trade: did the German presidency pass?' *Global Summitry* 3, 124–140. https://doi.org/10.1093/global/guy002.

Bickenbach, F., Liu, W.-H. (2015). The EU-China bilateral investment agreement in negotiation: motivation, conflicts and perspectives. Kiel Policy Brief No. 95.

Bonnitcha, J., Poulsen, L.N., Waibel, Mi. (2017). *The Political Economy of the Investment Treaty Tegime*. Oxford: Oxford University Press.

Cai, C. (2006). 'Outward foreign direct investment protection and the effectiveness of Chinese BIT practice'. *Journal of World Investment and Trade* 7, 621–652.

Chin, G. (2014). 'China's rising monetary power.' In Eric, H., Jonathan, K. (eds.), *The Great Wall of Money: Power and Politics in China's International Monetary Relations*. Ithaca, NY: Cornell University Press, pp. 184–212. https://doi.org/10.7591/9780801454677-011

Gallagher, N., Shan, W. (2009). *Chinese Investment Treaties: Policies and Practice*. Oxford: Oxford University Press.

Gao, H. (2011). 'China's ascent in global trade governance: from rule taker to rule shaker, and maybe rule maker?.' In Deere-Birkbeck, C. (ed.), *Making Global Trade Governance Work for Development*. Cambridge: Cambridge University Press, pp. 153–180.

Ikenberry, G.J. (2008). 'The rise of china and the future of the west: can the liberal system survive?' *Foreign Affairs* 87, 23–37.

Li, Y., Qi, T., Bian, C. (2019). *China, the EU and International Investment Law: Reforming Investor-State Dispute Settlement*. New York, NY: Routledge.

Perez-Aznar, F., Choer Moraes, H. (2017). The MERCOSUR protocol on investment cooperation and facilitation: regionalizing an innovative approach to investment agreements, EJIL:talk! (Report).

Poulsen, L.N. (2021). The E.U.-China investment deal and transatlantic investment cooperation. Perry World House, University of Pennsylvania.

Sauvant, K.P. (2019). 'China moves the G20.' In Chaisse, J. (ed.), *China's International Investment Strategy*. Oxford: Oxford University Press, pp. 311–328.

Sauvant, K.P., Hamdani, K. (2015). An international support programme for sustainable investment facilitation (Report). International Centre for Trade; Sustainable Development (ICTSD).

Schacherer, S. (2021). Facilitating investment through IIAs: the case of the regional comprehensive economic partnership agreement. Columbia FDI Perspectives No. 295, January 11, 2021.

Schill, S.W. (2007). 'Tearing down the Great Wall: the new generation investment treaties of the People's Republic of China.' *Cardozo Journal of International and Comparative Law* 5 (1): 73–118.

Schill, S.W. (2009). *The Multilateralization of International Investment Law, Cambridge International Trade and Economic Law*. Cambridge: Cambridge University Press. https://doi.org/ 10.1017/CBO9780511605451

Shen, W. (2010). 'Is this a great leap forward? A comparative review of the investor-state arbitration clause in the ASEAN-China investment treaty: from BIT jurisprudential and practical perspectives.' *Journal of International Arbitration* 27, 379–419.

Waibel, M. (2010). *The Backlash Against Investment Arbitration: Perceptions and Reality*. Alphen ann den Rijin, Netherlands: Kluwer Law International BV.

Wang, Z. (2017). 'The economic rise of China: Rule-taker, rule-maker, or rule-breaker?' *Asian Survey* 57, 595–617.

20

China and Investor-State Dispute Settlement

Experiences and Prospects

MANJIAO CHI

I Introduction

China's accession to the World Trade Organization (WTO) in 2001 is a milestone in its history.[1] Thanks to its WTO membership, China has grown into the world's second-largest economy,[2] a major global trading power,[3] and a leading investment-importing and investment-exporting state.[4] Chinese enterprises have also grown into major international business players.[5]

China and its investors also face a growing risk of investment disputes. China has concluded a large number of international investment agreements (IIAs), including around 140 bilateral investment treaties (BITs) and around 24 bilateral and regional free trade agreements (FTAs) with an investment chapter or section.[6] The majority of these IIAs allow

Thanks are due to Zhiyuan Yin for her valuable research assistance. The views and errors of this paper are solely the author's. Email: chimanjiao@uibe.edu.cn.

Unless otherwise indicated, all websites are last accessed on 1 September 2022.

1 The term "China" in the context of the WTO cover four different members, namely the People's Republic of China (Mainland China), the separate customs territories of Hong Kong, Macau and Taiwan Penghu, Kinmen and Macao. For the purpose of this paper, the term "China" in this paper only refers to Mainland China.

2 GDP data for all countries and economies is available at https://data.worldbank.org/indicator/NY.GDP.MKTP.CD?view=chart.

3 See WTO, *The Eighth Trade Policy Review Report of China* (WT/TPR/S/415), available at www.wto.org/english/tratop_e/tpr_e/s415_sum_e.pdf.

4 See UNCTAD, *World Investment Report 2021*, available at https://unctad.org/system/files/official-document/wir2021_en.pdf.

5 See Huiyao Wang and Lu Miao, *The Globalization of Chinese Enterprises: Trends and Characteristics* (Singapore: Springer, 2020).

6 A list of China's IIAs is available at https://investmentpolicy.unctad.org/international-investment-agreements/countries/42/china.

investor-state dispute settlement (ISDS), investor-state arbitration (ISA) in particular, though their ISDS clauses may be different.[7] Also, with the implementation of the Belt and Road Initiative (BRI), Chinese overseas investment has experienced a sharp expansion in recent years,[8] which exposes Chinese investors to more disputes with the host states. It would not be surprising that more ISDS cases will be initiated based on Chinese IIAs in the future.

In the meantime, since 2016, an unprecedented ISDS reform has been initiated under the auspices of the United Nations Commission on International Trade Law (UNCITRAL).[9] China is a major stakeholder in international investment governance and submitted a position paper on ISDS reform to UNCITRAL on 19 July 2019.[10] China's position on the ongoing ISDS reform could have a profound impact on both investors and the future ISDS landscape.

Against such a background, this chapter explores two interrelated issues: what could be learned from China's ISDS experience (Part II), and what China expects from the ongoing ISDS reform (Part III). Part IV is a brief conclusion.

II Looking into the Past: China's ISDS Experiences and Systematic Issues

According to the United Nations Conference for Trade and Development (UNCTAD),[11] China and its investors have encountered over a dozen ISDS cases relying on Chinese BITs in the past decade. All these cases arose in the new Millennium. As some legal issues relating to China's ISDS experiences have been broadly discussed, the focus will be put on a few systematic and unique issues.

[7] See Yuwen Li and Cheng Bian (2020). "China's Stance on Investor-State Dispute Settlement: Evolution, Challenges, and Reform Options", *Netherlands International Law Review* 67, at 503–51.

[8] See MOFCOM, "2020 Statistical Bulletin of China's Outward Foreign Direct Investment", available at http://images.mofcom.gov.cn/www/202109/20210929084957284.pdf (original in Chinese).

[9] See UNCITRAL, "Working Group III: Investor-State Dispute Settlement Reform", available at https://uncitral.un.org/en/working_groups/3/investor-state.

[10] UNCITRAL, "Possible reform of investor-State dispute settlement (ISDS): Submission from the Government of China" (A/CN.9/WG.III/WP.177).

[11] Available at https://investmentpolicy.unctad.org/investment-dispute-settlement/country/42/china.

(i) A Skeletal Review of ISDS Cases Relying on Chinese IIAs

During the past decade, China has been involved in the following six ISDS cases as the respondent state:

a. AsiaPhos Limited v. People's Republic of China (2020)(*ad hoc* arbitration under UNCITRAL Arbitration Rules), relying on the China-Singapore BIT (1985) (AsiaPhos v. China)[12];
b. Goh Chin Soon v. People's Republic of China (2020)(ICSID Case No. ARB/20/34), relying on the China-Singapore BIT (1985)(Goh v. China)[13];
c. Macro Trading Co., Ltd. v. People's Republic of China (2020)(ICSID Case No. ARB/20/22), relying on the China-Japan BIT (1988)(Macro v. China)[14];
d. Hela Schwarz GmbH v. People's Republic of China (2017)(ICSID Case No. ARB/17/19), relying on the China-Germany BIT (2003)(Hela Schwarz v. China)[15];
e. Ansung Housing Co., Ltd. v. People's Republic of China (2014)(ICSID Case No. ARB/14/25), relying on the China-Korea BIT (2007)(Ansung v. China)[16];
f. Ekran Berhad v. People's Republic of China (2011)(ICSID Case No. ARB/11/15), relying on the China-Malaysia BIT (1988)(Ekran v. China).[17]

The recent decade has also witnessed around a dozen ISDS cases initiated by Chinese investors against foreign states, including:

a. Qiong Ye and Jianping Yang v. Kingdom of Cambodia (2021)(ICSID Case No. ARB/21/42), relying on the ASEAN-China Investment Agreement (2009)(Ye and Yang v. Cambodia)[18];

12 Available at https://investmentpolicy.unctad.org/investment-dispute-settlement/cases/1106/asiaphos-v-china.
13 Available at https://investmentpolicy.unctad.org/investment-dispute-settlement/cases/1090/goh-v-china.
14 Available at https://investmentpolicy.unctad.org/investment-dispute-settlement/cases/1035/macro-trading-v-china.
15 Available at https://investmentpolicy.unctad.org/investment-dispute-settlement/cases/805/hela-schwarz-v-china.
16 Available at https://investmentpolicy.unctad.org/investment-dispute-settlement/cases/602/ansung-housing-v-china.
17 Available at https://investmentpolicy.unctad.org/investment-dispute-settlement/cases/427/ekran-v-china.
18 Available at https://icsid.worldbank.org/cases/case-database/case-detail?CaseNo=ARB/21/42.

b. Fengzhen Min v. Republic of Korea (2020)(ICSID Case No. ARB/20/26), relying on the China-Korea BIT (2007)(Min v. Korea)[19];
c. Wang Jing, Li Fengju, Ren Jinglin and others v. Republic of Ukraine (2020) (procedural details unknown), relying on the China-Ukraine BIT (1992)(Wang, Ren and others v. Ukraine)[20];
d. Jetion Solar Co. Ltd and Wuxi T-Hertz Co. Ltd. v. Hellenic Republic (2019)(*ad hoc* arbitration under UNCITRAL Arbitration Rules), relying on the China-Greece BIT (1992)(Jetion Solar et al. v. China)[21];
e. Sanum Investments Limited v. Lao People's Democratic Republic (II) (2017)(ICSID Case No. ADHOC/17/1), relying on the China-Laos BIT (1993) (Sanum v. Laos II)[22];
f. Beijing Urban Construction Group Co. Ltd. v. Republic of Yemen (2014) (ICSID Case No. ARB/14/30), relying on the China-Yemen BIT (1998)(BUCC v. Yemen)[23];
g. Sanum Investments Limited v. Lao People's Democratic Republic (2013)(PCA Case No. 2013-13), relying on the China-Laos BIT (1993) (Sanum v. Laos)[24];
h. Ping An Life Insurance Company of China, Limited and Ping An Insurance (Group) Company of China, Limited v. Kingdom of Belgium (2012)(ICSID Case No. ARB/12/29), relying on the China-BLEU BIT (1984) and the China-BLEU BIT (2007)(Ping An v. China)[25];
i. Beijing Shougang Mining Investment Company Ltd., China Heilongjiang International Economic & Technical Cooperative Corp., and Qinhuangdaoshi Qinlong International Industrial Co. Ltd. v. Mongolia (2010)(PCA Case No. 2010-20), relying on the China-Mongolia BIT (1991)(Beijing Shougang et al. v. Mongolia)[26];

19 Available at https://investmentpolicy.unctad.org/investment-dispute-settlement/cases/1098/min-v-korea.
20 Available at https://investmentpolicy.unctad.org/investment-dispute-settlement/cases/1105/wang-and-others-v-ukraine.
21 Available at https://investmentpolicy.unctad.org/investment-dispute-settlement/cases/975/jetion-and-t-hertz-v-greece.
22 Available at https://investmentpolicy.unctad.org/investment-dispute-settlement/cases/797/sanum-investments-v-laos-ii-.
23 Available at https://investmentpolicy.unctad.org/investment-dispute-settlement/cases/573/beijing-urban-construction-v-yemen.
24 Available at www.italaw.com/cases/2050.
25 Available at https://investmentpolicy.unctad.org/investment-dispute-settlement/cases/480/ping-an-v-belgium.
26 Available at https://investmentpolicy.unctad.org/investment-dispute-settlement/cases/367/beijing-shougang-and-others-v-mongolia.

j. Tza Yap Shum v. Republic of Peru (2007)(ICSID Case No. ARB/07/6), relying on the China-Peru BIT (1994)(Tza v. Peru).[27]

The above list should not be deemed exhaustive. It is possible that a few ISDS cases are not included, due to lack of sufficient transparency of ISDS cases.

Without going into the details of these cases, a few general observations could be drawn. First, though the current number of cases remains small, there is a clear trend that China's ISDS cases are on the rise. In 2020 alone, five ISDS cases were registered. As mentioned earlier, it is likely that more ISDS cases will be initiated. Second, somehow surprisingly, the majority of China's ISDS cases are initiated by Chinese investors against foreign states, including a few developed states, such as Belgium. There is no clear reason to explain this phenomenon, but it has been observed that Chinese investors, SOEs in particular, have become growingly affirmative of and accustomed to resorting to international adjudication to "defend" their overseas interests.[28] Third, most of these cases have been submitted to the ICSID. This is not surprising, since the majority of Chinese IIAs allow investors to select ICSID arbitration, in addition to or in lieu of *ad hoc* arbitration under UNCITRAL Arbitration Rules.[29]

An interesting observation is that China seems not frustrated by the ISDS cases against it. For instance, China's Ministry of Commerce (MOFCOM), the principal government agency responsible for handling China's ISDS and WTO cases for China, has never publicly commented on the ISDS cases; whereas MOFCOM spokesperson has frequently commented on China's WTO cases.[30]

China's silence in commenting ISDS cases could be attributed to several factors. First, China has not been "defeated" in any major ISDS cases in the legal sense up to date. Among the six cases against China, three are pending

[27] Available at https://investmentpolicy.unctad.org/investment-dispute-settlement/cases/255/tza-yap-shum-v-peru.

[28] See Manjiao Chi and Qing Ren. (2020). "China International Investment Arbitration Annual Watch (2020)", *Beijing Arbitration*, 02, at 1–47 (original in Chinese).

[29] See Manjiao Chi and Xi Wang. (2015). "The evolution of ISA clauses in Chinese IIAs and its practical implications: the admissibility of disputes for investor-state arbitration", *The Journal of World Investment and Trade*, 16 (5–6), at 869–98.

[30] See, *e.g.*, MOFCOM, "MOFCOM Spokesperson Speaks on Initiation a WTO Dispute against the U.S. on US 301 Tariff on Chinese Products", available at www.mofcom.gov.cn/article/ae/ag/202009/20200903001422.shtml (original in Chinese); "MOFCOM Department of Treaty and Law Person-in-Charge Speaks on China's Dropping the WTO Dispute against the EU relating to External Benchmark in Anti-dumping Investigation", available at www.mofcom.gov.cn/article/ae/sjjd/202007/20200702982154.shtml (original in Chinese).

(AsiaPhos v. China, Goh v. China, and Hela Schwarz v. China), two have been discontinued by a settlement agreement (Ekran v. China) or by the choice of the investor (Macro v. China), only one case has been decided (Ansung v. China) in the jurisdictional stage, in which the arbitral tribunal was in favor of China. Thus, from a practical perspective, these ISDS cases have not inflicted "real pain" on China in the sense of monetary compensation and legal defeat. There is no clear reason to explain China's "success" in handling ISDS cases. A possible explanation is the helpfulness of negotiation between investors and the state. Different from many states, China is a centralized state. There is no clear constitutional division of administrative authority between China's central and local governments. This essentially implies that the central government may deal with and even decide on investment issues that involve local governments. Thus, if necessary, China's central government may negotiate with foreign investors to solve the investment disputes. Such negotiation could be quite effective and efficient given the authority and resources of the central government.

Second, all ISDS cases against China involve disputes between foreign investors and China's local governments, most of these disputes relate to land-use rights issues. As a matter of fact, land disputes between private parties, both Chinese and foreign, and local governments have once been rampant in China in the past few decades, as a result of China's aggressive and underregulated urbanization measures.[31] Subsequent to China's revision of the relevant laws and regulations in around 2010, land disputes have decreased dramatically, and are less likely to be a major concern of investors.[32]

Third, China holds different perceptions of ISDS cases and WTO cases. To China, ISDS cases in general appear less sensitive than WTO cases. In WTO cases, what is challenged are China's laws, regulations, or measures or even measures of the Chinese Communist Party. Some cases involve sensitive issues, such as media censorship,[33] and the export

[31] See, *e.g.*, Eva Pils. (2005–2006). "Land Disputes, Rights Assertion, and Social Unrest in China: A Case from Sichuan", *Columbia Journal of Asian Law* 19, at 235–85; Xiaowen Lin et al. (2008). "Conflicts of Land Expropriation in China during 2006–2016: An Overview and its Spatiotemporal Characteristic", *Land Use Policy* 76, at 246–51.

[32] See Manjiao Chi and Zongyao Li. (2021). "Administrative Review Provisions in Chinese Investment Treaties: Gilding the Lily?", *Journal of International Dispute Settlement*, 12(1), at 138.

[33] See, *e.g.*, *China – Measures Affecting Trading Rights and Distribution Services for Certain Publications and Audiovisual Entertainment Products* (DS363), available at www.wto.org/english/tratop_e/dispu_e/cases_e/ds363_e.htm.

of strategic natural resources.[34] To China, these cases are not just trading disputes, but concern "national interests", which could have a "systematic impact" on China's economic and social governance.[35] Somehow, in contrast, China's ISDS cases were mainly caused by administrative conducts of local governments. Even if China loses cases, it will only need to pay monetary compensation to foreign investors.[36] Thus, ISDS cases are not deemed as a threat to China's national security and are less likely to have a systematic impact on China. This partly explains why, unlike some states that have been "hit" by ISDS cases, such as Australia, Germany, India, and Latin American states, China has not publicly commented on its ISDS cases.

On the other hand, China seems to hold a laissez-faire attitude towards ISDS cases initiated by its investors against foreign states. In practice, Chinese investors, similar to foreign investors, have discretion in initiating and handling investment disputes with the host states. In such cases, however, it is possible that the Chinese government be approached by investors or the foreign state for assistance. For instance, in Ping An v. Belgium, it is reported that Ping An has sought help from the Chinese Government to seek compensation from Belgium.[37] In *Sanum v. Laos*, as recorded in the judgment of the Court of Appeal of Singapore, the Laotian Ministry of Foreign Affairs sent a note to the Chinese embassy seeking China's views on a major legal issue, and the Chinese embassy replied to the note.[38] While these cases do not necessarily prove that China has formed a fixed pattern of practice, they give rise to an interesting question: whether and how China could be involved in investment disputes between Chinese investors and foreign

[34] See, *e.g.*, *China – Measures Related to the Exportation of Rare Earths, Tungsten and Molybdenum* (DS431), available at www.wto.org/english/tratop_e/dispu_e/cases_e/ds431_e.htm.

[35] See, *e.g.*, Manjiao Chi. (2013). "Trade-Plus Effects of WTO Dispute Settlement on China: An Ideal or Illusion?" *Journal of World Trade*, 47(6) at 1349–84; Joost Pauwelyn. (2010). 'The Dog that Barked but Didn't Bite: 15 Years of Intellectual Property Disputes at the WTO", *Journal of International Dispute Settlement*, 1(2), at 389–429.

[36] See, *e.g.*, Johnson L. Sachs, "Investment Treaties, Investor-State Dispute Settlement, and Inequality: How International Rules and Institutions Can Exacerbate Domestic Disparities". In José Antonio Ocampo (ed.), *International Policy Rules and Inequality* (New York: Columbia University Press, 2019), at 112–42.

[37] See New York Time, "Ping An seeks Beijing's Help over Nationalization of Fortis", available at www.nytimes.com/2008/11/28/business/worldbusiness/28iht-insure.1.18227245.html.

[38] See *Sanum Investments Ltd. v Government of the Lao People's Democratic Republic*, Judgement of the Court of Appeal of Singapore ([2016] SGCA 57), available at www.italaw.com/sites/default/files/case-documents/italaw7600.pdf, at 4.

states. It is too early to answer this question with meaningful accuracy, but it surely deserves further observation.

(ii) *Systematic Issues Raised in ISDS Cases Relying on Chinese IIAs*

Many of the decided ISDS cases relying on Chinese BITs have been broadly discussed. This chapter does not present a comprehensive study of all these cases, but only focuses on a few systematic issues.

The first systematic issue is the applicability of Chinese BITs in Hong Kong and Macao. While this issue has been discussed, almost all existing literatures take the perspective of treaty law, especially treaty interpretation and state succession in respective treaties.[39] They fail to explain why China has been reluctant in clarifying its position on this issue over the years, especially through BIT-making. This issue will be discussed *infra*.

Hong Kong and Macao were handed over to China by the United Kingdom (U.K.) and Portugal in 1997 and 1999 respectively. Following the "One Country Two Systems" (OCTS) policy, China established special administrative regions (SARs) in Hong Kong and Macao after their handover. An important legal issue relating to the handover is the application of treaties in the SARs. Take Hong Kong for example, before the handover, a number of treaties to which the U.K. is a party were also applied to Hong Kong through extension. While such an application should be terminated once Hong Kong becomes a Chinese territory, the termination does not lead to the automatic application of Chinese treaties to Hong Kong. To deal with this issue, the *Basic Law of the Hong Kong Special Administrative Region of the People's Republic of China* (HKBL) provides that the applicability of Chinese treaties to Hong Kong after the handover should be "decided by the Central People's Government, in accordance with the circumstances and needs of the Region, and after seeking the views of the government of the Region".[40]

Notwithstanding the arrangement in the HKBL, China's Central Government has never decided to apply its IIAs to Hong Kong. Besides, almost all Chinese IIAs are silent on their applicability to the SARs, with

[39] See, *e.g.*, Patrick Dumberry. (2018). "State Succession to BITs in the Context of the Transfer of Territory of Macao to China: Lessons Learned from the Sanum Saga", *Journal of International Arbitration*, 35(3), at 329–56, https://kluwerlawonline.com/journalissue/Journal+of+International+Arbitration/35.3/17374.

[40] Article 153, paragraph 2, HKBL.

the China-Russia BIT (2006) as the only exception, which expressly excludes the SARs from its scope of application.[41] As can be seen, the applicability issue is not only systematic as it pertains to almost all Chinese IIAs, but it is also unique and sensitive as it is linked with the OCTS policy.

The applicability issue has been discussed in two ISDS cases. In *Tza v. Peru*, the issue at dispute is, among others, whether the investors, Mr. Tza, a Hong Kong resident, could invoke the China-Peru BIT for protection. The tribunal essentially held that though Mr. Tza is a Hong Kong passport holder, he should be protected by the BIT as far as he has proven to be a Chinese national since the BIT protects "a national of a contracting state" as an investor.[42] In *Sanum v. Laos*, the issue at dispute is whether the investor, Sanum, a company registered in Macao, could rely on the China-Laos BIT for protection. The arbitral tribunal recognized that China has not extended the BIT to Macao.[43] Then, relying mainly on the international law principle of "moving treaty frontier" in the VCLT,[44] the arbitral tribunal ruled that since Macao has been incorporated as a territory of China after the handover, it falls in the application scope of Chinese BITs, unless the BITs exclude Macao from its application scope, which is not the case of the China-Laos BIT.[45] As can be seen, the arbitral tribunals in both cases recognized that Chinese BITs can be applied to the SARs, if the SARs are not excluded from their application scope.

Despite these arbitral awards, China has not publicly clarified the applicability issue until its embassy in Laos replied to the Laotian government following the arbitration of *Sanum v. Laos*. In its note, it is stated that China's concurrence with the Laotian view that the China-Laos BIT did not apply to Macao "unless both China and Laos make separate arrangements in the future".[46] This position has been reiterated by China's Ministry of Foreign Affairs. Referring to the HKBL, the Ministry confirmed that Hong Kong shall enjoy a high level of autonomy, including autonomy in concluding economic treaties with foreign

[41] Article 1, Protocol, China-Russian BIT.

[42] See *Tza v. Peru*, Decision on Jurisdiction and Competence (ICSID Case No. ARB/07/6), available at www.italaw.com/sites/default/files/case-documents/ita0880.pdf, at 16.

[43] See *Sanum Investments Ltd. v Government of the Lao People's Democratic Republic*, Award on Jurisdiction (PCA Case No. 2013-13), available at www.italaw.com/sites/default/files/case-documents/italaw3322.pdf (last accessed 10 October 2021), at 59.

[44] See Article 29, VCLT.

[45] See *supra* note 43, at 73.

[46] See *supra* note 38, at 4.

states in its own name.[47] Thus, Chinese BITs "in principle do not apply to the SARs, unless otherwise decided by the Central Government after seeking the views of the SAR governments and consulting with the other party of the BIT".[48]

Though the award in *Sanum v. Laos* does not have binding force as precedence, it is likely to be relied on or referred to by SAR investors and arbitral tribunals in future ISDS cases. Yet, China's diplomatic note seems to show a conflicting view on the applicability issue. China's view could not only profoundly influence the adjudication of the applicability issue in future ISDS cases, it also implies that China will have less flexibility in dealing with the issue. While it remains unclear why China chose to clarify the applicability issue during the set-aside proceedings of *Sanum v. Laos*, China's clarification does give rise to a number of interesting questions: why has China kept silent on the applicability issue for so long? Is China's silence intentional? What could China expect to get from its silence?

In retrospect, several facts could show that China's silence is intentional. Shortly before the handover of Hong Kong in 1997, some lawyers discussed whether Chinese treaties could be applied to Hong Kong after the handover, as the relationship between Hong Kong and China will have been changed from an "international" one to an "OCTS" one.[49] Such discussions imply that China and its lawyers have considered the applicability issue even before the handover. In addition, the China-Russian BIT (2006) explicitly stipulates that it shall not be applicable in the SARs unless otherwise agreed by the Parties.[50] Besides, the issue has been straightforwardly raised in 2008 by the initiation of *Tza v. Peru*. The above facts imply that China should have been aware of the applicability issue long before the initiation of *Sanum v. Laos*. Had China wished to clarify the issue, it could have had ample opportunities to do so. Yet, all of China's recent IIAs remain silent on the applicability issue, such as the China-Canada BIT (2012) and the ASEAN-China Investment Agreement (2009).

47 Article 151, HKBL.

48 Ministry of Foreign Affairs of the People's Republic of China, "Foreign Ministry Spokesperson Hua Chunying's Regular Press Conference on 21 October 2016", available at www.italaw.com/sites/default/files/case-documents/italaw7687.pdf (last accessed 10 October 2021).

49 See, *e.g.*, Ulrich G. Schroeter. (2004). "The Status of Hong Kong and Macao under the United Nations Convention on Contracts for the International Sale of Goods". *Pace International Law Review*, 16(2), at 307–32.

50 Article 1, *Protocol to the Agreement between the Government of the Russian Federation and the Government of the People's Republic of China on the Promotion and Reciprocal Protection of Investments.*

As mentioned, it was not until 2018 that China clarified its position on this issue in *Sanum v. Laos* upon the request of the Laotian government. And it remains unclear why China chose to clarify this issue after so many years of silence.

Practically speaking, China's silence is not without merits. It should be understood from a broader policy perspective, and could have an impact of "killing two birds with one stone". First, China's silence could be seen as "constructive vagueness" in IIA-making, which could be helpful to SAR investors, as this allows them to rely on Chinese IIAs for protection. Such helpfulness could be especially significant considering that China has concluded a large number of IIAs, while the SARs only host a limited number of IIAs. For instance, Hong Kong has concluded 21 BITs and seven FTAs.[51] Second, for historical reasons, the SARs, Hong Kong in particular, have played a key role in China's economic development and opening up. Many Chinese mainland investors use Hong Kong as a gateway for business convenience and overseas investment; foreign companies also use Hong Kong as a launchpad to expand in Mainland China.[52] In a sense, protecting SAR investment and investors have special significance to China.

A more complicated scenario of the applicability issue is where both the SAR and China have an IIA with a state. In such a case, are SAR investors allowed to select from a Chinese BIT and an SAR BIT? Up to the present, this treaty shopping issue has not emerged in reality. Thus, it remains unclear how arbitral tribunals, SAR investors, SAR Government, and China's Central Government will address the issue. Here, it is of interest to note that treaty shopping is not prohibited under international investment law, as IIAs have a purpose of encouraging and protecting foreign investment.[53] But treaty shopping should not be encouraged since it could go against the principle of reciprocity, create an undue regulatory chill on countries and even give rise to legitimacy concerns over IIAs.[54] As a matter of fact, various types of IIA provisions have been introduced to

[51] A list of Hong Kong IIAs is available at https://investmentpolicy.unctad.org/international-investment-agreements/countries/93/hong-kong-sar-china.

[52] Noah Sin, "Explainer: How Important is Hong Kong to China as a Free Finance Hub?", available at www.reuters.com/article/us-hongkong-protests-finance-explainer-idUSKBN2350VO.

[53] Julien Chaisse. (2015). "The Treaty Shopping Practice: Corporate Structuring and Restructuring to Gain Access to Investment Treaties and Arbitration", 11 *Hastings Business Law Journal* 225, at 228.

[54] See Jorun Baumgartner, *Treaty Shopping in International Investment Law* (Oxford: Oxford University Press, 2016), at 39–64.

help address the negative impacts of treaty shopping by investors, such as clauses of denial of benefits.[55] That said, however, if China clinches to its clarification made in *Sanum v. Laos*, it is unlikely to allow such treaty shopping practice.

To sum up, if China truly wishes to uphold its position on the applicability issue as clarified in *Sanum v. Laos*, it is advisable for China to consider revising the relevant IIA provisions when making or updating IIAs in the future. Preferably, an explicit language could be included to exclude IIAs to be applied to the SARs. Such exclusion could take the form of a refined definition of certain key terms, such as "territory" or "national", or an insertion of a statement similar to that in the China-Russia BIT. Up to the present, China has not made such revisions in its IIAs. Therefore, the real issue seems how much weight arbitral tribunals would give to China's clarification in *Sanum v. Laos* in future ISDS cases.

The second systematic issue relates to China's state-owned enterprises (SOEs). While SOEs are not unique to China, China hosts a large number of SOEs at central and local levels.[56] In recent years, China's SOEs have dramatically expanded their overseas investment as a result of BRI implementation. Because China's SOEs are active players in global market, it is unsurprising that they initiate ISDS cases against foreign states. Typical such cases include *BUCG v. Yeman* and *Beijing Shougang et al. v. Mongolia*.

That SOEs could be involved in ISDS cases is not a novel issue.[57] In such cases, arbitral tribunals have routinely adopted the "Broches test" in deciding whether the SOEs could be qualified claimants. According to this test, an SOE should not be disqualified as a "national of another Contracting State" unless it is acting as an agent for the government or is discharging an essentially governmental function.[58] For instance, in *BUCG v. Yemen*, Yemen argued that BUCG does not qualify as a "national of another Contracting State", since it as "a state-owned entity, is both an agent of the Chinese Government and discharges governmental functions

[55] See Bianca Böhme. (2021) "Recent Efforts to Curb Investment Treaty Shopping: How Effective Are They?", *Journal of International Arbitration* 38(4), at 511–32.

[56] A list of China's top central SOEs is provided by China's State-Owned Assets Supervision and Administration Commission of the State Council, available at www.sasac.gov.cn/n2588035/n2641579/n2641645/index.html.

[57] See, *e.g.*, Mark Feldman. (2016). "State-Owned Enterprises as Claimants in International Investment Arbitration", *ICSID Review* 31(1), at 24–35.

[58] See C. Schreuer, L. Malintoppi, A. Reinisch and A. Sinclair, *The ICSID Convention: A Commentary* (2nd edition) (Cambridge: Cambridge University Press, 2009), at 161.

even in its ostensible commercial undertakings".[59] The arbitral tribunal, however, based on the facts of the case, decided that BUCG is a qualified claimant and that it has *ratione personae* over BUCG.[60]

BUCG is but one of the many Chinese SOEs. In recent years, China seems to have strengthened its control over its SOEs. While the effectiveness and consequence of such control could only be evaluated on a case-by-case basis, China's growing control over its SOEs could make it easier for foreign states to prove that the SOEs are an agent of the Chinese government or play a governmental function. This could be a challenge to China's SOEs in proving themselves as qualified a claimant in future ISDS cases.

The third systematic issue relates to inconsistent treaty interpretation. This issue is not unique to China, as an inconsistent interpretation of IIAs is deemed a major reason for inconsistent arbitral awards and the legitimacy crisis of ISDS at a more fundamental level.[61] Since many Chinese BITs, early ones in particular, contain similar or identical terms, diverse interpretations of these terms would not only lead to inconsistent arbitral awards but also result in uncertainty and unpredictability of China's foreign investment protection standards in a broader sense.

In this respect, *Beijing Shougang et al. v. Mongolia*, *Tza v. Peru* and *Sanum v. Laos* are illustrative examples. All of these cases involve the interpretation of a key sentence in the ISDS clauses commonly seen in early Chinese BITs, namely "a dispute involving the amount of compensation for expropriation". According to some Chinese scholars, this is a narrowly defined jurisdictional requirement, which reflects China's cautious attitudes towards ISDS and grave concerns that ISDS could harm China's "judicial sovereignty".[62] With respect to this sentence, the arbitral tribunals in these cases made conflicting decisions. In *Tza v. Peru*, while resorting to the rules of treaty interpretation in the VCLT, the arbitral tribunal held the following:

[59] BUCG v. Yemen, Decision on Jurisdiction (31 May 2017), available at www.italaw.com/sites/default/files/case-documents/italaw8968.pdf, at 7.

[60] *Id.*, at 13.

[61] See *e.g.*, UNCITRAL, "Possible Reform of Investor-State Dispute Settlement (ISDS)" (A/CN.9/WG.III/WP.142), available at https://undocs.org/en/A/CN.9/WG.III/WP.142, at paras.9 and 31; Stephan W Schill (2017). "Reforming Investor-State Dispute Settlement: a Comparative and International Constitutional Law Framework", *Journal of International Economic Law* 20(3), at 649–72.

[62] See, *e.g.*, An Chen (2009). "Queries to the Recent ICSID Decision on Jurisdiction Upon the Case of Tza Yap Shum v Republic of Peru: Should China-Peru BIT 1994 Be Applied to Hong Kong SAR under the 'One Country Two Systems' Policy", *Journal of World Investment and Trade* 10(6), at 829–62.

> To give meaning to all the elements of the article, it must be interpreted that the words 'involving the amount of compensation for expropriation include not only the mere determination of the amount but also any other issues normally inherent to an expropriation, including whether the property was actually expropriated in accordance with the BIT provisions and requirements, as well as the determination of the amount of compensation due if any.[63]

In contrast, the arbitral tribunal in *Beijing Shougang et al. v. Mongolia* held the opposite opinion, stating that:

> Arbitration before an *ad hoc* arbitral tribunal would be available in cases where an expropriation has been formally proclaimed and what is disputed is the amount to be paid by the State to the investor for its expropriated investment. In other words, arbitration will be available where the dispute is indeed limited to the amount of compensation for a proclaimed expropriation, the occurrence of which is not contested.[64]

The interpretation issue is unlikely to be a major challenge in ISDS cases relying on China's recent IIAs since ISDS clauses in Chinese BITs concluded since the mid-1990s have been substantially broadened, so that "any dispute relating to an investment" may be submitted for ISA.[65] In retrospect, however, the interpretation of the ISDS clause in the China-Peru BIT was no less than a shock to China, especially because *Tza v. Peru* is the first case relying on a Chinese BIT. After the publication of the arbitral award, Chinese scholars have published a number of comments, and many argued that the arbitral tribunal's interpretation is wrong and that the interpretative power of arbitral tribunals should be properly limited.[66] Today, while scholarly discussions on these cases have largely diminished, China remains "bothered" by the issue of inconsistent interpretation of its IIA provisions and deems "inconsistent decisions" as a major concern over the existing ISDS regime.[67]

[63] See *Tza v. Peru*, *supra* note 42, at para.188.

[64] Beijing Shougang et al. v. Mongolia, Award (30 June 2017), available at www.italaw.com/sites/default/files/case-documents/italaw11026_0.pdf (last accessed 30 September 2021), at para.448.

[65] See Manjiao Chi and Xi Wang, *supra* note 28, at 884–8.

[66] See, *e.g.*, Wei Shen. (2011). "The Good, the Bad or the Ugly? A Critique of the Decision on Jurisdiction and Competence in Tza Yap Shum v. The Republic of Peru", *Chinese Journal of International Law* 10(1), at 55–95; Yanru Wei. (2006). "On the Impropriety of China's Recent Complete Acceptance of ICSID Jurisdiction", 13(1) *Chinese Journal International Economic Law*, at 109 (original in Chinese).

[67] See Part III, *infra*.

1 Looking into the Future: China's Position on ISDS Reform

Since the late 1990s, ISDS has been subject to growing criticisms on a number of grounds, such as high cost and long duration, unintended restraint on state regulatory rights, and inconsistent arbitral awards.[68] Such a legitimacy crisis of ISDS has been amplified by some high-profile cases, notably *Philip Morris Asia Limited v. The Commonwealth of Australia*,[69] and *Vattenfall AB and others v. Federal Republic of Germany*,[70] and has provoked unprecedented public debate during the course of the negotiations of some major FTAs, such as the *Transatlantic Trade and Investment Partnership between the U.S. and the EU* (TTIP) and the *Comprehensive Economic and Trade Agreement between Canada and the EU* (CETA).[71]

To respond to the legitimacy crisis of ISDS, various measures have been taken. At the national level, some Latin American countries have denounced the *Convention on Settlement of International Investment Disputes between States and the Nationals of Other States* (ICSID Convention) and terminating their BITs,[72] some have revised their existing BITs or IIA models with stress on domestic remedies for ISDS,[73] and some have proposed various ISDS alternatives, such as an investment court system.[74] At the international level, a global ISDS reform is in process, which features, among others, multilateral discussions and negotiations presided over by UNCITRAL Working Group III[75] and the fourth revision of ICSID Rules.[76]

Especially, the UNCITRAL ISDS reform is mandated as a government-led process that aims at identifying the inadequacies of the

68 See, *e.g.*, UNCITRAL, *supra* note 61, at para.20; Teresa Cheng. (2020). "The Search for Order within Chaos in the Evolution of ISDS." *ICSID Review*, 35(1–2), at 1–19.

69 Available at https://investmentpolicy.unctad.org/investment-dispute-settlement/cases/421/philip-morris-v-australia (last accessed 30 September 2021).

70 Available at https://investmentpolicy.unctad.org/investment-dispute-settlement/cases/329/vattenfall-v-germany-i- and https://investmentpolicy.unctad.org/investment-dispute-settlement/cases/467/vattenfall-v-germany-ii- (last accessed 30 September 2021).

71 See, *e.g.*, Michael Nienaber, "Tens of Thousands Protest in Europe against Atlantic Free Trade Deals", available at www.reuters.com/article/us-eu-usa-ttip-idUSKCN11N0H6 (last accessed 30 September 2021); DW, "Thousands Protest against CETA and TTIP in Brussels", available at www.dw.com/en/thousands-protest-against-ceta-and-ttip-in-brussels/a-19564581 (last accessed 30 September 2021).

72 See Teresa Cheng, *supra* note 68, at 1–2.

73 *Id.*, at 8.

74 See, *e.g.*, Yuwen Li and Cheng Bian, *supra* note 7, at 531–2.

75 Relevant information of the UNCITRAL ISDS reform process is available at https://uncitral.un.org/en/working_groups/3/investor-state (last accessed 30 September 2021).

76 Available at https://icsid.worldbank.org/resources/rules-amendments.

existing ISDS regime and exploring ways to improve this regime.[77] The reform offers a precious opportunity to observe how states evaluate the existing ISDS regime and how their preferred regime should look like. China is a major stakeholder of international investment governance and an active participant in the ISDS reform, China's position on ISDS reform thus deserves careful analysis.

2 China's Major Concerns and Proposals on ISDS Reform

In China, MOFCOM is responsible for negotiating China's IIAs and handling ISDS cases. It submitted a position paper on ISDS reform to UNCITRAL Working Group III on 19 July 2019, entitled "Recommendations of China Regarding Investor-State Dispute Settlement Reform" (Position Paper).[78] The Position Paper has three major parts, respectively explaining China's concerns over the existing ISDS regime, its proposals for reforming this regime, and its vision for the future ISDS regime.

The Position Paper at the outset explains China's major concerns over the current ISDS regime, which include the following:

a. arbitral awards lack an appropriate error-correcting mechanism;
b. arbitral awards lack stability and predictability;
c. arbitrators' professionalism and independence are questioned;
d. third-party funding affects the balance between parties' rights; and
e. time frames are overly long and cost overly high.[79]

After explaining its major concerns, the Position Paper puts forward a number of proposals for ISDS reform, including,

a. to explore the possibility of establishment of a permanent appellate mechanism;
b. to maintain the right of the parties to appoint arbitrators;
c. to improve the rules relating to arbitrators;
d. to encourage the use of alternative dispute resolution measures;
e. to include pre-arbitration consultation procedures; and
f. to enhance transparency discipline for third-party funding.[80]

77 UNCITRAL, *supra* note 61, at para.3.
78 UNCITRAL, "Submission from the Government of China" (A/CN.9/WG.III/WP.177) ("China Position Paper"), available at https://uncitral.un.org/sites/uncitral.un.org/files/wp_177_wgiii.pdf (last accessed 30 September 2021).
79 *Ibid.*, at 2–3.
80 *Ibid.*, at 4–5.

The Position Paper also clarifies that China welcomes UNCITRAL ISDS reform, and impliedly stresses that the reform should be progressed on a multilateral basis.[81]

While the Position Paper is not an exhaustive elaboration of China's view on ISDS reform, it is by far the only official document formally issued by MOFCOM on this important subject. Many of China's concerns and reform proposals stated in the Position Paper are shared by other states and have been discussed widely. That said, China's proposals do have some distinct features, which will be the focus of this Part.

3 China's Preference for a WTO-Style Appeal Mechanism

A major proposal of China is to establish an ISDS appeal mechanism. Such an idea is not entirely new.[82] Notably, it has been discussed during the third round of ICSID Rules revision between 2004 and 2006.[83] The major grounds for creating such an appeal mechanism include inconsistent treaty interpretation of IIA provisions and insufficiency of the existing award review mechanisms, particularly the annulment mechanisms under the ICSID Convention and the judicial review mechanism under the *Convention on Recognition and Enforcement of Foreign Arbitral Awards* (New York Convention).[84]

As discussed, China complains about the lack of predictability of arbitral awards in its Position Paper and shows a strong preference for an ISDS appellate mechanism. Though China does not elaborate on the proposed mechanism, it specifically points out that the mechanism should be "permanent" and "treaty-based". It is noteworthy that China expressly refers to the WTO appellate body as a model for the proposed ISDS mechanism. A WTO-style ISDS appeal mechanism is not only different from the optional arbitral appeal mechanisms incepted in some commercial arbitration rules,[85] but also seems unique among existing ISDS reform proposals. It is of interest to discuss the rationale underlying China's preference.

81 *Ibid.*, at 5–6.

82 See, *e.g.*, Chester Brown. (2017). "Supervision, Control, and Appellate Jurisdiction: The Experience of the International Court", *ICSID Review* 32(3), at 595–610.

83 Relevant information of ICSID Rules Revision is available at https://icsid.worldbank.org/sites/default/files/publications/Possible%20Improvements%20of%20the%20Framework%20of%20ICSID%20Arbitration.pdf.

84 See, *e.g.*, Albert Jan van den Berg. (2019). "Appeal Mechanism for ISDS Awards: Interaction with the New York and ICSID Conventions", *ICSID Review* 34(1), at 157–9.

85 See generally China Position Paper at 4.

First, China's preferred ISDS appeal mechanism is supposed to have a high degree of institutionality. The feature of "permanent" implies that the *ad hoc* ICSID annulment mechanism is not a desirable model for ISDS award review; while the feature of "treaty-based" implies that national courts (for award review under the New York Convention) or any other optional award review mechanism based on commercial arbitration rules would also be undesirable. Essentially, this proposal implies that existing award review mechanisms would not be considered by China for ISDS appeal.

Compared with existing award review mechanisms, the AB seems more "stable" and "predictable" for a number of reasons. The AB is a permanent adjudicative body composed of a fixed number of judges, the disputants are not allowed to "appoint" the judges, and the procedure is subject to a strict and clear statutory time limit,[86] while both ICSID annulment mechanism and judicial review mechanism lack such a level of procedural certainty. Besides, the AB also appears "powerful", since it has the authority to review substantive issues, including errors of treaty interpretation,[87] while both the ICSID annulment mechanism and judicial review mechanism only allow procedural issues to be reviewed. As such, despite all the criticisms, the AB seems to be in a better position to ensure the consistency of its decisions and the efficiency of its adjudicative work.

Second, China's preference for a WTO-style ISDS appeal mechanism is based on its nearly twenty-year experience of WTO litigation. Since its WTO accession in 2001, China has been involved in 63 WTO disputes as a complainant or respondent as of 30 September 2021.[88] All of these disputes involve China's major trading partners, especially the U.S., EU, and Japan, and around half of the disputes have been submitted to the AB for appeal.[89] China has invested massively in WTO litigation capacity building to effectively participate in the multilateral trading system centering around the WTO regime.[90] By its tenth year of WTO membership, China has already emerged from a reluctant participant in

86 See Art. 17 of WTO Dispute Settlement Understanding.

87 *Ibid.*

88 A list of China's WTO disputes is available at www.wto.org/english/tratop_e/dispu_e/dispu_by_country_e.htm (last accessed 20 Jan. 2019).

89 The information about the percentage of panel reports appealed is in Appellate Body Annual Reports, available at www.wto.org/english/tratop_e/dispu_e/ab_an_rep_e.htm.

90 See, *e.g.*, Pasha L. Hsieh. (2010). "China's Development of International Economic Law and WTO Legal Capacity Building", *Journal of International Economic Law* 13(4), at 997.

WTO litigation to an active and formidable player that used the system to defend its interests.[91] As China gets more experienced with WTO litigation, a WTO-style ISDS appeal mechanism seems to be a convenient option for China, as it could substantially save China's ISDS capacity-building efforts.

Third, China's such preference could also be understood as a potential support to its current foreign trade policy, especially in response to the unprecedented trade war with the U.S.[92] Since the Trump administration, the U.S. has shifted its foreign trade policy towards protectionism and unilateralism.[93] Notably, the U.S. has repeatedly blocked the appointment of new AB members, resulting in the dysfunction of the AB, which is deemed as a major hurt to the multilateral trade system.[94] While the U.S. is the chief designer of this system, China has stood out to be a supporter of this system.[95]Against this backdrop, China's preference for a WTO-style ISDS appeal mechanism not only conveys its view on ISDS reform but also impliedly enhances its self-portrayed image as a defender of trade multilateralism.

4 China's Preference for an "ISA Plus" Model

In its Position Paper, China also proposes that, in addition to ISA, other alternatives should be explored for ISDS. Two alternatives are highlighted by China, that is mediation and compulsory pre-ISA negotiation between host states and foreign investors. China also states that "investors' right of appointing arbitrators should not be denied". China's such statements send a clear signal, that is while China wants to have additional ISDS alternatives, it is not against ISA. To put it differently, China wants to keep ISA but hopes to provide certain flexibility by allowing other alternatives. In short, China has envisaged an "ISA plus" model for future ISDS. While

[91] Henry Gao, "China's Ascent in Global Trade Governance: From Rule Taker to Rule Shaker, and Maybe Rule Maker?", in Carolyn Deere Birkbeck (ed.), *Making Global Trade Governance Work for Development: Perspectives and Priorities from Developing Countries* (Cambridge: Cambridge University Press, 2011), at 167–72; Manjiao Chi. (2012). "China's Participation in WTO Dispute Settlement Over the Past Decade: Experiences and Impacts", *Journal of International Economic Law*, 15(1), at 22–49.

[92] See, *e.g.*, Manjiao Chi and Liang Qiao. (2019). "A Skeletal Review of the China-U.S. Trade War", *Canadian Foreign Policy Journal* 23(2), at 99–107.

[93] See *ibid.*

[94] See, *e.g.*, Hoekman Bernard and Petros C. Mavroidis. "Preventing the Bad from Getting Worse: The End of the World (Trade Organization) as We Know it?" *Robert Schuman Centre for Advanced Studies Research Paper* No. RSCAS 6 (2020).

[95] See Manjiao Chi and Liang Qiao, *supra* note 92, at 101.

this model is not entirely novel, it could have some unique implications on China and Chinese investors.

First, as mentioned earlier, despite that China has been sued in several ISDS cases by foreign investors, it has not encountered any major "defeat" up to the present. Unlike many other states, China seldom complains about the regulatory chill effects of ISA or the amount of compensation for ISDS cases. Given its successful ISDS experience, China does not need to hold a negative attitude towards ISA as a major ISDS alternative.

Second, China's implied support for ISA as a major ISDS option seems to reflect its growing interest as a leading investment-exporting state in the world. As early as the 1990s, China adopted the "Going Abroad Strategy" and started to encourage its enterprises, SOEs in particular, to invest abroad.[96] Since its initiation in 2013, the BRI has quickly become a priority on China's development and diplomatic agenda. While the BRI is not just an investment scheme, promoting trade and investment among BRI states is a major aspect of BRI implementation.[97] As Chinese overseas investment keeps expanding, disputes between Chinese investors and the host states are inevitable. Especially, as a large portion of Chinese investments is made in states that are environmentally vulnerable, politically unstable, economically underdeveloped, and culturally diversified,[98] effective and efficient ISDS seems imperative to China and its investors.

Third, in recent years, China is experiencing a dramatic deterioration of economic and diplomatic relations with many trade partners, especially leading economies in the world. As a result, Chinese investors nowadays face growing difficulty in acceding to and operating in many states.[99] And it is increasingly difficult for China to solve such difficulty with these states through diplomatic talks and bilateral negotiations. To many Chinese investors, ISA seems to be a reasonable choice for ISDS. It could particularly be the case as Chinese investors have got familiar with ISA and are affirmative in protecting their overseas interests. In light of this, it is pragmatic for China to support ISA as a major ISDS option, at least in the current situation.

[96] See Huiyao Wang and Lu Miao, *supra* note 5, at vii.

[97] See People's Republic of China National Development and Reform Commission, Ministry of Foreign Affairs, and Ministry of Commerce, "Vision and Actions on Jointly Building Silk Road Economic Belt and 21st-Century Maritime Silk Road", available at www.gov.cn/xinwen/2015-03/28/content_2839723.htm (original in Chinese).

[98] See Yuwen Li and Cheng Bian, *supra* note 7, at 525–26.

[99] See Huiyao Wang and Lu Miao, *supra* note 5.

Fourth, China's preference for ISA as a major ISDS option also reflects its support for the ongoing "ISDS adventure" of its leading arbitration institutions. With the growth of Chinese overseas investment, Chinese arbitration institutions also show a growing interest in the ISDS business.[100] While these Chinese arbitration institutions are not listed in Chinese IIAs as an optional ISA forum, it is possible for them to be selected for contract-based ISDS cases, especially by Chinese investors.[101] Since a decade ago, leading Chinese arbitration institutions, such as the China International Economic and Trade Arbitration Commission (CIETAC), the Beijing Arbitration Commission (BAC), and the Shenzhen Court of International Arbitration (SCIA) have embarked on an adventure of exploring opportunities in the ISDS business.[102] The ISDS adventure is not only prompted by commercial considerations but is also a measure of implementing China's development strategy. For instance, CIETAC has stated that its adventure is a measure of "serving China's BRI implementation".[103] A notable achievement of the ISDS adventure is the publication of specialized ISA rules by CIETAC in 2017,[104] and by BAC in 2019.[105]

Naturally, the historical ISDS adventure of Chinese arbitration institutions would only make sense if ISA remains to be a major ISDS option. Any ISDS reform proposal that could result in abandoning or marginalizing ISA would fundamentally go against the purpose of this adventure. In this sense, China's proposal of an "ISA plus" model renders implied support to the ISDS adventure of its arbitration institutions. Besides, as shown by the draft amendment of the Chinese Arbitration Law recently published by China's Ministry of Justice, China is considering removing some longstanding legal impediments to ISDS in its arbitration law, such

[100] See, *e.g.*, Manjiao Chi. (2021). "The ISDS Adventure of Chinese Arbitration Institutions: Towards a Dead End or a Bright Future?". *Asia Pacific Law Review* 28 (2), at 278; Tong Qi, "China's Policy on ISDS Reform: Institutional Choice in a Diversified Era". In Yuwen Li et al. (eds.), *China, the EU and International Investment Law* (London: Routledge, 2019), at 112–23.

[101] Manjiao Chi, *ibid.*, at 286.

[102] For the purpose of this chapter, it is unnecessary to elaborate on the "ISDS adventure" of Chinese arbitration institutions. For detailed discussions on this topic, see Manjiao Chi, *supra* note 100, at 279–96.

[103] See CIETAC, "Explanation on CIETAC International Investment Arbitration Rules (Trial Implementation)", available at www.cietac.org/index.php?m=Article&a=show&id=14469 (original in Chinese).

[104] Available at www.cietac.org/index.php?m=Article&a=show&id=15199&l=en.

[105] Available at www.bjac.org.cn/page/tz/guifan.html.

as the lack of capacity of foreign states as a disputing party in arbitration in China.[106] Such an amendment could help legitimize ISA under Chinese law, paving the way for Chinese and foreign arbitration institutions to engage in the ISDS business.[107]

III Conclusion

With a growing number of ISDS cases relying on Chinese IIAs, China and its investors have emerged as major stakeholders of ISDS. China's ISDS cases have given rise to a few systematic issues, such as the applicability of Chinese IIAs in the SARs, the legal status of Chinese SOEs in ISA proceedings, and the interpretation of some typical IIA provisions. China seems not very concerned over the possible increase in ISDS cases. Rather, it shows a clear preference for ISA as a major ISDS alternative. In its Position Paper, China proposes an "ISA plus" model with a WTO-style appeal mechanism for the future ISDS regime. Such proposals are realistic and beneficial to China, as they are based on China's ISDS and WTO litigation experiences, and also conform with its development strategy. As ISDS reform remains ongoing, it remains to be seen whether China will be challenged more profoundly in future ISDS cases, and whether China will change its position on ISDS reform.

106 Available at www.moj.gov.cn/pub/sfbgw/zlk/202107/t20210730_432958.html (original in Chinese).

107 See Manjiao Chi, *supra* note 28, at 10–11.

21

Chinese Firms in the US-China Trade War

SOO YEON KIM

How have Chinese firms responded to the US-China Trade War? The trade war between the world's two leading economies is first and foremost a political war. China, since its accession to the World Trade Organization (WTO) in 2001, grew by 2010 to supersede Japan as the second-largest economy in the world and is now positioned to challenge the leadership of the United States in the multilateral trading system. Against this backdrop, the US-China trade war tests the limits of the multilateral trading system under the WTO. Can the multilateral trading system continue to flourish if its two largest economies are engaged in a trade war, imposing tariffs on each other's exports and affecting supply chains as a result? This paper examines how Chinese firms have responded as the US imposed tariffs against imports from China. Responses can vary, from tariff-jumping FDI into the United States to shifting production to Southeast Asia, or even diverting economic exchange to other markets such as Europe. Even though the Phase One trade agreement, which was signed on 15 January 2020 and entered into effect the next month, on 14 February 2020, was expected to improve trade tensions, the US government has kept in place restrictive measures against Chinese firms, with more than 950 Chinese entities subject to sanctions.[1] In September 2022, the Biden administration announced it would maintain the tariffs imposed on Chinese imports pending an extended review.[2]

This chapter analyzes the shifts in the investment patterns of Chinese firms since 2010, focusing on changes since the official outbreak of the US-China trade war on 1 July 2018. The analysis tests four hypotheses concerning the response of Chinese firms. One is that Chinese firms have increased investments in the United States, much like the tariff-jumping investment activity observed in the 1980s during the US' trade conflict

[1] *Politico*, 13 January 2022.

[2] www.bloomberg.com/news/articles/2022-09-08/biden-delays-decision-on-china-tariffs-put-in-place-by-trump.

with Japan (Belderbos, 1997; Blonigen, 2002). Second, Chinese firms also have incentives to shift investments and consequently production to Southeast Asia, especially to those countries that have close economic links with the United States, and can help Chinese firms to avoid tariffs at the center of the trade war. The third possibility is that Chinese firms may direct greater attention to markets outside the United States, especially Europe, predated by extensive investments already undertaken after the global financial crisis in 2008 (Ma and Overbeek, 2015; Meunier, 2019). Finally, the fourth possibility is that China has turned inward to leverage its own massive population and the market opportunities it provides. This is akin to the trend of 'reshoring' or bringing production back to a firm's home country.

This analysis focuses on Chinese firms' investment activities, with the expectation that investment decisions shape firms' trading activities down the line. Data from the fDi Markets database on investment projects, which provides real-time information on greenfield foreign direct investment (FDI) projects around the world, are employed to investigate patterns in Chinese foreign direct investment in the years 2010–2020. The time frame covers the pre-trade war years 2010–2017 and the first three years of the trade war 2018–2020. Though the trade war does not officially start until July 2018, the trade tensions accompanying the International Trade Commission investigation were evident in the media and broader public domain. The analysis thus seeks to capture some of the behavior of Chinese firms in their investment activities that respond to these tensions and also anticipates the official actions to follow. As a contribution to this volume on China's 20 years in the WTO, this chapter contributes to our understanding of China as the world's second-largest economy, as a WTO member with obligations to comply with the rules of the multilateral trade regime, and its ability to influence trade and investment patterns in responding to its trade conflict and competition with the United States.

In terms of the main findings of this inquiry into Chinese firms' investment activities before and after the onset of the US-China Trade War, the results indicate the following patterns:

- In terms of major investment destinations, the US, India, and Indonesia were the top three destinations before the trade war. Since 2018, however, the top three greenfield investment destinations have shifted to countries such as Russia and Brunei. The United States, though still a major investment destination, experiences a sharp drop in greenfield investment from Chinese firms

- On sectoral patterns, real estate; coal, oil, and gas; and metals remain the top three sectors for Chinese firms' greenfield investment. Overall, however, there is a general decline in average annual Chinese overseas investments since 2018
- In investment activities, manufacturing, electricity, and construction are the top areas of investment activity, with investment in manufacturing rising sharply since 2018
- Chinese greenfield FDI has been concentrated in East Asia and Europe, which has seen significant gains with the onset of the trade war. Sub-Saharan Africa replaces South Asia as the third most popular investment destination for Chinese firms
- Over-time patterns across the regions show that the percentage of Chinese greenfield FDI declines for the US and rises for Europe in 2019. Chinese investment also increases substantially for East Asia and the Pacific in 2020 following a dip in 2019

I The Timeline

This section provides a brief chronology of the unfolding of the trade war. One general observation to offer at the start is that the US-China trade war is the formalization of a trade conflict that had already been ongoing since the beginning of this century. Trade tensions were apparent well before the election that brought Donald Trump to the White House. Signs that the trade conflict between the United States and China would be given greater attention were evident during Donald Trump's campaign. At a campaign stop at Alumisource, a metals recycling facility, in Monessen, Pennsylvania in June 2016, Trump delivered his jobs plan speech, in which he described China's accession to the World Trade Organization (WTO) as an event that enabled the 'greatest jobs theft in history'.[3] As part of his agenda to 'Make America Wealthy Again,' Trump laid out his plans, upon his election as President, to activate Sections 201 and 301 of the Trade Act of 1974 and Section 232 of the Trade Expansion Act of 1962. He intended to impose tariffs on Chinese exports to the United States, thus responding to 'illegal activities' in China's trade. Trump's speech also referred to the trade deficit with China, which had reached $800 billion by this time.[4]

[3] www.politico.com/story/2016/06/full-transcript-trump-job-plan-speech-224891.

[4] A fact check on this figure confirmed the accuracy of this statement, though the figure would be lower, at $500.361 billion, if taking into account services, where the US had a trade surplus. www.npr.org/2016/06/28/483883321/fact-check-trumps-speech-on-the-economy-annotated.

Donald Trump made good on his promise in Monessen, Pennsylvania. Once elected as President of the United States. Trump's first act in office, on 1 February 2017, was to withdraw the United States from the Transpacific Partnership (TPP) Agreement. He subsequently signed two executive orders in the next two months. They provided for stricter enforcement of tariffs imposed as part of anti-subsidy and anti-dumping measures. They also provided a full review of the United States' trade deficits and their causes. At his first summit in April 2017 with Chinese President Xi Jinping at Trump's Mar-a-Lago estate in Florida for a 24-hour visit, the two leaders agreed to 100 days of trade talks to address their differences on the United States' trade deficit with China. The talks led to an agreement on 11 May 2017, which provided market access for American beef producers, credit rating services, and credit card providers. For China, the agreement provided market access to the United States for Chinese producers of cooked poultry. This trade deal was beneficial for some US industries; however, it did not resolve broader structural issues at the center of US-China trade relations. These structural issues included China's requirements for technology transfer and the broader concerns and perception of US firms of unequal market access. The 100 days of trade talks, which ended on 19 March 2017, did not yield an agreement that addressed these structural problems in US-China trade relations.

On 14 August 2017, the Trump administration requested a Section 301 investigation on China to launch the US' first direct trade measure. The United States Trade Representative's (USTR) office announced the 'Initiation of Section 301 Investigation; Hearing; and Request for Public Comments: China's Acts, Policies, and Practices Related to Technology Transfer, Intellectual Property, and Innovation under Section 301 of the Trade Act'.[5] Rather than focusing on dumping or other quantitative dimensions of Chinese exports to the United States, the investigation was directed instead at China's behind-the-border practices in its trade regime.

In early 2018, while the USTR investigation was in progress, the Trump administration took additional trade measures, beginning with approval of global safeguard tariffs on imports of residential washing machines and solar cells and modules.[6] Tariffs under global safeguard measures were to be imposed on washing machines for three years. In the first year, there would be a 20% tariff on the first 1.2 million machines, and a tariff of 50%

[5] Docket No. USTR-2017-0016.

[6] USTR Press Release 22 January 2018.

would be imposed on machines above that number. For solar cells and modules, tariffs were approved for four years. There would be a tariff of 30% in the first year but it would be brought down to 15% by the fourth year. However, the approved measure also allowed for up to 2.5 gigawatts of unassembled solar cells to be imported annually with no tariffs. The approval and adoption of these global safeguard measures were the result of an earlier investigation that had already been ongoing. This investigation was undertaken by the independent and bipartisan U.S. International Trade Commission (ITC) under Section 201 of the US Trade Act.[7] The ITC investigation determined that imports of washers and solar cells and modules during the years 2012–2016 were 'a substantial cause of serious injury' to domestic producers. The recommendation of the ITC report was to apply global safeguard tariffs on these products. The global safeguard tariffs were officially to be applied to all trade partners. However, it was apparent that these safeguard tariffs were specifically targeting imports from South Korea and China.[8]

In March 2018, the Trump administration adopted additional protectionist trade measures. President Trump signed two proclamations on 8 March for tariffs on imports of steel and aluminum, and these tariffs were implemented approximately two weeks later, on 23 March. The proclamations exempted Canada and Mexico as partners of the North American Free Trade Agreement (NAFTA). Imports of steel from the rest of the world were to be charged with a tariff of 25%, and imports of aluminum were subject to a tariff of 10%.[8] These tariffs were imposed with the Trump administration's activation of Section 232 of the Trade Expansion Act of 1962. Under this provision, for reasons of national security, tariffs were allowed to be imposed for an indefinite period of time. The invocation of Section 232 justified the tariffs imposed on the imports of steel and aluminum as critical sectors for defense munitions and economic security as well as the protection of these domestic industries.

With the signing and implementation of these proclamations, Trump was fulfilling one of his key campaign promises, that is, to address unfair

[7] USTR Factsheet on Section 201 Cases.

[8] The ITC report named, in particular, Lucky Goldstar (LG) and Samsung. These firms had shifted their production of washing machines to China, Mexico, and then to Thailand and the Philippines to avoid anti-dumping duties that were earlier applied to them. Chinese firms producing solar cells and modules had also similarly shifted production earlier to Taiwan and then to Singapore, Malaysia, Korea, and Germany to avoid countervailing and anti-dumping duties that had been imposed on them. Argentina, Australia, Brazil and South Korea were later exempted from the steel tariff. Argentina and Australia were later exempted from the tariff on aluminum as well.

trade practices from trade partners. As such, the tariffs were strongly supported by pro-Trump groups. At the same time, the protectionist measures caused significant conflicts within both the Trump administration and the Republican Party. From the House of Representatives, 107 Republican members signed a letter in opposition to the tariffs. Gary Cohn, who was director of the National Economic Council, disputed with the Trump administration and subsequently resigned from his appointment. On the day before the tariffs on steel and aluminum were to take effect, the Trump administration, on 22 March 2018, announced the conclusion of the USTR's Section 301 investigation of China's Acts, Policies, and Practices Related to Technology Transfer, Intellectual Property, and Innovation, which had earlier been initiated through the US Trade Representative Robert Lighthizer. With the conclusion of the investigation, the Trump Administration announced also the trade measures to be taken specifically against China. The Memorandum signed by Donald Trump provided for three policy actions to be implemented to address 'China's acts, policies, and practices involving the unfair and harmful acquisition of U.S. technology'.[9] First, the Memorandum directed the US Trade Representative to initiate a case under the WTO dispute settlement mechanism. The case would involve a trade dispute over China's discriminatory technology licensing practices. Second, the Memorandum provided for an *ad valorem* duty of 25 per cent to be applied to Chinese exports to the United States. Products listed to be subject to this tariff included aerospace, information and communication technology, and machinery. Finally, the Memorandum also confirmed the investigation's recommendation that the U.S. Treasury Department, in cooperation with other relevant Departments and agencies, design a set of restrictions to combat China's investment strategy, which invariably sought to acquire sensitive technologies from the United States.

With the conclusion of the USTR Section 301 investigation and the subsequent proclamations adopting the recommendations of the report, the Trump Administration implemented the first set of China-specific tariffs on 6 July 2018. This day is regarded as the official start of the US-China Trade War. The trade conflict progressed with an escalation and exchange of tit-for-tat tariffs, all in all, a series of four rounds until September 2019. The Trump administration imposed significant tariffs on Chinese imports into the United States. Bown (2019) and Bown and Zhang (2019) estimate that through the reciprocal imposition of tariffs, the trade-weighted

[9] USTR Section 301 Fact Sheet.

average tariff rate increased more than six times in two years. In the following year, on 15 January 2020, the US and China successfully negotiated and signed the phase one agreement to suspend current tariffs on each other's exports. According to Chad Bown, who has been tracking trade flows throughout the trade war, tariffs remained high in March 2021. These higher tariffs appear to be the 'new normal' even with the signing and implementation of the phase one trade agreement (Bown, 2021).[10]

II Scholarship on Chinese Investment

Existing studies on Chinese foreign direct investment have highlighted how different Chinese investors are from investors from advanced industrial countries, especially those from the west (Buckley et al., 2007; Cheung and Qian, 2009; Han et al., 2014; Kang and Jiang, 2012; Ross, 2015; Yan et al., 2020). A common finding from these studies is that Chinese firms' overseas investment activities do not readily conform to the characteristics of the prevalent 'eclectic' paradigm in studies of investment (Dunning, 2000, 2001). The eclectic paradigm distinguishes between market-seeking, resource-seeking, strategic assets-seeking, and efficiency-seeking investments. Chinese investors organize their businesses in ways that are distinct and different from the investment activities of firms from the advanced industrial countries of the west. Chinese firms appear to favor long-term profits over short-term profits. This is observable, in particular, in investments in infrastructure, which inherently require a long horizon for reaping economic gains (Alon et al., 2014). Wei's (2010) study also notes that Chinese firms seek to exploit the country-specific advantages of investment locations more so than their own internal firm-specific advantages. This finding has been further supported by Wu's (2005) firm-level survey. Studies have also found that Chinese firms are less averse to the risks of investing in countries that have problems with political stability, social stability, and economic vitality (Chen et al., 2015, 2018; Li-Ying et al., 2013). The explanation may be that Chinese investors do not rely on local networks or institutions in carrying out their economic activities. Rather, Chinese firms are more inclined towards utilizing the network of home country firms in the host country, that is, other Chinese firms that are already established in the host country (Li et al., 2017; Peng, 2012). Finally, highlighting the role of the home country government, Chinese investors overseas are strongly supported by the institutional and policy support

[10] www.piie.com/system/files/documents/piie-chart-us-china-war-up-to-date.pdf.

of the Beijing central government. In this, the characteristics of Chinese firms' overseas investment activities are more consistent with 'institutional' approach to understanding foreign direct investment (Yang and Stoltenberg, 2014).

In the twenty-first century and in the years before the onset of the US-China trade war, China's overseas investment had been rapidly increasing. In the twentieth century, China's position in the global investment landscape was as a major recipient of FDI. China was not a major outbound investor, recording low levels of foreign direct investment. China shifted to a net investor in 2015 when its outward foreign direct investment exceeded foreign direct investment inward (Yan et al., 2020). Even as China's trade tensions with the United States were worsening, Chinese firms, both state-owned and private firms, remained active in their overseas investment activities. As noted above, consistent with the institutional paradigm of investment, Chinese firms' overseas investments received policy support from the central government, through both domestic policies and international economic agreements. Jiang (2010) notes that the Chinese government's various bilateral and plurilateral free trade agreement projects provided important institutional support and facilitated Chinese firms' investment activities. On the domestic front, the central government actively encouraged Chinese firms to invest overseas by introducing in 2001 its 'Go Out' policy (Buckley et al., 2007; Wei, 2010).

The Xi Jinping government's launch of the Belt and Road Initiative in 2013 also provided strong incentives for Chinese firms to coordinate their overseas expansion. The Chinese government's Belt and Road Initiative (BRI), formerly the 'One Belt One Road' initiative, is regarded as a key indicator of China's increasing assertiveness on the international stage (Chaisse and Matsushita, 2018; Cheng, 2016; Huang, 2016; Kim, 2022; Pencea, 2017). The BRI can be regarded as Beijing's grand strategy in the service of national interest. It emphasizes economic statecraft to further China's influence, both in the Asian region and globally (Callahan, 2016) to promote international economic cooperation centered on China. As such, BRI is compatible with Beijing's overall policy of encouraging and incentivizing Chinese firms to expand their economic presence overseas.

The impact of the US-China trade war so far has been strong and far-reaching. Amiti et al. (2020) advanced expectations that the trade conflict would lead to lower investment in 2020. This decline would be due to the shocks on the stock market from policies of the two adversarial countries, which would depress returns to capital. Scholarship has also linked the trade conflict with the impact of uncertainty on the stock market (Cai et al., 2020; Chengying et al., 2021). Wang et al.'s (2021) study also investigated the effect of the trade conflict on stock market movements. They found that Chinese private firms experienced the most negative reactions on the stock market, much more so than state-owned firms. As expected, Chinese firms directly impacted by the Trump administration's imposition of tariffs were especially vulnerable. Other studies such as Itakura (2020) as well as Li (2018) utilized computable general equilibrium models (CGE) to estimate the effect of the trade war on tariffs, investment, and productivity. Li found that the trade war had a negative impact on China's trade. Itakura's study found that both the United States and China had a lower gross domestic product (GDP), imports, and outputs as the trade war escalated. Itakura's analysis also showed that the trade war's impact on global value chains was even more significant. As the CGE model was further refined to account for agent-specific import demands, there was a drop in bilateral trade and a contraction of the global gross domestic product. Subsequent scholarship has largely corroborated the findings of studies using these simulations, focusing on the effects of the exchanges of tariffs between the United States and China on third parties that conduct trade along the international supply chain. Studies have found that third countries that are linked to China in the supply chain and also subject to US tariffs have been especially affected (Mao and Görg, 2020; Wu et al., 2021). The products from China subject to US tariffs were also likely to be intermediate inputs for goods produced in the United States. Such third countries were thus hurt downstream along the global supply chain. EU, Canada, and Mexico, the United States' closest trade partners, have been identified as the third parties most negatively affected by the trade conflict.

It should also be noted that the US-China trade war is more than a trade conflict. It is, more broadly, a political war, a competition between the world's leading economy and a rising challenger that is the second-largest economy in the world (Chong and Li, 2019; Kim, 2019; Liu and Woo, 2018). Concerns about the US' own hegemonic decline may well have sparked the US' initiation of the trade war by imposing the first set of tariffs. The trade conflict has effectively politicized China's sustained trade surplus with the United States, directing more attention to unfair trade practices that have resulted in the loss of jobs and China's acquisition of technology from the United States. Trade practices of Chinese firms and the Chinese central government have given rise to worries about national security and the standing of the United States as the leading economy in the world. On the other side, scholarship from China has even argued that the trade war is the Trump administration's attempt to place obstacles in the way of China's rise (Lai, 2019). In China's foreign economic activities, Beijing pursues economic statecraft that involves the promotion of export-related foreign direct investment, security in the supply of national resources, building up the competitiveness of Chinese firms' competitiveness, and maintaining strong and positive political ties with countries that are recipients of Chinese investment (Wei, 2010).

Finally, much of the existing scholarship has focused attention on the parties themselves, the United States and China, and how the trade conflict has impacted their trade. Chad Bown (2021) has tracked both the tariffs imposed by the two countries and their impact on bilateral trade. Tariffs and the resulting trade flows have been especially important since the negotiation and signing of the phase one agreement. The agreement was signed on 15 January 2020 and entered into effect on 14 February 2020.[11] As of 1 March 2021, Bown reported that Chinese tariffs on imports from the United States averaged 20.7%, and US tariffs on imports of Chinese goods averaged 19.3%. On the actual impact on US-China trade, as of 1 January 2021, 66.4% of US imports from China were subject to tariffs, and China imposed tariffs on 58.3% of goods imported from the United States. Bown's analysis of China's purchase commitments under the phase one agreement, namely to purchase US$200 billion worth of goods from the United States over two years and expected to reduce the US' trade deficit with China, fell significantly short of the goal. In fact, China's imports of goods from the United States were lower in 2020 than in 2017 and thus did not meet phase one targets. The COVID-19 pandemic may have affected these numbers. Nevertheless, even by July 2021, Bown's analysis reported that China's imports from the United States were still 30% lower than the phase one target, though this was still an improvement over 2020 when China's imports from the United States were 40% short of the phase one target.[12]

III Patterns in Chinese Investment, 2010–2020

This section reports patterns of greenfield investment by Chinese firms, with a view to the hypotheses elaborated in the above sections of this chapter. As noted earlier, the analysis draws on data on greenfield investments obtained from the FDi Markets database, which provides real-time

[11] US-China Trade War Tariffs: An Up-to-Date Chart.

[12] US-China phase one tracker: China's purchases of US goods.

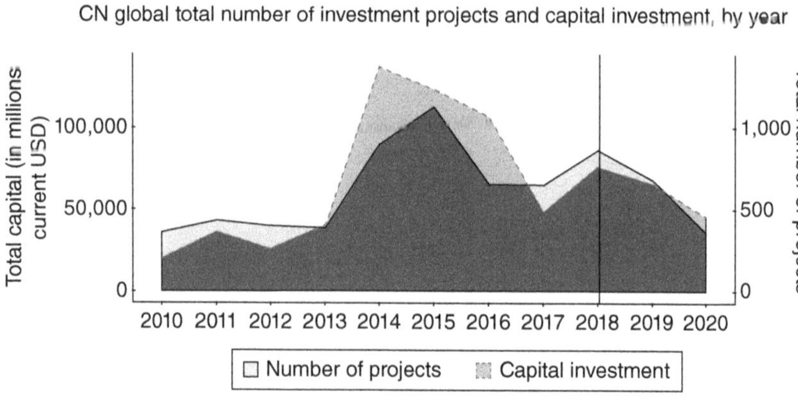

Figure 21.1 Chinese greenfield FDI, 2010–2020

information on cross-border investment flows by project and by firm.[13] The database includes a wide range of supplementary information at both the project and firm levels. The findings reported below take a descriptive approach to highlight the changes, if any, of patterns in the greenfield investment activities of Chinese firms since 2010. Firm-level data are aggregated at the national level to compare changes across states that are recipients of Chinese investments.

Figure 21.1 reports overall patterns in Chinese greenfield FDI in the years 2010–2020, inclusive. The data include both the total value of capital investment in current US dollars and the number of projects that have been undertaken by Chinese firms. For both the value of greenfield FDI and the number of projects, Figure 21.1 shows that Chinese firms' investment worldwide has declined since the onset of the trade war. The investment did peak in the years 2013–2017; however, there is a downward trend that is correlated with the time of the Trump administration.

The data indicate two interesting patterns in the investment behavior of Chinese firms. First, there is some anticipatory effect for the private sector ahead of the official start of the trade war in July 2018. There is a drop in the value of investment, and the number of projects also plateaus in 2017, as Trump begins his term and initiates Section 301 investigations against China. The launch of investigations signals the Trump administration's intent to fulfill earlier campaign promises to address China's unfair trade practices. The private sector may well have taken anticipatory action by

[13] www.fdimarkets.com/.

holding back investments. Second, the decline in investment activity by Chinese firms is notable already in 2018 and before the onset of the COVID-19 pandemic. Chinese firms invest less and in fewer projects in the years 2018 and 2019, with a further drop occurring in 2020, which is the first year of the pandemic. Thus, in addition to an anticipatory decrease in Chinese investment dollars and the number of projects in 2017, the subsequent two years marking the first and second of the trade war also show a downward trend in Chinese firms' investment activities. This pattern can also be associated directly with the trade war itself as it takes place before the onset of the COVID-19 pandemic.

With respect to the hypotheses concerning the increasingly inward orientation of the Chinese economy, Figure 21.1 provides indirect evidence. Figure 21.1 shows global totals for the value and number of projects in Chinese greenfield FDI, which have been declining since 2017. Assuming that the capital for investment available to Chinese firms has not changed significantly, one possibility is for this capital to be redirected to the domestic market. Though this claim would be stronger with data directly on Chinese firms' domestic investment activities, the patterns in global investment activities suggest the possibility of such a re-direction inward.

Investment destinations for Chinese firms also see a dramatic change before and after the official onset of the trade war in 2018. Figure 21.2 provides information on the top ten recipients of Chinese greenfield FDI, divided between the periods before and after the start of the trade war. In the years preceding the trade war, the top destination for investment by Chinese firms was the United States. This was followed by India, Indonesia, Malaysia, and Pakistan. Four Asian countries were thus among the top five recipients of Chinese greenfield in the pre-2018 years. This pattern shifts significantly in the years 2018 and later. Though the data are drawn only from three years, Figure 21.2 shows that Russia became the top recipient of Chinese greenfield FDI once the trade war began. Russia is followed by Brunei and, in third place, is the United States. The top ten recipients also include three other Asian countries, namely Indonesia, the Philippines, and India.

In terms of old and new destinations for Chinese greenfield FDI, the pre-trade war years include Malaysia, Pakistan, Egypt, South Africa, and the United Kingdom, which are not among the top ten recipients in 2018 and later. From Europe, the United Kingdom is displaced by Germany, in Africa, South Africa is displaced by Nigeria, and in Asia, Brunei, the Philippines, and Kazakhstan now figure among the top ten investment destinations for Chinese firms. The United States, India, Indonesia,

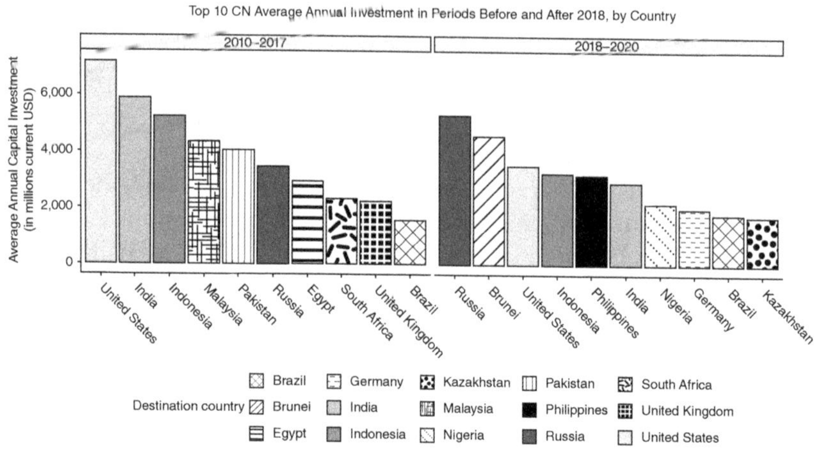

Figure 21.2 Top ten recipients of Chinese greenfield FDI, 2010–2020

Russia, and Brazil, though their ranking in terms of the value of capital investment received has shifted, remained among the top ten destinations for Chinese greenfield FDI.

(i) Sectoral Patterns

Figure 21.3 reports the top ten sectors in which Chinese firms have invested in the years 2010–2020, inclusive. The fDi Markets database classifies each project as belonging to one of 39 sectors. Figure 21.3 reports the sectors that received the largest capital investments from Chinese firms on an annual basis, between the periods 2010–2017 and 2018–2020. For the years 2010–2017, the top sectors for Chinese greenfield investment were real estate; coal, oil and gas; metals; renewable energy; automobiles original equipment manufacturing (OEM); communications; transportation and warehousing; chemicals; food and beverages; and electronic components. With the onset of the trade war, greenfield investment in coal, oil, and gas greatly increased while greenfield investment in real estate declined significantly in the amount of capital investment though it still remained among the top three sectors. Electronic components became the sector with the fourth-highest average annual greenfield FDI from Chinese firms, followed by communications, transportation and warehousing, automobiles OEM, textiles, and chemicals.

Overall, there was significantly less investment in automobiles OEM, and chemicals. Though transportation and warehousing ranked lower

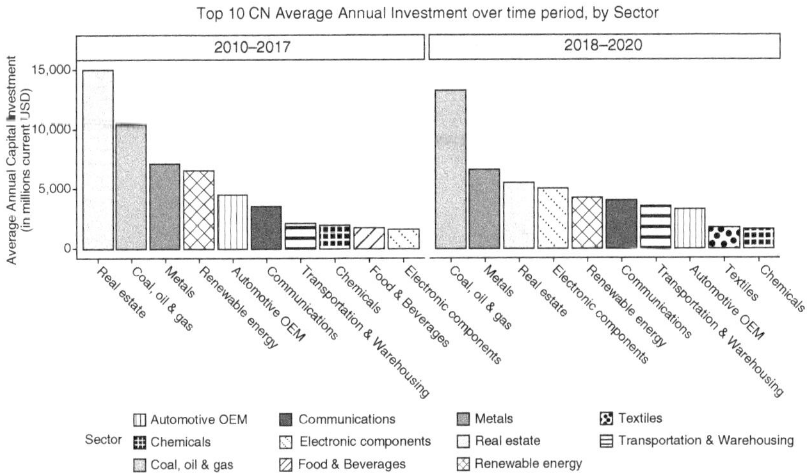

Figure 21.3 Chinese greenfield FDI by sector, 2010–2020

(seventh) in the trade war years, the average annual greenfield investment in this sector is higher in the value of the capital investment. Between the two periods, food and beverages, which ranked ninth in greenfield FDI, is replaced by investment in textiles in the first three years of the trade war. Food and beverages was the only sector that dropped out of the top ten from the pre-trade war years. Otherwise, the top ten sectors for Chinese greenfield FDI remained the same between the two periods though their relative ranking has shifted.

(ii) *Type of Activities*

Figure 21.4 reports the different types of business activities associated with Chinese firms' greenfield FDI projects. The fDI Markets database relies on a proprietary industry classification system that combines the industry or sector classification above with its closely associated business activities. Specifically, every project is classified as belonging to a particular cluster, sector, sub-sector and business activity. There are a total of 39 sectors, 270 sub-sectors, 17 clusters, and 18 business activities. A business activity refers to the actual function of a project's operations.

In Figure 21.4, the pre-trade war years' top ten business activities were, ordered according to the value of annual capital investments made by Chinese firms: manufacturing; construction; electricity; extraction; logistics, distribution and transportation; research and development; information, communication, and technology (ICT) and internet infrastructure;

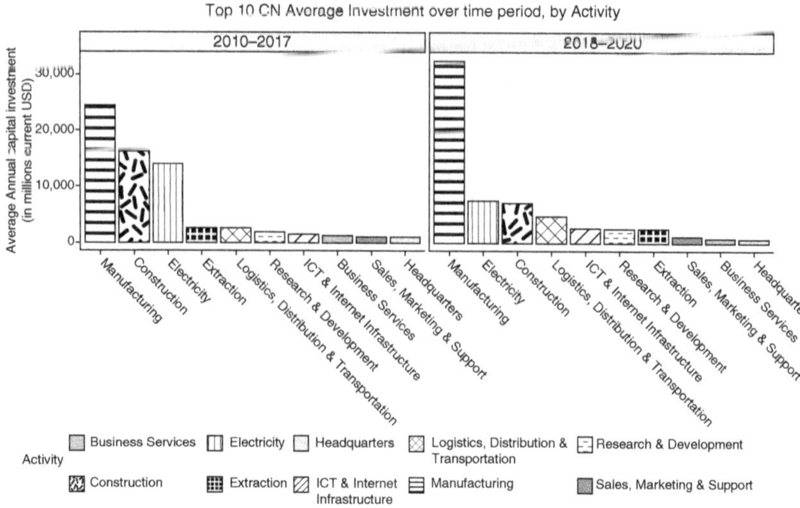

Figure 21.4 Chinese greenfield FDI activities, 2010–2020

business services; sales, marketing and support, and headquarters. In the years 2018 and later, manufacturing remains the top function and sees a significant boost in investment; electricity and construction remain within the top three functions but see a significant decline and a shift in ranking that makes them more or less equal in terms of the dollar value of capital investments. Extraction falls to seventh in capital investments as the trade war gets under way, while logistics, distribution, and transportation; ICT and internet infrastructure; and research and development, in this order, become more prominent as the functions undertaken in investment projects. The last three in the top ten functions of investment projects in the trade war years are sales, marketing, and support; business services; and headquarters. Interestingly enough, these last three functions are those that are not directly associated with production but rather come at the end of the production process as goods are moved to the market or an organizational function (headquarters) for the firm in locating their investments.

Overall, there is no change in the most common functions of Chinese greenfield FDI projects. The top ten business activities remain the same before and after the onset of the trade war. What has shifted is a sharp rise in manufacturing activities as the main function of Chinese FDI projects, substantial declines in construction and electricity as business activities in investment projects, and an increase in business activities associated with logistics, distribution, and transportation, ICT and internet infrastructure, and research and development. The shifts in these business activities may be a consequence of the COVID-19 pandemic, as the pandemic intensified electronic commerce and brought physical challenges in the delivery of international trade.

(ii) *Regional Patterns*

Figure 21.5 reports Chinese greenfield FDI across the eight regions of the world. Between the years 2010–2017, before the onset of the trade war, the regional distribution of Chinese greenfield FDI was as follows, in order of average annual capital investment: East Asia and the Pacific; Europe, South Asia, North America; Middle East and North Africa, Latin America and Caribbean, sub-Saharan Africa, and Central Asia.

Between the years 2018–2020 and the onset of the trade war, both East Asia and the Pacific and Europe saw large increases in Chinese FDI and also remained top destinations. Sub-Saharan Africa displaced South Asia as the third among regions receiving Chinese FDI, and Latin America and the Caribbean displaced North America as fourth among the regions in hosting Chinese investment. Chinese investments in South Asia fell steeply, from third to sixth among the regions. Chinese greenfield FDI in North America fell significantly and ranked fifth among the regions in the trade war years between 2018 and 2020. Similarly, Chinese investments in the Middle East and North Africa fell sharply in the amount of capital investment and from fifth to seventh among the eight regions. Finally, Central Asia remained last in rank among regions in receiving Chinese FDI; however, Figure 21.5 does indicate a rise in the average annual capital investment by Chinese firms in this region for trade war years, 2018–2020.

The regional patterns provide preliminary empirical support for the argument that Chinese firms have diverted their investment activities away from the United States, the adversary in the US-China trade war. Average annual capital investment in greenfield FDI from Chinese firms has declined in North America, which moved from the fourth to fifth most popular destination between the two periods, 2010–2017 and 2018–2020. There is also a notable drop in the quantum of investment as indicated in Figure 21.5. At the same time, Figure 21.5 shows large increases in Chinese FDI in East Asia and the Pacific, Europe, sub-Saharan Africa, and Central Asia. The patterns indicate that investments have intensified in regions that were already important destinations for Chinese FDI. East Asia and the Pacific and Europe have remained the top two regions for Chinese greenfield FDI. What is equally interesting to note is that sub-Saharan

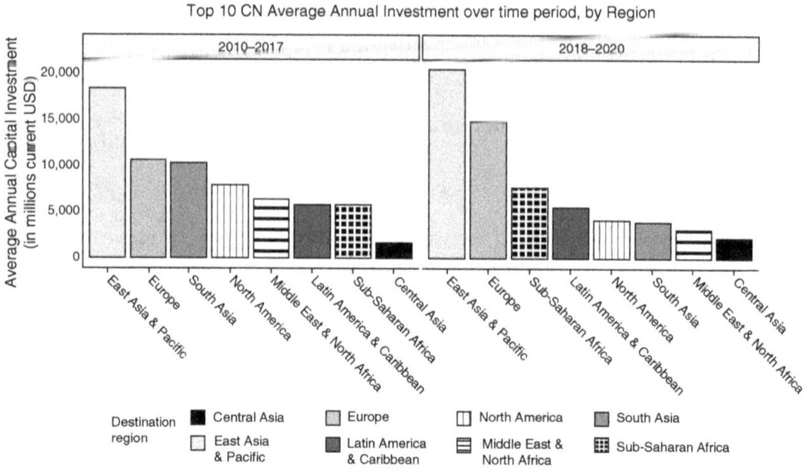

Figure 21.5 Chinese greenfield FDI by region, 2010–2020

Africa and Central Asia have also become more prominent as regional destinations for investment. Sub-Saharan Africa moved from sixth to third among the regions. Central Asia, though it is still ranked last among the regions, shows a significant increase in Chinese greenfield FDI in the trade war years.

(iv) Regional Patterns over Time

The distribution of Chinese FDI across the regions can be more closely examined on an annual basis across the years of the analysis sample. They provide more detailed information on how Chinese greenfield FDI activities have evolved between the pre-trade war years and since 2018. Figure 21.6 illustrates these over-time trends across the eight regions as discussed in the previous section. The figures capture FDI in each region as a percentage of total Chinese greenfield FDI, as contrasted with the trends in the value of the annual average capital investment that is presented in Figure 21.5.

Beginning with Central Asia, the region in terms of the percentage of total Chinese greenfield FDI sees a slight decline as the trade war begins. The high values of Chinese greenfield FDI that were observed in Figure 21.5 for East Asia and the Pacific are most notable for the period 2019–2020. For the first year of the trade war, 2018, there is a sharp drop

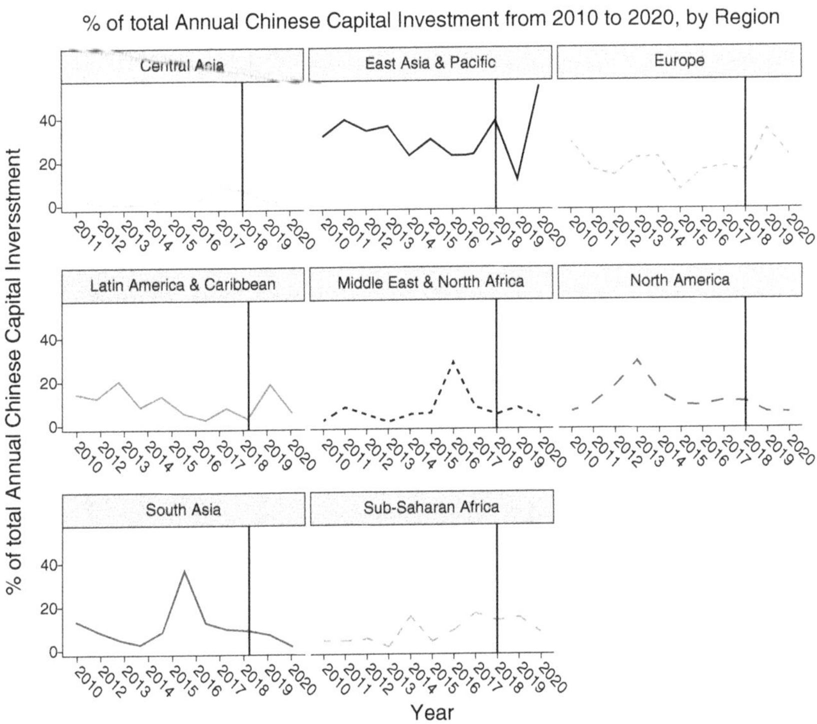

Figure 21.6 Longitudinal trends in Chinese FDI by region

in Chinese greenfield FDI in East Asia and the Pacific. The opposite pattern can be observed in Europe. Chinese greenfield FDI surged in 2018 but declined in the following year. There is nevertheless an overall upward trend in Chinese greenfield FDI in Europe. This trend is similar to Latin America and the Caribbean, where Chinese investment increased in the first year (2018) of the trade war but declined in the second year (2019). The Middle East and North Africa show no discernible change in the percentage of total Chinese FDI that they received. Following a significant decrease in 2017, Chinese investment levels out for the subsequent years as the trade war officially begins.

Chinese greenfield FDI patterns for North America are perhaps the most interesting. Figure 21.6 shows that Chinese greenfield investment peaked in 2013 but declined significantly in subsequent years. The onset of the trade war shows a further decline in Chinese investment, and it remains at the same level in 2019. In South Asia, the peak in Chinese greenfield FDI occurs in 2015; thereafter, the region receives far less Chinese investments and continues its decline through the trade war years. Finally, sub-Saharan Africa, though it does not receive a large percentage of Chinese greenfield investments, does show a consistent upward trend beginning in 2015. The trade war has maintained higher levels, but with a slight decline in 2019.

Overall, the longitudinal patterns in Chinese greenfield FDI reported in Figure 21.6 corroborate much of the distribution of Chinese FDI across the regions as reported in Figure 21.5. They provide more granular information on changes in Chinese greenfield FDI on an annual basis. They also apply a different measure of importance in the location of Chinese greenfield FDI, using the percentage of total Chinese greenfield FDI each year.

(v) *Investment Locations*

Figure 21.7 provides a visualization of Chinese FDI around the world, allowing for a comparison between the pre-trade war years and trade war years 2018–2020. The circles, in size and shade, represent the size of average annual capital investments made by Chinese firms. The maps put together information on both total Chinese greenfield FDI and their concentration in particular countries. As noted in Figure 21.1, overall Chinese greenfield FDI has declined with the onset of the trade war. The highest average in Chinese foreign capital investment before the trade war is recorded for the United States in the years 2010–2017, represented by the darkest large circle. In the years 2018–2020, there is no comparable level of Chinese greenfield FDI anywhere in the world.

In terms of regional concentration, average annual capital investments appears steady for Latin America. There is a greater distribution of greenfield FDI in Africa; that is, the map for 2018–2020 shows many more circles that indicate that Chinese firms have disbursed their investments in more countries with overall lower capital investments. Chinese greenfield FDI has also declined for Asia, though the value of average annual capital investments remains large relative to other regions. In Europe, the trade war resulted in some concentration of Chinese greenfield FDI as there are several larger circles representing larger values in capital investment. Consistent with information in previous figures, average annual capital investment in Chinese greenfield FDI has increased significantly in Russia in the trade war years 2018–2020, relative to the previous period, 2010–2017.

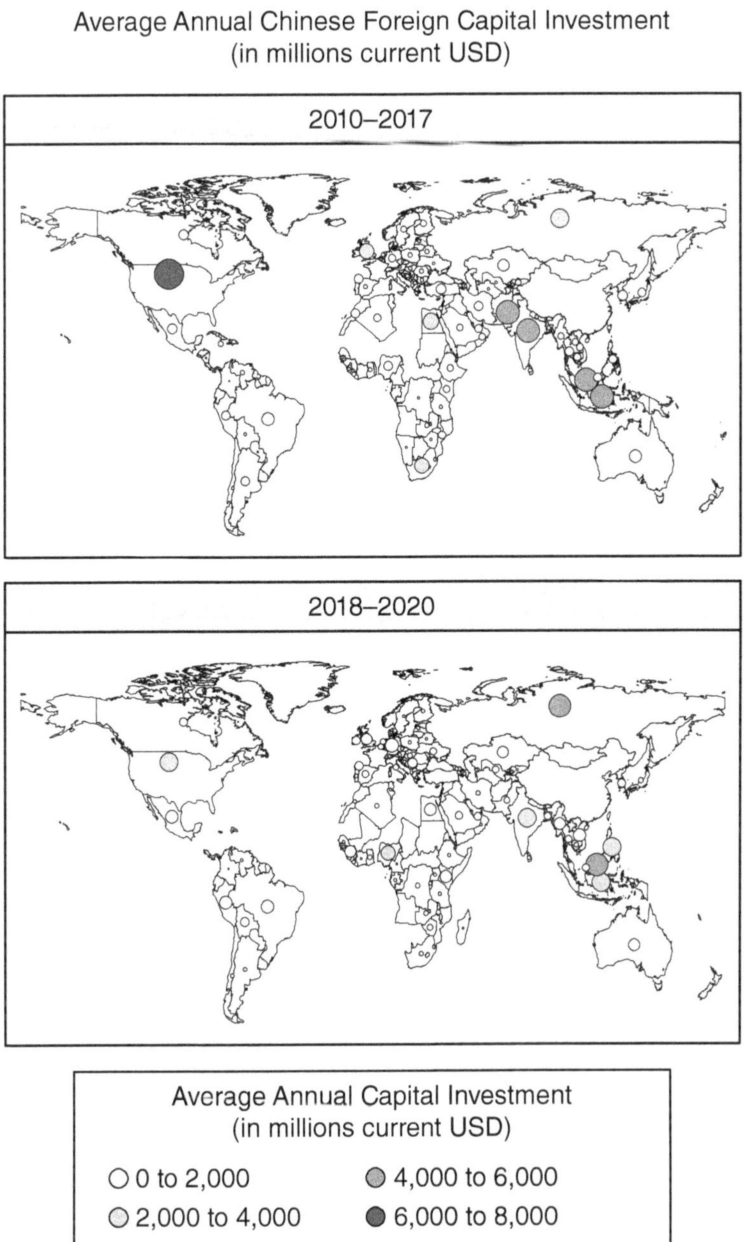

Figure 21.7 Map of Chinese greenfield FDI, 2010–2020

IV Conclusion

This chapter has examined China, a WTO member of twenty years that has grown to be the world's second-largest economy. The focus has been on Chinese investment, a key economic activity that is very closely related to trade, and how it has shifted since the onset of the trade war with the United States, the world's largest economy. This trade conflict extends well beyond the economic realm, of course, as it is emblematic of the political rivalry between the United States and China.

The analysis has examined several dimensions of China's investment activities, utilizing project-level data available on greenfield investments that reflect how Chinese firms have responded to the trade conflict. One notable behavior that is identifiable from the data is that investment patterns indicate some degree of anticipation from the private sector. That is, overall investment patterns drop sharply before the actual start of the trade war. The decline coincides more closely with the start of the Trump Presidency in the United States and the initiation of the Section 301 investigation. The overall pattern suggests that Chinese firms, and possibly firms more generally, respond first to the overall political climate and do so well ahead of concrete policy changes. Other notable changes in Chinese firms' investment patterns include regional distribution. Asia's attractiveness as an investment destination grows with the escalation of trade tensions, but also notable is the increased diversion to Europe for locating Chinese investment. There is a marked decline in greenfield investment in the United States, and Russia emerges as an important recipient of Chinese greenfield investment. Manufacturing, electricity, and construction continue as mainstays of Chinese investment choices, and similarly, real estate; coal, oil, and gas; and metals are top investment sectors for Chinese firms.

As the trade war continues to unfold, there has been a change in the executive office in the United States, with President Biden taking up office in 2021. The Biden administration appears largely to have continued with its predecessor's trade policy stance toward China. China also had its eighth trade policy review, as per the conditions of its accession to the WTO in 2001. While this chapter has identified some patterns in the investment activities of Chinese firms before and after the onset of the US-China trade war, there is much that remains uncertain about the role of both actors as the world's largest economies and members of the World Trade Organization.

References

Alon, I., H. Wang, J. Shen, and W. Zhang (2014). 'Chinese state-owned enterprises go global.' *Journal of Business Strategy* 35(6), 3–18.

Amiti, M., S. H. Kong, and D. Weinstein (2020). The effect of the US-China trade war on us investment. Technical report, National Bureau of Economic Research.

Belderbos, R. A. (1997). 'Antidumping and tariff jumping: Japanese firms' DFI in the European Union and the United States.' *Review of World Economics* 133(3), 419–57.

Blonigen, B. A. (2002). 'Tariff-jumping antidumping duties.' *Journal of International Economics* 57(1), 31–49.

Bown, C. P. (2019). 'US-China trade war: the guns of August.' Trade and Investment Policy Watch.

Bown, C. P. (2021). 'The US–China trade war and Phase One agreement.' *Journal of Policy Modeling* 43, 805–43.

Bown, C. P. and Y. Zhang (2019). Measuring trump's 2018 trade protection: five takeaways. PIIE, February 15.

Buckley, P. J., L. J. Clegg, A. R. Cross, X. Liu, H. Voss, and P. Zheng (2007). 'The determinants of chinese outward foreign direct investment.' *Journal of International Business Studies* 38(4), 499–518.

Cai, Y., Y. Tao, and Z. Yan (2020). 'Stock market trading volumes and economic uncertainty dependence: before and during sino-us trade friction.' *Economic Research-Ekonomska istraživanja* 33(1), 1711–28.

Callahan, W. A. (2016). 'China's "Asia dream" the belt road initiative and the new regional order.' *Asian Journal of Comparative Politics* 1(3), 226–43.

Chaisse, J. and M. Matsushita (2018). 'China's "Belt and Road" initiative: mapping the world trade normative and strategic implications.' *Journal of World Trade* 52(1), 163–86.

Chen, V. Z., J. Li, and D. M. Shapiro (2015). 'Subnational institutions and outward FDI by Chinese firms: the mediating role of firm-specific advantages.' *Multinational Business Review* 23(4), 254–76.

Chen, W., D. Dollar, and H. Tang (2018). 'Why is China investing in Africa? Evidence from the firm level.' *The World Bank Economic Review* 32(3), 610–32.

Cheng, L. K. (2016). 'Three questions on China's "belt and road initiative".' *China Economic Review* 40, 309–13.

Chengying, H., C. Rui, and L. Ying (2021). 'US-China trade war and China's stock market: an event-driven analysis.' *Economic Research-Ekonomska Istraživanja* 35(1), 3277–90.

Cheung, Y.-W. and X. Qian (2009). 'Empirics of China's outward direct investment.' *Pacific Economic Review* 14(3), 312–41.

Chong, T. T. L. and X. Li (2019). 'Understanding the China–US trade war: causes, economic impact, and the worst-case scenario.' *Economic and Political Studies* 7(2), 185–202.

Dunning, J. H. (2000). 'The eclectic paradigm as an envelope for economic and business theories of MNE activity.' *International Business Review* 9(2), 163–90.

Dunning, J. H. (2001). 'The eclectic (oli) paradigm of international production: past, present and future.' *International Journal of the Economics of Business* 8(2), 173–90.

Han, J., X. Chu, and K. Li (2014). 'China's ODI motivations, political risk, institutional distance and location choice.' *Theoretical Economics Letters* 4, 540–47.

Huang, Y. (2016). 'Understanding China's belt & road initiative: motivation, framework and assessment.' *China Economic Review* 40, 314–21.

Itakura, K. (2020). 'Evaluating the impact of the US–China trade war.' *Asian Economic Policy Review* 15(1), 77–93.

Jiang, Y. (2010). 'China's pursuit of free trade agreements: is China exceptional?' *Review of International Political Economy* 17(2), 238–61.

Kang, Y. and F. Jiang (2012). 'FDI location choice of chinese multinationals in East and Southeast Asia: traditional economic factors and institutional perspective.' *Journal of World Business* 47(1), 45–53.

Kim, M.-h. (2019). 'A real driver of US–China trade conflict: The Sino–US competition for global hegemony and its implications for the future.' *International Trade, Politics and Development* 3(1), 30–40.

Kim, S. Y. (2022). 'The politics of FTAs in Asia: the role of China and implications for EU trade policy.' In Johan Adriaensen and Evgeny Postnikov (eds.), *A Geo-Economic Turn in Trade Policy? EU Trade Agreements in the Asia-Pacific* (pp. 29–53). Palgrave Macmillan Ltd. The European Union in International Affairs.

Lai, E. L.-C. (2019). 'The US–China trade war, the American public opinions and its effects on China.' *Economic and Political Studies* 7(2), 169–84.

Li, C., C. He, and C. Lin (2018). 'Economic impacts of the possible China–US trade war.' *Emerging Markets Finance and Trade* 54(7), 1557–77.

Li, W., B. Guo, and G. Xu (2017). 'How do linking, leveraging and learning capabilities influence the entry mode choice for multinational firms from emerging markets?' *Baltic Journal of Management* 12(2), 171–93.

Li-Ying, J., T. Stucchi, A. Visholm, and J. S. Jansen (2013). 'Chinese multinationals in Denmark: testing the eclectic framework and internalization theory.' *Multinational Business Review* 21(1), 65–86.

Liu, T. and W. T. Woo (2018). 'Understanding the US-China trade war.' *China Economic Journal* 11(3), 319–40.

Ma, Y. and Overbeek, H. (2015). 'Chinese foreign direct investment in the European Union: explaining changing patterns.' *Global Affairs* 1(4–5), 441–54.

Mao, H. and H. Görg (2020). 'Friends like this: the impact of the US–China trade war on global value chains.' *The World Economy* 43(7), 1776–91.

Meunier, S. (2019). 'Chinese direct investment in Europe: economic opportunities and political challenges.' In Ka Zeng (ed.), *Handbook on the international political economy of China* (pp. 98–112). Cheltenham: Edward Elgar Publishing.

Pencea, S. (2017). 'A look into the complexities of the one belt, one road strategy.' *Global Economic Observer* 5(1), 142.

Peng, M. W. (2012). 'The global strategy of emerging multinationals from China.' *Global Strategy Journal* 2(2), 97–107.

Ross, A. G. (2015). 'An empirical analysis of Chinese outward foreign direct investment in Africa.' *Journal of Chinese Economic and Foreign Trade Studies* 8(1), 4–19.

Wang, X., X. Wang, Z. Zhong, and J. Yao (2021). 'The impact of US–China trade war on Chinese firms: evidence from stock market reactions.' *Applied Economics Letters* 28(7), 579–83.

Wei, Z. (2010). The literature on Chinese outward FDI. *Multinational Business Review* 18(3), 73–112.

Wu, F. (2005). 'The globalization of corporate China.' *NBR Analysis* 16(3). National Bureau of Asian Research.

Wu, J., J. Wood, K. Oh, and H. Jang (2021). 'Evaluating the cumulative impact of the US–China trade war along global value chains.' *The World Economy* 44(12), 3516–33.

Yan, S., S. Chandrasiri, and J. Karunaratne (2020). 'Globalisation of Chinese enterprises through outbound direct investment: evidence from Sri Lanka.' *Sri Lanka Journal of Economic Research* 8(1), 3–25.

Yang, X. and C. D. Stoltenberg (2014). 'A review of institutional influences on the rise of made-in-China multinationals.' *International Journal of Emerging Markets* 9(2), 162–80.

22

Technology Diffusion in the Triangle of China, the West and Developing Countries

The Contribution of Common Concerns of Humankind

THOMAS COTTIER

I Introduction

Technology drives the law, and the law inherently tends to lag behind specific technological innovations and changes. International conflicts arise due to alleged and real deficiencies in the law and legal protection. The US-China tariff war was initiated by the Trump Administration in 2017. Still unsettled today, concerns of inadequate protection of intellectual property and losing leadership in the field of information technology mainly induced it, in particular in the field of information technology. The alleged theft of intellectual property rights has been paramount (Eberhard Tundang, 2020). The row on the banning of G5 equipment originating in China but jointly developed with western companies (Malkin, 2020) was fuelled by fears of espionage and national security concerns. It strongly added to the geopolitical tensions, resulting in random hostage takings and incarceration by Chinese authorities of two innocent Canadian nationals in response to arresting the financial CEO of Huawei in Canada on behalf of the United States over alleged violations of sanctions. While the persons concerned have been released in the mean-time, tensions and concerns have further increased. The problem is unresolved. Differences in handling electronic data and data protection create uneven conditions for developing artificial intelligence, much to the advantage of China, given the mass of data available. Large technology companies are increasingly regulated in China to respond to the needs and aspirations of the communist party and the government. China seeks losing dependence on imported advanced technology, while the US is increasingly concerned about national security and the effort to rebuild an industrial base and repatriating production (see Chapters 8–10, 17, 21).

These concerns much influence bipartisan US trade policy today and restrict multilateralism. Unilateral measures, based upon safeguards are of increasing importance and explain the failure to restore the Appellate body in the WTO. The rows over Taiwan, the South China Sea, systematic human rights violations in Xinyang province, the suppression of civil liberties in Hong Kong, and the war in Ukraine offer a grim background to this paper. Epochal tensions between democracy and increasingly autocratic and oligarchic regimes inform the debate. Geopolitically, it would seem that there is no or little common ground left to reflect on issues of technology diffusion between the US and China, as well as the rest of the World affected by rivalry and conflict.

At the same time, many Western companies remain invested in China and hope to make large profits in a huge and increasing domestic market. China, vice versa, while increasing home markets, continues to depend upon foreign exports and needs to protect her foreign direct investment, securing access to advanced technologies and research. Global value chains strongly integrate China also in technology development (Malkin, 2020) and make it an important partner. Consumers around the world benefit from these arrangements and international trade offering enhanced competition and lower prices.

Thus, geopolitical and commercial interests in East and West alike are not in line. Ideological differences between the US and China and competing systems of governance rival economic interdependence and business and consumer interests (Wu, 2016). Most countries find themselves uneasily caught in between the struggle of the two superpowers. This is also true for the European Union. Germany in particular strongly depends upon exports to, and investments in, China in order to protect the welfare of its economy. The same is true for Switzerland. Developing countries cannot afford to take sides. Unlike the Cold War with the former Soviet Union and Eastern Europe, strong economic interdependence forces governments to maintain economic cooperation and ties wherever this is possible. Rationally, common interests persist, despite ideological differences. Common concerns, in particular abating and mitigating the pandemic and climate change make such cooperation indispensable and a necessity. The revolution in energy supply and the containment of pandemics cannot be addressed and succeed without cooperation and joint action in technology diffusion.

Technology has been the main driver not only of the law but also of international trade and investment over centuries. It will continue to do so despite political tensions. It opens channels of communication and cooperation. Technology diffusion is not a one-way street. It is a complex human transaction. Advanced technologies often depend upon local adaptation and recognition, in particular in agriculture. They benefit from recourse to traditional knowledge and expertise. They depend upon servicing and thus the transfer of knowledge and education. It offers the hope and potential to bridge differences, much to the advantage of individuals and families around the world which, at the end of the day, international law and relations must serve.

With this backdrop, the paper discusses the importance and potential of existing WTO law in multilaterally regulating the transfer and diffusion of technology. It seeks to identify shortcomings and common grounds which provide the basis for talks, negotiations, and amendments. The paper is less concerned with specific bilateral US-Sino relations. It focuses on what is of interest to the global community, including China and the US, in particular in the context of climate change mitigation and adaptation, biodiversity, and the global pandemic. While the basic struggle is about the epic tension between democracy, oligarchy, and tyranny ever since the typology was set out in classical Greek philosophy and history, the challenge in trade amounts to interfacing different systems of mixed economies within the multilateral trading system, including preferential trade and cooperation agreements.

II Taking Stock of WTO Law

It is worth recalling at the outset that WTO law, developed over a number of trade rounds, has increasingly addressed non-tariff barriers and thus issues of technology affecting international trade. WTO law, supplemented by preferential agreements building upon the common law of international trade (Cottier, 2015), has built a very substantial body of binding international law, comprising principles and rules applicable to technology (for a comprehensive analysis see Cottier, 2017). It essentially covers all areas of technology in the field of agriculture, industry, and services. It includes energy from electricity to fossil fuels. The constitutional principles of transparency, MFN, and national treatment in GATT apply to these fields. They allow addressing many problems relating to market access in the proliferation of technology, in particular where a new field has not been addressed by a more specialized agreement. Rules on tariffs and tariff reductions brought about greater access to foreign technology, and in some areas, such as information technology or chemical and pharmaceutical products, medical equipment, and information technology, members removed tariffs by means of sectoral initiatives and plurilateral agreements based upon critical mass. The following areas are of particular importance for the transfer and dissemination of technology.

(i) Intellectual Property

The WTO Agreement on Trade-related Aspects of Intellectual Property Rights (TRIPS Agreement) sets out the basic rules on ownership of technology in patent law and copyright (software) and the protection of trade secrets (see also Chapter 4). It establishes the legal framework for voluntary transfers by way of licensing. It allows countries to operate restrictions on contractual relations and abuse of dominant positions in competition law and policy. Fair use and compulsory licensing allow governments to protect public interests, mainly with their own territories. Overall, the multilateral IP system, including 26 WIPO treaties, offers a solid foundation for domestic law and commercial transactions, provided the law is properly implemented domestically and companies dispose of the necessary finance and funding (Lybecker and Lohnse, 2015). While skepticism against strong IP standards having adverse effects on to transfer of technology persists (Eberhard Tundang, 2020: 954), the TRIPS Agreement can be applied and construed in support of environmentally sound technologies (Zhuang, 2017). Unresolved challenges relate to developing and least-developing countries whose access to technology cannot be sufficiently secured by the TRIPS Agreement. Likewise, disciplines of protecting traditional knowledge supporting biodiversity have not yet materialized.

(ii) Technical Regulations

The Agreement on Technical Barriers to Trade (TBT Agreement) entails detailed disciplines on standards and regulations. It ensures that regulatory prescriptions and restrictions do not go beyond what is necessary to achieve a particular policy goal as defined by government and law. The Agreement on the Application of Sanitary and Phytosanitary Measures (SPS Agreement) addresses food standards and thus technology related to this sector. The Agreement on Government Procurement (GPA) offers a framework for defining technologies requirements and non-discriminatory procedures with which government purchases need to comply. The Agreement on Subsidies and Countervailing Duties (SCM Agreement) defines the scope and range of governmental support in the research and development of new technologies. The Agreement on the Implementation of Article VI of the General Agreement on Tariffs and Trade (Anti-dumping Agreement) and the Agreement on Safeguards allow for the protection of domestic industries threatened by imports of cheaper competitive products. Finally, the Agreement on Services (GATS) includes disciplines and conditions of market access for technology-related services, such as engineering or telecommunications.

The WTO is not itself a standard-setting organization. Technical standards and regulations are the subjects of specialized organizations, such as ITU or the Codex Alimentarius of WHO/FAO, to which WTO rules relate too. Most of the technical standards, essential for interoperability and the quality of products, are enacted by private standardization organizations, such as CEN, CENELEC, or ETSI (Delimatsis, 2015). Compliance with such norms essentially presumes compliance with basic security standards set out by law. More specific sectors of technology, such as navigation or aviation are addressed by specialized international standard-setting organizations, such as IATA and IMO. These standards, in turn, inform the application of WTO rules and principles.

(iii) Committees, Trade Policy Review, and Dispute Settlement

Overall, existing WTO law and additional agreements offer a broad and sound basis and guidance for regulating technology in domestic law. The work of Committees, reviewing the operation of Agreements, discusses and explores the implications for newer technologies. New issues are flagged in the process of periodical trade policy review. It offers the possibility of dispute settlement between Members of the WTO, in particular in applying special agreements and foremost general principles of non-discrimination to newer fields of technology so far unregulated in greater detail.

Geopolitical tensions should not obscure the potential of peaceful dispute resolution in the WTO as a way and means to address technology-induced differences and maintain peaceful relations among different political systems. Both the US and China as technological rivals have used it extensively (see Chapter 11). Dispute settlement offers a bridge that must not be withdrawn. It is able to address the interface of different governmental and administrative systems, all of which today are characterized as mixed economies entailing the role of government and the state which varies from country to country and from sector to sector. Dispute settlement offers a detailed analysis of the regulatory framework of a Member in a particular context. It allows applying the law and gaining insights also for areas not yet addressed by particular rules and disciplines. Jurisprudence relating to the protection of the environment convincingly demonstrates that WTO law is able to address new issues within the bounds of existing agreements. For example, discrimination relating to new technologies can be addressed by recourse to existing law. Or, claims of theft of intellectual property can be properly addressed on the basis of existing protection of undisclosed information, to the extent that the transfer does not result from joint ventures voluntarily engaged into by companies investing abroad. Recourse to unfair competition rules of the Paris Convention and incorporated in the TRIPS Agreement can be made.

The case law of the WTO strongly contributed to consolidating the law on technology and offering guidance in addressing emerging conflicts and difficulties, such as renewable energy. It allows for making new distinctions in product and production which will be crucial in addressing climate change mitigation and adaption (Conrad, 2011). Taxation and tariffs can be shaped accordingly (Cottier, 2014b; Holzer, 2014). It has come a long way and is not static. The law is a living thing even within the bounds of particular agreements. Recourse to general principles of law and other, relevant agreements further widen the potential to address new challenges in dispute settlement while fully respecting existing commitments.

(iv) Prospects

Today's WTO law essentially emerged from the 1995 Uruguay Round of multilateral trade negotiations, building upon eight previous rounds. Ever since, further progress in negotiations has been limited to government procurement, the revision of the TRIPS Agreement, and a new Agreement on Trade Facilitation. The Doha Development Agenda largely failed, leaving the impression of substantial loopholes and lacunae in the system. This in return informs the view that binding dispute settlement can only be resumed once these lacunae are successfully addressed. Current efforts, largely due to technological changes, no longer work on the basis of broad and comprehensive trade rounds, but incrementally address particular issues, such as fisheries subsidies. Some efforts are made formally outside the WTO, such as TISA or negotiations on electronic commerce and efforts for a framework of investment promotion. In sum, the law is not up to date, and much remains to be done on WTO reform (see Chapter 12) and, as suggested below, in developing a proactive agenda for negotiations on technology regulation and diffusion relating to climate change (Brewer, 2016; Brewer and Falke, 2012; Condon, 2009, 2017; Delimatsis, 2016). Yet, it is important to emphasize that the existing body of law amounts to an important solid foundation. It not only informs preferential trade agreements but also largely the legal status of new and emerging technologies.

Political stalemate, due to geopolitical tensions and a multipolar world dominated by US-Sino tensions, and the lack of progress in developing new disciplines in multilateral agreements today leads the US to reject binding dispute settlement by allowing for appeals to the void. The failure to reappoint Members of the Appellate Body, mainly induced by US criticism of a narrow reading of trade remedies, weakens the rule of law also in the field of technology management and diffusion. While panels continue to operate, binding arbitration today is limited to Members of the MPIA, the Multi-party Interim Appeal Arbitration Arrangement, to which 53 States, including the EU, today are members of and which is based on the arbitration clause of Art. 25 DSU. The first appeal based on the model took place in 2022. The US policy on WTO dispute settlement and all those following it ignore that both negotiations and dispute settlement work in tandem and are not a matter of sequencing, in particular in addressing issues of technology. They both contribute to solutions in tandem. Withdrawal from binding dispute resolution misses the potential to use international law in addressing tensions and differences. It forecloses a channel of communication in the courtroom and an instrument to apply rules and principles to emerging technologies in binding arbitration. It undermines multilateralism and fosters unilateralism and nationalism.

III A Focus on Common Concerns of Humankind

Given the geopolitical constraints and tensions among major powers and the end of an agenda dominated by a transatlantic alliance, which enabled the successful conclusion of multilateral trade rounds up to 1995, careful consideration should be paid to areas of common interest and concern shared by the global community. Specific bilateral and plurilateral problems among powers may be left to unilateral trade policy measures within the bounds of WTO law. Safeguards, the protection of human rights and labor standards, and recourse to national security are likely to increase unilaterally, in particular in areas of strategic importance to the balance of powers. In the field of technology regulation, cyberspace and the internet come to mind. Regulations strongly depend upon constitutional settings and political beliefs. It will be difficult to find common ground between democracy and autocracy in defining the rights and protection of individuals, or access to the internet and globally operating services. It will be difficult to agree on general and comprehensive rules of competition and antitrust, in particular for tech companies if such rules, on the one hand, protect markets and democracy, and control and primacy of state and party on the other hand. Perhaps, bilateral or plurilateral settlements may be found among those mainly affected by specific issues.

These caveats do not exclude addressing competition law and investment in future WTO negotiations. But here and elsewhere, the focus would need to be on shared and common interests in the fields and sectors of the economy where common ground and landing zones can be found. Foremost, the fields should be of interest to all the members of the WTO, and not limited to big powers.

It is submitted that the emerging principle of Common Concern of Humankind offers a foundation for future WTO negotiations. Areas covered by the principles inherently represent common problems and preoccupations, independently of a political system. All states share an interest to find common solutions. They cannot be found in isolation. Here, states inherently depend upon cooperation, comparable to the doctrine of comparative advantage which essentially relies upon reciprocity of trade concessions and is hardly sustainable in going unilateral and alone. Areas of common concern inherently require cooperation in producing global public goods (Cottier et al., 2014a). They are more narrowly defined than the shared and important principle of sustainability, balancing ecological, economic, and social interests (Bürgi-Bonanomi, 2015), or the broadly defined and comprehensive 2015 Sustainable Development Goals (SDGs). It is about addressing specific threatening problems, including by means of recourse to technology diffusion.

(i) Expressions in Treaty Law

The United Nations Framework Convention on Climate Change (UNFCCC) recognized climate change as a common concern of humankind. It was affirmed by the 2015 Paris Agreement and the 2021 Glasgow Climate Pact. The same holds true for the protection of biodiversity, and of preservation of cultural diversity. The WTO health regulations recognize the protection from pandemics a global concern. Other areas, such as the protection of the atmosphere, the problem of global migration, marine pollution, financial and monetary stability, or gross inequality within states come to mind (Cottier, 2021a). All these areas share the risk of serious threats to international peace and stability if left unattended. Most of them also share the trait of being transnational and cannot be addressed in isolation. It is of fundamental importance to note that measures are taken to benefit all and not only a single country. Vice versa, measures omitted harm all countries and the globe alike. Common Concern offers a fundamentally different logic from mercantilism and reciprocity underpinning the international trading system.

So far, the doctrine of Common Concern has been without any impact. A legal principle has not emerged, despite pressing needs. Policies on climate change have remained national and without sufficient coordination. Essential cooperation among the main emitters responsible for global warming, that is China, the United States, and the European Union, has not materialized in coordinating decarbonization and emission trading. As a result, the World in 2021 is heading for a 2.7°C increase in average global temperatures – far beyond the target of 1.5°C of the 2015 Paris Accord. In combating the pandemic, nations took recourse to trade restrictions and nationalism. Covax, the multilateral vaccine program of the World Health Organization is grossly underfunded and short of supplies, while industrialized countries have been hoarding vaccines way beyond their needs. It is obvious that neither climate change and biodiversity, nor the pandemic can be contained unilaterally and without effective international cooperation and coordination.

(ii) Toward a Legal Principle

It will be a long way to implement, recognize and establish a legal principle of Common Concern of Humankind (CCH) in response to policy failures and the fact that national jurisdictions cannot successfully address and solve certain problems on their own. Prospects are dim, but the principle as applied to specific areas is the only hope in times of increased international rivalry and nationalism. In anticipation of further failures detrimental to human welfare, it is imperative to push to the doctrine of common concern of humankind in civil society and politics, stress its recognition in respective fields, and work out legal implications, in particular for technology diffusion in fighting climate change and the pandemic. If States live up to commitments on human rights and sustainable development goals, much more needs to be done to disseminate essential vaccines and related technology to lower-income countries. Governments need to be reminded that they have accepted the areas of climate change, biodiversity, and international health as common concerns in treaties and are bound by them. The following legal implications are suggested and were developed (Cottier, 2021b):

Once a problem is recognized as a CCH in a process of claims and responses, legal doctrine suggests linking it to three types of obligations also applicable to technology diffusion (Ahmad, 2021a, 2021b) First, it entails an obligation to enhance cooperation beyond general public international law in addressing the shared problems. Secondly, it entails undertaking the necessary homework in addressing the problem at home; many of them require action locally, nationally, and internationally. Common Concerns are not limited to the realm of international law and relations. Climate change obviously informed this requirement. Thirdly, it entails obligations in compliance with international obligations. Failure to comply with obligations may trigger countermeasures and thus does not exclude unilateral measures against free-riding countries.

IV An Agenda of Common Concerns for the WTO

We submit that a future agenda for WTO negotiations should be placed under the realm of Common Concerns of Humankind. This essentially entails climate change mitigation and adaptation (Ahmad, 2021a, 2021b). It entails efforts in fighting global pandemics and diseases threatening mankind. It entails the protection of biodiversity. Fisheries negotiations, including technology and subsidy issues, made a good start.

The point is that in these areas all nations, despite the ideological divide, share a common problem. They share common interests to cooperate in trade and investment. They all are indirectly and directly affected. They cannot solve the problem on their own. They all depend upon cooperation and contributions made by others to successfully create public goods in the field. All benefit from negotiated results. They all share a common interest in compliance. Under the principle of Common Concern, WTO should develop a proactive agenda and take the lead on trade issues. Trade regulation amounts to a central, but not exclusive, component of an overall regime. Much of it entails access to, and dissemination of modern technology.

It is not a matter of addressing common concerns comprehensively and exclusively in the WTO. Goals and standards are set in other bodies and agreements. It is a matter of asking what contribution trade regulation can make. It is a matter of shaping the angles of international trade and investment in such areas of common interest with a view to supporting the attainment of goals and standards defined elsewhere. Principles and rules on trade and investment, subsidies, intellectual property, and possibly competition essentially address non-discrimination to, and on, foreign markets. This inherently entails disciplines on tariffs and taxation. They foster trade in products addressing the common concern and allowing for restrictions on harmful products. They make sure that restrictions are not overly broad and respond to the principle of necessity and proportionality. They focus on interconnecting different regulatory systems allowing for appropriate interfaces of technology. They contribute by fostering the dissemination of technology supporting sustainability by means of trade and investment abroad. While existing trade rules offer a solid basis, new disciplines are of particular importance in bringing about a proactive trade agenda and for the new field of sustainable investment promotion.

(i) *Climate Change Mitigation and Adaption*

Much of the issues on climate change mitigation and adaption relate to low-carbon technology (Ahmad, 2021a, 2021b, Brewer and Falke, 2012; Ockwell and Mallet, 2012; Ockwell et al., 2010). This is particularly true for energy, driving economies and the World, transportation, and agriculture. Central efforts on decarbonization and fostering renewable energy should be made at the WTO, in close cooperation with specialized international organizations. Such negotiations have not yet taken place as of 2021.

Decarbonization of the energy sector and the economy:

- The gradual reduction and elimination of fossil fuel subsidies in return for tangible benefits to consumers in health care and education of children. The agenda can build upon the model and modalities of the Agreement on Agriculture and negotiations on fisheries subsidies.
- Common Anti-trust rules on producer cartels in energy production and supplies.
- Defining the policy space for the financial support of research and development of renewable energy beyond the disciplines of the SCM Agreement. It entails the reactivation of well-defined non-actionable subsidies.
- Rules on the interconnection of renewable energy and the framework for a global electricity grid, enabling the rebalance of supply and demand of renewable electricity (wind, solar, hydropower, biomass, possibly nuclear energy) and derivatives (hydrogen, carbon-free kerosene, LNG).

- The creation of a multilateral framework on carbon tariffs for heavily polluting traded products, including reforming the HS, for border tax adjustment, and the interface of different emission trading systems or carbon taxes.
- Interfacing and mutual recognition of fuel efficiency standards of transportation (road, aviation, marine transportation).
- Policy space for tax incentives based upon carbon footprints.
- Policy space for the reduction of methane in agricultural production and tariffs based upon footprinting.
- The introduction of tax incentives for the transfer of technology to developing countries as a flanking measure to PPM-based measures (see below).
- Framework for the promotion of investment in technologies reducing greenhouse gas emissions in developing countries (see below).
- Liberalization of energy-related services (consulting, engineering), including mode 4.
- Framework on investment in renewable energy (see below).
- Modes of Cooperation with IEA, the Energy Charter, and other organizations.

Climate Change adaption in agriculture, trade in foodstuffs and nutrition:

- Climate change adaption requires negotiations revising the Agreement on Agriculture, bringing about better risk management, greater reliance on food imports, and equitable distribution in times of shortages, sourced from globally diverse sources.
- Disciplines on export restriction and fair sharing of food stuffs among countries in need.
- Support measures should be redirected to bring about diversity in crops, away from endangered monocultures in traded goods.
- A framework for trade in genetically engineered crops and food stuffs.
- Support of research and development for climate change-resisting plants.
- Disciplines on risk assessment and risk management in biotechnology regulation.
- Framework for investment in sustainable agriculture (see below).
- Liberalizing related services (consulting, engineering) including Mode 4.
- Modes of cooperation with FAO and other organizations.

(ii) Protecting Biodiversity

Trade-related efforts on protecting biodiversity have been limited at the WTO to intellectual property (Wager, 2008). They have not produced results, so far. Moreover, the list of issues to be addressed exceeds IPRs and entails rules on goods and services:

- Gradual reduction and phase out of fossil fuel subsidies for fisheries.
- Recognition of PPM-based rules on fishing techniques.
- Recognition of PPM-based rules on agricultural products, for example, palm oil production.
- Protecting traditional knowledge and cultural diversity in intellectual property.
- Recognition of agreed trade restrictions on endangered plant species.
- Disciplines on marine plastic pollution by way of limiting plastic packaging in international trade.
- Framework for rules and principles relating to the use and trade of pesticides and fertilizers in agriculture and trade products.
- Framework to encourage diversity of traded crops.
- Framework for labeling diversified foodstuffs.
- Framework of investment in crop and animal diversity (see below).
- Liberalizing related services (consulting, genetic engineering, plant, and animal breeding) including Mode 4.
- Modes of cooperation with UNEP, FAO, WIPO and Washington Treaty.

(iii) Combatting COVID-19 and Future Pandemics

A high-level dialogue between WTO and WHO commenced in 2021 (WTO, 2021a). A number of issues should be contemplated.

- Tightening rules on export restrictions on medical products and pharmaceuticals.
- Framework for financial support for research and development of vaccines.
- Regulatory and intellectual property framework for the production and international trade of vaccine and pharmaceutical components, value chains, and final products.
- Developing a legal framework for Private-Public-Partnerships (PPPs), in particular on IPRs.
- Recognition of framework requiring equitable distribution of, and access, to vaccines in terms of trade regulation.

- Liberalization of hospitals and services and access to jobs under Article VII:2 GATS, including mode 4.
- Liberalization of related services (vaccination, analytical, and testing), including mode 4.
- Framework for investment in health care services (see below).
- Modes of cooperation with WHO and International Health Regulation, international risk assessment, and national risk management in managing trade in medical products and equipment and movement of personnel.

V Strengthening Transfer and Dissemination of Technology to Developing Countries

Many of the issues and activities listed depend upon technology diffusion. Fundamental questions relating to access to technology have not been properly addressed in WTO law. While the framework is workable for commercial transactions, it fails to address the needs of lower-income countries short of finance and funding and a private sector able to engage forcefully by means of commercial acquisition of technology (Barton, 2017; Lybecker and Lohnse, 2015; Zhuang, 2017). As the dissemination of technology is at the heart of addressing common concerns of humankind, these issues move center stage. Two types of measures should be contemplated next to concessionary support programs:

(i) Tax Rebates for Technology Dissemination

Commitments and pledges on the transfer of knowledge and technology in international agreements ignore that governments rarely dispose of the technology that pertains to the private sector. Article 66:2 of the TRIPS Agreement obliges developed members "to provide incentives to enterprises and institutions in their territories for the purpose of promoting and encouraging technology transfer least-developed countries in order to enable them to create a sound and viable technological base." This provision has largely remained a dead letter. Special and differential treatment here has remained an empty promise. This is because most governments making such promises do not legally dispose of the technology. It is in the hand of companies and the private sector. Financial incentives may be qualified as export subsidies beyond export credits and thus contrary to the SCM Agreement (Ahmad, 2021a). It is submitted that industries engaging in low-income countries by investment or trade should benefit from domestic tax reductions, in order to offset financial risks and difficulties encountered. This idea, introduced by Hockman et al. (2005) still awaits implementation. Climate change is an excellent field, as such rebates can account for abatement measures abroad, contributing to agreed targets. It can also apply to other fields recognized as a common concern of humankind. This in return would require appropriate revisions in the SCM Agreement. A similar scheme could be extended to developing countries in general, or limited to particular sectors which are essential to commitments under the principle of common concern of humankind.

(ii) Tax and Tariff Revenues for Technology Dissemination

Tax revenues generated from import carbon tariffs and border tax adjustment should be used to fund technology dissemination to low and lower-income country producers with the aim to meet sustainable production standards and thus avoid further import restrictions. These funds could be accountable to abatement goals agreed upon by countries imposing tariffs and import restrictions in addressing the respective Common Concerns of Humankind. In addition, part of such income could be used to fund international programs supporting lower-income countries in readjusting to sustainable production standards.

VI Investment Promotion

While trade addresses cross-border activities, globalization entails the division of labor in producing components to products and thus the operation of global or regional value chains. Some 60% of all trade today is trade in components, sourced from a multitude of different sites and countries around the world. China plays a particularly important role in protecting corresponding investments (see Chapters 18–20, 21). Existing WTO rules on goods are almost silent on investment, while disciplines on services and intellectual property equally address and protect the foreign direct investment. Bilateral investment treaties address the protection of investment. In doing so, they indirectly promote investment. But they fall short of actively supporting it with a view to bringing about the sustainable production of exported products. Conditions of investment are largely left to transactional arrangements and projects, and multilateral disciplines are lacking. Developing countries are exposed to conditions imposed by major investors.

In superpower rivalry, it will be of interest to developing countries to develop a multilateral framework for investment and investment promotion which secures long-term benefits for their economies and people. Programs such as the Road and Belt Initiative of China, or the US response to the Build Back Better World Partnership should be subject to multilateral disciplines addressing conditions of investment for land use and natural resources, technology transfer and dissemination, local work content securing benefits accruing to the population. Developing countries – the vast majority of WTO members – are interested in bringing about the necessary safeguards against exploitation. Industrialized countries caught in between power blocks equally share an interest in creating level playing fields from the point of view of investors. Incentives and terms for sustainable technology diffusion in the context of global value chains and division of labor must be at the heart of the effort.

While negotiations, building upon the TRIMS Agreement, failed during the Doha Development Agenda, investment was taken up in bilateral cooperation and trade agreements. Since 2020, plurilateral negotiations on a framework of investment facilitation for development (MFIFD) are under way among WTO Members. They are supported by developing countries, China, and the EU. The effort addresses S&D, technical assistance, cross-border cooperation, facilitation of stay of personnel, and home country obligations for sustainable development (WTO, 2021a, 2021b). A comprehensive agreement should set the framework conditions which all investors need to respect and comply with in transactional agreements and investment programs in a transparent manner. Given geopolitical rivalries, this will be difficult to achieve. The framework agreement, however, could focus on recognized Common Concerns of Humankind, and expound on particular disciplines applicable to areas captured by this principle. The commonality of interests in addressing the concern should facilitate overcoming resistance to giving up power-based policy space and unilaterally imposing conditions to the benefit of addressing the concern, in particular climate change mitigation and adaption, the protection of biodiversity, and access to vaccines. An agreement addressing common concerns would address framework conditions for funding and returns, servicing loans, land rights, and use, labor conditions and mobility, protection of basic human rights, and finally for the transfer and dissemination of sustainable technology.

VII Conclusions

The existing body of multilateral trade rules offers a solid foundation for addressing the commercial dissemination of technology. Binding dispute settlement is able to authoritatively apply principles and rules to governmental regulation of emerging and new technologies. It offers a bridge to overcome superpower rivalries and protect the rights of Member States of the WTO, all being mixed economies in their own way. Shortcomings of the law relate to the dissemination of technology to developing countries lacking resources in the private sector. It is here that new disciplines are required and need to be developed. Given geopolitical rivalries, it is submitted that these efforts should focus on recognized Common Concerns of Humankind. It is here that we can identify globally shared common interests beyond power politics where Members of the WTO need to cooperate beyond unilateralism with a view to address these concerns effectively in their very own interest and thus allow for the dissemination and funding of appropriate technologies.

The WTO thus should develop a proactive trade and investment-related agenda for negotiations enabling and supporting recognized Common Concerns of Humankind, that is climate change mitigation and adaption, the protection of biodiversity, and the containment of global pandemics. Other topics may eventually be recognized and inform future negotiations. A substantial amount of topics for a proactive trade agenda of the WTO can be identified, and each of them is able to make a substantial contribution. They may result in amending existing agreements or bring about new treaties, in particular on energy and electricity, the reduction of fossil fuels subsidies, or the packaging of traded goods. Or they link up WTO law to agreements developed in other fora. Trade rules will increasingly distinguish products on the basis of sustainable modes of production. At the heart of this transition will have to be a mechanism to compensate for the necessary imposition of PPM-based trade restrictions by funding and allowing access to sustainable technology by developing countries with a view to leaving conventional modes of production behind. Such mechanism, using tax rebates or return of tax and tariff revenues will be accounted for the effort made in addressing the Common Concern and therefore is also in the interest of major markets and powers.

Given the structure of the world economy, additional rules need to address investment promotion for the benefit of developing countries, caught otherwise in between superpower rivalries. Agreed framework conditions, applicable to areas of Common Concern of Humankind, will create a level playing field for home countries, host countries, and investors. They secure that foreign direct investment is sustainable, non-exploiting with reasonable returns, and to the benefit of the population of the developing country concerned. Again, at the heart of this effort is that modern and sustainable technology is being deployed by foreign direct investors or donor countries in a cooperative manner and equally to the benefit of local welfare. Since such investment or financial support accounts for addressing a Common Concern, differences of interests and unilateralism, otherwise paramount in a World shaped by geopolitical rivalry, should rationally make way for international cooperation within the World Trade Organization and other international bodies. The emerging principle of Common Concern of Humankind offers the hope and potential that ideological differences and power play can cede to cooperation in limited areas of inherently shared interests and necessary cooperation in creating public goods in the pursuit of domestic and global welfare.

References

Ahmad, Z. (2021a). *WTO Law and Trade Policy Reform for Low-Carbon Technology Diffusion: Common Concern of Humankind, Carbon Pricing, and Export Subsidy Support.* Leiden/Boston: Brill.

Ahmad, Z. (2021b). 'Trade related measures to spread low carbon technologies: a common concern based approach'. In Thomas Cottier (ed.), *The Prospects of Common Concern of Humankind in International Law.* Cambridge: Cambridge University Press, pp. 95–152.

Barton, J.H. (2017). *Intellectual Property and Access to Clean Technologies in Developing Countries.* Geneva: ICTSD.

Brewer, T. (2016). 'International technology diffusion in a sustainable energy trade agreement'. In Gary C Hufbauer, Ricardo Melendenz-Ortiz and Richard Samans (eds.), *The Law and Economics of a Sustainable Energy Trade Agreement.* Cambridge: Cambridge University Press.

Brewer, T., Falke A. (2012). 'International transfers of climate friendly technologies: how the world trade system matters'. In David Ockwell and Alexandra Mallet (eds.), *Low Carbon Transfer: From Rhetoric to Reality.* London: Routledge.

Bürgi-Bonanomi, E. (2015). *Sustainable Development in International Law Making and Trade: International Food Governance and Trade in Agriculture.* Cheltenham: Edward Elgar.

Condon, B.J. (2009). 'Climate change and unresolved issues for climate change in WTO law'. *Journal of International Economic Law* 12: 895.

Condon, B.J. (2017). 'Disciplining clean energy subsidies to speed the transition to a low carbon world'. *Journal of World Trade* 51: 675.

Conrad, C.R. (2011). *Processes and Production Methods (PPMs) in WTO Law: Interfacing Trade and Social Goals.* Cambridge: Cambridge University Press.

Cottier, T. (2015). 'The common law of international trade and the future of the World Trade Organization'. *Journal of International Economic Law* 18: 3–20.

Cottier, T. (2017). 'Technology and the law of international trade regulation'. In Richard Brownsword et al. (eds.), *The Oxford Handbook of Law, Regulation and Technology.* Oxford: Oxford University Press, pp. 1017–51.

Cottier, T. (ed.). (2021a). *The Prospects of Common Concern of Humankind in International Law.* Cambridge: Cambridge University Press.

Cottier, T. (2021b). 'The principle of common concern of humankind'. In Thomas Cottier (ed.), *The Prospects of Common Concern of Humankind in International Law.* Cambridge: Cambridge University Press, pp. 1–94.

Cottier, T., Aerni, Ph., Karapinar, B., Matteotti, S., de Sépibus, J., Singal, A. (2014a). 'The principle of common concern and climate change'. *Archiv des Völkerrechts* 52: 293.

Cottier, T., Nartova, O., Shingal, A. (2014b). 'The potential of tariff policy for climate change mitigation: legal and economic analysis'. *Journal of World Trade* 48: 1007–37.

Delimatsis, P. (ed.). (2015). *The Law, Economics and Politics of International Standardisation.* Cambridge: Cambridge University Press.

Delimatsis, P. (ed.). (2016). *Research Handbook on Climate Change and Trade Law.* Cheltenham: Edward Elgar.

Eberhard Tundang, R. (2020). 'US-China trade war: an impetus for new norms on technology transfer'. *Journal of World Trade* 54: 943–60.

Hoekman, B.M., Maskus, K.E., Saggi, K. (2005). 'Transfer of technology to developing countries: unilateral and multilateral policy options'. *World Development* 33: 1587, 1593–94.

Holzer, K. (2014). *Carbon-Related Border Adjustment and WTO Law.* Cheltenham: Edward Elgar.

Lybecker, K.M., Lohnse, S. (2015). *Innovation and Diffusion of Green Technologies: The Role of Intellectual Property and other Enabling Factors.* Geneva: WIPO Global Challenges Report.

Malkin, A. (2020). *Getting beyond Technology Transfers: Analysis of and Recommendations on Intangible Economy Governance in China.* Waterloo: CIGI Papers 239.

Ockwell, D. Haum, R., Mallett, A., Watson, J. (2010). 'Intellectual property rights and low carbon technology transfer: conflicting discourses of diffusion and development'. *Global Environmental Change* 20: 729–38.

Ockwell, D., Mallett, A. (eds.). (2012). *Low Caron Technology Transfer: From Rhetoric to Reality.* London: Routledge.

Wager, H. (2008). 'Biodiversity, traditional knowledge and folklore: work on related IP matters in the WTO'. *International Human Rights Law Review* 3: 215.

WTO (2021a). 'WHO-WTO dialogue steps up efforts for increased COVID-19 vaccine production and equitable access'. www.wto.org/english/news_e/news21_e/igo_21jul21_e.htm (accessed October 29, 2021).

WTO (2021b). 'Investment facilitation for development news archives'. www.wto.org/english/news_e/archive_e/infac_arc_e.htm (accessed October 29, 2021).

Wu, M. (2016). 'The "China, Inc." challenge to global trade governance'. *Harvard International Law Journal* 57: 261–323.

Zhuang, W. (2017). *Intellectual Property Rights and Climate Change: Interpreting the TRIPS Agreement for Environmentally Sound Technologies.* Cambridge: Cambridge University Press.

INDEX

www.ingramcontent.com/pod-product-compliance
Lightning Source LLC
LaVergne TN
LVHW010339220926
848484LV00004BB/938
* 9 7 8 1 0 0 9 2 9 1 7 8 1 *